USING
MICROCOMPUTERS

APPLICATIONS FOR BUSINESS

**The Times Mirror/Mosby
Data Processing and Information Systems Series**

The Spence-Windsor System of Instruction

Instructor's Guide with Transparency Masters

Student Laboratory Manual

Data Diskettes

Test Items

Microtest Computerized Testing Package

All of these supplements were written by J. Wayne Spence and John C. Windsor. When combined with the **Using Microcomputers: Applications for Business** text, they provide a complete system of instruction for teaching introductory microcomputer applications. For more information see the Preface in this text or call Times Mirror/Mosby College Publishing at 800-325-4177.

USING MICRO COMPUTERS

Applications for Business

J. WAYNE SPENCE

JOHN C. WINDSOR

BOTH AT NORTH TEXAS STATE UNIVERSITY

 Times Mirror/Mosby College Publishing

St. Louis   Toronto   Santa Clara   1987

To Jan, Pat, and Cari. Thanks for your help, interest, and patience. Now—how about a vacation?

J.W.S.

To Eileen, Laura, and Rachel. Thanks for all your encouragement and support. We will go fishing this weekend.

J.C.W.

Editor: Susan A. Solomon
Developmental Editor: Rebecca A. Reece
Editorial Assistants: Pamela Lanam and Lisa Donohoe
Text and Cover Designer: Nancy Benedict
Production Coordinator: Stacey C. Sawyer, Montara, California
Illustrator: Bob Haydock
Typesetting: Progressive Typographers Inc.

FIRST EDITION
Copyright © 1987 by Times Mirror/Mosby College Publishing
A division of the C. V. Mosby Company
11830 Westline Industrial Drive,
St. Louis, MO 63146
Printed in the United States of America

Library of Congress Cataloging in Publication Data
Spence, J. Wayne.
  Using microcomputers.

  Bibliography: p.
  Includes index.
  1. Business—Data Processing. 2. Micro-computers—Programming. I. Windsor, John, 1946– . II. Title.
HF5548.2.S73   1986   650′.028′5416
    86-22986
ISBN 0-8016-4778-9

PR/VH/VH 9 8 7 6 5 4 3 2 1   02/A/290

CONTENTS IN BRIEF

v

COLOR HIGHLIGHTS

Two sections of full color photographs, located near Chapters 3 and 8, highlight microcomputer hardware and software and microcomputer graphics. The titles of the pages containing these photographs are:

CONTENTS IN DETAIL

All Chapters begin with Chapter Objectives and "What's Going on at ACE?" and end with Chapter Summary, Key Terms, and Chapter Questions. All Modules end with a Summary (that compares the packages discussed and offers guidelines for package evaluation), Module Questions, and Module Problems.

CONTENTS IN DETAIL, continued

5 Chapter Five
Applications Software:
Word Processing   93

M5 Modules/Chapter Five
Word Processing   115

M5a pfs:Write/Proof   118

CONTENTS IN DETAIL, continued

M6 Modules/Chapter Six
Spreadsheets   224

M6a pfs:Plan   227

M6b Lotus 1-2-3   249

CONTENTS IN DETAIL, continued

7 Chapter Seven
Applications Software: Databases 323

M7 Modules/Chapter Seven
Databases 346

M7a pfs:File and pfs:Report 349

CONTENTS IN DETAIL, continued

CONTENTS IN DETAIL, continued

CONTENTS IN DETAIL, continued

PREFACE

The Intended Audience for This Book

We wrote *Using Microcomputers: Applications for Business* for a practical, hands-on, first course on how to use the microcomputer as a business problem-solving tool. This course is typically taught at the freshman or sophomore level in two- or four-year colleges and is typically aimed at business majors, information systems majors, or MBAs. Our book assumes no previous microcomputer use or knowledge of computer concepts. It is appropriate for the introductory courses identified in the DPMA and ACM curricula, and it is consistent with the computer-fundamentals requirement of the AACSB.

Why We Wrote This Book

Several years ago our consulting work indicated increasing demand for microcomputer application systems and for instruc- tion on microcomputers and software packages. In response to this trend, we de- veloped one of the first college-level courses designed to provide students with hands-on use of computers.

Our book was originally written for our course to fill the void that the then-available books couldn't fill. It began as a locally pro- duced software manual, and, through ex- tensive class testing and marketing-based development, it evolved into a business-ori- ented microcomputer concepts and spe- cific applications textbook.

While we were writing our book, a num- ber of competing books were published. We've taken great care to ensure that our book does not have the deficiencies present in these currently available competitors. We specifically note the following:

Some Books Don't Address Specific Packages

A generic approach is fine for nonbusiness majors who need to "get their feet wet." Most businesses, however, now expect pro- spective employees to know how to use the popular packages to solve business problems.

Few Books Have a Business Orientation

When they do have any, it's "tacked on" in the form of exercises or boxed features. In general, our competitors do not integrate a business problem-solving theme but instead concentrate on package commands.

Some Books Are Incomplete

Students must often purchase two or more texts to cover general microcomputer concepts, data processing/information systems concepts, and specific applications packages. When a textbook makes claims to be complete and self-contained, the student often discovers too few commands with incomplete examples and is left to wade through confusing user documentation.

Some Books Are Inflexible

They usually cover only one package each for word processing, spreadsheet, and database applications. Instructors must have the three specific packages licensed in the lab or be forced to supplement. Conversely, some labs are equipped with more than one word processing package or more than one spreadsheet, and instructors want to let students choose the package they learn. This may require several different texts for classroom and lab.

Why We Think You Should Use This Book

Put quite simply, it works! The materials in our book have either been directly classroom tested or are based on a classroom-tested model. Furthermore, much of this text has been used at North Texas State and in seminars for business professionals, employees of governmental agencies, and members of professional associations. We have taught from this material, located its weaknesses, and altered its presentation so that it meets the following educational objectives:

Integration of Concepts and Hands-on Learning

This book presents both computer concepts and hands-on experience with many of the popular software packages. For example, a student not only learns how to use a particular database software package, but also why databases have replaced file management systems, how databases are structured, and how a database becomes an integrated part of the management information system of an organization.

Presentation of a Comprehensive Look at How Microcomputers Can Be Used to Solve Business Problems

Many of the existing microcomputer textbooks concentrate on the "big three"—word processing, spreadsheets, and database. Although these microcomputer applications are no doubt the most common ones, confining students to only these areas gives them a limited view of how to solve business problems they'll encounter on the job. We first present general software concepts, such as the levels of software and the relationships among machine language, operating systems, developmental languages, and software packages. After laying this foundation we show generic concepts, as well as specific package examples, of operating systems, word processing, spreadsheets, database, graphics, data communications, and integrated packages.

Provision of Instructors with a Flexible Teaching Tool

The Chapter/Module format allows maximum flexibility. The Chapters address generic concepts, whereas the Modules cover specific software packages. Beginning with Chapter 4, each Chapter is followed by two or more Modules. We realize that instructors may prefer particular software packages or may be limited to the software they currently have available. We have, therefore, included Modules describing a range of popular and currently available software packages:

MS-DOS	pfs:File and Report
CP/M	dBASE II and III
pfs:Write/Proof	R:base 4000 and
MultiMate	5000
WordStar	pfs:Graph
Multiplan	Chart Master
pfs:Plan	pfs:Access
Lotus 1-2-3	Crosstalk XVI
Symphony	Smartcom

Our approach enables maximum flexibility because:

- *You can choose the packages to be covered in your course.* We offer a number of packages from which to choose. Since we cover the packages most commonly used in colleges and universities, it's very likely you'll find all your choices in our book.

- *You may decide to teach a different package on short notice.* With other books, switching to a new package means switching texts, too. With our book, there is less chance that you'll pass up any opportunities to teach different packages.

- *You may decide to cover more than one package for a particular application.* Again, our wide selection of popular packages allows you to do this without buying another book or copying portions of the user's manual; you won't have to take the time to develop handouts and lecture notes or to create new exercises or cases.

Emphasis of Business Applications and a Problem-solving Orientation

Each Chapter begins with a "scenario"—a common business problem that may be either partially or fully solved by using a computer. In the scenarios we meet Chris Thompson, a new employee of American Consumer Electronics (ACE), Inc. The scenarios show Chris solving a variety of ACE's inventory problems. These business inventory problems are echoed in the Module Exercises, so that the student can actually solve the problems faced by Chris. In addition, each Module focuses on solving a problem associated with searching for and finding a job. The strength of this approach is that students see how business problems are solved rather than simply learning a list of commands.

How to Use This Book

The Chapters and Modules are self-contained and as such may be taught in any order without loss of continuity. We do recommend, however, that Chapters One through Four be taught first.

Chapters

The Chapters provide an understanding of generic concepts and functions as well as the uses of microcomputers and software packages. The Chapters set the stage for exploring one or more of the Modules that follow. Thus, the Chapters establish the essential foundations for the hands-on applications in the Modules.

Each Chapter contains:

- Objectives
- Key Terms
- Chapter Questions — end-of-chapter drill exercises and the more challenging "what if" questions

Modules

The Modules provide a step-by-step approach to solving business problems, and they are grouped by application type. Each group of Modules is preceded by a *Module Introduction* that identifies the details of the business problem to be solved within the individual Modules that follow. The Module(s) can be discussed in the classroom (ideally with a live demonstration), or students can work through a Module in the lab. Each group of Modules concludes with a *Module Summary,* which contains a general summary of all the packages discussed in that grouping, a comparison of those packages, and a checklist for evaluating software of that application type. Following the summary are *Module Questions,* which test students' knowledge of the specific commands of the software package, and *Module Problems,* which test students' ability to use the software to solve various business problems.

ACE Scenarios and the Job Hunting Problem

As mentioned above, realistic business examples are found throughout the book. The Scenarios about ACE begin each Chapter. The student reads "What's Going on at ACE?," in which Chris Thompson's business problem is described. This section sets the stage for the following Chapter and Modules and shows how Chris Thompson copes with the Chapter opening problem.

The Job Hunting Problem is carried throughout all of the Modules. Solving the same problem with different packages offers a building block approach not found in other texts.

Additional business problems to solve can be found in the Student Lab Manual that accompanies our text.

These Scenarios and Problems encourage student interest, reinfore concepts, and promote a problem-solving approach.

Additional Options

Microcomputer concepts are often taught in combination with computer concepts and/or BASIC programming. Thus this text may be used with:

- A computer concepts text
- A BASIC programming text

Times Mirror/Mosby's two offerings in this area are Floyd, *Essentials of Data Processing* (1987), and Cohen-Alger-Boyd *Business BASIC for the IBM PC with Cases* (1987).

Brief Version of Our Text

A version of our text that contains all the Modules for WordStar, dBASE II and III, and Lotus 1-2-3 is available from Times Mirror/Mosby. This book can also be used in combination with a concepts text or a BASIC text as described above.

Supplements

This text has a direct, practical approach. Likewise, our supplements package reflects a clear, useful business-oriented theme.

Instructor's Manual

Our Instructor's Manual provides the most complete assistance currently available to instructors of introductory microcomputing courses. Further, this guide was designed to allow instructors to add their own teaching notes and so tailor it for their use. It includes:

- Notes on establishing and managing a microcomputer laboratory facility
- A series of course syllabus suggestions for:
    semester/quarter-oriented courses
    courses with limited/extensive software use
    courses to be supplemented by other material
- Approximately 100 Transparency Masters, which include:
    key graphics that appear in the book
    adaptations of text graphics
    completely new illustrations
- Chapter components include:
    teaching tips and notes
    transparency master guide for each Chapter
    answers to all Chapter Questions

- Module components include:
    teaching tips and notes
    transparency master guide for each Module
    answers/solutions to all Module Questions and Problems
    additional Module Problems with solutions
- Sign-up sheet for those instructors wishing to be notified of Module Updates

Student's Laboratory Manual

This supplement, designed to facilitate students' use of the laboratory, is composed of:

- Hardware configuration guide—to record the types and locations of hardware available
- Software inventory—to keep track of the software packages and versions
- Restatement of all Module Problems with the appropriate data for each exercise
- "Test Yourself"—fill-in-the-blank and matching review questions and answers
- Quick response form—to be completed and submitted to the instructor for each exercise solved (minimizes amount of printout produced)
- Additional Module exercises, with the accompanying data for each exercise
- "Where do I find?" guide—to identify where items such as microcomputer magazines, hardware vendors, software vendors, and so on may be found
- Software summary sheets for each of the software packages presented in the text indicating the organization and

structure of menus and commands (reduces the need to have both text and lab manual in the lab at the same time)

Data Diskettes

A set of three data diskettes contains data sets for the Module Job Hunting Problem and the four additional problems in the Student Lab Manual as well as solutions for all Module exercises.

Testbank and Computerized Testing Package (MicroTest)

This includes over 1000 items with an average of over 50 items for each Chapter, an average of 20 items for each Module, and an average of 20 items that require knowledge of multiple Modules. The questions are predominately multiple choice, with the remainder distributed between true/false and matching. The testbank includes correct answers keyed to the appropriate Chapter or Module. This supplement is available to adoptors in printed and diskette version.

Module Updates

Our Modules will be updated and new Modules will be issued to adoptors based on a consensus of user needs. Instructors wishing to receive complimentary copies of our Module Updates should fill out the subscription form in the Instructor's Manual.

Software

This book is also accompanied by three Modules and educational versions of WordPerfect, SuperCalc4, and dBASE III PLUS. These Modules plus software supplement are available at no cost to adopters.

Acknowledgments

We are indebted to the many reviewers and market research telephone survey and personal interview respondents. Their input assisted us greatly.

Reviewers

Sarah Baker
Miami University of Ohio

Patricia Boggs
Wright State University

Samuel Coppage
Old Dominion University

Marilyn Correa
Polk Community College

Gary Erkes
Western Washington State

Sue Finch
Pima Community College

Al Garfinkel
Bergen Community College

Darrell Gobel
Catonsville Community
   College

George Grill
University of North Carolina

Don Henderson
Mankato State University

Russell Hollingsworth
Tarrant County Junior
   College

John Huhtala
Ferris State College

Santiago Ibarreche
University of Texas, El Paso

Richard Jarka
Oakton Community College

Donna Kizzier
Kearney State University

Buddy Krizan
Murray State University

Patrick Lamont
Western Illinois University

Jim LeBarre
University of Wisconsin,
    Eau Claire

Len Lindenmeyer
Anne Arundell Community
    College

Gary Marks
Austin Community College

Gerald Meyer
LeGuardia Community
    College

Micki Miller
Skyline College

Steve Murtha
Tulsa Community College

William O'Brian
Florida International
    University

William O'Hare
Prince Georges Community
    College

J. B. Orris
Butler University

Linda Rice
Saddleback Community
    College

Douglas Rippy
University of Dayton

Paul Ross
Millersville State College

Mark Sabet
California State University,
Los Angeles

Al Schroeder
Richland College

Richard Smith
Oregon State University

Tim Sylvester
College of DuPage

Linda Taylor
Gaskell & Taylor Engineering

John Tower
Oakland University

Richard White
University of California,
    Berkeley

Dean Whittaker
Ball State University

Market Research Respondents

Alabama: Steve Zimmerman. **Arizona:** Sue Finch. **California:** Ronald Cerruti, Jason Frand, Vivian Frederick, Professor Gessford, Shepperd Gold, Ko Isshiki, Bob Jones, David Patterson, Kevin Shannon, Bob Van Spyke, Gerald Wagner, Richard White. **Florida:** Bruce DeSautel. **Georgia:** Rod O'Connor. **Illinois:** Beverly Bilshausen, Jim Boyd, John Chandler, Janet Cook, Paul Dravillas, Dr. Duffy, Richard Jarka, Jean Longhurst, Linda Salchenburger, John Schrage, Richard Sosnowski, George Warren, Kurt White. **Indiana:** Tom Harris, Ruth Lankford, Dean Orris, Gloria Wagoner, Jeff Whitten, Jim Wilson. **Iowa:** Jerry Fottrah, Curtis Rawson. **Kentucky:** Bonnie Bailey. **Maryland:** Mike Ball, Al Hebner. **Michigan:** Randy Cooper, Clyde Hardman, Hans Lee, Al Polish, Dennis Severance, Sid Sysma, Donald Weinshank, Dave Wilson. **Minnesota:** Bernice Folz, Layne Hopkins. **Missouri:** David Bird. **New Jersey:** Al Garfunkel. **New Mexico:** James Menching. **New York:** William Hillman, Professor Minena. **North Carolina:** Rob Adler, John Gallagher, Richard Kerns, James Teng, Dale Williams, Don Williams. **Ohio:** Sarah Baker, Don Brazelton, Kenneth Dunning, Miles Kennedy, Ed Kosiewicz, Kathryn Murphy, Art Polan, Kathleen Preem, Clyde Randall, James Schefler, Thomas Schraber, Glenn Thomas, Professor Vernon. **Oklahoma:** Dr. Ackerman, Darryl Nord. **Oregon:** William Harrison, Mike Johnson, Jeanne Sloper, Rick Smith, David Sullivan. **Pennsylvania:** Darrell Craig, Ron Teichman, Clinton White. **South Carolina:** C. Brian Honess. **Tennessee:** Mohammed Ahrandi. **Texas:** Carl Ahlers, Maryam Alavi, Professor Friedich, Rod Hustenberg, Gary Marks, Mike Parks, Professor Ricketts, Dr. Les Rydl. **Virginia:**

Sam Coppage, Bob Gray, Art Hodge, Professor Pope, Rich Redmond, Howard Wilson, Jim Wynne. **Wisconsin:** Hank Bell, Susan Haugen, Robert Horton, Arthur Larson, Steve Ross.

We also wish to thank our colleagues and College of Business students at North Texas State, Nancy Benedict (Designer), Stacey Sawyer (Production Coordinator), Lisa Donohoe and Pam Lanam (Editorial Assistants), Rebecca Reece (Developmental Editor), and Susan Solomon (Executive Editor).

J. Wayne Spence

John C. Windsor

PROLOGUE

Welcome to the world of computers, especially microcomputers! You are about to learn how to use a computer to solve problems.

In the following chapters, you will become familiar with an individual — Chris Thompson — who is faced with a number of rather common business problems. You will follow Chris through the process of identifying the problems and learning how to use microcomputer equipment and computer programs to solve them.

As explained in Chapter 1, Chris works in the inventory control department of a large consumer electronics company; however, many of the problems that Chris faces are similar to ones you will have to face in the future. In Chapter 2, Chris learns about computer equipment. Someday you could be working for a company that uses microcomputers, or you might decide to purchase one for yourself.

In Chapter 3, you will have an opportunity to examine popular types of **software** (computer programs). Chapter 4 describes the computer **operating system,** which acts as a base for all other programs. Beginning with Chapter 4, each chapter is followed by a series of modules that illustrate the use of particular **software packages.** Each module describes how to use one program to solve particular problems related to the chapter topic.

Chapter 5 covers **word processing** programs. If you have to write textual material and want to be able to change it easily, word processing programs can solve the problem. As a student, you might want to use word processing to write letters, prepare class papers, or create outlines to assist you in studying for an exam.

Chapter 6 explores **spreadsheet** programs. Spreadsheets are used to solve problems dealing with sets of interrelated numbers. For example, you might want to keep track of your progress in the courses you are taking by creating a spreadsheet that computes course averages based on exam scores and grades on other assignments. You could also use a spreadsheet to maintain a personal budget and keep track of expenses. Thus, whereas word processing deals with words, spreadsheets generally deal with numbers.

Using Microcomputers: A List of Occupations or Professions and Possible Uses of Application Programs

Occupation or Profession	Word Processing (Using Words)	Spreadsheets (Manipulating Numbers)
Auto service/repair	Customer service report	Repair estimates
Broadcasting (radio and TV)	Script preparation	Projecting advertising revenues
Commercial and residential construction	Project description and specifications	Project cost estimates
Country club or pro shop	Member newsletter	Golf handicap computation
Educator	Preparing exams, lesson plans, student worksheets	Analysis of grades
Engineer	Project reports	Structural stress analysis
Entertainment (movie production)	Script preparation and modification	Project cost estimates
Equipment rental services	Customer contracts	Project cost estimates
Farmer	Financial report to bank	Crop rotation and planting mix analysis
Health and fitness studio	Membership renewal notices, advertising	Member performance analysis
Hotel/motel management	Registration confirmations	Conference/banquet cost projections
Investments and financial consultant	Investment portfolio	Analysis of investment performance

Database software is covered in Chapter 7. If you find it necessary to keep a list of many items and then search that list for particular entries (or combinations of entries), a database program can help you. For example, you could create a list containing all of your credit card accounts and names and addresses of persons to notify in case the cards are lost or stolen. You could create a household inventory that could be reported to an insurance company in the event of theft or damage by fire. You could record expenses in particular categories to assist you in preparing your federal or state income tax.

Sometimes "a picture is worth a thousand words"; therefore, it is often better to use a visual representation of data that

Database (Maintaining Lists)	Graphics (Creating Diagrams)	Communications (Interfacing with Others)
Appointment list, common problems list	Part specifications	Part location services
Advertising client list	Story diagrams, weather charts	Wire service contact
Project materials requirements list	Design diagrams	Link to suppliers, materials ordering
Membership list	Tournament competition brackets	Interclub reservations
Classroom inventory, assignment of textbooks	Class presentations	Classroom network, computer-assisted instruction
Parts list, bill of materials	Product design experimentation	Professional database inquiry
Prop management, scene requirements	Story board creation	Location-to-studio communication
Equipment inventory list	Equipment performance comparisons	Link to other rental services
Acreage inventory and historical crop performance	Historical production analysis	Commodity market link
Member profiles, membership list	Member progress comparisons	Link to parent company
Reservations, property inventory	Facility use analysis	Link to parent company
Client investment portfolio management	Investment plan performance comparisons	Link to Wall Street data services

▶

words or numbers cannot adequately describe. Chapter 8 describes the use of computer **graphics** programs that allow you to present information pictorially—by charts or graphs. Perhaps you want a visual representation of how you spend your money each month. You could produce a spreadsheet table that shows you, with numbers, where your money went, or you could produce a pie chart that demonstrates how your money was used. Perhaps you want to track your total income from year to year. One way of illustrating this type of comparison is to use a line or bar chart.

When it is either necessary or desirable for your computer to "talk" to another computer, you will use **communications** programs, as described in Chapter 9. Per-

Using Microcomputers (continued)

Occupation or Profession	Word Processing (Using Words)	Spreadsheets (Manipulating Numbers)
Janitorial service	Advertising, brochures	New client cost estimates
Journalist or reporter	Story preparation and production	Numerical analysis, expense reporting
Law enforcement	Neighborhood Watch program preparation	Call frequency analysis
Legal	Contracts, wills, brief preparation	Client charges
Limousine or taxi service	Vehicle operators guide book	Fleet cost analysis
Medical	Patient charts	Office budget
Preschool and day care center	Report to parents	Operating cost analysis
Property management	Tenant contracts	Utility usage tracking per unit
Real estate sales	Property description	Estimating client costs
Religious organization	Member newsletters, special program announcements	Operating budget analysis
Social worker	Case reports	Client financial needs analysis
Travel/tourism agency	Tour package preparation and advertising	Package cost projection, cost per party member

haps you want to plan a trip. Some commercial data services have airline schedules and fare information that can be accessed through your computer. These services also generally provide other data such as condensed versions of current news stories, stock market information, entertainment information, and so on. Your computer communications equipment, a communica-tions program, and your telephone will enable you to make contact with and use these services from your home or office. Thus, when your computer doesn't have all of the information you need, you may be able to get it from another computer.

Finally, Chapter 10 describes **integrated systems.** Integrated systems are collections of different types of programs

Database (Maintaining Lists)	Graphics (Creating Diagrams)	Communications (Interfacing with Others)
Type of services by client	Floor plan layout	Dispatch services
Story-line items	Story art	Transmission of story to publisher
Crime incidence data	Special program comparisons	Link to national law enforcement networks
Case disposition, client list	Crime/accident scene layout	Legal database inquiry
Client list, reservations	Area maps	Dispatch service
Diagnostic codes, insurance payment history	Patient therapy	Medical database inquiry
Client medical and emergency data	Learning aids and games	Computer assisted instruction network
Occupancy information	Tenant notices	Heating/air conditioning control
List of available properties	Floor plan layout	Link to national real estate service
Membership list	Board meeting presentations	National office links
Case assignment list and history	Demographic reporting	Link to departments of human services
Customer contact	Tour price comparisons	Airline reservations

capable of handling word processing, spreadsheets, databases, graphics, and communications. Thus, either one can buy individual programs capable of handling these functions independently, or one can buy a single package that does all of them.

But what of Chris Thompson in the inventory control department of a consumer electronics company? Chris will have to prepare a series of business letters to companies that make the products that the electronics company sells (word processing), determine the costs and profits associated with certain inventory items (spreadsheets), maintain a list of inventory items (database), produce charts for presentation at a business meeting (graphics), and transmit inventory information to a regional office (communications). Thus, Chris will learn to use—as you will—various computer programs to solve many types of common problems.

Although Chris works for a large company, this in no way limits the use of microcomputers and computer programs to large corporations. We have already identified a few personal uses of microcomputers and computer programs. The preceding table illustrates these and more. You will notice that the table lists a number of occupations or professions. Although the list is not exhaustive, see if your planned profession is in the list. Whether it is or not, you should examine the complete table; not only will you get an idea of how computers are being used in other occupations or professions, you might also get some new ideas about how computers could be used in your chosen career.

This text will take you on a journey full of challenges and rewards. The challenges will include becoming familiar with computers. However, the challenges don't stop there: You will learn how to make the computer a practical tool. The computer will not be your master! You will become not only **computer literate** but a **computer user,** capable of entering the business or professional world skilled in the use of a device no less threatening than the telephone. Good luck to you! We promise the journey is well worth the effort.

SCENARIO 1

An Introduction to the ACE Corporation

It was a bright September morning as I approached a tall, steel-and-glass building on a downtown Houston street. I had gotten up early because I wanted to be sure not to be late. As I walked up the steps, I noticed the sign on the side of the building: ACE, INCORPORATED. ACE stood for American Consumer Electronics.

Inside, I asked directions to room 410. I felt butterflies in my stomach as I rode the elevator. I glanced at my watch: 7:50. The elevator stopped on the fourth floor, and I walked to room 410. The sign said NEW EMPLOYEE ORIENTATION.

I opened the door. Inside were about 30 people sitting in desk-chairs, each about my age, and ready for the tasks that lay ahead. A folder had been placed on each desk. I found a folder with my name on it—Chris Thompson—and took my seat. In the folder were a pencil, a pen, a tablet, and a copy of a document labeled "Personnel Form." Thus began my first day on the job. ∎

Chapter One
Computers in Business:
An Introduction

Chapter Objectives

When you have completed this chapter, you will be able to:

- Discuss the functions of management and how they vary by level within an organization

- Describe the decision-making process and how it relates to management

- Distinguish between data and information

- Identify the characteristics of information

- Describe the relationship between management function, information characteristics, and type of information system used to support decision making

- Describe how microcomputers can be used to assist in the decision-making process

- Discuss the role of computers in business

The Nature of Management and Decision Making

ACE was started in 1952 by Mr. George Miller of Chicago. From his first store on Wacker Drive, he sold record players and TV sets. Soon thereafter, he opened a second store on the south side of Chicago. Both businesses went well, and by 1960 he had opened stores in Downers Grove, Schaumburg, and Waukegan. By 1965 Mr. Miller, then the sole owner of ACE, had decided to go public. So, by 1968 shares in ACE were listed on the New York Stock Exchange. By 1972, with the additional funds generated by stock offerings, ACE had spread over much of the Midwest, with regional offices in St. Louis, Minneapolis, and Cincinnati. Company headquarters remained in Chicago.

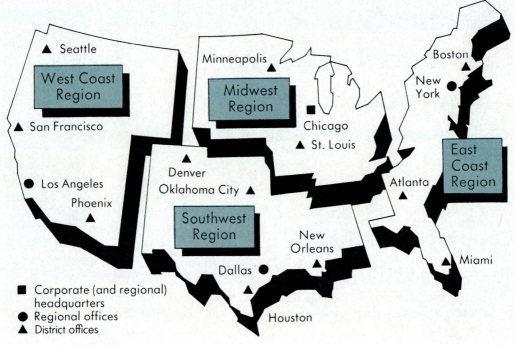

FIGURE 1.1
A geographic representation of ACE, Incorporated

Today, as illustrated in Figure 1.1, ACE does business throughout almost all of the United States. Regional offices exist in four major cities, with warehouse facilities in two of them; district offices are located in a dozen more cities; and sales facilities with approximately 750 showrooms are spread all over the country. ACE carries a complete line of consumer electronics products including a complete line of stereo and radio equipment, TV sets, tape players, video cassette recorders, and, most recently, computer products. Last year, the combined gross sales for the company were about 4.2 billion dollars.

ACE is organized along the lines shown in Figure 1.2. Mr. Miller is the president

and chief executive officer (CEO) of the company. Regional vice presidents head each of the major geographic regions—East Coast, Midwest, Southwest, and West Coast—and report directly to Mr. Miller. The Houston office reports to the regional vice president for the Southwest in Dallas—Mr. Sharp. The district office in Houston is managed by Ms. Fullerton. The 18 showrooms in the Houston district and the district administrative staff report to her. Mr. Jenkins, Chris's boss, is part of the administrative staff and reports to Ms. Fullerton.

As shown in Figure 1.3, ACE is made up of four management levels: (1) **strategic management,** the president and regional

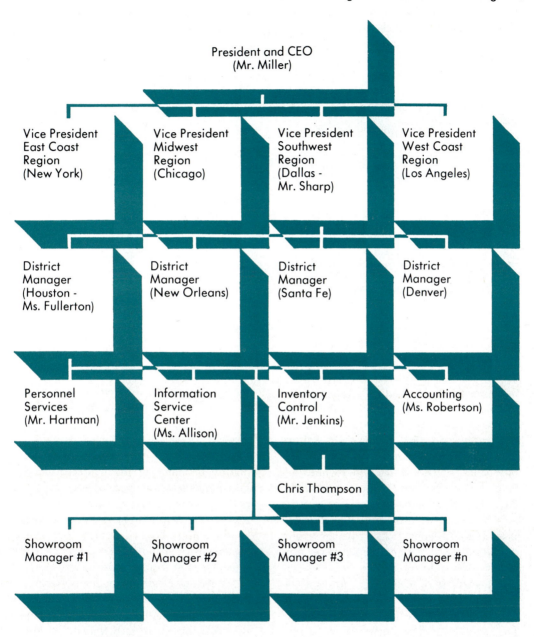

FIGURE 1.2

The internal organization of ACE, Incorporated, Southwest region, Houston district

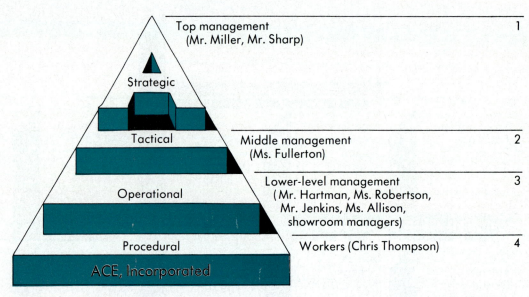

FIGURE 1.3
ACE management hierarchy; Southwest region, Houston

vice presidents; (2) **tactical management,** the district managers; and (3) **operational management,** local administrative staff and showroom managers. Below this level are the **procedural personnel** (workers)—the sales staff, warehouse stock personnel, office staff, and so on. Chris's job is at the "worker" level. Although workers are the lowest level in the company, the success of showroom managers, office managers, and the company in general depends on how well they do their jobs.

Regardless of which job you do, **decision making** is usually required to perform effectively. Everyone has to make decisions. The decisions may be far reaching, such as those often made by top executives, or they may have a limited effect. For example, Mr. Miller made the decision that ACE should be a public corporation. He, with the help of the vice presidents, decides when a new

showroom is to be opened or when to add new products, like computers, to the product line. In contrast, a sales clerk may be limited to deciding which customer to serve. Yet, all decision makers need information to make intelligent decisions. Mr. Miller needs to be aware of what the competition is doing and what new products are likely to be successful before increasing the product line. The sales clerk must know what a customer needs in order to perform satisfactory customer service.

When strategic management decides to sell a new product, that decision will affect the sales clerk. Although it may seem that the clerk has little influence on strategic management decisions, consider how strategic management might discover a possibly successful new product or a flaw in a current product: The sales clerk gives relevant product information to the showroom manager, who in turn passes this information—along with information provided by other sales clerks—to the district manager. The district manager collects and summarizes similar pieces of information from all showrooms and submits a report to the regional manager. Finally, the information, although greatly modified from its original form, reaches strategic management. If personnel at the lowest level are not interested in the success of the company and don't relay information—and if that same attitude is shared by coworkers—strategic management will ultimately have less information on which to base decisions. Furthermore, if decision making is not coordinated, the East Coast region might try to eliminate a product because it is having little success with it, while the West Coast region might be trying to acquire it. Decisions and decision-making processes must be shared.

By understanding decision making, one makes better decisions. You might say to yourself "I make decisions every day. Why do I need to know how to make a decision?" The real questions should be "Do I make decisions properly, do I make more good decisions than bad ones, and am I the person that should make the decisions?"

One poor decision could be fatal. For example, someone in the regional office makes a decision to decorate all of the Houston showrooms in a similar pattern—that is, using a theme of a field of five-pointed silver stars on a medium-blue background. It does not occur to anyone that these are the emblem and colors of the Dallas Cowboys. When sales decline sharply in the Houston showrooms (home of the Houston Oilers), the showrooms are closed. This example illustrates two bad decisions: to proceed with an inadequately researched decorating scheme and to close

the showrooms without proper analysis of all the factors contributing to the decline of sales. However, analyzing only the results of a decision doesn't always accomplish much. Decision making is more of a process than a single action.

The first step in the decision-making process is the identification of a problem (see Figure 1.4). In the preceding example, the problem is poor sales performance in the Houston showrooms. However, the decision maker should not jump to the conclusion that the problem has been identified *correctly*. In our example, the problem is showroom decoration, not products the customers don't want. In addition, the "problem" may not be as much an existing situation as the recognition of an opportunity. The "problem" could be when and if a new product should be introduced.

The second step in the decision-making process is the acquisition of information about the problem. After the information has been collected, one must analyze the information—step 3. This is done for two reasons: (1) to make sure the problem was identified correctly and (2) to provide the basis for identifying alternatives. If the problem has been inadequately defined or incorrectly identified, the process may return to step 1.

The fourth step is the creation of a list of **alternatives**—different ways to solve a problem. There is usually "more than one way to skin a cat," and there may be more than one reason for poor sales in the Houston showrooms. However, simply making a list of alternatives may in no way indicate which alternative is the best one. Thus, the fifth step is to collect information about each alternative and how, if implemented, it would affect the problem. For example, when one Houston sales clerk heard about the pending change of decor, he was heard

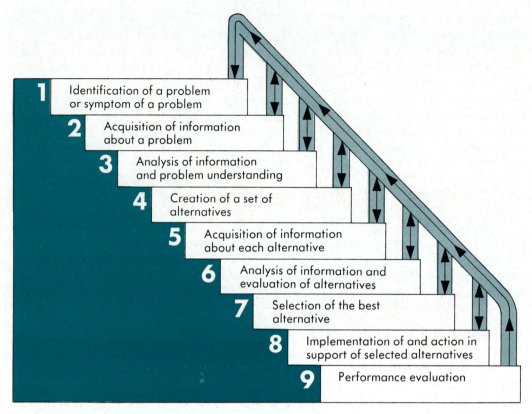

FIGURE 1.4
The nine steps of the decision-making process

to make a remark about the person in the regional office that made the decision. The remark was something like "The porch light is on, but I don't think anyone is home!" Thus, in this case, it doesn't appear that the people in the regional office collected sufficient information about decor alternatives —or maybe no information was gathered at all!

The sixth step is to analyze the information and evaluate each alternative so that the list of alternatives can be reduced. If no single alternative seems to be the best, step 5 may be repeated. If all alternatives are

rejected, the process may return to step 4. If all alternatives are rejected and no new alternatives can be established, the process may return to step 2.

Step 7 in the decision-making process is the selection of the "best" alternative. This may not be the most efficient or effective solution because the decision makers may not have had accurate and/or complete information about the alternatives (for example, information on the competitors' new projects). Also, the manager may use poor judgment in the evaluation of existing alternatives or even choose to do something that was not considered as an alternative. Thus, even under the best circumstances, not all decisions are "good" ones.

Once an alternative has been selected, it must be implemented—step 8. This requires management action in support of the decision. In the example, the decision is to modify the decor of the Houston showrooms, and the support action is an unscheduled sale to get customers back into the showrooms.

Finally, the ninth step is to measure and evaluate performances, which also requires the collection of information. Managers need to know the results of their decisions. Was the goal achieved? What went right? What went wrong? Can the decision-making process be improved? These are just a few of the questions to be asked when examining the **feedback**—timely reports of the results of a decision.

Levels of Management

Strategic Management As you have seen, **strategic management** represents the organization's top layer of management. The source of information for any level of management is a function of the level or position of the decision maker. Mr. Miller and other strategic managers receive a large portion of their information from external sources—that is, from outside the company (for example, information on competing electronics retail firms). This is called **external information.** In addition, the decisions they make are generally very broad and have a far-reaching impact on the company. Strategic managers set the long-range direction of the organization (for example, adding computers to the product line in place of increasing the list of portable radios). Finally, their decisions are geared toward the future (for example, opening offices in a new region on the basis of anticipated population growth).

Tactical Management The second, or middle, level of management is **tactical management.** Tactical managers can be identified by titles such as district director, general manager, or division supervisor. Tactical management reports to strategic management and is their most immediate source of **internal information**—information generated within the company. Tactical management decisions often represent adjustments of strategic management decisions to local situations. When Mr. Miller and the regional directors make the decision to open a new showroom, tactical management refines and implements the decision. For example, if a new showroom is to be added to the Houston district, Ms. Fullerton, the district manager for Houston, would collect information about customer buying patterns, city growth areas, and so on to determine the best location. Although some of their decisions are future oriented, tactical management is more concerned with the present. Tactical managers analyze historical information to determine the effectiveness of previous decisions (for themselves and subordinates) and to make current decisions.

Operational Management The lowest level of what a company normally considers to be management is **operational management.** This level is also called *line management,* and it carries titles such as supervisor, department manager, or office manager. The decisions at this level are more quantifiable (deal with numbers) than those made by tactical management and are relatively stable (highly structured). Furthermore, certain types of decisions are frequently repeated—such as when to order and how much of what (repetitive). Operational managers are often responsible for the immediate supervision and direction of workers. They are also the most immediate source of internal information for tactical management.

To better understand this management level, consider two functions of a showroom manager: inventory and ordering. One of the manager's responsibilities is to maintain an appropriate level of showroom inventory. For example, when the manager determines that the quantity of 19-inch black-and-white TV sets is low, more are ordered from the warehouse. This decision deals with numbers, and it is the type of decision that will be repeated frequently for this and other products. Also, this type of decision has a narrow range of impact (it affects only one showroom), and the results of the decision will be seen relatively quickly (the TV sets will arrive in a few hours or days).

Procedural Personnel   Workers, or **procedural personnel,** represent the last classification of employees within a company. This is where most people start, including Chris Thompson. Initially, these employees are not responsible for making wide-ranging decisions. Secretaries, sales clerks, warehouse workers, and so forth fall into this category. For the most part, workers carry out the decisions made by others and report directly to an operational manager. However, the fact that workers do not make wide-ranging decisions does not mean that they have no need for information. Their information needs will tend to be highly fixed, highly repetitive, and immediate.

The characteristics of each level of the management hierarchy of ACE have been briefly described. Table 1.1 gives more details about the types of decisions made and the information needed at each management level.

Functions of Management

Each management level performs the following four management functions in varying degrees:

- Planning
- Organizing
- Controlling
- Policy formulation

Planning   One of the elementary functions of management is **planning.** Organizational planning involves establishing objectives and the means to achieve them. It involves an assessment of both the present and the desired future positions of a company. Planning is one of the primary tasks performed by both strategic and tactical management. However, some basic planning does occur at the operational and procedural levels.

The decision to open a new showroom requires a significant amount of planning at all levels of the company. One aspect of planning is budgeting. Strategic managers must decide, based on the current budget, whether it is feasible to open a new showroom. If they decide to do so, they must consider the timing of the opening. For example, if they start planning to open the new showroom in March, they should be ready for business by the beginning of the Christmas buying season. The managers should also monitor the plan so that any midstream adjustments can be made. For example, if the electrical wiring was being installed in the new showroom and the electricians went on strike, could other construction activities be performed until wiring could resume?

TABLE 1.1 Dimensions of Decision Making by Hierarchical Level

Decision-making Parameter	Level of Personnel			
	Strategic	Tactical	Operational	Procedural
Orientation	Future	Past, present, and future	Past and present	Present
Impact of Decision	Extremely broad	Relatively broad	Relatively narrow	Extremely narrow
Decision Time Frame	Months and years	Weeks and months	Hours and days	Immediate
Type of Decision	Unstructured and nonrepetitive	Relatively unstructured and nonrepetitive	Relatively structured and repetitive	Completely structured and repetitive
Information Time Frame	Weeks and months	Days and weeks	Hours and days	Continuous
Source of Information	External and internal	Internal and external	Internal	Internal
Type of Information	Qualitative	Qualitative and quantitative	Quantitative	Quantitative
Form of Information	Abstract and summarized	Summarized	Detailed	Specific

Operational managers and procedural personnel are more involved in immediate planning than are strategic and tactical managers. For example, to meet the implementation schedule established by strategic management, the operational managers would have to develop a schedule for gathering information concerning a location for the new showroom. At the procedural level, a secretary would have to establish a daily plan for making contact with people at possible showroom sites to gather specific information (for example, square footage of building, lease terms, and so on). Thus, more specific, short-range plans would be developed by lower-level personnel, based on the more global, long-range plans of strategic management. Information gathering is only one activity associated with a new showroom opening that would require integrated planning among all levels of personnel within the organization.

Organizing Organizing requires the arrangement of company resources in support of a decision. In the preceding example, the decision is to open a new showroom. One of the functions of both strategic and tactical management is the organization of personnel, office space, funding, and so on associated with the new showroom. A number of organizing decisions would have to be made. Who is in charge? What is the chain of command, or who reports to whom? What additional personnel, physical space, funds, and so forth will be needed at the district level as a result of adding a showroom? The number of organizing decisions is seemingly endless. However, each of these organizing decisions is aimed at achieving a specific objective.

Controlling Once resources have been committed to a goal, it cannot be assumed that the goal will be achieved without supervision. Management must exercise **control** over the activities for which it is responsible. Strategic management may ask for a status report on the new showroom and measure progress toward the opening. Any additional directives issued by strategic management as a result of their assessment are usually control oriented. When tactical management asks for information regarding progress toward the completion of the showroom and makes decisions based on this information, these decisions are also control oriented. When a showroom manager consults with sales clerks concerning the progress of stocking TV sets, if the showroom manager instructs an employee to modify his or her activity in a particular way, these instructions are control oriented. Thus, management monitors and modifies the activities of subordinates by means of control.

Policy Formulation The establishment of rules and procedures to be followed by members of the organization is called **pol-**icy **formulation.** In the new showroom example, strategic management would have to establish a policy for passing information concerning the operation of the new showroom from the showroom to the district, to the region, and, finally, to corporate headquarters. This policy would identify the types of information needed by the district office, as well as the schedule for providing it. General work rules would be established by tactical management regarding length of work days, vacation schedules, discount purchases by employees, and so on. Finally, the showroom manager would establish policies regarding day-to-day operations of the showroom—for example, how to handle customer complaints, how to record individual sales, and who goes to lunch when. Policies are decisions that are made in anticipation of situations. They are guidelines established before an activity takes place.

The Nature of Data and Information

After lunch on the first day of work, Chris and the other new employees had to report to the **Information Center,** which had several connected microcomputers. Ms. Allison, the district director of computer services, explained that the facility was used for **user** training and development of user programs. This was just one of the computer facilities managed by Ms. Allison.

Although most of the new employees were unfamiliar with the computer equipment, in many jobs—including Chris's—using similar equipment would be an everyday occurrence. Because of the continued growth of ACE, there was no practical way for the company to do business without computers. There was just too much information to keep track of it by using only pencil, paper, and a filing cabinet.

Chris's first task on the computer was to complete a personnel form — something you may soon have to do. Ms. Allison instructed each employee on how to turn on the equipment and complete the necessary entries on a form that appeared on a TV-like screen. Then Ms. Allison demonstrated how the task was to be completed and told the employees how to turn off the machine. Chris later found out that all of the data entered on the forms was automatically collected and immediately transmitted to the district and regional computer centers. The next step would be to learn more about data and information and how to process them.

Characteristics of Data

Most management decisions are based on information. You might think that data and information are the same, but they aren't.

Data can be defined as unorganized facts and figures. These facts and figures do not, of themselves, convey information; they are the blocks with which information is built. Does the number 200 or the word *green* mean anything by itself? If you were told that 200 is the price of a TV set and green is the color of the company ID card, they would have meaning. Data is the raw material of information.

The entries that ACE's new employees made on their computer personnel forms became data that was transmitted to the company's main computer. Some of the data was obviously for payroll use. For example, data about Chris's dependents and health plan options is used by the payroll department to help determine paycheck deductions. Other data such as height, weight, brief medical history, telephone number, name and birth date of spouse and children is not needed to determine paycheck amounts but has a number of other uses. For instance, ACE's green employee identification cards — which are used to obtain discounts at any of the ACE showrooms — have a magnetic strip on the back that contains height, weight, and emergency medical data.

Data usually exists in a **data hierarchy** (see Figure 1.5). A **character** represents the lowest level in this hierarchy and means exactly what you think it means. A letter such as "A," or a digit such as "1," is a character. A **field** — also called a *data item* — is one character or two or more adjacent characters. The Social Security number, number of dependents, telephone number, and so forth on Chris's personnel form are fields. One field or two or more fields are combined into what is called a **record.** Chris's completed personnel form is a record. When related records are combined, the result is called a **file.** Data from Chris's personnel form is added to the data from the forms of all other employees to create a payroll file. Finally, a **database** is a collection of interrelated data — it may or may not be viewed as a collection of files. The data is cross-referenced to enable easy access and manipulation (databases will be discussed in detail in Chapter 7).

Characteristics of Information

Information was not mentioned anywhere in the data hierarchy. This is because **information** is the product or result of data manipulation. Common activities used to translate data into information include:

- **Classifying** — grouping like items together
- **Calculating** — performing mathematical operations

▶

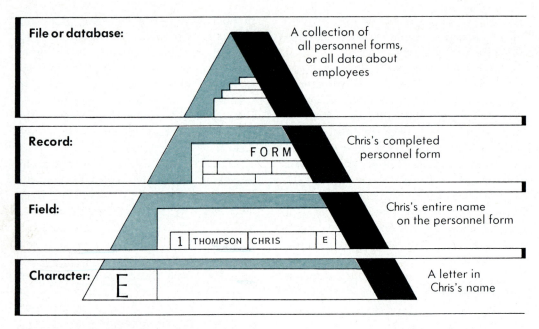

File or database: A collection of all personnel forms, or all data about employees

Record: Chris's completed personnel form

Field: Chris's entire name on the personnel form

Character: A letter in Chris's name

FIGURE 1.5
The data hierarchy

- **Summarizing**—reducing the amount of detail
- **Sorting**—arranging data in the desired order
- **Storing**—saving data for later use
- **Reporting**—producing the needed data

Information tells people something they didn't know before. The definition of information is linked to the structure of a company. What may be information at one level of the company—say, for a sales clerk—may be data at the next level—for a showroom manager. For example, when a sales clerk serves 50 customers in a day, that is information to the sales clerk but data to the showroom manager. The number of customers served by *all* the sales clerks is information to the showroom manager and data to the district manager. The performance of *all* the showrooms is information to the district manager, and so on up to the top of the company. Sometimes the distinction between data and information is subtle. In short, data must be manipulated in some way to become information.

Management Information Systems (MIS) and the Decision-making Process

Most large companies don't use a single computer system to manage information but, rather, a network of systems. A network of manual and computer-based systems is called a **management information**

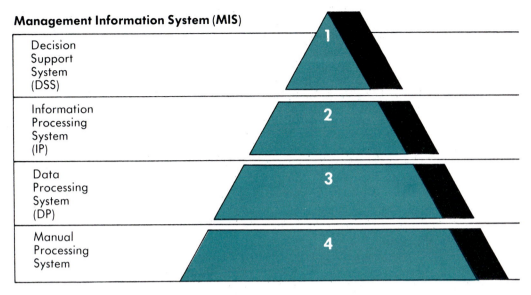

Management Information System (MIS)

Decision Support System (DSS)	1
Information Processing System (IP)	2
Data Processing System (DP)	3
Manual Processing System	4

FIGURE 1.6
Levels of information systems in a management information system (MIS), ranked from most sophisticated (top) to least sophisticated (bottom)

system, or **MIS.** Figure 1.6 shows that each processing system in the network has a particular level of performance sophistication, and all levels are used somewhere within the company. The real purpose of an MIS is to provide data and information to all levels of the company—management and workers.

Types of Systems in an MIS

The four main types of interdependent processing systems in a management information system are:

- Manual processing system
- Data processing system (DP)
- Information processing system (IP)
- Decision support system (DSS)

Manual Processing Systems   Many people assume that an information system must involve the use of computers; however, many historically successful systems have been based on manual methods of data manipulation. Until the early 1950s, all information systems were **manual processing systems.** These systems manipulate data without the use of a computer, and they are the least dependent on technology in general. Computers are not yet able to solve all types of problems. Indeed, some problems are much more easily solved by a human "processing" system. Manual processing systems are still being used, especially where computer access is limited.

Data Processing (DP) Systems   Also called **transaction processing systems, data processing systems** represent the first level of sophistication of systems that use a computer. DP systems first appeared in the late 1950s, with the advent of commercial computers. Data could now be manipulated — classified, calculated, and so on — much more quickly. In addition, the data storage capacity afforded by the computer became a very important consideration.

Under most circumstances, DP systems react rather than anticipate. When a transaction takes place — say, the sale of a TV set — the DP system reacts to that sale by performing the appropriate manipulations. As a consequence, DP system activities are generally governed by current events; however, at the same time, they maintain historical data. Furthermore, DP systems tend to manipulate internal data almost exclusively.

Data processing systems are clearly data based rather than information based. Any information that is produced is primarily a by-product of the DP activity.

Information Processing (IP) Systems As their name suggests, **information processing systems** produce information directly. The concept of IPs originated during the late 1960s; these systems are past, present, and future oriented. Although they rely heavily on internal data produced by DP systems, IP systems generally have the capability of anticipating at least some situations. For example, whereas a DP system might record the activity associated with the sale of a TV set, an IP system would forecast the future demand for this and other TV sets. Thus, this type of system can also use external data — for example, information about competitors or consumer buying habits — to refine forecasts.

Decision Support Systems (DSS)   Unlike most manual, DP, and IP systems, which involve more or less repetitive, predictable situations, **decision support systems** — introduced in the early 1970s — are oriented toward nonrepetitive, less predictable situations. They are sophisticated systems that provide a way of using information from all sources in new ways.

Strategic management must, from time to time, make one-time decisions — decisions that are not likely to be repeated in the foreseeable future. A decision of this type might be whether or not to introduce a new product. In this case, internal data may be of limited value; however, the use of external data is vital. And sometimes management must make a decision based on relatively little historical information. Furthermore, the decisions themselves may be unstructured or poorly structured — meaning the boundaries of the problem are somewhat "fuzzy." In such cases, the DSS often incorporates **decision models** — tools designed to approximate the decision-making environment and present hypothetical solutions to the problem and other recommendations. The DSS is capable of analyzing extremely complex management situations. In addition, these models may be able to modify the simulated environment in useful ways so the manager can keep track of or anticipate changes in the real business environment.

Decision models draw on information from all available sources, both within the company and outside. The DSS is highly sophisticated and requires the highest level of technology and skills of the managers who use them.

MIS and the Organizational Hierarchy

As you have seen, a company can be divided into at least four levels — strategic management, tactical management, operational

TABLE 1.2 Levels of Management and MIS Usage

Level of Management	Manual System	Data Processing System	Information Processing System	Decision Support System
Strategic	Limited use	Some use	Frequent use	High use
Tactical	Limited use	Frequent use	High use	Frequent use
Operational	Some use	High use	High use	Limited use
Procedural personnel	High use	High use	Limited use	No use

management, and procedural personnel. Furthermore, you have seen that the MIS can be divided into four levels—manual systems, DP systems, IP systems, and DSS. You're probably thinking "It's obvious that strategic management uses DSS, tactical management uses IP systems . . ." and so on. Although this may be true in a few cases, it is more likely that strategic management uses all levels of the MIS, as is shown in Table 1.2. Note that strategic management, tactical management, and operational management use all systems at some level, even though operational management might use DSS on a limited basis. Only procedural personnel have no access to DSS. The types of decisions they make generally don't require this level of sophistication. The primary user of DSS is strategic management. Tactical management uses information processing systems most. Operational management gets most of its support from data processing and information processing systems. Finally, procedural personnel get the greatest use from manual and data processing systems. You can see that each system

tends to be tailored more for a particular type of decision-making activity rather than for the company membership as a whole.

As Chris's first day of work drew to a close, Ms. Fullerton, the district manager, made a few closing remarks. She recounted many of the day's activities and reminded the new employees that they were an important, integral part of the company. Ms. Fullerton stressed that ACE was a rapidly growing company and that advancement to higher positions was limited only by the amount of dedication and initiative of the individual.

Each new challenge is coupled with a learning opportunity. As you read the following chapters, you will note that Chris is faced with several challenges, and you will be at Chris's side as new tools and techniques are learned to meet these challenges. View these challenges as learning opportunities, because you could find yourself in similar situations as you progress in your chosen field or profession.

Chapter Summary

This chapter introduced you to a business environment that has many of the same characteristics as most large organizations, regardless of the nature of the organization. As you have seen, the organization consists of identifiable personnel levels: strategic, tactical, operational, and procedural. The functions of management are planning, organizing, controlling, and policy formulation.

Different types of decisions are made at each level of the company hierarchy. Some decisions are future oriented, whereas others are concerned with past or present activity. Some decision-making processes require only internal data, while others use both internal and external data. Some decisions are mostly quantitative, whereas

others are primarily qualitative; some are structured, while others are rather ill-defined. Some decisions must be made immediately, whereas others are made over the course of months or years. Some decisions are very repetitive, while others are made only once. Finally, some decisions have an extremely broad impact, whereas others have a limited effect. There are nine basic steps in the decision-making process.

It is not surprising that a single business system cannot handle all of the aspects of the decision-making process. The MIS is a network of systems—manual, data processing, information processing, and decision support system—designed to make the decision-making process manageable. The sophistication of these systems depends on their level of computerization. All processing systems deal with data (unorganized, unrelated facts and figures) or information (the result of data processing).

Chapter Key Terms

Alternative
Calculating
Character
Classifying
Control(ling)
Data
Database
Data hierarchy
Data processing
   (DP) system
Decision making
Decision model
Decision support
   system (DSS)

External
   information
Feedback
Field
File
Information
Information Center
Information
   processing (IP)
   system
Internal
   information

Management
   information
   system (MIS)
Manual processing
   system
Operational
   management
Organizing
Planning
Policy formulation
Procedural
   personnel

Record
Reporting
Sorting
Storing
Strategic
   management
Summarizing
Tactical
   management
Transaction
   processing
   system
User (or end user)

Chapter Questions

1. Using your school as an organization, identify at least one position at each level of the organizational hierarchy. What types of decisions are made at each level? How are they different from one level to another?

2. Using a standard mailing label as an address record, identify all the data hierarchy characteristics that are associated with the data contained in the label.

3. Describe the difference between data and information. Give an example of a situation in which data for one individual would be information for another.

4. Describe the characteristics of the decision-making process. If your school were to open a new department, what types of decisions would have to be made? At what level do you think they would be made? What kinds of information would be needed?

5. Describe each of the systems that are part of an MIS. What is the primary characteristic of each of these systems?

6. How are the parts of an MIS related to one another and to the management hierarchy?

7. A manager is considering opening a new branch office. What level of management would most likely make this kind of decision? What are the characteristics of decisions made at this level? What kinds of information would be needed and where would the manager get the information? What other types of decisions would have to be made and at what level?

8. You are attempting to make a decision regarding entertainment for the evening (for example, whether to go to a movie). Assuming you are bored and wish to be entertained (step 1), list the remaining steps in the decision-making process, and describe how you would approach making a decision about an evening's entertainment relative to each of these steps.

9. You are about to enter the job market. First, identify the type of job in which you are interested. Then, identify the characteristics (type of company, location, and so on) of an organization having a job like the one you want. Why are these characteristics important to you?

10. Discuss what you know about computers and how they are used to solve problems. On the basis of your knowledge at this point, briefly describe the functions of word processing, spreadsheets, databases, graphics, and communications. (After you have completed the material in this text, check your answers to this question.)

SCENARIO 2

What's Going on at ACE?

Shortly after my first day at work, I happened to pass a computer store near the office. While I was looking at the window display, Ms. Allison, ACE's director of computer services, entered the store. I greeted her, and she explained that she was investigating microcomputers for her personal use at home as well as for ACE. In fact, she said I could expect to have a microcomputer on my desk in a couple of weeks. Since I didn't know much about the equipment, I decided to tag along and learn from an expert. ■

Chapter Two
The Anatomy of
Computer Hardware

Chapter Objectives

When you have completed this chapter, you will be able to:

- Outline the achievements that made microcomputers possible
- Identify the components of a computer system
- Describe the functions of the central processing unit and its association with internal memory

- Discuss common output devices and their characteristics
- Discuss common input devices and their characteristics
- Discuss the basics of the binary system
- Describe the types and uses of secondary storage devices

Historical Development of Computing Devices

The development of microcomputers began with the use of computing devices in general. One could go back as far as knots tied in strips of animal hide by prehistoric people or the abacus used by the ancient Chinese (although its invention is also claimed by the Italians and the Russians). As shown in Table 2.1, the development of modern computing devices began in the

1600s. Some of them have been refined— for example, an improved version of Pascal's adding machine is still used today. Computers came into existence in the late 1930s with the development of the first electromechanical computer—the MARK I. The MARK I used telephone relays to perform its computing and was stored in the basement of a building. At night, insects crawled into the basement and through the relays. The next morning, when the power was turned on and the relays closed, the insects would get caught. To get the com-

19

TABLE 2.1 The Historical Development of Computing Devices

Date	Person/Organization	Accomplishment
1642	Blaise Pascal (French)	Developed a mechanical adding and subtracting machine
1694	Gottfried Leibnitz (German)	Revised a mechanical adding machine to perform multiplication and division
1801	Joseph Jacquard (French)	Designed a weaving machine controlled by holes punched into cards
1822	Charles Babbage (English)	Developed the Analytical Engine to perform calculations based on instructions stored within the device
1843	Augusta Ada Byron (Lady Lovelace) (English)	Designed the first program for use by the Analytical Engine
1887	Herman Hollerith (American)	Developed tabulating machine using punched cards for U.S. Census Bureau (later formed a company that eventually became known as International Business Machines—IBM)
1911	James Powers (American)	Followed Hollerith at the Census Bureau and started a company eventually to be known as Sperry Univac
1937	Howard Aiken (American)	Developed electromechanical computer called the MARK I at Harvard University
1937	George Stibitz (American)	Developed electromechanical computer at the Bell Telephone Laboratories
1939	John Atanasoff and Clifford Berry (American)	Developed first electronic computer called the ABC (Atanasoff-Berry Computer); first computer to combine processor and memory storage devices
1944	John von Neumann (American)	Provided the ideas necessary to allow computers to store programs internally; also suggested use of the binary system for internal storage
1946	John Mauchly and J. Presper Eckert (American)	Developed the ENIAC—the first electronic digital computer—at the University of Pennsylvania, which was used to calculate ballistics tables for the U.S. Army during World War II
1949	Mauchly and Eckert (American)	Developed the EDVAC—the first stored-program computer

Date	Person/Organization	Accomplishment
1951	Mauchly and Eckert (American)	Developed the UNIVAC I — the first commercially used computer and the first to use the binary system; the first first-generation computer, all of which used vacuum tubes
1959	IBM Corporation	Developed the IBM 1401 — one of the second-generation computers, all of which used transistors
1964	IBM Corporation	Developed the IBM 360 — the first third-generation computer, which used miniature circuits
1969	M. E. Hoff, Jr. (American)	Developed the microprocessor — a computer on a chip — and formed the Intel Corporation
Early 1970s	—	Development of fourth-generation computers, characterized by the use of VLSI (very large scale integration) in circuit design
1974	Edward Roberts (American)	Developed the Altair 8800 — the first microcomputer — marketed through the MITS Corporation
1976	Tandy Corporation	Introduced the Radio Shack Model I microcomputer
1977	Apple Computer Corporation	Introduced their first microcomputer
1979	—	First 16-bit microcomputers available
1981	IBM Corporation	Entered the microcomputer market with the personal computer
1982	Motorola Corporation	16/32-bit microcomputers
1986	Intel Corporation Motorola Corporation National Semiconductor Texas Instruments	True 32-bit microcomputers and 256K RAM chips
What's next?	—	1 metabit RAM chips and fifth-generation, large computers

puter to work properly, someone would have to remove the insects—hence the term **debugging.**

The end of the 1930s and the 1940s saw major computer improvements. First, computers were all electronic, instead of electromechanical. Next, memory was added through the use of electromagnetic devices. Then computers were able to store instructions. With each improvement, computer speed increased and physical size decreased.

In 1951, the first computer for general use—the UNIVAC I—was produced, and it marked the beginning of what is called **computer generations.** The first generation of computers used vacuum tubes as their primary electronic component. The second generation used transistors; and the third generation used **miniature circuits (chips).** The forth generation simply shrank the size of the components by **VLSI** (very large scale integration) technology. The next generation has already been identified and will come into being with the birth of "thinking" computers that use **artificial intelligence.**

Microcomputers are the smallest computers. They use technology similar to that of **minicomputers**—medium-sized computers with greater storage capacity and speed—and **mainframes**—the largest and most powerful type of computer. Microcomputers were developed after the invention of the **microprocessor** by the Intel Corporation in 1969. (The *processor,* also called the *central processing unit,* is the internal hardware unit that basically runs the computer.) However, after Edward Roberts recognized that the microprocessor **chip** could be used to build a microcomputer, development activity became frantic. (A chip is a small—$\frac{1}{4}$-inch to less than $\frac{1}{8}$-inch square—piece of silicon that contains

hundreds of electronic components.) It seemed that everyone wanted to get in on the ground floor of this new technology, and by the late 1970s, as many as 300 companies were developing microcomputers or associated devices.

The first microcomputers were called *8-bit machines.* Essentially, they were capable of manipulating only a single, 8-bit character of data at a time. (A *bit* is a unit of internal storage and is discussed later.) However, by the late 1970s, the 16-bit micro came into being. If you double the amount of data that can be manipulated at one time, obviously you improve the speed with which a computer performs its activities. The next major achievement for microcomputers is the true 32-bit machine—the same internal size as most mainframe computers. The Apple MacIntosh and several other microcomputers already have some 32-bit capabilities. Although there are other characteristics of microcomputers, such as internal operating speed, that make them slower than mainframes, micros are quickly catching up to the technology used by their larger counterparts.

Microcomputer Hardware

A **computer system** is a collection of pieces of equipment, as illustrated in Figure 2.1. Each piece is designed to perform a particular function. The heart of the computer is the **central processing unit (CPU),** which manipulates data, and **internal memory,** which stores the data. These two components are sometimes referred to as the *computer;* however, other devices are necessary to make a computer usable. **Output** devices allow you to examine the results of the computer's activity. **Input** devices enable you to get data into the computer. **Storage de-**

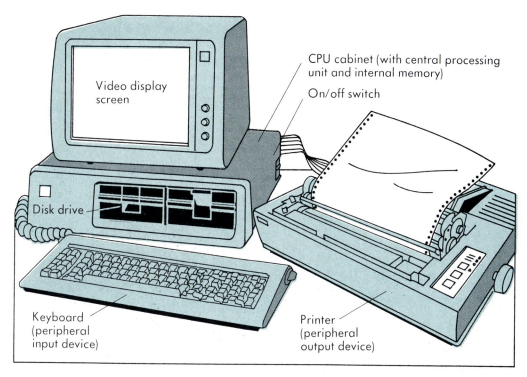

Video display screen

CPU cabinet (with central processing unit and internal memory)

On/off switch

Disk drive

Keyboard (peripheral input device)

Printer (peripheral output device)

FIGURE 2.1
A microcomputer system

vices give you the opportunity to save your work. Individually or collectively, all these devices (or pieces of equipment) are referred to as **hardware.** Output, input, and storage devices are also called **peripheral devices** because they are attached to the microcomputer by wires and are frequently located in an area adjacent to the microcomputer.

Processing Devices

Processing devices are usually thought of as the parts of a computer system that actually do the work. (We all know that you are the one who does the work. The computer is only a helper!) Processing devices can be said to have two parts—the central processing unit and internal memory.

Central Processing Unit (CPU)   The central processing unit controls the computer's activity and manipulates and communicates data. As shown in Figure 2.2, the CPU, sometimes called a *microprocessor*, can be divided into three parts, each performing a specific function. The **control unit** is responsible for controlling the activity of the computer itself. The **arithmetic unit** performs calculation functions. The **logic unit** is designed to make decisions based on data values (for example, is *A* greater than

Central Processing Unit Cabinet

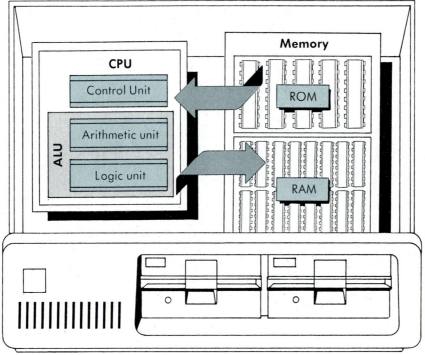

FIGURE 2.2
Inside the computer

B?). Sometimes the arithmetic and logic units are combined and are referred to as an **arithmetic/logic unit (ALU).**

Internal Memory   Also known as **internal storage** or **primary storage,** internal memory is usually in the same cabinet as the CPU. It is called *primary* because, unless instructed to do otherwise, the CPU uses only memory to save your results. It performs the functions of permanently retaining control information needed by the CPU or temporarily saving the work you are doing. Only the instructions and data in primary memory can be used directly by the CPU.

Most microcomputers use two different types of internal memory. **Read-only memory (ROM)** (see Figure 2.2) contains the control information needed to get the microcomputer started when you turn on the power. It may also be used to retain certain types of software (see Chapter 3 for an explanation of software). ROM is permanent; its contents are retained even when the power is off. The CPU is able to only read the contents of this memory—they cannot be changed by the CPU. The second type of memory is **random access memory (RAM).** RAM may also be called *user memory* because it is the part of memory you use most directly. This is where your work and most software are stored. Although it typically has a higher capacity than ROM, RAM is erased when the power is turned off. (However, there are some special types of RAM called *permanent memory* that use batteries or "bubble" memory to retain your work even when the power is turned off.) Thus, if you want to save your work for an indefinite period, you will normally need another type of storage device (as described in a later section).

Contents of Memory   Almost all computers are two-state devices because they function on the basis of electricity. For a computer, electrical current is either flowing or not flowing—two states: "on" and "off." While this is adequate for a computer, it presents some difficulty for humans. (Can you tell when electric current is flowing through a wire by looking at it?) To make it easier for humans to interpret what is in the computer's memory, a **binary numbering system** (base 2) is used. In this system, the binary digits (frequently referred to by the contraction **bits**) are 0 (off) and 1 (on). However, it is difficult to interpret data represented only by patterns of zeros and ones. Therefore, a coding structure was developed to make it easier for humans to interpret computer data. The most popular of these coding structures for microcomputers is called **ASCII (American Standard Code for Information Interchange).** ASCII (pronounced "as-key") uses groups of 8 bits (although 7-bit ASCII is also used) to represent characters as we know them. A group of 8 bits is a **byte,** which is essentially equivalent to an alphabetic character, a digit, or a special symbol. (The name sometimes attached to 4 bits is a "nibble." Thus, you have "bits," "nibbles," and "bytes"—whoever said that computer people don't have a sense of humor?)

Increments of internal storage (and disk storage, discussed later) are most frequently expressed in bytes. The most common of these expressions is in thousands of bytes, for which the symbol "K"—meaning *kilo*—is used to represent one thousand (actually 1,024). Thus, if you are using a computer with an internal storage capacity of 256K, this means that the equivalent of approximately 256,000 characters can be stored in RAM memory. Large microcomputers have an internal memory storage capacity of over one million bytes. This may be expressed as 1M, where the symbol "M"—meaning *mega*—is used to represent one million bytes (actually $K \times K$, or 1,048,576 bytes).

Output Devices

Once you have processed data, you will want to see at least part of the results. This is the primary function of output devices. They produce results in a humanly readable format.

Video Display Devices   There are many names for video display devices, including **video display terminal (VDT), cathode ray tube (CRT), display, screen,** and **monitor.** The new "flat screens" that are available on some microcomputers use plasma screen or **liquid crystal display (LCD)** technology. This is the same technology used for the display on digital watches. Regardless of the technology used, a video display device produces visual output on what is essentially a television-like screen. It is the most commonly used output device and is your most direct link with what the computer is doing.

Video display devices are typically capable of producing 24 lines of output, each containing up to 80 characters (although other capacities are not uncommon). It is

FIGURE 2.3
A sample of different printers: (top left) dot matrix (courtesy of Epson); (top right) daisy wheel (courtesy of Teletex); (bottom) laser (courtesy of Hewlett-Packard)

usually possible to access each character position on the screen through what is called **cursor addressing**. (A **cursor** is normally a blinking rectangle or underline that indicates the current character position on the screen.) Each character on the screen is composed of a number of illuminated dots, called **pixels** (for *picture elements*). Some video display devices permit **pixel addressing** (the ability to access a single picture element), which is frequently used to produce computer graphics. In addition, video display screens may be *monochrome* (one color) or *color* (meaning video output may be produced in a variety of colors). Monochrome screens may be black and white, green, amber, or other colors, but the screen will show only variations of the one color. Color screens may be *RGB* (red, green, blue color combinations) or *composite* (similar to a television).

Printers   The second most popular output device is the **printer,** which produces results on a piece of paper. As demonstrated in Figure 2.3, printers come in a variety of styles. The types of printers most frequently used with microcomputers are **dot matrix, daisy wheel** (letter quality), **ink jet,** and **laser** printers. Dot matrix printers produce characters as a series of dots, much like those produced on the video display screen. Daisy wheel printers produce fully formed characters, much like characters produced with a typewriter. (The term *daisy wheel* comes from the appearance of the printing element, which looks like a series of spokes of a wheel, with a character on each spoke. The spokes are petals, petals are on flowers, and hence the term *daisy*.) Dot matrix and daisy wheel printers are **impact printers** because the print element actually strikes the paper. Ink jet printers essentially spray dot patterns on the paper to produce different characters. Their biggest advantage is that they are much quieter and usually faster than either dot matrix or daisy wheel printers. Laser printers "burn" dot patterns on the paper much like a copying machine to produce different characters. Like the ink jet printers, laser printers are quieter than either dot matrix or daisy

wheel printers. Ink jet and laser printers are **nonimpact printers** because they do not strike the paper to print a character. Furthermore, dot matrix, ink jet, and laser printers can also produce color output.

All printers are **serial** or **parallel.** Serial printers receive one bit of data at a time. Parallel printers receive one character at a time. Thus, parallel printers are typically faster and simpler than serial printers. Printers are also **uni-** or **bidirectional.** Unidirectional printers print only left to right, whereas bidirectional printers print in both directions. Generally, bidirectional printers are faster than unidirectional models. Without reading the instructions that come with the printer it is impossible to tell whether it is a serial or parallel printer, or whether it prints unidirectionallly or bidirectionally. Finally, most printers are capable of producing a number of character **fonts.** (A *font* is a set of characters of the same size and shape.) Different fonts can be produced on dot matrix, ink jet, and laser printers by sending special signals to the printer or by using a special external switch. To change the font on a daisy wheel printer, you must change the printing element much like you would change the printing element of a typewriter.

Plotters   Graphics output often uses **plotters.** Although some printers are **dot addressable** (can produce a single dot, like a pixel, at a time) and can be used to produce graphics, plotters are specifically designed for this purpose. Essentially, a plotter "draws" the result rather than producing it as a series of dots. Thus, graphics produced by a plotter are generally superior to those produced by a printer. Plotters, as shown in Figure 2.4, come in two basic designs: *flatbed* and *drum*. On a flatbed plotter, the plotting paper is stationary and the drawing

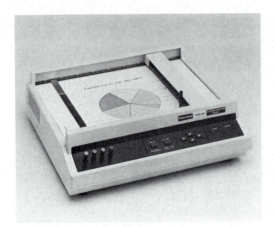 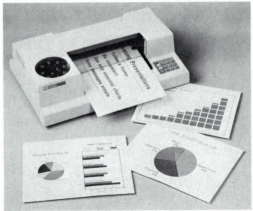

FIGURE 2.4
Plotters: (left) flat bed (courtesy of Radio Shack Division of Tandy Corporation); (right) drum (courtesy of Hewlett-Packard)

pens move. On a drum plotter, the pens move in one direction and the paper moves in the other direction (over a movable drum). Finally, plotters are frequently produced in *single-pen* and *multi-pen* versions. Multi-pen plotters are capable of producing multicolored graphics, changing pens automatically.

Input Devices

For the computer to do its work, you must have a way of communicating with it. Your communication with the computer will primarily consist of data (values to be manipulated) and instructions or commands. Among the devices used to enter data and instructions are keyboards, the mouse, light pens, voice recognition equipment, and bar code readers.

Keyboards The most popular means of communicating with the computer is the **keyboard.** As illustrated in Figure 2.5, it is arranged much like a typewriter in that the key positions of the central keyboard are in the same locations as on a typewriter. However, a number of additional keys appear on the computer keyboard. (The illustration shows the Keytronic 5151 and an IBM PC; if you are using a different computer, the keyboard arrangement may be different.) The easiest to recognize of these additional sets of keys is the **numeric key pad,** whose keys are arranged like a calculator's or a 10-key adding machine's. Although numeric (digit) keys appear across the top of the central part of the keyboard, the numeric key pad is easier to use for entering large amounts of numbers.

Most of the remaining keys on the keyboard are **control** keys that send special commands to the computer. (On some keyboards the numeric key pad keys also fulfill some control functions, which we will discuss later.) The most frequently used of these keys is the RETURN (or ENTER) key, which is the bent-arrow key on the IBM PC ⏎ . Some keyboards have both an

(a)

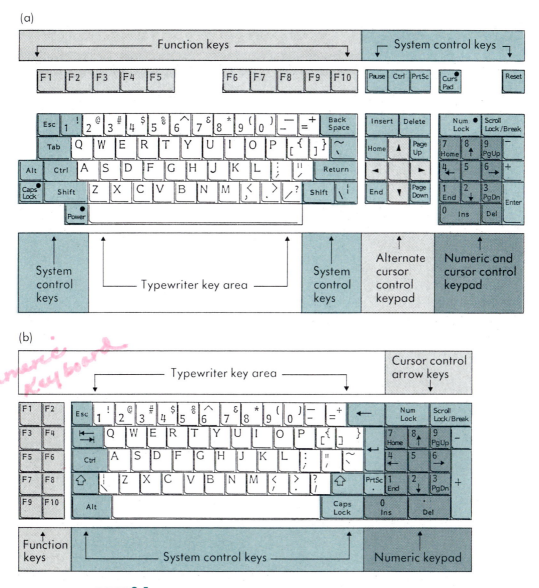

(b)

FIGURE 2.5
A computer keyboard: (a) Keytronic 5151; (b) IBM PC

ENTER and a RETURN key; the only difference is the location on the keyboard (both keys perform exactly the same function). The RETURN key, when pressed, transmits information to the computer. Be-

fore the RETURN key is pressed, entries you have typed using the keyboard can be corrected by using the BACKSPACE key (or the left-arrow key above the RETURN key, or the DELete and INSert keys located

 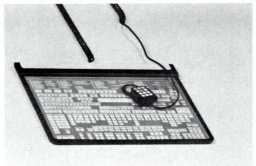

FIGURE 2.6
(left) The mouse (courtesy of the Microsoft Corporation); (right) advanced mouse and digitizing pad (courtesy of Intergraph Corporation)

at the bottom right corner of the IBM PC keyboard illustrated in Figure 2.5). The SHIFT key (or open up-arrow key on an IBM PC keyboard) serves the same purpose as on a typewriter. Other keys that surround the central part of the keyboard are ESCape, TAB ⇥ , CTRL (control), ALTernate, and CAPS LOCK (capital lock). ESC, CTRL, and ALT perform control-oriented functions, depending on the program being executed. TAB (the same as the tab key on a typewriter) and CAPS LOCK (like a shift lock on a typewriter) are used primarily for making the input operation a bit more convenient. Depending on the keyboard, the BREAK key and the PRINT (or PRTSC — print screen) keys may be adjacent to the central part of the keyboard. The BREAK key is used to interrupt the computer when it is performing a task. The PRINT key is used to produce a printed copy of the material that appears on the video display screen.

The numeric key pad keys also act as **cursor control keys,** used to manipulate the video display cursor. Depending on the

program in use, they can also be used for additional control operations. Finally, across the top or down the left side of the keyboard are **function keys.** The number and location of these keys vary from keyboard to keyboard, but their purpose is to perform specific functions as indicated by a particular program. Furthermore, because the keys are "programmable," you can change the functions assigned to individual keys. There is no such thing as a standard keyboard. In fact, some manufacturers make several different styles of keyboards for microcomputers.

The Mouse The **mouse,** a relatively recent innovation in input devices, is so called because the wire connecting it to the computer resembles a tail (see Figure 2.6). To move the cursor on the video display screen, the mouse is rolled around on a flat surface, like a desk top. Through this cursor movement, interpreted by a program, you can select functions for the computer to perform and otherwise manipulate data. Buttons on the mouse are used to indicate

LARGE COMPUTERS

① The Cray II is a "supercomputer" — a very large mainframe, which is the largest and most powerful type of computer.
② This Control Data Corporation (CDC) computer is a typical mainframe used by many large organizations. ③ The HP 3000 is a popular minicomputer and is considered typical in size. (The minicomputers are to the right of the video display terminals.)

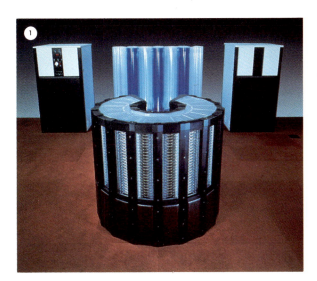

MICROCOMPUTERS

(4) The IBM PC (personal computer) is a "desktop" microcomputer, meaning that it is small enough to be used on the top of a desk. It is the standard by which other manufacturers label their machines as "PC compatible," which means that these machines can run most of the software produced for the IBM PC. (5) The TI PC (professional computer) is a PC compatible, not a "clone"; that is, it is compatible with the IBM PC, but it does not use exactly the same hardware and have the same hardware options as the IBM PC. (6) The Compaq has been a highly successful portable microcomputer and, although it looks different from the IBM PC on the outside, it is considered to be an IBM PC clone.

(7) The "lap top" microcomputer, so called because it can literally be used while on your lap, provides true portability. This photo shows an Epson lap top micro, an early model that used a cassette tape for data storage instead of a built-in disk drive as many current models do. Two peripheral devices are also shown: a printer and an external disk drive. Peripheral devices are attached to the lap top to produce printed output or to transfer data for storage. Most current lap tops are also PC clones.

INSIDE A MICROCOMPUTER

Chips are found almost everywhere today — not only in computers but also in telephones, airplanes, automobiles, microwave ovens, video games, and so on. A chip is a square of purified sand — silicon — that holds several layers of integrated electrical circuitry, depending on the complexity of design.
⑧ This integrated circuit chip schematic diagram was produced on a drum plotter, an output device that produces the chip image on paper and in color (see also photo ⑳).
⑨ Hundreds of microcomputer chips can be produced on a single silicon disk called a *wafer*. A wafer is only 4/1,000 of an inch thick. Wafers are sliced from silicon ingots two feet long and six inches in diameter that are produced in the purest form possible in the laboratory. ⑩ A single microprocessor chip is very small, often less than ¼ inch square. It controls and defines all the computer's activities, including input and output. Different types of chips are designed to fulfill different functions. For example, interface chips translate incoming signals, such as pressure on a keyboard key; ROM chips store instructions for the microprocessor chip to read. ⑪ A selection of chips can be assembled on a "board," or "card," such as this RAM expansion card, which "expands" the amount of random access memory in a computer.

PRODUCING RESULTS ON A DISPLAY SCREEN

⑫ Current monochrome (single-color) video display screens come in a variety of hues — for example, green and black, as shown here. Other varieties are black and white and amber and black. ⑬ Newer video display screens have enhanced pixel resolution, meaning that the number of <u>pic</u>ture <u>el</u>ements used to make up computer images have been increased, thereby producing a clearer image. These display screens are capable of producing a variety of colors. ⑭ Most lap top computers, including this Kaypro 2000, use LCD (<u>l</u>iquid <u>c</u>rystal <u>d</u>isplay) screens to conserve space and reduce power consumption. In LCD, a chemical (liquid crystal) is held between two pieces of clear glass. Light reflects off the bottom piece to show the shape of electrically charged liquid crystal molecules. The shape is changed by altering the electrical charge pattern. ⑮ The plasma screen — which uses gases that glow when electrically charged — will likely become the standard display screen of the future and may even replace the standard television screen of today. Both LCD screens and plasma screens are flat panel screens, meaning that they do not have the physical depth or the curvature of CRT (cathode ray tube) screens.

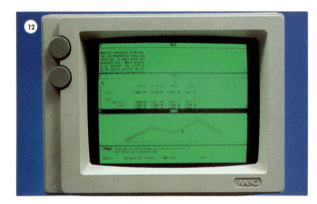

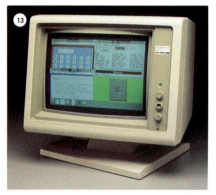

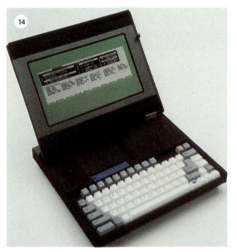

(16) Some of the more versatile printers are capable of producing a variety of fonts (character styles and sizes) and symbols by using special programs such as "Fancy Font."

(17) Some ink jet printers are capable of pro-ducing output in a variety of colors — a characteristic shared with newer dot matrix and laser printers. Earlier model printers produced output only in black and white.

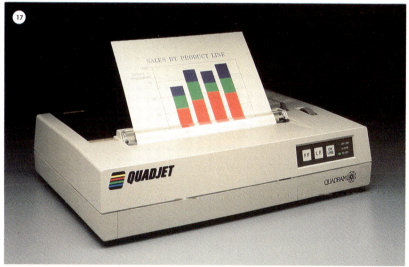

PRODUCING GRAPHIC RESULTS

(18) In a flatbed plotter, the paper is placed flat on the base of the machine. This multi-pen flatbed plotter is capable of producing several charts on the same page. Note the line of different colored pens on the far left side. (19) A digitizing graphics tablet and stylus can be used to enter graphic data into a computer. This method gives particular input flexibility to artists, engineers, and designers. Images can be drawn freehand on the tablet, which has an underlying grid of wires through which electrical pulses are transmitted to the stylus and then to the computer, or they can be traced. (20) In a drum plotter, paper is stretched across a drumlike mechanism. A combination of pen and paper movement is used to create charts. The pens are colored — as many as eight pens are used — and are positioned according to instructions from the computer.

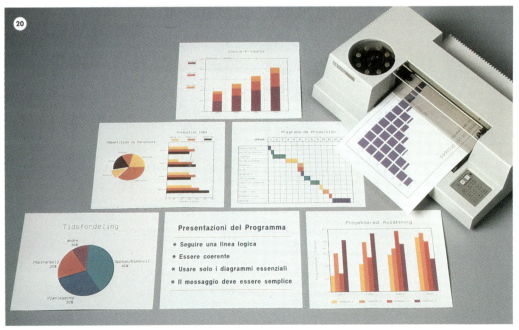

STORING RESULTS

(21) Although internal 5¼-inch disk drives remain the most popular, the HP Portable uses an external 3½-inch floppy disk drive.

(22) Hard disk drives (such as these 5¼-inch devices) often use no more space than 5¼-inch floppy disks but can store tens of millions of characters.

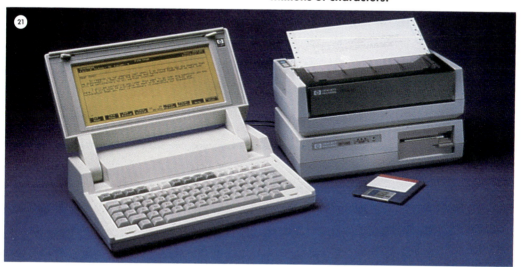

MICROCOMPUTERS AT WORK

(23) The HP Portable and other lap top micro-computers contain their own battery power supply and can be used away from the office. (24) The modern office frequently uses a variety of machines, sometimes interconnected, to get the job done.

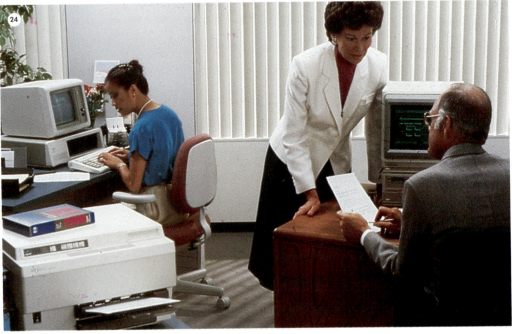

selections. **Game paddles, joy sticks,** and **roller balls** perform similar functions.

Light Pens   **Light pens,** which have been around for a while, are used to move the cursor around on the video screen or to draw a line. The tip of a light-reading pen placed on the sensitized screen surface closes a photoelectric circuit and allows the computer to identify the point. **Touch screens,** which have a grid of photoelectric cells, allow you to do the same thing using your finger instead of a pen. **Graphics tablets** are somewhat similar, but they use a grid on a flat surface rather than on the video screen.

Voice Recognition Equipment **Voice recognition equipment** allows people to talk to computers. By using a microphone that converts the human voice into electronic signals, one can tell the computer what to do. These input devices currently operate with a limited vocabulary— frequently less than one hundred words. However, in the future you will be able to speak directly to your computer in English language phrases, and the computer will respond. Conversely, **voice output devices** —a type of voice synthesizer—are already in use by the telephone company for directory assistance and by vending machines, allowing the computer to speak to you.

Bar Code Readers   To interpret the bar codes, called *universal product codes,* found on almost every consumer product, one needs a **bar code reader.** These devices transmit the value of the bar code to the computer and are frequently used to track inventory, whether at the warehouse or at the check-out counter at your local retail or grocery store.

Storage Devices

Not all data processed by the computer is entered from an input device or produced on an output device. Much of the data is available through the use of **storage devices** (sometimes called *secondary storage*) including disk and tape drives. Although tape drives (such as cassette recorders) have been used with microcomputers, most of today's microcomputer systems use disk drives. Whether the data is stored on tape or diskettes (the two most popular forms of magnetic storage media), it may be retrieved at a future time. Furthermore, data recorded on magnetic media is not lost when the power to the computer is turned off. However, just like your favorite musical performance recorded on cassette tape, data recorded on magnetic material can be erased or replaced. The computer places new data over the old data.

Floppy Disk(ette)s   The most popular secondary storage medium is the **floppy disk.** The floppy disk is so called because it is made of **flexible material.** There are many differences in disks including *size* (for example, 8 inch, $5\frac{1}{4}$ inch, and sub-4 inch, called *microfloppies*), *density* (data-recording capacity), and *single-sided* versus *dual-sided*. The higher the density and number of sides used (one or two), the more data a disk can hold; however, a disk may be less reliable because of the higher quality required.

Despite these differences, disks share many similarities. As shown in Figure 2.7, the floppy disk is covered by a protective jacket. An adhesive *external label* is normally attached to the jacket on which you (the user) can write the contents of the disk (use a felt-tip pen only). A **write-protect notch** safeguards the contents of the disk from

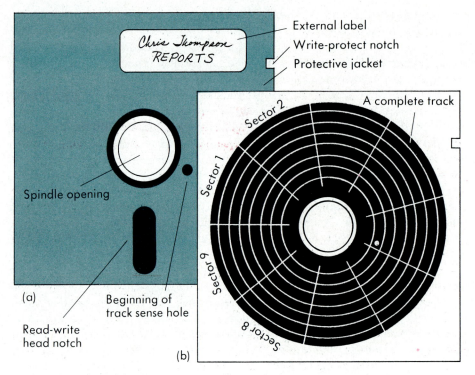

External label
Write-protect notch
Protective jacket

Chris Thompson
REPORTS

Spindle opening

Sector 2
Sector 1
A complete track
Sector 9
Sector 8

(a)

Beginning of
track sense hole

Read-write
head notch

(b)

FIGURE 2.7
**The floppy disk: (a) external view; (b)
internal view (recording surface)**

accidental erasure. (Some disk drives assume that the disk is write-protected—that
is, it can't be altered—if the notch is open.
Others assume the disk is protected if the
notch is covered.) A *beginning of* **track sense
hole** is cut in the jacket so that the disk drive
can determine where the tracks begin
(more on tracks later). A large notch cut in
the jacket, the **read-write head notch,**
allows the disk drive to read data from the
disk and write data on it. The circle cut out
of the middle of the jacket is the *spindle
opening.* When the disk is inserted into the
disk drive, the drive spindle shaft is inserted
into this opening, causing the disk to rotate
inside the jacket. Do not mistreat floppy

disks! Bending or folding the disk, touching
the recording surface with your fingers,
and getting dust on the recording surface
can damage the disk, making it unusable.

The recording surface of a floppy disk
is composed of a magnetic material much
like that used for recording or VCR tapes.
The disk surface is divided into concentric
rings called **tracks,** which are "read" or
"written on" by the computer's read-write
head as the disk rotates (see Figure 2.7b). As
the read-write head moves back and forth,
various tracks can be accessed. The tracks
are divided into **sectors.** When reading or
writing activity occurs, this is normally performed one sector at a time. The computer

"sends" the read-write head to the appropriate track and sector numbers — the sector "address."

To determine the capacity of a disk, you must know three things: (1) the number of tracks per side (an IBM PC disk drive allows 40 tracks per side); (2) the number of sectors in a track (for an IBM PC, each track is divided into 9 sectors); and (3) the number of bytes (characters) that a sector can hold (for an IBM PC, each sector can hold 512 bytes). Then, you simply multiply the numbers to determine the capacity of the disk. (For an IBM PC, this would be $40 \times 9 \times 512 = 184,320$ bytes for a single-sided disk; twice that amount for a double-sided disk.) This is how much data can be placed on a disk. (Over 210 double-spaced typed pages of text could be stored on one double-sided, dual-density, $5\frac{1}{4}$-inch disk.)

Hard Disk Drives   Although a floppy disk can hold a lot of data, many computer users find its capacity limiting. For example, suppose you wanted to store 200 characters of data for each of 4,000 inventory items. This would require 800,000 bytes of disk storage — more than will fit on one disk. To solve this problem, manufacturers have developed **hard disk drives.** (These devices are sometimes called *Winchester* drives, after the company that conceived the idea.) The recording medium (disk) is often rigid rather than "floppy." Also, the disk is frequently *nonremovable*, whereas floppy disks are easily removed from the disk drive. By placing the recording media in a sealed, protected environment, hard disk drives increase data storage capacity dramatically because of increased density, while minimizing the physical space required for the drive. Capacities of 5, 10, 20, and 40 million characters are not uncommon; some hard disks for microcomputers have capacities in

excess of 160 million characters. The area to the right of the disk drive shown in Figure 2.1 is large enough to hold a hard disk drive.

Hard disk systems are used because of the large amounts of data that they can hold. To protect this data from being lost or damaged, most hard disk systems use **tape streamers** to make **backups** (copies) of the data. A tape streamer, which looks something like a cassette tape player/recorder, is capable of quickly copying the data on a hard disk onto magnetic tape. A newer technology called the *Bernoulli Box* is replacing the combination of hard disks and the tape streamer backup. The Bernoulli Box is actually a nonremovable hard disk and a removable hard disk that can be used for backup or as an additional disk drive. Some microcomputer systems are even capable of using video disks or laser disks for high-density storage of data. However, this technology for microcomputers is still relatively new and very expensive.

Chapter Summary

In this chapter, you have seen how the developments in large computers led the way to the invention of the microcomputer. A microcomputer is a computer system comprising a central processing unit, memory, output devices, input devices, and secondary storage devices. Each of these devices performs an essential task in the computer system.

The central processing unit (CPU), which runs the computer, is made up of a control unit, an arithmetic unit, and a logic unit. In some computers, all three units may be in one piece (chip); in others, they can be two or even three separate chips. The CPU works with the internal memory, which usually comprises read-only memory (ROM) and random access memory (RAM). In general, ROM contains the control information, cannot be altered, and is permanent; RAM contains most of the programs (see Chapter 3), can be "written" on, and is temporary (work done may be lost if the power is turned off).

Common output devices, which give the computer user readable results, are CRTs, printers, and plotters. CRTs show results on a TV-like screen, printers give results "typed" on paper, and plotters draw graphics created on the computer. There

are four main types of printers: dot matrix, daisy wheel (letter quality), ink jet, and laser. Common input devices, which allow the user to communicate with the computer, are keyboards, the mouse, light pens, voice recognition equipment, and bar code readers.

Devices frequently used for secondary storage of data include floppy disks, hard disks, magnetic tape streamers, and the Bernoulli Box. Floppy disks have protective jackets, within which magnetic disks rotate; the data is recorded on and retrieved from track and sector addresses.

Chapter Key Terms

American Standard Code for Information Interchange (ASCII)	Control key	Laser printer	Read-only memory (ROM)
	Control unit	Light pen	
	Cursor	Liquid crystal display (LCD)	Read-write head notch
Arithmetic/logic unit (ALU)	Cursor addressing	Logic unit	Roller ball
	Cursor control key	Mainframe	Screen
Arithmetic unit	Daisy wheel printer	Microcomputer	Sector
Artificial intelligence	Debugging	Microprocessor	Serial
	Display	Miniature circuit	Storage device
Backup	Dot-addressable printer	Minicomputer	Tape streamer
Bar code reader	Dot matrix printer	Monitor	Timing hole
Bidirectional printer	Floppy disk(ette)	Mouse	Touch screen
	Font	Nonimpact printer	Track
Binary numbering system	Function key	Numeric key pad	Track sense hole
	Game paddle	Output device	Unidirectional printer
Bit	Graphics tablet	Parallel	
Byte	Hard disk drive	Peripheral device	Very large scale integration (VLSI)
Cathode ray tube (CRT)	Hardware	Pixel	
	Impact printer	Plotter	
Central processing unit (CPU)	Ink jet printer	Primary storage	Video display terminal (VDT)
	Input device	Printer	
Chip	Internal memory	Processing device	Voice output device
Computer generation	Internal storage	Random access memory (RAM)	Voice recognition equipment
	Joy stick		
Computer system	Keyboard		Write-protect notch

Chapter Questions

1. What characteristics do microcomputers and mainframes share?
2. What is ROM and how is it used by a microcomputer? What is RAM and how is it used?
3. Examine a computer system at your school. What output devices are attached to the microcomputer? What input devices?
4. What are the characteristics of the floppy disk drives (and disks) used by the computer at your school? A certain business has 300 employees; 500 characters of payroll data are to be retained for each employee. Determine the size of the payroll file. Can this be stored on a floppy disk?
5. Discuss purchasing a microcomputer for your private use. What hardware characteristics would be important to you and why? Don't forget peripheral devices.
6. How much would the microcomputer system in question 5 cost? Base you answer on ads found in computer magazines or newspapers, or on a visit to your local microcomputer store.
7. Which of the input devices discussed in this chapter would you expect to find at your school? Why? Which ones would you expect to find at the local game arcade? At a retail store (such as a grocery store)?
8. Where would each of the output devices discussed be used? Why?
9. For what tasks would you use each secondary storage device discussed in this chapter? When would you choose to use one device over the others?
10. Microcomputers have often been called "personal computers." Discuss whether or not you think this name is appropriate.

SCENARIO 3

What's Going on at ACE?

One morning at work I unexpectedly ran into an old friend—Fred Martin. During a brief conversation, I discovered that Fred had been hired a year ago and was working in the Software Development Group. Since I didn't understand much about this department, I asked Fred to join me during a coffee break and tell me about his job.

Fred explained that computer hardware cannot work alone—without software, hardware is just an expensive collection of silicon and wires. Software is the instruction set that tells the hardware what to do. Put another way, a computer program is a piece of software.

Chapter Three
The Nature of Computer Software

Chapter Objectives

When you have completed this chapter, you will be able to:

- Describe the three major types of software used on computers: system software, developmental software (programming languages), and applications software

- Explain basic software concepts
- Describe the differences among programming languages

Historical Development

Starting with the abacus, **software** was being developed along with calculating and computing equipment. During the early years, software was the set of procedures or instructions followed by the individual using a machine. [As advances were made in the design of these machines, more of the instruction processing was shifted from the individual (user) to the machine.] However, no major advances were made in software until 1801, when Joseph Jacquard transformed some of the instructions for a weaving loom into punched holes in paper cards.

Jacquard's punched cards were the first example of instructions put on a medium (or device) usable by a machine; by changing the program, one could change what the machine did. The principles behind the punched cards were used by Augusta Ada Byron, Countess of Lovelace, in the early 1840s to code the instructions for Charles Babbage's Analytical Engine, which was capable of doing certain types of mathematical computations. Lady Lovelace has since become known as the world's first programmer, and the codes she developed have been called the first software.

No further advances were made in software development until John von Neumann published his paper detailing the theory needed for the **stored-program concept.** The idea was to store instructions in the machine and change those instructions directly rather than write a new set each time the desired function changed. As the stored-program concept became better understood, and as computer hardware improved, modern software evolved.

Why Know About Software?

You may never write a computer program. Nevertheless, you should have an understanding of computer software. Software, after all, is the way to make the computer work for you. It is very likely that you will have to select certain types of software for your personal use, your use within an organization, or use by yourself and others within an organization. Furthermore, in some jobs you may have to help *design* software. Thus, the more you know about software, the better prepared you will be.

Making Decisions About Software

You have probably already been affected by computers in some way. Eventually you can expect to deal directly with a computer or with a person who uses a computer to make decisions that directly affect you. Although hardware decisions are usually made by computer specialists, software decisions involve both the people using the computer directly and those making decisions based on the information provided by the computer.

Helping to Design Software

Systems analysts, or **software engineers,** create software that will meet your needs. Although there are lots of programs available that perform specific tasks, they may not be able to solve the particular problem you need help with. Someone must design, develop, and implement a program for you. However, you will have to be involved in the design not only to ensure that the program does what it is supposed to do but also to ensure that it is easy for you to use and understand.

To accomplish these goals, you need to be familiar with the types of software available. Furthermore, you need to understand the functions of the various kinds of software, as well as their strengths and weaknesses.

Types of Software

This chapter has already used several terms in referring to software: **program, instructions,** and **code.** Several other names may also be used, including **language, package,** and **application.** All these terms refer to the same concept: a set of instructions used to make the computer perform a specific task. Although these terms may be interpreted somewhat differently, the name *software* covers all of them. Software can be divided into three groups, which will be discussed in this chapter: **system software, developmental software** (programming languages), and **applications software (packages).**

Software is also grouped by level. The first, or lowest, level language is the one used by the computer itself and is the farthest away from human language: **machine language,** the *first-generation computer language.* Because the computer is an electrical device, it receives instructions as a series of electrical signals or impulses. A set of signals that the computer can understand is called *machine-level instruction.* The computer can work on only one instruction at a time; therefore, the instructions are usually entered into the computer in the order they are to be used.

Because machine language is so difficult and tedious to work with, other languages have been developed using machine language as a foundation. Each of the higher-level languages builds on a lower level to make the language easier to understand. Although **high-level languages** are easier for people to work with, they have to be translated into equivalent machine-level instructions for the computer (more on this in the section on developmental software, or programming languages).

System Software

System software runs the computer; applications software and programming languages cannot be used without it. Sometimes these programs are on disk, but some newer computers may have all or part of the system software built in and stored in ROM. This is called **firmware.**

Control Programs   Control programs make sure all the parts of the computer are working together; they are frequently included in the computer's firmware. These programs do such tasks as: (1) checking the disk drive to make sure it is turning at the correct speed, (2) checking the other internal hardware components to make sure they are working correctly, and (3) checking

the computer's **clock** to mark the beginning and end of a **machine cycle** — the speed at which a computer performs a single operation. Microcomputer clocks usually operate at speeds of 2 to 12 million cycles per second (2 to 12 **megahertz**).

The control programs in a computer are usually collectively called the **supervisor.** These programs are stored in machine language form and are used by the computer operating system software to control the computer.

Operating System Software   The collection of programs used by the computer to run the supervisor and control the flow of other programs and data is called **operating system software** (see Figure 3.1). The operating system integrates the computer hardware with other software. It reduces the amount of user action required to perform specific tasks on the machine and allows the user to concentrate on the task to be performed rather than on the internal workings of the computer. Chapter 4 discusses operating systems in more detail.

Job Control Language   The fundamental language used to run the operating system is the **job control language.** Job control languages are different for each computer. For example, IBM calls its "JCL," whereas Hewlett-Packard uses "MPE" for its job control language. On large computers, job control languages are separate from the operating system; on most microcomputers, they are a part of the operating system. This combination makes the microcomputer easier to use.

Assembly Language   The language frequently used to develop operating systems is **assembly language.** Because program-

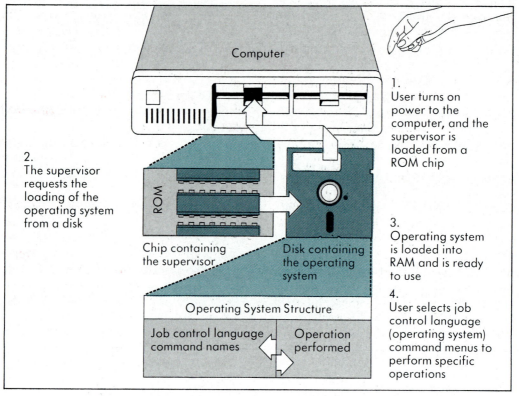

FIGURE 3.1
How system software works

ming in machine language is so difficult and easily subject to human error, **symbolic codes** were devised to represent machine language instructions. The codes of assembly language remind the programmer of what the instruction does, thus they are sometimes called **mnemonics.** Because assembly language is frequently used for operating system development and because it can also be used for other applications, it represents a bridge between system software and developmental software (programming languages) and may be referred to as a *second-generation language.*

Although assembly programs run faster than programs written in higher-level languages, assembly languages are **machine dependent;** that is, a program written for one type of computer will not run on another type. Figure 3.2 shows, in both machine language and assembly language, part of a program that accepts the prices of three purchased items, adds them together, calculates the sales tax (5%), adds the sales tax to the previous total, and produces a new total. (Figures 3.2–3.9 use the same example so you can see the similarities and differences among computer languages.)

Machine Language	Assembly Language
11100101 00000101	IN AH,5
11000101 00000101	IN AL,5
10000001 01100001 01000001	ADC AL,AH
11100101 00000101	IN AH,5
10000001 01100001 01000001	ADC AL,AH
11110111 01100001 00001101	IMUL AL,'1.05'
11000111 00000110	OUT AL,4
11110100	HLT

FIGURE 3.2
Machine and assembly language program examples (input and output operations deleted)

Developmental Software (Programming Languages)

Humans have a great deal of difficulty communicating with a computer in machine language, and computers cannot yet speak a human language, so several "intermediate" languages have been developed to allow humans to "converse" more easily with computers. These intermediate languages are called **developmental languages** because they are used to develop specific computer programs that apply to particular problem-solving situations (for example, developing an inventory program for ACE's main TV storerooms). In other words, these are the languages most frequently associated with the term computer **programming.** Because they use more easily recognized symbols, **programming languages** are easier to use than assembly languages. Programming languages, also known as **procedural languages,** represent a substantial improvement over assembly language—therefore, they are sometimes referred to as *third-generation languages.*

Each language has its own structure and set of rules. Instructions written in a particular language must follow those rules. In any computer language, a typical program statement or instruction is made up of two parts: an **operation code (op code)** and **operands.** The op code, sometimes called a **reserved word,** tells the computer what operation to perform (for example, add, subtract, multiply, divide). The operands tell the computer what data to use when performing the operation.

Some computers and computer languages (particularly assembly languages) may use many different operation codes in their instruction set. Although this may lead to some confusion, op codes consist of four general command types:

1. **Input-output:** reading or writing data
2. **Arithmetic:** using data in a calculation
3. **Branching:** going from one place in a program to another
4. **Logic:** making decisions based on data

The developmental languages used by a programmer will generally depend on the type of application being implemented. Because developmental languages were created with particular types of tasks in mind, they each have specific strengths that pro-

```
REAL ITEM1, ITEM2, ITEM3, TOTAL
READ* ,ITEM1, ITEM2, ITEM3
TOTAL = (ITEM1+ITEM2+ITEM3)*1.05
PRINT* '(1X,10X,F5.2)','TOTAL BILL =',TOTAL
STOP
END
```

FIGURE 3.3
FORTRAN language program example

grammers use to solve specific problems. Some popular programming, or developmental, languages are presented in the following sections.

FORTRAN (FORmula TRANslator) Developed in the mid-1950s, FORTRAN is the oldest of the high-level languages. Originally designed to meet the needs of engineers, mathematicians, and scientists, it is based on rules similar to those used to form expressions in algebra. Although FORTRAN can easily and quickly handle complex mathematical problems in **scientific applications,** it is not well suited for the large-scale input-output operations and data file manipulation common to **business applications.** Figure 3.3 shows the FORTRAN solution to the problem introduced in Figure 3.2.

COBOL (COmmon Business Oriented Language)   In the late 1950s, a group of people from private industry and the federal government met to devise a language that could process alphabetic as well as numeric data: COBOL (see Figure 3.4). This language was created to satisfy normal business application requirements. COBOL is relatively easy to understand because its commands are written like English-like statements. However, because of the rules and structure of the language, it is not one of the easiest languages to learn or use.

PL/I (Programming Language I) PL/I (see Figure 3.5) was designed for both scientific and business users. Although the language achieved some early success, it has the disadvantage of being very complex and difficult to use.

BASIC (Beginner's All-purpose Symbolic Instruction Code)   BASIC (see Figure 3.6) was originally developed at Dartmouth College as a high-level **interactive** language for instructional purposes, meaning that the language facilitated communication between computer and user. Because BASIC was designed to work in an environment where data can be easily and quickly entered into and retrieved from the computer, it became very popular, not only in education but also in industry. BASIC is also very flexible and is easy to learn. There are now over 128 different "dialects" or versions of BASIC; however, they are all fundamentally the same.

Pascal   Named after the French scientist and developed during the years 1968 through 1971, Pascal (see Figure 3.7) was

```
PROCEDURE DIVISION.
MAIN-PARAGRAPH.
    PERFORM 100-OPEN-FILES.
    PERFORM 200-READ-RECORD.
    PERFORM 300-CALC-NEW-TOTAL.
    PERFORM 400-PRINT-OUT.
    PERFORM 500-EXIT.
    STOP RUN.
100-OPEN-FILES.
    OPEN INPUT ITEM-FILE OUTPUT SALE-FILE.
200-READ-RECORD.
    READ ITEM-FILE AT END MOVE 'DONE' TO FILE-STATUS.
300-CALC-NEW-TOTAL.
    COMPUTE NET-PRICE = ITEM1 + ITEM2 + ITEM3.
    MULTIPLY NET-PRICE BY 1.05 GIVING TOTAL-PRICE.
400-PRINT-OUT.
    MOVE TOTAL-PRICE TO OUT-PRICE OF SALE-LINE.
    WRITE SALE-LINE AFTER ADVANCING 1 LINES.
500-EXIT.
    CLOSE ITEM-FILE, SALE-FILE.
```

FIGURE 3.4
COBOL language program example (file descriptions and data definitions deleted)

```
FINDPRICE: PROCEDURE OPTIONS (MAIN);
    DECLARE (ITEM1, ITEM2, ITEM3, TOTAL) FIXED DECIMAL;
    GET ITEM1, ITEM2, ITEM3;
    TOTAL = (ITEM1+ITEM2+ITEM3)*1.05;
    PUT LIST ('TOTAL PRICE = ',TOTAL);
END FINDPRICE
```

FIGURE 3.5
PL/I language program example

```
10 INPUT I1,I2,I3
20 LET T=(I1+I2+I3)*1.05
30 PRINT ''TOTAL PRICE = '';T
40 END
```

FIGURE 3.6
BASIC language program example

```
PROGRAM SALES (INPUT,OUTPUT);
CONST
    TAX: = .05;
VAR
    ITEM1,ITEM2,ITEM3,NET,TOTAL: REAL;
BEGIN
    READ(ITEM1,ITEM2,ITEM3);
    NET := (ITEM1+ITEM2+ITEM3);
    TOTAL := NET+NET*TAX;
    WRITELN ('TOTAL SALE = ',TOTAL);
END;
```

FIGURE 3.7
Pascal language program example

```
 BILL ()
{
    FLOAT ITEM1, ITEM2, ITEM3, NET, TOTAL;
    SCANF(''%2F %2F %2F'',&ITEM1,&ITEM2,&ITEM3);
    NET = ITEM1*ITEM2+ITEM3;
    TOTAL = NET*1.05;
    PRINTF(''%12S %2F'',TOTAL BILL =,&TOTAL);
}
```

FIGURE 3.8
C language program example

considered to have a great deal of potential because it facilitated **structured programming**—techniques used to standardize programming and make error detection easier. However, many of the applications for which Pascal was designed are now being written in newer programming languages such as C and Ada.

C A relatively new, general-purpose programming language, C (see Figure 3.8) is a low-level language. (The language was named "C" because it followed a language named "B.") Because it is useful in writing operating systems, it has been called a "system programming language." It does, how-

ever, work equally well as a major numerical and text-processing language. Although C has some similarity to assembly language and has the same advantage of running quickly, it does not depend on the computer's internal design, and with a little care in coding, it can be made **portable**—programs written in C can be executed on a variety of hardware without change.

Ada A high-level language, Ada—named after Augusta Ada Byron, the Countess of Lovelace—was developed under contract to the United States Department of Defense as their standard computer language. The language had to be simple, com-

```
WITH TEXT_IO; USE TEXT_IO;
PROCEDURE CALCULATE IS
    TYPE REAL IS DIGITS 10;
    PACKAGE IO_REAL IS NOW FLOAT_IO (REAL); USE IO_REAL;
    ITEM1,ITEM2,ITEM3,TOTAL: REAL;
BEGIN
    GET (ITEM1);GET(ITEM2);GET(ITEM3);
    TOTAL: = (ITEM1+ITEM2+ITEM3)*1.05;
    PUT (TOTAL); NEW_LINE;
END CALCULATE;
```

FIGURE 3.9
Ada language program example

plete, reliable, portable, and easy to maintain. It also had to work both on mainframe computers and on microcomputers. The latest version of Ada was released in July of 1982 and is the version used in Figure 3.9.

Table 3.1 presents a summary and comparison of some of the 250 or more developmental languages.

Applications Software

The term **applications software** refers to programs designed to accomplish a particular task for an individual user or a specified group of users. They are written in a developmental or assembly language, and they provide the user with the full power of the computer without requiring that he or she go through the laborious process of developing the program. Chapters 5 through 10 show you how to use this power.

How Does Software Work? Applications software comes in one of two forms on disk: **source code** or **object code.** Figure 3.10 shows the relationship between source code and object code. *Source code* is another name for a program written in a developmental language. It allows a user who is familiar with the language to read and understand the program's logic and to modify the program. For an applications program in this form to work on the computer, it first must be translated into machine language. This is done through either a **compiler** or an **interpreter.** A compiler translates the program into machine language all at once. An interpreter translates one statement at a time into machine language, allowing the user to check each statement for errors as it is executed. Although interpreters are slower than compilers, they are generally easier to use—they note errors for the user. Some developmental languages such as BASIC have both compilers and interpreters, although only one per language is more typical.

Object code is the machine language version of a program—in other words, the compiled version. Object code works faster than source code, and it usually requires less internal memory to store. However, the user cannot read it or modify the program to meet any special needs.

Who writes applications software? Perhaps you will some day. However, this can be a long and tedious process, especially if

TABLE 3.1 Developmental (Programming) Language Summary

Name	Language Characteristics
FORTRAN	*Meaning:* FORmula TRANslator *Main use:* Mini and mainframe computers *Strengths:* Ideal for scientific applications *Weaknesses:* Poor input-output processing
COBOL	*Meaning:* COmmon Business Oriented Language *Main use:* Mini and mainframe computers *Strengths:* English-like language, able to handle large files, handles input-output processing easily; language most used for business applications *Weaknesses:* Complex, handles arithmetic poorly, programs are long
PL/I	*Meaning:* Programming Language/I *Main use:* Mini and mainframe computers *Strengths:* Combines arithmetic and text processing *Weaknesses:* Very complex language
BASIC	*Meaning:* Beginner's All-purpose Symbolic Instruction Code *Main use:* Computers of all sizes; primary language of microcomputers *Strengths:* "Converses" with user, easy to learn, uses mathematics-like formulas, easy input-output file handling *Weaknesses:* Slow processing speed, difficult file handling
Pascal	*Meaning:* Named after Blaise Pascal *Main use:* Computers of all sizes *Strengths:* Scientifically oriented, uses structured programming techniques *Weaknesses:* Poor input-ouput processing, handles files poorly
C	*Meaning:* Named by Bell Labs (language after B) *Main use:* Computers of all sizes, primarily mini and microcomputers *Strengths:* A lot like assembly language, improves machine efficiency, can be used on a variety of machines *Weaknesses:* Complex language; programmer must handle machine details
Ada	*Meaning:* Named after Ada Byron, Countess of Lovelace *Main use:* Department of Defense language; primarily used on large computers *Strengths:* Complete, can be used on a variety of machines, easy to change or correct; does both arithmetic and text processing *Weaknesses:* New language, still evolving; complex to learn

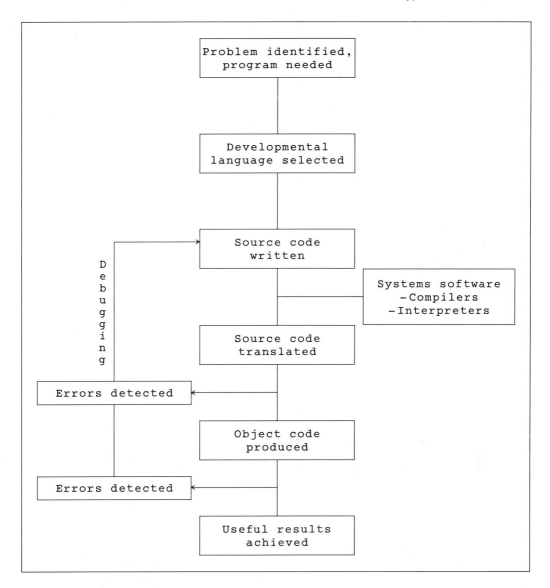

FIGURE 3.10
Relationship between source code and object code

the problem is very complex. In some cases, the need for the program may have disappeared long before the program is completed. Your company may have program-

mers who can develop programs for you, you may hire a consultant to develop programs, or you may buy *packaged* applications programs sold by a **software house** (a company specializing in software development) or a computer manufacturer.

No matter who develops the applications software, the steps involved in developing a program are the same:

1. **Plan the task solution**—identify the task and determine how to do it
2. **Prepare the program**—determine the logic and steps needed to make the computer perform the desired task in the chosen language
3. **Code the program**—write the program in the chosen language
4. **Make the program work (debugging)**—make sure the program is free of any errors
5. **Document the program**—finish writing the instructions for running and applying the program
6. **Implement the program**—make the applications software available to whoever is going to use it

Although all of these steps are important, documentation may spell the success or failure of a program. If a program is not documented or is poorly documented, all the work done will be for nothing. If a program is poorly designed and written, but does the job and is well documented, it can be used and improved. Ensuring the quality of applications software is difficult; however, well-designed and well-documented programs are needed by all users.

Packaged Software Sometimes called **user friendly** software, **packaged software** is the name given to software sold by software houses or other software suppliers. It is applications software that is produced for a general audience and can be used for a variety of tasks. Packaged software is the main topic of this text. The types of **packages** to be discussed include: word processing, spreadsheets, databases, computer graphics, communications, and integrated systems (packages designed to do more than one kind of task). There are also packages available for statistical analysis, bookkeeping, project management, and so on, as well as games.

A new type of software package—called **application generators**—is currently in development. On input of needs by the user, application generators would automatically produce applications software written in an appropriate programming language. If application generators are successful, programmers will no longer have to write individual programs directly in a programming language. However, even if this comes to be, the need for **nonprocedural languages** (languages that are stated in terms of general activities to be performed rather than as a specific sequence of instructions, as required by procedural languages) and **natural languages** (languages that resemble human languages) will still exist. These languages could be called *fourth-generation languages,* the group to follow the *third-generation languages* discussed earlier.

Software packages are typically **protected** (something is done to the software to prevent the user from copying it) and come in object code to speed their execution time. Because the packages are generally in object code, they are also somewhat machine dependent. To bypass this problem and make the packages work on as many different types of computers as possible, the packages frequently contain an **install program** (a special program that accompanies many software packages and that allows the user to tailor other programs in the package to the individual needs of the user or the user's equipment) that must be executed before the package will work on the computer being used.

Package Command Languages Every software package comes with a set of commands needed to use it. These command languages have been called many names, including **command language, macro language,** and **meta language.** (These languages are described more completely in later chapters.) They are usually fairly easy to use, and a single command accomplishes a lot (as you will see). Sometimes a set of instructions in these languages can be saved, producing a "program." This process might be more appropriately called **activity specification** rather than *programming* because it does not require extensive user training to perform.

To illustrate the concept of a command language, suppose you have entered a column of numbers—say, grades—in a spreadsheet package. To find the average of these grades manually, you would need to perform the following steps:

1. Add the numbers
2. Count how many numbers have been added
3. Divide the sum of the numbers by the count of the numbers
4. Display the results

In a spreadsheet package, all you would need to do is place the cursor where you want the results shown and type *average (r3:40c2)* (you'll learn why later). When you press the RETURN key, the average of the grades would be displayed—the computation is automatic. Similarly, rows or columns of numbers, such as stock prices, could be summed or otherwise manipulated.

The structure of the command language instruction in the example is the same as for all the other languages discussed. There is an *op code* (or *reserved word*) that tells the computer what to do (calculate the average) and one or more *operands* telling the computer what to operate on (the numbers in rows 3 through 40 in column 2—r3:40c2). Although not all command language instructions are this obvious, they are structured similarly.

Sometimes the op code or the operands are *implied,* which makes the package easier to use. Although they may not be visible, they are present. For example, if you are using a word processing package, you wouldn't want "background" operations to display on the screen as you type each letter. The package would then be hard to use, and nobody would want to buy it. Therefore, whenever you type a letter, the display command is "implied" at the cursor location.

A **menu** is another approach that is frequently used to facilitate the ease of use of a package. A menu is a list of functions that are displayed on the screen, from which the user makes a selection. Thus packages that require the user to enter the command to be executed are referred to as **command driven,** whereas packages that rely exclusively on menus for specification of activity are usually referred to as **menu driven.**

Packaged software is a rapidly growing part of the computer industry. Increasing competition is forcing manufacturers to lower the cost of software packages, sometimes dramatically, and motivating them to produce packages that are easier to use and more efficient. Packages are gradually bringing the full power of the computer to people who do not have the time or desire to learn a developmental language or programming.

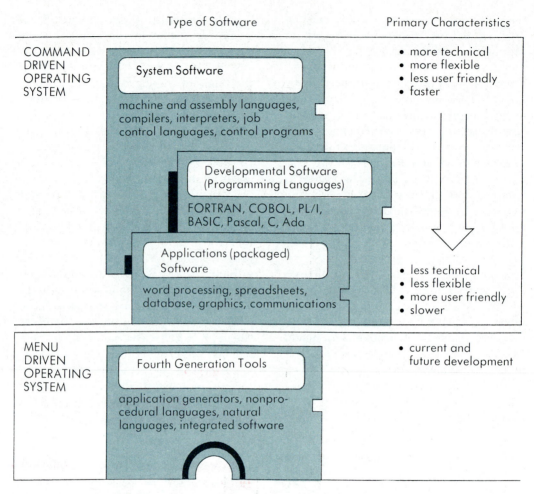

Type of Software   Primary Characteristics

COMMAND DRIVEN OPERATING SYSTEM

System Software

machine and assembly languages, compilers, interpreters, job control languages, control programs

- more technical
- more flexible
- less user friendly
- faster

Developmental Software (Programming Languages)

FORTRAN, COBOL, PL/I, BASIC, Pascal, C, Ada

Applications (packaged) Software

word processing, spreadsheets, database, graphics, communications

- less technical
- less flexible
- more user friendly
- slower

MENU DRIVEN OPERATING SYSTEM

Fourth Generation Tools

application generators, nonprocedural languages, natural languages, integrated software

- current and future development

FIGURE 3.11
Relationships among different levels of software

Chapter Summary

The choice of computer software depends on the user's knowledge and the type of applications required. Users familiar with programming languages, or developmental software, will select a language according to its strengths and weaknesses. If they choose not to develop their own program, they can select packaged software specific to their needs. Users must first identify the task to be done and then select the appropriate software, rather than select the software and then figure out what can be done.

This chapter presented an overview of the three basic types of software—system software, developmental software (programming languages), and applications software. It described the structure of commands used in all software and introduced you to several programming languages at different levels. Figure 3.11 summarizes the relationships among the different kinds and levels of languages.

The explanations in this chapter have been general and are appropriate for all microcomputers.

Chapter Key Terms

Activity specification
Application
Application generator
Applications software
Arithmetic operation
Assembly language
Branching operation
Business application
Clock
Code
Command driven
Command language
Compiler
Control program
Debugging

Developmental language
Developmental software
Firmware
High-level language
Input-output operation
Install program
Instruction
Instruction set
Interpreter
Job control language
Language
Logic operation
Machine cycle
Machine dependent
Machine language
Macro language

Megahertz
Menu
Menu driven
Meta language
Mnemonics
Natural language
Nonprocedural language
Object code
Operands
Operating system software
Operation code (op code)
Package
Packaged software
Portable
Procedural language
Program
Programmer

Programming
Programming language
Protected
Reserve word
Scientific application
Software
Software engineer
Software house
Source code
Stored-program concept
Structured programming
Supervisor
Symbolic code
Systems analyst
System software
User friendly

Chapter Questions

1. List the types of computer software. Give examples of each and tell how you would use them.
2. Discuss the differences between control programs and operating systems. Why is each needed?
3. Discuss the advantages and disadvantages of using developmental software to solve a problem on the computer.
4. Discuss the advantages and disadvantages of using packaged software to solve a problem on the computer. Which do you think is more useful to you, developmental software or applications software? Why?

5. Compare the steps you go through to solve a problem with the steps used to develop applications software using a programming language.

6. This chapter presented a number of programming languages. Which one do you feel would be the easiest to learn? Why? Which one do you feel would be the most difficult? Distinguish between scientific applications and business applications. What types of applications are you most likely to use?

7. Systems analysts, software engineers, and programmers are needed to develop applications software. What skills do you think these people must have?

8. Describe the process whereby source code is translated into object code. Why is this process necessary? How do compilers differ from interpreters?

9. Select one type of packaged software that you already know about. List ten questions you would ask before you decided to purchase it.

10. Compare the purposes of a job control language to a package command language? How are they similar? How are they different?

SCENARIO 4

What's Going on at ACE?

Soon after I started work at ACE, my boss, Mr. Jenkins, told me that some new microcomputers had arrived. He also said that, because I had had some experience with computers in high school and college, he had selected me to attend an orientation session to be conducted by the Information Center. The main topic of the session was to be operating systems.

■

Chapter Four
Introduction to
Operating Systems

Chapter Objectives

When you have completed this chapter, you will be able to:

- Define the term *operating system*
- Describe the purpose of an operating system

- Explain the general functions performed by an operating system
- Discuss the differences among types of operating systems

What Is an Operating System and Why Do You Need One?

Chapter 3 classified the **operating system** as a type of software called *system software.* An operating system is a program or a series of programs designed to control the computer system—that is, the CPU and attached peripheral devices. Without an operating system, computer hardware is essentially an expensive pile of junk.

A microcomputer operating systems is often referred to as **DOS (disk operating system).** This simply means that a copy of the operating system is stored on a disk and must be loaded into the computer's memory (RAM) before anything else is done. **MS-DOS** is the name of the disk operating system produced by the Microsoft Corporation. **PC-DOS** is the version of MS-DOS made for the IBM Personal Computer. However, not all operating systems have *DOS* in their name. For example, **CP/M (control program/microprocessor)** and UNIX are both operating system names.

You must find out which operating system you are using, because the functions ▶

and capabilities of each operating system are somewhat different. Furthermore, a single computer is not capable of using all operating systems. For example, TRS-DOS (Tandy/Radio Shack's disk operating system) will not work on an IBM PC, and PC-DOS cannot be used on the typical Apple computer, which uses Apple-DOS. There are many reasons for this lack of compatibility between computers and operating systems, but the simplest explanation is that each type of computer is different internally—the CPU is different, the signals sent to peripheral devices are different, the "internal" language is different, and so on.

Many applications software packages are written for particular operating systems. A software package (and data) written for one operating system typically will not work with a different operating system. To complicate matters even further, operating systems are frequently produced in several versions to reflect corrections or enhancements. These versions are usually "upwardly compatible." This means that software that works in version 1 of an operating system will also work in versions 2 and 3. However, software that works in version 2 may not work with version 1 of the same operating system.

An operating system performs three main types of functions: **job management, task management,** and **data management.** The job management function controls the transfer of programs to and from peripheral devices. It schedules a program for execution, locates the program on an external device, determines where it should be placed into RAM, and then passes control to the task manager. When the task manager completes its function, the job manager resumes control to schedule the next series of operations. Thus, all major activities begin and end with the job manager.

The task management function controls a program as it is executing. It initiates the execution, determines which program step should occur next, and helps the computer perform the specified activity. Thus, the task manager's primary function is to control what is going on within memory.

Finally, the data management function controls the flow of data within the computer system. It accepts instructions to perform an input or output (I/O) activity from the task manager. When an I/O is indicated, the data manager activates the specified device, transmits data to the device from memory or transmits data from the device to memory, interprets control messages sent from the device as the transfer takes place, and deactivates the device. The hardware linkage (or interface) between the CPU, memory, and peripheral devices is called a **system bus.** The bus is essentially a set of wires that provides a communications path between devices. The system bus is made up of a **command bus,** a **data bus,** and an **address bus.** Thus, the data manager's primary function is to control the activity that takes place on the system bus.

Historical Development

The first operating systems used by microcomputers were extremely primitive in comparison to the versions that are now available. The old systems were capable of performing only the most fundamental internal functions, accessed only a limited amount of memory (8K to 64K byte limitations were typical), and had limited access to peripheral devices. Because of operating system limitations, some of the very first microcomputers had to be programmed by flipping switches on the front of the computer. Fortunately, the capabilities of operating systems have been expanded, and the systems have been made easier to use. Current operating systems perform a wide range of easy-to-use functions, some can use memory in excess of 1M (mega)bytes, and all can access dozens of different devices.

Most of the operating systems in use today are called **single-user** operating systems. This essentially means that only one program can be executed at a time. These operating systems are relatively simple to use, but they may also limit the computer's capability. The original versions of most operating systems, including CP/M, were single-user operating systems.

A computer with a **multi-tasking** operating system is capable of performing more than one task at the same time. For example, the computer may be capable of executing more than one *program* at a time. **Concurrent processing,** which is also a form of multi-tasking, is multiple use of the *same program* at the same time. To perform more than one activity at a time, the memory of the computer is divided into two or more areas, called **partitions.** The operating system keeps track of a single program placed into each partition, and access to the CPU is shared by the partitions. This sharing activity is often called **time slicing.** Time slicing means that each partition receives access to the CPU only a part of the time. MS-DOS is an example of an operating system capable of multi-tasking (see Module 4a).

Operating systems that are single-user and multi-tasking are often divided into only two partitions. These partitions are usually labeled **foreground** and **background.** Activities that take place in foreground are high priority and are directly controlled by the user with the assistance of the operating system. Activities that take place in background are low priority; they are initiated by the user, but thereafter the operating system exclusively controls the activity until it is completed.

Spooling is an example of an activity that sometimes takes place in background: It allows you to print material and continue working on other tasks. If a report is printed in foreground, you must wait until the printing activity is completed before using the CPU again. In this case, the CPU is mostly idle while the printer is working. However, if the material to be printed is *spooled* (transmitted to a "holding area"—a disk or an available area of memory), the printing process can be performed in background. This means that you can continue to perform activities in foreground while unused CPU capacity is used to transmit the report to the printer in background.

All **multi-user** operating systems are multi-tasking. However, in a multi-user environment, more than one person may be working at the same time. Although each user is provided with a partition in which to operate, only one CPU is used. Of course, each user has a video display and keyboard, but memory and other devices (such as disks and printers) are shared. UNIX is an example of a multi-user operating system.

Fundamentals of Using an Operating System

When you turn your computer on, it does not yet have access to the operating system.

However, most microcomputers have a program that provides directions on how to get started. This program, sometimes called a **supervisor** or a **monitor,** is recorded in a special ROM in your microcomputer. This program will ask you to load the operating system and tell you how to do it.

Loading the Operating System

Normally an operating system is loaded by placing a disk containing an operating system into the first available disk drive (usually labeled drive A or drive 0). This disk drive is called the **default drive.** Once the operating system is loaded, you may be allowed to change the default drive. However, this change is not permanent and will be reset to the original default drive the next time you start the computer.

Some computers, like the IBM PC, assume that if the disk drive door is closed, the operating system is available. Others request that you press a key on the keyboard to indicate that the operating system disk has been placed in the drive. Upon the appropriate response, the disk drive "in-use" indicator light will come on, indicating that the operating system is being copied from the disk and placed in RAM. Once the operating system is loaded, a **prompt** (a character, symbol, word, or phrase that indicates the operating system is ready) appears on the video screen. A copy of the operating system will continue to reside within RAM until the power is turned off.

Loading the operating system is sometimes referred to as **booting** the system. However, the formal term for this operation is *bootstrapping* (as in "bringing one's self up by one's own boot straps").

When you are finished using the microcomputer, you should return to the operating system, remove any disks that may be in the disk drives, and then turn off the machine and the peripheral devices. This is called the **log-off** procedure, which is done to protect both the hardware and the software of the microcomputer system.

Reloading the Operating System

Loading the operating system in the "power up" mode is often called a **cold boot,** meaning that initially the computer's power was off and the computer was not in use when the operating system was loaded. However, it is sometimes necessary to reload the operating system while the power is still on. This operation is called a **warm boot,** meaning the computer was in use when it became necessary to start again essentially from scratch.

Although a warm boot is not frequently required, it is sometimes needed when the system gets "hung up." This happens when the computer cannot complete an activity or when you want it to stop what it is doing. For example, if you instruct the computer to print a file when the printer is not attached, the computer will stop until you either reboot the system or make a printer available. A warm boot might also be used to change from one version of an operating system to another. However, you should also realize that rebooting will erase the current contents of RAM.

Instructions for performing a warm boot vary from one computer and operating system to another. For example, some computers provide an external reset switch. To reboot such a computer, all that is necessary is to flip the reset switch. On other systems, a warm boot is performed by pressing a specific sequence of keys on the keyboard.

Files — Names, Types, and Access

Files are the primary means of communication between the operating system and the disk. Thus, you must know a little about files and their use before using the operating system to perform particular functions.

File Organization

You recall from Chapter 1 that a file represents the top-most level in a data hierarchy. Files are composed of records; records are composed of fields; and fields are composed of characters. Characters are produced either directly by a program or by your typing them on the keyboard. Most manipulations performed by an operating system are at the file level of the hierarchy.

Common Practices for Naming Files

Although some specific characteristics of file names vary from one operating system to another, a file name typically has three parts: a **disk drive designation,** a **label,** and an **extension.** The file name is generally made up of alphabetic characters and digits. The disk drive designation indicates which disk drive should be used. It is usually a letter (for example, A or B) or a number (for example, 0 or 1). If there is no disk drive designation, the currently active disk drive is used. The label is separated from the disk drive designation and the extension by some form of punctuation, such as a colon between the disk drive and the label and a period or slash between the label and the extension. For example, you might choose to identify a file with labels such as EXPENSES or SALES87. Normally, the label identifies the file by a particular name,

and the extension is used to indicate the type of file or how the file is to be used. Extensions such as COM or SYS, for example, usually identify operating system commands or system utilities, TXT or DOC may be used for textual files, and so on. (For instance, you might use a file name such as B:EXPENSES.DOC for an IBM PC, where B is the disk drive designation, EXPENSES is the label, and DOC is the extension.)

Some operating systems permit the manipulation of groups of files through what are called **wildcard** characters that are substituted for part of the file name. For example, the symbol * (asterisk) appearing as either the label or the extension is interpreted by some operating systems to mean any file with this label or extension. Thus, if an entry such as *.TXT was used with certain commands, the operating system would manipulate any file that had TXT as an extension. Other wildcard characters include the ? symbol, which means "I don't know" to the operating system. Thus, if an entry such as MICRO??.TXT was used with certain operating system commands, the operating system would manipulate any file containing TXT as the extension so long as the first five characters of the label were MICRO and the total length of the file name was seven characters.

All Files Are NOT Created Equal

As previously noted, file name extensions frequently identify particular types of files. Some of these files are created in a textual form; that is, you could actually look at and decipher what the characters mean if you viewed the file. Others are produced as "nonprintable" (machine language) characters—you could not read these, because they are in "computer form" (machine code), not "human form" (readable). If you attempt to view these files on the video screen or print them, you may cause your computer to "hang up," and it will be time for a "warm boot." For example, whereas some machine codes cause the keyboard to become "locked" or ignored, other codes might cause a disk drive to come on and stay on.

Getting to the Files You Need

Early versions of operating systems permitted only **sequential access** to files. This meant that you would have to access each file, in turn, until you came to the file you wanted. However, almost all current versions of operating systems permit **direct access** to files stored on a disk. This simply means that all you have to do is identify the file name you want, and the operating system will find it for you—the operating system will go directly to it. Furthermore, some operating systems will perform a **volume search,** going from one disk drive to the next looking for the specified file, in the event it does not find the file on the indicated (or first) disk drive.

Functions of an Operating System

Now that you have a general idea of what operating systems do, it is time to examine some of their specific functions. Although the command names and structures may vary from one operating system to another, the functions described in the following sections are common to almost all operating systems.

Finding Out What Is on a Disk — The DIRECTORY Command

Suppose you have an unlabeled disk and you want to know what is recorded on it, or suppose you want to manipulate a file but you cannot remember its name. This is the perfect time to display a **directory** of the disk. The name of the function may be called DIR (directory), CAT (catalog), or LIB (library), but the function is the same. When the directory command is entered from the keyboard (along with the specification of the disk drive), a list of the files recorded on the disk will be displayed on the video screen, as illustrated in Figure 4.1a. (Some operating systems use the same command to print out the directory.)

Normally, producing a list of the disk contents by file name is a relatively quick operation. Because the operating system does not scan the entire disk, but rather examines a special file recorded on the disk that contains a **volume table of contents** (sometimes called a *VTOC*), it can work quickly. The VTOC is usually a "hidden" (invisible) file, but it is vital for the operating system. (Only the operating system uses hidden files, but they do take up space on a disk.) In fact, if the VTOC is damaged or destroyed—say, because you put your fingers on the exposed area of the disk— the operating system cannot access the files on that disk (even though the files themselves may not be damaged). The VTOC contains not only the names of files but also their types, locations, and lengths.

Displaying the Contents of a File — The LIST or TYPE Command

You have seen the directory of files on a disk, and now you want to see what is in one

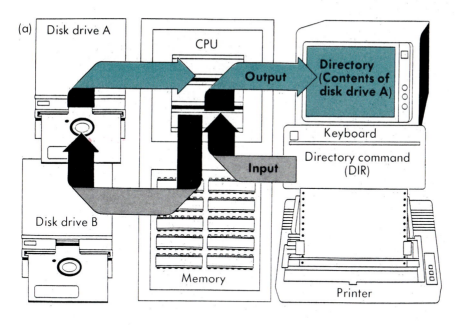

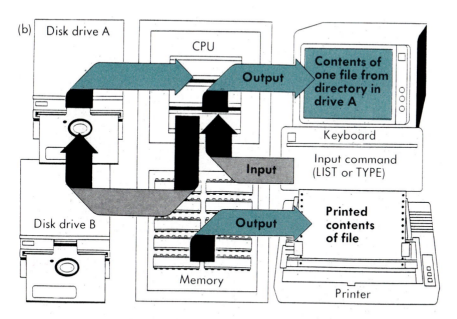

FIGURE 4.1
**Finding out what is on a disk: (a) displaying
the directory; (b) displaying and printing
contents of a file (black arrows =
commands; green arrows = data)**

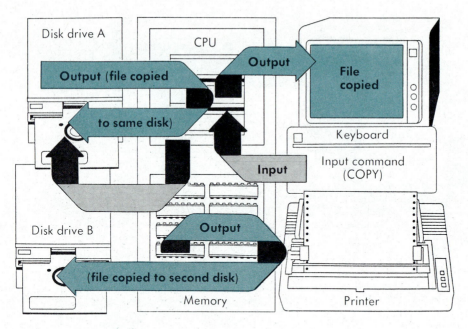

FIGURE 4.2
The COPY command

of the files. You can do this by entering commands such as LIST or TYPE followed by the file name. As shown in Figure 4.1b, these commands normally display the contents of the file on the video screen. The output will be produced rather rapidly; so if the entire file will not fit on the screen, you may have to use a PAUSE, HOLD, or BREAK key on your keyboard to interrupt the output long enough for you to read it. Also, remember that some files contain "computer form" (machine code) rather than "human form" (readable) characters, so you may not be able to read what is produced on the screen.

As illustrated in Figure 4.1b, some operating systems also provide an additional ability to produce a printed copy of the file with the LIST or TYPE command "print" option. Other operating systems use a specific command such as PRINT to produce a printed copy of a file. Still other operating systems require you to **log on** the printer by pressing a special key or a combination of keys on the keyboard to produce a printed listing. In this case, once the printer is logged on, any output produced on the display screen will also be produced on the printer. (The printer on these systems must be logged off when the listing is finished. This is usually performed by repeating the key sequence used to log on the printer.)

Copying a File on a Disk — The COPY Command

Suppose you have worked two or three hours to create a particular file. After that file has been saved, you probably don't want to run the risk of its being changed, erased, or destroyed. Even if you want to change it later, you might want to have a duplicate, or

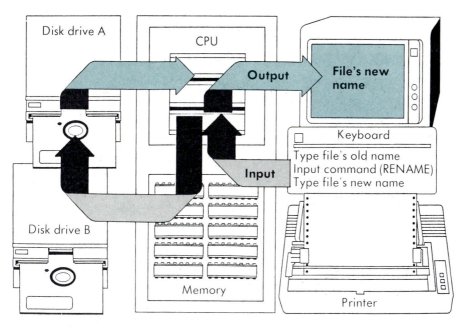

Disk drive A

CPU

Output

File's new name

Keyboard

Type file's old name
Input command (RENAME)
Type file's new name

Input

Disk drive B

Memory

Printer

FIGURE 4.3
The RENAME command

copy, of the original. If the file were on paper, you would simply use a photocopying machine to duplicate it. With a computer, copying is much quicker and simpler: All you do is use a command such as COPY. As shown in Figure 4.2, this command will make an exact duplicate of a file. The copy —often called a **file backup**—may be on the same disk as the original (provided you specify a different file name for the copy), or it may be copied to a disk in another disk drive. If the operating system permits the use of wildcard characters, groups of files can be copied from one disk to another with a single command.

Changing Your Mind About a File Name — The RENAME Command

What if you want to change the name of a file on a disk? You can't pull out your trusty

eraser and erase it. Of course, you could copy the file and give the copy the new name (and delete the old file). But by using a command such as RENAME, you can change the file name much more quickly. With the RENAME command, all you have to do is identify a file by its current name and then indicate what you want it to be called, as shown in Figure 4.3.

Removing a File from a Disk — The DELETE Command

What do you do when you really don't want a particular file that is on a disk? Figure 4.4 demonstrates that all you have to do is enter a command such as DELETE, ERASE, KILL, or PURGE followed by the name of the file, and the file disappears! (But don't change your mind and decide you want it back again. Most operating systems are not

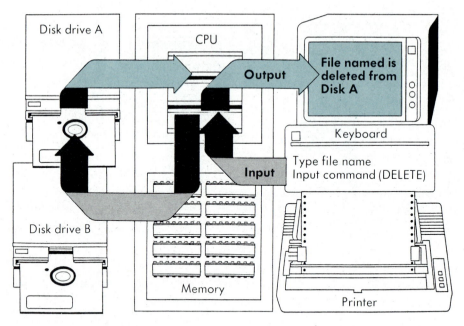

FIGURE 4.4
The DELETE command

that forgiving of mistakes.) Also, be extremely careful when using commands such as DELETE *.*. (After entering this command, a lump may rise in your throat as you realize that you have just wiped the disk clean—unless that is what you intended to do!)

Getting a Disk Ready for Use—The FORMAT Command

When you purchase blank disks (or you have decided that the material contained on an old disk is no longer needed), you use a command such as **FORMAT** to prepare the disk to accept information (and erase the old material, if applicable). The FORMAT command causes the operating system to "imprint" the disk with the proper pattern of tracks and sectors, and it prepares the directory area for use. The results of the FORMAT operation are usually reported on the screen (see Figure 4.5). By using the FORMAT command you can check to see whether a disk contains any bad or damaged sectors before you begin using it.

Creating a Backup Copy of a Disk— The DISKCOPY or BACKUP Command

When a disk is capable of accepting material—that is, after it has been formatted once—the complete contents of another disk may be copied onto it. This is called a **disk(ette) backup** and is shown in Figure 4.6. The COPY command deals with a file at a time, whereas commands such as DISKCOPY or BACKUP deal with complete disks. In some operating systems, commands such as COPY may be used to move only user files from disk to disk. A DISKCOPY or BACKUP command moves

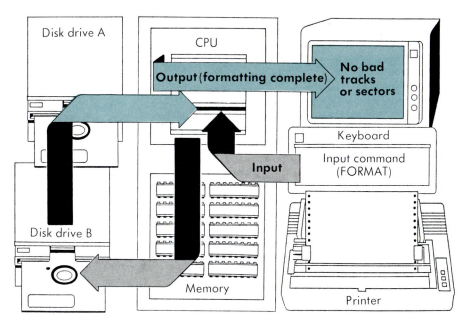

FIGURE 4.5
The FORMAT command

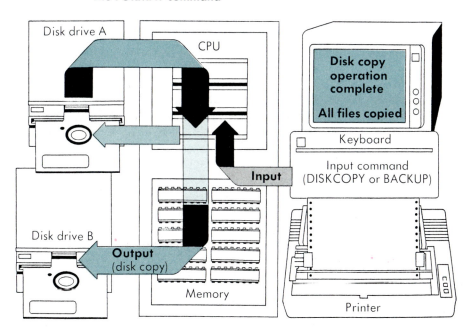

FIGURE 4.6
The DISKCOPY or BACKUP command

everything, including operating system files. However, you should be warned that the manufacturers of some software packages record applications files in a "protected" mode, meaning that the DISK-COPY or BACKUP command will not copy these files. There is no way to tell if a manufacturer's software is protected by looking at the disk; the documentation provided with the software will tell you what the copy limitations are.

Other Functions of Operating Systems

Almost all operating systems can do the operations just described. However, many operating systems can do more. Although they vary from one operating system to another, some of the additional operating-system functions are discussed in the following paragraphs.

Many operating systems request the user to specify the time and date when the operating system is initially loaded. The use of commands such as DATE and TIME allow the user to change these items without rebooting the operating system. These items may be important because some software packages use the time or date from the computer system while they are executing. For example, some COPY operations record the time and date a file was copied, so you can identify the most current version of the file.

As you work with a disk and add files to its directory, you use up more and more of its available space. Eventually, you will completely fill the disk. With commands such as CHKDSK (check disk) or STATUS, you can examine the disk's contents to determine how much space is left. If you were about to copy a large file to a disk, you might want to first determine the size of the file (determined by using a directory command) and

the amount of available space on the receiving disk (with a CHKDSK or STATUS command) before attempting to copy the file.

Operating systems also frequently provide a means of interacting directly with the peripheral devices such as the printer or the disk drive. These interaction procedures are usually established when the computer and devices are being set up or installed. For example, when interacting with a printer, the operating system may provide a **utility program** (a program that performs very specific, but limited, functions that are usually applied very infrequently) for setting the characteristics of a printed page, establishing the type of communication (also called **protocol**) between the computer and the printer, or instructing the printer to advance to the top of a new page.

One of the newer developments in operating systems is the addition of commands specifically designed to help you when you are using a hard disk, although they may also be used with floppy disks. Many of the new commands deal with what is referred to as a **subdirectory.** Imagine working with a disk containing hundreds of files. With this much data, producing even a list of file names would be a lengthy task. The use of subdirectories allows files on a hard disk to be divided into groups—each group represented by its own directory. Hard disk operating systems contain commands to create subdirectories, change from one subdirectory to another, and remove subdirectories. In addition, many of the previously discussed commands require that you identify the subdirectory name (between the disk drive designation and the file label) when referencing a file that is not in the subdirectory you are currently using. Thus, hard disk operating systems are designed to assist you in managing and using the large storage capacities of a hard disk.

Chapter Summary

This chapter described the main purpose and functions of the operating system. Operating systems fall into a category of software called *system software*, and their primary function is to manage the computer itself. There are several different kinds of operating systems, including single-user and multi-user systems. The single-user operating system, although serving only one user, may be capable of multi-tasking (performing more than one task at the same time) through the use of memory partitions. Multi-user operating systems, because they serve more than one user, are usually capable of multi-tasking operations and are at least capable of concurrent processing (multiple executions of the same program).

Finally, all operating systems perform three basic types of functions—job management, task management, and data management. Data management involves commands that list the contents of a disk, list the contents of a file, copy files, rename files, delete files, format disks, and create backup copies of disks.

Chapter Key Terms

Address bus
Background
Boot (bootstrap)
Cold boot
Command bus
Command driven
Concurrent
   processing
CP/M (control
   program for
   microprocessors)
Data bus
Data management
Default drive
Direct access

Directory
Disk drive
   designation
Disk(ette) backup
DOS (disk
   operating system)
Extension
File backup
Foreground
Formatting
Job management
Label
Log off (out)
Log on (in)

Menu driven
Monitor
MS-DOS (Microsoft
   disk operating
   system)
Multi-tasking
Multi-user
Operating system
Partitions
PC-DOS (Personal
   Computer disk
   operating system)
Prompt
Protocol

Sequential access
Single-user
Spooling
Subdirectory
Supervisor
System bus
Task management
Time slicing
Utility program
Volume search
Volume table of
   contents (VTOC)
Warm boot
Wildcard

Chapter Questions

1. What is an operating system, and why do you need one? What is the name of the operating system that you will probably use?

2. You are waiting in line at a supermarket check-out counter. Several customers are waiting in line, and the cashier is working on the purchases of one of the customers. In this situation, what or who represents the computer? What or who represents the operating

system? Can you provide an illustration of job management? Task management? Data management?

3. What is a file name, and how is it used by the operating system? What is the quickest way to find out what is on a disk?

4. Why is it important to make copies (backups) of your work? Give three reasons for doing so.

5. How can you determine the size of a file on a disk?

6. Explain the use of wildcard characters in a file name. What are the symbols used as wildcard characters? What does each mean?

7. What happens to a disk during a FORMAT operation?

8. Why is it important that you know how much free space is available on a disk? How can you find out this information?

9. How can you tell whether or not software has been protected so that you cannot make backup copies of it?

10. Why is it important for you to know what operating system your microcomputer system is using?

Modules/Chapter Four
Operating Systems

MS-DOS
Microsoft Disk Operating System
Microsoft Corporation
10700 Northup Way
Bellevue, WA 98004

CP/M
Control Program/Microprocessor
Digital Research Corporation
P.O. Box 579
Pacific Grove, CA 93950

Introduction to Operating System Modules

In the modules that follow, you will be given the opportunity to learn about one (or more) popular operating systems available for microcomputers. Module 4a discusses MS-DOS, and Module 4b covers CP/M. The problem statement that follows will acquaint you with the most-used features of operating systems and will prepare you to manage files and disks from the operating system rather than from a particular applications package.

Problem Statement for Operating System Modules

You have just uncrated your computer, and you are examining the manuals that came with your system. After you connect all of the peripheral devices, you decide that a test of the computer is in order to make sure all of the devices work properly. One of the first disks you come across indicates by its external label that it contains a copy of the operating system. You carry out your "system test" as follows:

1. Insert the operating system disk, boot the operating system, and list the file names contained on the disk.
2. Looking at the file names contained on the disk, you notice a file called MICRO.TXT. It looks like a text file, so you decide to list it on the screen. After listing it, you decide to produce a printed copy of the file.
3. You decide that you also want a copy of the MICRO.TXT file to "play" with. You make a copy on the operating system disk using the new file name MICRO.NEW.
4. You decide that you would much rather have a new name for the MICRO.NEW file, so you rename it MICRO.OLD.
5. You begin to think better of tampering with your only copy of the operating system, so you delete the file you have just created.
6. To be safe, you decide to make a backup copy of the operating system disk. (Depending on the operating system, you may first have to format the new disk.)
7. Finally, you may want to use the new disk later to store additional files, so you should determine how much space is available on the disk.

MS-DOS (Microsoft Disk Operating System)

Learning to Use MS-DOS

MS-DOS is one of the most popular disk-operating systems used with micro-computers. It was developed by Microsoft in the early 1980s, and it can be used on a wide variety of 16-bit microcomputer systems. For example, it is used with the IBM PC and compatible microcomputers.

Before you can perform functions with your computer, you must first load the operating system into memory.

Loading the MS-DOS Operating System

If your computer is off, do the following to load the operating system:

1. Insert the MS-DOS disk into drive A. Be sure the disk drive door that holds the disk in place is closed.
2. If you have a printer attached to your computer, be sure to turn it on as well as any other peripheral devices on the system. Next, turn on the monitor (or CRT) if it is a separate unit from the computer itself. Last, turn on the computer.
3. The disk drive indicator will come on (if your system has such an indicator), and the operating system will be loaded into memory.

Never open the disk drive door when the indicator light shows the disk drive is in use. You will damage your disk and possibly the disk drive.

When the operating system is completely loaded, you will be greeted by the message:

```
Command v. m.mm
Current date is Mon   1-12-87
Enter new date:
Current time is  8:00:09.10
Enter new time:
```

"m.mm" indicates the version of the operating system, and the "enter date" and "enter time" prompts indicate that you may supply the current date and time. After you have entered the date and time (in a format like that already shown on the screen) or you have pressed the RETURN key for both of these values (to use the system default values), you are ready to use the operating system and the computer.

Reloading the MS-DOS Operating System

If your computer is already on, you may want to reload the operating system. To perform a warm boot, do the following:

1. Remove the current disk from drive A and replace it with a disk containing the operating system. Then close the disk drive door.
2. Next, press and hold the CTRL (control) key, and, while holding it down, press both the ALTernate and DELete keys.
3. The disk drive indicator light will go on, and the operating system will be loaded into memory.

This procedure is sometimes called a *system reset* and can be useful under some circumstances. However, remember that each time the operating system is loaded (whether by a cold or a warm boot), the current contents of RAM are erased.

The last "message" produced on the screen after the operating system has been loaded is A>, indicating that the current default disk drive is A. (A: may appear if you have an older version of the operating system.) You can change the default drive by simply entering the disk drive designation, B:, and pressing RETURN while using the computer. Then the symbols B> would appear on the screen, meaning the B drive is the current default disk drive.

File — Names and Types

Each file should have a unique name (at least those files on a single disk). Because each disk can hold several files, you may want to create file names that remind you (by their names) of what they are.

File name labels in MS-DOS may be from one to eight characters long. These characters can be letters of the alphabet, digits, and special characters, including $ & # @ ! % ' ( ) – < > \ ^ { } ~ and ¦. The label may also be followed by an extension. An extension begins immediately after a period and may be one, two, or three characters long (using the same characters permitted for the file name).

The extensions BAS, EXE, BAT, and COM are special names for MS-DOS. The BAS extension is used to indicate that the file is a BASIC language program, and the extension EXE designates a file that contains an executable (machine language) program.

There are two types of commands in MS-DOS, as shown in Table 4a.1: Internal commands, which execute immediately because they are built into MS-

TABLE 4A.1 MS-DOS Internal and External Commands

Command Name	Type*	What Is It Used For?
DIR	Internal	Lists all the files on a disk
TYPE	Internal	Shows the contents of a file
DATE	Internal	Changes the current date
TIME	Internal	Updates the current time
COPY	Internal	Copies a file to any disk
RENAME	Internal	Changes the name of a file
ERASE	Internal	Removes a file from a disk
FORMAT	External	Prepares a disk to accept data
DISKCOPY	External	Makes a backup disk
DISKCOMP	External	Determines if two disks contain the same data
CHKDSK	External	Determines available space on a disk

* Internal commands are part of the MS-DOS file COMMAND.COM. External commands appear on an operating systems disk as individual files by the same name as the command name, with the extension COM.

DOS, and external commands, which must be loaded from the operating system disk each time they are used. A file that uses the BAT extension contains one or more commands that are executed by MS-DOS. COM extensions are used to indicate files that contain MS-DOS external commands.

In addition to the file label and its extension, a disk drive specification can be used to identify the file further. The disk drive is specified by using the disk drive letter (for example, A or B), followed by a colon—for example, A:COMMAND.COM and B:WORDSTAR.DOC. Wildcard symbols are also used to identify groups of files, as was indicated in Chapter 4.

Special Keys Used with MS-DOS

Locate the BREAK key. The BREAK key is used to tell the operating system to interrupt the current process. If you discover that you have made a mistake, or if you want the computer to do another task before it finishes what it is currently doing, you can use the BREAK key to stop whatever is happening, giving you the opportunity to enter new commands. On some keyboards (and some-

```
A>DIR

 Volume in drive A has no label
 Directory of  A:\

COMMAND  COM   15795  11-17-83   11:00a
CHKDSK   COM    6468  11-17-83   11:00a
PRINT    COM    3808  11-17-83   11:00a
CONFIG   COM    5764  11-17-83   11:00a
FORMAT   COM    6810  11-17-83   11:00a
DISKCOPY COM    3666  11-17-83   11:00a
DISKCOMP COM    1934  11-17-83   11:00a
SYS      COM    1902  11-17-83   11:00a
LIBRARY  DOC     940  11-17-83   11:00a
MICRO    TXT     384   1-12-85    8:00a
       10 Files     281600 bytes free
```

FIGURE 4A.1
The DIR command

times on the same key as the BREAK key), you will find a PAUS (pause) key (sometimes labeled SCROLL LOCK). This key is used to halt temporarily the activity being performed by the computer. The activity may be restarted by pressing the key again.

One of the most frequently used keys is the BACKSPACE key. Pressing this key deletes the current character from the display screen. Thus, the BACK-SPACE key is typically used to remove typing mistakes.

Solving the "System Test" Problem

The remaining sections in Module 4a are devoted to solving the system test problem. You may want to refer to the problem statement in the Introduction to Operating System Modules before you continue.

Now you are ready to begin using MS-DOS. As a starting point, you will be shown a list of commands and examples of how they work. The following discussion provides you with an introduction to the DIR, TYPE, COPY, REN-AME, DEL, FORMAT, DISKCOPY, TIME, DATE, and CHKDSK commands.

Finding Out What Is on a Disk — The DIR Command

The first operation frequently performed with a disk is to find out what is on it. You many use the DIR command for this purpose. As shown in Figure 4a.1,

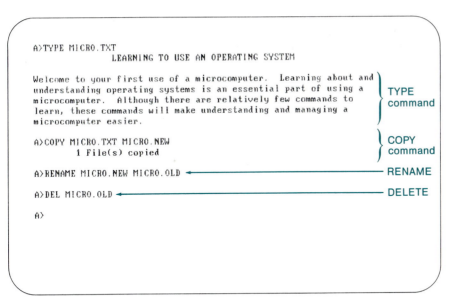

```
A>TYPE MICRO.TXT
              LEARNING TO USE AN OPERATING SYSTEM

Welcome to your first use of a microcomputer.  Learning about and
understanding operating systems is an essential part of using a
microcomputer.  Although there are relatively few commands to
learn, these commands will make understanding and managing a
microcomputer easier.

A>COPY MICRO.TXT MICRO.NEW
        1 File(s) copied

A>RENAME MICRO.NEW MICRO.OLD  ◄─────────────────────── RENAME

A>DEL MICRO.OLD  ◄─────────────────────────────────── DELETE

A>
```

TYPE command

COPY command

FIGURE 4A.2
Managing disk files

when you enter the DIR (an abbreviation of directory) command, a list of all the files on the disk will show up on the screen. Note that in Figure 4a.1, the current disk drive is identified, followed by a list of the files, their sizes, and creation dates. MS-DOS versions 2.0 and above will also show the amount of unused space remaining on the disk. Finally, the number of files on the disk is shown. The full format of this command is DIR [[d:]label.extension][/P][/W] ([ ]'s are used to indicate optional parts of the command), where d: indicates the disk drive and label.extension indicates the name of the desired file. If the /P option is used, only a page (screen) full of files is shown at a time. The list is continued by pressing any key. If the /W option is used, only the file names are shown, and they are listed horizontally rather than vertically. If you wished to see the files on drive B, you would enter the command DIR B:. Wildcard characters may also be used with the DIR command (for example, DIR *.* is equivalent to DIR showing all files, whereas DIR *.COM would show only files with a COM extension).

Displaying the Contents of a File — The TYPE Command

MS-DOS includes the command TYPE, which is specifically designed to show the contents of a file on the video display screen (see Figure 4a.2). The format of the TYPE command is TYPE d:label.extension, where d: is the disk drive, label is a file name on the disk in that drive, and extension is the file extension.

typo

(Wildcard characters are not permitted for this command.) When you enter the command TYPE MICRO.TXT, the contents of the file are produced only on the display screen. If you also want the file produced on the printer, you may log in the printer before using the TYPE command by pressing the PRINT key (if your keyboard has this key) or the CTRL and P keys simultaneously. (To log off the printer, simply repeat this sequence.) If you want only the current contents of the screen produced (instead of the whole file), press the SHIFT and PRINT or SHIFT and PRTSC (print screen) keys simultaneously.

Copying a File on a Disk — The COPY Command

To copy some (or all) of the files, use the COPY command (see Figure 4a.2). The simple format of the COPY command is COPY s:[oldfile] d:[newfile], where s: is the source disk drive, oldfile is the existing file name, d: is the destination disk drive, and newfile is the new file name (wildcard characters may be used with this command). If the destination and source disks are the same as the current disk drive, they may be omitted. Other options are available with the COPY command. Check your operating systems manual for additional details. To perform your copy operation, enter the command COPY MICRO.TXT MICRO.NEW, as shown in Figure 4a.2.

Changing Your Mind About a File Name — The RENAME Command

Sometimes you will change your mind about the name of a file. The RENAME command allows you to change the file name (see Figure 4a.2). The format of this command is RENAME d:oldfile newfile — this replaces an old file name (with an old extension) with a new file name (with a new extension). Note that a disk drive indication (d) is necessary only at the beginning of the command. (You cannot move a file from one disk to another with the RENAME command; this is what the COPY command does.) Also notice that you are not permitted to use wildcard characters with this command. Each file name and extension reference must be unique. The command RENAME MICRO.NEW MICRO.OLD, shown in Figure 4a.2, will rename your file.

Removing a File from a Disk — The DEL Command

Now that you can copy files from one disk to another and rename them, you should learn how to get rid of files you no longer want. As shown in Figure 4a.2, the DEL (an abbreviation for delete) command allows you to remove, or delete, a file from a disk. This function also has an alternate name, ERASE, or the abbreviation ERA. The format of these commands are DEL d:filename or ERA d:filename (either the file name or the extension may use wildcard characters). Thus, you may enter a command such as DEL MICRO.OLD or DEL *.OLD to delete files. The first example removes only the file MICRO.OLD. The second

```
A>FORMAT B:
MS-DOS Diskette Format Utility version 2.11

Insert new diskette for drive B:
and strike any key when ready


   362496 bytes total disk space
   362496 bytes available on disk

Format another (Y/N)?N
```

FIGURE 4A.3
Preparing a disk — the FORMAT command

example deletes all files with the extension OLD. (Obviously, you should be careful when using the command DEL *.*, because it eliminates *all* files on a disk).

Getting a Disk Ready for Use — The FORMAT Command

Before you begin to use a disk to store your own data, you must format it — that is, prepare it to receive the data. To do this, use the command FORMAT d:[/S][/1], where d indicates the disk drive containing the disk to be formatted. The /S option allows you to put a copy of the operating system on the disk after formatting is completed. The /1 option directs the system to format the disk for single-sided use only. (The default value is for double-sided use.)

As mentioned, the format command performs a "preparing" operation — also called *initializing*. The terms *to prepare, initialize,* or *FORMAT* a disk all mean the same thing. The FORMAT command will examine the data-recording area on the disk and determine whether or not it is usable by the computer system. In addition to checking the disk for bad spots, the FORMAT command also creates an empty directory on the disk.

To begin the formatting operation, select a new disk and place it in drive B. If you use an old disk, remember that the formatting operation will erase all files on it. Once you have selected a disk and entered the FORMAT B: command, you will see the messages shown in Figure 4a.3.

```
A>DISKCOPY A: B:

MS-DOS Diskette Copy Utility version 2.11

Insert source diskette in drive A:

Insert destination diskette in drive B:

Strike any key when ready

Copying 2 side(s), 9 sectors

Copy complete

Copy another (Y/N) ? N
A>
```

FIGURE 4A.4
**Creating backup files —
the DISKCOPY command**

Creating a Backup Copy of a Disk — The DISKCOPY Command

To create a backup or working disk containing all the files currently on another disk, enter DISKCOPY [s:][d:][/1][/F][/V], where s specifies the source disk and d identifies the destination disk. The /1 option causes only the first side of the source disk to be copied. The /F option indicates that the destination disk should be formatted while copying is being performed. The /V option indicates that the results of the copying operation are to be verified.

The DISKCOPY command differs from the COPY command in that it exactly duplicates the entire disk; the COPY command references individual files or groups of files on a disk. Figure 4a.4 illustrates the use of the DISK-COPY command. In this example, you entered the command DISKCOPY A: B:. You did not need to enter the /F option because you just finished formatting the disk in drive B in the previous section.

Changing the Current Date — The DATE Command

You are provided with an opportunity to indicate the current date when you load the operating system. However, if you find you either want to know the current date or want to change it later on, you simply enter the command DATE. The operating system will respond with the current date and the

```
A>DATE                                  ⌐
Current date is Mon  1-12-87            ⎬  DATE command
Enter new date:                         ⌐

A>TIME                                  ⌐
Current time is   8:13:46.60            ⎬  TIME command
Enter new time                          ⌐

A>CHKDSK                                ⌐

   362496 bytes total disk space        │
    29696 bytes in 2 hidden files       │
    51200 bytes in 10 user files        ⎬  CHKDSK command
   281600 bytes available on disk       │

   262144 bytes total memory            │
   223600 bytes free                    ⌐
```

FIGURE 4A.5
Other MS-DOS functions

prompt Enter new date: (see Figure 4a.5). If you wish to change the date, enter it in a mm-dd-yy format; that is, enter two digits for the month (mm), followed by a dash. Then enter two digits for the day of the month (dd), also followed by a dash. Finally, either two or four digits may be entered for the year (yy).

Changing the Current Time — The TIME Command

You are also provided with an opportunity to enter the current time when you load the operating system. If you decide you want to view the current time or change it later on, enter the command TIME. The operating system will respond with the current time and the prompt Enter new time: (see Figure 4a.5). If you wish to change the time, enter it in a hh:mm:ss.cc format; that is, hh represents the current hour (a value not greater than 24), mm represents the current minutes (between 0 and 59), ss indicates the seconds (between 0 and 59), and cc represents hundredths of seconds (between 0 and 99).

Finding Out How Much Space Remains on a Disk — The CHKDSK Command

Each file on your disk takes up space — how much space depends on the size of the file. Because the DIR command indicates the size of each file, you could approximate the amount of available space by adding up the file sizes. However, it is easier to use the CHKDSK (an abbreviation for check disk) command. The format of this command is CHKDSK [d:]. As illustrated in Figure 4a.5, the CHKDSK command not only provides the amount of remaining space on a disk but also gives information such as the amount of space used and available internal memory.

Other Features of MS-DOS

MS-DOS also provides many other useful commands. Through MS-DOS you can compare the contents of files (COMP) or entire disks (DISKCOMP). There is also a complete set of commands for use with a hard disk, giving you the ability to BACKUP and RESTORE the files on the disk, as well as create and remove subdirectories to make file handling easier. The most frequently used hard disk command allows you to change subdirectories. The CDIR (abbreviated CD) causes a change from one subdirectory to another; it is entered in the form [d:]CD\[directory name], where d indicates the disk drive and \ is required punctuation, unless you are currently using the initial disk directory (which is called the *main* or *root directory*). If a directory name is supplied, the operating system uses that directory rather than the directory previously used. If the command CD\ is entered, you will return to the main directory. Finally, MS-DOS provides a line editor that allows you to create, change, and display text files and program files that are in text format.

CP/M (Control Program/ Microprocessor)

Learning to Use CP/M

CP/M (and its more recent version, CP/M-86) is one of the oldest disk-operating systems used with microcomputers. It was developed by Digital Research in the early 1970s — the dawning of the microcomputer era. With CP/M, which at the time became an unofficial standard operating system, microcomputer software became transportable between machines.

Before you can do any task with your computer, you must first load the operating system into memory.

Loading the CP/M Operating System

If your computer is off, do the following to load the operating system:

1. Insert the CP/M disk into drive A. Be sure the disk drive door that holds the disk in place is closed.
2. If you have a printer attached to your computer, be sure to turn it on as well as any other peripheral devices on your system. Next, turn on the monitor (or CRT) if it is a separate unit from the computer itself. Last, turn on the computer.
3. The disk drive indicator will come on (if your system has such an indicator), and the operating system will be loaded into memory.

   Never open the disk drive door when the indicator light shows the disk drive is in use. You will damage your disk and possibly the disk drive.
   After the operating system has been loaded, you will be greeted by the message xxxK CP/M Ver m.m, where xxx indicates the amount of memory the operating system will access, and m.m indicates the version of the operating system. Now you are ready to use the operating system and the computer.

Reloading the CP/M Operating System

If your computer is already on, you may want to reload the operating system. To perform a warm boot, do the following:

1. Remove the current disk from drive A and replace it with a disk containing the operating system. Then close the disk drive door.
2. Next, press and hold the CTRL (control) key. At the same time, press the C letter key on the keyboard.
3. The disk drive indicator light will go on, and the operating system will be loaded into memory.

This procedure is sometimes called a *system reset* and can be useful under some circumstances. However, remember that each time the operating system is loaded (whether by a cold or a warm boot), the current contents of RAM are *erased*.

The last "message" produced on the screen after the operating system has been loaded is A>, indicating that the current default disk drive is A. You can change the default drive by simply entering the disk drive designation, B:, while using the computer. Then the symbols B> would appear on the screen, meaning the B drive is the current default disk drive.

Files — Names and Types

Each file should have a unique name (at least those files on a single disk). Because each disk can hold several files (up to 64), you may want to create file names that remind you (by their names) of what they are.

File name labels in CP/M may be from one to eight characters long. These characters can be letters of the alphabet, digits, and all special characters except < > . , ; : = ? * [and]. The label may also be followed by an extension. An extension begins immediately after a period and may be one to three characters long (using the same characters permitted for the file name).

CP/M uses 12 different extensions that have special meaning to the operating system. Among these are the extensions BAS, PRN, and COM. The BAS extension is used to indicate that the file is actually a BASIC language program, and the extension PRN designates a file that contains printer output (as if you instructed the computer to print, but, instead of having it sent to the printer, the output was sent to the disk).

There are two types of commands in CP/M: internal commands, which execute immediately because they are built into CP/M, and external commands (also called *transient files*), loaded into memory from the operating system disk each time the program is used. COM extensions are used to indicate files that contain CP/M external commands.

In addition to the file label and its extension, a disk drive specification can be used to identify the file further. The disk drive is specified by using the disk drive letter (for example, A or B), followed by a colon—for example, A:STAT.COM and B:WORDSTAR.DOC. Wildcard symbols are also used to identify groups of files, as was indicated in Chapter 4.

Special Keys Used with CP/M

Locate the BREAK key. The BREAK key is used to tell the operating system to interrupt the current process. If you discover that you have made a mistake, or if you want the computer to do another task before it finishes what it is currently doing, you can use the BREAK key to stop whatever is happening, giving you the opportunity to enter new commands.

One of the most frequently used keys is the BACKSPACE key (which may also be labeled RUBOUT). Pressing this key deletes the current character from the display screen. Thus, the BACKSPACE key is typically used to remove typing mistakes.

Solving the "System Test" Problem

The remaining sections in Module 4b are devoted to solving the system test problem. You may want to refer to the problem statement in the Introduction to Operating System Modules before you continue.

Now you are ready to begin using CP/M. As a starting point, you will be shown a list of commands and examples of how they work. The following discussion provides you with an introduction to the DIR, TYPE, PIP, ERA, REN, FORMAT, and STAT commands.

Finding Out What Is on a Disk — The DIR Command

The first operation frequently performed with a disk is to find out what is on it. You many use the DIR command for this purpose. As shown in Figure 4b.1, the DIR (an abbreviation of directory) command will list all the files on a disk on the screen. Note that in Figure 4b.1, each line begins with A:, which indicates that the files came from drive A. The full format of this command is DIR [[d:]label.extension] ([ ]'s are used to indicate optional items in the command), where d indicates the disk drive and label.extension indicates the name of the desired file. If you wished to see the files on drive B, you would enter the command DIR B:. Wildcard characters may also be used with the DIR command (for example, DIR *.* is equivalent to DIR showing all files, whereas DIR *.COM would show only files with a COM extension).

Displaying the Contents of a File — The TYPE Command

CP/M usually contains the transient program TYPE, which is specifically designed to show the contents of a file on the video display screen (see Figure 4b.1). The format of the TYPE command is TYPE d:label.extension, where d is the disk drive, label is a file name on the disk in that drive, and extension is the

```
A>DIR

A: COPY      COM : PIP      COM : FORMAT    COM : STAT      COM ⎞ DIR
A: BDIR      COM : CONFIG   COM : TOF       COM : INSTALL   COM ⎟ command
A: XWS       COM : WSMSGS   OVR : WSOVLY1   COM : MICRO     TXT ⎠
A>TYPE MICRO.TXT
               LEARNING TO USE AN OPERATING SYSTEM

Welcome to your first use of a microcomputer.  Learning about and ⎞ TYPE
understanding operating systems is an essential part of using a   ⎟ command
microcomputer.  Although there are relatively few commands to     ⎟
learn, these commands will make understanding and managing a      ⎟
microcomputer easier.                                             ⎠
A>
A>PIP MICRO.NEW=MICRO.TXT ←———————————————————————— PIP
A>
A>REN MICRO.OLD=MICRO.NEW ←———————————————————————— REN
A>
A>ERA MICRO.OLD ←—————————————————————————————————— ERA
A>
```

FIGURE 4B.1
Managing files on a disk

file extension. (Wildcard characters are not permitted for this command.) When you enter the command TYPE MICRO.TXT, the contents of the file are produced only on the display screen. If you also want the file produced on the printer, you may log in the printer before using the TYPE command by pressing the CTRL and P keys simultaneously. (To log off the printer, simply repeat the CTRL-P sequence.)

Copying a File on a Disk — The PIP Command

To copy some (or all) of the files, use the PIP (the peripheral interchange program) command. The format of the PIP command is PIP d:[newfile]=s:[oldfile], where d: is the destination disk drive, newfile is the new file name, s: is the source disk drive, and oldfile is the existing file name (wildcard characters may be used with this command). Note that the destination information is shown first, followed by the source information. If the destination and source disks are the same, they may be omitted.

The format presented above indicated a disk drive (possibly with file name and extension specifications) as the designation; however, PIP permits the use of device classes as the destination designation. Thus, the PIP command may appear as PIP CON:=s:[oldfile] or PIP LST:=s.[oldfile], where CON is an abbreviation for console — that is, the video display device — and LST is an abbreviation for list — that is, the printer. (Wildcard characters may also be used in this format). When CON is used as the destination designation, the PIP command is essentially the same as the TYPE command. However, when LST is the destination designation, the file is copied to the printer without being displayed on the screen. To perform your copy operation, enter the command PIP MICRO.NEW=MICRO.TXT, as shown in Figure 4b.1.

Changing Your Mind About a File Name — The REN Command

Sometimes you will change your mind about the name of a file. The REN (an abbreviation for rename) command allows you to change the file name (see Figure 4b.1). The format of this command is REN d:newfile=oldfile — this replaces an old file name (with an old extension) with a new file name (with a new extension). Note that a disk drive indication, d, is necessary only at the beginning of the command. (You cannot move a file from one disk to another with the REN command; this is what the PIP command does.) Also note that you are not permitted to use wildcard characters with this command. Each file name and extension reference must be unique. The command REN MICRO.OLD=MICRO.NEW, shown in Figure 4b.1, will rename your file.

Removing a File from a Disk — The ERA Command

Now that you can copy files from one disk to another and rename them, you should learn how to get rid of files you no longer want. As shown in Figure 4b.1, the ERA (an abbreviation for erase) command allows you to remove or delete a file from a disk. The format of the command is ERA d:filename (either the file name or the extension may use wildcard characters). Thus, you may enter a command such as ERA MICRO.OLD or ERA *.OLD to delete files. The first example removes only the file MICRO.OLD. The second example deletes all files with the extension OLD. (Obviously you should be careful when using the command ERA *.*, because it eliminates *all* files on a disk).

Getting a Disk Ready for Use — The FORMAT Command

Before you begin to use a disk to store your own data, you must format it — that is, prepare it to receive data. To do this, use the command FORMAT. This command performs a "preparing" operation — also called *initializing*. The terms *to prepare, initialize,* or *FORMAT* a disk all mean the same thing. The FORMAT command will examine the data-recording area on the disk and determine whether or not it is usable by the computer system. In addition to checking the disk for bad spots, the FORMAT command also creates a directory on the disk.

To begin the formatting operation, select a new disk and place it in drive B. If you use an old disk, remember that the formatting operation will erase all files on it. Once you have selected a disk and entered the FORMAT command, you will be presented with messages similar to those shown in Figure 4b.2.

```
A>FORMAT

Drive number            (A B C or D) ? B

Single, double or extended DENSITY (S, D, or X) ? S

Press <CR> to format SINGLE density disk in drive B

or "E" to EXIT, "N" for NEW parameters.

Disk now being formatted and verified.

RUN again, EXIT or NEW parameters (R E or N). E

To reboot: Insert CP/M system disk and press <CR>.
```

FIGURE 4B.2
The FORMAT command

Creating a Backup Copy of a Disk — The PIP Command (Again)

To create a backup or working disk containing all the files currently on another disk, enter PIP B:=A:*.*. Then, if you entered a DIR command — that is, DIR and DIR B: — both disks would appear to be exactly the same. If you are using CP/M-86, you could perform the same operation by entering the command COPYDISK and answering the questions that appear on the screen.

Finding Out How Much Space Remains on a Disk — The STAT Command

Each file on your disk takes up space — how much space depends on the size of the file. Unfortunately, the DIR command provides only the names of the files — not their sizes. Thus, you may want to use the STAT (an abbreviation of status) command, as illustrated in Figure 4b.3, to obtain this information.

If you enter the command STAT [d:][filename], the operating system will respond with either the message R/W, Space: nnnk or the message R/O, Space: nnnk, where nnn represents the remaining space on the disk (in thousands of bytes). Each message begins with either R/W (for a disk that can be read from and written to) or R/O (for a disk that can be read only — you can read from the disk, but you cannot write to it). If you want to examine a particular file or a group of files, you should supply a file name reference (including possible

```
A>STAT
A: R/W, Space: 456K  1-12-87

A>STAT MICRO.TXT

 Recs  Bytes  Ext Acc
   3     2k   1 R/W A:MICRO.TXT
Bytes Remaining On A: 456K

A>
```

FIGURE 4B.3
The STAT command

wildcard characters) with the STAT command. For example, if you entered the command STAT MICRO.TXT, the output shown in Figure 4b.3 would be the result.

Other Features of CP/M

CP/M also provides other useful commands. For example, both CP/M and CP/M-86 have an extensive HELP command that displays information on how to use each command that is available in the operating system. Additionally, CP/M provides a line editor that allows you to create, change, and display text files and program files that are in text format.

Summary of Operating System Modules

Modules 4a and 4b gave you a brief tour through MS-DOS and CP/M. First you were provided with a procedure for starting the computer under both cold and

TABLE 4S.1 A Comparison of MS-DOS and CP/M Operating Systems

	MS-DOS	CP/M	CP/M-86
Type of System	Single-user, multi-tasking*	Single-user*	Single-user, multi-tasking*
Computer Word Size Used	8- and 16-bit	8-bit	16-bit
Total Accessible Memory	Approximately 640K bytes	Approximately 64K bytes	Approximately 640K bytes
Memory Used by Operating System	12–25K bytes	8–12K bytes	12–25K bytes
Number of Available Commands	Approximately 30	Approximately 10	Approximately 20

* Available in multi-user versions

warm boot conditions. Then you were introduced to the file name structures permitted within MS-DOS and CP/M. After this general introduction, you were taken through the commands to (1) examine the contents of a disk (DIR), (2) look at the contents of a text file (TYPE), (3) copy files to a disk (COPY and PIP), (4) provide a new name for a file (RENAME and REN), (5) delete files from a disk (DEL and ERA), (6) create a usable disk (FORMAT), and (7) make a backup copy of a disk (DISKCOPY and COPYDISK). Also, you learned about commands to change the current date (DATE) and current time (TIME) in MS-DOS and to examine the space available on a disk (CHKDSK and STAT).

A Comparison of Operating Systems

Obvious areas of similarity between CP/M and MS-DOS include file names and wildcard characters and FORMAT, DIR, REN, and TYPE commands. The most significant difference is the reversal of source and destination names with commands that require two file names. Furthermore, some of the commands have different names (for example, STAT versus CHKDSK, PIP versus DISK-COPY and COPY, and ERA versus ERASE and DEL). Table 4s.1 provides other comparisons between MS-DOS and CP/M (and CP/M-86). By knowing and understanding more than one operating system, you should be able to learn quickly new, more advanced operating systems that may become popular in the future.

Guidelines for the Evaluation of Operating Systems

This is the first of a series of evaluation guidelines that will appear in each of the module summaries in this book. Typically, when you purchase a microcomputer system, the computer will come with the operating system that is recommended (and supported) by the manufacturer. However, in many cases you will have a choice of which operating system to use. Although there is not a long list of items you need be concerned with when selecting operating systems, some items are critical. In fact, because operating systems are tied so closely to the hardware being used, this same list could be used for hardware evaluation as well as the evaluation of operating systems.

- **Software supported** — Is the operating system capable of running the types of software you want to use? If you want to use specific vendor software packages, does the operating system run these packages?
- **Peripheral devices** — Does this operating system support the peripheral devices you want to use both now and in the future?
- **Functions (commands)** — Does this operating system have the functions (commands) that you want and will use most often?
- **Ease of use** — Try using the operating system. Are the functions easy to remember? Do the commands remind you of what the function is supposed to do? Are the keystrokes needed to carry out a function easy to enter, or does the operating system require a high use of simultaneous keystrokes (holding one key down while pressing another)?
- **Documentation** — Is the documentation for the operating system complete? Is it easy to read and understand?

Module Questions

1. What operating system does your computer use? When you load the operating system, what messages appear on the screen?
2. When you format a disk using your operating system, what is the number of bytes available?
3. According to your operating system's documentation, what are the internal commands available to you? What are the external commands?
4. Again, according to your operating system's documentation, what extensions have special meanings for your operating system?
5. What other operating systems (besides the one you are using) can be used on your microcomputer? (*Note:* Use the library or your local computer stores to find the answer to this question.)

Module Problems

1. Prepare a disk to hold the data for the work that will be done throughout the rest of the text using the following steps:
   a. Load your system.
   b. Turn on and log in the printer so that you can capture on paper everything that appears on the screen.
   c. Format the data disk.
   d. Reload the operating system.
2. You are going to make inquiries of your disk. First load your operating system and log in your printer so that you can capture the answers to your questions.
   a. List a directory of all the files on the disk in your default drive.
   b. List only those files using the COM extension.
   c. List the contents of a file having the TXT extension.
   d. Determine the amount of unused space on your disk by using the CHKDSK or STAT command (or a similar command, if you are using some other operating system).
3. You are going to look at the commands that manage the files on your disk. To do this, load your operating system and format a data disk. Now log in your printer so that you can turn in a printed copy of your work.
   a. Copy the file named MICRO.TXT from the system disk to your data disk.
   b. Compare the contents of the file named MICRO.TXT on your data disk with the same file on your system disk. Compare the files on your data disk with your system disk.
   c. Copy the file named MICRO.TXT on your data disk to a new file on your data disk.
   d. Rename the new file on your data disk INTRO.DOC.
   e. Delete the file name MICRO.TXT on your data disk.
   f. List the contents of the file named INTRO.DOC.

SCENARIO 5

What's Going on at ACE?

One day at the office, I overheard part of a conversation between Mr. Jenkins, my boss, and Ms. Fullerton, the district manager. They were discussing the fact that manufacturers annually update their products and introduce new models, and they mentioned the need to contact each of the manufacturers to find out what new products to expect.

Later in the day, Mr. Jenkins selected me to contact each of the companies that supplied ACE to get the latest information about current products and what new products would be introduced next year. Mr. Jenkins said that he would give me a draft of a letter to be sent to these companies and that a list of all the companies and their addresses was available on the office microcomputer. What was the easiest way to get the letters out? Mr. Jenkins suggested that I talk to Ms. Robertson, another office manager, who had used word processing to solve a similar problem. Ms. Robertson said that she had indeed used word processing and that she was so impressed with it that she was having all of her office staff trained in its use. She also invited me to attend a training seminar on word processing. ■

Chapter Five
Applications Software:
Word Processing

Chapter Objectives

When you have completed this chapter, you will be able to:

- Discuss the historical development of written communication
- Discuss the relationships among data elements used in word processing
- Describe the process of developing and modifying written text

- Identify many of the common features of word processing systems
- Describe how word processing is integrated with other types of processes to "communicate by computer"

Introduction to Word Processing

Suppose Ms. Fullerton is asked to prepare a sales analysis report for the Houston office to be presented to the president at the annual sales meeting in Chicago. Ms. Fullerton then asks the sales manager to prepare the report, and he gathers all the information and hands it to you. Once you have written and typed the report, the sales manager will read it, make corrections, and give it back to you to correct and retype. When you have

finally typed a version that the sales manager is happy with, the whole process will start again with Ms. Fullerton making the corrections. When the report is finally ready, it is sent to Chicago, but it gets lost in the mail, and you are asked to take your notes and retype the entire report, starting the process over again. Of course, you have only two weeks to complete the report.

There should be an easier way to complete this report, and there is. If you had used **word processing,** you could have simply made the necessary changes and printed a new copy instead of retyping the entire report every time there was a correction or change to make. When the report was lost, you could have simply pressed a few keys on your microcomputer and printed a new copy. Two weeks is plenty of time to write a report using word processing.

Historical Development

When humans first used a symbol to represent a thought or an idea, they made the first step toward establishing a method of communication. The first symbols were verbal, and you had to be there to get the message. Durable communication forms began with the use of visual symbols, such as drawings or paintings on cave walls, and portable written communication began with the use of papyrus (by the Egyptians). With the transfer of medium from stone to papyrus to paper, not only did written communication become more portable, it became quicker and easier to produce.

The next innovation was the development of printing methods. In the fifth century A.D., the Chinese began to use symbols carved out of blocks of wood to produce printed documents on paper. The invention of the movable-type press developed by Johann Gutenberg (producer of the Gutenberg Bible) in the early-to-mid-1400s was the first major improvement since the Chinese carved blocks. Other improvements have been made since then (for example the rotary press, lithography, and the use of metal character blocks), but few changes fundamentally altered the manner in which type was set until the advent of electronic (computer-based) typesetting devices.

Although the first patent for a typewriter was granted to Englishman Henry

Mills in 1714, the first working model wasn't produced until 1867. In that year, Christopher Sholes, an American printer, developed a working model of the modern mechanical typewriter. The product was finally manufactured and marketed in 1875, when it was produced by Remington and Sons. However, the devices were not immediately popular because most people were reluctant to try the new technology (people had the same initial reaction when word processing systems and microcomputers first appeared).

One of the most notable attempts to improve the Sholes typewriter involved the keyboard design. The **QWERTY keyboard** (named after the first six letters in the upper left corner of the keyboard) was designed to reduce key jamming—a problem with mechanical typewriters. The character placement was consciously arranged to be somewhat difficult to reach, thus slowing the speed of the most accomplished typist. Furthermore, because most people are right-handed, the most often used keys were positioned for striking by fingers of the left hand. Unfortunately, this legacy remains, although most typewriters and all currently manufactured keyboards attached to a computer are electronic and don't suffer from key jamming. Thus, although typewriters have been improved since the late 1800s, the process of typing is still basically the same. The **Dvorak keyboard,** designed in 1930 to increase typing speed by placing keys on the keyboard according to their frequency of use, has been slowly gaining acceptance.

During the late 1960s and the early 1970s, **word processing systems** were being developed. At first, these systems were single-user, **stand-alone, dedicated systems** (they could be used only by a single person at a time, they were not integrated with other office equipment, and they could perform only a word processing function), and they usually used magnetic tape or cards to store what was being typed. In the late 1970s, many of these systems were made more flexible, in that they supported multi-users, were integrated with other devices (for example disks, plotters, and computers), and could perform a variety of functions including, but not limited to, word processing. Today's modern office uses both typewriters and word processing systems (generally microcomputer based). However, the future will likely bring the demise of the typewriter, as word processing systems become even more flexible.

Definition of Word Processing

Chapter 1 introduced data processing systems, which are designed to manipulate data. Manipulation of data may include a variety of operations, such as classifying, calculating, summarizing, sorting, and storing. Data processing systems most frequently operate on numeric data, whereas word processing systems generally deal with alphabetic and alphanumeric data; that is, the data for a word processing system is words!

Some of the characteristics of data processing systems do not necessarily apply to word processing systems (for example, how do you "calculate" words?). Therefore, it is more meaningful to establish a new set of characteristics related to word processing systems. These characteristics include:

- **Word origination**—creating textual "data"
- **Editing**—correcting or otherwise modifying text

- **Formatting**—arranging text in a useful and meaningful form
- **Printing**—producing a hard-copy version of electronic text

Although many word processing systems have capabilities that are superior to these, all word processing systems, regardless of how limited, have at least these capabilities.

You recall the data hierarchy presented in Chapter 1. (A data file is composed of records, which are composed of fields, which are composed of characters.) The hierarchical structure used in word processing (see Figure 5.1) should be more familiar than the data hierarchy. At the highest level is the file. It is used to store a large body of text, such as a business letter, a project report, or a term paper. In some word processing systems, a file is also called a document. Thus, in the "creation" mode, you develop and save a file or document. In the processing mode, you retrieve a file or document. In fact, if any part of the text is known to the operating system, it would be the file or document name.

The second level in the word processing hierarchy is the page. This may be the same amount of text as the file for a single-page business letter; however, longer documents would consist of a number of pages. Depending on the word processing system, you will be given access to either the entire file at one time or a single page at a time. (Single-page-oriented word processing systems allow a single file to be larger than the amount of internal memory available on the computer, since only a small portion of the file is placed into memory at one time.) The third level of text is the block. A block is typically an amount of text defined by the person using the word processing package. It could be as large as several pages or as small as a few characters. A block is usually

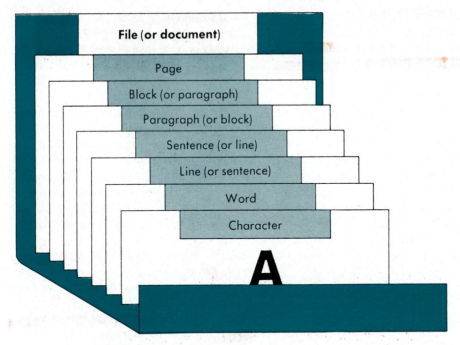

FIGURE 5.1
The word processing hierarchy

thought of as text that has the same format (for example, indented paragraphs versus paragraphs using regular spacing).

Each page is usually composed of a series of **paragraphs.** The paragraph level is one of the most significant levels associated with a file. Paragraphs will appear in a traditional form on a display screen or in a printed form, but they are generally stored as a continuous string of characters—from the first character of the paragraph to the end of the paragraph. In other words, a paragraph is composed of the characters entered between two RETURN keys. The reason for storing a paragraph in this manner, rather than as a series of lines, is fundamental to the way word processing works. When text changes are made within a paragraph, they typically affect all the text in the paragraph from the point of the change to the end of the paragraph, but they do not cause the format of the paragraph to change. Thus, regardless of the changes that may be made within a paragraph, it will continue to look like a paragraph and not a series of lines that are not associated with each other. The result is that when paragraphs are produced (either on the screen or on the printer), they are relatively well blocked; that is, they do not have severely jagged right margins.

Paragraphs are composed of one or more **sentences.** Each sentence may be composed of one or more **lines.** Almost all word processing systems permit some manipulation of sentences, and some systems even permit the manipulation of individual lines (regardless of whether they include complete sentences). The difference between sentences and lines is that a sentence is concluded with some form of punctuation (for example, a period or a question mark), whereas a line is the sequence of characters on one line display within a paragraph.

Sentences are composed of **words.** Words are one or more characters surrounded by spaces or some form of punctuation. Some word processing systems are capable of checking the spelling accuracy of words that appear in a file.

Finally, the last level of the word processing hierarchy is the **character.** The term *character* has its usual meaning. Words are made up of characters that may be alphabetic or numeric or of special characters (for example $, %, or &). Even a blank is a character, in this sense. In addition, some word processing systems use **control characters.** These are not characters as you usually think of them, but rather characters that can be used to control special features of the word processor, either in the way text is presented on the display screen or in the printed version of the text. An example of the use of control characters is at the beginning of this paragraph. The first sentence of this paragraph contains the word "character." Note that it looks different from the other words in the sentence: it is boldface. Control characters are often used to achieve this effect, as well as to do underlining.

Functions of Word Processing Software

Although word processing software may vary in terms of how specific functions may be performed, most word processing systems tend to support the same types of functions. The following sections cover many of the popular ones.

Providing Help

Most commercially produced software has some form of **HELP function.** As this term implies, this function supports your use of the software package. Thus, if you get "stuck" or you don't know what to do next, you simply ask for help. Obviously, this should be one of the first functions you look for in any software package. Until you learn the package well, the help function will be invaluable.

Help may be made available by topic, function, or level, depending on the software package. For example, some word processing packages require you to specify the topic you need help with. Then, depending on the package, the software will either provide all the information available for that topic or ask you to indicate which of the help elements for that topic you wish to view. If help is provided by function, the word processor keeps track of the function you are currently performing and provides assistance with that function. Again, you may have to indicate which aspect of that function you wish to investigate. Occasionally you may also be able to specify a help level. When you use a software package for the first time, you will be relatively unfamiliar with it. As you become more comfortable with the package, your needs for help will change. The less experience you have with a package, the more help you want. The more experienced you are, the less help you want. Typically, the higher the help level, the greater the amount of help information provided. At a lower level, the package would give less information, assuming that all you need is a hint to get you back on track.

Some word processing packages provide help through their basic structure. For example, the package can be either **menu** driven or command driven. In a menu-driven package, functions are performed according to options selected from a menu. The menu itself provides a first level of help, and it may be supplemented by help screens that provide explanations of the different options as well as instructions on how to carry them out. In a command-driven package, functions are performed according to commands entered from the keyboard. A command-driven system will usually have a menu that identifies the commands available; the size of the menu will depend on the help level selected. Finally, a command-driven package will almost always have a help function used to provide help screens that explain and illustrate the use of a command.

Margin Setting and Tab Stops

One of the first pieces of information your word processing system needs is the format of your text. When you produce a letter on a typewriter, you might begin by setting the left and right margins and tab stops. This is also required with word processing software. Just as you may use the current settings on a typewriter to produce a document, you may use the default settings—existing settings—of the word processing system. Furthermore, once new margin settings and tab stops have been established and saved, you may use them for other documents without resetting.

On a typewriter, the left margin setting establishes the text indentation from the left edge of a sheet of paper. The left margin setting in word processing establishes the indentation for both the printed and the electronic version of the product that appears on the screen. The right margin setting on a typewriter establishes the end of each line of type and, consequently, the

text indentation from the right edge of the paper. The right margin setting in word processing serves the same purpose. However, when you come to the end of a line on a typewriter, you are required to press the carriage return key or manually return the carriage to begin the next line. One of the significant differences between writing with a typewriter and entering text via word processing software is that word processing does not require a carriage return. As soon as the text hits the right margin setting, the software automatically begins a new line. Even if you are in the middle of a word when you come to the margin, the word processor will automatically scan backward on the current line to find the beginning of the word and move it to the next line. This feature of the word processor, called word wrapping, significantly improves entry speed for typists. Typists don't have to determine whether a word will fit on a line. They simply type the word, and the software decides if it will fit. Thus, touch typists never have to look up from their work. They simply continue to type until the end of the paragraph is reached. Then they press the RETURN (or ENTER) key to mark the end of the paragraph.

Tab stops are generally similar to those established for a line of type on a typewriter. In a word processor, however, these tab stops are set and modified electronically. As with a typewriter, using a tab key causes you to move from one tab stop to the next. Depending on the software package, these tab stops are either hard tabs or soft tabs. If hard tabs are used by the software, spaces are inserted to adjust the line to the next available tab stop. If soft tabs are used, although the line will appear to have the appropriate number of spaces, an embedded (invisible) character is inserted to make the left-to-right adjustment. Although hard tab markers will give the visual impression that the tab key has been used on both the screen and the printed text, the soft tab can be changed later and the document reformatted. In this case, new tab stops could be used to replace old tab stops and give the document a different appearance. All the space used by a soft tab can be removed by eliminating a single character, whereas hard tabs require that individual spaces be removed.

Other features may be included with the margin settings and tab stops. For example, some word processing systems require you to state what type of right margin will be used—**ragged,** like typewritten text (this is typically the default setting); **right-justified,** or *blocked,* where equal space is added between words so that the right margin is even (a straight line, just like the left margin); or **proportionately spaced,** where individual character widths are adjusted to make the right margin even.

Many word processing systems use **decimal-point alignment** tab stops (called *decimal tabs*). These stops automatically align the decimal points in columns of numbers. When typing normally, characters appear from left to right. When using decimal-point alignment, characters will move from right to left until the decimal point is entered; then the left-to-right sequence is resumed. Finally, some word processing systems require the specification of page length and line spacing (for example, single-spaced or double-spaced) when determining margins and tab stops.

Word Origination and Text Editing Functions

Many of the advantages of word processing are based on the ability of the software package to create text easily and, as a part of that process, to change **(edit)** it. This text was written using a word processing package.

Word origination implies the creation of text, whether it is in the form of a business letter, a project report, or a term paper. In word processing, words are entered via a keyboard. But even this simple task is not entirely the same as typing the document. As words are entered into the word processor, they are placed in a file in electronic form. No physical product is obtained until a printing option is selected. As text is entered, the word processor ensures that it fits within the selected margin requirements. As one line becomes full, the word processor automatically begins another line and adjusts the previous line as necessary so that it contains complete words. Finally, the BACKSPACE key is used to correct keying ("typing") errors by backing the cursor up to the location of the error and then entering the new character to replace the old one (this is somewhat like using "lift off" tape to make corrections on a typewriter).

Many word processing packages have a **status area,** which is usually always present on the screen. Generally, this area will indicate the current line (consecutively numbered from the top to the bottom of a page), the current character position (column position on a left-to-right basis on a line), and the margin and tab settings. Other information in this area may include the file name, page number, and mode of operation. Thus, the status area is used to tell you where you are in the text and what is going on there.

The real power a word processor gives you is the ability to change text. Suppose you were typing a term paper, and, after finishing, you discovered that you had accidentally left out a critical paragraph (or a sentence or a word). The paper must look

Before   **After**

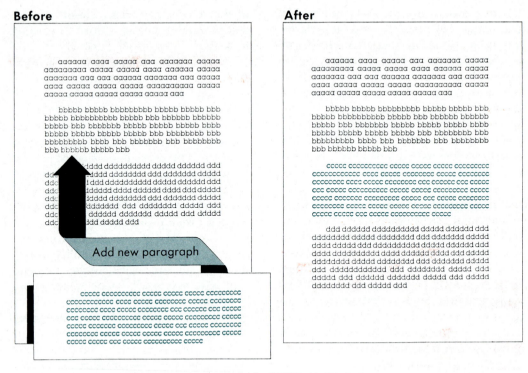

FIGURE 5.2
The insertion operation

clean and professional, so you retype the text from the point of the omission. With a word processor, you don't have to go to anywhere near the trouble of retyping a document. Remember that the document is in electronic form; even if it has already been printed, it is no big problem to correct it and reprint it.

To add a paragraph to a document (see Figure 5.2), you must first move the cursor to the point in the document where you want the paragraph to go. One way of doing this is to use the cursor control keys that are on most keyboards (discussed in Chapter 2). These are the keys with arrows on them.

When you press the arrow that points to the left, the cursor moves left. If you press the arrow that points to the right, the cursor moves right. The up and down arrows work in the same way. The arrow keys can also be used to perform **scrolling** operations. For example, if you continue to press the down arrow key, text farther along in the document appears at the bottom of the screen, and text at the top of the screen disappears. This does not mean that the text that disappeared off the top of the screen is lost. It has only disappeared from view. If you are near the bottom of a block of text, using the up arrow key may cause scrolling in the opposite direction. In addition, if the text is wider than will fit on the screen, left and right scrolling is sometimes possible.

Some packages provide ways to move around within a document. One of these methods is through the use of a **split screen.** A split-screen function divides the screen in half either vertically or horizontally, with the two halves of the screen being used to show two different views of the document. Special key sequences are used to move the cursor from one half of the screen to the other. A **window** is sometimes used as another name for a split screen; however, there usually can be more than two windows (some packages allow up to eight windows). Windows can be of any size, and they do not have to present views of the same document. One window may have a view of the letter that was entered, while the other views the list of names and addresses where the letter should be sent.

Whatever method is used to move the cursor around in the document, once you have reached the point where you left text out, you simply select the **insert** function and enter the omitted text. Again, the omission could be of any size, from a paragraph or more down to and including individual characters.

If the problem was a repeated paragraph, (easy enough to do, especially when you get interrupted while typing), the solution is similar to adding missing (or new) text. You simply move the cursor to the location of the error (by using the cursor control keys), select the delete function, and remove the unwanted text (regardless of its size), as shown in Figure 5.3. This function differs from one word processing package to another. Some packages require you to simply repeat the delete function until the unwanted text disappears, whereas others

will delete complete lines, sentences, or paragraphs at once.

The last of the basic functions performed in the text editing mode is **replacement.** This simple operation usually does not require the selection of a specific function. In the replacement mode, you simply move the cursor to the location of the problem and begin typing. The characters that you enter replace the existing characters on a one-for-one basis. For example, suppose the word *weak* appeared in a document. If you had intended to indicate a seven-day period of time, you used the wrong word. You could move the cursor to the letter "a" in *weak* and press the "e" key. Then *weak* would become *week* with very little effort on your part. Transposition errors (swapping two or more letters of a word) are common, but with little effort *there* becomes *three, form* becomes *from, gas* becomes *sag,* and so on. Such problems are easily solved by replacement.

Cut/Paste and Copy Functions

Suppose your paragraphs, sentences, and words are correct, but they are in the wrong order. If you wrote on a typewriter, you can solve the problem as follows: With a pair of scissors and glue or tape, you can cut the pieces of the document apart and paste them back together in the correct order. This is somewhat laborious, but it can be done. However, if your document is stored electronically, it is a rather simple matter to move elements of the text from one place to another. As indicated in Figure 5.4, you first locate the portion of the text that needs to be moved. Then you identify how much text—say, a paragraph—is to be moved. Next, you "cut and lift" the paragraph from its present location. The re-

Before

After

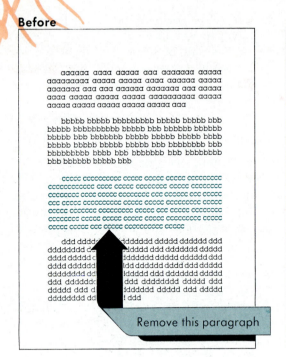

Remove this paragraph

FIGURE 5.3
The deletion operation

maining text moves up to fill the hole. Then, you move to the location where the "lifted" paragraph is to be placed. Finally, you insert (paste) the copied paragraph into its new location, and the text below the new paragraph moves down to allow enough room for it. You have just completed a **cut-and-paste** operation electronically!

Fundamentally, the **copy** function is highly similar to a cut-and-paste operation. The difference lies in the fact that, with the copy operation, the original version of the text is not affected by the operation; that is, if you want to duplicate a paragraph, you simply locate the paragraph, designate how much text is to be copied (not lifted), move to the new location, and insert the copied paragraph. Not only is this function handy

for duplicating single paragraphs, but it is especially useful when you want to duplicate specific pieces of text over and over again. Even if there are some differences in the individual lines of the repeated material, it may take less time to duplicate the block of text and then make the necessary individual changes than to type everything anew.

Find and Replace Functions

The longer the document, the more difficult and time consuming it is to locate particular text references. Furthermore, when you are relying on your eyes to locate each occurrence of a word or phrase, you may

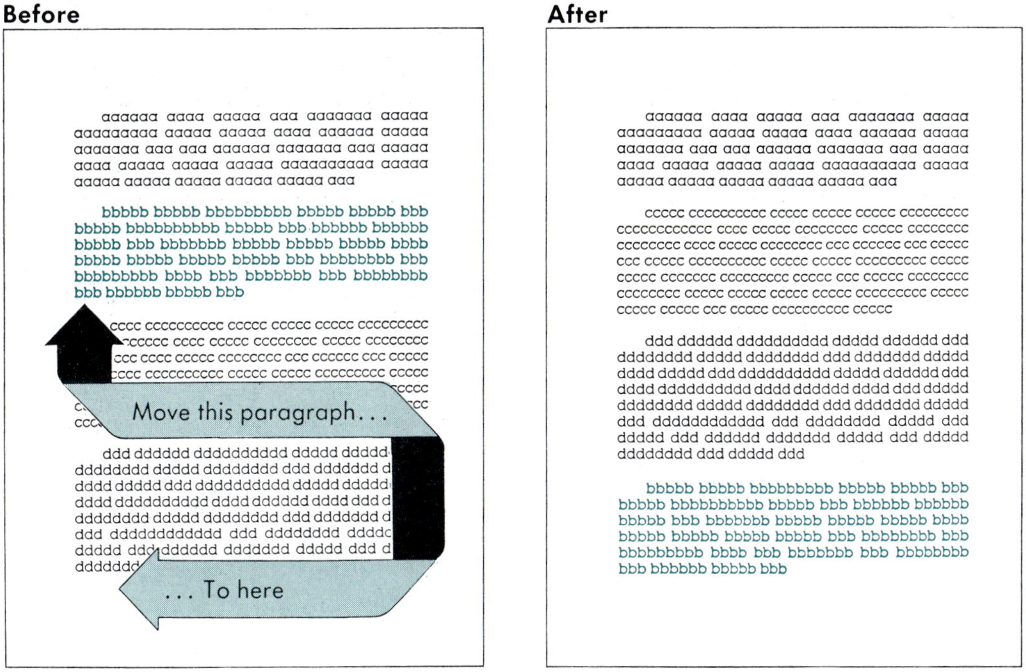

Before

After

aaaaaa aaaa aaaaa aaa aaaaaaa aaaaa
aaaaaaaaaa aaaaa aaaaa aaaa aaaaaa aaaaa
aaaaaaa aaa aaa aaaaa aaaaaaa aaa aaaaa
aaaa aaaaaa aaaaa aaaaa aaaaaaaaaa aaaaa
aaaaa aaaaa aaaaa aaaaa aaaaa aaa

bbbbb bbbbb bbbbbbbbb bbbbb bbbbb bbb
bbbbb bbbbbbbbbb bbbbb bbb bbbbbb bbbbbb
bbbbb bbb bbbbbbbb bbbbb bbbbb bbbbb bbbb
bbbbb bbbbb bbbbb bbbbb bbb bbbbbbbb bbb
bbbbbbbbb bbbb bbb bbbbbbbb bbb bbbbbbbbb
bbb bbbbbb bbbbb bbb

ccc cccccccc ccccc ccccc ccccc ccccccccc
ccccc cccc ccccc ccccc ccccccc ccc ccccc
ccc cccc ccccc ccccccc ccc ccccc ccc cccc
cccc cccccccccc ccccc ccccc ccccccccc ccccc

Move this paragraph...

ddd dddddd ddddddddd ddddd dddddd d
dddddddd ddddd ddddddddd ddd ddddddd d
dddd dddddddddd ddddd dddddd dddd ddd d
dddddddd ddddd ddddddddd ddd ddddddd d
ddd dddddddddd ddd ddddddddd ddddd
ddddd ddd dddddd ddddddd ddddd ddd d
ddddddd

... To here

aaaaaa aaaa aaaaa aaa aaaaaaa aaaaa
aaaaaaaaaa aaaaa aaaaa aaaa aaaaaa aaaaa
aaaaaaa aaa aaa aaaaa aaaaaaa aaa aaaaa
aaaa aaaaaa aaaaa aaaaa aaaaaaaaaa aaaaa
aaaaa aaaaa aaaaa aaaaa aaaaa aaa

ccccc cccccccccc ccccc ccccc ccccc ccccccccc
cccccccccccc cccc ccccc ccccccc ccccc ccccc
cccccccccc cccc ccccc ccccccc ccc ccccc ccc ccccc
ccc ccccc cccccccccc ccccc ccccc ccccccccc ccccc
ccccc ccccc cccccccccc ccc ccc ccccc ccccccccc
cccccccccc ccccc ccccc ccccc ccccc ccccccccc ccccc
ccccc ccccc ccc ccccc ccccccccccc ccccc

ddd dddddd ddddddddd ddddd dddddd ddd
dddddddd ddddd ddddddddd ddd ddddddd ddddd
dddd ddddd ddddd ddddddddd ddddd dddddd ddd
dddd dddddddddd ddddd ddddddddd ddd ddddddd
dddddddd ddddd ddddddddd ddd ddddddd ddddd
ddd ddddddddddd ddd ddddddd ddddd ddd
ddddd ddd dddddd ddddddd ddddd ddd
dddddddd ddd ddddd ddd

bbbbb bbbbb bbbbbbbbb bbbbb bbbbb bbb
bbbbb bbbbbbbbbb bbbbb bbb bbbbbb bbbbbb
bbbbb bbb bbbbbbbb bbbbb bbbbb bbbbb bbbb
bbbbb bbbbb bbbbb bbbbb bbb bbbbbbbb bbb
bbbbbbbbb bbbb bbb bbbbbbbb bbb bbbbbbbbb
bbb bbbbbb bbbbb bbb

FIGURE 5.4
The cut-and-paste operation

overlook some of them, especially if part of the phrase is on one line and the remainder of it is on another line. The **find** function makes it easy to locate such specific text references.

Suppose you were working on a 20-page document, and you discovered that a word was misspelled throughout the document. It would take you a while to locate each occurrence of the misspelled word, and there is no guarantee that you would find them all. With the find function, all you must do is specify the word or phrase to be located. The word processing software does the rest. It will search through the text until it locates the specified word, and then it will stop and show you the word in context. You may choose to terminate the find function

at this point or instruct the software package to proceed. However, one word of CAUTION. Be careful how you specify the word or text to be found. When you specify a search text string (a series of characters representing a word or phrase to be located within an existing body of text) such as *the*, most software packages will find not only *the* but also *they, them, there, their, theory,* and other words beginning with the same specified characters as the search string. Some word processing packages will even find *weather, either, another, blithe,* and other words that have the search string embedded within them. Thus, you should carefully delimit — specify characters that surround the search string, including **blanks** when possible — the text being sought.

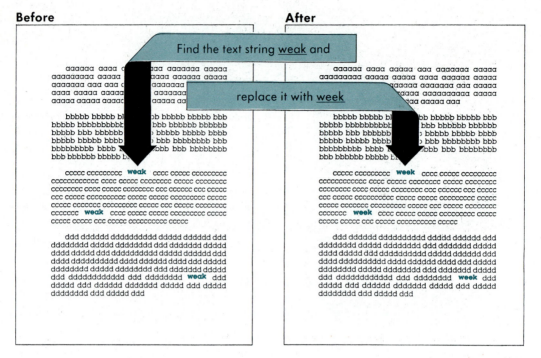

FIGURE 5.5
The find and replace operations

The **replace** function is often coupled with the find function. Not only do you want to find an incorrect word or phrase, but you want to replace it with another word or phrase (assuming that you are not just deleting a mistake). In most cases, the combined find and replace functions begin the same way the find function does. However, you must specify a replacement. In this case, the software package examines the text for each occurrence of the search string and replaces it with the replacement string (see Figure 5.5). Most software packages allow the search and replacement strings to be of different lengths. Furthermore, most packages provide for an affirmative replacement; that is, the search string, when found each time, will not be replaced by the replacement string unless you so indicate.

Page Formatting and Printing Functions

The text you have been working on so far probably looks rather messy. The insertion and deletion, cut-and-paste, copy, and find and replace operations have left you with either short or long pages. In some cases, even the paragraphs look a bit ragged. However, most word processing packages provide a **page formatting** function, frequently called **pagination.** This function simply reformats the existing text so that it fits neatly within page boundaries. In some cases, you will supply the characteristics of the pagination process immediately before the execution of the process. In other cases, as previously mentioned, page characteristics are established at the same time that margins and tab stops are set. In addition, the page formatting function frequently permits you to specify the beginning page number (which usually defaults to page 1), line spacing (single or double space between lines), whether continuous or cut (single sheet) forms are to be used, and so on. Frequently, page formatting is done immediately before printing. Some of the paging characteristics may even be a part of the print function.

Headers and Footers

When you are dealing with a multiple-page report, you may want to put special information at the top and/or bottom of each page—that is, provide a **page header** or a **page footer,** or both. For example, look at the border area of this page and the facing page. Note that the page numbers, the chapter title, and the section title appear in the top margin area. These are page headers. Some books have this information at the bottom of the page—page footers. As shown in Figure 5.6, page headers can be the name of a report (this information could also go at the bottom of the pages). At the bottom of the pages in the example, page numbers are printed; however, these could also be printed at the top of the pages. To produce page numbers, a **page number code** is usually added to the header or footer information to indicate the location and form of the page number. In addition, most word processors support the use of a date code for printing the current date.

Finally, some word processors allow left and right page headers and footers and alternating-page headers and footers (for example, only on odd-numbered pages).

Look at the page headers on this page and the facing page: two header specifications were used. The header on the left page is even with the left margin. The header on the right page is even with the right margin. This makes it convenient for the reader to flip through the text and still see the page numbers and chapter titles. If a single header specification had been used to produce the page numbers at the margin, half of the page numbers would have been on the inside of facing pages and not easily seen by a person flipping through the pages. Thus, the use of headers and footers is based on the type of document being produced and whether or not the pages will face each other.

Output and Font Specifications

Because the primary purpose of word processing software is to produce printed documents, most packages have the capability of varying the appearance of printed text (see Figure 5.7). Many of these special printing functions are highly dependent on the printer used; thus all of the special features may not be available even if supported by your software. Some of the fundamental special printing features are **underlining, double underlining,** and **boldface** type. These options are used to stress a word or phrase visually. Underlining causes a word or phrase to have a line drawn under it. Double underlining causes two sets of lines to be printed under the text (for example, for totals). **Boldface** requires the printer to backspace and print a character or series of characters repeatedly. The result is a bolder—meaning darker (and perhaps wider)—set of characters.

Another feature that may be available is the printing of **subscripts** and **superscripts.** Subscripts are letters, numbers, or

Before

After

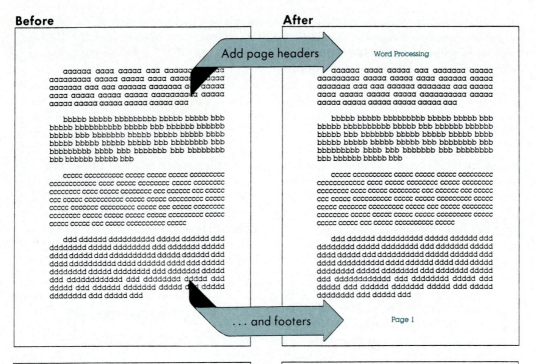

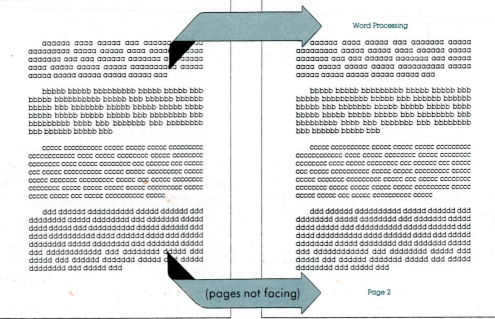

Add page headers

Word Processing

... and footers

Page 1

(pages not facing)

Word Processing

Page 2

FIGURE 5.6
Page headers and footers

```
      What you are looking at is the actual printout
from a word processor produced by a dot matrix printer
in draft mode.   Note that many of the special features,
such as underline and boldface, are illustrated here.

      Some dot matrix printers can create 'letter
quality' output, and some word processing software
can produce text below a line called a subscript
and text above a line, called a superscript.

      Some languages also require the use of overprints
(for example, the word 'señor' or the digit '7').   The
legal profession sometimes uses strike-throughs.

      Finally, it is possible to alter the type style of the
output by choosing a variety of print
fonts. The possible print fonts are limited only by your
imagination.
```

FIGURE 5.7
Controlling printer functions

other symbols that appear slightly below the line of print—like this $_3$. Superscripts appear slightly above the line of print—like this ^{3}. To perform this function, the printer must be capable of both forward and backward movement to a fraction (usually one-half) of the line width. In addition, to print a subscript, the printer would move down a fraction of a line, print the subscript, and move back up to the original line position. Superscripts are produced in the opposite fashion.

Word processing software may also support other features, such as **overstrike** and **strike through.** Overstrikes are used to enhance the appearance of one or more characters. For example, some international languages require the printing of a tilde (˜) above a character. In other cases, it might be desirable to overstrike zeros and sevens (∅ and 7̸). Strike throughs are used to overprint a word or a series of words that must clearly appear in printed form as having been deleted. This is frequently used in legal documents (see Figure 5.7).

A printer may also be able to skip to the top of a new page before it has filled the preceding page; this is called the **forced end-of-page** function. This function can be very handy when you are creating a report element, such as a table, that should not be split across pages.

To ensure exact left-to-right spacing, such as when entering tables, a **soft blank** or a **hard blank** can be used. When printing, some word processors will ignore (suppress) spaces that appear at the beginning of a line. This is done so that the left margin is square. If the spaces are ignored or affected by reformatting, they are soft blanks. However, when report elements such as tables are being produced, spaces at the beginning of lines are often desirable. Thus, hard blanks are placed at the beginning of lines to ensure left-to-right position of these items—hard blanks are not influenced by reformatting.

The **printer stop** feature is used to halt the printer for operator intervention. This may be required to change the paper, the printer spacing, the printing element on a daisy wheel printer, and so on. Other printer controls may be used to begin or end some of the printer functions from within the document itself, rather than using manual means to select the functions. While some controls may be used to select the number of characters per inch **(pitch)** on a line, others may be used for **font** selection. A font is a typeface style. Thus, you may choose to change the type style within the text to *italicize* words or phrases for greater emphasis. Other font controls are used to generate half-size or double-size characters or to change to an international language character set. Additionally, some word processing packages will produce documents in **draft quality,** with a single pass of the print head of a dot matrix printer, or **letter quality,** with two passes of the print head to approximate the quality achieved with daisy wheel printers.

Spelling Verification

If you have difficulty with spelling, the **spelling verification** feature will be a "life saver." This feature is typically available as an option on word processing packages. To use it, first you write your document, then you call for the execution of the "spelling checker." That part of the word processing package then begins to examine every word in the document to see if it appears in its dictionary. If a word is not in its dictionary, the spelling verification feature marks it so that you can see it in the text. It also marks words that appear in the dictionary but that seem to be misspelled. Frequently, the program will ask you if you want to change the spelling of the word or continue to the next word. Some packages allow you to build your own personal dictionary, so that frequently used words, such as technical vocabulary that is not included in the package's own spelling dictionary, will not continue to be marked, and some suggest locations for hyphens (for example, if the word breaks at the end of a line).

The spelling verification feature will not correct bad grammar or incorrect word use. Neither will it correct the spelling of "bad" words—words that are correct but misused (for example, *to* and *too*). However, it will identify words that seem to be spelled incorrectly. It is up to you to make the corrections. Furthermore, proper names (of persons, places, and things) are generally not part of the spelling dictionary and so will be marked by the spelling verification feature. If a name, such as a location (for example, Chicago), is used frequently, it could be placed in your personal dictionary.

Boilerplating

Boilerplating typically means that a document is created from stored textual elements (for example, paragraphs) rather than treated as conventional electronic text (see Figure 5.8). In this case, original text may be fragmented and stored in a number of different files. By using the boilerplating

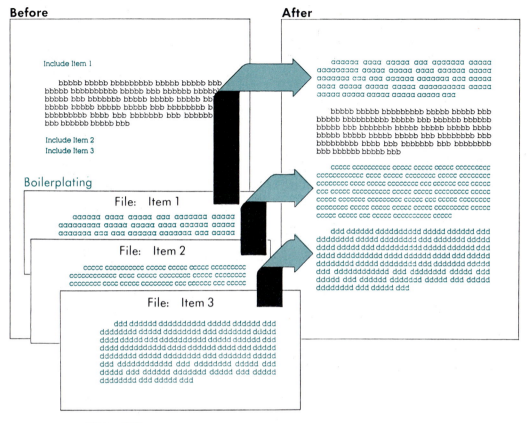

FIGURE 5.8
Boilerplating

feature, these text fragments—all or some of them—are collected into a working document for editing and printing.

To illustrate this feature, suppose you go to a lawyer's office to set up a personal will. Your lawyer has previously studied common legal wills and testaments and has determined which parts of them are relatively standard. Your lawyer has also electronically stored these standard paragraphs and saved them as separate files. When you come in to get your will done, you answer some questions to determine what type of will you need. After the question-and-answer period, the lawyer instructs a typist to enter any specific information on the computer and combine it with the appropriate general paragraphs already stored—boilerplate paragraphs.

In Figure 5.8, the "before" document shows a paragraph that has just been written that is supposed to be combined with three other files that have been stored. When the complete document is put together, the boilerplate paragraphs will be inserted. The result is a will that looks like it has been prepared specifically for you. However, only certain parts are tailored to the individual — the bulk of the document is boilerplate. This technique is also frequently used to produce **form letters.**

Other Word Processing Features

Two common additional features are **multiple column** breaking and **mail merge.** Text that might normally extend for the entire width of a page can be reformatted into multiple columns — like the format used by many newsletters. Multiple columns of text are arranged on the page to minimize the distance the eye has to travel to read an entire line. The number of columns per page depends on the width of the paper. With wide paper or a small font size, it is possible to place three or more columns on a single page. Sometimes the pages are completely arranged electronically and printed as **camera ready copy** — meaning that they are shot by camera to prepare film for printing plate preparation.

The mail merge feature is frequently used for mass mailing purposes. Some word processors permit you to develop a form letter that indicates another file is to be merged during the printing process. For example, names and addresses may be merged into multiple copies of a form letter, as shown in Figure 5.9. Thus, for each copy of the letter that is printed, new name and address information is supplied from the merge file. This feature may also be used to "fill in the blanks" within a document. Thus, if the merge operation is shown inside a paragraph, the insertion would be made at that point.

Mail merging is not the same as boilerplating. In true boilerplating, the only item inserted into your document is an *instruc-*tion to include another document or file at a particular point in the text. When you merge a document, a copy of the document or file to be merged is actually in your document.

Integration with Other Software Packages

Sometimes it is desirable to use products (for example, charts, graphs, tables, or numerical and other data) of another type of software package within a document being written on a word processing package. Unless the word processing function is integrated (combined) with other functions, such as graphics, a special technique must be used to combine these features. This technique is often called the **import** function.

To perform the import function, the product of another software package must be a **text file** (recorded in ASCII — American Standard Code for Information Interchange — character format, or perhaps **DIF — data interchange format** — character format, but not in machine language). Files created by one software package are not necessarily directly accessible by another software package unless they are text files. Each package typically uses its own particular way of formatting and storing data. However, the creation of text files is a common feature of many packages. So, before importing, the first step is to load the data of the other package and create a text file. (You will need to look this up in the package's user manual to determine what function to use to produce material as a text file.) Once the text file is available, you perform the import function, which creates a new file — a duplicate of the text file — in the format used by the word processor.

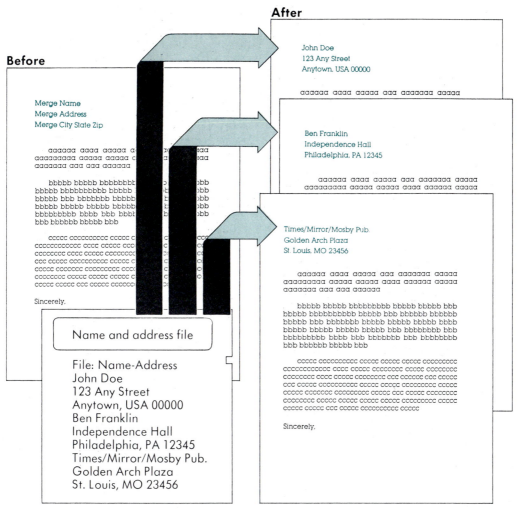

FIGURE 5.9
The mail merge operation: mass mailing

From that point on, all you have to do is perform the normal word processing functions (such as text editing).

Sometimes you will want to do the reverse of importing. If you want to use a word processing file in some other software

package, you will **export** it. The export function creates a text file from a document currently in the format of the word processor. This text file could then be exported into other packages that could use such textual data. Thus, the import function is used to "bring in" a text file, and the export function to "send" or create and store a text file.

Uses of Word Processing

Many of the uses of word processing are obvious. Any secretary primarily responsible for maintaining correspondence with others could use this type of package. By using word processing software, a secretary could transcribe a dictated letter, transmit a draft copy of the letter to the boss, alter the letter on the basis of changes made by the boss, and produce a "letter perfect" copy for mailing. Furthermore, a copy of the letter could be stored electronically, rather than tying up file cabinet space. However, in some companies, even the boss produces letters and other documents such as memos, notices, and reports. The idea is for the document to be produced as quickly as possible. If the boss has the necessary keyboard skills, the document could probably be produced more quickly than if sent to a secretary for typing and later review.

The necessity of producing printed reports is not unique to a business environment. For example, students write reports and résumés. Many people make shopping lists, Christmas card lists, insurance inventories, credit card accounts lists, personal financial statements for bank loan applications, and so on.

Some professions use word processing heavily. For example, the use of the boilerplating feature by the legal profession has been previously mentioned. In other areas of the legal profession, word processing is now being used to produce the final version of trial transcripts.

Most large news agencies use word processing to maintain notes about news events or stories. Many newspapers even have the ability to transmit word processing files directly into newsprint, thus shortening the time required to get the latest edition out. Many publishing firms also have this capability; that is, many authors now write on a word processor, and the publisher typesets the book from the electronic text (disks), thereby facilitating a quick and correct transcription process. This reduces both the number of typesetting errors and the necessity of proofreading the final product.

In the television and movie industries, writers are now using word processing systems to produce scripts. In fact, one writer for a television soap opera credits word processing for the improvement of scripts over the years. This is because scripts can now be rewritten and made available to the actors almost immediately.

In the advertising area, word processing is being used to produce catalogs and other advertising matter. In the mass mailing area, the mail merge feature of word processing systems is singularly responsible for making "personalized" contact possible with millions of potential customers annually. Using the same concept, country clubs can send lists of special events to members, political candidates can seek contributions from or send campaign literature to people in election districts, and amusement parks and tourist resorts can reach target markets for their services.

Word processing usually represents an improvement over any other method of dealing with words. Look around you. You can probably identify a dozen ways to use word processing that haven't yet been mentioned!

Chapter Summary

This chapter introduced word processing. Obviously, words and ideas have been transmitted in various ways throughout history. However, the advent of computers and word processing software has revolutionized the process of creating, editing, and reproducing text—clearly and quickly.

Functions common to most word processing software packages include word origination and text editing: formatting, setting margin and tab stops, deleting/inserting, cut/paste and copy, blocking, scrolling, find and replace, underlining, boldfacing, and so on. Features such as spelling verification are usually options. Other features may also be available for printer control, boilerplating, multiple-column printing, and mail merging. Finally, you have seen that word processing has a number of very useful applications.

Chapter Key Terms

Alignment
Blank
Block
Block buffer
Boilerplating
Boldface
Camera ready copy
Character
Command driven
Control character
Copy
Cut-and-paste
Data interchange format (DIF)
Decimal-point alignment
Dedicated system
Default setting
Document
Double underlining
Draft quality

Dvorak keyboard
Editing
Embedded character
Export
Find
Font
Forced end-of-page
Form letter
Formatting
Hard blank
Hard tab
HELP function
Help screen
Insert
Import
Letter quality (near letter quality)
Line
Mail merge
Margin setting
Menu driven

Multiple column
Overstrike
Page
Page header
Page footer
Page number code
Pagination (page formatting)
Paragraph
Pitch
Printer stop
Printing
Proportionately spaced
QWERTY keyboard
Ragged right
Replace
Right-justified
Ruler
Scrolling
Sentence

Soft blank
Soft tab
Spelling verification
Split screen
Stand-alone system
Status area
Strike through
Subscript
Superscript
Tabs (tab stops)
Text
Text file
Underlining
Window
Word
Word origination
Word processing
Word processing system
Word wrapping

Chapter Questions

1. You are currently a student. Identify the types of text that you are required to produce to fulfill particular assignments. How could word processing be used to fulfill these requirements? Would word processing be a practical alternative for all of your written assignments? If not, which ones could be done more easily in some other way?

2. Select a printed document (use the title page for the next chapter of this text if necessary). See if you can identify the following characteristics of that document:
   a. margin settings
   b. tab stops
   c. page characteristics
   d. page headers
   e. page footers
   f. font changes or special print control functions

3. Describe potential problems with find and replace functions. What happens when your search string is not unique? Discuss ways in which a document can be recovered (returned to its original form) after an accidental replacement caused a number of incorrect modifications of your text. Would your recovery be any different if you had accidentally erased an entire paragraph?

4. Some professions use typed text more frequently than others. Identify ten professions, professional groups, or job classifications that produce text as a major part of their activity. How might word processing be used in your chosen career field?

5. What capabilities must a word processing package have to meet your needs?

6. Explain the difference between the FORMAT command in an operating system and the format function in word processing.

7. What is the difference between hard and soft characters? Specifically, what is the difference between hard tabs and soft tabs, and between hard and soft blanks?

8. What is the difference between the way tab stops and decimal tabs are handled by a word processing package?

9. Explain the difference between merging an "outside" document into your document and boilerplating.

10. What is the difference between word processing and data processing?

Modules/Chapter Five
Word Processing

pfs:Write/Proof
Software Publishing Corporation
1901 Landings Drive
Mountain View, CA 94043

MultiMate
MultiMate International Corporation
52 Oakland Avenue
East Hartford, CT 06108

M5c
WordStar
MicroPro International Corporation
33 San Pablo Avenue
San Rafael, CA 94903

Introduction to Word Processing Modules

The following modules give you the opportunity to learn about one (or more) of three popular word processing packages available for microcomputers. Module 5a covers pfs:Write/Proof, Module 5b introduces MultiMate, and Module 5c discusses WordStar.

Problem Statement for Word Processing Modules

Find the job hunting data in Appendix A. You will use the job hunting problem as an example of how word processing can help you create documents useful in the job hunting process.

The data in Appendix A reveals that you are in contact with a number of companies. The status of this contact varies depending on how far the contact process has progressed. In some cases, you have not yet established a date for an on-site interview (for example, with Champion Cowboy Supply). You will eventually want to write letters to the companies confirming the interview date, so you have decided to develop a business letter that can be modified for each company. The initial draft of this letter is as follows:

```
                          Letterhead
                       (Your Address)


                                              Letter Date

        Company Address

        Salutation

            According to your (telephone call on or
        letter dated) (response date), it appears that
        (interview date) is an acceptable date for my
        visit to your company. Thank you very much for
        expressing an interest in my qualifications
        for your job position at (company name).

            I look forward to visiting you at your
        company. I am excited about the prospect of
        being employed by a company with such an
        excellent reputation.

            Again, let me express my apprecaition for
        your interest and prompt reply to my job
        inquiry. If you need to contact me before our
        meeting, please feel free to call me at
        427-1964.

                                              Closing
```

With this draft in hand, you are ready to start working on your word processing package to produce a business letter that can be used repeatedly. The following list represents the types of operations you may use in the development and production of this letter.

1. Load the word processing package and enter the letterhead information. This information should consist of:

```
(Your Name)
1427 Shannon Lane
Carrolton, TX 75343
```

Once the text for the letterhead has been entered, center the lines.

2. Enter the general information related to the date, company address, and salutation. The date entry should begin in a column position that is at least halfway across the page.

3. Enter the text of the letter and the closing, as shown earlier.

4. After examining the structure of the letter, you decide that the first and second paragraphs should be joined and that the first paragraph should begin with what is currently the second sentence. Thus, you need to alter the separation of the first and second paragraphs and move the second sentence so that it becomes the first sentence. You will probably have to adjust the text afterward to make the letter more visually appealing. You also decide to modify the line margins to produce a 65-character space line.

5. You want the letterhead to stand out, so you decide to boldface it.

6. To verify your spelling, use the spelling checker.

7. Now that the general format of the letter has been established, customize the letter for sending to Champion Cowboy Supply. Their address is:

```
Mr. Joe Garcia
Champion Cowboy Supply
126 Hollyhill Road
Garland, TX 75342
```

8. After you print the letter to Champion Cowboy Supply, prepare letters to the Mosteq Computer Company and the Kelly Construction Company.

Use one (or more) of the following modules and learn to use word processing by working through the preceding steps. This is your opportunity for more hands-on experience with the computer. The steps are not difficult, and the results can be rewarding (and achieved faster than by doing the work by hand).

M5a

pfs:Write/Proof

Learning to Use pfs:Write

Pfs:Write is the word processing package for the pfs Software Series of applications packages. It is available for a variety of microcomputer systems using the MS-DOS or PC-DOS operating systems. The pfs:Write package combines the features of a modern typewriter with the capabilities of a microcomputer. It has many powerful features that allow you quickly and easily to prepare, print, and store the documents you need in your daily work and personal life.

When you are prepared to begin working with pfs:Write, start with the computer's system disk in drive A. If you are using a system that has two disk drives, a disk prepared to hold your documents should be in drive B. After you have booted your system, replace the system disk with the pfs:Write disk, and enter the command WRITE. When the package is loaded into memory, it will respond by placing the MAIN MENU on the screen, as shown in Figure 5a.1. Now press the 1 key, followed by the F10 key, to cause the screen to change to the initial text workspace, as shown in Figure 5a.2. You can return to the MAIN MENU at any time by pressing the ESCape key. By pressing the 1 key and the F10 key, you will return to the text workspace exactly as you left it.

The pfs:Write package makes extensive use of the function keys to perform special operations. One of these special functions is the HELP command. While you are in the text workspace, press the F1 key and the initial help screen will appear (see Figure 5a.3). The help screen explains the function keys and the methods of moving around the text workspace.

Defining the Page — Margin Settings

Now press the F10 key to return to the text workspace. After you become familiar with the cursor control keys and know how to move around the workspace, you are ready to write letters setting up interviews with prospective employers. Press the ESCape key to return to the MAIN MENU, and then press the 2 key, followed by the F10 key. You are now looking at the DEFINE PAGE

Remember

```
            PFS:WRITE MAIN MENU
            -------------------


        1   TYPE/EDIT        4   GET/SAVE/REMOVE

        2   DEFINE PAGE      5   CLEAR

        3   PRINT            6   EXIT



              SELECTION NUMBER:



        (C) 1983 Software Publishing Corporation


F1-Help                                      F10-Continue
```

FIGURE 5A.1
The pfs:Write MAIN MENU

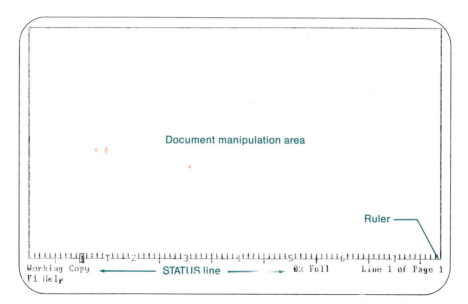

Document manipulation area

Ruler

```
Working Copy    ←——— STATUS line ———→    0% Full    Line 1 of Page 1
F1 Help
```

FIGURE 5A.2
The initial text workspace

Remember

```
         Function Keys                      Cursor Movement

 ┌──────────────┬──────────────┐                  Up
 │              │              │                   ↑
 │ Help    F1   │ F2   Set Tabs│           Left ←    → Right
 │              │              │                   ↓
 ├──────────────┼──────────────┤                 Down
 │ Beg. of Line │ End of Line  │
 │         F3   │ F4           │       Next Tab              ──▶|
 │ Prev. Word   │   Next Word  │       Previous Tab          Shift |◀──
 ├──────────────┼──────────────┤
 │ Delete Word  │ Delete Line  │       Next Screen           PgDn
 │         F5   │ F6           │       Previous Screen       PgUp
 │ Label        │   Duplicate  │
 ├──────────────┼──────────────┤       Beg. of Document      Home
 │ Underline    │ Boldface     │       End of Document       End
 │         F7   │ F8           │
 │ Search & Replace │   Format │       Insert/Overstrike     Ins
 ├──────────────┼──────────────┤       Delete Chars/Blocks   Del
 │              │              │       BackSpace             ←
 │ Append  F9   │ F10 Continue │       Return to Main Menu   Esc
 └──────────────┴──────────────┘

              Press F10 to continue
```

FIGURE 5A.3
Help screen showing the use of function keys

```
                    DEFINE PAGE MENU




            LEFT MARGIN: 10    RIGHT MARGIN: 70

            TOP  MARGIN: 6     BOTTOM MARGIN: 6

            PAGE LENGTH: 66



 HEADING:

 FOOTING:



 F1-Help                                   F10-Continue
```

FIGURE 5A.4
The page definition menu

MENU shown in Figure 5a.4. With this menu, you can set the page margins as well as enter headings and footings that will be printed automatically on each page. Note that all of the margin settings are in characters rather than inches. This is so that pfs:Write will be able to work with a wide variety of printers.

A standard sheet of paper is $8\frac{1}{2}$ inches wide and 11 inches long and has 66 lines of text on the page. The 6-line margins at the top and bottom of the page will be approximately 1 inch. The right and left margins are a little more difficult to keep track of. Pfs:Write allows the left margin to be as small as 1 character and the right margin to be as large as 78. The value for the left margin must be smaller than the value for the right margin.

On a standard sheet of paper, the number of characters per line is generally 85. The number depends on the pitch (number of characters per horizontal inch) of the type and the kind of printer being used. Normally, the number of characters per line of text (after subtracting the right and left margins) should be approximately 65. All of these numbers are estimates; their values can be adjusted to meet your particular needs.

The existing margin settings will meet your needs, so press the F10 key to return to the MAIN MENU. Now press the 1 key, followed by the F10 key, and you will be ready to enter the text for your document.

Finishing the Page Definition — Setting the Tab Stops

Interview letters should have an acceptable form or design. For example, your name and address should be at the top of the first page, the date should also be near the top, and the body of the letter should be easy to read. Although you are sending the letter to several companies, it should appear to be a personal letter, not a form letter. There are several methods that can be used to meet these objectives, and you will need to decide which ones to use.

One of the first decisions you will have to make is where to put the tab stops in your letter. Pfs:Write supports two types of tab stops: the first is the common typewriter tab; the second, a decimal tab, is used when you are entering numbers in a column and you want the decimal points in all the numbers to be in a vertical line.

Press the F2 key to set the tabs for your letter. The cursor will move to the line at the bottom of your page called the *ruler*. The left and right brackets ([and]) on this line mark the left and right margins for the page that you set when you used the DEFINE PAGE MENU. The T on this line is the only automatic tab stop created by pfs:Write. It is five spaces to the right of the left margin and is the normal beginning-of-paragraph tab. To set other tabs for the document, use the left and right arrow keys to move to the position of the desired tab, and press the T key. A new tab will be defined at that location. Moving the cursor to position 45 on the ruler and pressing the T key will set the tab shown in Figure 5a.5.

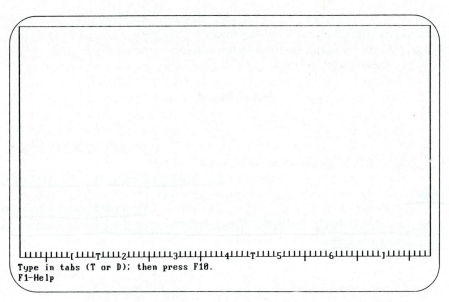

Type in tabs (T or D); then press F10.
F1-Help

FIGURE 5A.5
Setting the tab stops

The decimal tab works a little differently. You still use the arrow keys to move to the place where you want the decimal tab to appear, but you press the D key to enter the decimal tab. When you use the TAB key to move to this tab stop, characters you enter are placed to the left of that stop until a decimal point is entered. After that, any additional characters are placed to the right of the tab stop. After setting all your tabs, press the F10 key to return to the document.

Solving the Job Hunting Problem

The remaining sections in this module are devoted to solving the job hunting problem. You may want to refer to the problem statement in the Introduction to Word Processing Modules before you continue. Also, remember that the data used in this problem can be found in Appendix A.

Entering Text

To start your letter, simply enter your name. After pressing the RETURN key, the cursor will move to the first position of the next line. Now enter your address and press the RETURN key to enter the city, state, and zip code. Pressing the RETURN key twice will move the cursor down two lines, where

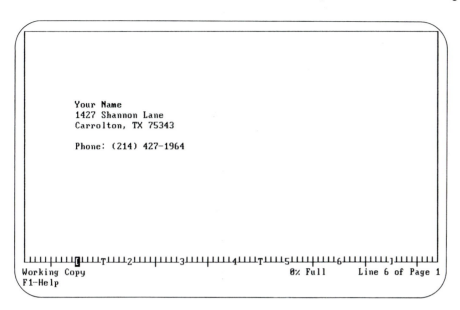

FIGURE 5A.6
Entering the letterhead

you can enter your telephone number. When you have finished entering this part of the text, the screen will look like the one illustrated in Figure 5a.6.

The address you just entered is the top of the letter. To make the letter look more professional, center each line of the address. You can change the position of text on a line by simply moving the cursor to the line you want to change and pressing the F8 key. The line the cursor is on will be highlighted, and a prompt will appear on the status line asking how you want the line formatted, as shown in Figure 5a.7. Pressing an L moves the line so the first character in the line is at the left margin; pressing a C centers the text between the left and right margins; and pressing an R moves the line so the last character in the line is at the right margin. As soon as you enter your choice, the desired adjustment is made and the line is redisplayed. Centering the text for your name, address, and telephone number results in the screen in Figure 5a.8.

Now you are ready to continue writing the letter. Because some parts of the letter will change every time you redo it for a different company, you need to be able to find them quickly. To make this easier, enclose in parentheses all of the parts of the letter that might change. With this in mind, press the TAB key twice to move the cursor to the tab stop at position 45 that was set earlier and enter (date). Continue to enter the letter until you reach the end of the first line. The screen will look like Figure 5a.9.

As you continue writing the letter through the first two sentences, two operations will occur: First, when the cursor arrives at the right margin of the

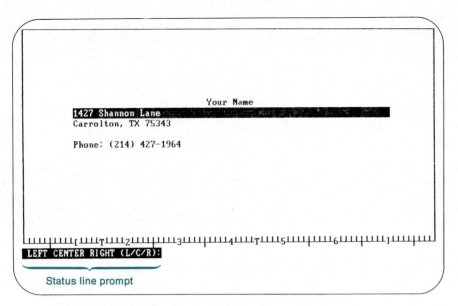

FIGURE 5A.7
Centering your name and address on a line

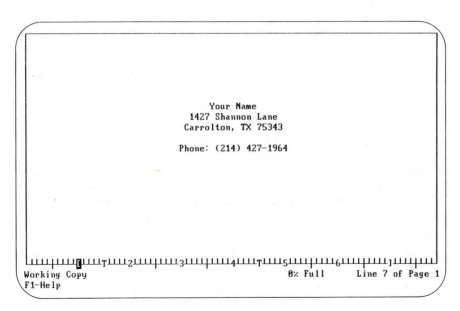

FIGURE 5A.8
Centering the letterhead

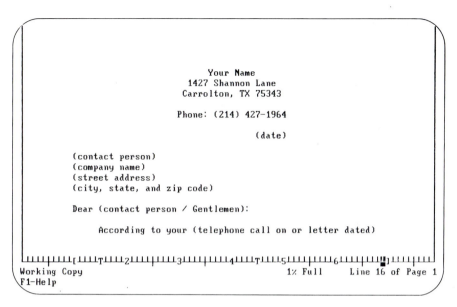

```
                        Your Name
                    1427 Shannon Lane
                    Carrolton, TX 75343

                    Phone: (214) 427-1964

                                (date)

    (contact person)
    (company name)
    (street address)
    (city, state, and zip code)

    Dear (contact person / Gentlemen):

        According to your (telephone call on or letter dated)
```

FIGURE 5A.9
When you reach the bottom of the screen

page, it automatically moves to the left margin of the next line and displays what you have typed. This is called *word wrapping*. The word wrapping operation allows you to enter the text without worrying about when you reach the end of a line. If you have not reached the end of a word when the right margin is encountered, pfs:Write will scan backward until it finds the beginning of the word and then move the complete word to the new line. This operation greatly simplifies and speeds up the process of entering text material.

The second operation that occurs when you enter the complete first two sentences of the letter is that your name disappears off the top of the screen. However, your name is still a part of the letter; the package has just moved the screen's view of the letter further down the page so that you can see what you are currently typing. This operation is called *scrolling*, and it enables you to view the part of the document you are working on. If you wish to see the top of the letter, simply press the up arrow key, the PG UP key, or the HOME key. After entering the first two sentences, your view of the letter is the same as the one in Figure 5a.10. Once you have entered the completed letter, the screen will look like the one illustrated in Figure 5a.11.

Editing Text

If you make mistakes while entering the letter — whether you notice them when you make them or later on — you can correct them easily. Use the cursor

```
                        1427 Shannon Lane
                        Carrolton, TX 75343

                    Phone: (214) 427-1964

                              (date)

      (contact person)
      (company name)
      (street address)
      (city, state, and zip code)

      Dear (contact person / Gentlemen):

           According to your (telephone call on or letter dated)
      (response date), it appears that (interview date) is an
      acceptable date for my visit to your company.  Thank you very
      much for expressing an interest in my qualifications for your
      job position at (company name).




|||||||||||||█|||T|||2|||||||||||3|||||||||||4|||T||||5|||||||||6|||||||||||]|||||||||
Working Copy                                   1% Full      Line 21 of Page 1
F1-Help
```

FIGURE 5A.10
Continuing the letter—the first paragraph

```
      Dear (contact person / Gentlemen):

           According to your (telephone call on or letter dated)
      (response date), it appears that (interview date) is an
      acceptable date for my visit to your company.  Thank you very
      much for expressing an interest in my qualifications for your
      job position at (company name).

           I look forward to visiting you at your company.  I am
      excited about the prospect of being employed by a company
      with such an excellent reputation.

           Again, let me express my apprecaition for your interest
      and prompt reply to my job inquiry.  If you need to contact
      me before our meeting please feel free to call me at 427-
      1964.

                         Sincerely,


                         Your Name

|||||||||||||█|||T|||2|||||||||||3|||||||||||4|||T||||5|||||||||6|||||||||||]|||||||||
Working Copy                                   3% Full      Line 33 of Page 1
F1-Help
```

FIGURE 5A.11
The complete letter

control keys to move the cursor to where you want to make a correction. There are now several options available to you. If you enter characters, whatever is on the screen will be replaced with what you type. If you press the INSERT key before entering characters, then whatever you type will be inserted at the cursor location—moving the rest of the text to the right.

You also have two methods of erasing text. If you press the BACKSPACE key, the cursor will move one position to the left, deleting the character to the left. This will not move the text that is to the right of the cursor. Pressing the DELETE key will delete the character under the cursor and move the text to the right of the cursor one position to the left. If you need to erase more than a few characters, you can use the SHIFT and F5 keys to delete the entire word the cursor is on. The SHIFT and F6 keys can be used to delete the complete line the cursor is located on.

Through the use of these keys, mistakes can be corrected quickly. This can give you a professional-looking document without the necessity of retyping an entire page as you would have to do if you were using a typewriter.

A Cut-and-Paste Operation

When you are reading a document after it has been completely entered, you may change your mind about how you want the text to read. For example, the first and second paragraphs of the letter you just wrote would read better if they were combined. To accomplish this, move the cursor to the left margin of the first line in the second paragraph; press the DELETE key until the letter I appears under the cursor. Move the cursor up one line and press the DELETE key again to move the paragraph up one line. Finally, move the cursor to a position two spaces past the period at the end of the first paragraph and press the DELETE key one more time; the paragraphs will be joined, as shown in Figure 5a.12. Note that you have done more than remove the spaces that separated the end of the first paragraph from the beginning of the second. The two paragraphs have actually been joined, forming one paragraph, and the resulting paragraph has been reformatted.

Reviewing the letter again, you note that the first paragraph is very positive. This is good practice when writing business letters. However, the paragraph would flow better if the second sentence were used as the opening. To exchange the first sentence with the second, you need to perform a cut-and-paste operation. In pfs:Write, this is called a *block move*.

The first step in a block move is to label the block you want to work with. Since it is easier to move the second sentence, move the cursor so that it is positioned over the "T" in "Thank you" at the beginning of the second sentence, and press the F5 key. Now move the cursor to the last character in the second sentence, the period. Figure 5a.13 shows what the screen will look like now that the second sentence has been "labeled."

```
Dear (contact person / Gentlemen):

     According to your (telephone call on or letter dated)
(response date), it appears that (interview date) is an
acceptable date for my visit to your company.  Thank you very
much for expressing an interest in my qualifications for your
job position at (company name).  I look forward to visiting
you at your company.  I am excited about the prospect of
being employed by a company with such an excellent
reputation.

     Again, let me express my appreciation for your interest
and prompt reply to my job inquiry.  If you need to contact
me before our meeting please feel free to call me at 427-
1964.

                         Sincerely,


                         Your Name


Working Copy                      3% Full     Line 20 of Page 1
F1-Help
```

FIGURE 5A.12
Joining the first and second paragraphs

```
Dear (contact person / Gentlemen):

     According to your (telephone call on or letter dated)
(response date), it appears that (interview date) is an
acceptable date for my visit to your company.  Thank you very
much for expressing an interest in my qualification for you
job position at (company name).  I look forward to visiting
you at your company.  I am excited about the prospect of
being employed by a company with such an excellent
reputation.

     Again, let me express my appreciation for your interest
and prompt reply to my job inquiry.  If you need to contact
me before our meeting please feel free to call me at 427-
1964.
                         Sincerely,


                         Your Name


Working Copy    Labelling         3% Full     Line 20 of Page 1
F1-Help
```

FIGURE 5A.13
Marking a sentence for moving

```
Dear (contact person / Gentlemen):

      Thank you very much for expressing an interest in my
qualification for you job position at (company name).
According to your (telephone call on or letter dated)
(response date), it appears that (interview date) is an
acceptable date for my visit to your company.  I look forward
to visiting you at your company.  I am excited about the
prospect of being employed by a company with such an
excellent reputation.

      Again, let me express my appreciation for your interest
and prompt reply to my job inquiry.  If you need to contact
me before our meeting please feel free to call me at 427-
1964.
                        Sincerely,


                        Your Name
```

```
Working Copy                              3% Full    Line 16 of Page 1
F1-Help
```

FIGURE 5A.14
The new letter with the move completed

After the block has been labeled, you may remove, copy, or move it. To move a block to another location, you must first remove it from its current location. To do this, simply press the DELETE key. When you press the DELETE key, the block is removed from the text of your document and placed in a special memory area known as the *block buffer* (or holding area). The block remains in the block buffer until it is replaced by another block or until the computer is turned off. Now move the cursor to the place where you want the block to begin—to the "A" in "According" at the beginning of the first sentence. By pressing the F6 key, you will duplicate the contents of the block buffer beginning at the location of the cursor. The second sentence now begins the paragraph (see Figure 5a.14).

To copy the sentence—that is, to repeat it rather than move it—in another location, the steps are similar. After labeling the block, press the F6 key instead of the DELETE key to copy the block into the block buffer. Then move the cursor to the desired location and copy the contents of the block buffer by pressing the F6 key again.

Page Formatting—Redefining the Page

Your letter appears to be a little too short. Rather than trying to think of additional text to add, it would be easier to make the letter appear longer by

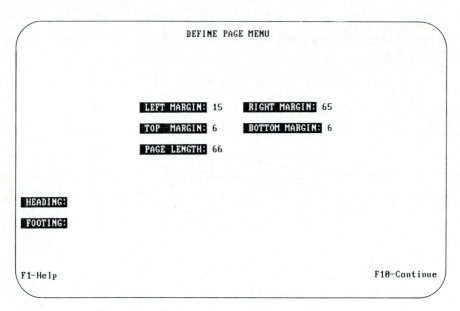

FIGURE 5A.15
Setting new margins — the DEFINE PAGE MENU

making the lines shorter. The way to reformat the complete page is through the DEFINE PAGE MENU that you used earlier. Press the ESCape key to return to the MAIN MENU, the 2 key to indicate you want to define your page, and the F10 key to enter the DEFINE PAGE MENU. Now change the left margin to 15 and the right margin to 65, as illustrated in Figure 5a.15. Return to your document by first pressing the F10 key, then the 1 key when you are in the MAIN MENU, and the F10 key again: your letter will look like the one in Figure 5a.16.

After redefining your letter, recenter the heading and reset the items that where entered at position 45. The change in the left margin moved all of the text you entered to the right five characters.

Enhancing the Letter for Effect — Output Specifications

Pfs:Write supports the use of three print enhancements directly from the package: forced page break, underlining, and boldface. Other enhancements supported by your printer can be used by placing commands for the printer in your document. To send commands to your printer, enter the command *PRINTER code 1, code 2, and so on*, or *P code 1, code 2, and so on*. Note that the codes used will be specifically for the printer you are using and not pfs:Write.

```
         Dear (contact person / Gentlemen):

              Thank you very much for expressing an interest
         in my qualification for you job position at
         (company name).  According to your (telephone call
         on or letter dated) (response date), it appears
         that (interview date) is an acceptable date for my
         visit to your company.  I look forward to visiting
         you at your company.  I am excited about the
         prospect of being employed by a company with such
         an excellent reputation.

              Again, let me express my apprecaition for your
         interest and prompt reply to my job inquiry.  If
         you need to contact me before our meeting please
         feel free to call me at 427-1964.
                             Sincerely,


                             Your Name


 Working Copy                        3% Full      Line 32 of Page 1
 F1-Help
```

FIGURE 5A.16

The letter with new margin definitions

One printer code that is supported by pfs:Write and changes the way the document is printed is the forced page break. If you wish to start a new page at a particular location in your document, simply enter the command *NEW PAGE* or *N*. The line following the new-page command will begin on the next page of the printed output.

To underline a character, move the cursor to the character you want to underline and press the SHIFT and F7 keys. To underline several characters, press the SHIFT and F7 keys repeatedly. The status line will identify these print enhancements whenever the cursor is on the enhanced character.

The final print enhancement supported by pfs:Write is boldface. This feature works exactly the same as the underline feature, except that you use the SHIFT and F8 keys to boldface the character. Use boldface to enhance your name, address, and telephone number in the letter, as illustrated in Figure 5a.17.

Checking for Spelling Errors

The pfs Software Series provides a companion package to pfs:Write called pfs:Proof. Pfs:Proof is designed to proofread all text documents created by pfs:Write. It finds misspelled words using a 100,000-word dictionary. It also identifies repeated words, run-together words, and irregularly capitalized

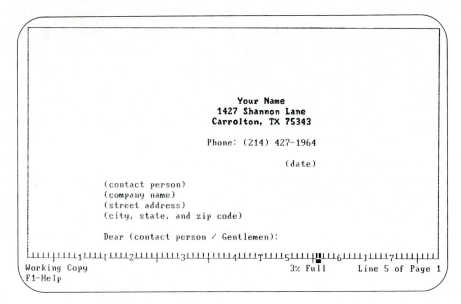

FIGURE 5a.17
Boldfacing the letterhead

words, and it allows you to correct them on the spot. Additionally, pfs:Proof allows you to add words to the dictionary through the use of a personal dictionary.

Before using pfs:Proof, you must save your letter on your data disk. To save the letter, press the ESCape key to return to the MAIN MENU, and then press the 4 key, followed by the F10 key, to enter the GET/SAVE/REMOVE MENU. This menu allows you to retrieve a file that has been previously saved, to erase a file from your data disk, or to save the document you have been working on.

Once the screen displays the GET/SAVE/REMOVE MENU, to save the letter press the 2 key and the TAB key and enter the name of the file you want to use for saving the letter. Saving the file as B:JOBS is illustrated in Figure 5a.18. If you cannot remember the names that you have already used for files on the data disk, enter B: and press the F10 key. Pfs:Write will display a list of the file names on the disk in drive B.

To use pfs:Proof on the letter you have just completed and saved, exit the pfs:Write program by pressing the 6 key, followed by the F10 key, while in the MAIN MENU. Replace the pfs:Write disk in drive A with the pfs:Proof disk. Now enter the command PROOF. The pfs:Proof MAIN MENU, shown in Figure 5a.19, will appear on the screen.

To begin proofing your letter, press the 1 key, followed by the RETURN key. Pfs:Proof will display a directory of the contents of drive B, as illustrated in

```
                    GET/SAVE/REMOVE MENU



                   1   GET DOCUMENT

                   2   SAVE DOCUMENT

                   3   REMOVE FILE



              SELECTION NUMBER: 2
              DIRECTORY OR FILE NAME: B:JOBS




  F1-Help                                        F10-Continue
```

FIGURE 5A.18
**Saving your letter — the GET/SAVE/
REMOVE/MENU**

```
                    PFS:PROOF MAIN MENU
                    -------------------


                   1   PROOF DOCUMENT

                   2   UPDATE DICTIONARY

                   3   EXIT


                   SELECTION NUMBER:


           Copyright 1984, fut·heuristix Inc.

         Copyright 1984, Software Publishing Corporation


  F1-Help                                        ↵ Continue
```

FIGURE 5A.19
pfs: Proof MAIN MENU

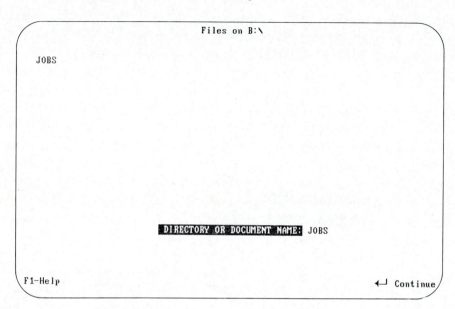

FIGURE 5A.20
Getting the document for spelling checking

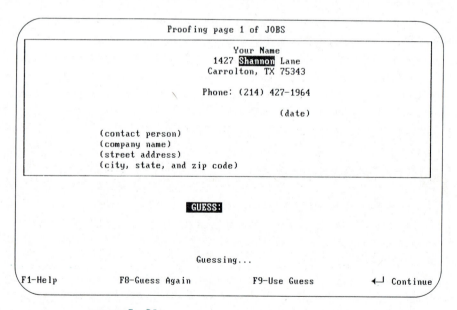

FIGURE 5A.21
Finding misspelled words

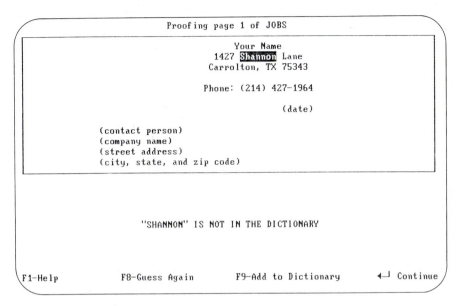

FIGURE 5A.22
Adding your street name to the dictionary

Figure 5a.20. You simply enter JOBS, and the package will begin proofing your letter. Pfs:Proof assumes that the document is located in drive B.

The first word that pfs:Proof finds that is not in the dictionary is your name. If you have spelled your name correctly, press the RETURN key. The message (your name) IS NOT IN THE DICTIONARY will be displayed; you can press the F1 key for help, press the F8 key to have the package "guess again," press the F9 key to add your name to the dictionary, or press the RETURN key to continue checking the letter without making any changes. The next word not in the dictionary is "Shannon," as illustrated in Figure 5a.21. Pressing the RETURN key gives you the opportunity to add this word to the personal dictionary, as shown in Figure 5a.22. Pressing the RETURN key again will cause pfs:Proof to continue checking the letter.

The package will now go on to find that it does not recognize "Carrolton," "TX," or "apprecaition." When pfs:Proof arrives at the word "apprecaition," which is indeed misspelled, it will guess what the correct spelling should be, as in Figure 5a.23. Press the F9 key to use the guess to correct the word, and you have the results in Figure 5a.24.

When pfs:Proof has finished checking your letter, the screen in Figure 5a.25 will be displayed; pressing the RETURN key will display the MAIN MENU. Now that your letter has been checked, you can exit pfs:Proof by

```
          Proofing page 1 of JOBS

    that (interview date) is an acceptable date for my
    visit to your company.  I look forward to visiting
    you at your company.  I am excited about the
    prospect of being employed by a company with such
    an excellent reputation.

        Again, let me express my  apprecaition  for your
    interest and prompt reply to my job inquiry.  If
    you need to contact me before our meeting please
    feel free to call me at 427-1964.
                                Sincerely,




            GUESS:  appreciation




 F1-Help        F8-Guess Again        F9-Use Guess      ↵ Continue
```

FIGURE 5A.23
Finding the last misspelled word

```
          Proofing page 1 of JOBS

    that (interview date) is an acceptable date for my
    visit to your company.  I look forward to visiting
    you at your company.  I am excited about the
    prospect of being employed by a company with such
    an excellent reputation.

        Again, let me express my  appreciation  for your
    interest and prompt reply to my job inquiry.  If
    you need to contact me before our meeting please
    feel free to call me at 427-1964.
                                Sincerely,




            GUESS:  appreciation




 F1-Help        F8-Guess Again        F9-Use Guess      ↵ Continue
```

FIGURE 5A.24
pfs:Proof's best guess

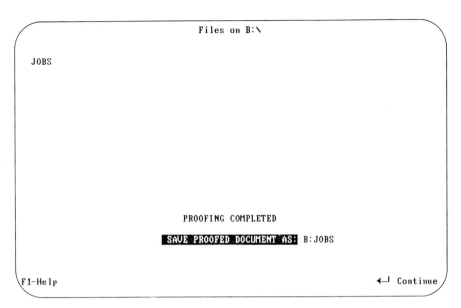

FIGURE 5A.25
Saving the proofed document

pressing the 3 key, followed by the RETURN key. Remove the pfs:Proof disk from drive A and place the pfs:Write disk back in drive A. You are ready to finish the letters.

Personalized Messages — Find and Replace Functions

With the pfs:Write disk in drive A and your data disk in drive B, enter the command WRITE to load the package and get the MAIN MENU. By selecting option 4 and pressing the F10 key, you display the GET/SAVE/REMOVE MENU that was shown in Figure 5a.18. To retrieve your document, select number 1, press the TAB key, and enter B:JOBS. Pressing the F10 key will retrieve and display your letter on the screen, placing you in the edit mode.

Now that you are ready to send the three letters needed to set up your interviews, the phrases marked with parentheses in the master letter need to be personalized. Looking over the letter, you note that you have used (company name) twice. Rather than entering the company name for each letter twice, you can use the Search and Replace functions in pfs:Write to change this text. To use this function, press the F7 key to display the search options shown in Figure 5a.26.

F7 - search options

```
                          Your Name
                       1427 Shannon Lane
                     Carrolton, TX 75343

                    Phone: (214) 427-1964

                                    (date)

      (contact person)
      (company name)
      (street address)
      (city, state, and zip code)

      Dear (contact person / Gentlemen):

 SEARCH FOR:
 REPLACE WITH:                        MANUAL OR AUTOMATIC (M/A): M
```

FIGURE 5A.26
Search and replace text in the letter

```
      (contact person)
      Champion Cowboy Supply
      (street address)
      (city, state, and zip code)

      Dear (contact person / Gentlemen):

          Thank you very much for expressing an interest
      in my qualification for you job position at
      (company name).  According to your (telephone call
      on or letter dated) (response date), it appears
      that (interview date) is an acceptable date for my
      visit to your company.  I look forward to visiting
      you at your company.  I am excited about the
      prospect of being employed by a company with such
      an excellent reputation.

          Again, let me express my appreciation for your
      interest and prompt reply to my job inquiry.  If
      you need to contact me before our meeting please
      feel free to call me at 427-1964.
 SEARCH FOR: (company name)
 REPLACE WITH:Champion Cowboy Supply          REPLACE (YES/NO/QUIT):
```

FIGURE 5A.27
Replacing (company name)

The first item that should be entered is the word or phrase that you want to search for. In your case, this is (company name). However, you can also enter characters followed by two periods (abc..) to find words beginning with those characters, two periods followed by characters (..abc) to find words ending with those characters, a set of characters preceded and followed by two periods (..abc..) to find words containing those characters in any position, or simply two periods (..) to find the next word in the letter, no matter what it is.

After pressing the TAB key, you can enter the word or phrase to be used for replacement. In your case, for the letter going to Mr. Joe Garcia, the phrase would be "Champion Cowboy Supply." Pressing the TAB key again gives you the choice of making the replacements Automatic (A) or Manual (M) (see Figure 5a.26). If you choose to use manual replacement, when the search phrase is found, you will need to enter a Y to do the replacement, or an N to leave the text as it is.

Once you have decided how you want to operate the search options, press the F10 key to begin the search. Pressing the Q key will stop the search operation and return you to normal editing. Figure 5a.27 illustrates the manual replacement of the phrase (company name) with Champion Cowboy Supply.

Printing Your Letter — The Print Function

You have replaced the phrases marked by parentheses with the appropriate entries, so now you are finally ready to print the letters. The PRINT MENU in pfs:Write is used to produce a paper copy of the document that is currently in memory. The package will print to any printer that is properly connected to your computer system. It will allow you to print the entire document, a range of pages, or a single page from the document. If needed, pfs:Write will print multiple copies of the document or selected pages. It will also allow you to choose to print the document in single-space or double-space format, pause at the end of each page to position a new sheet of paper, or shift the entire document to the right, allowing for variations in the printer's left margin. Pfs:Write will even search your letter for an address and print an envelope for you. Additionally, the PRINT MENU will allow you to combine data from pfs:File with the document to produce form letters or insert a graph from pfs:Graph, a report from pfs:Report, or other pfs:Write documents while printing.

All of these operations are accomplished by using the print enhancements mentioned earlier or by using the options available in the PRINT MENU shown in Figure 5a.28. Since none of these options is needed to print your letter, simply bring up the PRINT MENU from the MAIN MENU by pressing the 3 key, followed by the F10 key. Pressing the F10 key will cause the package to print your letter, as shown in Figure 5a.29. To stop the printing operation, press the SPACE BAR. Pressing the F10 key will cause the printing to

```
                          PRINT MENU


            FROM PAGE: 1   TO PAGE: 1

            PRINT TO: LPT1:

            PAUSE BETWEEN PAGES (Y/N): N

            NUMBER OF COPIES: 1

            SINGLE/DOUBLE/ENVELOPE (S/D/E): S

            INDENT: 0

            JOINING PFS:GRAPH (Y/N): N

            PFS FILE NAME:




F1-Help                                        F10-Continue
```

FIGURE 5A.28
Printing the letter — the PRINT MENU

resume. You can stop printing and return to the MAIN MENU by pressing the
ESCape key.

Other Features of pfs:Write

Although all of the functions available with pfs:Write have already been mentioned, some of the special features should be emphasized. Pfs:Write is one of
the few word processing packages that allow for true boilerplating. You can, as
with most word processing packages, add a document to the text you are
working on by using the F9 key for the Append function. Additionally, you can
have another document printed as a part of the text you are working on without
having to actually add it to your current text. This is done by using the command *JOIN file name*.

Pfs:Write also has the capability of printing graphs created by pfs:Graph
(discussed in Chapter 8) through the use of the command *GRAPH picture file
name*.

The package will also use the contents of specific fields found in a file
created by pfs:File (discussed in Chapter 7). The interface between pfs:Write,
pfs:Graph, and pfs:File is discussed in Module 10a — the pfs series.

```
                              Your Name
                           1427 Shannon Lane
                           Carrolton, TX 75343

                         Phone: (214) 427-1964

                                          January 12, 198x

          Mr. Peter Hoague
          Mosteq Computer Company
          1420 Wozniak Way
          Farmers Branch, TX 76331
```

```
                              Your Name
                           1427 Shannon Lane
                           Carrolton, TX 75343

                         Phone: (214) 427-1964

                                          January 12, 198x

          Mr. Joe Garcia
          Champion Cowboy Supply
          126 Hollyhill Road
          Garland TX 75342
```

```
                              Your Name
                           1427 Shannon Lane
                           Carrolton, TX 75343

                         Phone: (214) 427-1964

                                          January 12, 198x

          Kelly Construction Company
          1414 Jupiter Rd.
          Garland, TX 75242

          Dear Gentlemen:

              Thank you very much for expressing an interest
          in my qualifications for your position at
          Kelly Construction Company.  According to your
          letter dated December 11, 198x, it appears that
          January 22, 198x is an acceptable date for my visit
          to your company.  I look forward to visiting you at
          your company.  I am excited about the prospect of
          being employed by a company with such an excellent
          reputation.

              Again, let me express my appreciation for your
          interest and prompt reply to my job inquiry.  If
          you need to contact me before our meeting please
          feel free to call me at 427-1964.

                              Sincerely,

                              Your Name
```

FIGURE 5A.29
The final letters setting interview dates

MultiMate

Learning to Use MultiMate

MultiMate is the professional word processing package from Multimate International Corporation. It is available for a variety of microcomputer systems using the MS-DOS or PC-DOS operating system. The MultiMate package combines the features of a modern typewriter with the capabilities of a microcomputer. It has many powerful features that allow you quickly and easily to prepare, print, and store the documents you need in your daily work and personal life.

When you are prepared to begin working with MultiMate, start with the MultiMate disk in drive A. If you are using a system that has two disk drives, a disk prepared to hold your documents should be in drive B. After you have booted your system, enter the command WP. When the package is loaded into memory, it will respond by placing the MultiMate copyright notice on the screen. Pressing the SPACE BAR will cause the main menu to appear on the screen, as shown in Figure 5b.1. Now press the 2 key, followed by the RETURN key, to cause the screen to change to the initial new document screen shown in Figure 5b.2. Pressing the RETURN key after entering a name, jobsmm, for the new document will change the screen to the DOCUMENT SUMMARY SCREEN shown in Figure 5b.3. After entering the information needed for this screen, press the F10 key to get the MODIFY DOCUMENT DEFAULTS shown in Figure 5b.4, and press the F10 key again to get the initial text workspace shown in Figure 5b.5.

You can return to the main menu at any time by pressing the F10 key. When you press the F10 key, your document is automatically saved on the disk in drive B. To return to your document, you must choose option 1 in the main menu and go through the same three screens that were used in creating a new document.

The MultiMate package makes extensive use of the function keys to perform special operations. One of these special functions is the HELP command. While you are in the text workspace, press the SHIFT and F1 keys, and the initial help screen will appear (see Figure 5b.6). The screen explains the general HELP topics available and gives instructions for obtaining help about a partic-

```
            ┌─────────────────────────┐
            │    M U L T I M A T E     │
            │  Word Processor  Ver 3.22│
            └─────────────────────────┘


            1) Edit an Old Document
            2) Create a New Document

            3) Print Document Utility
            4) Printer Control Utilities
            5) Merge Print Utility

            6) Document Handling Utilities
            7) Other Utilities
            8) Spell Check a Document
            9) Return to DOS

               DESIRED FUNCTION: ▪


     Enter the number of the function; press RETURN
        Hold down Shift and press F1 for HELP menu

                                            S:↑ N:↓
```

FIGURE 5B.1
The MultiMate main menu

```
                    CREATE A NEW DOCUMENT

              Enter the Name of the New Document

         Drive :  B          Document : ▒▒▒▒▒▒▒▒▒▒▒▒

Approximately 00362496 characters [00144 Page(s)] available on Drive B












        Press return to continue, PgDn to switch drive directory    S:↑ N:↓
```

FIGURE 5B.2
Creating the document

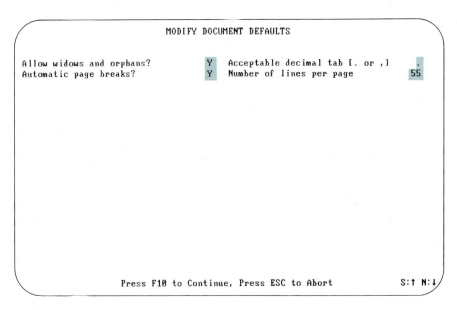

```
                        DOCUMENT SUMMARY SCREEN


  Document   JOBSMM                    Total pages    0
  Author     your name
  Addressee  companies
  Operator   your name

  Identification key words :
             letter
             interview


  Comments :
      letter to set up interviews with companies




  Creation Date    04/08/86          Keystrokes last session    0
  Modification Date 04/08/86         Total keystrokes           0

         Use tab keys to change fields - Press F10 when finished
         If creating a Library press F5   (Do not fill in screen)      S:↑ N:↓
```

FIGURE 5B.3
Entering document summary information


```
                        MODIFY DOCUMENT DEFAULTS


  Allow widows and orphans?        Y   Acceptable decimal tab [. or ,]     .
  Automatic page breaks?           Y   Number of lines per page           55
```



```
              Press F10 to Continue, Press ESC to Abort        S:↑ N:↓
```

FIGURE 5B.4
Setting the document defaults

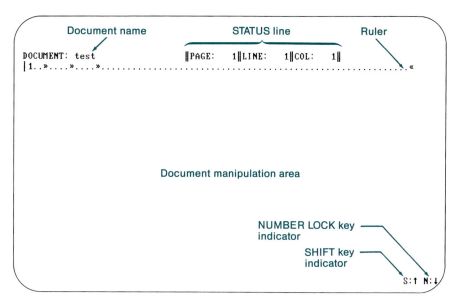

FIGURE 5B.5
The initial text work space

```
DOCUMENT: JOBSMM              ‖PAGE:    1‖LINE:    1‖COL:    1‖

HELP MENUS

        Press the function key for the help desired.
        Example: Press the F8 key for help on the Copy function.
                 Press Alt F for help on the Footer function.
        To get help on more general topics, press one of the following keys:

        HELP DESIRED                          PRESS
        ------------------------------        -----
        CURSOR POSITIONING                      1
        EDITING FUNCTIONS                       2
        FORMAT LINE CONTROLS                    3
        PRINTING FUNCTIONS                      4
        MISCELLANEOUS FUNCTIONS                 5
        LIST OF ALL HELP TOPICS AND KEYS        6




Press Escape to exit                                        S:↓ N:↓
```

FIGURE 5B.6
The initial HELP MENU

```
DOCUMENT: JOBSMM                 ‖PAGE:    1‖LINE:    35‖COL:    1‖

COPY

1.  Move the cursor on the first character or symbol to be copied.
2.  Press the Copy function key F8.
    (You will be prompted from this point on.)
    To copy the current Format Line along with the text, press the Format
    function key F9.
3.  Use the Highlighting Process to identify the text to be copied.
4.  Press the Copy function key F8.
5.  Move the cursor to the new location where the text is to be inserted.
6.  Press the Copy function key F8.




                                                                    S:↓ N:↓
Press Escape to exit, Return to go to previous menu
```

FIGURE 5B.7
Help instructions for the COPY command

ular command. If you press the F8 key, you will receive instructions on how to use the COPY command, as shown in Figure 5b.7. Now press the ESCape key to return to the text workspace.

Table 5b.1 provides a summary of the keys used to move the cursor around the text work area. After you become familiar with the cursor control keys and know how to move around the workspace, you are ready to write letters setting up interviews with prospective employers. Interview letters should have an acceptable form or design. For example, your name and address should be at the top of the first page, the date should also be near the top, and the body of the letter should be easy to read. Although you are sending the letter to several companies, it should appear to be a personal letter, not a form letter. There are several methods that can be used to meet these objectives, and you will need to decide which ones to use.

One of the first decisions you will have to make is where to put the tab stops. MultiMate supports two types of tab stops: the first is the common typewriter tab; the second, a decimal tab, is used when you are entering numbers in a column and you want the decimal points in the column to be in a vertical line.

Press the F9 key to set the tabs for your letter. The cursor will move to the line at the top of your page called the *ruler*. The length of this line indicates the length of a line of text that can be entered into your document. The >>'s on the line are the only automatic tab stops created by MultiMate. They are located

TABLE 5B.1 MultiMate Cursor Commands

Key	Function	Moves to
Shift Tab	Back tab	Beginning of current line
Down Arrow	Cursor down	Down one line
Left Arrow	Cursor left	Previous character
Right Arrow	Cursor right	Next character
Up Arrow	Cursor up	Previous line
End	End of screen	Last character of screen
Ctrl End	End of page	Last character of page
F1	Go to page	Beginning of entered page
Alt T	Go to tab	First character after a tab
Home	Home	First character of screen
Ctrl PgDn	Next page	First character of next page
Ctrl Right Arrow	Next word	First character of next word
PgDn	Page down	Down 18 lines
PgUp	Page up	Up 18 lines
Ctrl PgUp	Previous page	Last character of previous page
Ctrl Left Arrow	Previous word	First character of previous word
Alt F3	Scroll left	First character of line
Alt F4	Scroll right	Last character of line
Tab	Tab	Next tab
Ctrl Home	Top of page	Beginning of current page

five, ten, and fifteen spaces to the right of the left margin and are the normal beginning-of-paragraph tabs. To set other tabs for the document, use the left and right arrow keys to move to the desired position of the tab and press the TAB key. A new tab will be defined (and >>'s will appear) at that location. To remove the tab stops, move the cursor to the location of a current tab indicator and press the SPACE BAR. Remove the tabs at positions 10 and 15, move the cursor to position 45 on the ruler, and press the TAB key to set the tab shown in Figure 5b.8.

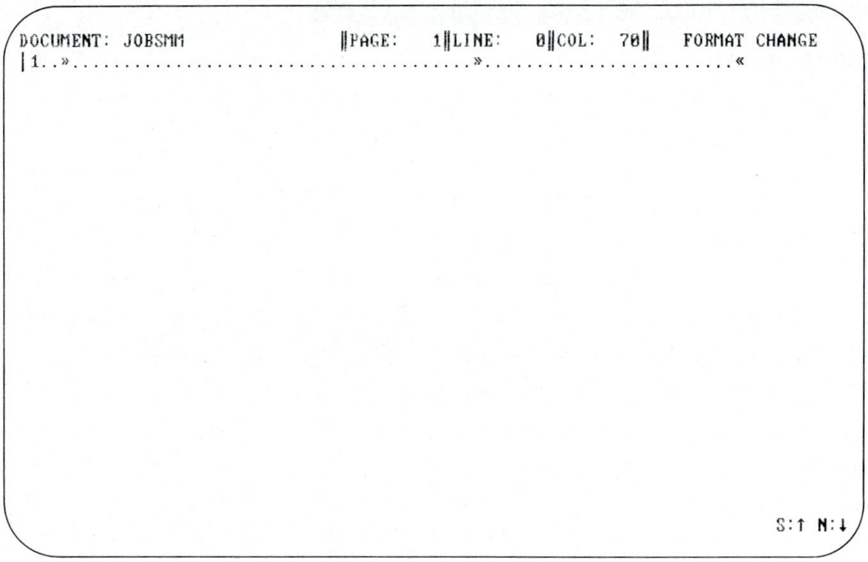

```
/ DOCUMENT: JOBSMM              ‖PAGE:   1‖LINE:   0‖COL:  70‖   FORMAT CHANGE
| 1..».........................................».........................«




































                                                              S:↑ N:↓
```

FIGURE 5B.8
Setting the tab stops

The decimal tab works a little differently. You still use the arrow keys to move to the place where you want the decimal tab to appear, and you press the TAB key as if you were entering a normal tab. When you use the TAB key to move to the tab stop and enter numbers, press the SHIFT and F4 keys. Now the characters that you enter are moved to the left of that stop until a decimal point is entered. After that, any additional characters are placed to the right of the tab stop. After setting all your tabs, press the F9 key to return to the document.

Solving the Job Hunting Problem

The remaining sections in this module are devoted to solving the job hunting problem. You may want to refer to the problem statement in the Introduction to Word Processing Modules before you continue. Also, remember that the data used in this problem can be found in Appendix A.

Entering Text

Your address should appear at the top of the letter. To make the letter look professional, center each line of the letterhead. You can center any text you enter on a line by simply pressing the F3 key and typing the text. To start your letter, press the F3 key and enter your name. After pressing the RETURN key,

```
DOCUMENT: JOBSMM              ‖PAGE:   1‖LINE:   6‖COL:    1‖
|1..»..............................»...........................«
                         «Your Name«
                       «1427 Shannon Lane«
                      «Carrolton, TX 75343«
  «
                      «Phone: (214) 427-1964«




                                                    S:1 N:↓
```

FIGURE 5B.9
Entering the centered letterhead

the cursor will move to the first position of the next line. Now press the F3 key, enter your address, and press the RETURN key. The same procedure can be used to enter the city, state, and zip code. Pressing the RETURN key twice will move the cursor down two lines, where you can enter your telephone number. When you have finished entering this part of the text, the screen will look like the one illustrated in Figure 5b.9.

Now you are ready to continue writing the letter. Because some parts of the letter will change every time you redo it for a different company, you need to be able to find them quickly. To make this easier, enclose in parentheses all of the parts of the letter that might change. With this in mind, press the TAB key twice to move the cursor to the tab stop at position 45 that was set earlier and enter (date). Continue to enter the letter until you reach the end of the first line. The screen will look like Figure 5b.10.

As you continue writing the letter, two actions will happen: First, when the cursor arrives at the right margin of the page, it automatically moves to the left margin of the next line and displays what you have typed. This is called *word wrapping*. Word wrapping allows you to enter the text without worrying about when you reach the end of a line. If you have not reached the end of a word when the right margin is encountered, MultiMate will scan backward until it finds the beginning of the word and then move the complete word to the new line. This operation greatly simplifies and speeds up the process of entering text material.

```
DOCUMENT: JOBSMM                 ‖PAGE:    1‖LINE:  16‖COL:  75‖
|1..»..............................................»............................«
                          «Your Name«
                      «1427 Shannon Lane«
                      «Carrolton, TX 75343«
«
                      «Phone: (214) 427-1964«
«
    »                                    »(date)«
«
(contact person)«
(company name)«
(street address)«
(city, state, and zip code)«
«
Dear (contact person / Gentlemen):«
«
    »According to your (telephone call on or letter dated) (response date),



                                                              S:↑ N:↓
```

FIGURE 5B.10
When you reach the end of the first line

The second action that occurs when you enter the complete letter is that your name disappears off the top of the screen. However, your name is still a part of the letter; the package has just moved the screen's view of the letter further down the page so that you can see what you are currently typing. This operation is called *scrolling*, and it enables you to view the part of the document you are working on. If you wish to see the top of the letter, simply press the up arrow key, the PG UP key, or the HOME key. After entering the first two sentences, your view of the letter is the same as the one in Figure 5b.11. Once you have entered the completed letter, the screen will look like the one illustrated in Figure 5b.12.

Editing Text

If you make mistakes while writing the letter—whether you notice them when you make them or later on—you can correct them easily. Use the cursor control keys to move the cursor to where you want to make a correction. There are now several options available to you. If you enter characters, whatever is on the screen will be replaced with what you type. If you press the INSERT key before entering characters, then whatever you type will be inserted at the cursor location—moving the rest of the text to the right.

```
DOCUMENT: JOBSMM                ‖PAGE:   1‖LINE:  21‖COL:   1‖
│1..»..................................»...........................«
                        ↵Your Name«
                      ↵1427 Shannon Lane«
                      ↵Carrolton, TX 75343«
«
                      ↵Phone: (214) 427-1964«
«
     »                                    »(date)«
«
(contact person)«
(company name)«
(street address)«
(city, state, and zip code)«
«
Dear (contact person / Gentlemen):«
«
    »According to your (telephone call on or letter dated) (response date),
it appears that (interview date) is an acceptable date for my visit to
your company.  Thank you very much for expressing an interest in my
qualifications for your job position at (company name).«
«
                                                         S:↑ N:↓
```

FIGURE 5B.11

**When you reach the bottom of the screen
—entering the first paragraph**

```
DOCUMENT: JOBSMM                ‖PAGE:   1‖LINE:  35‖COL:   1‖
Dear (contact person / Gentlemen):«
«
    »According to your (telephone call or letter dated) (response date),
it appears that (interview date) is an acceptable date for my visit to
your company.  Thank you very much for expressing an interest in my
qualifications for your job position at (company name).«
«
    »I look forward to visiting you at your company.  I am excited about
the prospect of being employed by a company with such an excellent
reputation.«
«
    »Again, let me express my apprecaition for your interest and prompt
reply to my job inquiry.  If you need to contact me before our meeting,
please feel free to call me at 427-1964.«
«
«
     »                                    »Sincerely,«
«
«
«
     »                                    »Your Name«
                                                         S:↓ N:↓
```

FIGURE 5B.12

The completed letter

```
DOCUMENT: JOBSMM                ‖PAGE:    1‖LINE:   19‖COL:   58‖
Dear (contact person / Gentlemen):«
«
    »According to your (telephone call on or letter dated) (response date),
it appears that (interview date) is an acceptable date for my visit to
your company.  Thank you very much for expressing an interest in my
qualifications for your job position at (company name).  I look forward to
visiting you at your company.  I am excited about the prospect of being
employed by a company with such an excellent reputation.«
«
    »Again, let me express my apprecaition for your interest and prompt
reply to my job inquiry.  If you need to contact me before our meeting,
please feel free to call me at 427-1964.«
«
«
    »                                     »Sincerely,«
«
«
«
    »                                     »Your Name«
                                                            S:↓ N:↓
```

FIGURE 5B.13
Joining the first and second paragraphs

You can also erase text. Pressing the DELETE key twice will delete the character under the cursor and move the text to the right of the cursor one position to the left. If you need to erase more than a few characters, you can use the DELETE key to mark the beginning of the text you want to delete. When MultiMate asks: DELETE WHAT? use the arrow keys to move to the last character you want to delete and press the DELETE key again. The text you just "highlighted" by moving the cursors will be deleted.

Through the use of these keys, mistakes can be quickly corrected. This can give you a professional-looking document without the necessity of retyping an entire page as you would have to do if you were using a typewriter.

A Cut-and-Paste Operation

When you are reading a document after it has been completely entered, you may change your mind about how you want the text to read. For example, the first and second paragraphs in the letter you just wrote would read better if they were combined. To accomplish this, move to the RETURN MARK at the end of the first paragraph. Press the SPACE BAR twice, followed by the DELETE key. Now "highlight" all the characters between the cursor and the "I" in the next sentence, press the DELETE key again, and the paragraphs will

```
DOCUMENT: JOBSMM              ‖PAGE:    1‖LINE:  18‖COL:  16‖      MOVE WHAT?
Dear (contact person / Gentlemen):«
«
   »According to your (telephone call on or letter dated) (response date),
it appears that (interview date) is an acceptable date for my visit to
your company.  Thank you very much for expressing an interest in my
qualifications for your job position at (company name).  I look forward to
visiting you at your company.  I am excited about the prospect of being
employed by a company with such an excellent reputation.«
«
   »Again, let me express my apprecaition for your interest and prompt
reply to my job inquiry.  If you need to contact me before our meeting,
please feel free to call me at 427-1964.«
«
«
   »                              »Sincerely,«
«
«
«
   »                              »Your Name«



                                                        S:↓ N:↓
```

FIGURE 5B.14
Marking a sentence for moving

be joined, as shown in Figure 5b.13. Note that you have done more than remove the spaces that separated the end of the first paragraph from the beginning of the second. The two paragraphs have actually been joined, forming one paragraph, and the resulting paragraph has been reformatted.

Reviewing the letter again, you note that the first paragraph is very positive. This is good practice when writing business letters. However, the paragraph would flow better if the second sentence were used as the opening. To exchange the first sentence with the second, you need to perform a cut-and-paste operation. In MultiMate, this is called a *Move operation*.

The first step in a Move operation is to tell MultiMate you want to move some text. This is done by pressing the F7 key. Since it is easier to move the second sentence, move the cursor so that it is positioned over the "T" in "Thank you" at the beginning of the second sentence, and press the F7 key. Now move the cursor to the last character in the second sentence, two spaces past the period, and press the F7 key again. Figure 5b.14 shows what the screen will look like now that the second sentence has been "highlighted." This highlighted area is called a *block*.

After the block has been highlighted, you can move it. To move a block to another location, move the cursor to the location where you want the first letter of the highlighted area to be—to the "A" in "According" at the beginning of

```
DOCUMENT: JOBSMM              ‖PAGE:   1‖LINE:  16‖COL:   5‖
|1..»............................».........................«
                         ↔Your Name«
                    ↔1427 Shannon Lane«
                    ↔Carrolton, TX 75343«
 «
                      ↔Phone: (214) 427-1964«
 «
     »                                 »(date)«
 «
(contact person)«
(company name)«
(street address)«
(city, state, and zip code)«
 «
Dear (contact person / Gentlemen):«
 «
    »Thank you very much for expressing an interest in my qualifications
for your job position at (company name).  According to your (telephone
call on or letter dated) (response date), it appears that (interview date)
is an acceptable date for my visit to your company.  I look forward to
visiting you at your company.  I am excited about the prospect of being
employed by a company with such an excellent reputation.«
 «
                                                          S:1 N:↓
```

FIGURE 5B.15
The new letter with the move completed

the first sentence. By pressing the F7 key, you will move the contents of the highlighted area to the new location. The second sentence now begins the paragraph (see Figure 5b.15).

Page Formatting — Redefining the Page

Your letter appears to be a little too short. Rather than trying to think of additional text to add, it would be easier to make the letter appear longer by making the lines shorter. The way to reformat the complete page is through the F9 key that you used earlier to set the tab stops.

Press the F9 key to return to the ruler. Now use the arrow keys to move along the ruler until the cursor is at column 65. Press the RETURN key to mark the end of the line, and press the F9 key to record the change and return to the document. The letter will be reformatted to meet the new margin specifications, as shown in Figure 5b.16.

Enhancing the Letter for Effect — Output Specifications

To improve the presentation of your text material, MultiMate allows you to use several print enhancements directly — for example, underlining, boldface, and forced page break.

```
DOCUMENT: JOBSMM              ‖PAGE:    1‖LINE:    1‖COL:   28‖
|1..»..................................................».....................«
                          ↔Your Name«
                      ↔1427 Shannon Lane«
                      ↔Carrolton, TX 75343«
  «
                      ↔Phone: (214) 427-1964«
  «
     »                                    »(date)«
  «
(contact person)«
(company name)«
(street address)«
(city, state, and zip code)«
  «
Dear (contact person / Gentlemen):«
  «
   »Thank you very much for expressing an interest in my
qualifications for your job position at (company name).
According to your (telephone call on or letter dated) (response
date), it appears that (interview date) is an acceptable date
for my visit to your company.  I look forward to visiting you at
your company.  I am excited about the prospect of being employed
by a company with such an excellent reputation.«
                                                     S:↑ N:↓
```

FIGURE 5B.16

Setting new margins — making the letter longer

To underline a character, move the cursor to the space before the character you want to underline and insert the underline command by pressing the ALTernate and - keys. To stop the underline command, insert the underline command again by pressing the ALTernate and - keys after the last character you want underlined.

The boldface feature works exactly like the underline feature, except that you press the ALTernate and Z keys to mark the beginning and end of the boldface operation. Use the boldface command to enhance your name, address, and telephone number in the letter, as illustrated in Figure 5b.17.

The forced page break changes the way the document is printed. If you wish to start a new page at a particular location in your document, simply press the ALTernate and B keys. The line following the New Page command will begin on the next page of the printed output.

Checking for Spelling Errors

The MultiMate software package provides a dictionary designed to proofread all text documents created by MultiMate. It finds misspelled words using an extensive dictionary provided by Merriam-Webster, Inc. Additionally, Multi-Mate allows you to add words to the dictionary through the use of a Custom Dictionary.

```
DOCUMENT: JOBSMM                   ‖PAGE:   1‖LINE:   5‖COL:   43‖
│1..»...................................».................«
                          ◆▓Your Name«
                        ◆1427 Shannon Lane«
                        ◆Carrolton, TX 75343«
«
                    ◆Phone: (214) 427-1964▓«
«
    »                               »│date│«
«
(contact person)«
(company name)«
(street address)«
(city, state, and zip code)«
«
Dear (contact person / Gentlemen):«
«
    »Thank you very much for expressing an interest in my
qualifications for your job position at (company name).
According to your (telephone call on or letter dated) (response
date), it appears that (interview date) is an acceptable date
for my visit to your company.  I look forward to visiting you at
your company.  I am excited about the prospect of being employed
by a company with such an excellent reputation.«
                                                   S:↑ N:↓
```

FIGURE 5B.17
Boldfacing the letterhead

```
                  SPELL CHECK AN OLD DOCUMENT

            Enter the Name of the Document to be checked

        Drive :  B           Document : JOBSMM

Approximately 00360448 characters [00144 Page(s)] available on Drive B
JOBSMM







        Press return to continue, PgDn to switch drive directory   S:↑ N:↓
```

FIGURE 5B.18
Naming the document to check for spelling errors

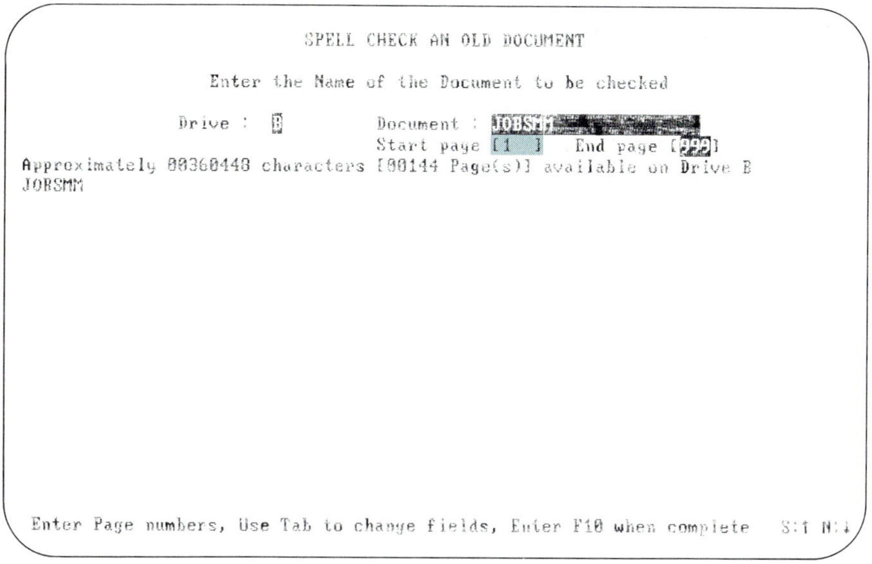

```
                       SPELL CHECK AN OLD DOCUMENT

              Enter the Name of the Document to be checked

         Drive :  B        Document :  JOBSMM
                           Start page [1  ]    End page [999]
Approximately 00360448 characters [00144 Page(s)] available on Drive B
JOBSMM








Enter Page numbers, Use Tab to change fields, Enter F10 when complete   S:1 N:1
```

FIGURE 5B.19

Entering the part of the document to check

To SPELL CHECK the letter you have just completed, press F10 and select option 8 while in the main menu. Enter the name of the document you want to check, as shown in Figure 5b.18. MultiMate will ask for the starting and ending pages of the document to be checked, as illustrated in Figure 5b.19. Now replace the disk in drive A with the dictionary disk. When the document has been completely checked for spelling errors and all the errors have been "marked" in the document, the screen in Figure 5b.20 will be displayed.

To correct the marked misspellings, you will use the Spell Edit feature. To begin Spell Edit, insert the MultiMate system disk in drive A and select option 1 to edit an old document. Once you have gone through the screens defining the document, and the screen shows the text work area, press the ALTernate and F10 keys. Now insert the dictionary disk in drive A as instructed by the message on the screen and press any key.

The first word that MultiMate finds that is not in the dictionary is your name. If you have spelled your name correctly, press the 2 key. The next word not in the dictionary is "Shannon," as illustrated in Figure 5b.21. Pressing the 0 key gives you the opportunity to add this word to the Custom Dictionary. Pressing the 2 key again will cause MultiMate to continue checking the letter.

The package will now go on to find that it does not recognize "Carrolton," "TX," and "apprecaition." When MultiMate arrives at the word "apprecai-

```
                    SPELL CHECK AN OLD DOCUMENT

               Enter the Name of the Document to be checked

          Drive : B          Document : JOBSMM
                              Start page [1]      End page [999]
    Approximately 00360440 characters [00144 Page(s)] available on Drive B
    JOBSMM
```

```
                    OPERATION COMPLETE - PRESS ANY KEY TO CONTINUE
                    [00004] WORDS MISSPELLED  [00149] WORDS TOTAL      S:1 N:1
```

FIGURE 5B.20
Completing the SPELL CHECK operation

```
DOCUMENT: JOBSMM              |PAGE:   1|LINE:   2|COL:  30|
|1..»..............................»..................«
                      «Your Name«
                 «1427 Shannon Lane«
                 «Carrolton, TX 75343«
«
                 «Phone: (214) 427-1964«
«
    »                                  »(date)«
«
(contact person)«
(company name)«
(street address)«
(city, state, and zip code)«
«
Dear (contact person / Gentlemen):«
«

                    Please enter desired function
          0)    Add this word to the Custom Dictionary
          1)    Ignore this place mark and find the next mark
          2)    Clear this place mark and find the next mark
          3)    Find a list of possible correct spellings
          Esc)  End Spell Edit and resume Document Edit
                                                      S:1 N:1
```

FIGURE 5B.21
**Finding the misspelled words, using the
SPELL EDIT function — adding your street
name to the dictionary**

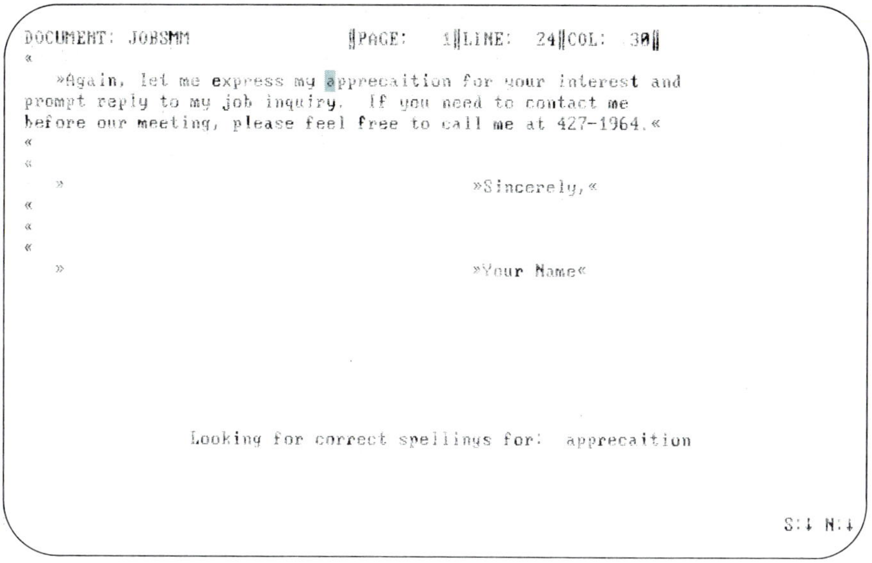

```
DOCUMENT: JOBSMM          ‖PAGE:    1‖LINE:  24‖COL:  30‖
«
   »Again, let me express my appreciaition for your interest and
prompt reply to my job inquiry.  If you need to contact me
before our meeting, please feel free to call me at 427-1964.«
«
«
   »                                   »Sincerely,«
«
«
«
   »                                   »Your Name«




          Looking for correct spellings for:  apprecaition



                                                   S:↓ N:↓
```

FIGURE 5B.22
Finding the last misspelled word

tion,'' which is indeed misspelled, it will look for the correct spelling after you press 3, as shown in Figure 5b.22. MultiMate will display a list of words to replace the misspelled word, as illustrated in Figure 5b.23. Since none of the choices are the correct spelling of the word you intended to enter, press the ESCape key and correct the spelling to ''appreciation.'' Replace the dictionary disk with the MultiMate system disk and enter the correction. Now move the cursor to any position before ''appreciation,'' and press the ALTernate and F10 keys and place the dictionary disk in drive A to continue the Spell Edit operation. Once MultiMate has finished checking the document, your screen will look like Figure 5b.24. To continue using MultiMate, press any key and exchange the disk in drive A for the MultiMate system disk.

Personalized Messages — Find and Replace Functions

Now that you are ready to send the three letters needed to set up your interviews, the phrases marked with parentheses in the master letter need to be personalized. Looking over the letter, note that you have used (company name) twice. Rather than entering the company name for each letter twice, you can use the Replace function in MultiMate to change this text. To use this function, press the SHIFT and F6 keys to display the replace options shown in Figure 5b.25. Choose option 1 for GLOBAL (to be done in the entire document)

```
DOCUMENT: JOBSMM              ‖PAGE:   1‖LINE:   24‖COL:   30‖
«
   »Again, let me express my apprecaition for your interest and
prompt reply to my job inquiry.  If you need to contact me
before our meeting, please feel free to call me at 427-1964.«
«
«
   »                                   »Sincerely,«
«
«
«
   »                                   »Your Name«




            Enter the number of the word to replace the misspelled word
                or press Esc to return to Document Edit.
1) abrogation           4) practicing          7) precautions
2) precaution           5) practising          8) preachifying
3) abrogations          6) predation           9) preclusion
                                                         S:↑ N:↓
```

FIGURE 5B.23
MultiMate's best guess

```
DOCUMENT: JOBSMM              ‖PAGE:   1‖LINE:   24‖COL:   30‖
«
   »Again, let me express my appreciation for your interest and
prompt reply to my job inquiry.  If you need to contact me
before our meeting, please feel free to call me at 427-1964.«
«
«
   »                                   »Sincerely,«
«
«
«
   »                                   »Your Name«




            UNABLE TO FIND NEXT MISSPELLING - PRESS ANY KEY      S:↑ N:↓
```

FIGURE 5B.24
Finishing the SPELL EDIT operation

```
DOCUMENT: jobsmm              ‖PAGE:   1‖LINE:   1‖COL:  27‖    REPLACE MODE
 1..»..............................»..................«
                         ↔ Your Name«
                      ↔1427 Shannon Lane«
                   ↔Carrolton, TX 75343‖«
 «
                   ↔Phone: (214) 427-1964«
 «
    »                                »(date)«
 «
(contact person)«
(company name)«
(street address)«
(city, state, and zip code)«
 «
Dear (contact person / Gentlemen):«
 «
   »Thank you very much for expressing an interest in my
qualifications for your job position at (company name).
According to your (telephone call on or letter dated) (response
date), it appears that (interview date) is an acceptable date
for my visit to your company.  I look forward to visiting you at
your company.  I am excited about the prospect of being employed
by a company with such an excellent reputation.«
TYPE OF REPLACE:       1) GLOBAL   2) DISCRETIONARY   3) ABORT      S:↑ N:↓
```

FIGURE 5B.25
Search and replace text in the letter

replacement. The first item to be entered is the word or phrase that you want to replace. In your case, this is (company name), as shown in Figure 5b.26. Now press the SHIFT and F6 keys again, and enter the word or phrase to be used as replacement, as illustrated in Figure 5b.27. When you press the SHIFT and F6 keys a final time, the screen will look like Figure 5b.28. After replacing all the phrases marked by parentheses with the appropriate entries in each of the three letters, you are ready to print the letters.

Printing Your Letter — The Print Function

The print menu in MultiMate is used to produce a paper copy of the document that is currently in memory. The package will print to any printer that is properly connected to your computer system. It will allow you to print the entire document, a range of pages, or a single page from the document. If needed, MultiMate will print multiple copies of the document or selected pages. It will also allow you to choose the top margin of a page, pause at the end of each page to position a new sheet of paper, or shift the entire document to the right allowing for variations in the printer's left margin. You can also specify whether your document is to be printed in draft quality or letter quality.

These print functions, plus others, are accomplished by using the print menu shown in Figure 5b.29. To make the changes needed to print your letter,

```
DOCUMENT: JOBSMM                    ‖PAGE:    1‖LINE:    1‖COL:   27‖    REPLACE MODE
|1..»..............................................»..................«
                          +▮Your Name«
                          +1427 Shannon Lane«
                          +Carrolton, TX 75343▮«
«
                          +Phone: (214) 427-1964«
«
     »                                      »(date)«
«
(contact person)«
(company name)«
(street address)«
(city, state, and zip code)«
«
Dear (contact person / Gentlemen):«
«
    »Thank you very much for expressing an interest in my
qualifications for your job position at (company name).
According to your (telephone call on or letter dated) (response
date), it appears that (interview date) is an acceptable date
for my visit to your company.  I look forward to visiting you at
your company.  I am excited about the prospect of being employed
by a company with such an excellent reputation.«
REPLACE WHAT?  (company name)                                      S:↑ N:↓
```

FIGURE 5B.26

What do you want to replace?

```
DOCUMENT: JOBSMM                    ‖PAGE:    1‖LINE:    1‖COL:   27‖    REPLACE MODE
|1..»..............................................»..................«
                          +▮Your Name«
                          +1427 Shannon Lane«
                          +Carrolton, TX 75343▮«
«
                          +Phone: (214) 427-1964«
«
     »                                      »(date)«
«
(contact person)«
(company name)«
(street address)«
(city, state, and zip code)«
«
Dear (contact person / Gentlemen):«
«
    »Thank you very much for expressing an interest in my
qualifications for your job position at (company name).
According to your (telephone call on or letter dated) (response
date), it appears that (interview date) is an acceptable date
for my visit to your company.  I look forward to visiting you at
your company.  I am excited about the prospect of being employed
by a company with such an excellent reputation.«
REPLACE WITH?  Champion Cowboy Supply                             S:↑ N:↓
```

FIGURE 5B.27

What do you want to replace it with?

```
DOCUMENT: jobsmm              ‖PAGE:   1‖LINE:   15‖COL:    1‖
                        ↔1427 Shannon Lane«
                        ↔Carrolton, TX 75343█«
«
                        ↔Phone: (214) 427-1964«
«
   »                                 »(date)«
«
(contact person)«
Champion Cowboy Supply«
(street address)«
(city, state, and zip code)«
«
Dear (contact person / Gentlemen):«
«
   »Thank you very much for expressing an interest in my
qualifications for your job position at Champion Cowboy Supply.
According to your (telephone call on or letter dated) (response
date), it appears that (interview date) is an acceptable date
for my visit to your company.  I look forward to visiting you at
your company.  I am excited about the prospect of being employed
by a company with such an excellent reputation.«
«
   »Again, let me express my appreciation for your interest and
                                                          S:↑ N:↓
```

FIGURE 5B.28

The results of the search and replace operation—(company name)

```
                  Submit a Document for Printing

                 Drive : B        Document: JOBSMM

Start print at page number       001   Stop print after page number       001
Left margin                       010   Top margin                         006
Pause between pages?                N   Right justification?                 N
Draft print?                        N   Default pitch (4 = 10 cpi)           4
Lines per inch (6 or 8)             6   Header/footer first page number    001
Printer number                    001   Parallel or Serial (P or S)          P
Document page length              066   Number of original copies          001
First page bin number (0,1,2,3)     0   Middle pages bin number (0,1,2,3)    0
Last page bin number (0,1,2,3)      0   Printer type                   EPSONFX
                                        Sheet Feeder type


Print document summary screen?      N   Print spooling statistics?           N
Delete spooler entry when done?     Y   Print in (B)ackground or (F)oreground? B

Current Time is:   21:00:07          Delay Print until Time is:   21:00:07
Current Date is:   06/10/1986        Delay Print until Date is:   06/10/1986

Press F1 for Printers, F2 for Sheet Feeders - only the first 16 are displayed
BROTHR1    BROTHR15  CITOHF10  DAISYWRT  DIABL620  DIABL630  EPSON    EPSONMX
EPSONFX    GEMINI    IBM       M1550     NEC3510   NEC3515   NEC3550  NEC5510
                 Press F10 to Continue, Press ESC to Abort         S:↓ N:↓
```

FIGURE 5B.29

Submitting your letter for printing—the Print menu

```
                        Your Name
                    1427 Shannon Lane
                    Carrolton, TX 75343

                   Phone: (214) 427-1964

                                        January 12, 198x

        Mr. Peter Hoague
        Mosteq Computer Company
        1428 Wozniak Way
        Farmers Branch, TX 76331
```

```
                        Your Name
                    1427 Shannon Lane
                    Carrolton, TX 75343

                   Phone: (214) 427-1964

                                        January 12, 198x

        Kelly Construction Company
        1414 Jupiter Rd.
        Garland, TX 75242
```
                                                            it
                                                          visit

                                                          by a

                                                          and

                                                            .

```
                        Your Name
                    1427 Shannon Lane
                    Carrolton, TX 75343

                   Phone: (214) 427-1964

                                        January 12, 198x

        Mr. Joe Garcia
        Champion Cowboy Supply
        126 Hollyhill Road
        Garland, TX 75342

        Dear Mr. Garcia,

            Thank you very much for expressing an interest in my
        qualifications for your job position at Champion Cowboy Supply.
        According to your letter dated January 10, 198x, it appears that
        January 20, 198x is an acceptable date for my visit to your
        company.  I look forward to visiting you at your company.  I am
        excited about the prospect of being employed by a company with
        such an excellent reputation.

            Again, let me express my appreciation for your interest and
        prompt reply to my job inquiry.  If you need to contact me
        before our meeting, please feel free to call me at 427-1964.


                                        Sincerely,


                                        Your Name
```
                                                            it
                                                          visit

                                                          by a

                                                          and

                                                            .

FIGURE 5B.30
The final letters setting interview dates

```
DOCUMENT: JOBSMM               ‖PAGE:    1‖LINE:    1‖COL:   27‖
|1..».............................................».................«
                           ↔▉Your Name«
                         ↔1427 Shannon Lane«
                         ↔Carrolton, TX 75343«
«
                         ↔Phone: (214) 427-1964▉«
«
    »                                       »⊦date⊦«
«
⊦contact⊦⊦ob⊦«
⊦company⊦«
⊦address⊦«
⊦city⊦, ⊦state⊦ ⊦zip⊦«
«
Dear ⊦greeting⊦«
«
   »Thank you very much for expressing an interest in my
qualifications for your job position at ⊦company⊦. According to
your ⊦call⊦ ⊦response⊦, it appears that ⊦interview⊦ is an
acceptable date for my visit to your company.  I look forward to
visiting you at your company.  I am excited about the prospect
of being employed by a company with such an excellent
reputation.«
                                                        S:↓ N:↓
```

FIGURE 5B.31
**Setting up the letter to accept merge
information**

simply bring up the print menu from the main menu by pressing the 3 key, followed by the RETURN key. After entering the name of the document you want to print in the DOCUMENT FOR PRINTING screen, press the RETURN key and make the changes shown in Figure 5b.29, using the TAB key or the arrow keys to move through the menu. Pressing the F10 key will cause the package to print your letters, as shown in Figure 5b.30.

Other Functions of MultiMate

Although not all of the functions available with MultiMate have been mentioned, Module 5b covered the basic functions needed to prepare a document. Several advanced features that may prove useful should be mentioned before finishing an explanation on how to use MultiMate. The Merge option allows you to extract text from one file and place it in the proper location in another file. For example, you just printed three different letters to prospective employers to set up interviews. To print these letters with the needed changes all at one time, you could use the Merge feature. Write the letter as shown in Figure 5b.31, with the areas of text that change for each letter marked by pressing the ALTernate and M keys at the beginning and end of each phrase. Save this document and then create a second document, called the *Merge File,* contain-

```
DOCUMENT: JOBSMERGE              ‖PAGE:    1‖LINE:   22‖COL:    1‖
|1..»....»....»..........................................................«
|-date|-«
January 12, 198x|-«
«
|-contact|-«
Mr. Joe Garcia|-«
«
|-company|-«
Champion Cowboy Supply|-«
«
|-address|-«
126 Hollyhill Road|-«
«
|-city|-«
Garland|-«
«
|-state|-«
TX|-«
«
|-zip|-«
75342|-«
«
|-greeting|-«                                            S:↓ N:↓
```

FIGURE 5B.32
Entering the merge information

ing the information to be substituted for the names in the primary document, as shown in Figure 5b.32. The information for each letter should be on a separate page.

After pressing F10 to return to the main menu, choose option 5, the MERGE PRINT utility, and fill in the requested information, as illustrated in Figure 5b.33. Now press the F10 key, and each of the three letters will be printed with the information you entered in the Merge File substituted for the names in the primary document.

MultiMate provides another feature that is similiar to the Merge function. This feature is called *Key Procedures.* With Key Procedures, you can save a document as a series of keystrokes. When the Key Procedure is executed, the keystrokes are played back into your document, pausing where you have indicated that you wish to enter additional text.

MultiMate also has many printer controls available. You are acquainted with some of them (boldface, underline, and page break). Other printer controls include the ability to use subscripts and superscripts, using the CONTROL (CTRL) and F2 keys to repaginate (reset the page breaks in a document), and using the SHIFT and F2 keys to combine pages (combine the current page with the preceding page).

MultiMate will also allow you to print both headers and footers on the page. A header is placed in the document by moving the cursor to the top of the

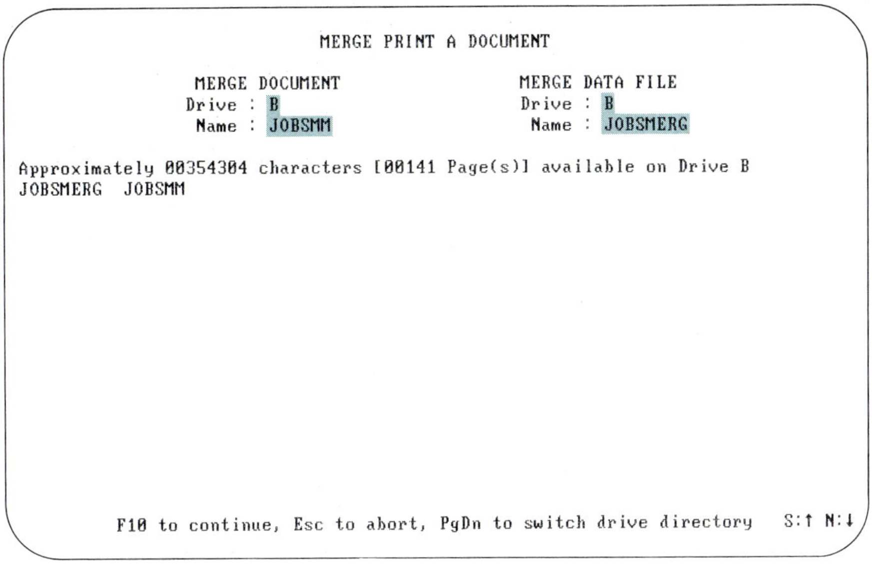

```
                    MERGE PRINT A DOCUMENT

        MERGE DOCUMENT              MERGE DATA FILE
        Drive : B                  Drive : B
        Name : JOBSMM              Name : JOBSMERG

Approximately 00354304 characters [00141 Page(s)] available on Drive B
JOBSMERG  JOBSMM




           F10 to continue, Esc to abort, PgDn to switch drive directory   S:↑ N:↓
```

FIGURE 5B.33
Merging the two documents, using the
MERGE PRINT option

page where you want the header to begin and then pressing the ALTernate and H keys, entering the header, and pressing the ALTernate and H keys a second time to end the header. Footers are entered in much the same manner: Place the cursor at the bottom of the page, and use the ALTernate and F keys to begin and end the footer. Headers and footers can be printed on each page of the document, on all the odd-numbered pages, or on all the even-numbered pages. You may even set up one header and footer for odd-numbered pages and a second header and footer for even-numbered pages. Page numbering can be controlled in either the headers or the footers of a document.

Finally, MultiMate can do simple arithmetic. It is capable of doing both horizontal and vertical addition on rows and columns of numbers.

WordStar

Learning to Use WordStar

WordStar is one of the most popular word processing packages. In part, this stems from the fact that WordStar has been around for a while. However, its popularity is probably due more to the fact that WordStar is among the most versatile word processing packages. It is available on a wide variety of microcomputer hardware and can be used with a variety of operating systems, including CP/M and MS-DOS.

Once you have started your computer and the operating system is ready to go, all you have to do to load WordStar is enter the command WS. WordStar will respond with the log-on screen, as shown in Figure 5c.1. The version of WordStar used in this module is one that can be used with the IBM PC and IBM-PC compatible microcomputers.

Momentarily, the log-on screen will disappear and will be replaced with the WordStar OPENING MENU, or general command menu, as shown in Figure 5c.2. At this point, you can begin working on a document file. Note that the command screen is arranged in sections. You may select any of the commands on the screen by simply pressing the letter associated with the indicated function. You do not have to press the RETURN key to complete the entry. If you find you have selected the wrong function, press the ESCape key, and you will be returned to the previous command screen.

In the Preliminary Commands section, you may change the currently logged disk drive. The typical default disk drive is A, but it can be changed with the L command. Unless you specify otherwise, WordStar will use this disk drive when retrieving and saving documents. If the File directory option is ON, WordStar will display the directory of the default disk drive at the bottom of the command screen. Thus, if you are unsure of the names of the documents on the disk in drive B, you need only change the default drive to view the directory. Among the WordStar Options shown in the lower right corner of the screen are MailMerge and CorrectStar. These options will be discussed later.

The final option available from Preliminary Commands is the one that selects the help level (H). WordStar, like many software packages, has a built-in way of assisting you to use the package. This is usually called a *Help function*. However, unlike most software packages, WordStar permits you to establish the level of help that you desire. If you press the H key, you will see the screen

FIGURE 5C.1
The WordStar log-on screen

FIGURE 5C.2
WordStar OPENING MENU

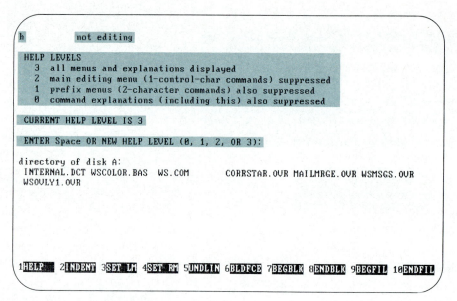

FIGURE 5C.3
Setting the help level

shown in Figure 5c.3. Normally, WordStar begins with a help level of 3, the level that provides you with the most information. However, as you become more familiar with using WordStar, you may decide you want less help. Later, you will see that the help level can be changed as you are working on a document. This is done to provide you with "less visible help" and "more visible document."

The File Commands section of the screen permits you to perform manipulations of complete documents (see Figure 5c.2). You can print a document (P), create a new name for a document (E), make a copy of an existing file (O), or delete a file from a disk (Y). Of these options, Print and Copy are probably the most used. The P option will be discussed after you have had a chance to build your document.

The Copy option, however, is worth talking about now. If you have a document with which you want to "experiment," you might decide to save a copy of the original document in case the one you are experimenting with is lost or altered to the extent it cannot be recovered. If your work pattern involves repeated modifications of existing documents, you can use the WordStar Copy option to make a duplicate of the document. (However, you could always use the operating system's copy function to make a duplicate of a file on your data disk before you load WordStar.)

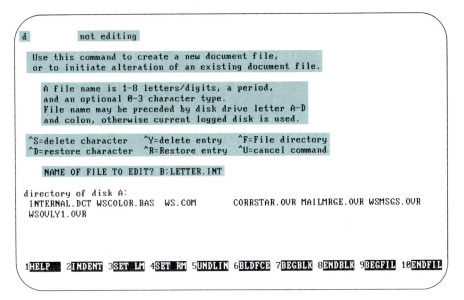

FIGURE 5c.4
Opening a document file

The System Commands section of the screen (Figure 5c.2) permits you to run a program (R) or to exit WordStar (X) and return to the operating system. Among other functions, the R option will permit you to execute operating system commands without leaving WordStar. The X option gets you out of WordStar.

The final section of the WordStar OPENING MENU deals with opening files. (The terms *file* and *document* may be used interchangeably.) To begin the manipulation of a document in WordStar, you would normally select the D option (Figure 5c.2). This means either that you are going to work on a document that WordStar has built or that you wish to create a new document. However, WordStar is capable of manipulating documents that have been created by other packages; so long as the document has been saved as a text (ASCII) file, the file can be retrieved by WordStar using the N option.

Figure 5c.4 shows the screen after using the D option. WordStar will prompt you with information at this point that should enable you to create a valid document name. For the job hunting problem, you may want to create a file called B:LETTER.INT. This document will be placed on drive B and will be called LETTER.INT — the letter that is used to establish an interview date. The same process is also used to retrieve an existing document when you are using the OPENING MENU screen.

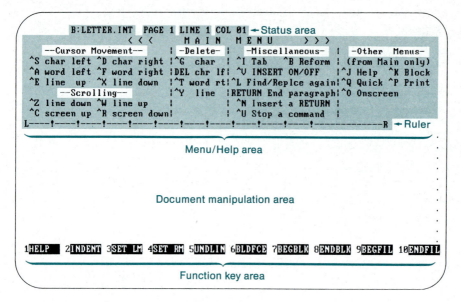

```
        B:LETTER.INT  PAGE 1 LINE 1 COL 01 ← Status area
                  < < <    M A I N   M E N U    > > >
    --Cursor Movement--    ¦  -Delete-  ¦   -Miscellaneous-   ¦  -Other  Menus-
 ^S char left ^D char right ¦^G  char   ¦ ^I Tab   ^B Reform  ¦ (from Main only)
 ^A word left ^F word right ¦DEL chr lf¦ ^V INSERT ON/OFF      ¦^J Help  ^K Block
 ^E line up   ^X line down  ¦^T word rt¦^L Find/Replce again¦^Q Quick ^P Print
    --Scrolling--           ¦^Y  line   ¦ RETURN End paragraph¦^O Onscreen
 ^Z line down ^W line up    ¦          ¦ ^N Insert a RETURN   ¦
 ^C screen up ^R screen down¦          ¦ ^U Stop a command    ¦
L----!----!----!----!----!----!----!----!----!----!--------------R ← Ruler
```

            Menu/Help area

            Document manipulation area

 1HELP   2INDENT 3SET LM 4SET RM 5UNDLIN 6BLDFCE 7BEGBLK 8ENDBLK 9BEGFIL 10ENDFIL

            Function key area

FIGURE 5C.5
WordStar's MAIN MENU

Some Preliminaries About Working with Documents

If you have set help to the highest level, you will see a screen like the one in Figure 5c.5 when you enter the document mode. This is called the MAIN MENU, and it will stay on the screen as you work with a document. The MAIN MENU is divided into four parts. The first part appears across the top of the screen and might be called a "status area." It identifies the current document name, page number, line number, and column position. The document name will be fixed while working on a document; however, the page number, line number, and column position will change as you move about the document. The page number identifies a page for printing purposes. The line number indicates the line position on a page. The column number indicates which character position you are addressing on the indicated line. Any character typed on the keyboard exists at the indicated page, line, and column position.

The second part of the MAIN MENU screen might be called the "available operations area" (left section of Figure 5c.5), because it identifies the types of operations that can currently be performed. All of the operations shown in this area require a two-key combination. The symbol ^ indicates that the CTRL key must be used in conjunction with the associated character. For example, the first combination shown at the upper left corner of the screen is ^S. This means that to perform this function you must press the CTRL key and, while holding it, press the S key. (Hereafter, unless stated to the contrary, it will be assumed that the CTRL key is also pressed when selecting a particular operation.)

TABLE 5C.1 WordStar Cursor Movements (IBM-PC and IBM-PC Compatibles)

Operation or Function	Control Key Combination	Other Key Combinations
Move left one character	^S	Left Arrow
Move right one character	^D	Right Arrow
Move up one line	^E	Up Arrow
Move down one line	^X	Down Arrow
Move left one word	^A	
Move right one word	^F	
Move display screen up one line	^W	
Move display screen down one line	^Z	
Move to previous display screen	^R	Pg Up
Move to next display screen	^C	Pg Down
Move to the top of the screen	^QS/^QE*	Home
Move to the bottom of the screen	^QX*	End
Move to the right end of the current line	^QD*	
Move to the beginning of the document	^QR*	
Move to the end of the document	^QC*	

* Available through the QUICK MENU. Check your version of WordStar for other useful key combinations; some versions may differ.

The first section of the operations area is labeled Cursor Movement. For example, ^S is used when you want to move one character position to the left. Cursor movement operations such as this (using the CTRL key in combination with another key) may be a bit tedious and unnatural. However, if arrow keys are available on your keyboard, you may find that they are much more convenient to use to perform the same function. The cursor control operations that are possible with WordStar are summarized in Table 5c.1, but because there are a number of varieties of WordStar, you should check your version to determine which "control code" (control key combination) to use to perform a particular operation. The second section of the MAIN MENU, Scrolling, also deals with cursor movement, but in larger "jumps."

The third section, Delete, allows you to delete text on the screen. ^G deletes the current character (the character in the same position as the cursor). The DEL key can be used to delete the character immediately to the left of the current cursor position. (It can also be used to eliminate paragraph markers, as will be discussed shortly.) ^T deletes the word immediately to the right of the cursor, and ^Y deletes the entire line in which the cursor appears. ^QY deletes all characters from the cursor position to the right end of the line. ^Q DEL deletes all characters from the cursor position to the left end of the line. (All ^Q functions are a part of the QUICK MENU, identified in the right corner of the OPENING MENU shown in Figure 5c.2)

The fourth section of the MAIN MENU is called *Miscellaneous.* It indicates that ^I may be used to tab from one tab marker to another. However, the TAB key can also be used for this purpose. ^B is used to reformat a paragraph. Reformatting means to manipulate the text, usually after a modification, so that it fits within the left and right margin positions. ^V is a "toggle switch" that turns the text insertion mode on or off (this can also be accomplished by using the INS key). ^L is used to indicate whether the last find or replace operation is to be continued to the next occurrence or whether Spell Check is to continue. The RETURN key is used to mark the end of paragraphs. ^N is used to insert a RETURN (end of paragraph marker) within currently existing text. ^U or the BREAK key is used to interrupt an operation that is in progress.

The final section of the operations area identifies Other Menus that may be selected from the MAIN MENU. The first of these is the HELP MENU selected by pressing ^J. The HELP MENU provides additional information on a wide variety of topics and may be used to determine how a particular function works or to learn about other functions. By pressing ^Q, the QUICK MENU is presented. The general functions associated with the QUICK MENU are moving through blocks of text (for example, a few words or several paragraphs of text) and performing find and replace operations. The ONSCREEN MENU is selected by pressing ^O. The Onscreen functions control the appearance of the document, both on the screen and in terms of what is printed. Onscreen functions include such operations as setting left and right margins, centering text, setting line spacing (for example, single-space or double-space), and so on. ^K is used to select the BLOCK MENU. The BLOCK MENU deals with functions such as saving a document, cut-and-paste operations, and merging other documents into the current file. Finally, the PRINT MENU is selected by pressing ^P. The Print functions generally specify special printing effects, such as boldface and underline.

The next major area indicated on the MAIN MENU screen is called a *ruler.* It begins with the character L (Figure 5c.5), which indicates the position of the left margin. The character R on the other end shows the position of the right margin. Along the line between the left and right margins are hyphens and exclamation points. The position of each ! marks the position of a tab stop.

The final area of the MAIN MENU screen is currently blank. It is the area of the screen where your document will be shown. It could be called the document manipulation area or text area, because most changes to the document will be shown here. Note that each of the lines of the text area ends with a period—indicating that no text has been entered on these lines—you are at the bottom of the document area. Other symbols that might appear in this area are : —lines preceding the document, < —paragraph marker, + —line exceeds screen width, and ---, current line to overprint previous line. Thus, when you view your document through the document manipulation area, you will see more than just the document itself. You will also see certain control symbols, such as the markers at the ends of lines and special printing symbols.

Getting Help from WordStar

Depending on your hardware and the version of WordStar you are using, the bottom line on your screen may show function key designations (Figure 5c.5). If your system does not show this line, you will have room for an extra line of text in your document manipulation area. In addition, your function key designations may be different from those shown in Figure 5c.5 because the functions these keys control can be selected when WordStar is installed. The function key designations, although present on the initial WordStar screen, are not usable until you enter a document. The function keys and the designations shown in Figure 5c.5 specify functions that select the HELP MENU (F1), indent or reformat a paragraph (F2), set the left margin (F3), set the right margin (F4), underline (F5), boldface (F6), mark the beginning of a block (F7), mark the end of a block (F8), go to the beginning of the file (F9), and go to the end of the file (F10).

Select ^J from the MAIN MENU (or press F1). As previously indicated, this key sequence selects the HELP MENU, as shown in Figure 5c.6. Note that even though you leave the document manipulation area when you get help (or perform other functions), the status line remains unchanged, the Other Menus area is presented, the ruler is visible, and perhaps a portion of your document is shown. When you select certain functions, your document may totally disappear from view. However, after the function has been completed, you will return to the MAIN MENU and the document manipulation area. In other words, even though your document may momentarily disappear, WordStar is saving it for you until you return to the MAIN MENU.

Solving the Job Hunting Problem

The remaining sections in this module are devoted to solving the job hunting problem. You may want to refer to the problem statement in the Introduction

```
^J       B:LETTER.INT  PAGE 1 LINE 1 COL 01
            < < <    H E L P    M E N U      > > >
                                      !       --Other  Menus--
  H  Display & set the help level  !  S  Status line    !  (from Main only)
  B  Paragraph reform (CONTROL-B)  !  R  Ruler line      !  ^J  Help  ^K  Block
  F  Flags in right-most column    !  M  Margins & Tabs  !  ^Q  Quick ^P  Print
  D  Dot commands, print controls  !  P  Place markers   !  ^O  Onscreen
  I  Index of commands             !  V  Moving text     !  Space Bar returns
                                   !                     !  you to Main Menu.
  L----!----!----!----!----!----!----!----!----!----!----!----------R

  1HELP   2INDENT 3SET LM 4SET RM 5UNDLIN 6BLDFCE 7BEGBLK 8ENDBLK 9BEGFIL 10ENDFIL
```

FIGURE 5C.6
The HELP MENU

to Word Processing Modules before you continue. Also, remember that the data used in this problem can be found in Appendix A.

Entering Text

When you begin the problem (creating your interview letters), the MAIN MENU should be visible. Enter your name on the first line and press the RETURN key to indicate that the line has been completed. Note that the < symbol appears at the end of the line. Continue the process by entering your address on the next line, and your city, state, and zip code on the third line. Then press the RETURN key twice and enter your phone number. Be sure to complete the last line by pressing the RETURN key. You now have your letter-head at the top of the document. However, each of these lines begins at the left margin. To center the text of each of these lines, first move the cursor to the line to be centered and press the key sequence ^OC. This selects the ON-SCREEN MENU, and, as you can see from Figure 5c.7, the character C performs the centering function. Repeat the cursor movement and ^OC key sequences for each of the remaining lines to be centered.

Next, you need to specify the location for the date. Move the cursor to the line after your phone number. You need a couple of blank lines before you enter the date, so press the RETURN key twice. Since you want the date to

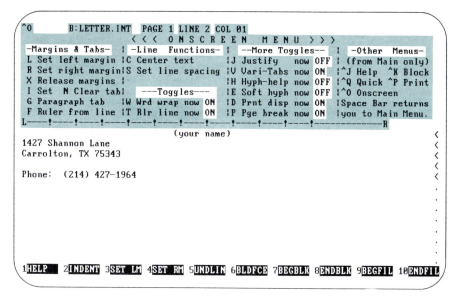

FIGURE 5C.7
The ONSCREEN MENU and centering text

appear toward the right side of the line, press the TAB key (or use ^I) to move across the line to approximately column 45. (Watch the status line, and you will see the column position indicator change each time you perform the tab operation.)

Since you are creating a general letter, you have decided to use brackets ([ ]) to enter all information that will be changed. This will make these items easier to find and replace later on when you get ready to send the letter to different companies on a specific date. Thus, you should enter the characters [Date].

Continue the letter by entering a general reference (in brackets) for the contact name, company name, company address, city, state, and zip code and a salutation. Make sure you press the RETURN key an extra time between the date and the contact name and between the city, state, and zip code and the salutation. Now, your letter should look like Figure 5c.8. Note that as you have entered these lines, your name has disappeared from the document manipulation area. It has not been lost, it has simply disappeared from view. You may want to make sure that your name is still present by moving the cursor to the top of the document. It would be quicker to do this by entering ^R (or pressing F9)—previous screen. However, to continue with your letter, remember to move back to the bottom again—possibly by using ^C a few times (or pressing F10).

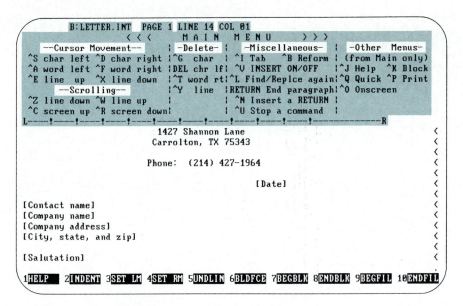

FIGURE 5C.8
Working on the interview letter—the initial heading

Now that the heading for your letter has been completed, continue with the body of the letter. Move to the second line below the salutation area and begin to type the remaining text. Remember, cursor movement will take you only to the bottom of the existing text. You will need to add a blank line between the salutation and the body by pressing the RETURN key.

As you type, mistakes can be corrected by using a series of keys. For example, you may delete characters by using the ^G and DEL keys. You may also use the BACKSPACE key to move backward and then overtype existing characters or use the ^V or INS keys to turn the insertion mode on and off. This will allow you to insert characters between existing characters on a line. However, remember to turn the insertion mode off after you have completed the operation by pressing ^V or the INS key again.

Start the first paragraph with a tab operation. This will cause the first line of the paragraph to be indented. Then continue by simply typing the text of the first paragraph. As you approach the end of the first line of the paragraph, your screen will look similar to the one in Figure 5c.9. As you approach the end of the line, resist the temptation to press the RETURN key. WordStar is equipped with a word wrapping function, and it will automatically break each line of text as you enter a paragraph so that it fits within the specified margins. Thus, you should continue typing as though all of the text of the paragraph were a single line—WordStar will fit it within the margins. When you reach the end of the

```
        B:LETTER.INT   PAGE 1 LINE 16 COL 71
                   < < <    M A I N   M E N U    > > >
       --Cursor Movement--    ¦ -Delete- ¦  -Miscellaneous-  ¦  -Other Menus--
 ^S char left ^D char right ¦^G  char  ¦ ^I Tab   ^B Reform ¦ (from Main only)
 ^A word left ^F word right ¦DEL chr lf¦ ^V INSERT ON/OFF   ¦^J Help  ^K Block
 ^E line  up  ^X line down  ¦^T word rt¦^L Find/Replce again¦^Q Quick ^P Print
       --Scrolling--        ¦^Y  line  ¦RETURN End paragraph¦^O Onscreen
 ^Z line down ^W line up    ¦          ¦ ^N Insert a RETURN ¦
 ^C screen up ^R screen down¦          ¦ ^U Stop a command  ¦
 L----!----!----!----!----!----!----!----!----!----!--------------R
                                                                        <
                   Phone:  (214) 427-1964                               <
                                                                        <
                               [Date]                                   <
                                                                        <
 [Contact name]                                                         <
 [Company name]                                                         <
 [Company address]                                                      <
 [City, state, and zip]                                                 <
                                                                        <
 [Salutation]                                                           <
                                                                        <
      According to your [telephone call on or letter dated] [response d  .
 1HELP   2INDENT 3SET LM 4SET RM 5UNDLIN 6BLDFCE 7BEGBLK 8ENDBLK 9BEGFIL 10ENDFIL
```

FIGURE 5c.9
The word wrap feature on paragraphs

first paragraph, press the RETURN key twice. This will end the current paragraph and will produce a blank line between the first and second paragraphs. Continue typing the remainder of the text, using a similar mode of operation, until you reach the closing area of the letter. Place the closing toward the right end of the line by using the tab operation to move the text over so that it is aligned with the date entry. Now your letter should look like Figure 5c.10.

Editing Text

Now that you have written the letter, you decide to make a few changes. First, you think the letter would read better if the first and second paragraphs were joined. Move the cursor to the beginning of the second paragraph, and begin pressing the DEL key. You will notice that the < paragraph-marker character disappears and the first line of the second paragraph is joined to the last line of the first paragraph. You may need to turn the insertion mode on and add a couple of blanks between the sentences after you have joined the paragraphs (depending on where you started the cursor at the beginning of the second paragraph).

Now that the paragraphs have been joined, note that the + symbol appears at the end of the line where the two paragraphs were merged (see Figure 5c.11). This means that the current text does not fit within the existing margins. To

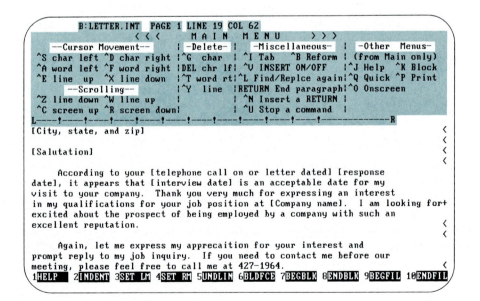

FIGURE 5C.10
Completing the first draft of the interview letter

FIGURE 5C.11
Joining paragraphs

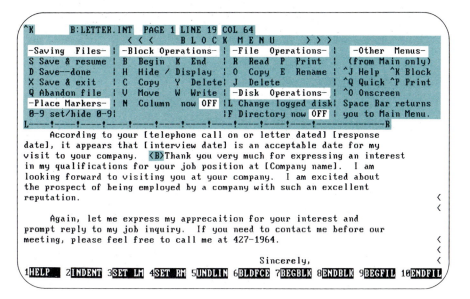

^K   B:LETTER.INT PAGE 1 LINE 19 COL 64
                  < < <   B L O C K   M E N U   > > >
-Saving Files- ¦ -Block Operations- ¦ -File Operations- ¦ -Other Menus-
S Save & resume ¦ B Begin K End   ¦ R Read P Print   ¦ (from Main only)
D Save--done   ¦ H Hide / Display   ¦ O Copy E Rename ¦ ^J Help ^K Block
X Save & exit   ¦ C Copy   Y Delete ¦ J Delete   ¦ ^Q Quick ^P Print
Q Abandon file   ¦ V Move   W Write ¦ -Disk Operations- ¦ ^O Onscreen
-Place Markers- ¦ N Column now OFF ¦L Change logged disk¦ Space Bar returns
0-9 set/hide 0-9 ¦   ¦F Directory now OFF ¦ you to Main Menu.
L----!----!----!----!----!----!----!----!----!----!----!----!--------------R
      According to your [telephone call on or letter dated] [response
date], it appears that [interview date] is an acceptable date for my
visit to your company. <B>Thank you very much for expressing an interest
in my qualifications for your job position at [Company name]. I am
looking forward to visiting you at your company. I am excited about
the prospect of being employed by a company with such an excellent
reputation.   <
                                                                         <
      Again, let me express my appreciaiton for your interest and
prompt reply to my job inquiry. If you need to contact me before our
meeting, please feel free to call me at 427-1964.   <
                                                                         <
                             Sincerely,   <
1HELP   2INDENT 3SET LM 4SET RM 5UNDLIN 6BLDFCE 7BEGBLK 8ENDBLK 9BEGFIL 10ENDFIL

FIGURE 5C.12
**Moving the second sentence to the
beginning of the letter**

correct this problem, make sure the cursor is on this line and press ^B (or press
F2). This function reformats the text of the paragraph to conform to the
current margin settings. You may use this operation at other times, such as
when you add or delete words or sentences within a paragraph.

A Cut-and-Paste Operation

Now you decide that the new first paragraph would flow better if it began with
the second sentence. It is quicker to perform a cut-and-paste operation than to
delete and retype the sentence. To cut and paste, move the cursor to the first
character of the second sentence and press ^K to enter the BLOCK MENU.
Press the letter B to mark the beginning of the block to be manipulated at this
position (or press F7). Now the symbol <B> will appear in your document to
mark the location of the beginning of the block (see Figure 5c.12). Move the
cursor to the first letter of the next sentence and press the ^K key again. To
mark the end of the block at this position, press the letter K (or press F8). You
will immediately be returned to the MAIN MENU, and the entire block will be
highlighted. The highlighted area marks the text to be manipulated—in this
case, the second sentence of the letter. To move this sentence to the beginning
of the letter, move the cursor to the first letter of the first sentence. Now press

the key sequence ^KV—perform a block move. The highlighted text will disappear from its original position and will reappear at the location of the cursor. To remove the highlighting, simply press the key sequence ^KH—hide block. The first paragraph is again a bit ragged, so press ^B to reformat it. This should result in the text shown in Figure 5c.13.

Page Formatting—Redefining the Page

Your letter has only about 20 lines of text, and it looks too short. Rather than adding more text, reformat the document so that it appears to be longer. One means of performing this alteration is to change the margins. As shown in Figure 5c.13, you enter the ONSCREEN MENU by pressing ^O and select R—set right margin. Note that the new right margin is to be set at column 65. After you press the RETURN key to enter the right margin, the right margin marker in the ruler will move to column 65. (You may also move the cursor to column 65 of any existing line of text and press F4). However, you still need to reformat the existing paragraphs to conform to this new line format. Thus, move to the beginning of each paragraph and press ^B; each paragraph will be restructured to conform to the new line length.

Enhancing the Letter for Effect—Output Specifications

Now that you have changed the line length, recenter the text of the letterhead to conform to the new format. To enhance the letterhead, print it in boldface. To do this, move to the first character of your name, turn the insertion mode on, and press ^P. You will be provided with the PRINT MENU; the letter B signifies boldface. After pressing B (or F6) to indicate where boldface printing is to begin, move the cursor to the end of your phone number and enter the PRINT MENU again (see Figure 5c.14). ^B appears before your name to indicate that boldface is now on. By entering B again, you indicate where boldface printing is to end.

Checking for Spelling Errors

Now that all of the modifications have been made, it is time to save the work you have done. By entering ^KD, you indicate that you have finished the document and you wish to save it. This will also return you to the OPENING MENU. (There are other means of ending a work session. For example, you may enter a document and later decide you don't want to work on it or save any changes you might have made. You can abandon changes made to a file by using ^KQ to terminate a session.)

Now that your document is saved, it is time to verify the accuracy of your spelling. From the OPENING MENU, select the S option—Run CorrectStar.

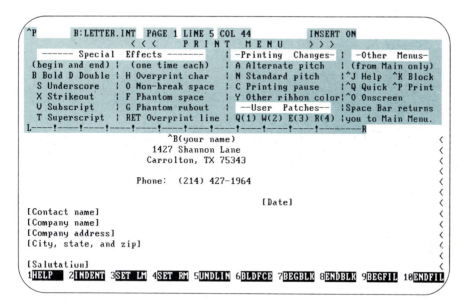

```
^Or        B:LETTER.INT  PAGE 1 LINE 23 COL 01
              < < <  O N S C R E E N   M E N U  > > >
-Margins & Tabs- ¦ -Line Functions- ¦ --More Toggles-- ¦ -Other Menus-
L Set left margin ¦C Center text     ¦J Justify   now OFF ¦ (from Main only)
R Set right margin¦S Set line spacing¦V Vari-Tabs now ON  ¦^J Help  ^K Block
X Release margins ¦                  ¦H Hyph-help  now OFF ¦^Q Quick ^P Print
I Set  N Clear tab¦  ---Toggles---   ¦E Soft hyph  now OFF ¦^O Onscreen
G Paragraph tab   ¦W Wrd wrap now ON ¦D Prnt disp  now ON  ¦Space Bar returns
F Ruler from line ¦T Rlr line now ON ¦P Pge break  now ON  ¦you to Main Menu.
RIGHT MARGIN COLUMN NUMBER (ESCAPE for cursor column)? 65
L----!----!----!----!----!----!----!----!----!----!----!----R
qualifications for your job position at [Company name].  According to
your [telephone call on or letter dated] [response date], it appears
that [interview date] is an acceptable date for my visit to your
company.  I am looking forward to visiting you at your company.  I am
excited about the prospect of being employed by a company with such an
excellent reputation.                                                <
                                                                     <
    Again, let me express my appreciaiton for your interest and
prompt reply to my job inquiry.  If you need to contact me before our
meeting, please feel free to call me at 427-1964.                    <
                                                                     <
                                    Sincerely,                       <
1HELP   2INDENT 3SET LM 4SET RM 5UNDLIN 6BLDFCE 7BEGBLK 8ENDBLK 9BEGFIL 10ENDFIL
```

FIGURE 5C.13
Resetting the right margin — making the letter longer

```
^P       B:LETTER.INT  PAGE 1 LINE 5 COL 44          INSERT ON
              < < <  P R I N T   M E N U  > > >
------ Special  Effects ------- ¦ -Printing  Changes- ¦ -Other Menus-
(begin and end) ¦ (one time each) ¦ A Alternate pitch ¦ (from Main only)
B Bold D Double ¦ H Overprint char ¦ N Standard pitch  ¦^J Help  ^K Block
S Underscore    ¦ O Non-break space¦ C Printing pause  ¦^Q Quick ^P Print
X Strikeout     ¦ F Phantom space  ¦ Y Other ribbon color¦^O Onscreen
V Subscript     ¦ G Phantom rubout ¦ --User  Patches-- ¦Space Bar returns
T Superscript   ¦ RET Overprint line¦ Q(1) W(2) E(3) R(4) ¦you to Main Menu.
L----!----!----!----!----!----!----!----!----!----!----!----R
                    ^B(your name)                           <
                    1427 Shannon Lane                       <
                    Carrolton, TX 75343                     <
                                                            <
                Phone:  (214) 427-1964                      <
                                                            <
                             [Date]                         <
                                                            <
[Contact name]                                              <
[Company name]                                              <
[Company address]                                           <
[City, state, and zip]                                      <
                                                            <
[Salutation]                                                <
1HELP   2INDENT 3SET LM 4SET RM 5UNDLIN 6BLDFCE 7BEGBLK 8ENDBLK 9BEGFIL 10ENDFIL
```

FIGURE 5C.14
Boldfacing the letterhead

```
s            not editing

To begin spelling check, enter name of file to be checked
To review last file edited, type ^R

^S=delete character    ^Y=delete entry    ^F=File directory
^D=restore character   ^R=Restore entry   ^U=cancel command

    NAME OF FILE TO CHECK? B:LETTER.INT




directory of disk A:
 INTERNAL.DCT WSCOLOR.BAS  WS.COM      CORRSTAR.OVR MAILMRGE.OVR WSMSGS.OVR
WSOVLY1.OVR




1HELP   2INDENT 3SET LM 4SET RM 5UNDLIN 6BLDFCE 7BEGBLK 8ENDBLK 9BEGFIL 10ENDFIL
```

FIGURE 5C.15
Entering CorrectStar

```
         CorrectStar      Release 3.30  I.D. # 26334Q4-001
  Copyright (c) 1983, 1984, MicroPro International Corporation.
                 All Rights Reserved

       (c) Copyright 1983, 1981, Houghton Mifflin Company.
          Based upon The American Heritage Dictionary.


Please check your CorrectStar options

 <ESC>=start spelling check   ^S=delete character   ^Y=delete entry
 ^U=cancel spelling check     ^D=restore character  ^R=restore entry

Document: B:LETTER.INT
Personal Dictionary:
 A:PERSONAL.DCT
Auto Reform (Y/N):
 Y
Soft Hyphen Insertion (Y/N):
 N
<RET> - to begin:

Please wait...loading internal dictionary
```

FIGURE 5C.16
Selecting spell checking options

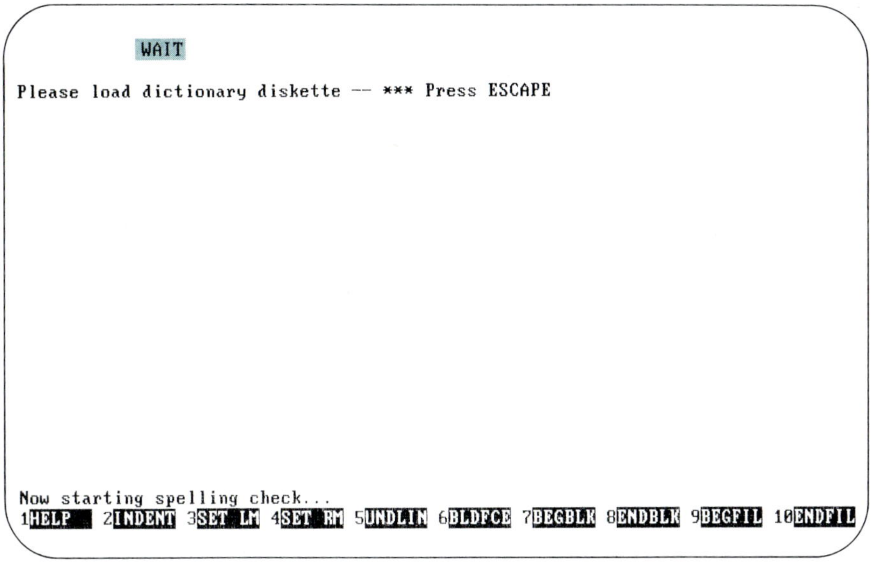

```
        WAIT
Please load dictionary diskette -- *** Press ESCAPE
```

```
Now starting spelling check...
1HELP    2INDENT  3SET LM  4SET RM  5UNDLIN  6BLDFCE  7BEGBLK  8ENDBLK  9BEGFIL  10ENDFIL
```

FIGURE 5C.17
Loading the main dictionary

As shown in Figure 5c.15, CorrectStar will request the name of the document to be checked. You should enter B:LETTER.INT. CorrectStar will then ask you to specify the options to be used during the spell checking operation (see Figure 5c.16). The first option, which has a default value of A:PER-SONAL.DCT, is to specify the disk drive and the file name containing your personal dictionary. CorrectStar actually uses three dictionaries—a personal dictionary containing a list of words that you may frequently use that are not in the other CorrectStar dictionaries, an internal dictionary (INTERNAL.DCT) that contains approximately 30.000 commonly used words, and a main dictionary (MAIN.DCT) that contains approximately 100,000 words (see Figure 5c.17). The personal dictionary is tailored to your use; the internal dictionary is placed directly into memory, and it contains words like *it, the, and,* and so on. The main dictionary is used when a word is not found in either the personal or the internal dictionary.

The other options you control from the screen (shown in Figure 5c.18) are automatic reformatting and hyphenation. If you use the default value of Y for Auto Reform, CorrectStar will adjust the text of a paragraph so that it fits between the margins when spelling corrections result in either longer or shorter words. Otherwise, line lengths are not adjusted. When the Soft Hyphen Insertion is selected, words at the end of each line will automatically be hy-

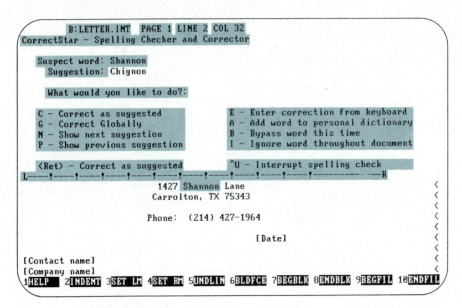

FIGURE 5c.18
When CorrectStar makes a spelling suggestion

phenated in such a way that the maximum line length is used. If the default value of N is used, only full words will appear at the end of each line.

Once you have selected the CorrectStar options, your screen will look like the one in Figure 5c.19. At this point, CorrectStar verifies the presence of the main dictionary. If you are working on a microcomputer that has only floppy disk drives, you will find it necessary to remove the WordStar disk from drive A and replace it with the main dictionary disk.

After a momentary pause, your screen will look like Figure 5c.20. You are now ready to begin correcting the spelling in your document. The first word that is marked by CorrectStar is *Shannon,* which is not included in the personal, internal, or main dictionaries. However, for many words, CorrectStar will search dictionaries and suggest other words with similar spellings or sounds — one such suggestion is *Chignon.*

Once a dictionary search has been completed, you are provided with a list of actions, including the following: use the suggested correction for the current word (C or the RETURN key), use the suggested correction for the current word wherever it appears in the document (G), select another suggestion (N), recall a previous suggestion (P), enter a correction from the keyboard (E), add the word to the personal dictionary (A), ignore the occurrence of the word (B), and ignore all occurrences of the word (I). CorrectStar can be interrupted by

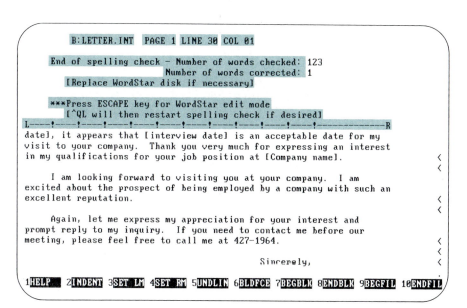

```
        B:LETTER.INT  PAGE 1 LINE 25 COL 31
CorrectStar - Spelling Checker and Corrector

    Suspect word: apprecaition
Type correction: appreciation

    What would you like to do?: E

                                   E - Enter correction from keyboard
                                   A - Add word to personal dictionary
                                   B - Bypass word this time
                                   I - Ignore word throughout document

                                   ^U - Interrupt spelling check
L----!----!----!----!----!----!----!----!----!----!----R
excellent reputation.                                          <
                                                               <
    Again, let me express my apprecaition for your interest and
prompt reply to my inquiry.  If you need to contact me before our
meeting, please feel free to call me at 427-1964.              <
                                                               <
                            Sincerely,                         <

1HELP  2INDENT 3SET LM 4SET RM 5UNDLIN 6BLDFCE 7BEGBLK 8ENDBLK 9BEGFIL 10ENDFIL
```

FIGURE 5c.19
Correcting apprecaition

```
        B:LETTER.INT  PAGE 1 LINE 30 COL 01

    End of spelling check - Number of words checked: 123
                            Number of words corrected: 1
    [Replace WordStar disk if necessary]

    ***Press ESCAPE key for WordStar edit mode
       [^QL will then restart spelling check if desired]
L----!----!----!----!----!----!----!----!----!----!----R
date], it appears that [interview date] is an acceptable date for my
visit to your company.  Thank you very much for expressing an interest
in my qualifications for your job position at [Company name].   <
                                                                <
    I am looking forward to visiting you at your company.  I am
excited about the prospect of being employed by a company with such an
excellent reputation.                                           <
                                                                <
    Again, let me express my appreciation for your interest and
prompt reply to my inquiry.  If you need to contact me before our
meeting, please feel free to call me at 427-1964.               <
                                                                <
                            Sincerely,                          <

1HELP  2INDENT 3SET LM 4SET RM 5UNDLIN 6BLDFCE 7BEGBLK 8ENDBLK 9BEGFIL 10ENDFIL
```

FIGURE 5c.20
Returning to normal WordStar operations

using ^U, should you find the need to make other changes to a document while checking for correct spelling. To restart CorrectStar, enter ^L. For the suspect word in Figure 5c.18, you could select the A, B, or I option. (If this were your actual street name, you would probably want to add it to your personal dictionary rather than ignore it.)

Other words that do not appear in any of CorrectStar's dictionaries are "Carrolton," "TX," and "apprecaition." You would probably choose to bypass corrections for Carrolton and TX. However (as shown in Figure 5c.19), *appreciation* is misspelled. Furthermore, CorrectStar provides no suggestion for a correction. As a result, the first four choices (C, G, N, and P) are not shown on the screen. In this case, enter the correction from the keyboard (E). Simply type the correction and press the RETURN key.

Since *appreciation* is the last suspect word in the letter, the next step is to return to the WordStar edit mode (see Figure 5c.20). If you are using a floppy disk system, you will have to replace the CorrectStar disk in drive A with the WordStar disk. Once this is done, press the ESC key, and you will continue in the normal WordStar mode. Remember to save the corrected document if you made any corrections.

Personalized Messages — Find and Replace Functions

Your next task is to prepare your general letter so that it can be sent to Mr. Joe Garcia at Champion Cowboy Supply. First, go to the [Date] area of the letter and enter the appropriate date. Then change [Contact name] to Mr. Joe Garcia. Next, change [Company name] to Champion Cowboy Supply. However, this name appears both in the address area and within the body of the letter. Thus, it might be quicker to find each reference to [Company name] and replace them all at once. To perform this operation, enter the QUICK MENU by pressing ^Q and select the A option — find and replace.

Figure 5c.21 illustrates how this process works. First, WordStar will ask for the character string you wish to find. You should supply the exact text — [Company name]. Next, WordStar will ask for the replacement: all occurrences of [Company name] are to be replaced with Champion Cowboy Supply. Finally, the find and replace operation needs information on how the operation is to be handled through a request for options. Note that NG has been specified in Figure 5c.21, which means "perform the operation without stopping each time to ask if the replacement is correct in this circumstance" (N) and "perform the operation for the entire file" (G). Once the RETURN key is pressed, all of the occurrences of [Company name] are replaced.

After this operation has been completed, continue to make changes for other items contained in brackets ([ ]). You may find it more convenient to use the find operation than looking for them yourself. This can easily be done by entering ^QF and entering [as the text to be found. The finding operation can be easily repeated by entering ^L for the next occurrence of the character

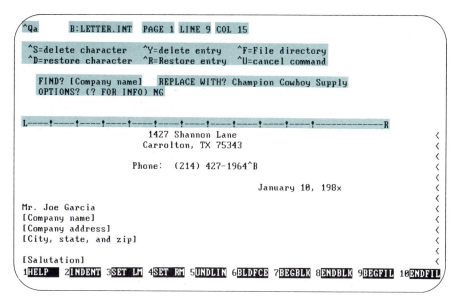

FIGURE 5C.21
Using the find and replace functions

string [. (The ^L operation also works for the replacing function when you have not specified G—global—as one of the options.) After all the substitutions have been made, your letter should look like the one in Figure 5c.22.

Printing Your Letter — The Print Function

Once you have modified the letter, save it and return to the OPENING MENU. Once this is done, select P—the print function. As shown in Figure 5c.23, you will be asked a series of questions, beginning with "Which document do you want to print?" You should enter B:LETTER.INT. You will be asked a number of additional questions, including "Do you want the output to be placed on a disk file rather than printed?" This option allows you to save the document as a print (ASCII) file in addition to a WordStar document. This might be a desirable format for interfacing with other applications packages. In addition, you will be asked to supply the beginning page number and the ending page number. On a long document, you could select only a portion of the file—particular page ranges—for printing.

Other questions include the use of form feeds (control of vertical printing, suppression of page formatting), automatic formatting to a saved description of individual pages, and stopping between individual pages—so that single sheets of paper may be fed into the printer. As shown in Figure 5c.23,

```
    B:LETTER.INT  PAGE 1 LINE 19 COL 17
                 < < <    M A I N   M E N U   > > >
   --Cursor Movement--  : -Delete- :  -Miscellaneous-  : -Other  Menus-
^S char left ^D char right :^G  char  :^I Tab   ^B Reform :(from Main only)
^A word left ^F word right :DEL chr lf:^V INSERT ON/OFF  :^J Help  ^K Block
^E line  up ^X line down :^T word rt:^L Find/Replce again:^Q Quick ^P Print
    --Scrolling--        :^Y  line  :RETURN End paragraph:^O Onscreen
^Z line down ^W line up   :          : ^N Insert a RETURN :
^C screen up ^R screen down:         : ^U Stop a command  :
L----!----!----!----!----!----!----!----!----!----!----!------R
                                    January 12, 198x              <
                                                                  <
Mr. Joe Garcia                                                    <
Champion Cowboy Supply                                            <
126 Hollyhill Road                                                <
Garland, TX 75342                                                 <
                                                                  <
Dear Mr. Garcia,                                                  <

    Thank you very much for expressing an interest in my
qualifications for your job position at Champion Cowboy Supply.
According to your letter dated January 10, 198x, it appears that
January 20, 198x is an acceptable date for my visit to your
company.  I am looking forward to visiting you at your company.
1HELP   2INDENT 3SET LM 4SET RM 5UNDLIN 6BLDFCE 7BEGBLK 8ENDBLK 9BEGFIL 10ENDFIL
```

FIGURE 5C.22
**The interview letter after the find and
replace operation**

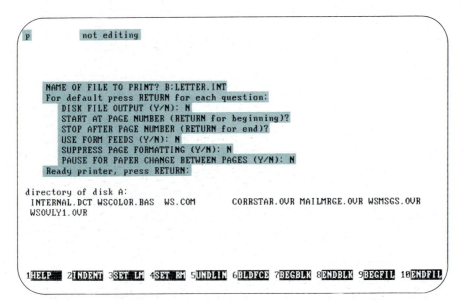

```
p           not editing




   NAME OF FILE TO PRINT? B:LETTER.INT
   For default press RETURN for each question:
      DISK FILE OUTPUT (Y/N): N
      START AT PAGE NUMBER (RETURN for beginning)?
      STOP AFTER PAGE NUMBER (RETURN for end)?
      USE FORM FEEDS (Y/N): N
      SUPPRESS PAGE FORMATTING (Y/N): N
      PAUSE FOR PAPER CHANGE BETWEEN PAGES (Y/N): N
   Ready printer, press RETURN:

directory of disk A:
 INTERNAL.DCT WSCOLOR.BAS  WS.COM        CORRSTAR.OVR MAILMRGE.OVR WSMSGS.OVR
WSOVLY1.OVR




1HELP   2INDENT 3SET LM 4SET RM 5UNDLIN 6BLDFCE 7BEGBLK 8ENDBLK 9BEGFIL 10ENDFIL
```

FIGURE 5C.23
Entering the print function

```
                         (your name)
                       1427 Shannon Lane
                       Carrolton, TX 75343

                 Phone:  (214) 427-1964

                                        January 12, 198x

        Mr. Joe Garcia
        Champion Cowboy Supply
        126 Hollyhill Road
        Garland, TX 75342

        Dear Mr. Garcia,

            Thank you very much for expressing an interest in my
        qualifications for your job position at Champion Cowboy Supply.
        According to your letter dated January 10, 198x, it appears that
        January 20, 198x is an acceptable date for my visit to your company.
        I am looking forward to visiting you at your company.  I am excited
        about the prospect of being employed by a company with such an
        excellent reputation.

            Again, let me express my appreciation for your interest and
        prompt reply to my job inquiry.  If you need to contact me before
        our meeting, please feel free to call me at 427-1964.

                                        Sincerely,
```

FIGURE 5c.24
**The interview letter to Champion Cowboy
Supply**

each of these questions has a default response generated by pressing the RE-
TURN key. (If you press the ESCape key after entering the document name,
WordStar will immediately begin printing your document using the default
values without asking you additional questions.)

Align the printer to the top of the page before the document begins
printing. If for some reason you want to stop the printing function, press the
letter P, which halts the printing process and asks you what you want to do next.
(These prompts will appear on your screen after printing begins.) The result of
printing the document B:LETTER.INT is shown in Figure 5c.24.

Other Features of WordStar

In addition to sending a letter to Champion Cowboy Supply, you are also to
send letters to Kelly Construction Company and Mosteq Computer Company.

You could repeat the find and replace and printing operations just described, but you might find it easier to use the MailMerge function of WordStar. To use this function, you must alter the interview letter. As shown in Figure 5c.25, B:LETTER.INT has been altered to include a number of new lines. The top three lines now contain what are known as *dot commands*—each of these lines begins with a period in column 1.

Dot commands are used to control the printing and MailMerge functions. For example, .HE at the beginning of a line is used to specify a page heading; .FO designates a page footing. Additional text would accompany each of these dot commands to specify the content of the page heading or the page footing.

In Figure 5c.25, the first dot command is .OP, which means that page numbers are to be omitted. The second dot command is .DF—define file. This command indicates that when the document is printed, it should use the contents of B:JOBS.DTA in the process. For your problem, the file B:JOBS.DTA will contain the company information (names, addresses) necessary to print all three interview letters. The third dot command is only partially visible. The .RV command indicates that a list of variables (for example, Date, Contact-name, Company-name) are to be read during the printing process. Each of these names appears later in the document and is used in a kind of "fill in the blank" operation. For example, when the letter is being printed, a certain value will be retrieved from B:JOBS.DTA for Date, and it will be substituted for each entry in the letter marked &Date&. The locations of data values that match the list provided in the .RV command are marked by field names beginning and ending with the & symbol. Furthermore, these field names do not have to be listed in the same order in the .RV command as they are used in the document. (Note that the &Company-name& field appears twice in the letter.)

The last dot command goes at the bottom of the page, as shown in Figure 5c.26. The .PA indicates that a new page is to begin at this position. This ensures that each letter will begin on a new page when multiple copies of it are printed. Remember to save this version of the letter before continuing.

The next step is to create the B:JOBS.DTA file (see Figure 5c.27). This file must be created using the nondocument (ASCII) mode. Thus, you must select N, rather than D, from the OPENING MENU when creating or editing this file. Also, it is recommended that the .DTA file extension be used. This will avoid any conflict between this file and any other WordStar-related file.

The data values to be used in the B:LETTER.INT document must be in exactly the same order as specified in the .RV command. Thus, the Date value should be first, followed by the Contact name, Company name, and so on. Each data value should be separated by a comma (missing or omitted values should be accounted for by a comma indicating the location of the missing value). Any data value containing a comma should be enclosed within quotation (") marks, as in the Date field.

Finally, each line of a document or file cannot exceed 240 characters, and each data line should be terminated by pressing the RETURN key.

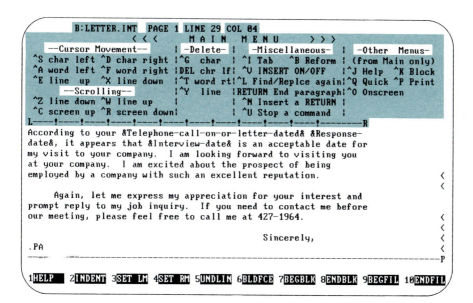

```
     B:LETTER.INT  PAGE 1 LINE 10 COL 15
              < < <    M A I N   M E N U    > > >
  --Cursor Movement--  ¦ -Delete- ¦  -Miscellaneous-  ¦ -Other  Menus-
^S char left ^D char right ¦^G  char ¦ ^I Tab    ^B Reform ¦ (from Main only)
^A word left ^F word right ¦DEL chr lf! ^V INSERT ON/OFF  ¦^J Help  ^K Block
^E line  up ^X line down  ¦^T word rt!^L Find/Replce again¦^Q Quick ^P Print
      --Scrolling--       ¦^Y  line ¦RETURN End paragraph¦^O Onscreen
^Z line down ^W line up   ¦         ¦ ^N Insert a RETURN ¦
^C screen up ^R screen down¦         ¦ ^U Stop a command  ¦
L----!----!----!----!----!----!----!----!----!----!----!---------R
.OP                                                              <
.DF B:JOBS.DTA                                                   M
.RV Date, Contact-name, Company-name, Company-address, City-state-zip, Salutati+
              ^B(your name)                                      <
              1427 Shannon Lane                                  <
              Carrolton, TX 75343                                <
                                                                 <
        Phone:  (214) 427-1964^B                                 <
                                                                 <
                           &Date&                                <
                                                                 <
&Contact-name&                                                   <
&Company-name&                                                   <
&Company-address&                                                <
1HELP   2INDENT 3SET LM 4SET RM 5UNDLIN 6BLDFCE 7BEGBLK 8ENDBLK 9BEGFIL 10ENDFIL
```

FIGURE 5c.25

Setting up the letter for a MailMerge operation

```
     B:LETTER.INT  PAGE 1 LINE 29 COL 04
              < < <    M A I N   M E N U    > > >
  --Cursor Movement--  ¦ -Delete- ¦  -Miscellaneous-  ¦ -Other  Menus-
^S char left ^D char right ¦^G  char ¦ ^I Tab    ^B Reform ¦ (from Main only)
^A word left ^F word right ¦DEL chr lf! ^V INSERT ON/OFF  ¦^J Help  ^K Block
^E line  up ^X line down  ¦^T word rt!^L Find/Replce again¦^Q Quick ^P Print
      --Scrolling--       ¦^Y  line ¦RETURN End paragraph¦^O Onscreen
^Z line down ^W line up   ¦         ¦ ^N Insert a RETURN ¦
^C screen up ^R screen down¦         ¦ ^U Stop a command  ¦
L----!----!----!----!----!----!----!----!----!----!----!---------R
According to your &Telephone-call-on-or-letter-dated& &Response-
date&, it appears that &Interview-date& is an acceptable date for
my visit to your company.  I am looking forward to visiting you
at your company.  I am excited about the prospect of being
employed by a company with such an excellent reputation.         <
                                                                 <
    Again, let me express my appreciation for your interest and
prompt reply to my job inquiry.  If you need to contact me before
our meeting, please feel free to call me at 427-1964.            <
                                                                 <
                           Sincerely,                            <
.PA                                                              <
----------------------------------------------------------------P
1HELP   2INDENT 3SET LM 4SET RM 5UNDLIN 6BLDFCE 7BEGBLK 8ENDBLK 9BEGFIL 10ENDFIL
```

FIGURE 5c.26

Forcing an end-of-page

```
       B:JOBS.DTA  FC=533 FL=4 COL 01
               < < <     M A I N   M E N U     > > >
    --Cursor Movement--    !  -Delete-   !  -Miscellaneous-    !  -Other  Menus-
 ^S char left ^D char right !^G  char    ! ^I Tab   ^B Reform  ! (from Main only)
 ^A word left ^F word right !DEL chr lf! ^V INSERT ON/OFF      !^J Help  ^K Block
 ^E line  up  ^X line down  !^T word rt!^L Find/Replce again!^Q Quick ^P Print
    --Scrolling--           !^Y  line  !RETURN End paragraph!^O Onscreen
 ^Z line down ^W line up    !          ! ^N Insert a RETURN !
 ^C screen up ^R screen down!          ! ^U Stop a command   !
"January 12, 198x", Mr. Joe Garcia, Champion Cowboy Supply, 126 Hollyhill Road,+
"January 12, 198x", Mr. Peter Hoague, Mosteq Computer Company, 1428 Wozniak Way+
"January 12, 198x", Personnel Division, Kelly Construction Company, 1414 Jupite+
                                                                              .
                                                                              .
                                                                              .
                                                                              .
                                                                              .
                                                                              .
1HELP   2INDENT 3SET LM 4SET RM 5UNDLIN 6BLDFCE 7BEGBLK 8ENDBLK 9BEGFIL 10ENDFIL
```

FIGURE 5c.27
Creating the JOBS.DTA file

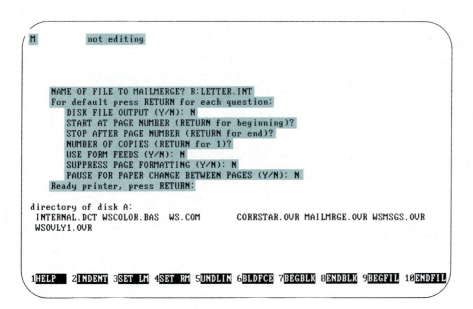

FIGURE 5c.28
Entering the MailMerge function

As shown in Figure 5c.28, using the MailMerge function is similar to printing a document. Select the M—MailMerge—option from the OPEN-ING MENU and supply B:LETTER.INT as the MailMerge file. Thereafter, you may either respond to the individual prompts for additional information or press the ESCape key to begin printing the documents immediately. The results of this operation are shown in Figure 5c.29 on the next page.

Of course, WordStar has other means of performing merging operations. As illustrated in Figure 5c.30, you can use the .AV dot command to insert data values into a document. The .AV command "ask for a value" is entered from the keyboard as the document is being printed. Thus, while printing B:LET-TER.INT, the screen will appear as shown in Figure 5c.31.

Finally, to complete your WordStar session, leave WordStar and return to the operating system by selecting X from the OPENING MENU screen.

Summary of Word Processing Modules

The modules in Chapter 5 have given you the opportunity to learn about one (or more) of three popular word processing packages available for microcom-puters: pfs:Word/Proof (Module 5a), MultiMate (Module 5b), and WordStar (Module 5c). You learned about these word processing packages by writing interview letters in connection with the job hunting problem.

Comparison of Word Processing Packages

Before attempting to answer the questions and work on the problems at the end of this section, study Table 5s.1 on page 198, which provides a quick compari-son of the different word processing packages. Although there are similarities among the packages (for example, each is capable of use with only one disk drive), there are a number of rather distinct differences. (The table covers only a few of these differences.)

An example of one difference among word processing packages is the means for selecting special printing functions. In WordStar, a print function is selected by using a control character that may be hidden from view. In Multi-Mate, print functions are selected by using the ALTernate key, followed by a letter code, that cannot be hidden. Finally, pfs:Write print functions are se-lected by using function keys that are not visible on the screen.

If you compare the capabilities of the packages presented, you will find that some are easier to use than others. Further, some packages are specifically designed to solve particular types of word processing problems.

```
                              (your name)
                           1427 Shannon Lane
                           Carrolton, TX 75343

                        Phone:  (214) 427-1964

                                              January 12, 198x

            Personnel Division
            Kelly Construction Company
            1414 Jupiter Road
            Garland, TX 75242
```

```
                              (your name)
                           1427 Shannon Lane
                           Carrolton, TX 75343

                        Phone:  (214) 427-1964

                                              January 12, 198x

            Mr. Peter Hoague
            Mosteq Computer Company
            1428 Wozniak Way
            Farmers Branch, TX 76331
```

any.
t
pany.
ited

d
re

```
                              (your name)
                           1427 Shannon Lane
                           Carrolton, TX 75343

                        Phone:  (214) 427-1964

                                              January 12, 198x

        Mr. Joe Garcia
        Champion Cowboy Supply
        126 Hollyhill Road
        Garland, TX 75342

        Dear Mr. Garcia,

            Thank you very much for expressing an interest in my
        qualifications for your job position at Champion Cowboy Supply.
        According to your letter dated January 10, 198x, it appears that
        January 20, 198x is an acceptable date for my visit to your company.
        I am looking forward to visiting you at your company.  I am excited
        about the prospect of being employed by a company with such an
        excellent reputation.

            Again, let me express my appreciation for your interest and
        prompt reply to my job inquiry.  If you need to contact me before
        our meeting, please feel free to call me at 427-1964.

                                Sincerely,
```

y.
hat
mpany.
cited

nd
ore

FIGURE 5c.29
Interview letters produced by MailMerge

```
    B:LETTER.INT  PAGE 1 LINE 1 COL 01
              < < <   M A I N   M E N U   > > >
    --Cursor Movement--    |  -Delete- |  -Miscellaneous-  |  -Other  Menus-
 ^S char left ^D char right | ^G  char | ^I Tab   ^B Reform | (from Main only)
 ^A word left ^F word right |DEL chr lf| ^V INSERT ON/OFF   |^J Help  ^K Block
 ^E line  up  ^X line down  |^T word rt| ^L Find/Replce again|^Q Quick ^P Print
    --Scrolling--          |^Y  line  |RETURN End paragraph|^O Onscreen
 ^Z line down ^W line up    |          | ^N Insert a RETURN  |
 ^C screen up ^R screen down|          | ^U Stop a command   |
L----!----!----!----!----!----!----!----!----!----!----R
.DM Below, enter the values to be printed in the Interview Letter        M
.AV "Enter the letter Date............. ", Date                          M
.AV "Enter the Contact name........... ", Contact-name                  M
.AV "Enter the Company name........... ", Company-name                  M
.AV "Enter the Company address........ ", Company-address               M
.AV "Enter the City, state and zip code ", City-state-zip               M
.AV "Enter the Salutation............. ", Salutation                    M
.AV "Was the contact by Phone or Letter ", Telephone-call-on-or-letter-dated  M
.AV "Enter the Response date.......... ", Response-date                 M
.AV "Enter the Interview date......... ", Interview-date                M
                  ^B(your name)                                         <
                  1427 Shannon Lane                                     <
                  Carrolton, TX 75343                                   <
1HELP    2INDENT 3SET LM 4SET RM 5UNDLIN 6BLDFCE 7BEGBLK 8ENDBLK 9BEGFIL 10ENDFIL
```

FIGURE 5C.30
Using the "Ask for Value" command

```
      MailMerge-printing B:LETTER.INT    not editing


      P= Stop PRINT


Below, enter the values to be printed in the Interview Letter
Enter the letter Date............. January 12, 198x
Enter the Contact name........... Mr. Joe Garcia
Enter the Company name........... Champion Cowboy Supply
Enter the Company address........ 126 Hollyhill Road
Enter the City, state and zip code Garland, TX 75342
Enter the Salutation............. Dear Mr. Garcia,
Was the contact by Phone or Letter letter dated
Enter the Response date.......... January 10, 198x
Enter the Interview date......... January 20, 198x

directory of disk A:
 INTERNAL.DCT WSCOLOR.BAS  WS.COM      CORRSTAR.OVR MAILMRGE.OVR WSMSGS.OVR
 WSOVLY1.OVR




1HELP    2INDENT 3SET LM 4SET RM 5UNDLIN 6BLDFCE 7BEGBLK 8ENDBLK 9BEGFIL 10ENDFIL
```

FIGURE 5C.31
Printing an interview letter containing
"Ask for Value" commands

TABLE 5S.1 A Comparison of Word Processing Applications Packages

Characteristic	pfs:Write	MultiMate	WordStar
Operating system	PC-DOS, MS-DOS	PC-DOS, MS-DOS	PC-DOS, MS-DOS, CP/M
Main memory (RAM) (minimum)	128k bytes	256k bytes	64k bytes
Disk drives	1	1	1
Printer (optional)	80- or 132-column ASCII	80- or 132-column ASCII	80- or 132-column ASCII
View on screen	Compressed to single space	Compressed to single space	Shown as printed
Selectable HELP	No	No	Yes, 4 levels
Ruler location	Bottom of screen	Top of screen	Top of screen
Function selected primarily by	Function key	Function key	CTRL key followed by one or more letters/symbols
Visible control codes	No	Yes	Yes, but can be hidden
Special printing			
Boldface	Yes	Yes	Yes
Doublestrike	No	Yes	Yes
Underline	Yes	Yes	Yes
Subscript	No	Yes	Yes
Superscript	No	Yes	Yes
Overprint	No	Yes	Yes
Strikeout	No	Yes	Yes
Spell-checking	Yes, with pfs:Proof (recommends spelling change/substitution)	Yes (recommends spelling change/substitution)	Yes, with SpellStar or CorrectStar
MailMerge	Yes, with pfs:File	Yes, from file	Yes, from file or keyboard
Boilerplating	Yes	No, can merge	No, can merge
Multicolumn print	Yes	No	Yes, possibly
Interface method	Print file, SYLK	Print file	Print file

Thus, you should determine which package to use based on the problem to be solved.

Guidelines for the Evaluation of Word Processing Packages

Before you select a word processing package for your own use, answer the following questions:

- **Typing speed**   Are special function and control character keys easy to reach? Does the package provide automatic word wrapping? Can you "get ahead" of the word processor during normal text entry? (You should not be able to.)

- **Automatic reformatting**   Are paragraphs automatically reformatted when you make corrections, or must you reformat by hand? Can different paragraphs have different formats?

- **Copying text**   How easy is it to mark the text to be copied and then move it to another location within the document?

- **Margin settings**   How far can the right margin be moved? Does the package scroll to the right?

- **Cursor control**   How easy is it to move around in the document? Is it possible to move directly from paragraph to paragraph? From page to page? Can you move directly to a specified page?

- **Search and replace**   Can you replace parts of words as well as whole words? Can you control whether replacement is automatic or determined by you? Must you reenter the command every time a replacement is made? Can you search and replace from the bottom to the top of the document as well as from top to bottom?

- **Text editing**   How easy is it to edit a document? (Remember, this is the true power of a word processor.) Are you required to switch modes in order to perform editing operations?

- **Type styles**   Does the package provide the different type styles you need (for example, boldface, italic, underline, subscripts, superscripts)?

- **Text formatting**   Is it easy to change the margins for the text? Can you easily change from single-spacing to double-spacing or triple-spacing? Does the package easily change between ragged, right-justified, and centered text?

- **Hardware compatibility**   Will this word processor run on your microcomputer? Does it work with your brand of printer, and is it able to use the full capabilities of the printer?

- **Saving documents**   Does the package automatically save documents before you quit? Does it automatically keep backups of the documents? What is the format used to save a file (ASCII or DIF)?

What Happened at ACE?

The training seminar on word processing was interesting. Of course it took a little time to learn to use the package. After the seminar Chris used the list of suppliers and the word processing package to get Mr. Jenkins's letters out on time. And, because Chris made the deadline, ACE was able to get the new products ahead of some of the competition, and profits showed an increase that month.

Module Questions

1. What word processing package are you using? Is it command driven or menu driven? Does it have a help function? How is the help function used?
2. What is the maximum size of a document that your word processing system can handle? What is the "word processing hierarchy" of your word processing package?
3. Check your word processing package's documentation: What are the additional features available to you? How do you select and use them?
4. How are the control characters handled by your word processing package?
5. What other word processing packages (besides the one you are using) can be used on your microcomputer? (*Note:* Use the library or your local computer store to find the answer to this question.)

Module Problems

1. The goal of the job hunting process is to find a single suitable job. However, during your job hunt, you have received a number of offers. Ultimately, you will refuse all but one of them. Of course, when you decide to refuse an offer, you should write a letter to the company indicating your decision. Currently, you have decided to refuse the offer made by Matt's Films, Incorporated. Write them a letter, thanking them for their offer but indicating that you have decided to accept another opportunity. Because this letter will be sent to other companies as you decide to refuse their offers, make the letter sufficiently general, so that it can be used again.
2. You must prepare a letter to each showroom manager in the district asking him or her to supply sales information on all audio equipment (radios and stereos) sold during the last month. Your letter should contain a list of all the

audio items. This list is located in the inventory data for ACE, Incorporated (found in Appendix B).

3. Using the inventory data for ACE, Incorporated (found in Appendix B), prepare a letter to be sent to each supplier (vendor). This letter should request information about all products available from that supplier. It should also inquire about currently available discounts for quantity purchases and any promotional or display items that might be useful for the grand opening of a new store in south Houston.

SCENARIO 6

What's Going on at ACE?

One Friday about 4:30 in the afternoon, just when I was looking forward to the weekend, the phone rang. It was my boss, Mr. Jenkins. He said that he was going to make a trip to the regional office in Dallas at the end of next week and he needed some information on sales performance of the inventory items from one of our district stores. Some of the sales figures would need to be adjusted when he got updated information, but he wasn't expecting the update until about Wednesday. So, he asked me to get the inventory information set up for some quick calculations that could be easily changed when the update arrived.

I immediately called Ms. Allison and explained the problem to her in the hope that she could give me some direction on how to use a computer to solve it. She said that the problem looked like it could be solved by using something called a *spreadsheet*. I wasn't really sure what she was talking about, so I asked how to learn quickly about spreadsheets. Ms. Allison said that several store managers were to be in her training facility on Monday, and one of her staff, a Mr. Cotterman, was going to conduct a one-day seminar on spreadsheets and their application. So, on Monday I was in the seminar and ready to go. ■

Chapter Six
Applications Software:
Spreadsheets

Chapter Objectives

When you have completed this chapter, you will be able to:

- Discuss the general historical development of electronic spreadsheets
- Give a general description of an electronic spreadsheet
- Explain the basic functions of electronic spreadsheets
- Describe some of the uses of electronic spreadsheets

Introduction to Spreadsheets

Suppose you are planning a ski trip during the next break in classes; you know that some of your friends will go with you, but you don't know how many. You need to calculate the total shared expenses for the trip, as well as each person's cost. To do this, you have gathered the following information:

1. **Getting there**
   You have available a van that can carry 8 people and gets 14 miles per gallon and a car that can carry 4 people and gets 26 miles per gallon. The travel distance is 821 miles one way, and you can expect to add another 200 miles while you are there.

2. **Staying there**
   Even if you drive straight through by rotating drivers, you will need a place to stay while skiing. You can rent a condominium that will hold 6 people for $60.00 a night double occupancy plus $20.00 a night for each additional person. You will need the condominium for 6 nights. Food for the 6 days that you will be there will cost about $50.00 per person for breakfast and dinner. Lunch, if not a bag lunch, will be about $8.00 per day.

```
SKI TRIP              NUMBER OF PEOPLE
                   2        3        4        5        6
==================================================================
Transportation   83.53    83.53    83.53   155.12   155.12
Lodging          60.00    80.00   100.00   120.00   140.00
Food            100.00   150.00   200.00   250.00   300.00
                -------------------------------------------------
Total           243.53   313.53   383.53   525.12   595.12

Cost per person 121.76   104.51    95.88   105.02    99.19
Ski cost        320.00   320.00   320.00   320.00   320.00
                -------------------------------------------------
Total per person 441.76  424.51   415.88   425.02   419.19
```

```
        SKI TRIP              NUMBER OF PEOPLE
                        7        8        9       10       11       12
        =======================================================================
        Transportation 155.12   155.12   238.65   238.65   238.65   238.65
        Lodging        200.00   200.00   220.00   240.00   260.00   280.00
        Food           350.00   400.00   450.00   500.00   550.00   600.00
                       ----------------------------------------------------
        Total          705.12   755.12   908.65   978.65  1048.65  1118.65

        Cost per person 100.73   94.39   100.96    97.87    95.33    93.22
        Ski cost        320.00  320.00   320.00   320.00   320.00   320.00
                       ----------------------------------------------------
        Total per person 420.73 414.39   420.96   417.87   415.33   413.22
```

FIGURE 6.1
The cost calculations for the ski trip

3. **Equipment**
   Lift tickets will be $17.00 per day, and ski rental will cost $15.00 per day, if you rent skies for all 6 days.

   Clearly, as people decide to go, you could calculate the cost per person with a pencil and paper. Doing the calculations in this manner would require a lot of arithmetic and time, whereas using one of the spreadsheet packages would quickly and easily give you the results shown in Figure 6.1.

   Obviously, using the computer to do these calculations is easier and faster than doing them by hand. If you were presented with a complex problem—for example, developing monthly budgets for a company or

an organization—the ability to use electronic spreadsheets would be even more valuable. This chapter will cover the basics of electronic spreadsheets and examine some of their uses in business.

Historical Development

Electronic spreadsheet packages are currently the best-selling business applications software for microcomputers. Originally conceived as a simple replacement for a blackboard and a calculator, electronic spreadsheets have been used for applications from personal expense account budgeting to drawing up budgets for large corporations.

The original idea for electronic spreadsheets was developed by a Harvard MBA student in 1978. He was tired of adding rows and columns of numbers over and over again for his homework assignments. The software package developed to relieve the student of this tedious work was called *VisiCalc*, co-authored by Dan Bricklin and Bob Frankston. In 1984, VisiCalc, the original commercial spreadsheet package for microcomputers, was the best-selling applications software ever written, having sold over 700,000 copies worldwide.

Shortly after VisiCalc was introduced to the microcomputer world, other competitors entered the market. These applications packages were called **visiclones** and included *Lotus 1-2-3*, *Multiplan*, and *Supercalc*, as well as others.

For people too busy to develop their own solutions to specific problems through the use of an electronic spreadsheet, there is now a growing industry providing preprogrammed spreadsheet models for particular applications (called **templates**) as supplements to the electronic spreadsheet package.

Definition of Spreadsheets

Electronic spreadsheets have been called many names; the most common of these are **worksheets** and **scratchpads**. Conceptually, a spreadsheet is nothing more than a large sheet of paper divided into rows and columns. With an electronic spreadsheet, the "paper" is the memory of the computer, with part of the spreadsheet shown on the computer screen.

Matrix Terminology

A **work space** (the part of a spreadsheet where data is displayed) that is divided into rows and columns, as shown in Figure 6.2, is usually thought of as a **matrix.** In a matrix, an individual cell (a specific row and column position in the work space capable of retaining a series of characters or a value) containing data is referenced by indicating the row and column identifiers for the desired cell; that is, rows are usually identified by numbers (1, 2, 3, and so on), and columns may be identified by numbers (1, 2, 3, and so on) or letters (A, B, C, and so forth). By pressing the arrow keys on your keyboard, you can move the cursor around within the work space and look at different cells. When the cursor accesses portions of the spreadsheet that are not yet visible on the screen, this movement is called **scrolling.**

The type of cell-referencing system previously described is fairly common. If you look at a city map, you will find numbers down both sides indicating the rows and letters across the top and bottom of the map indicating the columns. These row and column indicators are used to show the location of streets and public buildings on the map. Your seat in a concert hall is also indicated by a row number or letter and a seat number in that row—a column indicator.

Although the term *matrix* may be new to you, the use of row and column identifiers to indicate a position or cell is not. When using row and column identifiers to indicate a position in a matrix, there are a couple of rules that must be followed. First, when identifying a particular cell—for example, the cell in the third row of column D, as shown in Figure 6.2—you normally indicate the column first and the row second. If you don't provide the row indicator, then you have identified the entire column as a

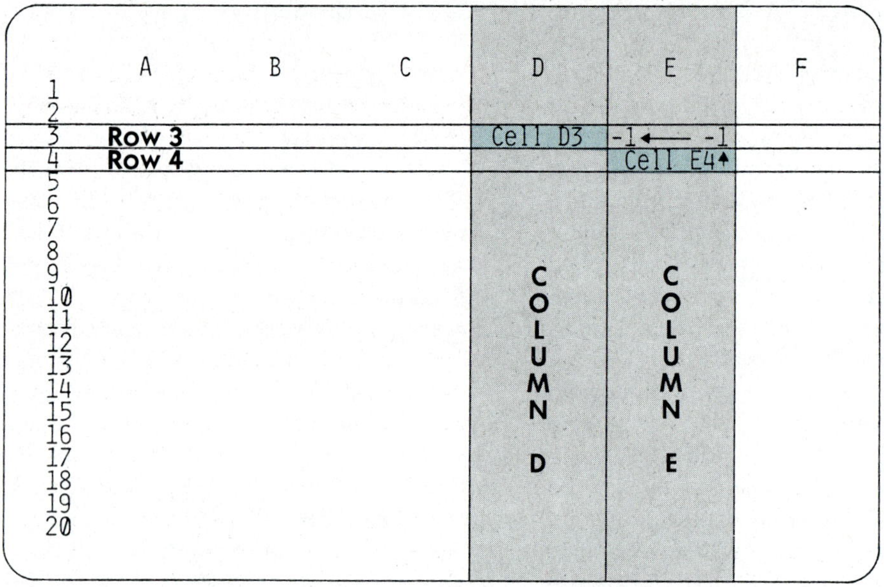

FIGURE 6.2
Rows and columns of a spreadsheet on a screen

cell; conversely, eliminating the column indicator identifies the entire row as a cell.

Second, a cell can be identified by its **absolute address** — that is, row 3 column D — or by its **relative address** — that is, its position relative to another cell. For example, if the current cursor location is on row 4 column E, then row 3 column D would be row −1 column −1 (see Figure 6.2). This relative position is indicated by the number of rows and columns and the directions you would have to move the cursor to arrive at the indicated cell (usually "+" for down or right and "−" for up or left).

Arithmetic Operations

Although the spreadsheet is structured as a matrix, it does not use advanced **matrix arithmetic** operations, such as matrix multi-

plication, inversion, or the calculation of determinants. Instead, it uses **scalar arithmetic** — the set of operations that you learned in elementary school. These arithmetic operations are addition, subtraction, multiplication, and division, plus some special functions that have proven useful, such as squares, square roots, averages, and logarithms.

Although specific arithmetic operations are discussed later, it is important to mention how an arithmetic operation is entered in a spreadsheet. To do arithmetic, move the cursor to the location in which you want the answer to appear. The equation or arithmetic operation is then entered, indicating the address of cells, if any, to be used in the operation. For example, suppose you had entered the values 97, 85, and 88 in cells row 1 column A, row 2 col-

To add figures

umn A, and row 3 column A, as shown in Figure 6.3. To add these three numbers together and place the result in row 4 column A, place the cursor in the cell row 4 column A and type either +97+85+88 or +A1+A2+A3, and the number 270 will appear in row 4 column A. The advantage of using cell references rather than the actual values can be seen when one or more of the actual values change. If the value 97 is changed to 87, the arithmetic operations based on the values would have to be changed to be correct. However, if cell references are used to indicate the locations of the actual values, the resulting sum based on this operation would automatically be changed by the software to reflect the new value in cell A1.

There are, of course, many other arithmetic operations that can be done with these numbers. However, before you learn about the functions of spreadsheets, you need to know a little about the characteristics of the data you can use in spreadsheets.

There Are Different Kinds of Data — Data Types

In general, **data types** are forms of data representation inside the computer. Although there are many different ways to represent data in spreadsheets, you are concerned with only two types: **character data** and **numeric data.**

Character Data

Typically, when you think of character data, you think of the letters of the alphabet — A through Z. However, when a computer uses character data, it can be the letters of the alphabet — A through Z — special charac-

ters — such as —, +, $, @, and # — and the "characters" 0 through 9.

Because character data, often referred to as **alphanumeric data,** is represented differently than numeric data, you cannot perform arithmetic operations on it. In fact, the only operations you can do directly with character data is sorting it into alphabetical order.

Numeric Data

Numeric data is any combination of the digits 0 through 9 used to represent a numeric value. Numeric data can also contain a minus symbol and a decimal point. For example, a quantity such as 50 or a price such as 1.95 is usually considered numeric data. Cells containing numeric data can be used in arithmetic operations. In fact, in most spreadsheets, formulas and mathematical functions are treated as numeric data. Although this may seem a little confusing now, because mathematical functions are considered numeric data, you can perform arithmetic operations on cells containing other arithmetic operations. For example, in Figure 6.1, the "Total per person" is the sum of the "Cost per person" and the "Ski cost." The "Cost per person" is the "Total" divided by the number of people, and the "Total" is the sum of "Transportation," "Lodging," and "Food." To calculate the "Total per person," you will perform three levels of arithmetic operations, some of which depend on arithmetic operations in other cells.

Functions of Spreadsheets

Now that you have examined the structure of a spreadsheet, learned how to identify

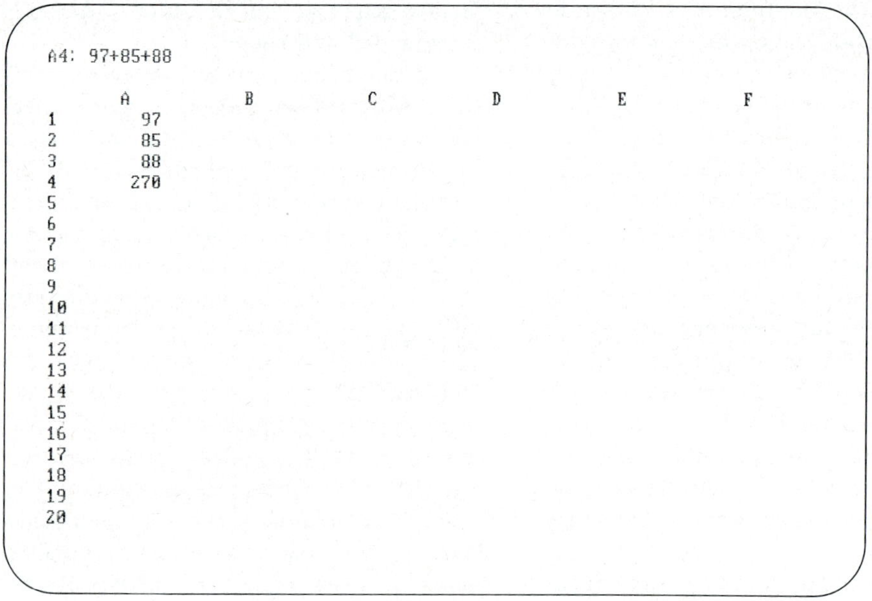

A4: 97+85+88

	A	B	C	D	E	F
1	97					
2	85					
3	88					
4	270					
5						
6						
7						
8						
9						
10						
11						
12						
13						
14						
15						
16						
17						
18						
19						
20						

a

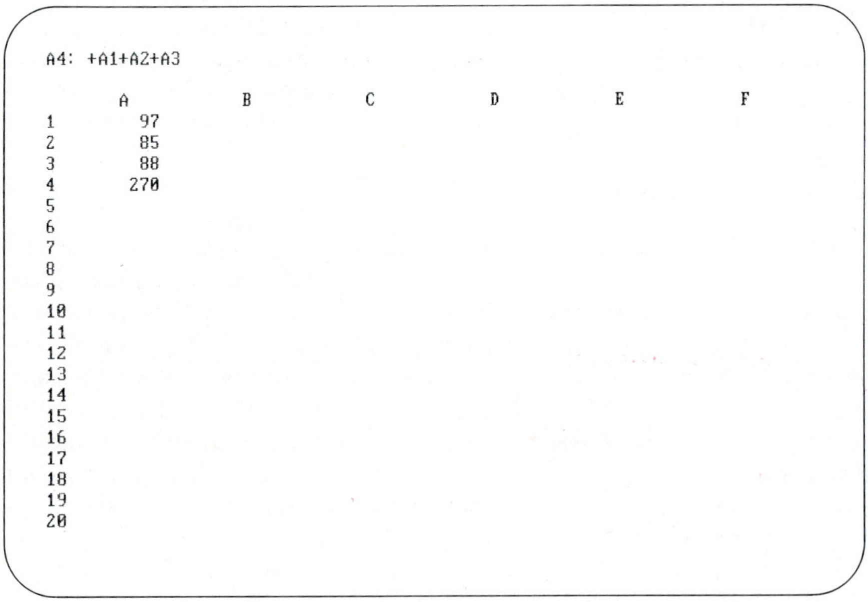

A4: +A1+A2+A3

	A	B	C	D	E	F
1	97					
2	85					
3	88					
4	270					
5						
6						
7						
8						
9						
10						
11						
12						
13						
14						
15						
16						
17						
18						
19						
20						

b

FIGURE 6.3
Using a spreadsheet to add three numbers

cell locations, and learned the difference between character and numeric data, you are ready to look at the functions of a spreadsheet. The functions discussed here are the general functions included in almost all spreadsheet packages. Although your package may not include all the functions mentioned in this chapter, it probably has other special capabilities.

Now What Do You Do? — Getting HELP

Every spreadsheet application package you use will provide a user's manual as the primary source of assistance for working with the package. However, when you're in the midst of an operation and can't remember a small item of information, it isn't very convenient to find and read a manual for help. For this reason, most spreadsheet packages provide a special HELP command that you can use to refresh your memory. The information provided by the HELP command is not as complete as the manual's information; however, the HELP command does provide enough information to remind you how to do a particular operation. It is almost always faster and easier to use the spreadsheet HELP command than to use the manual.

Efficient Traveling — Moving Around in the Spreadsheet

What you see on the screen when you first enter a spreadsheet program is similar to Figure 6.4a and represents only a part of your total work space. In general, there are two ways to move around in your spreadsheet so that you can view and work with all of the cells in your work space. The first method is through the use of the computer's cursor control keys. These keys are

used to move the cursor up, down, right, and left to an adjacent cell. As you move to a row or column not shown on the screen, the entire spreadsheet shown on the screen moves up or down, or right or left, by adding the row or column to one side of the screen and removing the row or column at the opposite side of the screen. Figure 6.4b shows the movement of the spreadsheet across a work space that has been moved to the right two columns beyond the initial screen and down two rows beyond the initial screen.

The second method of movement around your work space is through the use of a GO TO command. All spreadsheet packages have some form of this command. Simply enter the spreadsheet package's GO TO command and the address of the cell to which you want to move the cursor. The package will automatically scroll the screen so that the desired cell is shown. The HOME command is a special version of the GO TO command. It moves the cursor to the cell located at the first row and first column of the spreadsheet from any cell in the work space.

Although most of the movement around a spreadsheet can be achieved by employing special-use keys (for example, arrow keys and the HOME key) on the keyboard, the GO TO command and similar commands, are executed differently. The execution of these commands is usually performed by one of two means, depending on the design of the package: by *immediate command* or by *menu*. When using a package that employs the immediate-command concept, you simply enter the command from the keyboard, and the package interprets and executes the command — the package is **command driven.** For example, to execute a GO TO command, the immediate

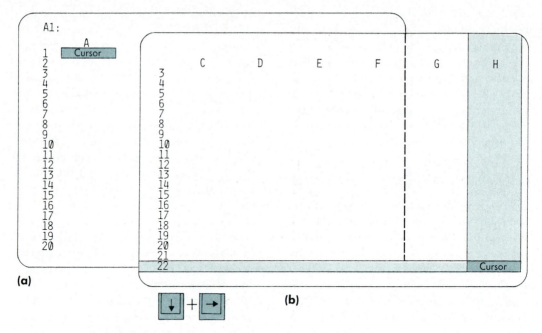

FIGURE 6.4
(a) The initial screen of a spreadsheet and (b) scrolling (moving the screen using the down- and right-arrow keys)

command could be /G, where the character / indicates that a command (rather than data) follows. The most common means of selecting commands is by the use of menus. In this case, the package presents a list of available commands, and you select the one you want from that list—the package is **menu driven.** If the command is complicated, you will be provided with additional menus (sometimes called *submenus*) from which you select other options. The more complicated the command, the more levels of menus involved. Finally, some packages use both types of command execution; that is, you can either enter the command sequence directly from the keyboard or select options from available menus.

What Do the Numbers Mean?— Titles and Labels

When you first start working on a spreadsheet, you will be viewing a screen that has the rows and columns identified. The rest of the work space will be totally blank, as in Figure 6.4. The first operation you should perform is to title the spreadsheet, the rows, and the columns by typing in characters, often called **text.** With most packages, all you need to do is start typing to enter text. When you type an alphabetic character, the package will automatically enter text-entry mode.

If the title you want to enter begins with a numeric character, the package must be told that what you really want is a character and not a number. For example, suppose you are entering month and year titles. When you type in 8/85, the computer will show .09411765 in the cell (the "/" symbol is used for divide in spreadsheets). This occurs because you didn't type a letter first. To handle this problem, spreadsheet packages use a special character—usually a '—that you type first to indicate that what follows is to be treated as characters. To title a column "8/85," all you need to type is '8/85, and 8/85 will appear in the cell. But remember, numbers that are entered in this form are treated as characters and cannot be mathematically manipulated.

If you are working with a large spreadsheet, as you work down the rows the screen will scroll up and your column titles will scroll off the screen. As you move to the right across the columns, the screen will scroll to the left and the row titles in column 1 will leave the screen. This means you won't know what the titles are for the rows or columns, and you might enter a value in the wrong cell. To overcome this problem, you can establish fixed TITLES (or LABELS) for your spreadsheet (the name depends on the package you are using). TITLES can be either horizontal or vertical, or both. The command locks the title rows or columns in place on the screen so that, as you move around on your spreadsheet, the top rows or first columns containing the titles will not scroll off the screen. This concept is demonstrated in Figure 6.5.

Once you have labeled the rows and columns in your spreadsheet, some packages permit you to take advantage of the **LABEL names.** In some of the newer spreadsheet packages, you can use the row or column names (sometimes called **range names**) instead of their row and column

identifiers. For example, if you are adding the contents of row 1, row 2, and row 3 together, you would use a command like +r1 + r2 + r3. If these rows had been named "January," "February," and "March," you could enter a command such as +January + February + March and get the same results.

Getting the Numbers into a Spreadsheet — Numeric Values and Formulas

The original purpose of spreadsheets was to relieve the user of the tedious arithmetic involved in adding and subtracting rows and columns of numbers. With this goal in mind, the requirements for entering values and formulas are usually very simple. To enter a numeric value, all you need to do is place the cursor in the cell where the value should be recorded and type the number. The spreadsheet package will automatically recognize that you are entering a numeric value.

A formula is also treated as a numeric value by spreadsheet packages. When you enter a formula, start with a + (plus symbol) (although most spreadsheet packages will allow you to start with any digit). The following arithmetic operators are used to define the arithmetic operations performed between numeric operands (numbers): + for addition, − for subtraction, * for multiplication, / for division, ^ or ** for an exponent, and (and) (parentheses) as grouping symbols.

The numeric operand can be a number (value) or a cell address containing a numeric value. The arithmetic operators are evaluated according to a set order of operations called **algebraic precedence.** The sequence of operations performed is:

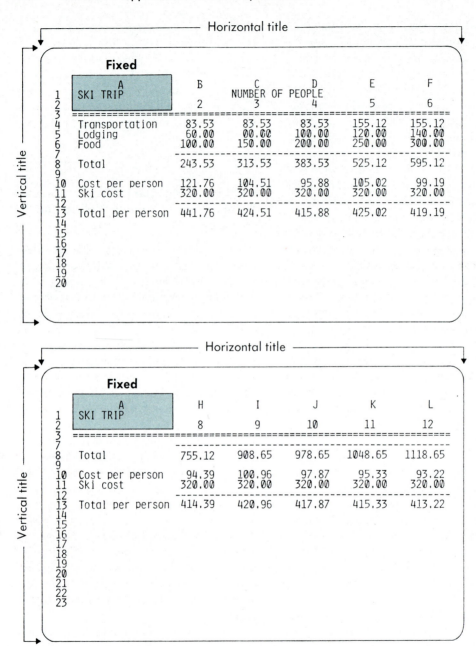

```
┌──────────────────── Horizontal title ────────────────────┐
│                                                           │
│      Fixed                                                │
│   ┌───────────┐  B       C        D        E        F     │
│ 1 │    A      │      NUMBER OF PEOPLE                      │
│   │ SKI TRIP  │  2       3        4        5        6      │
│ 2 └───────────┘                                           │
│ 3 ═══════════════════════════════════════════════════════│
│ 4 Transportation  83.53    83.53    83.53   155.12   155.12│
│ 5 Lodging         60.00    00.00   100.00   120.00   140.00│
│ 6 Food           100.00   150.00   200.00   250.00   300.00│
│ 7 ──────────────────────────────────────────────────────│
│ 8 Total          243.53   313.53   383.53   525.12   595.12│
│ 9                                                         │
│10 Cost per person 121.76   104.51    95.88   105.02    99.19│
│11 Ski cost        320.00   320.00   320.00   320.00   320.00│
│12 ──────────────────────────────────────────────────────│
│13 Total per person 441.76  424.51   415.88   425.02   419.19│
│14                                                         │
│15                                                         │
│16                                                         │
│17                                                         │
│18                                                         │
│19                                                         │
│20                                                         │
└───────────────────────────────────────────────────────────┘
```

```
┌──────────────────── Horizontal title ────────────────────┐
│                                                           │
│      Fixed                                                │
│   ┌───────────┐  H       I        J        K        L     │
│ 1 │    A      │                                           │
│   │ SKI TRIP  │  8       9       10       11       12      │
│ 2 └───────────┘                                           │
│ 3 ═══════════════════════════════════════════════════════│
│ 7 ──────────────────────────────────────────────────────│
│ 8 Total          755.12   908.65   978.65  1048.65  1118.65│
│ 9                                                         │
│10 Cost per person  94.39   100.96    97.87    95.33    93.22│
│11 Ski cost        320.00   320.00   320.00   320.00   320.00│
│12 ──────────────────────────────────────────────────────│
│13 Total per person 414.39  420.96   417.87   415.33   413.22│
│14                                                         │
│15                                                         │
│16                                                         │
│17                                                         │
│18                                                         │
│19                                                         │
│20                                                         │
│21                                                         │
│22                                                         │
│23                                                         │
└───────────────────────────────────────────────────────────┘
```

FIGURE 6.5
Row and column titles in a spreadsheet

```
Step 0:    (2*(3+8/2-4^2/8)+16)/2 (original formula--begin within the
                                   inner-most set of parentheses)

Step 1:    (2*(3+8/2-16/8)+16)/2 (evaluation of exponent)

Step 2:    (2*(3+4-16/8)+16)/2 (first division--left to right)

Step 3:    (2*(3+4-2)+16)/2 (second division--left to right)

Step 4:    (2*(7-2)+16)/2 (addition--left to right)

Step 5:    (2*5+16)/2 (subtraction--inside set of parentheses
                       completely evaluated)

Step 6:    (10+16)/2 (multiplication)

Step 7:    26/2 (addition--final set of parentheses completely
                 evaluated)

Step 8:    13 (division--evaluation of expression complete)
```

FIGURE 6.6
**The evaluation sequence for a mathematical expression
(underlined operation means "performed next"; boldface
indicates operation just performed)**

1. Evaluation of arithmetic expressions (formulas) from left to right
2. Determination of the value of groupings, beginning with the innermost grouping first
3. Computation of any exponents
4. Evaluation of multiplication and division
5. Completion of addition and subtraction

For example, if the computer were to evaluate the expression $(2*(3+8/2-4^2/8)+16)/2$, it would work from left to right, performing the operations according to the rules for the order of operations. With each sequential step in evaluating the expression, the changes shown in Figure 6.6 would take place.

Removing Entries from a Spreadsheet —Blanking Cells

When you are entering data into or making changes to a spreadsheet, you may want to remove the contents of a cell. If the cell contains character data, pressing the SPACE BAR will replace the contents of the cell with a single space. However, entering a space to remove the contents of a cell containing a numeric value, an arithmetic formula, or a mathematical function will result in an error during the evaluation, or it will be ignored. The solution to this problem is to blank the contents of the cell. When you blank the cell, be careful of the commands you use. Some packages will use a BLANK command to clear the contents of the cell, whereas others will use the BLANK command to clear the contents of the *spreadsheet*. If your package has a CLEAR or ERASE command, it will generally eliminate the contents of the entire spreadsheet —so be careful when you use this one! In those packages with a CLEAR or ERASE command, a BLANK command is used to clear the contents of a cell. Check your package's use of these commands fully before you start work to avoid getting an awful surprise.

All Numbers Do Not Look the Same — Formatting

In this section, you will find out about two types of formatting. Spreadsheets may call these two types of formatting by different names and even have different command sequences for accomplishing the operations. However, both operations are found in all spreadsheet packages. These formats are **column-width formats** and **number formats.**

Column-width formats are used to increase or decrease the size of the cells in a column. When you enter the titles for the rows and columns in your spreadsheet, you may find that the default size (the normal column width for the package) of the cell is too small to hold all of the name. Conversely, you may find that you don't want the cell to be as large as the default size. Through the use of column-width formats, you can specify the character width of a column (number of characters in the column). Column-width formats can be used to adjust the width of all the columns in a spreadsheet or, in most of the newer spreadsheet packages, the width of individual columns.

Number formats — also called **display formats** — are used to define the visual appearance of cells. You can set the format for the entire spreadsheet, a column, or an individual cell. The format options generally available in a spreadsheet package are **integer, floating point, fixed point, currency, left-justified,** and **right-justified.** *Integer* formats are used to present whole numbers and do not display decimal fractions. In fact, if a decimal value is entered into a cell that is set for an integer format, the number is automatically rounded, and only the integer is displayed.

A *floating point* format means that the decimal-fraction part of a number fills up the entire cell, no matter where the decimal point is. As the number of digits in the decimal fraction varies from cell to cell, depending on the position of the decimal point (its position is allowed to vary among cells), the maximum number of digits will be shown. Thus, values such as 12345678, 1234.5678, and .12345678 could all appear in the same column. With *fixed point* numbers, the decimal-fraction part of a number is displayed, but only for as many places as you have specified. For example, suppose you have set the column width to nine characters and want to show the number 378.169357. The floating point display would be 378.16936 — using all of the spaces in the cell. If you had set the display format of the cell to fixed point with two decimal places specified, the cell would contain the number 378.17.

The *currency* format would show a number that is fixed point with two decimal places and begins with a currency ($) symbol. The left- and right-justified formats tell the spreadsheet package whether the number should be shown lined up on the left edge or on the right edge of the column.

Data May Come and Data May Go — Inserting and Deleting

While in the process of building your spreadsheet, it is likely that you will need to either insert or delete a row or a column. This can occur for many reasons: an error was made, additional information needs to be added, you no longer need some of the information, or you just want to make the spreadsheet look better. No matter what the reason, the ability to insert and delete complete rows or columns makes these adjustments quick and easy.

A few words of warning are needed here. Although all spreadsheets will adjust your formulas and mathematical functions when you add or delete rows or columns, you need to be very careful. When the row or column inserted or deleted includes the first or last cell addressed by a formula or mathematical function, the adjustment to the cells referenced by the formula or function may not be correct.

Furthermore, insertions and deletions can cause a problem called **circular reference.** This problem occurs when a cell uses the contents of another cell to determine its contents and the referenced cell refers to the first cell. For example, suppose cell A4 contains the formula $+D5 - E3$, and cell D5 contains the formula $+A4 + E3$. When the spreadsheet attempts to determine the value of cell A4, it encounters a reference back to itself. If the package allowed this to happen, it would continuously recalculate the value of A4, because, for each evaluation of A4's value, it creates a new value for cell D5, which causes a new value for A4, which causes a new value for D5, and so on—a circular reference. To avoid continuous recalculation, spreadsheet packages produce an error message when a circular reference is created.

Why Type It All Again? — Copying

To speed up the process of building your spreadsheet, most packages provide the capability of copying the contents of one cell into another cell or range of cells. Although the copy function can be used to duplicate the contents of any cell, its major advantage is in copying an arithmetic formula or mathematical function from one cell to another. When copying a formula or function, the contents of the original cell are copied into the receiving cell or cells. If you want the formula or function adjusted for changes in the cell addresses of those cells involved in the calculations as the duplication takes place, you must declare the copy as a *relative operation.* Declaring a copy operation *relative* (adjusting cell addresses) or *absolute* (no adjustment of cell addresses) is normally handled by having you respond to questions asked by the spreadsheet package during the execution of the COPY command.

That Is Not Where You Want It — Moving Data

Spreadsheet packages also provide the ability to move rows and columns from one location in a spreadsheet to another. This allows you to place rows and columns in whatever order you want them, to make the spreadsheet easier to use. As with the insertion and deletion of rows or columns, you will need to check arithmetic formulas and mathematical functions after the move. Furthermore, some spreadsheet packages (for example, Lotus 1-2-3) assume that you are moving rows or columns into "available" space. If you specify moving a row or column to the location of a row or column containing data, the data will be replaced!

When You Can't See All of Your Spreadsheet at One Time — Windows

Suppose you want to view two widely separated areas of your spreadsheet at the same time. Or perhaps you've titled your rows and you want to keep those titles on the screen as you move through your spreadsheet, but because the titles may change, you do not want to set up vertical titles. The **window** command splits the screen, either vertically or horizontally, so that two areas of the spreadsheet can be viewed through two windows simultaneously. The number of windows available depends on the package you are using. Two windows, as shown in Figure 6.7, are the most common.

When the screen is split, the windows can be scrolled together (**synchronized**) or independently (**unsynchronized**). Spreadsheet cells can be displayed in different formats in each window, and each window can have different column widths.

Rearranging the Rows — Sorting

Another way to arrange the contents of a spreadsheet is to use a *sorting* function. Although the SORT command is available in most spreadsheet packages, it may not be included in early versions.

The sort feature rearranges a spreadsheet on the basis of the contents of a column. The column can contain either character or numeric data, which can be ordered on either an ascending (smallest to largest) or a descending (largest to smallest) basis. To use the command, you need to specify the column to be sorted (sometimes called a *sort key*) and the sorting order. With most packages, the entire row is moved during the sort operation. However, some packages (for example, Lotus 1-2-3) require that you specify the range of the data to be sorted.

When you have performed a sort operation, or whenever you have changed the order of your row or columns, be sure you check the formulas and functions in your spreadsheet. When moving rows and columns used in calculating the values for formulas and functions, cell references may not be correctly adjusted. This can lead to incorrect and confusing results.

You Can Do a Lot with Numbers — Mathematical Functions

Mathematical functions are included in all spreadsheet packages. These functions perform more complex calculations than the simple arithmetic operations available through formulas. Functions are used to save the effort of typing frequently used formulas (such as adding a long list of numbers), to perform calculations that are frequently necessary (such as finding averages), and to produce results (such as of a trigonometric function) that are not easily achieved by formulas.

A function can be used in any cell where you would use a formula or a value. It consists of the name of a function followed by a value or list of values (often called **arguments**) in parentheses. Although the name of a function uses letters, the spreadsheet package must be in "value" mode when you enter the function's name. Some spreadsheet packages require that the function name be preceded by a special character, whereas other packages require you to enter only an arithmetic operator (a plus symbol is usually the easiest to use).

You Do Not Always Have to Do the Arithmetic — Logical Functions

Suppose you wanted to do a calculation only if a certain condition existed. For example, suppose you are calculating the income of a company and you have one row labeled PROFIT and another labeled LOSS. For the row labeled PROFIT, you would like to give the computer the following instructions: **If my revenues are greater than my expenses, then calculate profit as revenues minus expenses, or else print a**

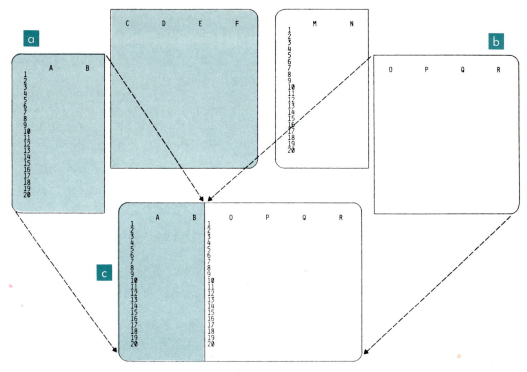

FIGURE 6.7
Splitting the screen, using windows

zero. For the row labeled LOSS, the following instructions would be needed: **If my revenues are less than my expenses, then calculate loss as expenses minus revenues, or else print a zero.** These instructions can be given to the spreadsheet package through the use of **logical functions.**

A logical function is a relational comparison connected by a **relational operator** (for example, greater than, less than, equal to). Logical functions are often called *if-then* conditions. Their structure is as follows: **If a stated condition is true, then return the first value, otherwise return the second value.** The general form is this:

IF(condition, value1, value2). Again, to use a logical function, the spreadsheet must be in the "value" mode. This still requires the typing of a special character or an arithmetic operator (for example, a plus symbol). In the preceding example, for the row labeled PROFIT, the condition is **my revenues are greater than expenses,** value 1 is **calculate profit as revenues minus expenses,** and value 2 is **or else print a zero.** The values in the logical function may be a number (some spreadsheet packages allow characters), an arithmetic formula, a mathematical function, or another logical function. The **logical condition** in this function consists of a value, followed by a relational operator, and a value. The values used in the conditional part of the logical function may be an address, a value, an arithmetic function, or a mathematical function. The condition for the row labeled PROFIT consists of a first value (**my revenues**), a relational operator (**are greater than**), and a second value (**my expenses**). Using the capabilities of the spreadsheet package, which may include the AND, OR, and NOT **logical operators** (key words used to connect two or more relational comparisons), complex logical functions can be developed to return the desired value.

Do It All Again — Recalculation

Every time you enter a value into a spreadsheet, all arithmetic formulas, mathematical functions, and logical functions are automatically recalculated. As the spreadsheet gets bigger, the amount of time required for this recalculation gets larger. To minimize the amount of time you have to wait during this operation, most packages provide you with the ability to "turn off" the recalculation feature. This means that you will have to remember — after you have entered all the numeric values, arithmetic formulas, and functions — to enter the RECALCULATION command to bring your spreadsheet up to date.

Showing Off Your Work — Printing

The PRINT or OUTPUT command is used to make a copy of all or part of your spreadsheet to the printer or a disk file. The print option allows you to designate what part of the spreadsheet is to be printed and to set up the printing features. The available features will depend on the package you are using; however, you can generally specify page length, page width, and double or single spacing. Other features of this function might include the ability to produce page headings and footings, select an area of the spreadsheet to print, and print the actual contents of each cell (for example, formulas and functions) instead of just the resulting values.

Choosing the option of producing output to the printer will cause your spreadsheet, as you have set it up, to be printed. Choosing the option of "printing" to the disk will send your spreadsheet to the disk file in the same form as it would have appeared on the printer (a "print" file).

Saving Your Work — File Handling

All spreadsheet packages allow you to save and retrieve files containing your spreadsheets. You have just seen that a spreadsheet can be saved in a print file. Print files, however, cannot be retrieved by the spreadsheet package for use by the package. In other words, you cannot do any more calculations on a spreadsheet that has been saved on a disk as a print file. To save and retrieve a spreadsheet, you must save it as a "spreadsheet" file. This is a file that contains all of the spreadsheet information, including cell formats, arithmetic formulas, mathematical functions, and window definitions.

Some packages also give you the capability to save and retrieve DIF (data interchange format) and SYLK (symbolic link) files. The rules for saving these types of files are usually the same as those for saving spreadsheet files. These files provide one of the means by which data can be transferred between different types of applications packages, including different spreadsheet packages.

Where Can You Go from Here? — Integration with Other Software

It is very important that spreadsheet packages be able to interface (share data) with other applications packages. If you are writing a report for class or for your boss, you may need to create a spreadsheet file that can be read by a word processing package. If you are dealing with a large amount of data that is already in a database, it would be helpful to be able to read the data from the database rather than re-enter it all at the keyboard. If your spreadsheet package does not have graphics capabilities, you may need to save the data in a form that can be read by a graphics package.

The standard method of interfacing different types of software packages is by making the saved files shareable by the various packages. Although several software packages are written so that they can read files created by many of the spreadsheet packages, the usual method of sharing data is to use DIF files. For interfacing with word processing packages, it is usually easier to create print files from the spreadsheet data. This type of file can be read by almost all word processing packages, allowing for greater flexibility in the selection of software for your use.

Finally, some spreadsheet packages come with a procedural language or a means by which spreadsheet commands can be entered, saved, and retrieved. When you employ this type of feature, the result is often called a **macro**. A macro is used to retain a series of operations that are frequently performed, saving you a considerable amount of time, as compared with entering the command sequence from the keyboard each time it is needed. When these macros are produced to help solve specific types of problems, they may be referred to as a spreadsheet *template* or *model*.

Uses of Spreadsheets

Because spreadsheets are designed to make arithmetic using large amounts of data easier to handle, many of the initial uses of these types of packages were accounting related. However, the purposes for which the packages were written and the purposes for which they are actually used can be very different. In general, you could say that the use of spreadsheet packages is limited only by the limitations of the user's imagination.

Perhaps the easiest and most common use of spreadsheet packages is for personal checkbook balancing. When your checking account statement arrives in the mail and you start to reconcile the bank's records with what you have recorded in your checkbook, there always seem to be problems. Some checks you have written have not cleared the bank, the bank has added service charges for checks written, deposits have been processed, and charges may have been posted for the use of the bank's ATM (Automatic Teller Machine). In addition, you may have made errors in arithmetic over the last month. Spreadsheets can quickly be set up to record all deposits, checks, and service charges and do the arithmetic required to balance your checkbook. If you create a separate column to keep a running balance, much like in your checkbook, you can even find the arithmetic errors that usually take hours to locate manually.

Another common use of the spreadsheet is as a teacher's grade book. Although entering grades into a spreadsheet package takes as long (or slightly longer) as entering grades in a grade book, there are several advantages for the teacher. The students can be recorded in any order the teacher wants (usually alphabetically by the students' names) and later changed to another order (may be ordered by course average). The average grade on an assignment or test can be calculated automatically. The student records can be sorted by student number, assignment grade, or test grade for printed reports. Finally, at the end of the term, the students' final averages and grades can be calculated automatically, saving the teacher a great deal of time and work. Another advantage to the teacher, which the student can share, is the ability of a spreadsheet package to calculate automatically a student's average after each grade is entered. This way both teacher and student can determine what the student's grade is at any time during the term.

The owner of a mountain resort uses a spreadsheet to keep track of sales and cash flow. Profits depend on a high volume of small sales ($50 to $200) at several profit centers, such as restaurant, boat dock, gift shop, and landing strip. When all the accounting was done by hand, the owner got reports on a monthly basis only and then often after several weeks' delay. Using a spreadsheet package, daily reports with year-to-date and month-to-date sales figures in 23 different categories are produced on demand. The package also produces monthly sales tax and alcohol tax reports. The use of a spreadsheet package has shortened the reporting time between the owner and the resort's accountant and allowed for better cash-flow control, which means that excess funds can be quickly identified and invested in certificates of deposit to maximize profits.

A specialty print shop also uses spreadsheets to control its profits. Because of the many variables involved, it used to take the owner of the print shop several hours to estimate the cost of printing jobs. Job prices would vary based on the amount of art work and the number of colors used, the type of press used, and the grade of paper, as well as several other factors. Using a spreadsheet package and a series of formulas and functions developed over a weekend, the owner now enters the data into the spreadsheet and can quote a price that includes the profit margin in a matter of seconds.

Banks and savings and loan companies use spreadsheets in a similar manner. When a customer applies for a loan to buy a house or a car, the loan application information is entered into a spreadsheet package. The analysis done by the spreadsheet package determines whether the customer is qualified for the loan and the amount of the monthly payments needed to pay off the loan. Although the loan approval process still takes a couple of days, the customer now has immediate information about the terms of the loan.

City governments use spreadsheets to help their citizens. A small town in Ohio used a spreadsheet package to analyze the effects of a rate increase for a natural gas company on the company's profits and on the company's customers. As a result of the analysis, the amount of the rate increase was reduced, and methods of billing the customers were changed. This action resulted in only small increases in the citizens' gas bills, while at the same time it improved the company's ability to meet its expenses.

A financial planner uses a spreadsheet to investigate investment alternatives and strategies. The financial analyst determines the current value of an investment, such as the market price and quantity of stocks, and determines at what point, as the price falls, it would be worthwhile to change to another investment, discounting the amount of brokerage fees. In the same fashion, the analyst uses the spreadsheet to determine when investments should be altered as stock prices increase. Thus, the analyst uses the spreadsheet to solve "what if" problems, such as "what if the value of commodity A rises and that of commodity B remains the same?" By using a spreadsheet, the analyst improves the performance of the investment portfolio.

These are just some of the ways to use spreadsheets. There are many others. In fact, several books have been written on spreadsheet application. The number and variety of applications will increase as these packages continue to evolve and become even more powerful. However, spreadsheets cannot solve *all* numeric data manipulation problems. The more mathematically elaborate and logically complex the process, the more likely the solution of the problem lies with programs written in a developmental language. Although you might find someone using a spreadsheet to perform payroll processing, this type of application is still better suited to more specific software produced in a developmental language.

Chapter Summary

Electronic spreadsheets can be an effective tool for handling large volumes of data and repetitive calculations. In fact, the original spreadsheet package was developed because one student was tired of adding rows and columns of numbers.

Spreadsheets use a matrix format (rows and columns) to address specific locations of character (alphanumeric) and numeric data. Arithmetic formulas and mathematical functions are treated as numeric data by a spreadsheet package, and these formulas and functions are evaluated using a set of rules for the order of operations called *algebraic precedence.*

This chapter discussed the basic functions available on most spreadsheet packages; Table 6.1 provides a summary of these functions, as well as a brief description of their use.

Some of the popular uses of spreadsheet packages were also described — ranging from balancing personal checkbooks to assisting in the operation of a resort and city governments. There are many other areas where spreadsheets can be used. These applications are virtually without limits.

Chapter Key Terms

Absolute address	Column-width	Integer	functions
Algebraic	format	Label name	Matrix
precedence	Command driven	Left-justified	Matrix arithmetic
Arguments	Currency	Logical condition	Menu driven
Character data	Data type	Logical function	Number format
(alphanumeric	Display format	Logical operator	Numeric data
data)	Fixed point	Macro	Range name
Circular reference	Floating point	Mathematical	Relational operator

Relative address	**Scrolling**	**Text**	**Window**
Right-justified	**Synchronized**	**Unsynchronized**	**Worksheet**
Scalar arithmetic	**movement**	**movement**	**Work space**
Scratchpad	**Template (model)**	**Visiclones**	

TABLE 6.1 Summary of Spreadsheet Functions

Function	Domain	Purpose
Help	Global	Provides assistance and instructions
Windows	Global	Splits spreadsheet into multiple visible parts
Print	Global	Produces a copy of all or part of a spreadsheet on a printer or into a disk file (print file)
File	Global	Saves or retrieves a spreadsheet file from disk
Recalculate	Global	Re-evaluates all cell values, including formulas and functions
Label	Row or column	Sets special titles or headings for rows or columns of the spreadsheet
Format	Column or cell	Sets the column width or the display format for a column or cell
Move	Row or column	Changes the location of one or more rows or columns to another position
Sort	Column	Orders or sequences the spreadsheet on the basis of cell values in a column
Insert	Row or column	Adds one or more new empty rows or columns at a desired location
Delete	Row or column	Removes one or more rows or columns and adjusts the locations of other rows or columns to fill in the empty space
Value	Cell	Specifies that the contents of a cell are to be numeric data
Text	Cell	Specifies that the contents of a cell are to be character data
Formula	Cell	Causes the resulting value of an arithmetic expression to be entered into a cell
Function (Math and Logical)	Cell	Causes the resulting value of a special (mathematical) operation to be placed into a cell
Copy	Cell	Duplicates the contents of one cell into another
Blank	Cell	Erases the contents of a cell

Chapter Questions

1. Using an organization with which you are familiar (for instance, a student club, church, or business), identify several problems that could be solved by using a spreadsheet. Give a brief explanation of how a spreadsheet could be used for each problem.
2. Describe how you would set up a spreadsheet to balance your bank statements.
3. Use your imagination and name some other uses you could make of a spreadsheet application program at home, school, or work.
4. What are the differences between character data and numeric data? Give an example of each. Why do you think the computer uses the two different data types?
5. What is your major course of study? List ten ways a spreadsheet could be used to assist you in your career.
6. List the display formats for numeric data. Give an example of a type of data that would use each format.
7. Describe, in your own words, the concept of spreadsheet windows. Why are they a desirable feature of spreadsheets?
8. Many spreadsheet packages include a sorting function. List five reasons that you might want to have the data presented in a spreadsheet sorted in a particular order. Which of these sets of sorted data would be most useful if ordered in an ascending sequence? In a descending sequence?
9. Describe the differences between absolute addresses (cell references) and relative addresses. When do you think you should use absolute addresses in the creation of a spreadsheet? Relative addresses?
10. The formula for computing the total repayment value of a loan when interest is compounded semiannually is

$$P(1 + R)^2$$

where P is the principal (amount borrowed) and R is the interest rate. Write this formula as it might appear in a cell of a spreadsheet. Check your formula by indicating which mathematical operation would be evaluated first, second, and so on. Use the letters in the loan formula as cell references.

Modules/Chapter Six

 pfs:Plan
Software Publishing Corporation
1901 Landings Drive
Mountain View, CA 94043

M6b **Lotus 1-2-3**
Lotus Development Corporation
161 First Street
Cambridge, MA 02142

M6c **Multiplan**
10700 Northup Way
Bellevue, WA 98004

Introduction to Spreadsheet Modules

In the modules that follow, you will be given the opportunity to learn about one (or more) of the popular spreadsheet packages available for microcomputers. Module 6a will cover pfs:Plan, Module 6b will present Lotus 1-2-3, and Module 6c will cover Multiplan.

Problem Statement for Spreadsheet Modules

Find the data for the job hunting problem in Appendix A. You will use this data and the problem stated as an example of how spreadsheets can be used to manipulate data and produce interesting results.

When ready to seek employment, everyone is interested in evaluating job offers in as many ways as possible. What is the salary offered? Does it include certain benefits (life insurance, health insurance, paid vacation days, and retirement contributions paid by the company)? Will I have to commute? How far? Do I really want to work for that company?

Once you have an idea of what you want, you can build a spreadsheet and use it to compare companies and job offers. The following list represents the types of manipulations and comparisons you might want to make once the spreadsheet has been built.

1. Across the top of your spreadsheet, set up the following titles:

   ```
   Company Name
   Salary Offer
   Life Benefits
   Health Benefits
   Retirement
   Commuting Distance
   Vacation Days
   Job Preference
   ```

2. After setting up the column headings (you will probably need more than one row for the headings) and making them TITLES so that they will always appear at the top of your spreadsheet, format the cell sizes in each of your columns so that your spreadsheet will be readable and will hold the data you are going to enter.

3. Now enter the data for all the companies listed in Table A.2, **Offers from Companies,** found in Appendix A. Form two windows by splitting the spreadsheet between the columns labeled Company Name and Salary Offer. Be sure these windows are synchronized.

4. Before you start manipulating the data, insert a new column after the column labeled Vacation Days and label it Vacation Value. To fill in the values for Vacation Value, use the formula Vacation Days times Salary Offer divided by 250.

5. Add a new column to your spreadsheet. This column should be labeled Actual Offer and is the sum of Salary Offer, Health Benefits, Life Benefits, and Retirement.

6. Set up a row for an Average Company and calculate averages for each of the columns.

7. You have received a letter of acceptance from First State National Bank. You need to enter this information in your spreadsheet. Enclosed with the letter of acceptance was a description of the job containing the following details:

```
Salary Offer: $22,000.00
Life: $210.00
Health: $325.00
Vacation Days: 14
Retirement: $2950.00
```

You have established that the commuting distance is 25 miles, and your preference for the job is 2. After inserting a new row with this information, recalculate the totals and averages.

8. Now sort the companies in your spreadsheet by your preference ranking. Remember, when you perform the SORT, do not include Average Company in the sort area.

pfs:Plan

Learning to Use pfs:Plan

Pfs:Plan is the electronic spreadsheet package for the pfs series of applications software. It is available for a variety of microcomputers with the MS-DOS or PC-DOS operating system. The pfs:Plan package combines the convenience and ease of use of a pocket calculator with the memory and display capabilities of a microcomputer. It has many powerful features, including calculating and recalculating values easily and quickly and formatting or tailoring the spreadsheet to meet your needs.

When you are prepared to begin working with pfs:Plan, start with the operating system disk in drive A. If you are using a system that has two disk drives, a disk prepared to hold your data should be in drive B. After you have booted your system, replace the operating system disk in drive A with the pfs:Plan disk and enter the operation PLAN. When the package is loaded into memory, it will respond by placing the Main Menu on the screen, as shown in Figure 6a.1. Now press the 1 key, followed by the RETURN key, to cause the screen to change to the initial spreadsheet work space, as shown in Figure 6a.2. You can return to the Main Menu at any time by pressing the ESCape key. By pressing the 1 key, followed by the RETURN key, you will return to the spreadsheet, which is exactly as you left it.

The Arrangement — What a pfs:Plan Spreadsheet Looks Like

Look at the spreadsheet in Figure 6a.2. Note that none of the rows or columns is identified with either letters or numbers — a common practice with most spreadsheet packages. Pfs:Plan uses a special row and column labeled "Headings" for identification. This row and column can accept character (text) data or numeric data as an identifying label. The remainder of the spreadsheet work space is used for numeric data. Any letters typed in this area are treated as comments, and the package will not allow you to do any operations on them.

A pfs:Plan spreadsheet is capable of handling up to 255 rows and 70 columns, depending of the internal memory of your computer. The initial (default) width of each cell is 9 characters, but a cell can be modified to as few as 1 character or as many as 25 characters. In fact, pfs:Plan will automatically

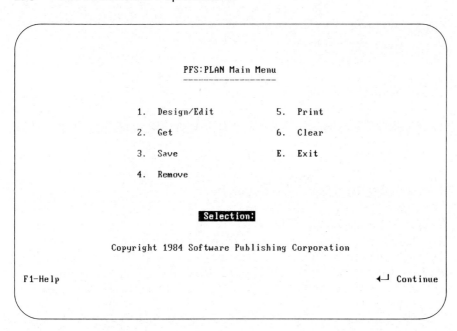

```
                    PFS:PLAN Main Menu
                    ------------------

        1.   Design/Edit          5.   Print

        2.   Get                  6.   Clear

        3.   Save                 E.   Exit

        4.   Remove



                        Selection:


     Copyright 1984 Software Publishing Corporation


 F1-Help                                          ↵ Continue
```

FIGURE 6A.1
pfs:Plan initial screen — Main Menu

adjust the size of the cell as you enter the information to be presented in that cell.

Making pfs:Plan Work for You — The Operation Structure

The pfs:Plan package uses a *tiered* or *multileveled* menu structure. When you enter an operation, pfs:Plan will either carry out that operation or ask you to enter additional operations until the package has enough information to execute the operation. "Immediate" operations in pfs:Plan require that you type either a letter or a number. Typing a letter or a number does not require any additional information for execution, and the letter or number will be placed in the cell referenced by the cursor. Pfs:Plan uses function keys to begin additional operations, as described in Figure 6a.3.

Learning About Your Keyboard — Cursor Movement and Function Keys

The pfs:Plan package makes extensive use of the function keys to perform special operations, such as calling up the Help screen. While you are still in the Main Menu, press the F1 key, and the initial Help screen will appear. By

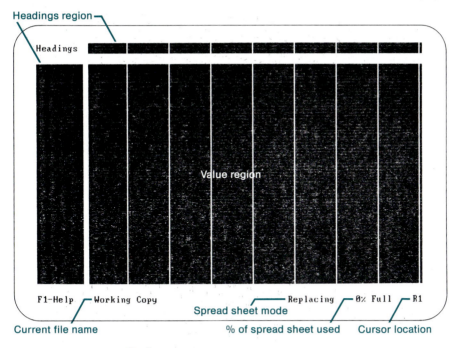

FIGURE 6A.2
The pfs:Plan screen layout — work space

pressing the RETURN key, you will see Figure 6a.3. Now press the RETURN key and return to the spreadsheet.

Now you should become familiar with how to move the cursor from one cell to another. If you press the TAB key, the cursor moves to the beginning of the column to the right until it reaches the right edge of the screen. If you continue to press the TAB key, the spreadsheet will appear to move to the left — off the screen. Actually, the cursor is still moving to the right, but for the cursor to continue to appear on the screen, the work space must also move. By pressing the SHIFT and TAB keys, you can move back to the left. Note that the screen scrolls in the same manner as it did before. You can also use the up- and down-arrow keys to move up and down in the spreadsheet.

Sometimes moving to the desired cell by using the TAB key is too slow, particularly if you are moving a long distance through the spreadsheet. You can use the PgUp and PgDn keys to move to the next screen full of data or to the previous screen full of data. Pressing the END key, followed by one of the four arrow keys, will move you to the end of the spreadsheet in the direction of the arrow key. After you are familiar with moving around the spreadsheet, press the HOME key or use the END key and the arrows to return to the top of the first column. You are now ready to begin building your spreadsheet.

```
        Function Keys              Return to Main Menu   Esc

   ┌─────────────┬─────────────┐
   │        F1   │ F2          │        Cursor Movement
   │ Help        │ Quick-Entry │
   │             │             │   Next column        CTRL → or →|
   ├─────────────┼─────────────┤   Previous column    CTRL ← or Shift |←
   │        F3   │ F4          │   Screen up          PgUp
   │ Erase Entry │   Calculator│   Screen down        PgDn
   ├─────────────┼─────────────┤
   │ Restore R/C │ Remove Row/Col│ Upper left value   Home
   │        F5   │ F6          │   Top row            END followed by ↑
   │ Copy Row/Col│ Insert Row/Col│ Bottom row         "    "    "  ↓
   ├─────────────┼─────────────┤   First column       "    "    "  ←
   │  Target     │    Format   │   Last column        "    "    "  →
   │        F7   │ F8          │
   │ Recalculate │     View    │           Editing
   ├─────────────┼─────────────┤
   │ Variables   │             │   Backspace delete   ←
   │        F9   │ F10         │   Delete character   Del
   │ Formulas    │    Continue │   Insert/Replace     Ins
   └─────────────┴─────────────┘
   Use shift to get top functions
                                              ↵ Continue
```

FIGURE 6A.3
The Help menu showing a summary of keys

Solving the Job Hunting Problem

The remaining sections of this module are devoted to solving the job hunting problem. You may want to refer to the problem statement in the Introduction to Spreadsheet Modules before you continue. Also, remember that the data used in this problem can be found in Appendix A.

What's in a Name? — Entering Headings and Labels

One of the first activities you will want to perform in a spreadsheet is to label your rows and columns. To do this, you must use the arrow keys to move the cursor to the Headings row. Since entering any data into this cell is considered an immediate operation for entering labels, simply type in the labels for the columns. Having done some planning before starting to work on the spreadsheet, you know that the labels will be more helpful if you use more than one row for a label. Even though only one row is shown for Headings, don't worry. Simply type the bottom line of the labels, shown in Figure 6a.4, across the spreadsheet. Pressing the TAB key will move the cursor one column to the right, and you can enter the label for the next column.

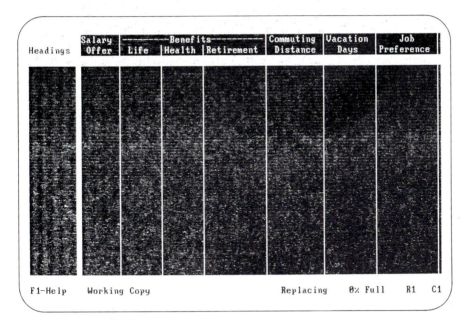

FIGURE 6A.4
Column headings for the job offers problem

Now return the cursor to the first Headings cell. Press the F6 key and the R key, followed by the RETURN key, to insert another row above the row you just entered. Pfs:Plan will allow you to insert up to two additional rows in the Headings row for a total of three rows of column labels. You can now continue entering the column labels as shown in Figure 6a.4. Notice the label "---------Benefits----------." This is called a *group label* by pfs:Plan. To enter this label, move the cursor to the first cell belonging to that group and enter a —, followed by the group label. Now enter -'s (hyphens) until the cursor reaches the right edge of the cell you want to include in the group. Pressing the RETURN key will automatically center the group label over the cells contained within the group. Once you have all the labels entered, press the HOME key to return to the top of the first column.

Two Views of the Spreadsheet — Using Windows

Unfortunately, pfs:Plan will not allow you to create windows. However, the Headings row and column will always appear on the screen, eliminating much of the need for windows.

Entering the Company Names — Entering Row Labels

Now that the spreadsheet columns are fully labeled, you are ready to enter company names from the jobs problem. These are actually row labels. Pfs:Plan uses *indents* to group row labels. The main row label is a group label. Every label below the group label that has been indented at least one character is considered a part of that group. The group ends when you enter another label without indenting. It works like an outline for a report or a speech, and you can enter a number of groups and subgroups. Because the column is only 25 characters wide, only 24 indentations are possible; hence, you can have only 25 grouping levels.

The simplest way to enter the company names is to place a group label in the first row. To do this, enter "Company" in the first row starting at the left edge of the column. Press the RETURN key to move to the beginning of the next row. Now press the SPACE BAR and enter the name of the first company. When all the company names have been entered, the spreadsheet will look like the one shown in Figure 6a.5.

What Is Your Offer? — Placing Numeric Values in the Spreadsheet

To enter the information about the job offers, press the HOME key to move the cursor to the top of the first column in the value region. Now enter the job offer information from the first company, pressing the TAB key after each entry to move to the next column. When you have finished the first row of data, use the HOME key and the down-arrow key to move the cursor to the beginning of the next row. Continue entering the data for each company until the spreadsheet has all of the data entered; at this point, it will look like Figure 6a.6.

Mistakes Will Happen — Making Corrections

If you make a mistake while entering the data into your spreadsheet, you can easily correct it. When the mistake is made during the entry of data into a cell, simply press the BACKSPACE key to delete the character immediately to the left of the cursor.

If you have already entered the data into a cell and moved on, corrections are even easier. Move the cursor back to the cell containing the data you wish to change, and enter the correct data. The correction will be made automatically. If the data item is so long that you don't want to re-enter the value of the entire cell, you can use the left and right arrow keys to move to the characters you want to change. To replace a character, simply type over that character. To remove a character, place the cursor over the character you want to delete and press the DELete key. To insert a character, use the arrow keys to place the cursor where you want to add the character, press the INSert key, and type the characters to be inserted. To erase the entire cell entry, simply press the F3 key.

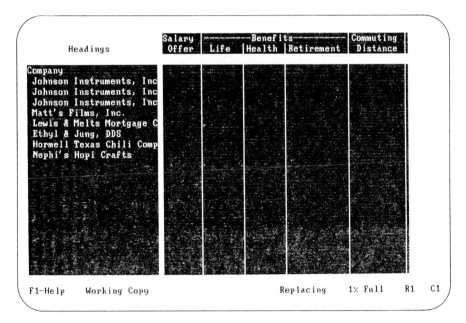

Headings	Salary Offer	Benefits			Commuting Distance
		Life	Health	Retirement	
Company					
Johnson Instruments, Inc					
Johnson Instruments, Inc					
Johnson Instruments, Inc					
Matt's Films, Inc.					
Lewis & Melts Mortgage C					
Ethyl & Jung, DDS					
Hormell Texas Chili Comp					
Nephi's Hopi Crafts					

F1-Help   Working Copy   Replacing   1% Full   R1   C1

FIGURE 6A.5
Entering the company names

Headings	Salary Offer	Benefits			Commuting Distance
		Life	Health	Retirement	
Company					
Johnson Instruments, Inc	19,000	135	354	3,333	45
Johnson Instruments, Inc	19,200	135	354	3,333	35
Johnson Instruments, Inc	19,100	135	354	3,333	25
Matt's Films, Inc.	18,950	155	456	5,000	33
Lewis & Melts Mortgage C	22,000	500	600	4,400	35
Ethyl & Jung, DDS	20,000	325	950	6,000	95
Hormell Texas Chili Comp	19,300	164	320	2,202	53
Nephi's Hopi Crafts	15,670	250	425	1,333	47

F1-Help   Working Copy   Replacing   1% Full   R1   C1

FIGURE 6A.6
Entering the job offer data

A View with Numbers — The Format Operation

In Figure 6a.6, you can see that although most of the numbers that were entered are dollar values, they don't have any decimal points. This makes the spreadsheet difficult to read. It would be much better if the numbers showed dollars and cents rather than just dollars. To add decimal points, you can use the Format operation. The Format operation is available at two levels. First, you can format each individual column through the use of the Format row. Second, you can use the Global format operation to set the format for the entire spreadsheet.

Because most of the numbers in the spreadsheet are in dollars, use the Global format operation to change the cell formats to dollars. To issue a Format operation, press the SHIFT and the F8 keys at the same time. Four new areas will appear on the screen, as shown in Figure 6a.7. Two of these, Minimum column width and Global format, appear at the top of the screen. The Minimum column width determines the smallest size to which any column is allowed to shrink, and the Global format determines how pfs:Plan displays and prints values in the spreadsheet. By pressing the up-arrow key, the TAB key, and the SHIFT and TAB keys simultaneously, you can move the cursor back and forth between the new areas and the spreadsheet.

Now move the cursor to the Global format area and enter the Format operation 2,$. All the numbers in the spreadsheet are now represented as dollars and cents. However, there are three columns — "Commuting Distance," "Vacation Days," and "Job Preference" — whose data is not represented by dollars. To change these values back to whole numbers, move the cursor to the cell in the Format row above the column containing the title "Commuting Distance" and enter 0. You have just formatted that column as INTEGER. The Format row at the top of the spreadsheet and the column at the left side of the spreadsheet are used to set the formats for individual rows and columns.

Now you can move to the column labeled "Vacation Days" and enter a 0 for its format. You should also repeat this function for the column labeled "Job Preference."

A Spreadsheet with Room to Grow — The Insert Function

The first task to be accomplished with the spreadsheet is to calculate the value of the vacation days for the different jobs. However, space needs to be specified to store the results of the calculations. To create a new column for the value of vacation days, move the cursor to the column to the right of where you want the new column to appear. This would be the column labeled "Job Preference." Now press the F6 key to tell the package you want to do an insertion. Press the C key to indicate you want to add a column to the spreadsheet, and a new column will be added to the left of the cursor, as in Figure 6a.8.

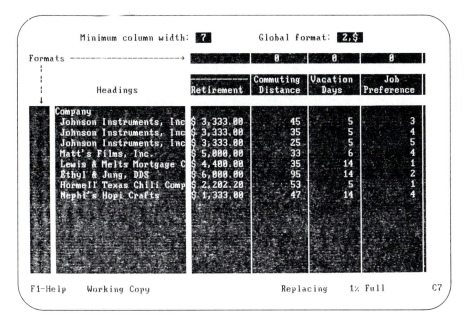

FIGURE 6A.7
Selecting the currency presentation format—it makes cents

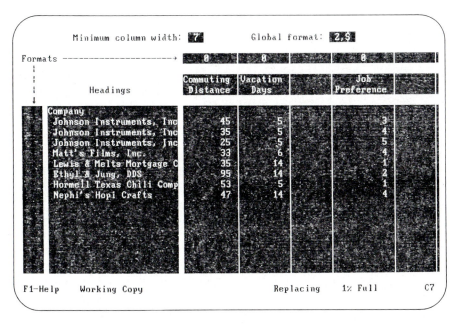

FIGURE 6A.8
Inserting a new column

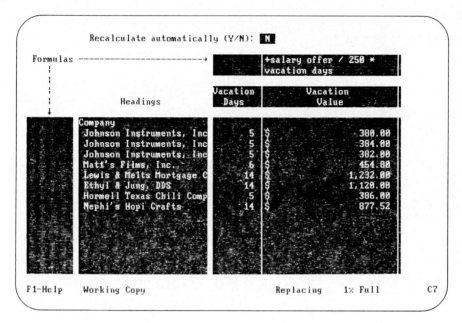

FIGURE 6A.9
Entering the formula for "Vacation Value"

The new column needs to be labeled. Press the F10 key to enter the Continue operation, returning the spreadsheet to its normal view. Now move the cursor to the Headings row above the new column and enter the label "Vacation" in the first row and "Value" in the second row (see Figure 6a.9).

Figure It This Way — Using a Formula

After setting up the new column, you need to do the calculations necessary to fill the cells with the proper values. Doing these calculations will entail the use of an arithmetic formula. To enter a formula or a mathematical function, press the F9 key, and the Formula region will appear on the screen. This region comprises a row across the top of the spreadsheet for entering formulas for the columns and a column at the left edge of the spreadsheet for entering formulas that operate on the rows (see Figure 6a.9). The automatic recalculation status is displayed at the top of the screen. You should first move the cursor to the recalculation region and press N to turn the automatic recalculation off.

Position the cursor in the Formulas row and at the column labeled "Vacation Value" and prepare to enter the formula needed for this column. You have determined that on the average you would work approximately 250 days in a calendar year (365 days less weekends and holidays). Thus, the "Salary Offer" of each company can be established on a per-day basis (salary divided by 250). Since "Vacation Days" is stated in terms of number of days, you could then determine the "Vacation Value" for each company. This is a perfect place to use a formula.

To enter this formula into the spreadsheet, first enter the name of the column containing the salary offer, followed by a space. Now enter the / (to indicate division), followed by a space, the number 250, an * (for multiplication), followed by another space, and the name of the column containing the number of vacation days for the job offer. When you press the RETURN key and the F7 key to recalculate the spreadsheet, it will look like Figure 6a.9. The formula will be displayed in the Formula row at the top of the column, and all the values calculated on the basis of that formula will appear in the column. Note that the format for the new column is dollars and cents. This is because you set the Global format at 2,$ — so all new rows will automatically have that format. Also note that when you return to the normal view by pressing the F10 key, the formulas are no longer displayed on the screen, and the column width returns to the size necessary to hold the label and values in that column.

Now that you have entered a formula, it is time to look at pfs:Plan's rules for formulas. Row and column formulas are written in the same way and are entered in the same manner. When writing a formula you should use the following rules:

1. Type row and column headings exactly as they appear in the Headings region (except for use of capitalization)
2. Use space between the operators and the headings if you desire (spaces are optional)
3. Enclose headings containing mathematical operators in quotation marks
4. Enclose headings consisting of only numbers in quotation marks

Now you can calculate the "Actual Offer" of the companies. Move the cursor to the right of the column labeled "Salary Offer" and insert a new column. This is done by pressing the F6 key to start the Insert operation and the C key to insert a new column. The new column is inserted between the column labeled "Salary Offer" and the column labeled "Life"—the remainder of the spreadsheet has been shifted one column to the right. You need to finish setting up the spreadsheet for the new column by entering the new column labels.

To calculate the actual offer, press the F9 key to get the Formulas region, move the cursor to the cell in the Formulas row above the new column, and enter the following formula: +salary offer + @total benefits. After entering the formula, press the RETURN key and the F7 key to recalculate the spreadsheet. Your spreadsheet will now look like Figure 6a.10. Note that the other columns referenced by the formula are on the right and left sides of this column. This fact made no difference in the calculations; however, you need to be very careful and check calculations when referencing cells that are to the

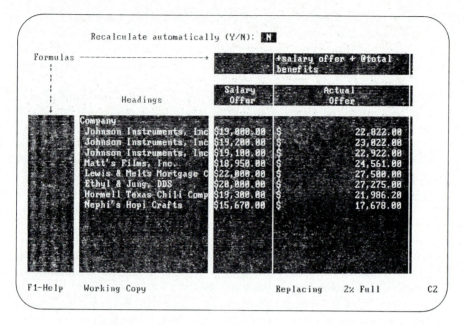

FIGURE 6A.10
Another formula — computing the value of the "Actual Offer"

right of your formula. Referencing these cells may create circular referencing problems or cause incorrect calculations.

The formula you just entered used two special features of pfs:Plan. First, you entered a mathematical function in the formula. This function was @total. (Table 6a.1 describes the functions available in pfs:Plan.) Second, you referenced the company contributions for "Life," "Health," and "Retirement" through the use of their group label — "Benefits." The ability to use group names in formulas greatly simplifies many of the calculations done on pfs:Plan spreadsheets.

Providing a Visual Break — Creating a Dividing Line

Now that all the values have been entered for all the companies, it is time to start thinking about what else you might want to do. First, you might decide to place a visual break across the bottom of the list of companies. To do this, move the cursor down the Headings column until it is positioned at the row below the last company entered. To create a dividing line horizontally across a spreadsheet, type a —, a =, or a _ in the Headings region, and press the TAB key. A line of the selected symbol will appear across that row of the spreadsheet, as illustrated in Figure 6a.11.

TABLE 6A.1 pfs:Plan Functions

Function Name	Meaning and Operation
AVG	Averages groups of rows or columns; averages rows or columns with the same heading (in different groups); averages all rows or columns
CUM	Gives cumulative totals of values in a row or column
FV	Gives future value of money in a row or column
GROW	Enters values in a row or column where each successive value is a certain amount greater (or smaller) than the one before it
MAX	Finds the largest value in a group of rows or columns; finds the largest value in rows or columns with the same heading (in different groups); finds the largest value in all rows or columns
MIN	Finds the smallest value in a group of rows or columns; finds the smallest value in rows or columns with the same heading (in different groups); finds the smallest value in all rows or columns
NPV	Gives net present value of a row or column
PAYMENT	Calculates payments to retire a loan
PREV	Returns a row or column to its previously given value
START	Creates a starting value for CUM, PREV, and GROW functions
TOTAL	Totals groups of rows or columns; totals rows or columns with the same heading (in different groups); totals all rows or columns

Letting pfs:Plan "Compute"—Using a Function

Most spreadsheet packages provide a number of very useful functions, such as the @total function previously used. Although the result of many of the functions could be achieved by using formulas, often it is much easier to use a function than to create just the right formula or set of formulas. (Return to Table 6a.1 for a list of functions that are available with pfs:Plan.)

In the job offers problem, you might want to establish averages (for comparison purposes) for many of the columns that contain numeric values. To do this, begin by entering the title "Average Company" in the Headings column below the dividing line you just created. Now press the F9 key to get to the Formulas region, and move the cursor down the Formulas column until it is at the row labeled "Average Company." Because you entered all of the company

FIGURE 6A.11
Creating a visual break

names by indenting them under the group label "Company," you simply have
to enter the formula @AVG COMPANY. Pressing the F7 key to recalculate the
spreadsheet will result in the screen shown in Figure 6a.12. Pressing the F10
key to return to the normal view of the spreadsheet will cause the screen to
appear as shown in Figure 6a.13.

New Information on a Job Offer — Adding a New Row

The new offer that you just received from the First State National Bank needs
to be entered into the spreadsheet. Since the companies are entered in no
special order, the new offer can be inserted in the last row of company names
just before the dividing line. To insert a new row, move the cursor to the
dividing line row and press the F6 key to enter the Insert operation. Now press
the R key, and a new row will appear in the spreadsheet at the tenth row. The
old row containing the dividing line and the average company have been moved
down one position.

   To enter the data on the new job offer, move the cursor to the Headings
column for the new row and begin entering the data. After the data has been
entered, the spreadsheet will look like Figure 6a.14. To finish entering the data,
you have to calculate the values for "Vacation Value" and "Actual Offer." To

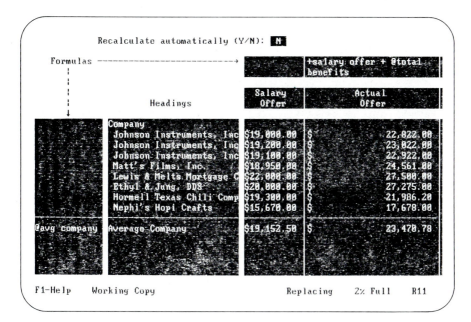

Recalculate automatically (Y/N): N

Formulas ------------------------> +salary offer + @total benefits

Headings	Salary Offer	Actual Offer
Company		
Johnson Instruments, Inc	$19,000.00	$ 22,822.00
Johnson Instruments, Inc	$19,200.00	$ 23,022.00
Johnson Instruments, Inc	$19,100.00	$ 22,922.00
Matt's Films, Inc.	$18,950.00	$ 24,561.00
Lewis & Melts Mortgage C	$22,000.00	$ 27,500.00
Ethyl & Jung, DDS	$20,000.00	$ 27,275.00
Hormell Texas Chili Comp	$19,300.00	$ 21,986.20
Nephi's Hopi Crafts	$15,670.00	$ 17,678.00
@avg company Average Company	$19,152.50	$ 23,470.78

F1-Help   Working Copy   Replacing   2% Full   R11

FIGURE 6A.12
Creating an "Average Company"—using the AVG function

Headings	Salary Offer	Actual Offer	Benefits		
			Life	Health	Retirement
Company					
Johnson Instruments, Inc	$19,000.00	$22,822.00	$135.00	$354.00	$ 3,333.00
Johnson Instruments, Inc	$19,200.00	$23,022.00	$135.00	$354.00	$ 3,333.00
Johnson Instruments, Inc	$19,100.00	$22,922.00	$135.00	$354.00	$ 3,333.00
Matt's Films, Inc.	$18,950.00	$24,561.00	$155.00	$466.00	$ 5,000.00
Lewis & Melts Mortgage C	$22,000.00	$27,500.00	$500.00	$600.00	$ 4,400.00
Ethyl & Jung, DDS	$20,000.00	$27,275.00	$325.00	$950.00	$ 6,000.00
Hormell Texas Chili Comp	$19,300.00	$21,986.20	$164.00	$320.00	$ 2,202.20
Nephi's Hopi Crafts	$15,670.00	$17,678.00	$250.00	$425.00	$ 1,333.00
Average Company	$19,152.50	$23,470.78	$224.88	$476.63	$ 3,616.78

F1-Help   Working Copy   Replacing   2% Full   R12

FIGURE 6A.13
The normal view of the "Average Company"

Headings	Salary Offer	Actual Offer	Benefits		
			Life	Health	Retirement
Company					
Johnson Instruments, Inc	$19,000.00	$22,822.00	$135.00	$354.00	$ 3,333.00
Johnson Instruments, Inc	$19,200.00	$23,022.00	$135.00	$354.00	$ 3,333.00
Johnson Instruments, Inc	$19,100.00	$22,922.00	$135.00	$354.00	$ 3,333.00
Matt's Films, Inc.	$18,950.00	$24,561.00	$155.00	$456.00	$ 5,000.00
Lewis & Melts Mortgage C	$22,000.00	$27,500.00	$500.00	$600.00	$ 4,400.00
Ethyl & Jung, DDS	$20,000.00	$27,275.00	$325.00	$950.00	$ 6,000.00
Hormell Texas Chili Comp	$19,300.00	$21,986.20	$164.00	$320.00	$ 2,202.20
Nephi's Hopi Crafts	$15,670.00	$17,670.00	$250.00	$425.00	$ 1,333.00
First State National Ban	$22,000.00				
Average Company	$19,152.50	$23,470.70	$224.88	$476.63	$ 3,616.78

| F1-Help   Working Copy | | Replacing   2% Full   R10 C2 |

FIGURE 6A.14
Entering a new row — the values for First State National Bank

do this, simply press the F7 key to recalculate the spreadsheet. The spreadsheet now appears like the one shown in Figure 6a.15.

Putting Rows in Order — The Move Operation

Your final task on the spreadsheet is to sort the companies by "Job Preference." The list of companies is functional, but you will probably want the jobs you prefer at the top of the list. Unfortunately, pfs:Plan does not have a sort function. The only way these rows can be rearranged is to use the *remove/restore* sequence. Move the cursor over to the column labeled "Job Preference" and look at the data, (see Figure 6a.16). The easiest way to rearrange the rows is to move the rows containing a "1" to the top of the spreadsheet. Then move the rows containing a "2" to the next rows and so on until the spreadsheet is in the order you want.

To perform the move sequence, first remove a row by placing the cursor on the row that you want to move and press the SHIFT and F6 keys, followed by the R key, to indicate you want to remove a row. Then move the cursor to the place you want the row to be and press the SHIFT and F5 keys to restore the row at this location. After you have performed all the movement (remove and

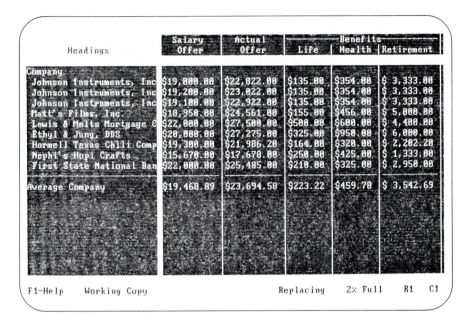

FIGURE 6A.15
Recalculating the spreadsheet

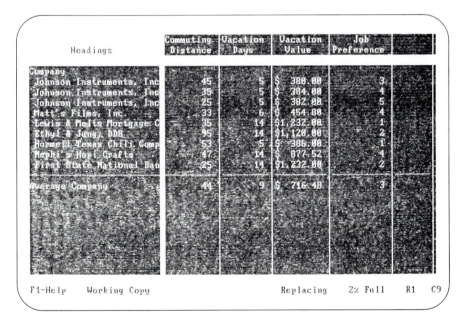

FIGURE 6A.16
Checking the order of "Job Preference"

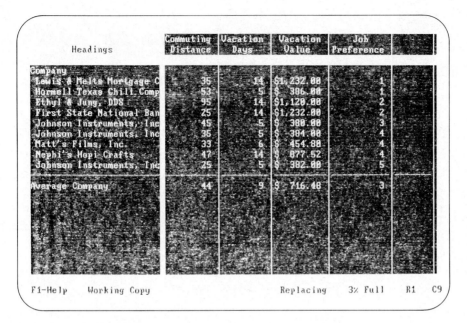

FIGURE 6A.17
Getting the job preferences in sorted order

restore) operations, the spreadsheet will look like the one shown in Figure 6a.17. Now press the HOME key to move the cursor to the top of the first row in the value region and press the F7 key to recalculate the spreadsheet.

Holding On to What You've Got — The Save and Get Options

Now that all your work has been done and you have a spreadsheet you can be proud of, it's time to save the work. First you must return to the Main Menu. Press the ESCape key, and you will see the Main Menu shown in Figure 6a.1. To save the spreadsheet, press the 3 key to get the Save Menu shown in Figure 6a.18. Press the 1 key to indicate that you want to store a spreadsheet. Now you need to enter the file name you want to use to store the spreadsheet. Pfs:Plan has three simple rules for a valid file name:

1. It can be up to 8 characters long.
2. The first character must be a letter.
3. Only letters and numbers can be used.

The file name may also include a three-letter extension after the file name. To add the extension, type a period followed by the three letters.

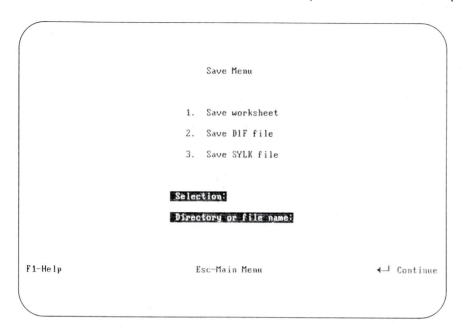

```
                    Save Menu


            1.   Save worksheet

            2.   Save DIF file

            3.   Save SYLK file



          Selection:

          Directory or file name:



F1-Help                Esc-Main Menu                    ◄─┘ Continue
```

FIGURE 6A.18
The pfs menu for saving the spreadsheet

If your computer system has two disk drives and you have a data disk in drive B, then enter B: followed by the file name. If the file name you want to use is JOBS, then when pfs:Plan moves the cursor to the line "Directory or file name:," enter the operation B:JOBS, and the spreadsheet will be saved on the data disk in drive B. If a file of the same name has already been stored on the disk, pfs:Plan will display a warning message and ask you whether or not you want to replace the previously existing file. Once a spreadsheet has been saved, you can exit pfs:Plan by returning to the Main Menu and entering operation E.

To recall a spreadsheet that has been previously saved, you again start with the Main Menu. This time, after loading pfs:Plan into memory, press the 2 key to access the Get Menu and press the 1 key to retrieve a spreadsheet. When the cursor moves to the line with the message "Directory or file name:," enter the file name. If you want to retrieve the file that was just saved, enter B:JOBS, and the spreadsheet will be "loaded" into your work space exactly as it was saved.

Showing Off Your Spreadsheet — The Print Operation

The Print operation is used to produce an image on paper of the spreadsheet as it appears on the screen. To start the printing operation, return to the Main

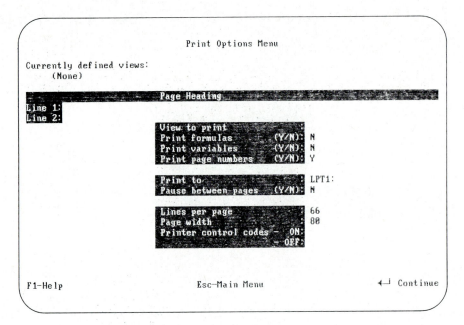

FIGURE 6A.19
So you want it on paper — the Print Options Menu

Menu by pressing the ESCape key. Now press the 5 key to get the Print Options Menu shown in Figure 6a.19. Using the Print Options Menu, you can tell pfs:Plan what to print and how you want it printed. In addition, you can enter up to two lines of title for the spreadsheet.

After setting the print options the way you want them, press the RETURN key. Figure 6a.20 shows the spreadsheet as it is printed by pfs:Plan. Note the page numbering used by the print option. If the spreadsheet is too long to fit on one page, the remainder of the spreadsheet is printed on page 2, page 3, and so on.

Other Features of pfs:Plan

Pfs:Plan has several additional features that can be helpful. One commonly used feature is the Clear operation. This option is available from the Main Menu by entering a 6 to get the Clear Menu. From this menu, you can clear the entire spreadsheet or only the variables in the spreadsheet.

Pfs:Plan has the ability to store and load DIF (data interchange format) files and SYLK (symbolic link) files. Through the use of these two types of files,

	Salary Offer	Actual Offer
Company		
Lewis & Melts Mortgage C	$22,000.00	$27,500.00
Hormell Texas Chili Comp	$19,300.00	$21,986.20
Ethyl & Jung, DDS	$20,000.00	$27,275.00
First State National Ban	$22,000.00	$25,485.00
Johnson Instruments, Inc	$19,000.00	$22,822.00
Johnson Instruments, Inc	$19,200.00	$23,022.00
Matt's Films, Inc.	$18,950.00	$24,561.00
Nephi's Hopi Crafts	$15,670.00	$17,678.00
Johnson Instruments, Inc	$19,100.00	$22,922.00
Average Company	$19,468.89	$23,694.58

	Benefits			Commuting
	Life	Health	Retirement	Distance
Company				
Lewis & Melts Mortgage C	$500.00	$600.00	$ 4,400.00	35
Hormell Texas Chili Comp	$164.00	$320.00	$ 2,202.20	53
Ethyl & Jung, DDS	$325.00	$950.00	$ 6,000.00	95
First State National Ban	$210.00	$325.00	$ 2,950.00	25
Johnson Instruments, Inc	$135.00	$354.00	$ 3,333.00	45
Johnson Instruments, Inc	$135.00	$354.00	$ 3,333.00	35
Matt's Films, Inc.	$155.00	$456.00	$ 5,000.00	33
Nephi's Hopi Crafts	$250.00	$425.00	$ 1,333.00	47
Johnson Instruments, Inc	$135.00	$354.00	$ 3,333.00	25
Average Company	$223.22	$459.78	$ 3,542.69	44

	Vacation Days	Vacation Value	Job Preference
Company			
Lewis & Melts Mortgage C	14	$1,232.00	1
Hormell Texas Chili Comp	5	$ 386.00	1
Ethyl & Jung, DDS	14	$1,120.00	2
First State National Ban	14	$1,232.00	2
Johnson Instruments, Inc	5	$ 380.00	3
Johnson Instruments, Inc	5	$ 384.00	4
Matt's Films, Inc.	6	$ 454.80	4
Nephi's Hopi Crafts	14	$ 877.52	4
Johnson Instruments, Inc	5	$ 382.00	5
Average Company	9	$ 716.48	3

Page 1-3

FIGURE 6A.20
A printed report from the job offers spreadsheet

pfs:Plan can create spreadsheets that can be transferred to other packages that can accept this type of file. The use of DIF and SYLK files also allows pfs:Plan to transfer data from one spreadsheet to another. This enables you to consolidate data from several different spreadsheets for special calculations and reports.

The package also provides for disk maintenance through the use of option 4 in the Main Menu. The Remove Menu allows you to remove files from your data disk.

Finally, pfs:Plan has the option of interfacing directly with two other packages in the pfs series. Pfs:Plan can read data into a spreadsheet format from a file saved by pfs:File (presented in Module 7a). If you print a spreadsheet to a disk file, it can be read directly by the pfs series word processor, pfs:Write (presented in Module 5a).

Lotus 1-2-3

Learning to Use Lotus 1-2-3

Lotus 1-2-3 is one of the more recently developed spreadsheet packages. It is designed to overcome some of the shortcomings of earlier spreadsheet packages by providing additional capabilities. In fact, Lotus 1-2-3 may be considered an integrated package, because it possesses capabilities far beyond those of a simple spreadsheet package. 1-2-3 represents the spreadsheet portion of the Lotus package and thus is used to identify the spreadsheet function. It is one of the easiest packages to learn and use. Furthermore, it is currently one of the most popular software packages ever produced.

When you begin to use 1-2-3, start by booting the operating system. If you are using a computer with two disk drives, place a disk that has been prepared to hold your data in drive B. Once the operating system has been loaded, all that is required is to place the Lotus system disk in drive A and type LOTUS. Press the RETURN key, and you will be greeted by the Lotus log-on menu, as shown in Figure 6b.1. Note that the version number is shown on this screen (V.1A) — if you have any questions about which version of Lotus you are using, you can check the log-on screen.

In the Access System menu, Lotus identifies the other functions the package is capable of performing. The discussion presented in this module addresses only the spreadsheet functions of Lotus. As noted at the bottom of the screen, you may select other functions by using the arrow keys to identify the function. In any case, after you have made your selection, press the RETURN key. If you desire information on the other aspects of Lotus, see Module 7b (databases), Module 8b (graphics), and Module 10b (integrated packages). Before the first 1-2-3 screen appears, you will see a screen that identifies which release number of 1-2-3 you are using. As indicated toward the bottom of the screen, you may press any key on the keyboard to enter the spreadsheet function.

The Arrangement — What a 1-2-3 Spreadsheet Looks Like

After the log-on screens disappear, you will be presented with an empty spreadsheet, as shown in Figure 6b.2. Whether you have previously built and

```
Lotus Access System  V.1A  (C)1983 Lotus Development Corp.          MENU
------------------------------------------------------------------------
1-2-3  File-Manager  Disk-Manager  PrintGraph  Translate  Exit
Enter 1-2-3 -- Lotus Spreadsheet/Graphics/Database program
========================================================================




                          Thu  01-Jan-87
                          8:28:02am







          Use the arrow keys to highlight command choice and press [Enter]
       Press [Esc] to cancel a choice; Press [F1] for information on command choices
```

FIGURE 6B.1
**The Lotus Access System command menu
(log-on menu)**

saved other spreadsheets or not, this is always the starting point. The initial screen is divided into two basic areas. The bottom of the screen represents the spreadsheet work space, and the top is the command menu area.

A 1-2-3 spreadsheet is capable of handling a spreadsheet of up to 2048 rows and 256 columns, depending on the internal memory capability of your computer (some later versions support a much larger work space). The initial (default) width of each cell is 9 characters, but a cell can be modified to be as few as 1 character or as many as 72 characters. However, do not confuse the column width (which determines the cell size) with the data length. The width of a column may be narrower or wider than the data shown in that column. The width of each column can be expanded or contracted independently of the others to provide the clearest picture of what is in the spreadsheet.

The highlighted portion of the screen at the upper-right corner, the status indicator, will contain the word READY, which indicates that 1-2-3 is ready to proceed and that you are in data-entry mode. As you perform different types of operations, the status indicator changes to reflect your current state of operation. For example, when you enter the command selection mode, the status changes to MENU (as in Figure 6b.2). When you place a number into a cell, the status is VALUE. When you enter text into a cell, the status is LABEL. When

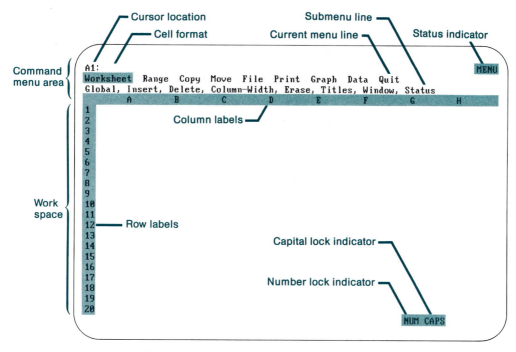

FIGURE 6B.2
The 1-2-3 screen layout — work space

you are in a cell-addressing mode, the status will be POINT. When 1-2-3 is in the process of completing an activity, the status will temporarily be WAIT. (In the automatic recalculate mode, you must WAIT until the function has been performed before you proceed.)

The status in Figure 6b.2 is MENU. To move from the log-on screen to this screen, press the slash (/) key. This causes the initial command menu to appear. In the MENU mode, the first line under the current cell marker identifies the types of functions that can be performed. The second line provides an additional explanation of the functions (or directions on how to complete a selected function, as will be shown later). A brief description of each of these functions is presented in Table 6b.1. The function to be used will be highlighted, as shown in Figure 6b.2. Many of the functions, when selected, will provide additional menus that more fully describe the operation to be performed. A function can be selected either by pressing the first letter of the function (for example, "R" for the Range function) or by pressing the right- or left-arrow key, which causes the highlighted area to move from one function to the next. If you continue to press the right-arrow key when Quit is reached, the highlighted area will return to the Worksheet function, and you may restart the selection process. As you select command functions (which may in turn have subfunctions), you could

TABLE 6B.1 General Lotus 1-2-3 Commands

Function	Operation

Worksheet	Performs operations that affect the entire spreadsheet, including:
	    Global — modification of all cells
	    Insert — add new rows or columns
	    Delete — remove new rows or columns
	    Column-Width — change the default size of cells
	    Erase — delete the entire spreadsheet
	    Titles — establish a "title" window
	    Window — establish a "general" window
	    Status — provide current operational information

Range	Performs operations that affect a cell or a specified range of cells, including (many available under Worksheet/Global as well):
	    Format — modify the presentation mode
	    Label-Prefix — modify cell alignment
	    Erase — remove the contents of a cell or range of cells
	    Name — provide an identifying name for a cell or range of cells
	    Justify — adjust width of text paragraph
	    Protect — turn cell "locking" on
	    Unprotect — turn cell "locking" off
	    Input — turn on/off entry access to protected cell

Copy	Reproduces the contents of one or more cells into another area of the spreadsheet
Move	Reproduces the contents of one or more cells into another area of the spreadsheet while erasing the contents of the original cells

File	Performs disk file manipulations, including:
	    Retrieve — get a spreadsheet file from disk
	    Save — retain the current spreadsheet on disk
	    Xtract — save a portion of the current spreadsheet on disk
	    Erase — remove a file from disk

make a mistake and enter the wrong function or supply an incorrect response. However, 1-2-3 performs a "return to previous step" operation when you press the ESCape key. Thus, if you have entered the Worksheet function and you decide you should have selected another function, press the ESCape key, and the menu (as shown in Figure 6b.2) will return to the screen. If you are currently looking at the command screen and you want to return to the data-entry mode, press the ESCape key again and you will be back to the original appearance of the command area.

Function	Operation
File, cont.	List — show the names of disk files and available disk space Import — get a spreadsheet "print" file from disk Directory — set the default disk drive
Print	Produces a printed copy of the spreadsheet, including: Print — produce output on the printer File — produce output to a disk file Page — advance to the top of the next page Options — establish headers, footers, margins, and so on Setup — send special print codes to the printer Page-Length — establish the number of lines per page Other — indicate the cell characteristics desired Clear — erase previously established print options Align — reposition the top of page Go — produce the indicated output Quit — terminate the print function
Graph	Creates a graphic presentation of the material contained in the spreadsheet (see Graphics, Module 8b)
Data	Performs general functions on existing data, including: Fill — fill the cells of the spreadsheet with a set of predetermined-determined values Table — perform table manipulations Sort — arrange the specified cells in the designated order Query — perform database retrieval functions (see Database, Module 7b) Distribution — calculate frequency distribution
Quit	Terminates the 1-2-3 session and returns to the Lotus menu of general functions

Learning About Your Keyboard —
Cursor Movement and Function Keys

When you enter an "empty" spreadsheet, your cell reference will be "A1"—row 1 and column A. However, as you build your spreadsheet, you will want to reference other cells. As you move from place to place in the spreadsheet, the highlighted area also moves, and the current cell marker in the command area of the screen is updated.

TABLE 6B.2 Function Key Designations for 1-2-3

Function Key	Operation Performed
F1	Enter the Help mode
F2	Enter the Edit mode for current cell contents
F3	List the currently specified range names
F4	Identify the current cell as an absolute address
F5	Go To a specified cell position
F6	Move to the next available window
F7	Repeat most recently specified data query
F8	Repeat most recently specified table operation
F9	Perform recalculation
F10	Create the most recently specified graph
F11*	Change meaning of arrow keys from cell-addressing to window-addressing
F12*	Move to the end of a block of cells, an entry, or a menu

* Not available on all versions of Lotus or certain keyboards.

The simplest way of moving from one cell to another is by using the cursor-movement or arrow keys. If using the arrow keys is not quick enough for you, you can traverse the spreadsheet more rapidly if you press the ALTernate key and a cursor-movement key at the same time. If you press the ALTernate key and the right-arrow key together, the entire screen scrolls to reveal the next full set of columns to the right of the current screen. If the last column identified in the current screen is column H, the first column in the next screen presentation will be column I. Of course, similar operations may be achieved by using the left-, up-, and down-arrow keys.

Suppose you are at the bottom-right corner of a spreadsheet and you want to get back to cell A1. All that is necessary is to press the HOME key. Regardless of where you are in the spreadsheet, you will go to cell A1. However, if you want to reference a cell other than A1, you may want to use the Go To function. This function requires the use of one of the function keys, as identified in Table 6b.2. When you press the F5 key, you will be asked to supply a cell reference. On completing this entry, 1-2-3 will move directly to that cell regardless of its direction from the previous location. Alternately, you are permitted to access a "named" portion of the spreadsheet by selecting the Name option of the Range function. If you don't know which cells have a designated name, you can find out by pressing the F3 key. On those keyboards equipped with "extra" function keys, you can press the F12 and HOME keys together to address the last cell of the active spreadsheet—the lower-right corner.

Trying to Remember — The Help Function

The Help function is selected by pressing the F1 function key. If you are currently working in the READY mode and you press F1, you will be provided with general information in the first help screen. From this point, you may select the highlighted topic or use the arrow keys to move through the list to select any of the other topics. When you make a selection, the list of topics changes so that you can reach other Help information. When you are ready to return to what you were doing, simply press the ESCape key. When you return, your spreadsheet is at exactly the position you left it.

If you are using one of the many command menus and you press the F1 function key, you will receive information related to the previously highlighted command selection. At any time, whether you are currently using the command menu or some lower-level menu, you can press the F1 key and retrieve information about that specific topic or operation.

Solving the Job Hunting Problem

The remaining sections of this module are devoted to solving the job hunting problem. You may want to refer to the problem statement in the Introduction to Spreadsheet Modules before you continue. Also, remember that the data used in this problem can be found in Appendix A.

What's in a Name? — Entering Headings and Labels

Now you are ready to put the job offer data into the spreadsheet. Examine Figure 6b.3. The contents of cell A2 are entered by first pressing the down-arrow key so that cell A2 is the currently active cell. Since no command menu is currently on the screen, as you enter the letter "C" of "Company Name," the status mode changes to LABEL. Thus, the label "Company Name" is to be placed in cell A2. Initially, the complete text ("Company Name") of cell A2 is visible. As you enter the contents of adjacent cells, the original text will be truncated to the width of the cell ("Company"), as in Figure 6b.3. However, 1-2-3 retains the complete length of the text even though you may not be able to see all of it in the spreadsheet. When numeric values are too long for the cell, the cell is filled with the * symbol.

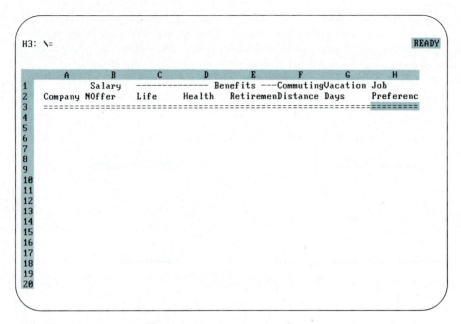

FIGURE 6B.3
Column headings for the job offers problem

After you enter the text "Company Name," you can press the RETURN key. However, you will then have to use the arrow keys to move to the next cell into which a value is to be placed. Entering text in this manner will take a while to complete. As an alternative, 1-2-3 permits you to move the cursor without pressing the RETURN key — that is, by using the cursor-movement keys. 1-2-3 assumes that as soon as you move from the current cell, you want what you have entered for that cell to be stored in that cell. Thus, by pressing a cursor-movement key, you store the contents of the previous cell and move to another cell. This requires fewer keystrokes than pressing RETURN for each entry.

While you are in the data entry mode, if the first character you enter for a cell is a digit or an arithmetic operation, 1-2-3 assumes you want to enter a numeric value, formula, or function in that cell. An examination of Figure 6b.3 reveals that some of the cells begin with what would normally be considered a numeric value or an arithmetic operation (for example, - in cell C1 or = in cell A3). If you want to enter digits or arithmetic operation symbols but want to have them treated as text, begin the entry with an apostrophe ('), which indicates that the characters are to be treated as text. If you want to fill a cell completely with a character or symbol, press the Backslash (\) key and the symbol you want to use. This option was used for the cells in row 3.

Too Large or Too Small? — Changing Column Widths

Now that you have entered the column headings for the job offers problem, it's time to tidy up a bit. You ought at least to increase the size of the "Company Name" column. After all, the company names that will be entered later will all be longer than 9 characters. You should plan to make a column as wide as the longest piece of data you want to see in the spreadsheet in that column, although you may change the column width at any time without losing any of the data.

Look at the top of Figure 6b.4. Note that the command menu now reflects that you have selected the Worksheet function and you are currently referencing the column containing the "Company Name" heading. By selecting the Column-Width option, the command screen will change, and you will be asked if you want to Set (create a new width) or Reset (return to the default setting) the column. If the Set option is selected, you will be asked to supply the number of character positions for cells in the current column. Note that as you change the default width from 9 to 25 characters, the status mode changes to EDIT, indicating that you are changing the current value.

Although many of the other columns in the spreadsheet might be wide enough to contain the data you plan to place in them, you may decide to make them wider so that visible breaks exist between the columns after the data has been entered. Move the cursor to cell B1 and re-enter the Worksheet function. This time, select the Global option. You may still select a Column-Width option within the Global operation. Now increase the column width to 12 characters per column. Since this is a global operation, all of the columns from the current column position to the right are modified to a width of 12 characters. Figure 6b.5 shows that each of the column headings is now at the desired width. Thus, you may change the column width of a single column or a range of columns, depending on the options selected from the Worksheet function.

Creating a New Look! — Formatting Cells for Text

When looking at Figure 6b.5, you might have noticed that all of the text you have supplied occupies the left-most portion of each of the cells — that is, it is left-justified. This is acceptable, but it might be more visually appealing if you adjusted these headings so they are centered within the character positions of the columns. This time, you should select the Range function. Within the Range function, select the Label-Prefix option. As a result of this selection, you will be asked for the desired alignment of the cell contents — Left, Right, or Center. If Left is specified, the cell contents will be left-justified. If Right is selected, the contents of the cell will be right-justified — will occupy the right-most columns. If Center is chosen, the contents will be centered within the available character positions. For the job offers problem, you might want to

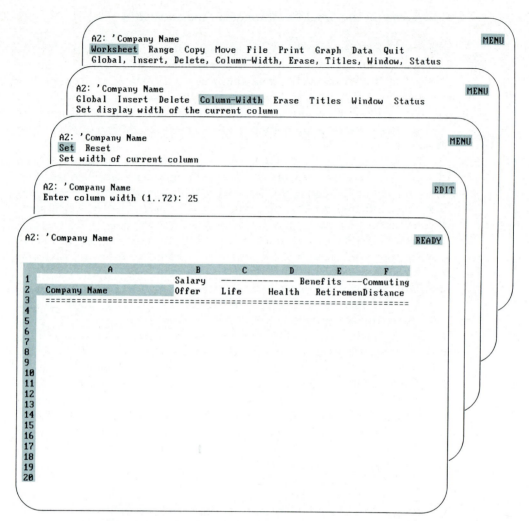

FIGURE 6B.4
Changing the width of one column

center all the column headings, beginning with the "Salary Offer" heading, within the 12-character width of these columns. After you have selected the Center option, 1-2-3 will ask you to "Enter range of labels." This entry is followed by the cell range "B1..B1." This means that unless you indicate otherwise, the only cell to be affected by the operation is cell B1. However, note that the status mode has changed to POINT. This means that you can modify this reference at this time.

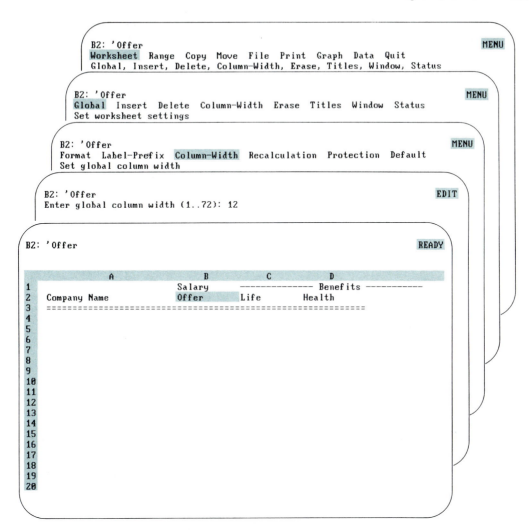

FIGURE 6B.5
Changing the width of all the columns

Before you proceed with a modification, however, one important question needs to be answered. If a range is to be indicated, where does the range begin? If the range begins at B1, simply press the period (.) key. (Actually, two periods will appear in the command line.) This provides an "anchor" for the beginning cell reference. If you would like an anchor at a position other than the current cell, simply enter the beginning cell reference or use the arrow keys to move to the desired cell. Once the initial position has been identified, you may enter the ending point of the range or use the arrow key to address the ending cell. If you use the arrow key for this addressing operation, the entire area to be affected by the operation is highlighted. Anytime the status mode is POINT, cell addressing (or identifying a range of cells) can be performed in this manner. The range for this particular operation is from B1 to H2, including all cells bounded by B1 in the "northwest" and H2 in the "southeast." The results of this operation and of adjusting the group headings are shown in Figure 6b.6.

A View with Numbers — Formatting Cells for Numeric Values

Now that you have had a chance to see how cells can be manipulated when they contain text, it is time to examine the type of presentations you might want to see under each of the column headings. Look at Figure 6b.7. Note that the data to be recorded under the "Company Name" heading could easily be entered in the default mode — the company names are text and would be satisfactory in appearance if they were left-justified. However, many of the other columns need some special treatment. For example, you would expect the values placed under the "Salary Offer" heading to represent dollars and cents. Thus, you might begin your definition of the values to be presented in this column by changing the format. The command screen portion of this figure indicates that cell B4 is currently being referenced — the location of the first salary amount. The default alignment (right-justified for numeric values) is satisfactory, but you might want to change the format style. Figure 6b.7 indicates that the Range function has been selected, along with the Format option. Once in the Format option, you can choose from a rather wide range of format styles. For your problem, the Currency presentation is desirable, an illustration of which is shown in the command message area when you move the cursor to the Currency option. The default number of decimal positions for the Currency mode is 2, but it can be modified. Finally, a range of cells is specified. (B4 to E11 is the area of the spreadsheet expected to contain dollar values from your job offers). After the operation has been completed, note that the cell format (at the top of the screen, adjacent to the cell location) now shows C2 — Currency format with two decimal places.

Entering the Company Names — Another Example of Entering Text

Now that all the column headings have been established and all the numeric cells are in an appropriate format, it is time to begin to enter the data associated with each of the companies in the job offers spreadsheet. The first company is "Johnson Instruments, Inc.," which should appear in row 4 column A. All that is necessary to enter the company name, or other character data, is to place the cursor in the appropriate cell and type the needed text. After the first company

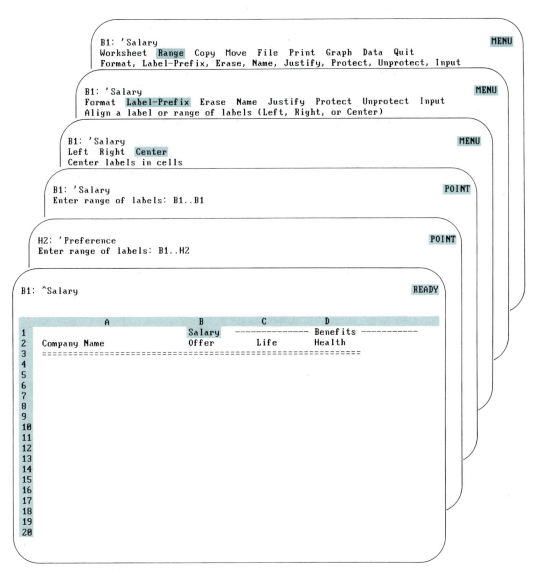

FIGURE 6B.6
Centering the column headings

name has been entered, you may decide it is easier to enter all company names first and later enter the numeric values associated with each company. If this is the case, simply press the down-arrow key and continue typing individual company names in column A of each new row. The result of this activity is shown in Figure 6b.8.

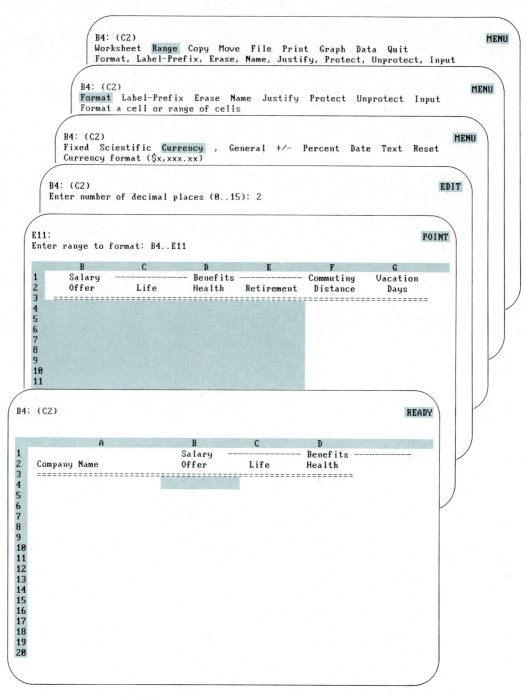

FIGURE 6B.7

Selecting the currency presentation format — it makes cents

```
A12:                                                        READY

                    A                B       C       D
                                  Salary   ------------ Benefits ----------
1                                 Offer     Life    Health
2   Company Name
3   =================================================================
4   Johnson Instruments, Inc.
5   Johnson Instruments, Inc.
6   Johnson Instruments, Inc.
7   Matt's Films, Inc.
8   Lewis & Melts Mortgage Co
9   Ethyl & Jung, DDS
10  Hormell Texas Chili Co.
11  Nephi's Hopi Crafts
12
13
14
15
16
17
18
19
20
```

FIGURE 6B.8
Entering the company names

Two Views of the Spreadsheet — Using the Window Function

Now that you have entered all the company names, it is time to enter the numeric values associated with them. However, before you proceed, stop for a moment and think about how you might enter these numbers. If you decide to enter the values a row at a time, the spreadsheet will scroll to the left when you reach the right edge of the screen. When this happens, the company name will no longer be visible. To avoid confusion and possible incorrect placement of numbers in the spreadsheet (associating a numeric value with the wrong company name), it would be desirable to have the company name always on the screen. This is exactly what spreadsheet windows are designed to support.

In Figure 6b.9, the Worksheet function and the Window option have been selected, producing the third command menu. As you begin the screen-splitting operation, note that the current cell indicates a position in column B. As you examine the current menu, you will be asked to select a Horizontal (left-to-right) or Vertical (up-and-down) split. For the job offers problem, you want to split the screen vertically at column B. This means that all columns to the left of column B, the company names, will be in one window, and the columns to the right will be in another window. Horizontal and vertical windows are normally synchronized — linked so that they move together. However, after a window has been established, you may later decide that the window should be unsyn-

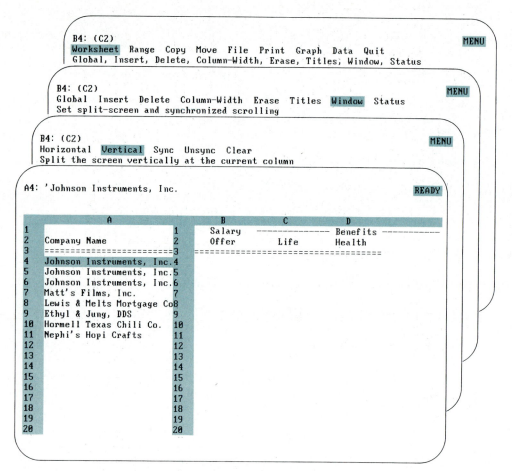

FIGURE 6B.9
Creating a vertical window

chronized (Unsync), resynchronized (Sync), or removed (Clear) to make viewing the spreadsheet easier.

The results of establishing a new window are shown in Figure 6b.9. Note that a break now exists between the "Company Name" and the "Salary Offer" headings and a new set of row numbers appears on the screen. The currently active window is based on the current cell reference. In this figure, cell A4 is identified as the current cell. If you find that you need to move between windows, arrow keys won't help you. However, remember that the function key F6 will allow you to move between (among) windows. Based on the current screen, if you pressed F6, you would be in the area identified as columns B

```
B12:                                                              READY

              A                    B         C          D
 1                        1     Salary   ----------- Benefits ----------
 2   Company Name         2     Offer      Life      Health
 3   =================    3   ========================================
 4   Johnson Instruments, Inc.4  $19,000.00  $135.00   $354.00
 5   Johnson Instruments, Inc.5  $19,200.00  $135.00   $354.00
 6   Johnson Instruments, Inc.6  $19,100.00  $135.00   $354.00
 7   Matt's Films, Inc.  7  $18,950.00  $155.00   $456.00
 8   Lewis & Melts Mortgage Co8  $22,000.00  $500.00   $600.00
 9   Ethyl & Jung, DDS   9  $20,000.00  $325.00   $950.00
10   Hormell Texas Chili Co. 10  $19,300.00  $164.00   $320.00
11   Nephi's Hopi Crafts 11  $15,670.00  $250.00   $425.00
12                       12
13                       13
14                       14
15                       15
16                       16
17                       17
18                       18
19                       19
20                       20
```

FIGURE 6B.10
Entering the job offer data

through D. By pressing F6 again, you return to the window containing column A.

What Is Your Offer? — Placing Numeric Values in the Spreadsheet

Now it is time to place numeric values in the spreadsheet. The process is basically the same as entering text. So long as you begin the contents of a cell with a digit, an arithmetic operator (for example, + or −), or an "@" symbol (which identifies functions), 1-2-3 will interpret the data as a numeric value and the status mode changes to VALUE. Thus, in Figure 6b.10, as soon as the 1 in 19200 was pressed on the keyboard, the status indicator changed to VALUE.

As you proceed down the length of row 4, entering the values under each column heading, the value 19200 is automatically converted to $19,200.00. (Remember that you are using the Currency format for each of these cells.) Then, as you enter the value under the "Retirement" heading and proceed to the right, the screen scrolls to the left, but the company names still appear in the first window. Finally, note that the values under "Commuting Distance," "Vacation Days," and "Job Preference" are single digits rather than in a dollars and cents format. (Remember, you stopped formatting columns of values with the "Retirement" column—column E.) Thus, these columns remain in the default format. Note also that the company names are still visible on the screen even though you are far to the right of column A.

After entering the first row, all that remains is to repeat this activity (entering numeric values) until all the job offer data has been placed in the spreadsheet. However, since you are now far away from column A, you may decide to return rapidly to the beginning columns by using the HOME key or ALTernate and left-arrow keys rather than return one cell at a time.

Holding on to What You've Got — Saving the Spreadsheet

Although you will want to perform other operations in this spreadsheet, you may decide to save the work you have done up to now. To save a spreadsheet, enter the File function. As shown in Figure 6b.11, the File function permits you to Retrieve (load) a saved spreadsheet, Save a spreadsheet (record the current spreadsheet on a disk), Xtract (save) a portion of a spreadsheet, Erase (delete) an existing spreadsheet on a disk, List (view) the spreadsheet names on a disk, Import (retrieve) a nonspreadsheet file, and produce a Directory of a disk.

Because you want to save or record the current spreadsheet, select the Save option. 1-2-3 will then ask for a file name by which the spreadsheet will be saved on the disk. If you want the spreadsheet saved on your data disk, you will have to supply the disk drive designation. The file name must be a "legal" file name for the operating system in use. However, 1-2-3 provides its own extension (WKS for WorKSheet). Hereafter, your spreadsheet will be called "JOBS," and it will be on drive B. When the spreadsheet is saved, not only are the individual cells saved, but your current cell position and windows are saved as well. Thus, if you were to exit 1-2-3 at this point and later retrieve the jobs spreadsheet, when the first screen appeared, B11 would be the current cell, and it would appear in the second window. This process allows you to begin again at some later time at exactly the position in which you last saved the spreadsheet.

A Spreadsheet with Room to Grow — The Insert Function

It is often difficult, if not impossible, to predict the exact layout that will be needed in a spreadsheet when you begin. Such is the case with the jobs spreadsheet. Now you need a new column between "Vacation Days" and "Job Preference" in which to place an estimate of the value of your vacation time. You begin by moving the current cell pointer to the location in the spreadsheet where the new column is to appear. Then you select the Insert option of the Worksheet function. Note that the Insert option allows you to insert either a column or a row. You currently need a column, so you can select this option by pressing the RETURN key, since "Column" is already highlighted. Then you will be presented with other menus that control the insertion process. First, you are requested to indicate where the insertion process is to begin. As shown in Figure 6b.12, when cell H4 is identified, the new column is to appear before

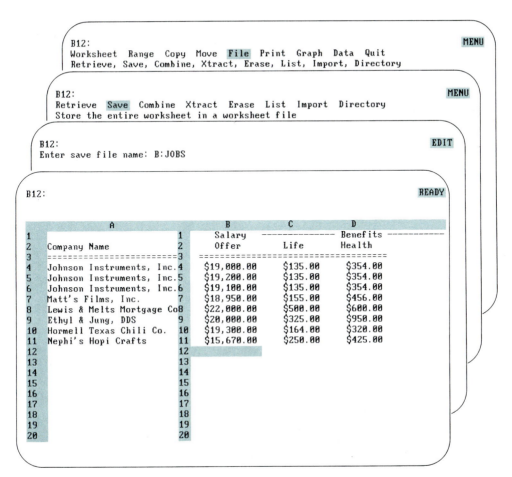

```
B12:                                                          MENU
Worksheet  Range  Copy  Move  File  Print  Graph  Data  Quit
Retrieve, Save, Combine, Xtract, Erase, List, Import, Directory

    B12:                                                      MENU
    Retrieve  Save  Combine  Xtract  Erase  List  Import  Directory
    Store the entire worksheet in a worksheet file

        B12:                                                  EDIT
        Enter save file name: B:JOBS


            B12:                                              READY


                        A                 B        C          D
            1                       1    Salary  ---------- Benefits ----------
            2  Company Name         2     Offer    Life      Health
            3  =====================3  =================================
            4  Johnson Instruments, Inc.4  $19,000.00  $135.00   $354.00
            5  Johnson Instruments, Inc.5  $19,200.00  $135.00   $354.00
            6  Johnson Instruments, Inc.6  $19,100.00  $135.00   $354.00
            7  Matt's Films, Inc.   7  $18,950.00  $155.00   $456.00
            8  Lewis & Melts Mortgage Co8  $22,000.00  $500.00   $600.00
            9  Ethyl & Jung, DDS    9  $20,000.00  $325.00   $950.00
           10  Hormell Texas Chili Co. 10  $19,300.00  $164.00   $320.00
           11  Nephi's Hopi Crafts 11  $15,670.00  $250.00   $425.00
           12                      12
           13                      13
           14                      14
           15                      15
           16                      16
           17                      17
           18                      18
           19                      19
           20                      20
```

FIGURE 6B.11
Saving the spreadsheet

column H. Next you are asked to specify the range of columns to be inserted. If more than one column is to be added, the number of columns represented by the range corresponds to the number of columns to be added. The columns that follow this position will be shifted to the right. Column H is now empty, and the other columns to the right of this position now have new column identifiers (for example, "Job Preference" is now in column I).

Figure It This Way — Using Formulas

You intend column H to hold approximate values of vacation time. You have determined that on the average you would work approximately 250 days in a

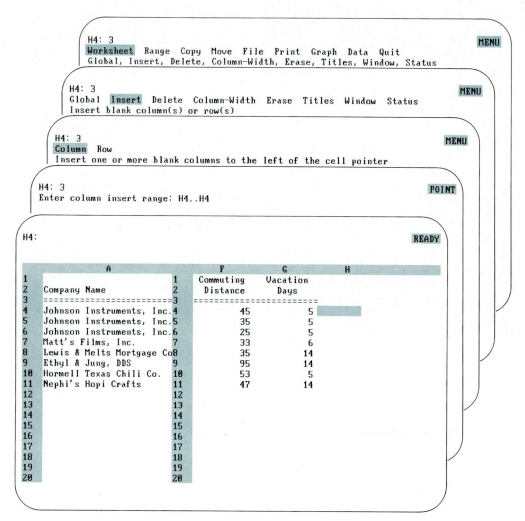

FIGURE 6B.12
Inserting a new column

calendar year (365 days less weekends and holidays). Thus, the "Salary Offer" of each company can be established on a per-day basis (salary divided by 250). Since vacation time is stated in terms of number of days, you could then determine the "Vacation Value" for each company. You can see this is a perfect place to use a formula. To enter a formula into a cell, begin with a digit or an arithmetic operator. (A formula will ultimately result in a numeric value.) Thus, + is entered first, to which 1-2-3 responds with the VALUE status. (1-2-3 will try to designate the formula as text if it begins with B—a column reference.)

```
H4: (C2) +B4/250*G4                                                    READY

                    A              1    Commuting    Vacation    Vacation
1                                       Distance     Days        Value
2   Company Name                   2
3   ===============================3    ==================================
4   Johnson Instruments, Inc.      4        45          5           $380.00
5   Johnson Instruments, Inc.      5        35          5
6   Johnson Instruments, Inc.      6        25          5
7   Matt's Films, Inc.             7        33          6
8   Lewis & Melts Mortgage Co      8        35         14
9   Ethyl & Jung, DDS              9        95         14
10  Hormell Texas Chili Co.       10        53          5
11  Nephi's Hopi Crafts           11        47         14
12                                12
13                                13
14                                14
15                                15
16                                16
17                                17
18                                18
19                                19
20                                20
```

FIGURE 6B.13
Entering the formula for "Vacation Value"

The formula is +B4/250*G4. The cell reference B4 addresses the cell in this row containing the salary offered. Salary offered is divided by 250 ("/" means to divide). The result is then multiplied ("*" means to multiply) by the contents of cell G4 — the value of vacation days.

Note that spaces are not permitted in formulas. When the RETURN key is pressed, rather than the formula being placed in the cell, its value is placed there, as shown in Figure 6b.13. However, if you look at the command area, you will see that the formula, not the value, is the actual contents of cell H4. Since column H is now associated with column G, any change in the value of "Vacation Days" will result in an automatic change in "Vacation Value."

Note that cell H4 is formatted in dollars and cents. Several functions have been performed between Figures 6b.12 and 6b.13. Some of these functions include entering the column heading, increasing the width of the column, centering the heading, and changing the format of cell H4 to a Currency format.

Duplicating — The Copy Function

Now that cell H4 has an established format, you might want to replicate (copy) the contents of that cell and its format to other cells. For the screen setup in

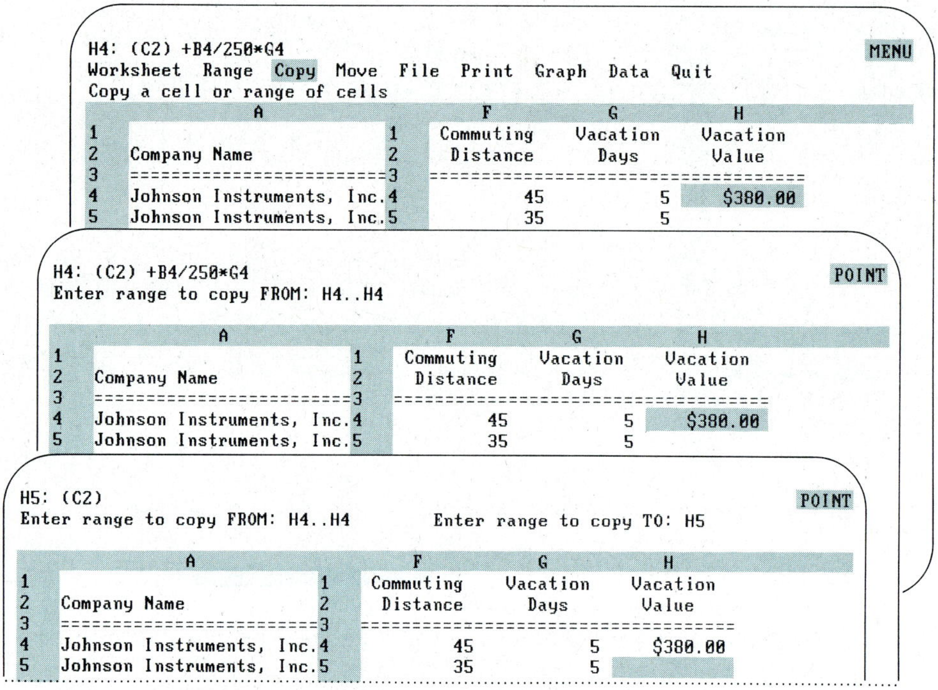

FIGURE 6B.14
Copying a formula to other cells in the same column

Figure 6b.13, the Copy function is used to copy the contents and format of H4 to other cells in the same column of the spreadsheet. The first command menu of the Copy function asks you to provide the anchor position. Cell H4 is the point from which you wish to copy. Since you are not copying a range of cells to another range of cells, "H4" is the only entry necessary. When you press the RETURN key, you can then enter the "range of cells to copy TO." The receiving range is established in exactly the same way as when you were centering the heading. After you have established the range to copy "FROM" and the range to copy "TO," as soon as the Copy function is completed, you will see the

```
H11: (C2)                                                              POINT
Enter range to copy FROM: H4..H4      Enter range to copy TO: H5..H11

                    A                       F          G          H
1                                   1    Commuting   Vacation   Vacation
2    Company Name                   2    Distance    Days       Value
3    =============================  3    ==================================
4    Johnson Instruments, Inc.      4       45          5        $380.00
5    Johnson Instruments, Inc.      5       35          5
6    Johnson Instruments, Inc.      6       25          5
7    Matt's Films, Inc.             7       33          6
8    Lewis & Melts Mortgage Co      8       35         14
9    Ethyl & Jung, DDS              9       95         14
10   Hormell Texas Chili Co.       10       53          5
11   Nephi's Hopi Crafts           11       47         14
```

```
H4: (C2) +B4/250*G4                                                    READY

                    A                       F          G          H
1                                   1    Commuting   Vacation   Vacation
2    Company Name                   2    Distance    Days       Value
3    =============================  3    ==================================
4    Johnson Instruments, Inc.      4       45          5        $380.00
5    Johnson Instruments, Inc.      5       35          5        $384.00
6    Johnson Instruments, Inc.      6       25          5        $382.00
7    Matt's Films, Inc.             7       33          6        $454.80
8    Lewis & Melts Mortgage Co      8       35         14      $1,232.00
9    Ethyl & Jung, DDS              9       95         14      $1,120.00
10   Hormell Texas Chili Co.       10       53          5        $386.00
11   Nephi's Hopi Crafts           11       47         14        $877.52
12                                 12
13                                 13
14                                 14
15                                 15
16                                 16
17                                 17
18                                 18
19                                 19
20                                 20
```

FIGURE 6B.14
(continued)

results, as indicated in Figure 6b.14. When a formula is copied in this manner, the cell reference H4 is changed to H5 for row 5, H6 for row 6, and so on.

Figure 6b.15 illustrates the process of adding another column, further to the left than before, which is essentially the same as entering "Vacation Value." In fact, when the "Actual Offer" column is added, the previously used relative addresses (used in the "Vacation Value" column) are adjusted so that the operation is still accurate. The formula to be used in the "Actual Offer" column is relatively the same as the one used before. The formula is +B4+D4+E4+F4, where B4 indicates the salary offer cell, D4 the life insur-

FIGURE 6B.15
Another formula—computing the value of
the "Actual Offer"

ance cell, E4 the health insurance cell, and F4 the retirement contribution cell. Thus, cell references that appear in formulas can indicate cells that are either left or right (up or down) from the current column, or both. The result of this formula is placed in cell C4, formatted to the Currency presentation mode, and copied to the remaining cells in the same column, as shown in Figure 6b.15.

Providing a Visual Break — The Copy Function Again

Now that all the values have been entered for all the companies, it is time to start thinking about what else you want to do. First, you might decide to place a visual break across the bottom of the list of companies similar to the one immediately under the column headings. To do this, you could duplicate the contents of cell A11 (see Figure 6b.16). Select the Copy function and indicate that you want to copy the contents FROM that cell TO another cell or, as shown in Figure 6b.16, a range of cells.

Letting 1-2-3 "Compute"—Using Functions

Most spreadsheet packages provide a number of very useful functions. Although the result of many of the functions could be achieved by using formulas,

```
B12: \-                                                              READY

              A                     B         C          D
                           1     Salary    Actual  ------------ Benefits
1  Company Name            2     Offer     Offer     Life
2  ===================     3     =========================================
3  Johnson Instruments, Inc.4   $19,000.00 $22,822.00  $135.00
4  Johnson Instruments, Inc.5   $19,200.00 $23,022.00  $135.00
5  Johnson Instruments, Inc.6   $19,100.00 $22,922.00  $135.00
6  Matt's Films, Inc.      7    $18,950.00 $24,561.00  $155.00
7  Lewis & Melts Mortgage Co8   $22,000.00 $27,500.00  $500.00
8  Ethyl & Jung, DDS       9    $20,000.00 $27,275.00  $325.00
9  Hormell Texas Chili Co. 10   $19,300.00 $21,986.20  $164.00
10 Nephi's Hopi Crafts     11   $15,670.00 $17,678.00  $250.00
11 -------------------     12   ------------
12                         13
13                         14
14                         15
15                         16
16                         17
17                         18
18                         19
19                         20
20
```

FIGURE 6B.16
**Creating a visual break with the Copy
function**

often it is much easier to use a function than to create just the right formula or set of formulas. The functions that are available with 1-2-3 are presented in Table 6b.3.

For the job offers problem, you might want to establish averages (for comparison purposes) for many of the columns that contain numeric values. As shown in Figure 6b.17, you can begin by entering the title "Average Company" in A12. Then move to B12 and indicate the function you want to enter. You then enter @AVG(list), where "list" is a range of cell references including all of the salary offers. Of course, you could simply type in a range reference, but many of the 1-2-3 functions permit you to address the cells by using the arrow keys. For example, if you entered AVG(and began to move the cursor, you would see that a cell reference is added after the left parenthesis. As you move, the cell reference is updated until you enter .. (two periods), indicating that the first part of the range has been established. Then you proceed downward (using the arrow keys) to establish the ending position of the range—B11 for your problem. When you have reached the ending position, conclude the cell function by entering the closing parenthesis. When the RETURN key is pressed, the function is stored in cell B12, and 1-2-3 determines the value of the function and places it in the cell. The result of using the average function is shown in

TABLE 6B.3 Lotus 1-2-3 Functions

Function Name	Meaning and Operation
@ABS(n)	Absolute value, where "n" is a numeric value, a cell reference, or a formula
@ACOS(n)	Arc cosine "n," where "n" is a numeric value, a cell reference, or a formula
@ASIN(n)	Arc sine "n," where "n" is a numeric value, a cell reference, or a formula
@ATAN(n)	Arc tangent "n," where "n" is a numeric value, a cell reference, or a formula (2-quadrant)
@ATAN2(n)	Arc tangent "n," where "n" is a numeric value, a cell reference, or a formula (4-quadrant)
@AVG(list)	Average, where "list" is a series of numeric values, a series of cell references, or a range of cell references
@CHOOSE(n,list)	Selects the "nth" value from a "list" of values, where "n" is a numeric value, a cell reference, or a formula and "list" is a series of numeric values, cell references, or formulas
@COS(n)	Cosine "n," where "n" is a numeric value, a cell reference, or a formula
@COUNT(list)	Counts the number of values in a designated list, where "list" is a series of numeric values, a series of cell references, or a range of cell references
@DATE(value1,value2,value3)	Determines the number of days elapsed since the turn of the century, where "value1" is a year, "value2" is a month, and "value3" is a day
@DAY(value)	Determines day number (1 to 31) based on a "value" representing the number of days elapsed since January 1, A.D. 1
@ERR	Returns the special value "ERR"—error
@EXP(n)	Calculates "e to the nth," where "n" is a power and may be a numeric value, a cell reference, or a formula
@FALSE	Returns the value 0, if "false"
@FV(value1,value2,value3)	Determines the Future Value of an investment, where "value1" represents the payment amount, "value2" represents the interest rate, and "value3" represents the investment period
@HLOOKUP(value,area,number)	Searches a designated "area" composed of rows, columns, or both for the indicated "value," where "value" is a numeric value, a cell reference, or a formula and "number" is the initial row value

Function Name	Meaning and Operation
@IF(logical,value1,value2)	Determines if the "logical" expression is true. If true, "value1" is assigned to the cell. If false, "value2" is assigned to the cell.
@INT(n)	Integer value of "n," where "n" is a numeric value, a cell reference, or a formula
@ISERR(value)	Indicates if indicated value is an error and returns the value 1 if true
@ISNA(value)	Indicates if indicated value is not available and returns the value 1 if true
@IRR(value,list)	Internal Rate of Return for an initial estimated "value" of the rate for the specified "list" of cells, where "list" is a range of cells
@LN(n)	Natural logarithm of "n," where "n" is a numeric value, a cell reference, or a formula
@LOG(n)	Logarithm (base 10) of "n," where "n" is a numeric value, a cell reference, or a formula
@MAX(list)	Maximum value in a "list," where "list" is a series of numeric values or a range of cells
@MIN(list)	Minimum value in a "list," where "list" is a series of numeric values or a range of cells
@MOD(value1,value2)	Returns the remainder when "value1" is divided by "value2," where "value1" and "value2" are numeric values, cell references, or functions
@MONTH(value)	Determines month number (1 to 12) based on a "value" representing the number of days elapsed since January 1, A.D. 1
@NA	Returns the special value "NA"—not available
@NPV(value,list)	Net Present Value of a "list," where "value" is the interest rate and "list" is a series of numeric values, a series of cell references, or a range of cell references
@PI	Returns the mathematical value of "pi"
@PMT(value1,value2,value3)	Determines the amount of a loan Payment, where "value1" represents the principal amount, "value2" represents the interest rate, and "value3" represents the loan period
@PV(value1,value2,value3)	Determines the Present Value of an annuity, where "value1" represents the payment amount, "value2" represents the Interest rate, and "value3" represents the investment period
@RAND	Generates a random number between 0 and 1

TABLE 6B.3 *(continued)*

Function Name	Meaning and Operation
@ROUND(n,digits)	Rounds "n" to a value indicated by "digits," where "n" is a numeric value, a cell reference, or a formula and "digits" is the number of decimal points in the desired result (if positive) or position to the left of the decimal point (if negative)
@SIN(n)	Sine of "n," where "n" is a numeric value, a cell reference, or a formula
@SQRT(n)	Square root of "n," where "n" is a numeric value, a cell reference, or a formula
@STD(list)	Standard Deviation of a "list," where "list" is a series of numeric values, a series of cell references, or a range of cell references
@SUM(list)	Sum (total) of a "list," where "list" is a series of numeric values, a series of cell references, or a range of cell references
@TAN(n)	Tangent of "n," where "n" is a numeric value, a cell reference, or a formula
@TODAY	Determines the number of days elapsed since January 1, A.D. 1
@TRUE	Returns the value 1, if "true"
@VAR(list)	Variance (differences) of a "list," where "list" is a series of numeric values, a series of cell references, or a range of cell references
@VLOOKUP(value,area,number)	Searches a designated "area" composed of rows, columns, or both for the indicated "value," where "value" is a numeric value, a cell reference, or a formula and "number" is the initial column value
@YEAR(value)	Determines year number (0 to 99) based on a "value" representing the number of days elapsed since January 1, A.D. 1

Figure 6b.17. Be careful when specifying the range (for a function in this case and for other commands that use ranges): Make sure the first cell reference is above the last cell reference, if you are copying down a column. If you are copying a row, the beginning position must be to the left of the ending position.

Look at Figure 6b.18. Note that the presentation format of cell B13 has been altered to the Currency form, and the contents of B13 have been copied to the remaining cells in this row. However, this causes a bit of a problem. The averages for "Commuting Distance," "Vacation Days," and "Job Preference"

```
B13: (F2) @AVG(B4..B11)                                           READY

                    A                 B          C          D
1                                1  Salary    Actual    ------------- Benefits
2   Company Name                 2  Offer     Offer     Life
3   ========================== 3  ==================================
4   Johnson Instruments, Inc. 4  $19,000.00 $22,822.00 $135.00
5   Johnson Instruments, Inc. 5  $19,200.00 $23,022.00 $135.00
6   Johnson Instruments, Inc. 6  $19,100.00 $22,922.00 $135.00
7   Matt's Films, Inc.         7  $18,950.00 $24,561.00 $155.00
8   Lewis & Melts Mortgage Co 8  $22,000.00 $27,500.00 $500.00
9   Ethyl & Jung, DDS          9  $20,000.00 $27,275.00 $325.00
10  Hormell Texas Chili Co.   10  $19,300.00 $21,986.20 $164.00
11  Nephi's Hopi Crafts       11  $15,670.00 $17,678.00 $250.00
12                            12  -----------------------------------
13  Average Company           13  19152.50
14                            14
15                            15
16                            16
17                            17
18                            18
19                            19
20                            20
```

FIGURE 6B.17
Creating an "Average Company"—using the AVG function

```
B13: (C2) @AVG(B4..B11)                                           READY

                    A                 B          C          D
1                                1  Salary    Actual    ------------- Benefits
2   Company Name                 2  Offer     Offer     Life
3   ========================== 3  ==================================
4   Johnson Instruments, Inc. 4  $19,000.00 $22,822.00 $135.00
5   Johnson Instruments, Inc. 5  $19,200.00 $23,022.00 $135.00
6   Johnson Instruments, Inc. 6  $19,100.00 $22,922.00 $135.00
7   Matt's Films, Inc.         7  $18,950.00 $24,561.00 $155.00
8   Lewis & Melts Mortgage Co 8  $22,000.00 $27,500.00 $500.00
9   Ethyl & Jung, DDS          9  $20,000.00 $27,275.00 $325.00
10  Hormell Texas Chili Co.   10  $19,300.00 $21,986.20 $164.00
11  Nephi's Hopi Crafts       11  $15,670.00 $17,678.00 $250.00
12                            12  -----------------------------------
13  Average Company           13  $19,152.50 $23,470.78 $224.88
14                            14
15                            15
16                            16
17                            17
18                            18
19                            19
20                            20
```

FIGURE 6B.18
Averages after formatting and copying

are shown in the Currency format, but they are not dollars and cents. Thus, for these cells, it is necessary to re-enter the Format function and change their presentation format code back to the Fixed mode.

New Information on a Job Offer — Adding a New Row

Next, you need to add the new job offer from First State National Bank. Insert a new row at row 11 of your spreadsheet for the new job information. Figure 6b.19 shows the data entered in row 12 for First State National Bank. Note that the formula for "Actual Offer" (and "Vacation Value") has been copied into this row from row 11 and that the format has been set to Currency. Also note that none of the averages have changed and that no message currently exists in the error line area.

Since the new row is outside the range of cells used to calculate the average company values, the numbers you have entered had no effect on the values in row 14. To get the new averages for row 14 that include First State National Bank, you must re-enter the average function and copy it across the entire row, and again change the formats for "Commuting Distance," "Vacation Days," and "Job Preference." When you have finished, your screen should be the same as the one in Figure 6b.20.

Putting Rows in Order — The Sort Function

The last requirement of this problem is to order the job offers by your job preference. The list of companies is adequate, but you will probably want the jobs you prefer (the smaller numbers) at the top of the list. To accomplish this, you can use the Move function to specify the cells you wish to move and then specify the location to which you wish to move them. One word of caution: When you move cells that are used in a mathematical function — in this case, the "Average" function — the cells involved in the calculations may change, giving you incorrect results.

There is an alternative to the Move function, as indicated in Figure 6b.21; you can select the Data function and from this function select the Sort option. When the next menu appears, you should specify both a Data-Range and a Primary-Key before executing the sorting operation. First, the Data-Range is selected, and the range of cells representing the computational area (A4 through J12) is identified. Since you must specify a Data-Range, you can sort only a portion of the spreadsheet; that is, columns can be sorted independently. Second, you must identify the Primary-Key. The Primary-Key consists of the cell values in Column J — the values representing job preference. After the key has been identified, you will be asked to indicate whether you want the order of sorting to be ascending (A). [Select descending (D) for a largest to smallest

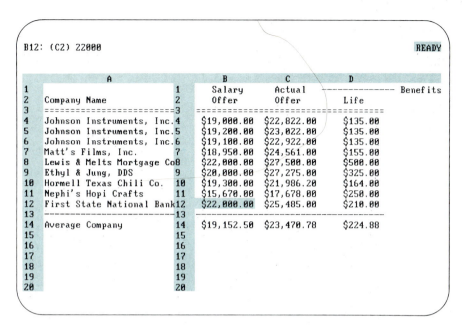

B12: (C2) 22000   READY

	A		B	C	D	
1		1	Salary	Actual	-------------	Benefits
2	Company Name	2	Offer	Offer	Life	
3	=========================	3	===			
4	Johnson Instruments, Inc.	4	$19,000.00	$22,822.00	$135.00	
5	Johnson Instruments, Inc.	5	$19,200.00	$23,022.00	$135.00	
6	Johnson Instruments, Inc.	6	$19,100.00	$22,922.00	$135.00	
7	Matt's Films, Inc.	7	$18,950.00	$24,561.00	$155.00	
8	Lewis & Melts Mortgage Co	8	$22,000.00	$27,500.00	$500.00	
9	Ethyl & Jung, DDS	9	$20,000.00	$27,275.00	$325.00	
10	Hormell Texas Chili Co.	10	$19,300.00	$21,986.20	$164.00	
11	Nephi's Hopi Crafts	11	$15,670.00	$17,678.00	$250.00	
12	First State National Bank	12	$22,000.00	$25,485.00	$210.00	
13	-------------------------	13	---			
14	Average Company	14	$19,152.50	$23,470.78	$224.88	
15		15				
16		16				
17		17				
18		18				
19		19				
20		20				

FIGURE 6B.19

Entering a new row — the values for First State National Bank

B14: (C2) @AVG(B4..B12)   READY

	A		B	C	D	
1		1	Salary	Actual	-------------	Benefits
2	Company Name	2	Offer	Offer	Life	
3	=========================	3	===			
4	Johnson Instruments, Inc.	4	$19,000.00	$22,822.00	$135.00	
5	Johnson Instruments, Inc.	5	$19,200.00	$23,022.00	$135.00	
6	Johnson Instruments, Inc.	6	$19,100.00	$22,922.00	$135.00	
7	Matt's Films, Inc.	7	$18,950.00	$24,561.00	$155.00	
8	Lewis & Melts Mortgage Co	8	$22,000.00	$27,500.00	$500.00	
9	Ethyl & Jung, DDS	9	$20,000.00	$27,275.00	$325.00	
10	Hormell Texas Chili Co.	10	$19,300.00	$21,986.20	$164.00	
11	Nephi's Hopi Crafts	11	$15,670.00	$17,678.00	$250.00	
12	First State National Bank	12	$22,000.00	$25,485.00	$210.00	
13	-------------------------	13	---			
14	Average Company	14	$19,468.89	$23,694.58	$223.22	
15		15				
16		16				
17		17				
18		18				
19		19				
20		20				

FIGURE 6B.20

Correcting the "Average Company" row

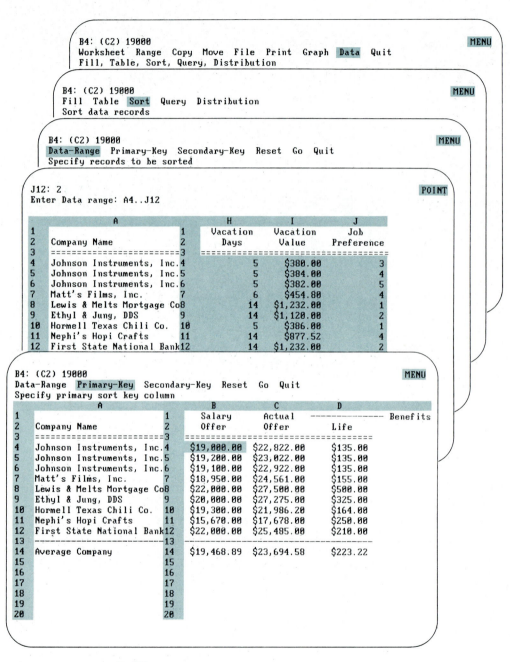

```
B4: (C2) 19000                                                        MENU
Worksheet  Range  Copy  Move  File  Print  Graph  Data  Quit
Fill, Table, Sort, Query, Distribution
```

```
B4: (C2) 19000                                                        MENU
Fill  Table  Sort  Query  Distribution
Sort data records
```

```
B4: (C2) 19000                                                        MENU
Data-Range  Primary-Key  Secondary-Key  Reset  Go  Quit
Specify records to be sorted
```

```
J12: 2                                                               POINT
Enter Data range: A4..J12
```

	A		H Vacation Days	I Vacation Value	J Job Preference
1		1			
2	Company Name	2			
3	=======================	3	=========	=========	=========
4	Johnson Instruments, Inc.	4	5	$380.00	3
5	Johnson Instruments, Inc.	5	5	$384.00	4
6	Johnson Instruments, Inc.	6	5	$382.00	5
7	Matt's Films, Inc.	7	6	$454.80	4
8	Lewis & Melts Mortgage Co	8	14	$1,232.00	1
9	Ethyl & Jung, DDS	9	14	$1,120.00	2
10	Hormell Texas Chili Co.	10	5	$386.00	1
11	Nephi's Hopi Crafts	11	14	$877.52	4
12	First State National Bank	12	14	$1,232.00	2

```
B4: (C2) 19000                                                        MENU
Data-Range  Primary-Key  Secondary-Key  Reset  Go  Quit
Specify primary sort key column
```

	A		B Salary Offer	C Actual Offer	D -------------- Benefits Life
1		1			-------------- Benefits
2	Company Name	2	Salary Offer	Actual Offer	Life
3	=======================	3	=========	=========	=========
4	Johnson Instruments, Inc.	4	$19,000.00	$22,822.00	$135.00
5	Johnson Instruments, Inc.	5	$19,200.00	$23,022.00	$135.00
6	Johnson Instruments, Inc.	6	$19,100.00	$22,922.00	$135.00
7	Matt's Films, Inc.	7	$18,950.00	$24,561.00	$155.00
8	Lewis & Melts Mortgage Co	8	$22,000.00	$27,500.00	$500.00
9	Ethyl & Jung, DDS	9	$20,000.00	$27,275.00	$325.00
10	Hormell Texas Chili Co.	10	$19,300.00	$21,986.20	$164.00
11	Nephi's Hopi Crafts	11	$15,670.00	$17,678.00	$250.00
12	First State National Bank	12	$22,000.00	$25,485.00	$210.00
13	-------------------------	13			
14	Average Company	14	$19,468.89	$23,694.58	$223.22
15		15			
16		16			
17		17			
18		18			
19		19			
20		20			

FIGURE 6B.21
Getting the job preferences in sorted order

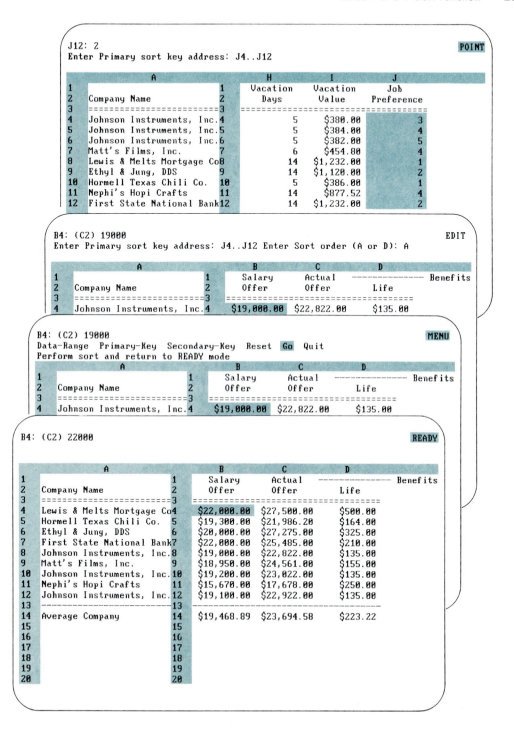

```
J12: 2                                                                  POINT
Enter Primary sort key address: J4..J12

                    A              H          I           J
 1                         1    Vacation   Vacation      Job
 2  Company Name           2      Days       Value    Preference
 3  ======================3    =======================================
 4  Johnson Instruments, Inc.4      5       $380.00         3
 5  Johnson Instruments, Inc.5      5       $384.00         4
 6  Johnson Instruments, Inc.6      5       $382.00         5
 7  Matt's Films, Inc.     7        6       $454.80         4
 8  Lewis & Melts Mortgage Co8     14      $1,232.00        1
 9  Ethyl & Jung, DDS      9       14      $1,120.00        2
10  Hormell Texas Chili Co. 10      5       $386.00         1
11  Nephi's Hopi Crafts    11      14       $877.52         4
12  First State National Bank12    14      $1,232.00        2
```

```
B4: (C2) 19000                                                          EDIT
Enter Primary sort key address: J4..J12 Enter Sort order (A or D): A

                    A                 B          C          D
 1                         1       Salary     Actual    ----------- Benefits
 2  Company Name           2       Offer      Offer        Life
 3  ======================3    =======================================
 4  Johnson Instruments, Inc.4  $19,000.00  $22,822.00   $135.00
```

```
B4: (C2) 19000                                                          MENU
Data-Range  Primary-Key  Secondary-Key  Reset  Go  Quit
Perform sort and return to READY mode

                    A                 B          C          D
 1                         1       Salary     Actual    ----------- Benefits
 2  Company Name           2       Offer      Offer        Life
 3  ======================3    =======================================
 4  Johnson Instruments, Inc.4  $19,000.00  $22,822.00   $135.00
```

```
B4: (C2) 22000                                                          READY

                    A                 B          C          D
 1                         1       Salary     Actual    ----------- Benefits
 2  Company Name           2       Offer      Offer        Life
 3  ======================3    =======================================
 4  Lewis & Melts Mortgage Co4  $22,000.00  $27,500.00   $500.00
 5  Hormell Texas Chili Co.  5  $19,300.00  $21,986.20   $164.00
 6  Ethyl & Jung, DDS      6    $20,000.00  $27,275.00   $325.00
 7  First State National Bank7  $22,000.00  $25,485.00   $210.00
 8  Johnson Instruments, Inc.8  $19,000.00  $22,822.00   $135.00
 9  Matt's Films, Inc.     9    $18,950.00  $24,561.00   $155.00
10  Johnson Instruments, Inc.10 $19,200.00  $23,022.00   $135.00
11  Nephi's Hopi Crafts    11   $15,670.00  $17,678.00   $250.00
12  Johnson Instruments, Inc.12 $19,100.00  $22,922.00   $135.00
13  ---------------------13
14  Average Company        14   $19,468.89  $23,694.58   $223.22
15                         15
16                         16
17                         17
18                         18
19                         19
20                         20
```

order.] Finally, after all of the characteristics of the sorting operation have been specified, the Go option is selected and the operation is executed. The sorted spreadsheet is shown in Figure 6b.21.

Note that the company names are now ordered by job preference. At this point it is probably a good idea to save your work again. However, this time the spreadsheet file JOBS already exists, and you will be asked if you want the new spreadsheet to Replace the old one.

Showing Off Your Spreadsheet — The Print Function

Your spreadsheet is now complete. Perhaps you would like to see the entire spreadsheet in printed form. To print the spreadsheet, select the Print function. This function then produces the Print menu, as shown in Figure 6b.22. Your choices are to send the spreadsheet to the Printer or send the spreadsheet to a print File. The next menu provides output controls. First, specify the portion of the spreadsheet to be printed by using the Range option and indicating the range of cells. Next, select the Options from the menu. As a result of entering the Go mode, the contents of the spreadsheet are printed, as illustrated by Figure 6b.23.

Getting Out of Lotus — The Quit Function

When your spreadsheet work has been completed, terminate 1-2-3 by using the Quit function and return to the Lotus Access System menu. From there, you may decide to select another Lotus function or return to the operating system. When you select the Quit function, you will be asked if you are sure that you want to exit 1-2-3. Remember to save your spreadsheet now if you plan to use it later — this is your last chance before you leave 1-2-3. Once you exit from 1-2-3, you will again see the initial menu, and you will be able to select the Exit function. Finally, you will be asked to confirm an exit to the operating system. If you indicate "Yes" to this question, the next set of symbols to appear on the screen will be produced by the operating system. You are now successfully out of Lotus.

Other Features of Lotus 1-2-3

Lotus is an integrated package and so includes a number of features that are not covered in this module. Additional presentations on Lotus are found in Modules 7b, 8b, and 10b. However, there are some other features of 1-2-3 that need to be mentioned here. The first of these is selected through the Status option, Worksheet function. This option permits you to examine some default characteristics that help control the way 1-2-3 operates. One of the features

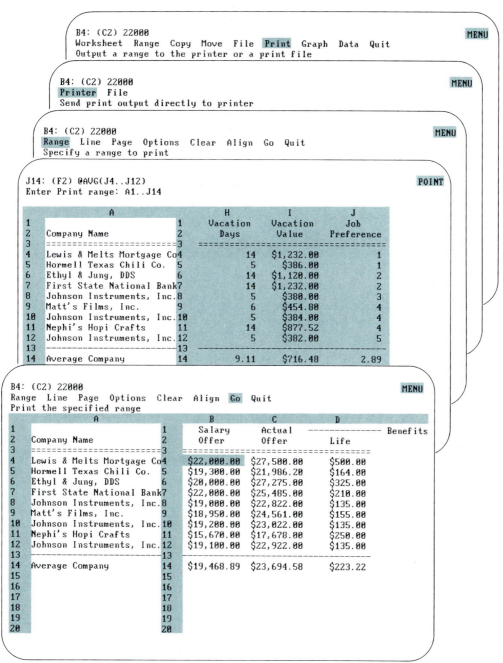

B4: (C2) 22000
Worksheet Range Copy Move File **Print** Graph Data Quit
Output a range to the printer or a print file   MENU

B4: (C2) 22000
Printer File   MENU
Send print output directly to printer

B4: (C2) 22000
Range Line Page Options Clear Align Go Quit   MENU
Specify a range to print

J14: (F2) @AVG(J4..J12)   POINT
Enter Print range: A1..J14

	A		H	I	J
1		1	Vacation	Vacation	Job
2	Company Name	2	Days	Value	Preference
3	======================	3	============	============	============
4	Lewis & Melts Mortgage Co	4	14	$1,232.00	1
5	Hormell Texas Chili Co.	5	5	$386.00	1
6	Ethyl & Jung, DDS	6	14	$1,120.00	2
7	First State National Bank	7	14	$1,232.00	2
8	Johnson Instruments, Inc.	8	5	$380.00	3
9	Matt's Films, Inc.	9	6	$454.80	4
10	Johnson Instruments, Inc.	10	5	$384.00	4
11	Nephi's Hopi Crafts	11	14	$877.52	4
12	Johnson Instruments, Inc.	12	5	$382.00	5
13	----------------------	13			
14	Average Company	14	9.11	$716.48	2.89

B4: (C2) 22000
Range Line Page Options Clear Align **Go** Quit   MENU
Print the specified range

	A		B	C	D	
1		1	Salary	Actual	------------- Benefits
2	Company Name	2	Offer	Offer	Life
3	======================	3	============	============	============
4	Lewis & Melts Mortgage Co	4	$22,000.00	$27,500.00	$500.00
5	Hormell Texas Chili Co.	5	$19,300.00	$21,986.20	$164.00
6	Ethyl & Jung, DDS	6	$20,000.00	$27,275.00	$325.00
7	First State National Bank	7	$22,000.00	$25,485.00	$210.00
8	Johnson Instruments, Inc.	8	$19,000.00	$22,822.00	$135.00
9	Matt's Films, Inc.	9	$18,950.00	$24,561.00	$155.00
10	Johnson Instruments, Inc.	10	$19,200.00	$23,022.00	$135.00
11	Nephi's Hopi Crafts	11	$15,670.00	$17,678.00	$250.00
12	Johnson Instruments, Inc.	12	$19,100.00	$22,922.00	$135.00
13	----------------------	13			
14	Average Company	14	$19,468.89	$23,694.58	$223.22
15		15			
16		16			
17		17			
18		18			
19		19			
20		20			

FIGURE 6B.22
Controlling the printed output

Company Name	Salary Offer	Actual Offer	Life
Lewis & Melts Mortgage Co	$22,000.00	$27,500.00	$500.00
Hormell Texas Chili Co.	$19,300.00	$21,986.20	$164.00
Ethyl & Jung, DDS	$20,000.00	$27,275.00	$325.00
First State National Bank	$22,000.00	$25,485.00	$210.00
Johnson Instruments, Inc.	$19,000.00	$22,822.00	$135.00
Matt's Films, Inc.	$18,950.00	$24,561.00	$155.00
Johnson Instruments, Inc.	$19,200.00	$23,022.00	$135.00
Nephi's Hopi Crafts	$15,670.00	$17,678.00	$250.00
Johnson Instruments, Inc.	$19,100.00	$22,922.00	$135.00
Average Company	$19,468.89	$23,694.58	$223.22

Benefits Health	Retirement	Commuting Distance	Vacation Days	Vacation Value	Job Preference
$600.00	$4,400.00	35	14	$1,232.00	1
$320.00	$2,202.20	53	5	$386.00	1
$950.00	$6,000.00	95	14	$1,120.00	2
$325.00	$2,950.00	25	14	$1,232.00	2
$354.00	$3,333.00	45	5	$380.00	3
$456.00	$5,000.00	33	6	$454.80	4
$354.00	$3,333.00	35	5	$384.00	4
$425.00	$1,333.00	47	14	$877.52	4
$354.00	$3,333.00	25	5	$382.00	5
$459.78	$3,542.69	43.67	9.11	$716.48	2.89

FIGURE 6B.23
A printed report from the job offers spreadsheet

shown through the Status option is the Recalculation mode. When you begin working on a large spreadsheet, it is often desirable to have the Recalculation mode turned "off" so that individual cell entries can be made more quickly. You can change the Recalculation mode through the Global option of the Worksheet function. You can, of course, have the Recalculation performed anytime by pressing the F9 key. The default Recalculation sequence is "Natural" (it first evaluates cells that contain formulas and functions from which other cells derive their values), although this may be changed to sequences (such as Columnwise, Rowwise, or Manual).

Other character default characteristics of the worksheet that are presented through the Status menu are values of General cell format, label entries prefixed by an apostrophe ('), cell width of 9 characters, and Protection mode "off." These features may be changed to new values, most by using the Global option of the Worksheet function. Finally, the Status menu indicates the amount of available memory for your spreadsheet. This is one way to determine how much work space you have left.

Another handy feature of 1-2-3 is available through the Name option of the Range function. Suppose you have a series of cells that are frequently used as a group. This could be a row, a column, several rows, or several columns. If you select the Name option, you are permitted to refer to this group of cells by a *range name*. For example, the Name function can be used to name the column of values representing the "Salary Offer" as "Salary." "Salary" could now be used to reference this group of cells for the purposes of computation. To establish the average salary offered, it would be possible to use the function @AVG(Salary). The range name itself must be a continuous string of characters, without blanks or hyphens. However, the underline character may be used in place of blanks or hyphens. Also remember that the F3 key can be used to provide a list of the range names for your spreadsheet.

These are but a few of the additional capabilities of 1-2-3. As you explore this package more fully, you will become familiar with still other features, such as macros, that you can develop and use to assist you in solving particular types of problems or reducing the time it takes to create a spreadsheet. As you encounter unfamiliar features of the package, remember that the Help function (F1) provides explanations of how they work.

Multiplan

Learning to Use Multiplan

Multiplan is a recently developed spreadsheet package designed to overcome some of the shortcomings of earlier spreadsheet packages by providing additional capabilities. Thus, although Multiplan does not possess the extended capabilities of still other packages developed since its realease, it remains one of the easiest packages to learn and use.

When you begin to use Multiplan, start by booting the operating system. If you are using a computer with two disk drives, place a disk that has been prepared to hold your data in drive B. Once the operating system has been loaded, all that is required is to place the Multiplan disk in drive A and type MP. Press the RETURN key, and you will be greeted by the Multiplan log-on message, as shown in Figure 6c.1. Note that the version number is shown here (1.20), so if you need to know the version of Multiplan you are using, you can find out from this screen.

The Arrangement — What a Multiplan Spreadsheet Looks Like

After the log-on message disappears, you will see an empty spreadsheet, as shown in Figure 6c.2. Whether you have previously built and saved other spreadsheets or not, this is always the starting point. The initial screen is divided into two basic areas. The top of the screen represents the spreadsheet work space and is divided into rows and columns, whereas the bottom is the command area, which shows a command menu and current status information. Depending on which operations you perform, the appearance of each of these parts of the screen is subject to change.

The work space portion of the spreadsheet designates both rows and columns by number (1, 2, 3, and so on across the top of the screen represent the column numbers; 1, 2, 3, and so forth down the left side of the screen represent row numbers). A Multiplan spreadsheet is capable of handling up to 255 rows and 63 columns. The initial (default) width of each cell is 10 characters, but a cell can be modified to be as narrow as 3 characters or as wide as 32 characters. The width of a column may be narrower or wider than the data placed in that

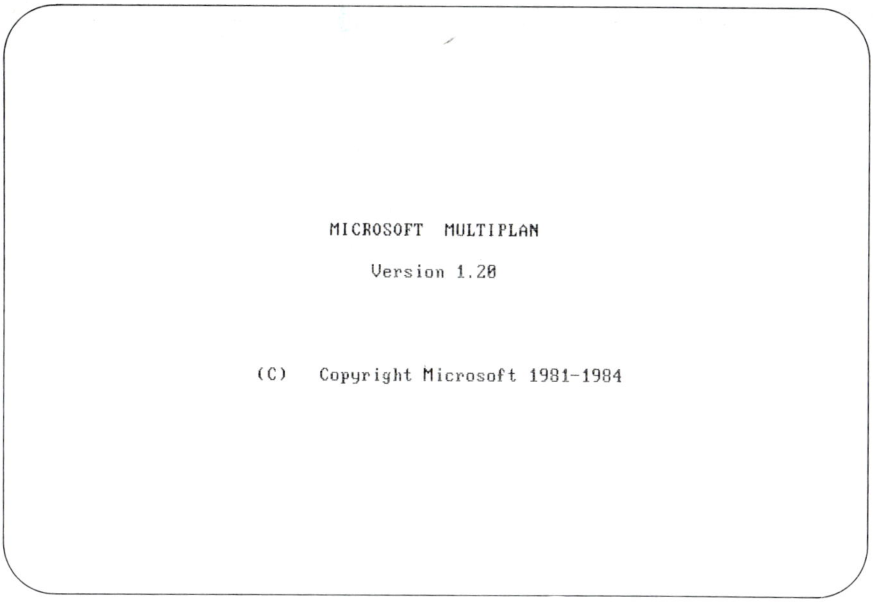

```
            MICROSOFT  MULTIPLAN
              Version 1.20



   (C)   Copyright Microsoft 1981-1984
```

FIGURE 6c.1
Multiplan log-on message

column. Thus, the width of each column can be expanded or contracted independently of the others without loss of data to provide the clearest picture of what is in the spreadsheet.

The Multiplan command menu takes up a major part of the command area. The menu consists of

```
Alpha Blank Copy Delete Edit Format Goto Help Insert Lock Move

Name Options Print Quit Sort Transfer Value Window Xternal
```

These are the functions that Multiplan can perform. A brief description of each of these functions is presented in Table 6c.1. The function to be used will be highlighted, as shown in Figure 6c.2. Many of the functions, when selected, will provide additional menus that more fully describe the operation to be performed. A function is selected by either pressing the first letter of the function (for example, "F" for the Format function) or pressing the TAB key, which causes the highlighted area to move from one function to the next. If you continue to press the TAB key when Xternal is reached, the highlighted area will return to the Alpha function, and you can restart the selection process.

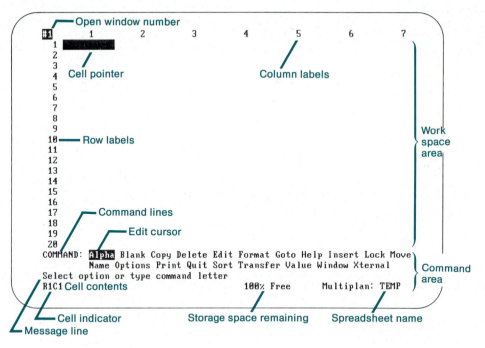

FIGURE 6C.2
The Multiplan screen layout

Getting from Here to There — Cursor Movement and the Goto Function

The initial cell reference for an empty spreadsheet is "R1C1"—row 1 and column 1. However, as you build your spreadsheet, you will want to reference other cells. As you move from place to place in the spreadsheet, the highlighted area also moves, and the current cell marker of the command portion of the screen is updated.

The simplest way of moving from one cell to another is by using the cursor movement or arrow keys. If using the arrow keys is not quick enough, you can traverse the spreadsheet more rapidly if you press the ALTernate key and a cursor-movement key at the same time. If you press the ALTernate key and the right-arrow key together, the entire screen scrolls to reveal the next full set of columns to the right of the current screen. Therefore, if the last column identified on the current screen is column 7, the first column on the next screen presentation will be column 8. Similar operations are done by using the left-, up-, and down-arrow keys.

Suppose you are at the bottom-right corner of a spreadsheet and you want to get back to R1C1. Just press the HOME key. Regardless of where you are on the spreadsheet, you will go to R1C1. On those keyboards equipped with

TABLE 6C.1 General Multiplan Commands

Function	Operation
Alpha	Enters a series of characters into a cell that is not to be used for computation
Blank	Erases the current contents of a cell
Copy	Reproduces the contents of one or more cells into another area of the spreadsheet
Delete	Removes a row or a column
Edit	Modifies the current contents of a cell without completely re-entering it
Format	Modifies the appearance of a cell or a series of cells
Goto	Locates and references a particular cell in another part of the spreadsheet
Help	Provides additional information about a particular topic
Insert	Adds a new row or column within the currently used spreadsheet area
Lock	Retains the current cell or cells with their present contents regardless of other changes that may affect surrounding parts of the spreadsheet
Move	Reproduces the contents of one or more cells into another area of the spreadsheet and removes the original cell or cells
Name	Provides a label for a cell or a group of cells that may be referenced by that label
Options	Modifies the characteristics that control how the spreadsheet operates (for example, recalculation)
Print	Transmits the contents of the spreadsheet to an output device (for example, a printer)
Quit	Terminates the Multiplan session
Sort	Reorders the contents of a spreadsheet into a specified sequence
Transfer	Performs file operations (for example, loading and saving spreadsheets)
Value	Enters a series of characters into a cell that are numeric or that are to produce a numeric value that can be used for computation
Window	Splits the spreadsheet into multiple parts for the purposes of viewing the spreadsheet
Xternal	Performs functions related to the operating system or operations on spreadsheets that are not currently active

function keys, the F9 key permits you to address the last cell of the active spreadsheet — the lower-right corner. If you want to reference a particular cell other than R1C1, you may want to use the Goto function. Select this function from the command menu by pressing the letter G or by using the TAB key to move the highlighted area of the command menu to the Goto function and then pressing the RETURN key.

Trying to Remember — The Help Function

There are two ways to use the Help function. The first way is probably already obvious. You can select the Help function from the command menu by pressing the letter H or using the TAB key to reference the Help function. This could be called a *general* approach to using the Help function. From this point, you may select the Resume, Start, Next, or Previous options. This list of choices will appear on each screen. The Resume option returns you to your spreadsheet at exactly the position you left it. The Start option allows you to return to the beginning of the Help information. The Next option allows you to see the next screen of help information. The last option, Previous, allows you to go backward through the help material. Other choices will also be shown, depending on where you are currently located within the help file.

The second way to use the Help function provides specific information about a particular command or function. Instead of using the Help function directly, you use the ? symbol (or, alternatively, the F10 key, if your keyboard is so equipped). At any time, whether you are currently using the command menu or a lower-level menu, you can press the ? key and retrieve information about that specific topic or operation.

Solving the Job Hunting Problem

The remaining sections of this module are devoted to solving the job hunting problem. You may want to refer to the problem statement in the Introduction to Spreadsheet Modules before you continue. Also, remember that the data used in this problem can be found in Appendix A.

What's in a Name? — Entering Headings and Titles

Now you are ready to put the job offer data into the spreadsheet, starting with the column headings. Look at Figure 6c.3. Enter the contents of cell R2C1 by first pressing the down-arrow key so that cell R2C1 is the current active cell. Next, select Alpha (see Table 6c.1) from the command menu and enter the text to appear in the current cell. (Be careful: You must first select a function and then enter the text associated with that function.) Note that the text you supply may actually be longer (wider) than the current cell width. However, the complete length of the text is retained by Multiplan even though you may not be able to see all of it on the spreadsheet. When numeric values are too long for the cell, the cell is filled with the # symbol.

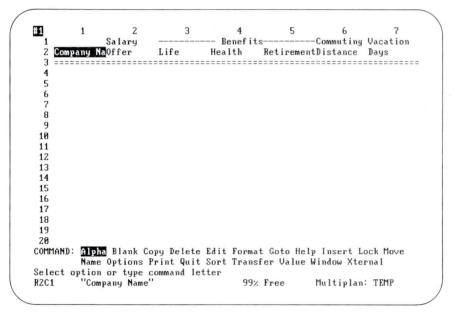

FIGURE 6C.3
Column headings for the job offers problem

After you enter the text "Company Name," you may want to press the RETURN key; however, this action will return you to the command menu, and you will have to move to the next cell (perhaps R2C2) and re-enter the Alpha function. Entering text in this manner will take a while to complete. Instead, you can move the cursor without pressing the RETURN key. Multiplan assumes that as soon as you move from the current cell, you want the previously entered text stored in that cell. Thus, by pressing a cursor-movement key, not only do you store the contents of the previous cell and move to another cell, but you also stay within the Alpha function—the command line will be modified from ALPHA: to ALPHA/VALUE:. This means that either alphabetic data or numeric data can be entered at this time. Multiplan assumes that if the first character is alphabetic, you want to enter text. If the first character is a digit or an arithmetic operation, you want to enter a numeric value, formula, or function. An examination of Figure 6c.3 reveals that some of the cells begin with what would normally be considered a numeric value or an arithmetic operation (for example, - in cell R1C3 or = in cell R3C1). If you want to enter digits or arithmetic operation symbols and have them treated as text, you should begin the character string with an apostrophe ('), which indicates that the following characters are to be treated as Alpha (text) characters.

Too Large or Too Small? — Changing Column Widths

Now that you have entered the column headings for the job offers problem, it is obvious that the spreadsheet's appearance could be improved. You ought at least to increase the size of the "Company Name" column. After all, the company names that will be entered later will be longer than 10 characters. You should plan to make the width of a column at least as long as the longest piece of data you want to see in that column, although you may change the column width any time you feel it is necessary.

Look at Figure 6c.4. Note that the command menu shows that you have selected the Format function, and you are currently referencing the column containing the "Company Name" heading. By selecting the Width option, the command screen will change, and you will be permitted to specify the number of character positions to be reserved for this column. In this illustration, you want to increase the width of column 1 to 25 characters. If you enter "d," the column width will return to the default setting of 10 characters.

Although many of the columns that currently appear on the spreadsheet are wide enough to contain the data you plan to place in them, you may decide to make them still wider so that visible breaks exist between the columns after the data has been entered. Figure 6c.5 shows columns 2 through 10 at the desired width — 12 characters. Thus, you may change the column width of a single column or a range of columns with the Width option of the Format function.

Creating a New Look — Formatting Cells for Text

You may have noticed that all of the text you have supplied in Figure 6c.5 occupies the left-most portion of each of the cells; that is, it is left-justified. This is satisfactory, but it might be more visually appealing if you adjusted the column headings so they are centered within the 12-character column width. Again, re-enter the Format function, but this time select the Cells option. This selection produces the Format cells menu from which you can select the cells to be altered, the desired alignment (positioning), the format code (type of presentation), and the number of decimal places.

To center the column heading "Salary Offer," first press the TAB key to move from the "cells" reference area to the "alignment" area. Within the alignment (or format code) area, you can move from one option to another by pressing the SPACE BAR or by pressing the first letter of the option. The current or selected option within the alignment (or format code) area is shown in parentheses after you move to another area. After the option has been selected, the next area is addressed by pressing the TAB key. When all selections have been made, the function is performed by pressing the RETURN key. Note that only "Salary" has been centered. Of course, you could repeat this function for each cell by moving to that cell and centering its contents; how-

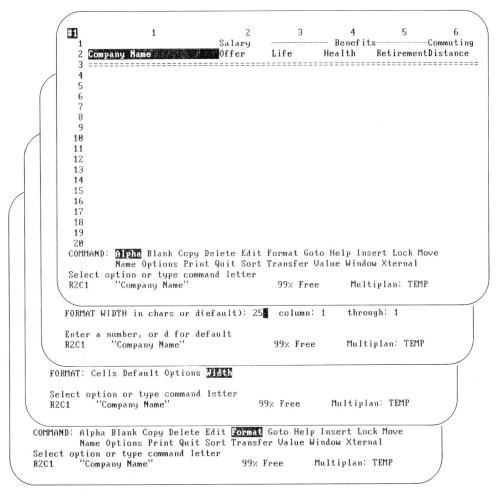

FIGURE 6C.4
Changing the width of one column

ever, a quicker way to do this is to re-enter the Format function for formatting cells but specify a range of cells to be centered, instead of a single cell. First, check the command menu: the current cell reference (R1C2) will be indicated. Then press the colon (:) key and indicate the range of cells to be affected by the operation. The last heading you want to center is located at row 2 and column 8 (R2C8). Multiplan assumes that the range reference includes all cells within the rectangle that begins at R1C2 and ends at R2C8—about 14 cells in all. Thus, after the cell-range reference has been completed, all that is necessary is to press the RETURN key for the function to take place, as shown in Figure 6c.6.

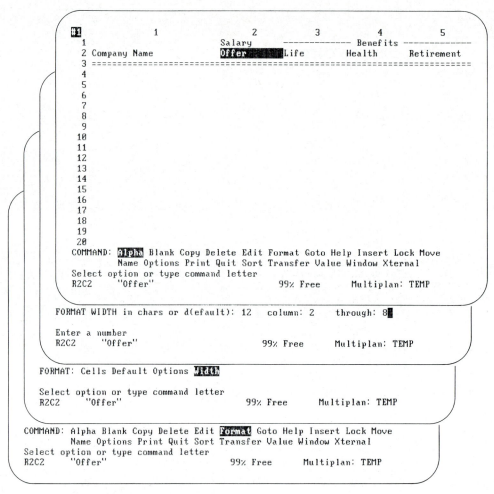

FIGURE 6C.5

Changing the width of all the columns

A View with Numbers—Formatting Cells for Numeric Values

Now that you have had a chance to see how cells can be manipulated when they contain text, it is time to learn how to work with numbers. The data to be recorded under the "Company Name" heading (see Figure 6c.7) could easily be entered in the default mode—the company names are text and could

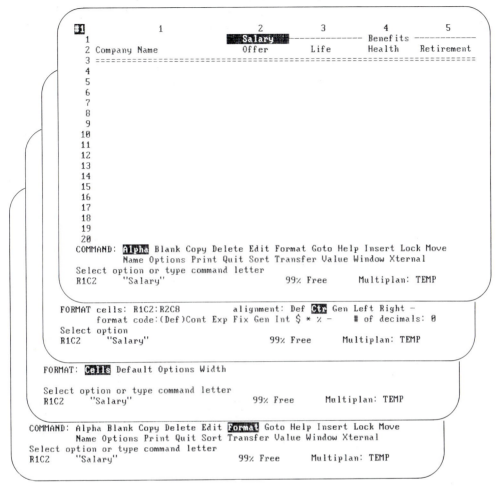

FIGURE 6c.6
Centering the column headings

remain left justified. However, many of the other columns need some special treatment. For example, you expect the values to be placed under the "Salary Offer" heading to represent dollars and cents—so this column's format needs to be changed. The command screen portion of Figure 6c.7 indicates that cell R4C2 is currently being referenced—the location of the first salary amount. The default alignment (right-justified for numeric values) is satisfactory, but,

```
#1              1              2         3 ------------ Benefits ------------ 5
1                                      Salary    ------------
2 Company Name                         Offer     Life    Health    Retirement
3 =========================================================================
4                                   ████████████
5
6
7
8
9
10
11
12
13
14
15
16
17
18
19
20
COMMAND: Alpha Blank Copy Delete Edit Format Goto Help Insert Lock Move
         Name Options Print Quit Sort Transfer Value Window Xternal
Select option or type command letter
R4C2                                    99% Free        Multiplan: TEMP
```

```
COPY RIGHT number of cells: 3█     starting at: R4C2

Enter a number
R4C2                                 99% Free      Multiplan: TEMP
```

```
COPY: Right Down From

Select option or type command letter
R4C2                                 99% Free      Multiplan: TEMP
```

```
COMMAND: Alpha Blank Copy Delete Edit Format Goto Help Insert Lock Move
         Name Options Print Quit Sort Transfer Value Window Xternal
Select option or type command letter
R4C2                               99% Free       Multiplan: TEMP
```

```
FORMAT cells: R4C2            alignment:(Def)Ctr Gen Left Right -
         format code: Def Cont Exp Fix Gen Int($)* % -    # of decimals: 2
Enter a number
R4C2                           99% Free       Multiplan: TEMP
```

```
FORMAT: Cells Default Options Width

Select option or type command letter
R4C2                            99% Free       Multiplan: TEMP
```

```
COMMAND: Alpha Blank Copy Delete Edit Format Goto Help Insert Lock Move
         Name Options Print Quit Sort Transfer Value Window Xternal
Select option or type command letter
R4C2                            99% Free       Multiplan: TEMP
```

FIGURE 6C.7
**Selecting the currency presentation
format—it makes cents**

for dollars and cents, you must change the format code (by using the SPACE BAR) to a "$" format with 2 decimal places. After this has been done, any value placed into this cell will be displayed in a dollars and cents format.

Using It Again — The Copy Function

Now that cell R4C2 has an established format, you can replicate (copy) the contents of that cell and its format into other cells. In Figure 6c.7, the Copy function is used to copy the cell contents and format of R4C2 into other cells of the spreadsheet. The first command menu of the Copy function asks you in which direction (either Right or Down) you want the contents of the current cell copied or if you want the contents copied From a cell other than the current cell. In the first pass through this menu, Right is indicated, which brings you to the next menu. You are then asked to indicate the number of cells to the right that are to contain the current cell contents and format of R4C2. In the illustration, 3 is selected — the next three cells, including the "Retirement" column. The Copy function is then repeated, and the Down option is selected. (The Right option copies from column to column; Down copies from row to row.) After the format has been copied down 7 rows, all rows between and including row 4 to row 11 will be formatted for dollars and cents for column 2. The Copy function then has to be repeated for each of the remaining columns that will display values in a dollars and cents format (columns 3, 4, and 5). Of course, you could have done all this simply with the Format cells option by specifying R4C2:R11C5 — a range of cells — when cell R4C2 was formatted!

Entering the Company Names — Another Example of Entering Text

Now that all the column headings have been established and all the numeric cells are in an appropriate format, it is time to begin to enter the data associated with each of the companies in the job offers spreadsheet. The first company is "Johnson Instruments Inc.," which should be entered in row 4 column 1. (Remember that you have to select the Alpha function first and then enter the text.) After this company name has been entered, you may decide it is easier to enter all the company names first and enter the numeric values associated with each company later. If this is the case, simply press the down-arrow key, and you will be able to enter a company name in each row of the first column without re-entering the Alpha function. The result of this activity is shown in Figure 6c.8.

Two Views of the Spreadsheet — Using the Window Function

Now that you have entered all of the company names, it is time to enter the numeric values associated with them. However, before you proceed, stop for a

FIGURE 6C.8
Entering the company names

moment and think about how you might enter these numbers. If you decide to enter the values a row at a time, the spreadsheet will scroll to the left when you reach the right edge of the screen. When this happens, the company name will no longer be visible. To avoid confusion and the possible incorrect placement of numbers in the spreadsheet (associating values with the wrong company name), it is desirable to have the company name on the screen during the data entry process. This is exactly what spreadsheet windows are designed to support.

In Figure 6c.9, the Window function has been selected, and the first command menu is presented. At this point, you can indicate that you want to Split the screen into an additional part, put a Border around the currently active window, Close an open window, or Link two existing windows so that they scroll together. For our problem, you want to Split the current screen into two windows — one containing the company names and another containing all other values. Note that the current cell indicates a position in column 2. After you indicate that the screen should be split, you will be asked if the screen is to be split on a Horizontal (left-to-right) or Vertical (up-and-down) basis or if you want only Titles (for example, headings) to be split. For this problem, you want to split the screen vertically at column 2. This means that all columns to the left of column 2 — that is, the company names — will be in one window, and all

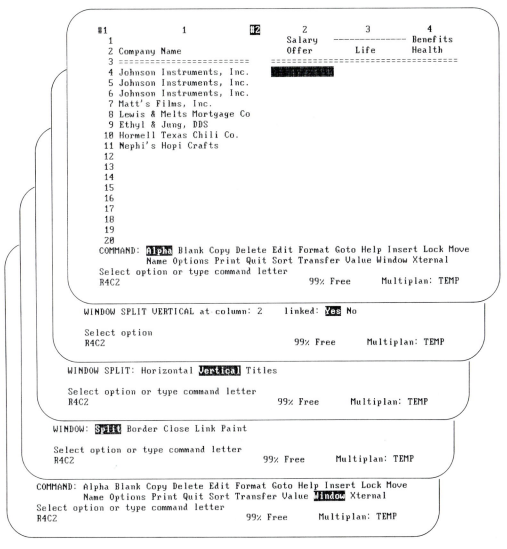

FIGURE 6C.9
Creating a vertical window

columns to the right (including column 2) will be in another window. Finally, indicate that the windows should be Linked—the windows are to move (up and down) together. (Otherwise, each window would move independently of the other.)

Figure 6c.9 shows how the screen looks after you have split it into two windows. Note that a visual break now exists between the "Company Name"

```
#1            1           #2      2         3         4
 1                                Salary    ---------  Benefits
 2 Company Name                   Offer     Life      Health
 3 =========================      ============================
 4 Johnson Instruments, Inc.      $19000.00 $135.00   $354.00
 5 Johnson Instruments, Inc.      $19200.00 $135.00   $354.00
 6 Johnson Instruments, Inc.      $19100.00 $135.00   $354.00
 7 Matt's Films, Inc.             $18950.00 $155.00   $456.00
 8 Lewis & Melts Mortgage Co      $22000.00 $500.00   $600.00
 9 Ethyl & Jung, DDS              $20000.00 $325.00   $950.00
10 Hormell Texas Chili Co.        $19300.00 $164.00   $320.00
11 Nephi's Hopi Crafts            $15670.00 $250.00   $425.00
12                                ███████████
13
14
15
16
17
18
19
20
ALPHA/VALUE: █

Enter text or value
R12C2                            99% Free     Multiplan: TEMP
```

FIGURE 6c.10
Entering the job offer data

and "Salary Offer" headings, and the designation "#2" appears in the gap. Furthermore, the "#2" is highlighted. This indicates that the currently active window is the "#2" window.

If you find that you need to move between windows, arrow keys won't help you. To move between windows (for example, from 2 to 1 or vice versa), you can either use the Goto function, previously used to move between single cells, or simply press the semicolon (;) key.

What Is Your Offer? — Placing Numeric Values in the Spreadsheet

Now it is time to place numeric values in the spreadsheet. The process is somewhat easier than entering text values. When you are at the command menu screen and you press a numeric digit or arithmetic operator (for example, + or −), Multiplan assumes that you wish to enter a numeric value. Thus, as in Figure 6c.10, as soon as you press the 1 (in 19200) on the keyboard, VALUE appears in the command menu area.

As you leave column 2 and proceed across row 4, entering the values under each column heading, the values in columns 2 through 5 are automatically converted to a dollars and cents format (for example, 19200 becomes

$19200.00). As you enter the value under the "Retirement" heading and proceed to the right, note that although the screen scrolls to the left, the company names still appear in window #1. Finally, note that the values under "Commuting Distance," "Vacation Days," and "Job Preference" appear as single digits (default format) rather than in a dollars and cents format. (You stopped formatting columns of values using the dollars and cents format with the "Retirement" column.) Even though you are now far to the right of column 1, the company names are still visible on the screen.

You have entered the first row of numeric values; now repeat this activity until all the job offer data has been placed in the spreadsheet. Rather than moving back to column 2 one cell at a time, you can return rapidly by using the HOME key or the ALTernate and left-arrow keys.

Holding On to What You've Got — Saving the Spreadsheet

Although you will want to perform other operations on this spreadsheet, it is time to save the work you have done up to now. To save a spreadsheet, enter the Transfer function. As shown in Figure 6c.11, the Transfer function permits you to Load (retrieve) a saved spreadsheet, Save a spreadsheet (record a copy on a disk), Clear (erase) the current spreadsheet in internal storage, Delete an existing spreadsheet on a disk, indicate Options (how the spreadsheet should be loaded or saved), and Rename an existing spreadsheet on a disk.

Because you want to save your spreadsheet, select the Save option. Multiplan will then ask for a file name by which the spreadsheet will be saved on the disk. The file name must be a "legal" file name for the operating system in use. Hereafter, your spreadsheet will be called "JOBS," and it will be on disk drive B. When the spreadsheet is saved, not only are the individual cells saved, but your current cell position and windows are saved as well. Thus, if you were to exit Multiplan at this point and later retrieve the B:JOBS spreadsheet, when the first screen appeared, R12C2 would be the current cell, and it would appear in window #2. This process allows you to begin again at some later point at exactly the position in which you last saved the spreadsheet. Also note that the file name at the bottom of the screen changes from TEMP to B:JOBS.

A Spreadsheet with Room to Grow — The Insert Function

It is often difficult, if not impossible, to predict the exact layout of a spreadsheet when you begin. Such is the case with the JOBS spreadsheet. Now you need a new column between "Vacation Days" and "Job Preference" in which to place an estimated value of your vacation time. Begin by moving the current cell pointer to the location on the spreadsheet where the new column is to appear. Then select the Insert function. Note that the Insert function allows you to insert either a Row or a Column. You currently need a column, so select

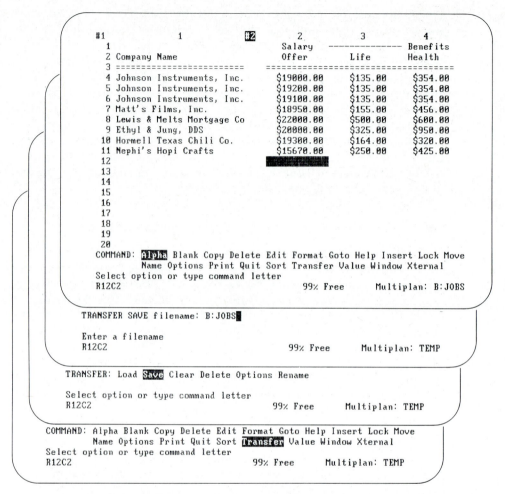

```
#1                 1            #2        2          3          4
 1                                     Salary    ------------ Benefits
 2  Company Name                       Offer       Life      Health
 3  =========================          ========================================
 4  Johnson Instruments, Inc.          $19000.00  $135.00   $354.00
 5  Johnson Instruments, Inc.          $19200.00  $135.00   $354.00
 6  Johnson Instruments, Inc.          $19100.00  $135.00   $354.00
 7  Matt's Films, Inc.                 $18950.00  $155.00   $456.00
 8  Lewis & Melts Mortgage Co          $22000.00  $500.00   $600.00
 9  Ethyl & Jung, DDS                  $20000.00  $325.00   $950.00
10  Hormell Texas Chili Co.            $19300.00  $164.00   $320.00
11  Nephi's Hopi Crafts                $15670.00  $250.00   $425.00
12
13
14
15
16
17
18
19
20
COMMAND: Alpha Blank Copy Delete Edit Format Goto Help Insert Lock Move
         Name Options Print Quit Sort Transfer Value Window Xternal
Select option or type command letter
R12C2                                  99% Free      Multiplan: B:JOBS
```

```
TRANSFER SAVE filename: B:JOBS

  Enter a filename
R12C2                                  99% Free      Multiplan: TEMP
```

```
TRANSFER: Load Save Clear Delete Options Rename

Select option or type command letter
R12C2                                  99% Free      Multiplan: TEMP
```

```
COMMAND: Alpha Blank Copy Delete Edit Format Goto Help Insert Lock Move
         Name Options Print Quit Sort Transfer Value Window Xternal
Select option or type command letter
R12C2                                  99% Free      Multiplan: TEMP
```

FIGURE 6c.11
Saving the spreadsheet

this option by pressing C. Then you will be presented with a command menu that controls the insertion process. From this menu, indicate how many columns are to be inserted (# of columns), where the insertion is to begin (before which column) if other than at the current cell position, and how many rows are to be added. The result of the column-insertion operation is shown in Figure 6c.12. Note that a completely new column has been added, and all columns that previously followed column 8 have been shifted to the right, in terms of both position and column number.

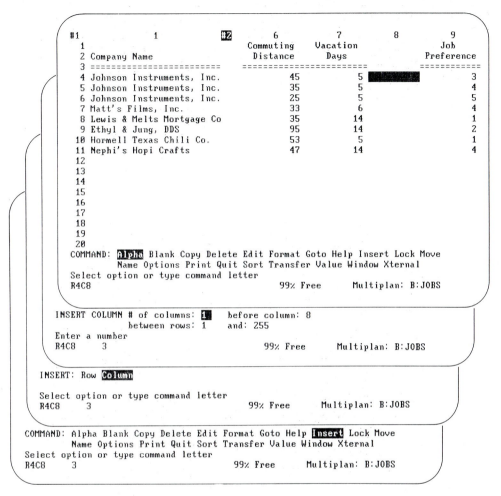

FIGURE 6C.12
Inserting a new column

Figure It This Way — Using a Formula

You intend column 8 to hold approximate values of vacation time. You have
determined that on the average you would work approximately 250 days in a
calendar year (365 days less weekends and holidays). Thus, the "Salary Offer"
of each company can be established on a per-day basis (salary divided by 250).
Since vacation time is stated in terms of number of days, you could then
determine the "Vacation Value" for each company.

```
#1              1           #2      6          7           8           9
 1                               Commuting   Vacation    Vacation      Job
 2  Company Name                 Distance      Days        Value    Preference
 3  =========================    ================================================
 4  Johnson Instruments, Inc.       45          5       $380.00        3
 5  Johnson Instruments, Inc.       35          5                      4
 6  Johnson Instruments, Inc.       25          5                      5
 7  Matt's Films, Inc.              33          6                      4
 8  Lewis & Melts Mortgage Co       35         14                      1
 9  Ethyl & Jung, DDS               95         14                      2
10  Hormell Texas Chili Co.         53          5                      1
11  Nephi's Hopi Crafts             47         14                      4
12
13
14
15
16
17
18
19
20
COMMAND: Alpha Blank Copy Delete Edit Format Goto Help Insert Lock Move
         Name Options Print Quit Sort Transfer Value Window Xternal
Select option or type command letter
R4C8     +RC[-6]/250*RC[-1]           99% Free        Multiplan: B:JOBS
```

FIGURE 6C.13
Entering the formula for "Vacation Value"

To enter a formula (in this case, salary divided by 250) into a cell, you must use the Value function. (A formula will ultimately result in a numeric value.) Of course, you could press V to enter this function, but it is usually easier to indicate that you want to work with a numeric value by entering "+" first, to which Multiplan responds with the VALUE prompt. (Multiplan will not know what to do with "R"—a row reference—if it is the first character in the formula.)

Enter the formula +RC[−6] / 250 * RC[−1] (note that the use of blanks has no effect on the formula). The cell reference RC[−6] means use the value in the same row but 6 columns to the left (minus means left for columns and up for rows; plus means right for columns and down for rows). This is the location of the column containing the salary offer. Salary offer is then divided by 250 ("/" means to divide). The result of this computation is then multiplied ("*" means multiply) by the contents of cell RC[−1] — the value in the same row, but one column to the left — the value of vacation days.

When the RETURN key is pressed, rather than the formula being placed in the cell, its value is placed there, as shown in Figure 6c.13. However, look at the command area: The formula, not the value, is shown as the actual contents of cell R4C8. Columns 2 and 7 are now associated with column 8, so any change in

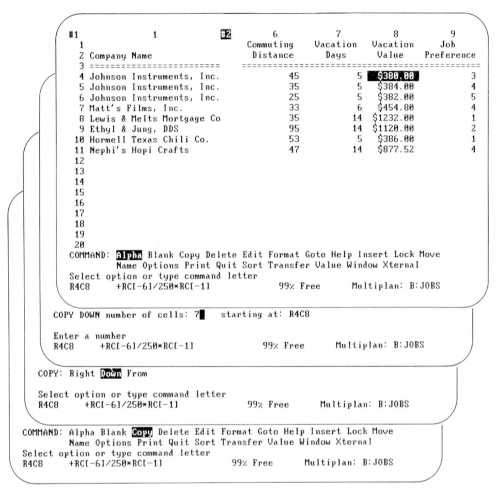

```
#1              1           #2      6         7         8         9
1                              Commuting  Vacation  Vacation    Job
2 Company Name                  Distance    Days     Value    Preference
3 ========================      ======================================
4 Johnson Instruments, Inc.        45        5    $380.00        3
5 Johnson Instruments, Inc.        35        5    $384.00        4
6 Johnson Instruments, Inc.        25        5    $382.00        5
7 Matt's Films, Inc.               33        6    $454.80        4
8 Lewis & Melts Mortgage Co        35       14   $1232.00        1
9 Ethyl & Jung, DDS                95       14   $1120.00        2
10 Hormell Texas Chili Co.         53        5    $386.00        1
11 Nephi's Hopi Crafts             47       14    $877.52        4
12
13
14
15
16
17
18
19
20
COMMAND: Alpha Blank Copy Delete Edit Format Goto Help Insert Lock Move
         Name Options Print Quit Sort Transfer Value Window Xternal
Select option or type command letter
R4C8     +RC[-6]/250*RC[-1]              99% Free      Multiplan: B:JOBS
```

```
COPY DOWN number of cells: 7     starting at: R4C8

Enter a number
R4C8     +RC[-6]/250*RC[-1]              99% Free      Multiplan: B:JOBS
```

```
COPY: Right Down From

Select option or type command letter
R4C8     +RC[-6]/250*RC[-1]              99% Free      Multiplan: B:JOBS
```

```
COMMAND: Alpha Blank Copy Delete Edit Format Goto Help Insert Lock Move
         Name Options Print Quit Sort Transfer Value Window Xternal
Select option or type command letter
R4C8     +RC[-6]/250*RC[-1]              99% Free      Multiplan: B:JOBS
```

FIGURE 6C.14
**Copying a formula to other cells in the
same column**

the value of salary offer or vacation days will result in an automatic change in
the vacation value.

Note that cell R4C8 is formatted in dollars and cents. Several functions
have been performed between Figure 6c.12 and 6c.13. These functions include entering the column heading, increasing the width of the column, centering the heading, and changing the format of cell R4C8 to a $ format code.

The values shown in column 8 of Figure 6c.14 are the result of having
copied the contents of cell R4C8 into the remaining cells in that column. Note

```
#1              1          #2      2        3        4           5
 1                                Salary   Actual  ------------- Benefits
 2 Company Name                   Offer    Offer    Life        Health
 3 ========================        ================================================
 4 Johnson Instruments, Inc.      $19000.00 $22822.00   $135.00     $354.00
 5 Johnson Instruments, Inc.      $19200.00 $23022.00   $135.00     $354.00
 6 Johnson Instruments, Inc.      $19100.00 $22922.00   $135.00     $354.00
 7 Matt's Films, Inc.             $18950.00 $24561.00   $155.00     $456.00
 8 Lewis & Melts Mortgage Co      $22000.00 $27500.00   $500.00     $600.00
 9 Ethyl & Jung, DDS              $20000.00 $27275.00   $325.00     $950.00
10 Hormell Texas Chili Co.        $19300.00 $21986.20   $164.00     $320.00
11 Nephi's Hopi Crafts            $15670.00 $17678.00   $250.00     $425.00
12
13
14
15
16
17
18
19
20
COMMAND: Alpha Blank Copy Delete Edit Format Goto Help Insert Lock Move
         Name Options Print Quit Sort Transfer Value Window Xternal
Select option or type command letter
R4C3      +RC[-1]+RC[+1]+RC[+2]+RC[+3]   99% Free     Multiplan: B:JOBS
```

FIGURE 6c.15
Another formula—computing the value of
the "Actual Offer"

that the value was not copied from cell to cell; rather, the formula was copied. Since the values of salary offer and vacation days are different, the corresponding vacation values are different.

Figure 6c.15 shows another new column—"Actual Offer." This column was inserted in essentially the same manner as "Vacation Value." In fact, when the "Actual Offer" column was added, any cells to the right containing relative addresses (for example, the vacation value formula) are adjusted so that computations are still accurate.

The formula used in the "Actual Offer" column is slightly different from the one used before. The formula is +RC[−1]+RC[+1]+RC[+2] +RC[+3], which indicates that the value stored in the same row and 1 column to the left ("Salary Offer") is to be added to the values in the cells that are 1 column to the right ("Life"), 2 columns to the right ("Health"), and 3 columns to the right ("Retirement"). After the value of the initial cell (R4C3) has been determined, it can be formatted and copied to the other cells in the same column.

Duplicating—The Copy Function Again

Now that all the values have been entered for all the companies, it is time to start thinking about what else could be done to improve the appearance of the

```
#1         1              #2    2        3        4         5
  1                             Salary   Actual  ---------- Benefits
  2 Company Name                Offer    Offer    Life      Health
  3 ======================     ==================================
  4 Johnson Instruments, Inc.  $19000.00 $22822.00 $135.00  $354.00
  5 Johnson Instruments, Inc.  $19200.00 $23022.00 $135.00  $354.00
  6 Johnson Instruments, Inc.  $19100.00 $22922.00 $135.00  $354.00
  7 Matt's Films, Inc.         $18950.00 $24561.00 $155.00  $456.00
  8 Lewis & Melts Mortgage Co  $22000.00 $27500.00 $500.00  $600.00
  9 Ethyl & Jung, DDS          $20000.00 $27275.00 $325.00  $950.00
 10 Hormell Texas Chili Co.    $19300.00 $21986.20 $164.00  $320.00
 11 Nephi's Hopi Crafts        $15670.00 $17678.00 $250.00  $425.00
 12 ----------------------     ---------------------------------
 13
 14
 15
 16
 17
 18
 19
 20
COMMAND: Alpha Blank Copy Delete Edit Format Goto Help Insert Lock Move
         Name Options Print Quit Sort Transfer Value Window Xternal
Select option or type command letter
R12C2     "-----------"              99% Free     Multiplan: B:JOBS
```

FIGURE 6c.16
Creating a visual break with the Copy function

spreadsheet. First, you might decide to place a visual break across the bottom of the list of companies like the one immediately under the column headings. To do this, you could duplicate the contents of cell R3C1 (see Figure 6c.16). Select the Copy function and indicate that you want to copy the contents From that cell To another cell or, as shown in Figure 6c.16, a range of cells.

Letting Multiplan "Compute"—Using Functions

Most spreadsheet packages provide a number of very useful functions. Although the result of many of the functions could be achieved by using formulas, often it is much easier to use a function than to create just the right formula or set of formulas. The functions that are available with Multiplan are presented in Table 6c.2.

For the job offers problem, you might want to establish averages (for comparison purposes) for many of the columns that contain numeric values. As shown in Figure 6c.17, you can begin by entering the title "Average Company" in R13C1. Then move to R13C2 and indicate that you want to enter the Value function. Next, enter AVERAGE(list), where AVERAGE is the name of a Multiplan function and "list" is a range of cell references including all of the salary offers. Of course, you could simply type in a range reference, but many

TABLE 6C.2 Multiplan Functions

Function Name	Meaning and Operation
ABS(n)	Absolute value, where "n" is a numeric value, a cell reference, or a formula
AND(list)	Returns "true" when all of the logical expressions in the "list" of logical expressions are true
ATAN(n)	Arc tangent "n," where "n" is a numeric value, a cell reference, or a formula
AVERAGE(list)	Average, where "list" is a series of numeric values, a series of cell references, or a range of cell references
COLUMN()	Identifies the column number of a column reference used in a function
COS(n)	Cosine "n," where "n" is a numeric value, a cell reference, or a formula
COUNT(list)	Counts the number of values in a designated list, where "list" is a series of numeric values, a series of cell references, or a range of cell references
DOLLAR(n)	Converts the format to a "$" format code, where "n" is a numeric value, a cell reference, or a formula
EXP(n)	Calculates "e to the nth," where "n" is a power and may be a numeric value, a cell reference, or a formula
FALSE()	Returns the "logical" value "false"
FIXED(n,digits)	Converts the format to a "Fix" format code, where "n" is a numeric value, a cell reference, or a formula and "digits" is the number of positions following the decimal point
IF(logical,[THEN] value1, [[ELSE] value2])	Determines if the "logical" expression is true. If true, "value1" is assigned to the cell. If false, "value2" is assigned to the cell. The words THEN and ELSE are optional; punctuation is required.
INDEX(area,subscripts)	Permits the selection of a cell from a specific "area," where "subscripts" indicate the row and/or column in the specified area
INT(n)	Integer value of "n," where "n" is a numeric value, a cell reference, or a formula
ISERROR(value)	Indicates if indicated value is an error
ISNA(value)	Indicates if indicated value is not available
LEN(string)	Resulting length, in number of characters, based on a "string," where "string" is a text value or a cell reference
LN(n)	Natural logarithm of "n," where "n" is a numeric value, a cell reference, or a formula
LOG10(n)	Logarithm (base 10) of "n," where "n" is a numeric value, a cell reference, or a formula
LOOKUP(n,area)	Searches a designated "area" composed of rows, columns, or both for "n," where "n" is a numeric value, a cell reference, or a formula

Function Name	Meaning and Operation
MAX(list)	Maximum value in a "list," where "list" is a series of numeric values or a range of cells
MID(text,start,count)	Selects a series of characters from the designated "text" beginning at the "start" character position for a length of "count" characters
MIN(list)	Minimum value in a "list," where "list" is a series of numeric values or a range of cells
MOD(value1,value2)	Returns the remainder when "value1" is divided by "value2," where "value1" and "value2" are numeric values, cell references, or functions
NA()	Returns the special value #N/A — not available
NOT(logical)	Reverses the "logical" expression
NPV(value,list)	Net Present Value of a "list," where "value" is the interest rate (expressed as a whole number or a decimal fraction) and "list" is a series of numeric values, a series of cell references, or a range of cell references
OR(list)	Returns "true" if any of the logical expressions in a "list" of logical expressions are true
PI()	Returns the mathematical value of "pi"
REPT(text,count)	Repeats the value of "text" characters "count" times
ROUND(n,digits)	Rounds "n" to a value indicated by "digits," where "n" is a numeric value, a cell reference, or a formula and "digits" is the number of decimal points in the desired result (if positive) or positions to the left of the decimal point (if negative)
ROW()	Returns the row number of a row reference in a function
SIGN(n)	Sign of "n," where "n" is a numeric value, a cell reference, or a formula and the sign is reported as "1" if positive, "0" if zero, or "−1" if negative
SIN(n)	Sine of "n," where "n" is a numeric value, a cell reference, or a formula
SQRT(n)	Square root of "n," where "n" is a numeric value, a cell reference, or a formula
STDEV(list)	Standard Deviation of a "list," where "list" is a series of numeric values, a series of cell references, or a range of cell references
SUM(list)	Sum (total) of a "list," where "list" is a series of numeric values, a series of cell references, or a range of cell references
TAN(n)	Tangent of "n," where "n" is a numeric value, a cell reference, or a formula
TRUE()	Returns the logical value "true"
VALUE(text)	Determines the numeric value of "text," where "text" is a character string composed, at least in part, of digits — otherwise the value is 0

```
#1          1          #2    2        3         4          5
 1                            Salary   Actual  ----------- Benefits
 2 Company Name               Offer    Offer    Life       Health
 3 =========================  ======== ======== ========== ==========
 4 Johnson Instruments, Inc.  $19000.00 $22822.00 $135.00  $354.00
 5 Johnson Instruments, Inc.  $19200.00 $23022.00 $135.00  $354.00
 6 Johnson Instruments, Inc.  $19100.00 $22922.00 $135.00  $354.00
 7 Matt's Films, Inc.         $18950.00 $24561.00 $155.00  $456.00
 8 Lewis & Melts Mortgage Co  $22000.00 $27500.00 $500.00  $600.00
 9 Ethyl & Jung, DDS          $20000.00 $27275.00 $325.00  $950.00
10 Hormell Texas Chili Co.    $19300.00 $21986.20 $164.00  $320.00
11 Nephi's Hopi Crafts        $15670.00 $17678.00 $250.00  $425.00
12                           ------------------------------------------
13 Average Company               19152.5
14
15
16
17
18
19
20
COMMAND: Alpha Blank Copy Delete Edit Format Goto Help Insert Lock Move
         Name Options Print Quit Sort Transfer Value Window Xternal
Select option or type command letter
R13C2     AVERAGE(R[-9]C:R[-2]C)        99% Free       Multiplan: B:JOBS
```

FIGURE 6C.17
Creating an "Average Company"—using the AVERAGE function

```
#1          1          #2    2        3         4          5
 1                            Salary   Actual  ----------- Benefits
 2 Company Name               Offer    Offer    Life       Health
 3 =========================  ======== ======== ========== ==========
 4 Johnson Instruments, Inc.  $19000.00 $22822.00 $135.00  $354.00
 5 Johnson Instruments, Inc.  $19200.00 $23022.00 $135.00  $354.00
 6 Johnson Instruments, Inc.  $19100.00 $22922.00 $135.00  $354.00
 7 Matt's Films, Inc.         $18950.00 $24561.00 $155.00  $456.00
 8 Lewis & Melts Mortgage Co  $22000.00 $27500.00 $500.00  $600.00
 9 Ethyl & Jung, DDS          $20000.00 $27275.00 $325.00  $950.00
10 Hormell Texas Chili Co.    $19300.00 $21986.20 $164.00  $320.00
11 Nephi's Hopi Crafts        $15670.00 $17678.00 $250.00  $425.00
12                           ------------------------------------------
13 Average Company            $19152.50 $23470.78 $224.88  $476.63
14
15
16
17
18
19
20
COMMAND: Alpha Blank Copy Delete Edit Format Goto Help Insert Lock Move
         Name Options Print Quit Sort Transfer Value Window Xternal
Select option or type command letter
R13C2     AVERAGE(R[-9]C:R[-2]C)        99% Free       Multiplan: B:JOBS
```

FIGURE 6C.18
Averages after formatting and copying

of the Multiplan functions permit you to indicate cell ranges by using the arrow keys. For example, if you entered AVERAGE(and began to move the cursor, you would see that a cell reference is added after the opening parenthesis. As you move, the cell reference is updated until you press the RETURN key. Then you are returned to the cell in which you began. You would then enter a colon (:) and begin moving the cursor again to establish the ending point of the range. Once you have reached this position, press RETURN again, and Multiplan will supply the cell reference and return to the original cell. All you need to do now to obtain the column averages is enter the closing parenthesis and press RETURN.

The result of using the AVERAGE function for cell R13C2 and copying the function to the remaining cells in the row is shown in Figure 6c.18. Of course, this figure also indicates that the format of the cell has been changed to a "$" format code, which has been copied to the other cells in the same row. The averages for commuting distance, vacation days, and job preference are shown in a $ format. Thus, for these cells, it is necessary to re-enter the Format function and change the format code back to the Default setting.

New Information on a Job Offer — Adding a New Row

Next, you need to add a new job offer from First State National Bank. Insert a new row at row 12 of your spreadsheet for the new job information (see Figure 6c.19). Note that the formulas for "Actual Offer" and "Vacation Value" have been copied from row 11 and that the Format has been set to $. Also note that none of the averages has changed and that no error message currently exists in the command menu area.

Since the new row is outside the range of cells used to calculate the average company values, the numbers you have entered had no effect on the values in row 14. To get the new averages for row 14 that include First State National Bank, you must re-enter the average function and copy it across the entire row, and again change the formats for "Commuting Distance," "Vacation Days," and "Job Preference." When you have finished, your screen should be the same as the one in Figure 6c.20.

Putting Rows in Order — The Sort Function

The last requirement of this problem is to order the job offers by your job preference. The list of companies is adequate, but you will probably want the jobs you prefer at the top of the list. To accomplish this, you can use the Move function to specify the cells you wish to manipulate and then specify the location to which you wish to move them. One word of caution: When you move cells that are used in a mathematical function — in this case, the "Average" function — the cell references involved in the calculations may change, giving you incorrect results. This may occur when the cells at the ends of a range are

```
#1            1           #2      2         3          4            5
 1                                Salary    Actual   -------------- Benefits
 2 Company Name                   Offer     Offer       Life        Health
 3 ===========================   ==============================================
 4 Johnson Instruments, Inc.     $19000.00 $22822.00  $135.00      $354.00
 5 Johnson Instruments, Inc.     $19200.00 $23022.00  $135.00      $354.00
 6 Johnson Instruments, Inc.     $19100.00 $22922.00  $135.00      $354.00
 7 Matt's Films, Inc.            $18950.00 $24561.00  $155.00      $456.00
 8 Lewis & Melts Mortgage Co     $22000.00 $27500.00  $500.00      $600.00
 9 Ethyl & Jung, DDS             $20000.00 $27275.00  $325.00      $950.00
10 Hormell Texas Chili Co.       $19300.00 $21986.20  $164.00      $320.00
11 Nephi's Hopi Crafts           $15670.00 $17678.00  $250.00      $425.00
12 First State National Bank     $22000.00 $25485.00  $210.00      $325.00
13                               -----------------------------------------------
14 Average Company               $19152.50 $23470.78  $224.88      $476.63
15
16
17
18
19
20
COMMAND: Alpha Blank Copy Delete Edit Format Goto Help Insert Lock Move
         Name Options Print Quit Sort Transfer Value Window Xternal
Select option or type command letter
R12C2    22000                    99% Free        Multiplan: B:JOBS
```

FIGURE 6C.19
Entering a new row — the values for First State National Bank

```
#1            1           #2      2         3          4            5
 1                                Salary    Actual   -------------- Benefits
 2 Company Name                   Offer     Offer       Life        Health
 3 ===========================   ==============================================
 4 Johnson Instruments, Inc.     $19000.00 $22822.00  $135.00      $354.00
 5 Johnson Instruments, Inc.     $19200.00 $23022.00  $135.00      $354.00
 6 Johnson Instruments, Inc.     $19100.00 $22922.00  $135.00      $354.00
 7 Matt's Films, Inc.            $18950.00 $24561.00  $155.00      $456.00
 8 Lewis & Melts Mortgage Co     $22000.00 $27500.00  $500.00      $600.00
 9 Ethyl & Jung, DDS             $20000.00 $27275.00  $325.00      $950.00
10 Hormell Texas Chili Co.       $19300.00 $21986.20  $164.00      $320.00
11 Nephi's Hopi Crafts           $15670.00 $17678.00  $250.00      $425.00
12 First State National Bank     $22000.00 $25485.00  $210.00      $325.00
13                               -----------------------------------------------
14 Average Company               $19468.89 $23694.58  $223.22      $459.78
15
16
17
18
19
20
COMMAND: Alpha Blank Copy Delete Edit Format Goto Help Insert Lock Move
         Name Options Print Quit Sort Transfer Value Window Xternal
Select option or type command letter
R14C2    AVERAGE(R[-10]C:R[-2]C)  99% Free        Multiplan: B:JOBS
```

FIGURE 6C.20
Correcting the "Average Company" row

```
#1              1            #2      7        8        9        10
 1                               Commuting Vacation Vacation   Job
 2 Company Name                   Distance   Days    Value  Preference
 3 ========================       ===================================
 4 Lewis & Melts Mortgage Co         35       14   $1232.00          1
 5 Hormell Texas Chili Co.           53        5    $386.00          1
 6 Ethyl & Jung, DDS                 95       14   $1120.00          2
 7 First State National Bank         25       14   $1232.00          2
 8 Johnson Instruments, Inc.         45        5    $380.00          3
 9 Johnson Instruments, Inc.         35        5    $384.00          4
10 Matt's Films, Inc.                33        6    $454.80          4
11 Nephi's Hopi Crafts               47       14    $877.52          4
12 Johnson Instruments, Inc.         25        5    $382.00          5
13 -----------------------        ----------------------------------
14 Average Company                35.00     9.50   $806.00       2.50
15
16
17
18
19
20
COMMAND: Alpha Blank Copy Delete Edit Format Goto Help Insert Lock Move
         Name Options Print Quit Sort Transfer Value Window Xternal
Select option or type command letter
R4C10    1                         99% Free       Multiplan: B:JOBS
```

```
SORT by column: 10    between rows: 4    and: 12   order: > <

Select option
R4C10    3                         99% Free       Multiplan: B:JOBS
```

```
COMMAND: Alpha Blank Copy Delete Edit Format Goto Help Insert Lock Move
         Name Options Print Quit Sort Transfer Value Window Xternal
Select option or type command letter
R4C10    3                         99% Free       Multiplan: B:JOBS
```

FIGURE 6c.21
Getting the job preferences in sorted order

moved. Another problem that may occur is circular reference — two or more cells involved in a computation that refer to each other.

There is an alternative to the Move function: the Sort function (see Figure 6c.21). Since the current cell reference is R4C10, you don't have to specify the column (the default column is 10 at this cell position) whose data is to be sorted or the beginning cell in this column (because row 4 is the current row reference). You want to limit the ending position of this range at row 12, and you must select an ascending sort sequence (>) or a descending sort sequence (<). Ascending is the default value.

Note that in Figure 6c.21 the company names are not in the previous order; rather, they are ordered by your job preference. Also note that all of the averages changed. Because the sort operation moved the rows at the beginning

```
#1               1              #2    2         3          4           5
 1                                  Salary    Actual   ----------- Benefits
 2 Company Name                     Offer     Offer      Life       Health
 3 ==============================   ======== ======== =========== ===========
 4 Lewis & Melts Mortgage Co        $22000.00 $27500.00  $500.00    $600.00
 5 Hormell Texas Chili Co.          $19300.00 $21986.20  $164.00    $320.00
 6 Ethyl & Jung, DDS                $20000.00 $27275.00  $325.00    $950.00
 7 First State National Bank        $22000.00 $25485.00  $210.00    $325.00
 8 Johnson Instruments, Inc.        $19000.00 $22822.00  $135.00    $354.00
 9 Johnson Instruments, Inc.        $19200.00 $23022.00  $135.00    $354.00
10 Matt's Films, Inc.               $18950.00 $24561.00  $155.00    $456.00
11 Nephi's Hopi Crafts              $15670.00 $17678.00  $250.00    $425.00
12 Johnson Instruments, Inc.        $19100.00 $22922.00  $135.00    $354.00
13 ------------------------------   -------- -------- ----------- -----------
14 Average Company                  $19468.89 $23694.58  $223.22    $459.78
15
16
17
18
19
20
COMMAND: Alpha Blank Copy Delete Edit Format Goto Help Insert Lock Move
         Name Options Print Quit Sort Transfer Value Window Xternal
Select option or type command letter
R14C2    AVERAGE(R[-10]C:R[-2]C)        99% Free        Multiplan: B:JOBS
```

FIGURE 6c.22
**Correcting the "Average Company" one
more time**

and end of your list in the average function, the formula cell references are now
incorrect and will need to be re-entered, as in Figure 6c.22.

At this point, it is probably a good idea to save your work again. However,
note that this time the spreadsheet file B:JOBS already exists, and you will be
asked if you want the new spreadsheet to replace the old one—you should
answer yes to this question.

Showing Off Your Spreadsheet — The Print Function

Your spreadsheet is now complete. Perhaps you would like to see the entire
spreadsheet in printed form. To print the spreadsheet, select the Print function. This function then produces the Print menu, as shown in Figure 6c.23.
Your choices are to send the spreadsheet to the Printer, send the spreadsheet
to a print File, adjust the Margins of the printed page, and select printing
control Options. Many spreadsheets are physically wider than the printer
paper or wider than the printer is capable of handling. Thus, the spreadsheet
may be produced on several pages, as illustrated for the job offers problem in
Figure 6c.24. Therefore, it is sometimes necessary to do a physical "cut and
paste" operation to reassemble the rows to recreate the appearance of the
stored spreadsheet.

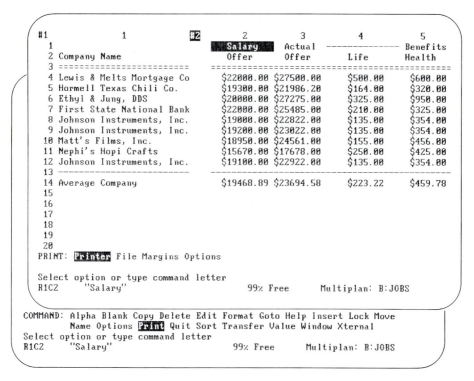

```
#1              1            #2      2        3        4        5
 1                                 Salary   Actual  ─────────── Benefits
 2 Company Name                    Offer    Offer     Life     Health
 3 ======================          ===================================
 4 Lewis & Melts Mortgage Co       $22000.00 $27500.00 $500.00  $600.00
 5 Hormell Texas Chili Co.         $19300.00 $21986.20 $164.00  $320.00
 6 Ethyl & Jung, DDS               $20000.00 $27275.00 $325.00  $950.00
 7 First State National Bank       $22000.00 $25485.00 $210.00  $325.00
 8 Johnson Instruments, Inc.       $19000.00 $22822.00 $135.00  $354.00
 9 Johnson Instruments, Inc.       $19200.00 $23022.00 $135.00  $354.00
10 Matt's Films, Inc.              $18950.00 $24561.00 $155.00  $456.00
11 Nephi's Hopi Crafts             $15670.00 $17678.00 $250.00  $425.00
12 Johnson Instruments, Inc.       $19100.00 $22922.00 $135.00  $354.00
13 ─────────────────────────       ───────────────────────────────────
14 Average Company                 $19468.89 $23694.58 $223.22  $459.78
15
16
17
18
19
20
PRINT: Printer File Margins Options

Select option or type command letter
R1C2      "Salary"                  99% Free      Multiplan: B:JOBS
```

```
COMMAND: Alpha Blank Copy Delete Edit Format Goto Help Insert Lock Move
         Name Options Print Quit Sort Transfer Value Window Xternal
Select option or type command letter
R1C2      "Salary"                  99% Free      Multiplan: B:JOBS
```

FIGURE 6C.23
Controlling the printed output

Leaving Multiplan—The Quit Function

When your spreadsheet work has been completed, terminate Multiplan by using the Quit function, and return to the operating system. When you select the Quit function, you are provided with the message "Enter Y to confirm": press Y for "Yes." One word of caution about the Quit function: Multiplan will not warn you that you have changed the contents of the spreadsheet since you last saved it. If you have made changes, save them before you quit. Don't forget!

Other Features of Multiplan

Multiplan's Option function controls "recalc," which automatically recalculates cell values when the value in any cell has been changed. Although the default for "recalc" is "yes," as the spreadsheet gets larger you may want to change the code to "no." Remember, the larger the spreadsheet, the longer it takes to recalculate the value in each cell. However, if you find you need to

```
                                Salary      Actual    ------------
          Company Name          Offer       Offer        Life
          ==================================================================
          Lewis & Melts Mortgage Co  $22000.00 $27500.00    $500.00
          Hormell Texas Chili Co.    $19300.00 $21986.20    $164.00
          Ethyl & Jung, DDS          $20000.00 $27275.00    $325.00
          First State National Bank  $22000.00 $25485.00    $210.00
          Johnson Instruments, Inc.  $19000.00 $22822.00    $135.00
          Johnson Instruments, Inc.  $19200.00 $23022.00    $135.00
          Matt's Films, Inc.         $18950.00 $24561.00    $155.00
          Nephi's Hopi Crafts        $15670.00 $17678.00    $250.00
          Johnson Instruments, Inc.  $19100.00 $22922.00    $135.00
          ------------------------------------------------------------------
          Average Company            $19468.89 $23694.58    $223.22
```

```
     -- Benefits ------------ Commuting   Vacation   Vacation      Job
        Health   Retirement   Distance      Days      Value     Preference
     ==================================================================================
        $600.00   $4400.00        35          14     $1232.00         1
        $320.00   $2202.20        53           5      $386.00         1
        $950.00   $6000.00        95          14     $1120.00         2
        $325.00   $2950.00        25          14     $1232.00         2
        $354.00   $3333.00        45           5      $380.00         3
        $354.00   $3333.00        35           5      $384.00         4
        $456.00   $5000.00        33           6      $454.80         4
        $425.00   $1333.00        47          14      $877.52         4
        $354.00   $3333.00        25           5      $382.00         5
     ----------------------------------------------------------------------------------
        $459.78   $3542.69       43.67        9.11     $716.48        2.89
```

FIGURE 6C.24
A printed report from the job offers spreadsheet

perform a recalculation when the "recalc" mode is "no," all you have to do is press the ! key. On those keyboards that support function keys, the F8 key is used to perform recalculation.

Another handy feature of Multiplan is available through the Name function. Suppose you had a series of cells that were frequently used as a group. This could be a row, a column, several rows, or several columns. If you select the Name function, you can refer to a group of cells by a name. For example, the Name function can be used to name the column of values representing the salary offers "Salary." "Salary" can then be used to reference this group of cells in the Goto function, or the cells could be collectively identified for the purposes of computation. In this case, to establish the average salary offer, it is possible to use the function AVERAGE(Salary). The Name itself must be a continuous string of characters, without blanks or hyphens. (However, the underline character can be used in place of blanks or hyphens.)

Summary of Spreadsheet Modules

The modules in Chapter 6 have given you the opportunity to learn about one (or more) of three popular spreadsheet packages available for microcomputers. They are pfs:Plan (Module 6a), Lotus 1-2-3 (Module 6b), and Multiplan (Module 6c). You learned about these spreadsheet packages by building spreadsheets with data involved in the job hunting problem.

Comparison of Spreadsheet Packages

Before using the spreadsheet package that you have available to answer the questions and solve the problems at the end of this section, study Table 6s.1, which presents a quick comparison of the different spreadsheet packages. Some of the differences between the packages are quite dramatic (for example, the memory requirements).

However, Table 6s.1 does not include all of the differences between spreadsheet packages. For example, pfs:Plan is designed specifically for business applications, whereas the other two packages are designed for general application. Lotus 1-2-3 provides both graphics and database capabilities, which are not available with the other spreadsheet packages. Pfs:Plan interfaces directly with the other application packages in the pfs series, whereas Lotus 1-2-3 and Multiplan can generate files that are usable by other packages. There are also price differences among the packages. However, the prices change so rapidly that comparisons are difficult.

In short, if you compare the capabilities of the different spreadsheet packages, you can find the one that most closely meets your needs. A software package that doesn't meet your needs is worthless to you, regardless of how elegant it is. So let your applications dictate your software purchases.

Guidelines for the Evaluation of Spreadsheet Packages

Before you select a spreadsheet package for your own use, try to answer the following questions:

- **Completeness of documentation**   Are the manuals well written, understandable, and easy to use? Are tutorials on package use available?

TABLE 6S.1 A Comparison of Spreadsheet Application Packages

| Characteristics | Requirements | | |
	pfs:Plan	Lotus 1-2-3	Multiplan
Operating system	MS-DOS or PC-DOS	MS-DOS or PC-DOS	CP/M, MS-DOS, or PC-DOS
Main memory (RAM)	128k bytes minimum	192k bytes minimum	64k bytes minimum
Disk drives	1	1	1
Printer (optional)	80- or 132-column ASCII files	80- or 132-column ASCII files	80- or 132-column ASCII files
Size of spreadsheet	20 columns × 48 rows	256 columns × 2048 rows (minimum)	63 columns × 255 rows
Number of special functions	11	44, excluding database	40
Number of windows	0	2	8
Command structure	Multi-level command	Multi-level menu or command	Multi-level menu
Default column width	9	9	10
Minimum column width	3	1	3
Maximum column width	25	72	32
Interface method	DIF, SYLK, print files	DIF, print files (also Transfer function)	SYLK, print files

- **Operating characteristics**   What is the maximum size of the spreadsheet supported by the package? How fast does the package perform calculations on a small, a medium, and a large spreadsheet? Is the speed affected by particular combinations of formulas and functions? How fast does it save and retrieve files? What flexibility do you have in terms of file storage?

- **Ease of setup**   When using the package, how easy is it to enter data? How do you address cells, and how easy is it to reference a cell or a range of cells? Are range labels available?

- **Command structure**   Is the package command or menu driven? How easy is it to select and execute a command? Are menus understandable and given in a logical sequence?

- **Internal help facility**   Is the Help option available? How easy is it to use? How complete is it? How quickly can you find the information you need?

- **Cursor movement**   Can you easily move around the spreadsheet using the arrow keys? Can you scroll easily? Are additional keys or key combinations available to move around the spreadsheet more quickly?

- **Cell formatting**   Can you format a single cell, or must you format a complete column or section? What are the minimum and maximum cell widths? What kinds of text formatting are available (for example, left-justified, right-justified, centered)? Can the contents of cells be adjusted to cell lengths? What kinds of number format options are available? Are standard formats (integer, floating point, and so on) available? Are special formats (dates, percentages, and so forth) available?

- **Editing cell values**   Is an editing feature available? How easy is it to use? What kinds of editing operations can be performed (for example, character insertion and deletion)?

- **Windows**   How many windows are available? What controls do you have on synchronized versus unsynchronized scrolling? Are these controls assigned by window or to the whole spreadsheet? How easy is it to go from one window to another?

- **Printing flexibility**   What controls do you have on printing? Can you "print" to a file as well as to a printer? Can you print only a portion of the spreadsheet? Do you have page controls, including top and bottom margins, left and right margins, headings, footings, and page numbering? Can you print formulas and functions as well as cell values? Are special routines available to take advantage of special printer features?

- **Completeness of functions**   Do you have adequate mathematical and logical functions? How easy are the functions to use? How flexible are they? Are any of the functions related to identifying and interpreting errors?

- **Interfacing characteristics**   Are the files produced by the package directly compatible with any other software? Can the package produce print files? DIF files? SYLK files? Are there any special interfacing provisions, like automatic conversion of data from another package? Does this version of the package accept data produced by a previous version, or is there a translation process?

- **Other characteristics**   Can the package produce graphics on the screen and on the printer? What, if any, provisions have been made for word processing? Database uses? Communications?

What Happened at ACE?

On Monday, Chris attended Mr. Cotterman's seminar on spreadsheets and got some very useful training about spreadsheets and how to use them. On Tuesday, Chris managed to get all of the inventory data into a spreadsheet and perform the necessary calculations. Then, when Mr. Jenkins dropped off the updated inventory information Tuesday afternoon, Chris was able to correct a few entries in the spreadsheet, which automatically produced updated calculations. By 4:30 that day, the assignment was complete and a printed report was on Mr. Jenkins' desk. Mr. Jenkins was pleased with Chris, and Chris was pleased about completing the task on such short notice. That spreadsheet package really helped!

Module Questions

1. Select one of the spreadsheet packages. Explain how absolute cell references are identified in this package. How is relative addressing performed?
2. Select one of the spreadsheet packages. List all of the number formats available and provide an example of each. Does this package have any format options for character data? If so, what are they?
3. Select one of the spreadsheet packages. Are windows available? How many? What controls are available for the windowing operations? How do you transfer from one window to another?
4. Select one of the spreadsheet packages. How many mathematical functions are available in this package? If you wanted to compute a total for the values in rows 3 through 20 in the second column, what would the function look like, and how would you enter it from the keyboard? Can you use a range label with this function?
5. Create a comparison table for Lotus 1-2-3 and Multiplan. This table should include the following items: maximum spreadsheet size, default cell width, keys used to move around in the work space, means of identifying cell ranges, types of number formats, procedures for inserting and deleting rows and columns, and operation of the Sort function. Which package, in your opinion, most nearly meets your needs for spreadsheet software? Why?

Module Problems

1. You have just received information on another job offer for the job hunting problem. You are provided with the following information:

   Company Name: Regal Products, Inc.
   Salary Offer: $27,000.00
   Life Insurance: $315.00
   Health Insurance: $450.00
   Retirement Contribution: $3,550.00
   Vacation Days: 14
   Commuting Distance: 45 miles
   Job Preference: 1

   Enter this information into the spreadsheet for the job hunting problem. Compute all totals and adjust averages, as necessary.

2. Using the inventory data for ACE, Incorporated (found in Appendix B), set up a spreadsheet based on the store sales. Use this spreadsheet to calculate the monthly and annual profit for each of the items carried in inventory, the profit for each class of items, and for the entire store.

3. Use a spreadsheet package to develop a monthly budget for the coming year. You have accepted the job offer from Lewis & Melts Mortgage Company from the job hunting problem, and you are paid at the end of each month. Although the company provides many benefits, you still have to pay federal and state income tax on the money you earn, as well as make contributions to Social Security. Assume that federal income tax is 15% of your gross earnings, and state income tax is 2%. Social Security is 6.75% of your first $35,000 of gross income (income before taxes). Insert a row labeled "Net Income after Taxes," which is your gross monthly income less all taxes. Then enter your expenses in the following categories: Housing (mortgage payment or rent), Food, Clothing, Utilities (electricity, gas, and telephone), Auto Insurance (if any), Transportation (car payment, gasoline, oil, and periodic maintenance or costs related to other modes of transportation), Charitable Contributions (5% of your net income), Savings (2% of your net income), and Miscellaneous Expenses (4% of your net income). Your final entry should be labeled "Excess Funds or Deficit" and should be calculated as your net income less all expenses. You may assume that you start with $1,000 in savings. At the end of each month, any deficit must be covered from previous savings. When excess funds are available, they should be deposited in the next month's savings amount. At the end of the year, can you save enough money (via your savings) to take a trip that will cost you $2,000? Would your situation be any different if you had taken the job with Regal Products, Inc. (from Problem 1)?

SCENARIO 7

What's Going on at ACE?

One morning I was called to Mr. Jenkins' office. I had no idea what Mr. Jenkins wanted; it turned out that he had a very demanding project in mind!

Mr. Jenkins showed me the inventory records room. Inside the room were row upon row of filing cabinets. Mr. Jenkins said that he wanted me to begin working on getting all the records organized in some useful fashion. The reason for this, he said, was because when a report was needed, someone had to come to these files and retrieve the needed data by hand. Sometimes it took two or three days of hard work to produce a good report. However, some reports are needed the same day, and others are needed in no more than one day. So, ACE had a problem!

At first, I couldn't even imagine how to tackle this job. Then I remembered something that Ms. Allison had mentioned. When she was discussing the company's computer system, she suggested that employees call her whenever they had a problem that looked like it could be handled by a computer. So I called Ms. Allison, who said that there were a couple of ways of handling the problem: one was by using software called a *database*. I knew little about databases, but Ms. Allison said that a one-day seminar on databases was going to be held at the local university that coming weekend. I called the university and enrolled.

Chapter Seven
Applications Software: Databases

Chapter Objectives

When you have completed this chapter, you will be able to:

- Explain the difference between a file management system and a database system

- Provide a working definition of a database and how a database is organized

- Describe the various basic structures commonly found in current, readily available database packages

- Discuss the basic functions of a database

- Explain how a database can be used in a personal and in an organizational environment

Introduction to Databases

Suppose you are given the problem of collecting and organizing all the data about players on a professional football team. For each player you would have to collect volumes of data—for example, the data illustrated in Figure 7.1.

Over the course of each player's career, you will need to produce many reports for the team. For example, each coach needs a player roster for his area of responsibility,

the front office needs a list of contracts that expire in the coming year so that contract negotiations can be planned, the team physicians need a list of injuries resulting from last week's game, and so on; there are many more reports needed by the organization.

Putting all this collected data into filing cabinets is not a particularly efficient way of handling data. Going through all the records every time you need to prepare a report is not very efficient either. Instead, you can use a computer and a **database** ▶

FIGURE 7.1 Data Required for a Professional Football Player

Social Security Number	Expiration Date of	Position(s) Played:	Heart Rate/Blood
Name	Contract	Offense	Pressure:
Street Address	Terms of Contract	Defense	At Rest
City	Physical Performance:	Special Teams	Mild Stress
State	Time/10 Yards	Medical Data:	Playing Level
Zip Code	Time/40 Yards	Data of Last Physical	Maximum Stress
Phone Number	Time/100 Yards	Results of Physical	.
Date of Birth	Weight/Dead Lift	Current Medical	.
Height	Weight/Bench Press	Status	.
Weight	Weight/Curl	Injuries:	
Jersey Number	Weight/Squat Thrust	Head	
Years in Pro-Football	.	Chest	
College Attended	.	Back	
College Position(s)	.	Arms/Shoulders	
Played		Wrists/Hands/	
		Fingers	
		Upper Leg	
		Knee	
		Lower Leg	
		Ankles/Feet/Toes	
		Internal	

FIGURE 7.1
Data required for a study of professional football players

management system (DBMS) to manage the data efficiently. A DBMS is a group of common utility programs designed to allow the user to interface with a vast collection of data, called a **database.**

Historical Development

As shown in Figure 7.2, we have come a long way since the days when it was necessary to maintain the bulk of an organization's data in filing cabinets. However, even in the early days of computing, handling data was problematic; all file-handling operations (including input and output) were a direct consequence of programmer action, and not everyone possessed programming skills.

As programming became more sophisticated, procedures for handling large amounts of data were developed. In the 1960s, computer companies developed **file management systems (FMS)** to deal with the problems of large collections of data. The use of magnetic tape on early computers gave way to the **direct (random) access** approach using magnetic disk. It was during the 1960s that many business organizations put together huge information-handling systems. These information systems were built for individual functional

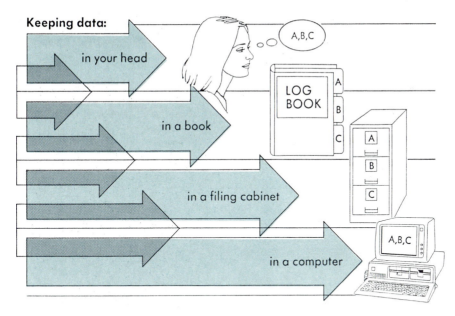

FIGURE 7.2
Developments in data storage and retrieval

application areas, such as accounting, payroll, inventory, and personnel. What became very obvious was that there was significant duplication in the data, referred to as **data redundancy**, being stored. For example, both payroll and personnel files stored the names of all of an organization's employees.

File and Data Management Systems

As a result of the inefficiency associated with handling data by traditional means, many new companies were formed whose primary focus was to improve the methods of working with large amounts of data. These firms began by defining and identifying the need for **data independence** (a sep-

aration of how data is stored from how it is used), flexibility of data types, performance of file types, and security of data in the stored media. Based on the efforts of these companies, file management systems (FMS) and data management systems (DMS) eventually evolved. In both file and data management systems, data is the basic element. Data comprises a collection of facts, concepts, or instructions necessary for the operation of an organization. Figure 7.3 shows the data hierarchy for these systems.

File Management Systems (FMS)

A file management system is a self-contained system integrating all of the facilities needed for file handling. The intent of a file system is to eliminate the use of high-level programming languages for handling the data. The file system is designed to commu-

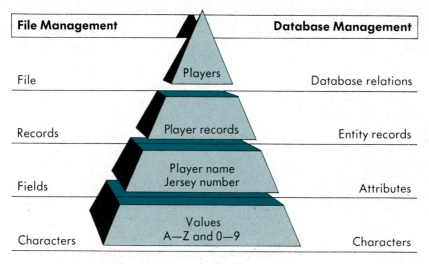

File Management		Database Management
File	Players	Database relations
Records	Player records	Entity records
Fields	Player name Jersey number	Attributes
Characters	Values A—Z and 0—9	Characters

FIGURE 7.3
Data hierarchy for files and databases

nicate directly with the "best" possible data-handling method for the particular type of file.

Sequential Files   Sequential file systems, one of the first methods of handling data, are stored files in either ascending (smallest to largest) or descending (largest to smallest) order, by a selected field. For example, if you stored the data for a football team sequentially, the field used to access a player's data later could be the player's NAME. Storing the data in ascending order by NAME means that it will be stored alphabetically. Alternatively, the player data could be retrieved by the JERSEY NUMBER field, where the records have been ordered on an ascending basis by JERSEY NUMBER value. To access a particular record in a sequential file, all preceding records have to be read. Thus, if you have a 52-record file, and you want the tenth record, you have to bypass the first nine records before you get to the one you want.

Direct Files   **Direct file** systems, a more modern file-storage method, can use only disk storage devices (including floppy disks and hard disks used with microcomputers). This method stores records at unique locations (addresses) on the disk. The locations are derived from a mathematical manipulation (called **hashing algorithms**) performed on specific fields, called **keys,** within each record. A key uniquely identifies a record. **Primary** and **secondary keys** are used to identify a record by two or more fields. The primary key is the most important field, and the secondary keys represent the less important fields.

To retrieve a record, the same manipulation that is used to place the record in the file is performed, and the system goes directly to the calculated location. For the football team example, the primary key might be the JERSEY NUMBER field. The value of the JERSEY NUMBER field is unique for each player, whereas the NAME field might contain duplicates (for example,

Smiths and Johnsons). However, jersey numbers may range from 00 to 99 — that is, 100 positions. A hashing algorithm is used to reduce the number of record positions necessary to store the data for all the players on a 50-man roster. To retrieve the tenth record (not necessarily jersey number 10), the computer calculates the location within the file where the desired data is stored and makes "one" read — the tenth record position. It does not first read nine other records.

Indexed-Sequential Files

Indexed-sequential files use the best traits of both the sequential- and the direct-file methods. Records are stored in ascending order by a primary key. As the record is stored, its address is written to an **index** (also called a **directory**) that is also recorded on the disk. If most of the records are needed for a particular report, the records are simply read sequentially. If only a few of the records are needed, records can be accessed directly by searching the index. It is not necessary to perform calculations to determine a record's location.

Data Management Systems (DMS)

In the late 1960s, the use of large collections of data had increased so much that more advanced concepts of data storage and retrieval were needed. It was during this period that many vendors and large organizations began their development of the large-scale data-handling systems known as **data management systems (DMS).** These systems eventually came to be known as database management systems (DBMS). The early data management systems followed a very rigid design, known as a **hierarchical (tree) structure.** This structure (discussed later) is still used today, but it has given way to other structures, which, from a user's standpoint, are less formal and much easier to use.

Data Views

While companies were developing new and better ways to handle data, an important change was taking place: fewer programmers and more and more senior managers and office clerks were using the database management systems. However, the data had to be provided to these different types of users in different ways. Most users didn't want to know about the particular methods used in handling the data. In addition, all users didn't need the same data, and even if they did, they didn't want to examine the data in the same ways.

How can a database serve different functional areas? To answer this, look at the example of the football team: How can a database about the players serve different functions? The illustrations in Figure 7.4 show that each functional area of the franchise has access to the database for its own needs. This approach makes the database very effective. Because all the data is in one place, it is easier to control **data integrity** (the data is complete, accurate, and not misleading), reduce data redundancy, and share the data among all interested users (data independence).

In practice, you can view data in a database system in three ways: *conceptually, logically,* and *physically.* The diagram in Figure 7.5 and the following discussion will help you to understand the different ways of viewing data.

Conceptual View

The **conceptual view** of data represents the general view of the overall flow of data within an organization

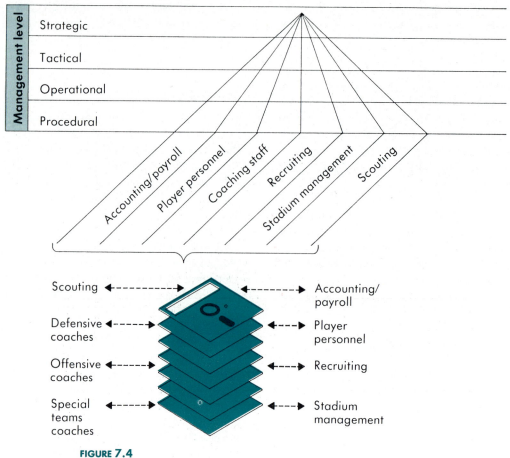

FIGURE 7.4
A football team database

such as a bank, hospital, farm, retail store, or football team. The purpose of this view is to identify all entities (record types) used in the organization and to identify the relationships among those entities. At the conceptual level, you are not concerned about which database management system to use, how the data itself will be used specifically, or how the system will be implemented (placed into operation). Thus, the purpose of the conceptual view is to gain an overall grasp of the organization's data.

Logical View   The **logical view** of data represents the application stage in the process of understanding the way data is organized and creating a database system. Thus, it represents the individual user's view of the database. (However, this view is always based on the conceptual view.) It is possible to have as many different logical views of a database as there are users.

For example, typical information needs of particular football franchise users of the database might be:

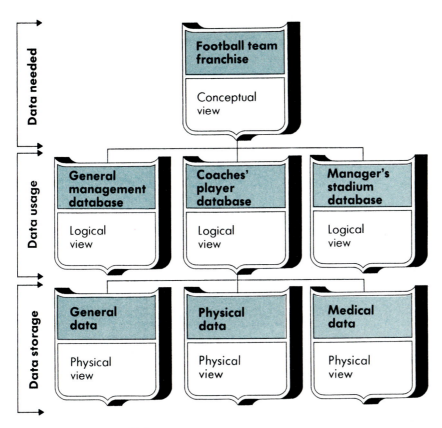

FIGURE 7.5
Different views of data

1. **Special teams coaches**—"Provide me with a list of players arranged according to their time over 40 yards who are not first string players on either offense or defense."

2. **Recruiting**—"What offensive team positions are currently manned by players who have been in professional football for more than five years?"

3. **Advertising and promotions**—"Which players have previously been involved in advertising or promotions for the franchise? Which players have been involved in commercial advertising?"

In each of these examples of database use, the player's name is used; however, in each case, it serves a different function, depending on the needs of the user.

Physical View   The **physical view** of data represents the view that is closest to the actual machine representation of the data. It deals with the storage of data within the computer system—where the data is stored and what medium is used, as well as the format of the stored data. The data is no longer described only in terms of concepts and logic; it can also be accessed and manipulated physically (or electronically). Generally speaking, the physical formats of the data are not important to the user or the programmer, but they are important to the computer system. What is important to the user is that the bridge or linkage between the logical view and the physical view is the database management system.

Database Systems

Before you proceed, you need more formal definitions of a database and its components. A database is an integrated collection of related computer data files. It is through integration that databases are able to solve two major problems normally associated with the more traditional data storage techniques of file processing: data independence and data redundancy. The goal of any database system is to increase data independence, reduce data redundancy, increase the speed of data handling, and improve the ease of data access.

Figure 7.3 showed how file management systems can be viewed on a file-record-field-character hierarchy, as presented in Chapter 1. If you were to extend the hierarchical view of data, you would see that groups of related files would constitute a database.

The value of the database rests entirely on the quality of the data collected and stored. If you've been careless in the data collection operation, the data may contain errors, making the data worthless for use in future decision making. In the computer industry, this has been referred to as "**gar-bag̲e-i̲n, g̲arbage-o̲ut,**" **GIGO** for short.

Definition of a Database

Databases are made up of entities, attributes, entity records, and keys. An **entity** is any identifiable object, concept, or activity belonging to an organization. Organizations can have many different entities. For example, if the organization is a football team, one of the entities within the football franchise structure is the PLAYER. Other entities could be COACHES, STADIUM SEATING, EQUIPMENT, BUDGETS, and so on. Thus, a database entity is similar to a record in a file management system.

An **attribute** (also referred to as a **field, data item,** or **data element**) is a property of an entity and is represented by a name and a set of values. Like an organization, an entity may have several attributes. For the football team example, the attribute POSITION could have several values, including QUARTERBACK, TIGHT END, OUTSIDE LINE BACKER, STRONG SAFETY, and so on. Thus, an attribute of an entity is similar to a field of a record in a file management system.

An **entity record** is a set of attributes and their associated values that describe a particular entity occurrence. If you have the entity called PLAYER with attributes of NAME, JERSEY NUMBER, POSITION, YEARS-PROFESSIONAL, and COLLEGE ATTENDED, three entity records could be

JAMES SMITH, 85, Flanker, 3, Baylor University
ROY O'NEILL, 54, Defensive Tackle, 2, University of Nebraska
LARRY HAND, 34, Running Back, 0, Miami (Florida)

A key, as mentioned previously, is an attribute that uniquely identifies the attribute values for that entity record. Keys can be thought of as being primary or secondary. Primary keys, such as JERSEY NUMBER, are considered the most important and are generally used to search for a particular entity record.

Relationships within a Database

A **relationship,** in database terms, represents the way two pieces of data—that is, entities and attributes—are tied together. This relationship can be one-to-one, one-to-many, or many-to-many.

One-to-One (1:1) Relationships

When a single value in one entity can be related to only a single value in a second entity and a single value in the second entity relates to only one value in the first, it is called a **one-to-one (1:1) relationship.** For example, if a unique JERSEY NUMBER is assigned to each PLAYER NAME, the relationship between JERSEY NUMBER and PLAYER NAME is said to be one-to-one, as shown in Figure 7.6a.

One-to-Many (1:m) Relationships

When a value in one entity relates to many values in the second entity but a value in the second entity can relate to only one value in the first, it is called a **one-to-many (1:m) relationship.** At any given point in time, zero, one, or many player names can be associated with a time over 40 yards. Thus, a given time over 40 yards can be assigned to many player names, and there is a "many" relationship between time and player names, as shown in Figure 7.6b.

Many-to-Many (m:m) Relationships

When entity #1 references many values in entity #2 and a value in entity #2 relates to many values in entity #1, it is called a **many-to-many (m:m) relationship.** In the football team example, any PLAYER NAME could be associated with several different POSITIONs, and any POSITION could be performed by several PLAYER NAMEs. In this case, you have a many-to-many relationship between PLAYER NAME and POSITION, as illustrated in Figure 7.6c. For example, LARRY HAND is normally a RUNNING BACK but could also play as a PUNTER. However, he is not the only running back on the team, nor is he the only one capable of being a punter.

Types of Database Structures

This section will introduce you to the advantages and disadvantages of three **database structures** in common use today: **hierarchical, network,** and **relational.** The different structure types are referred to as **models,** or *database models.*

Hierarchical Structure

The concept of hierarchy is relatively easy to understand, especially in the area of organizations. For example, in a football team there are a head coach, unit coaches, positions, and players, as shown in Figure 7.7. Hierarchical databases are arranged in the same fashion. The topmost entity is referred to as the **dominant entity,** and lower entities in the structure are called **subordinate.** The relationship between the dominant entity and the subordinate entities is one-to-many. For every subordinate entity there can be only one dominant entity. Hierarchical databases are used mostly for

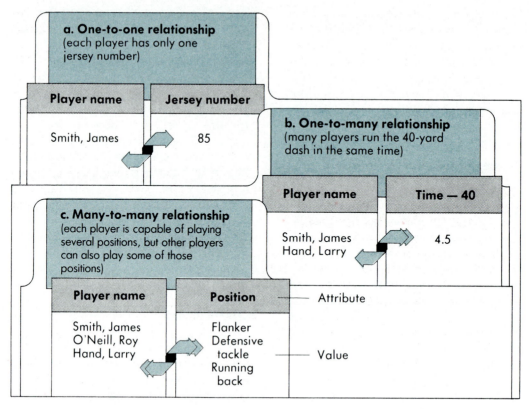

a. One-to-one relationship
(each player has only one jersey number)

Player name	Jersey number
Smith, James	85

b. One-to-many relationship
(many players run the 40-yard dash in the same time)

Player name	Time — 40
Smith, James Hand, Larry	4.5

c. Many-to-many relationship
(each player is capable of playing several positions, but other players can also play some of those positions)

Player name	Position
Smith, James O'Neill, Roy Hand, Larry	Flanker Defensive tackle Running back

Attribute

Value

FIGURE 7.6
**Relationships between attribute values
(single arrowhead = one relationship; dual
arrowhead = many relationships)**

large computers and are not generally found on programs for microcomputers.

The major advantage associated with the hierarchical structure is the ready availability of proven hierarchical DBMS packages. Other advantages include its relative simplicity and ease of use. Also, data-handling speed is predictable because all relationships between entities are known and do not frequently change.

The disadvantages include the lack of easy ways to implement many-to-many relationships and the fact that the insertion and deletion of entities are complex. Finally, when using a hierarchical DBMS, you are allowed to access subordinate entities only through the dominant entity.

Network Structure

In network structures, the concepts of dominant and subordinate entities are expanded. All entities are allowed to be both dominant and subordinate at the same time. Like the hierarchical models, these DBMS packages are used on large computers.

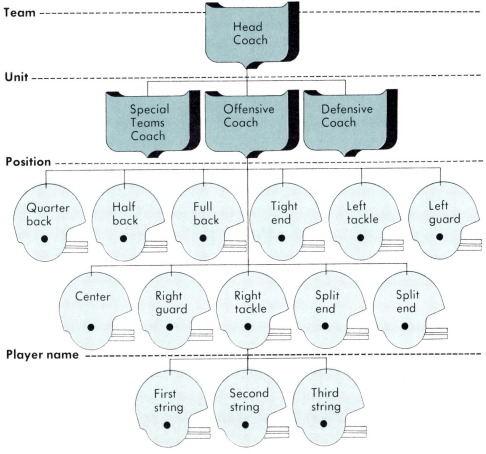

FIGURE 7.7
Hierarchy of a football team

The basic concept involved in this structure is the interconnection of entities as a "network." The terms *dominant* and *subordinate* are not used; instead, you use the terms **owner record** and **member record,** as shown in Figure 7.8. Note that the figure introduces a new term: **set type.** The set type gives the relationship between an owner record and member records. In the football team example, a set type of OFFENSIVE TEAM could exist within a framework composed of an owner record of OFFENSIVE COACH and member records identified by POSITIONs Furthermore, a single POSITION (for example, quarterback) is an owner record of several member records known as PLAYER NAMEs.

Network models allow easy implementation of one-to-many relationships and

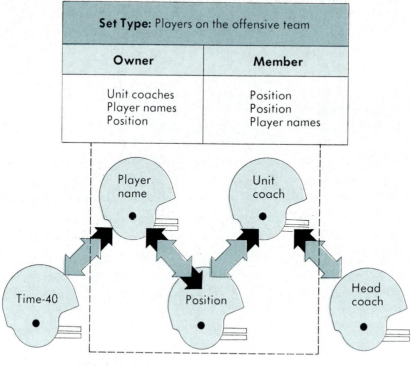

Set Type: Players on the offensive team	
Owner	**Member**
Unit coaches Player names Position	Position Position Player names

FIGURE 7.8
Network structure

many-to-many relationships. Perhaps the biggest advantage of the network model is that it is the only structure with a recognized set of standards.

The major disadvantage of the network structure is that to use the database effectively, the user must be very familiar with the record types and set types involved in the structure. In short, the network model is very complex to use, and the user is generally required to have programming skills.

Relational Structure

Software packages using the relational model are not only found on the large machines, but they are also available on micro-

computers. This type of structure is very easy to use, primarily because the relationships between entities are shown in table formats rather than organized like the diagrams shown for the hierarchical and network models. Tables like those illustrated in Figure 7.9 are common in relational models. Every table represents an entity type, every column represents an attribute of the entity, and every row represents an entity record. In more technical terms, rows are called **tuples.**

Relational models offer great flexibility in accessing data, because the relationship structure can be changed very easily. Records (rows) can easily be inserted or deleted, and complex relationships can be cre-

Player Database						
Player name	Position	Jersey number	College attended	Height	Weight	_ _ _

Position Database					
Position	Minimum height	Minimum weight	Minimum speed	Minimum strength	_ _ _

FIGURE 7.9
Relationships within a relational database

ated and used. The only possible disadvantage is that data access may be slightly slower when compared to the other database models. Relational models also require that the primary keys used in the database uniquely specify each entity record. Relational databases that meet the unique-key criterion are said to be in **domain/key normal form** — there are no ambiguous record references.

Major Functions of a Database Management System (DBMS)

All database management systems allow the user to do certain types of activities. In the past, the user was always the programmer, who would have to "code" the necessary instructions to access the desired data.

Today, DBMS systems, particularly those found on microcomputers, are very **user friendly,** which means that the system, usually through a series of questions and answers or by simple English-like instructions, will allow even a beginning user to access data. Although each DBMS package has its own unique instructions, you will find that in almost every instance, an extensive HELP facility is available in case you forget a command. Because most microcomputer database packages use the relational model, the major functions discussed in the following sections will be specific to a relational database.

Organization and Structure — Creation of a Database and Storage of Data

All database packages allow you to create a database. Initially, the process of creating a

FIGURE 7.10 Characteristics of Data Used in the Creation of a Database

Entity: PLAYER

Attribute	Type	Length*
PLAYER NAME	Alphabetic	30
SOCIAL SECURITY NUMBER	Alphabetic	11
ADDRESS	Alphabetic	30
CITY	Alphabetic	20
STATE	Alphabetic	2
ZIP CODE	Alphabetic	10
JERSEY NUMBER	Numeric	2
TIME-10 YARDS	Numeric	4.2†
TIME-40 YARDS	Numeric	4.2†
TIME-100 YARDS	Numeric	5.2†

* Total length of the attribute including decimal places
† .2 indicates how many decimal places

FIGURE 7.10
Characteristics of data used in the creation of a database

database means that you will "reserve" space on the disk in which to place your data. Creation also includes the process of defining the structure of your data. This structure should not be confused with database structures, but instead should be thought of as "characteristics" of your particular data or as an entity definition. These characteristics include the name of the attribute, the data type (alphabetic, numeric, or logical) and the length of the data value. The length of a data value is supplied to tell the DBMS how many characters should be reserved for each attribute; therefore, it should specify the maximum number of characters to be reserved for the attribute. Examples of data characteristics are shown in Figure 7.10.

Note that the figure shows that the attribute PLAYER NAME is alphabetic and may contain values up to a maximum length of 30 characters. Of course, you can enter names shorter than 30 characters if you want. Names over this length will be **truncated** (cut off) at the 30-character limit. For example, if you entered a name such as "Christopher Frederick Stubblefield," the application package would truncate it to "Christopher Frederick Stubblef" (30 characters). The "ield" would be missing. The truncation operation also takes place for numeric attributes. However, alphabetic data values are generally truncated from the rightmost characters of the attribute, while numeric values may be truncated from the left. The numeric attribute TIME-40 YARDS is shown to have a length of 4.2. This means that the total length of TIME-40 YARDS will be 4 digits. The ".2" portion of the length indicator specifies that two of those 4 digits will be to the right of the decimal point.

Once the structure of your data has been established through commands such as CREATE, STORE, or DEFINE, most packages will ask you to enter your data. The system will ask you to enter one entity record at a time, attribute by attribute. Many of the packages will also provide a form into which the data is to be entered. This form will appear on the screen and may indicate the attribute name, data type, and maximum length, as specified in the structure.

When Data Has Errors — Maintaining Data

One of the most important activities associated with a database is keeping the data accurate and up-to-date. Depending on the database, this activity can be an occasional operation or a constant vigil. For example, if you were working on a football team database, changes to the COACHES portion might be relatively infrequent, whereas keeping player records accurate could be very time consuming.

Data editing is the process of examining particular attributes and making changes in the attribute values as necessary. Some data editing is usually necessary immediately after a database is built. There is not much chance that even an expert data-entry person could enter a thousand entities and not make at least one mistake. For example, it would probably be a constant irritation if Jack Smith had to put up with being called "Jack Smythe" simply because of a data-entry error. In addition, Jack Smith's playing position might change, and you would want to modify the POSITION attribute value accordingly. Any database package ought to be able to handle this type of change easily. Commands such as EDIT or CHANGE are frequently used to perform these types of editing tasks.

More or Less Data — Adding and Deleting Entities

Database packages generally allow you to add and delete entities. In the football team environment, new players are periodically acquired, and they have to be added to the player database. Other players retire or are cut from the team and must be removed from the player database and possibly archived (saved) in a "former players" database.

To add entities to a database, you might use a command like INSERT or APPEND. The functions of these two commands are slightly different. A command like INSERT typically causes an item to be added to a specific location in the database. APPEND, instead, usually causes a new entity to be added to the end of the database. Finally, some database packages do not permit you to choose the location of new entities. In these packages, getting an entity placed at a particular location is usually achieved by reorganizing the database.

The deletion of entities from a database frequently requires a two-step operation. The first step "marks" the data (usually at the entity level) to be deleted, and the second step removes the data from the database. With this two-step operation, it would be possible, for example, to "mark" players who have been placed on waivers or injured reserves without physically removing the players' data. Any data marked for deletion is usually **transparent** (not available) to other operations. Commands such as DE-LETE or MARK perform this function.

It is also possible to "unmark" data that had previously been marked for deletion. In the football team example, if a player who has been placed on injured reserves returns to active status, the data could be recovered with little difficulty by "unmark-ing" it; this is done by using a command such as RECALL or UNMARK.

Finally, when it becomes obvious that the "marked" records should be removed from the database, another command, such as PACK, causes the entity to be physically removed.

Finding the Answers — Retrieval and Query of Data

Once accurate data has been organized and placed into a database, you will want to **re-trieve** particular pieces of data in the database. Database retrieval simply means that you wish to have the database management system get particular pieces of data and show them to you. A database **query** (or

inquiry) is another name for this process. Usually, a query indicates that a portion of the database is to be retrieved, but only if specified conditions are met.

To illustrate the retrieval process, suppose you have built a football team database. One of the pieces of data you want to retrieve is information about a particular player. To get this information, you might simply enter a command such as "show me information about offensive players." The database management system would then produce the information. However, the request could be more specific. For example, you might say "show me information about offensive players, but only if they are backs."

Whenever you are retrieving records from a database, you will want to use an option that lets you retrieve the particular records you are interested in. This is accomplished through the use of retrieval command options such as FOR or WHERE. These options require the use of a **relational expression.** A relational expression states the condition on which an entity record is to be retrieved. If the relational expression is "true" (the stated condition is met), the record is retrieved. A relational expression takes the form of:

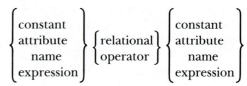

Table 7.1 presents the common relational operators and their meanings.

For example, if the special teams coach was trying to establish a list of desirable players to use on a punt return team, he could get a list of players from the PLAYER database by entering a retrieval command with the selection option, such as

TABLE 7.1 Relational Operators Used in the FOR or WHERE Option

Relational Operator	Meaning
>	Greater than
>=	Greater than or equal to
=	Equal to
<>	Not equal to
<=	Less than or equal to
<	Less than

TIME-40 $<$ 4.5. In this relational expression, "TIME-40" is an attribute name representing the amount of time it takes the player to run 40 yards, "$<$" (less than) is a relational operator, and "4.5" is a constant. Thus, the PLAYER database would now be searched, and only the names of players who run the 40-yard dash in less than 4.5 seconds would be retrieved.

Complex retrievals can be done through the use of the logical operators AND and OR. These logical operators are used to chain relational expressions together creating **logical expressions.** A logical expression may take the form of:

{relational expression} {logical operator}
{relational expression}

The retrieval criterion is still the same; whenever the logical expression is "true," the record is retrieved. This time, however, when the OR logical operator is used, either relational expression may be true to create a "true" condition. When the AND logical operator is used, both relational expressions must be true to create a "true" condition.

For example, suppose the special teams coach really wanted newer players for the punt return team. He would still want a certain time over 40 yards, but he would also want to limit the retrieval to players who were in their first or second year — that is, YEARS-PRO of 0 (rookie) or 1. If he specified the retrieval condition TIME-40 $<$ 4.5 AND YEARS-PRO $<$ 2, he would receive a list of all players who met the time criterion, but only if they were first- or second-year players. However, a simple change in the logical expression could create a vastly different result. Suppose the coach indicated the retrieval condition TIME-40 $<$ 4.5 OR YEARS-PRO $<$ 2. This time the list would include all the players who met the time criterion (regardless of the number of years they had played) and all first- and second-year players (regardless of their time over 40 yards). Therefore, be extremely careful when using logical operators, because the results of your retrieval could be vastly different based on your use of AND and OR.

Retrieval (query) functions on data within a database could be produced using commands such as SELECT, LIST, or DISPLAY, followed by a list of attribute names to be produced and a list of conditions that must be met. With such a command, you could also specify the primary and secondary keys (to establish an order or sequence for the results), along with the database or databases you want searched.

Right Data, Wrong Order — Sorting and Indexing

Another extremely useful feature of most database packages is the ability to sort data into different orders. Imagine having a database whose data had to stay in the order in which it was entered. You wouldn't expect jersey numbers to be assigned alphabetically by a player's name or the player's name to be associated with his time in the 40-yard dash! Yet different users will want data reported by each of these attributes.

Sorting (the ordering of data) can be performed on any of the attributes of a database. Frequently, sorting can be performed on an attribute in either an ascending (smallest to largest) or a descending (largest to smallest) sequence. Some packages will allow you to sort multiple attribute fields in one operation. Typical sorting commands might be called SORT or ORDER.

Sorting is useful in some situations, but it is probably more useful to index the database. Indexing may look just like a sorting operation, but, for the computer, these functions are not the same. Sorting physically moves entity records from one place to another on the disk so they are in proper order; indexing moves only the index (or directory) entries (the data is not moved or physically rearranged). You will find that with some packages indexing is much faster than sorting. Commands that perform an indexing operation might be referred to as INDEX or ORDER.

For your football team example, the special teams coach might want the players ordered alphabetically by the player's name, jersey number, or time in the 40-yard dash. Whereas there are probably multiple uses for the PLAYER database with entity records ordered alphabetically by name or numerically by jersey number, there would be a limited number of uses for a database organized by time in the 40-yard dash. Thus, the PLAYER database could be sorted (and stored) by name or jersey num-

ber. However, it is likely that the data would be indexed to create a sequence by time in the 40-yard dash.

Extending a Database for New Uses — Modifying the Database Structure

Whereas it is usually easy to load data into a database and change attribute values, it is sometimes difficult or impossible to rearrange the locations of attribute fields within an entity record. But suppose you want to change the structure of your database to include another attribute. Depending on the flexibility of the database package, this may be possible by using a command such as MODIFY or ALTER.

Even in the most limited database packages, you could always create another database, based on data already available in a current database, and add new attributes. For relational databases, there are special commands, shown in Table 7.2, for just this type of problem. These commands tend to be extremely powerful. If you wanted to separate data in one database into two databases, you could do it by using a command such as PROJECT. If you currently have data in two databases and you want to bring them together, you could do so by using a command such as JOIN.

For example, suppose you are maintaining a RECRUIT database containing the names of all the prospective players for the coming season. At the end of the recruiting season, your team will acquire some of these players — others will be deleted from the RECRUIT database. At the beginning of the season, as the recruits are actually added to the players' roster, the PLAYER database from the previous season could be JOINed to the RECRUIT da-

TABLE 7.2 Relational Model Modification Commands

Command Type	Function Performed
INTERSECT	Forms a new database containing the entity records from two databases that have common matching attributes
UNION	Is used to combine databases or to add a new attribute to an existing database
SUBTRACT	Forms a third database composed of the entity records from a second database that do not have any matching attributes in the first database
PROJECTION	Creates a new database that is a subset of an existing database
JOIN	Forms a third database by combining entity records from two other databases
APPEND	Takes entity records from one database and appends them to the end of another database

tabase to form a new PLAYER database for the coming season.

Putting the Pieces Together — Producing Reports

After you've created a database and manipulated the data, it is likely that you want to produce a report showing your results. Most database packages allow you to prepare and produce reports on the display screen, the printer, or both by using such commands as REPORT, LIST, and PRINT.

To prepare a report, the database package will normally ask you to specify the format in which you want the data to be displayed. Some packages allow very complex formats to be specified, whereas others allow only simple specifications. Typical kinds of specifications include report title, page length, column headings, attribute names desired in the report, attribute lengths (these may be different from those specified when you created the database), and whether you want arithmetic totals for numeric attributes. Thus, it is normally a relatively easy task to produce a formal report about the data contained in a database.

Other Features

Almost all database packages will allow some type of totaling, counting, or summing operations; however, a few will allow arithmetic calculations to be performed on the database itself. Some packages will allow very extensive calculations, including operations such as simple mathematics — add, subtract, multiply, divide, and exponentiation (raising a number to a power). Other mathematical functions may include determining absolute values and averages.

Some database packages will allow you to change uppercase characters into lowercase characters and vice versa. Others will allow you to convert alphabetic characters into numeric characters and numeric characters into alphabetic characters. Many database packages permit data to be defined in a "date" mode, allowing dates to be checked and manipulated in a somewhat different fashion. A few of the more advanced packages will even allow you to compare characters logically, using the same format discussed in the section on Retrieval and Query of Data. The logical operators, such as AND and OR, may also be used in this extended type of relational expression.

In certain situations, it is desirable to be able to store data in formats that will increase flexibility in sharing them. Some database packages use only DIF files to transport data to other software packages, whereas others use only ASCII files. Some of the more advanced packages allow you to store the data you've created in either format. Others will store the data in only one format but will allow you to convert the data into other formats by using a special utility program.

Finally, some database packages have extended features that deal with data integrity and security. For example, some packages are accompanied by a set of rules that can be attached to attribute fields. The purpose of these rules is to minimize errors when entering data and to notify you when a mistake is made. Thus, these rules can be used to increase the accuracy of data that is placed into the database. **Security** features —included in some of the more advanced packages—are designed to minimize access to the database by unauthorized individuals. The use of **passwords** is one of the more popular means of providing security. Depending on the package, passwords may be available at the database level, the entity level, the attribute level, or at all levels within the database structure.

Uses of Databases

Now that you have been introduced to many of the characteristics of databases and database management systems, you're probably asking yourself: What good are they? Who can use them? Are they limited to those companies or organizations with large amounts of data to store and maintain? How can they be used in the world in which you live? The answer to all these questions is quite simple: Anyone can use a database package to store and manipulate data, whether the data needs are great or small.

Brokerage firms use databases to keep records of stock activities. In some cases, the information obtained from these historical records is used to "predict" growth stocks and stocks that will be taking a turn for the worse.

Many organizations use databases to keep track of their inventory. For example, libraries frequently use databases to maintain inventories of books and other holdings. By using a database, the librarian can keep track of when books are checked out and returned, determine what types of books are frequently used (for example, mysteries, fiction, and nonfiction), determine usage patterns for particular types of books, establish which users frequent the library and which ones tend to be delinquent in returning books, perform searches for particular types of references, and so on.

Banks use databases to keep track of your checking account, savings account, IRAs, and loans. They also keep track of your credit history and the amount of money due the federal government because of the interest you earned on the money you invested.

Hospitals use databases to keep track of patients, bed utilization, drug distribution, physician performance, and billing. In some cases, hospitals are using databases to keep track of intensive-care patients not only by monitoring their progress but also by scheduling needed resources for their care. Resources like drug administration, physician visits, diet preparation, and physical therapy routines can also be monitored and scheduled.

Police units throughout the nation are using databases to track criminal patterns, types of crimes, and various violations, such as parking tickets. This data is stored and shared with law enforcement departments nationwide, including the FBI.

Museums use databases to keep track of their inventory. Some art galleries keep track of their artists, clients, holdings, and show schedules. Of course, like other organizations, museums and galleries also keep record of billing and accounts payable.

What about the individual? How can *you* use a database? How about keeping a log of all the checks you've written? You could keep track of your individual investments. Or how about a list of all the companies you have written to in search of a job? Or, perhaps, you could keep records on the books in your personal library—author, title, and person who has borrowed the book. Maybe you want to keep track of your classmates, maintain a list of credit cards and account numbers, have a mailing list for Christmas cards, and so on.

No matter what line of work you are in, no matter how large an organization you belong to, you will find that using databases will help you in keeping track of the data you will need to make decisions. Databases and database management systems are useful today; they are not coming into use, they are in use.

Chapter Summary

This chapter introduced you to databases and database management systems. Database management systems began as file management systems that supported sequential, direct, and indexed-sequential access to data. The chapter described what data is and how it is used. You learned about the various views of data, from the conceptual view (how data is thought of) and the logical view (how data is examined and evaluated) to the physical view (how data is stored).

You also learned about the concepts of relations among attribute values (one-to-one, one-to-many, and many-to-many) and how these relations are represented in different database models. The models discussed included three structural forms: hierarchical, network, and relational. Of the three, only the relational model is currently available on the microcomputer.

Next, this chapter covered the general functions of a database and functions that are common to all database management systems. Some of the common commands used by different database systems were also discussed.

The last section described some of the ways in which databases can be used. It's up to you to use your imagination to visualize their countless applications.

Chapter Key Terms

Attribute	Direct file	Key	Query (inquiry)
Conceptual view	Domain/key	Logical expression	Relational
Database	normal form	Logical view	expression
Database	Dominant entity	Many-to-many	Relational structure
management	Entity	(m:m)	Relationship
system (DBMS)	Entity record	relationship	Retrieve
Database structure	Field	Member record	Secondary key
(model)	File management	Model	Security
Data editing	system (FMS)	Network structure	Sequential file
Data element	Garbage-in,	One-to-many (1:m)	Set type
Data independence	garbage out	relationship	Subordinate entity
Data integrity	(GIGO)	One-to-one (1:1)	Transparent
Data item	Hashing algorithms	relationship	Truncate
Data management	Hierarchical (tree)	Owner record	Tuple
system (DMS)	structure	Password	User friendly
Data redundancy	Index (directory)	Physical view	
Direct (random)	Indexed-sequential	Primary key	
access	file		

Chapter Questions

1. Using an organization in your town, list several entities that might be used in a database. Now list the attributes that would be used to define those entities. Are those attributes alphabetic, numeric, or logical?

2. Make a trip to your local hospital. Check with the chief administrator for permission to talk with the people in the data processing department. Ask them what kind of database system they are using. Is it hierarchical, network, or relational? Are they using databases on microcomputers? What software package are they using? Do they see any reason for changing their current database system to another package? Why or why not?

3. Make a trip to your local bank and arrange for a tour of its computer center. During the tour, ask to see how the database system works. Ask how it was created and how data is stored, retrieved, and manipulated. Explain in a short report all that you've seen.

4. Prepare a short paper on the difference between sorting and indexing in a database environment.

5. Prepare an oral presentation on one of the three access methods presented in this chapter: sequential, direct, or indexed-sequential. Which is best to use in the database environment? Why?

6. Describe the differences among the three views of a database: conceptual, logical, and physical. As the chief executive of an organization, which view do you think would be of most interest to you? As a database user, which view is most important?

7. Compare the database structures known as hierarchical, network, and relational. Identify at least one advantage and one disadvantage of each structure.

8. Define the terms *entity, entity record, attribute,* and *attribute value.* Give an example of each of these items as it would apply to a student database at your school.

9. What is a tuple? What kind of database structure identifies relationships in terms of tuples? What kind of relationship (for example, one-to-one) most closely approximates a tuple?

10. In the football team example, you are requested to retrieve data that identifies all quarterbacks. Write, in an English-like statement, a relational expression that satisfies this request. What constants, attribute names, expressions, and relational operators did you use? Expand this request to include those players who played quarterback in college. Write the logical expression. What constants, attribute names, expressions, relational operators, and logical operators did you use?

Modules/Chapter Seven
Databases

M7a   **pfs:File** *and* **pfs:Report**
Software Publishing Corporation
1901 Landings Drive
Mountain View, CA 94043

M7b   **Lotus 1-2-3 Database**
Lotus Development Corporation
161 First Street
Cambridge, MA 02142

M7c   **dBASE II** *and* **dBASE III**
Ashton-Tate
10150 West Jefferson Boulevard
Culver City, CA 90230

M7d   **R:base Series 4000 and 5000**
Microrim, Inc.
3925 159th Ave. N.E.
Redmond, WA 98052

Introduction to Database Modules

In the modules that follow you will be given the opportunity to learn about one (or more) of the popular database packages available for microcomputers: pfs:File and pfs:Report (Module 7a), Lotus 1-2-3 (Module 7b), dBASE II and dBASE III (Module 7c), and R:base Series 4000 and 5000 (Module 7d).

Problem Statement for Database Modules

To illustrate the use of database packages, this chapter will use the job hunting problem. This problem will require you to build a database and maintain the contents of the database by adding new records, modifying attribute values, and deleting unwanted records. In addition, you will be required to query the database and produce reports based on the contents of the database.

As a job seeker, you are interested in keeping track of interviews and offers (or rejection letters) as they come in. Items to keep track of include company name and address, contact person within the company, date the company responded to the application, and the scheduled interview date or notice of "no openings." Once you get an interview, you want to be able to keep track of the salary offered, the amount of certain benefits (life insurance, health insurance, vacation days, and retirement contributions). You may also want to know the commuting distance to the job site and to order the job offers according to your personal job preferences.

Once you know what information you want to keep track of, you can build a database and use it to produce reports and comparisons. The data needed for this problem is presented in Appendix A. The following list represents the types of activities you will perform on the database once it has been built. (Note that some database packages permit the use of only one database at a time. Thus, steps 1 and 2 below may be combined because of this limitation.)

1. Build the structure of the COMPANY part of the database and enter the data.
2. Build the structure of the JOBS part of the database and enter the data.
3. You have just received a letter of rejection from WTBS Channel 5 TV. You need to enter the COMPANY part of the database and change the status of the offer from that company from "Ongoing" to "Rejected."
4. You have received a letter of acceptance from First State National Bank. You need to enter the COMPANY part of the database and change the status of the offer from that company from "Ongoing" to "Offered." Enclosed with the letter of acceptance was a description of the job containing the following details:

   Site: North
   Amount of Offer: $22,000.00
   Life Insurance: $210.00
   Health Insurance: $325.00
   Vacation: 14 Days
   Retirement contribution: $2950.00

You have established that the commuting distance is 25 miles, and your preference for the job is 2. This information needs to be added to the JOBS database.

5. Find all companies that have rejected your employment application. You want to delete any job details that appear in the database for these companies.

6. Find all the jobs in the COMPANY part of the database for which offers have been extended. The report is to contain the company name, contact person, city, state, and zip code. You want the companies listed in order by zip code. You also want a count of the number of job offers.

7. Find all companies in the COMPANY part of the database for which you have an offer and for which the amount of the offer (from the JOBS database) is greater than $19,000. You want to produce a report containing the company name, the amount of the offer, your preference for the job, and the "net" offer (the amount of the offer plus life, health, and retirement contributions). You want these jobs listed by preference (and also by company name if the preferences happen to be the same for two or more jobs).

pfs:File and pfs:Report

Learning to Use pfs:File and pfs:Report

Pfs:File is the file-handling application package for the pfs series of application packages. The package is available for a variety of microcomputer systems using the MS-DOS or PC-DOS operating system. Pfs:File is not a database package. However, pfs:File is an advanced file-handling package that performs a number of useful functions. This means that although the package does not have all of the features found in a database package, it allows you to organize, store, and retrieve information in a fast, easy, and reliable manner.

Pfs:Report is a companion application to pfs:File. It is used to generate reports designed to your specifications from the files created and stored by pfs:File. Pfs:Report is designed to provide the user with additional report features not available in pfs:File.

Before you start working with pfs:File, you need to become familiar with its terminology. Because pfs:File is a file-handling application package, rather than a database application package, the terms it uses are based on the file-processing concepts presented in the first part of this chapter. The collection of data you want to save about a particular subject is called a *file* rather than a *database,* an *entity* or *record* is called a *form,* and an *attribute* or *field* is an *item.* Thus, if you are familiar with the conventional terminology used in database or file management systems, you should be familiar with the terminology used in pfs:File and pfs:Report.

When you are ready to begin working with pfs:File, start with the computer system disk in drive A. If you are using a system that has two disk drives, a disk prepared to hold your data should be in drive B. After you have booted your system, replace the system disk in drive A with the pfs:File disk, enter the command FILE, and press the RETURN key.

When the package is loaded into memory, it will respond by placing the FUNCTION MENU on the screen, as shown in Figure 7a.1. The FUNCTION MENU lists the seven main functions provided by pfs:File. Whenever you press the ESCape key, pfs:File will stop whatever it is doing and return to this menu. One of the first functions you will want to perform in any file-handling package is to create your own file.

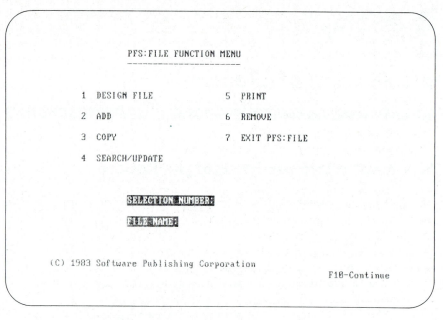

FIGURE 7A.1
pfs:File FUNCTION MENU

Solving the Job Hunting Problem

The remaining sections of this module are devoted to solving the job hunting problem. You may want to refer to the problem statement in the Introduction to Database Modules before you continue. Also, remember that the data used in the problem can be found in Appendix A.

Building a File — The DESIGN Function

To define a file, select function 1 from the FUNCTION MENU, press the TAB key to move to the next item in the menu, enter the name of the file you wish to define, and press the F10 key to perform the function selected. A file name may be one to eight characters long and may use the letters A through Z, the digits 0 through 9, and the characters $ # & @ ! % ' ( ) – < > _ \ ^ and ~. A file name can also have an extension—a period followed by one, two, or three characters. If a file name has an extension, the extension must always be used when referring to that file. A file name also indicates the disk drive where the file is stored. Thus, if you specify a file named JOBS, pfs:File will work on a file named JOBS on the system default drive—usually drive A. If you specify a file named B:JOBS, pfs:File will work with a file named JOBS on drive B.

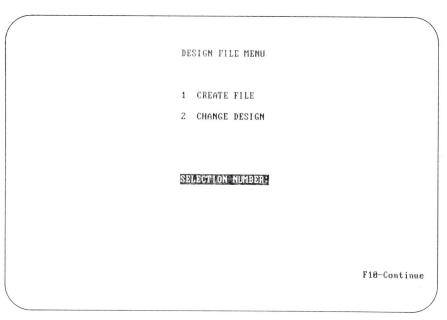

```
DESIGN FILE MENU


1   CREATE FILE

2   CHANGE DESIGN




    SELECTION NUMBER:




                                    F10-Continue
```

FIGURE 7A.2
pfs:File DESIGN FILE MENU

For the sample problem, enter the file name B:JOBS, press the F10 key, and the DESIGN FILE MENU shown in Figure 7a.2 will appear on the screen. If the JOBS file already exists and you want to change its design, select function 2. However, since you are designing the file for the first time, select function 1 to create the file. Pressing F10 to continue will cause a blank form to be displayed on the screen, like the one in Figure 7a.3.

A form is made up of items that describe the data you want to place in the file. Each item should have a name that ends with a colon (:). Be sure to leave spaces after the item name so that you can enter the data when you have completed the form design.

To create a form like the one shown in Figure 7a.4, use the arrow, the HOME, and the RETURN keys to move the cursor around the screen. To indicate the location of an item, place the cursor where you want an item to begin and enter the item label. Each form can hold a maximum of 100 items and can contain up to 32 pages. You can move back and forth between pages by using the PgUp (Page Up) and the PgDn (Page Down) keys. If you create a form with more than one page, the page number in the lower-right corner of the screen will be followed by an asterisk (*) to indicate that there are additional pages in the form.

If you want to erase a page of the form design, display that page on the screen and press the CTRL (Control) and HOME keys. The page that is dis-

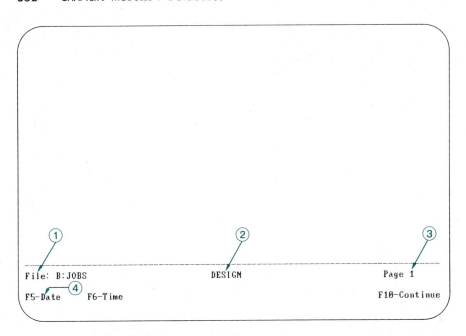

FIGURE 7A.3
**pfs:File blank form DESIGN screen: message area contents
([1] name of file you are working with; [2] what information
you should be entering; [3] number of the page for this
form displayed on the screen; [4] the function keys available
and what they do)**

played will be erased but not removed from the form. To remove a page from a form, select function 2 (change design) from the DESIGN FILE MENU.

When you have finished designing the form, press the F10 key to save the form and return to the FUNCTION MENU. If you press the ESCape key, you will return to the FUNCTION MENU; however, the form you were working on will not be saved.

Entering Data — The ADD Function

Now that the form for the file has been designed, it is time to enter the data you want to save. To do this, simply select function 2 from the FUNCTION MENU. If you just finished entering the form design, the name of the file will still be on the screen, and you don't need to reenter it. After pressing the F10 key to continue, you will see an empty form like the one shown in Figure 7a.5. Note that this form is "form 1," and it contains the material you created earlier. Whenever you choose the ADD function, pfs:File will display the first empty form in your file.

```
Company Name:

Address:

City:                State:      Zip:

Contact Person:

Responded:           Interview:          Status:

Worksite:            Commuting Distance:  Vacation Days:

Offer:          Life:           Health:          Retirement:

Job Preference:




-------------------------------------------------------------
File: B:JOBS               DESIGN              Page 1

F5-Date      F6-Time                          F10-Continue
```

FIGURE 7A.4
JOBS File form DESIGN

```
Company Name:

Address:

City:                State:      Zip:

Contact Person:

Responded:           Interview:          Status:

Worksite:            Commuting Distance:  Vacation Days:

Offer:          Life:           Health:          Retirement:

Job Preference:




-------------------------------------------------------------
File: B:JOBS               FORM 1              Page 1

F2-Print Form      F5-Date      F6-Time        F10-Continue
```

FIGURE 7A.5
Blank input form for the JOBS File

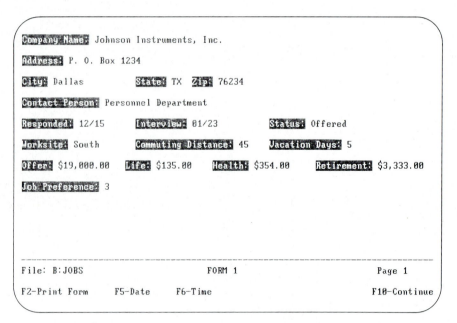

FIGURE 7A.6
Input data for the first form in the JOBS File

To enter the job hunting data, use the TAB key to move to the first space after an item name and type the appropriate entry. Use the PgUp and PgDn keys to move between pages. When you have entered all of the data for the first form, as shown in Figure 7a.6, press the F10 key to move to the next form. Once you have entered the data for all of the forms, press the ESCape key to return to the FUNCTION MENU. Pfs:File will automatically save your forms (and data) in the file. (You will need to enter the three job offers from Johnson Instruments, Inc., as three different forms. This is because pfs:File is a file-handling package rather than a database. Also note that Lewis & Melts Mortgage Company should be entered as Lewis & Melts Mortgage Co. [the maximum usable item length] because of the length of the name. Although the length will not cause problems now, when you are creating reports later the length of the name could be a problem.)

Correcting Errors When Entering Data

If you make a mistake while entering the data, press the BACKSPACE key to erase the entry and enter the correct data. When you notice a mistake in a previous item, use the TAB or the arrow keys to move the cursor back to the incorrect data and alter the entry by entering the correct data over the error. If

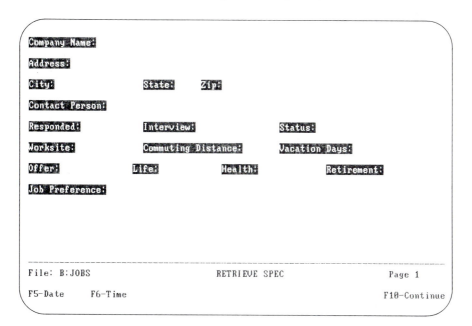

```
Company Name:

Address:

City:                State:       Zip:

Contact Person:

Responded:           Interview:              Status:

Worksite:            Commuting Distance:     Vacation Days:

Offer:          Life:           Health:            Retirement:

Job Preference:




   ------------------------------------------------------------------
File: B:JOBS               RETRIEVE SPEC                   Page 1

F5-Date     F6-Time                               F10-Continue
```

FIGURE 7A.7
pfs:File RETRIEVE SPECifications screen

you suddenly realize that you made an error on a previous form, you will have to use the SEARCH/UPDATE function in the FUNCTION MENU to make the correction.

Changing the Contents of a File — The SEARCH/UPDATE Function

The SEARCH/UPDATE function is used to retrieve specific forms from your file and display them, one by one, on the screen. When a form is displayed on the screen, you can use the special function keys available with the SEARCH/UPDATE function to modify the contents of the form. To use this function, select number 4 from the FUNCTION MENU and press F10 to continue.

Pfs:File will display RETRIEVE SPECifications, as shown in Figure 7a.7. You can now enter the specifications that a form must meet in order to be displayed on the screen. Use the TAB key to move the cursor to the item that you want to set the specifications for and enter the desired conditions. The conditions you can set for each item fall into six categories: (1) blank, (2) full item match, (3) partial item match, (4) numeric item match, (5) numeric range match, and (6) the "not" match.

Leaving a blank for the retrieval specifications indicates that pfs:File should ignore this item. In other words, there is no condition set on the item. A full item match specification indicates that you want those forms displayed where the item matches exactly the characters you have entered. For a full item match, pfs:File uses the following rules:

- Spaces before the first character and after the last character are ignored.
- Multiple spaces within the item are treated as a single space.
- There is no distinction made between uppercase and lowercase letters.

If you want to use a full item match method to select the form for WTBS Channel 5 TV, enter the entire name in the item labeled "Company Name."

If you do not want to enter the entire name for WTBS, you could use a partial item match specification. A partial item match specification is entered by using two periods .. (ignore unwanted characters). To specify WTBS Channel 5 TV, enter the partial match specifications wtbs .., .. tv, or .. channel ... You may even use the two periods (..) by themselves to search for forms (records) with any data entered in a specific item. This is different from leaving an item blank, because the specification requires that the item contain data. If you don't remember the TV station's call letters, you can even use the "at" symbol (@). This symbol will match any character in the position of the @ symbol in the item. For example, the retrieve specification could be entered as wt@s .. in order to retrieve the desired form.

There are two ways to match numeric data. One way is to enter digits as if they were characters. For example, you could enter the partial match specification .. 5 .. to find the form for WTBS Channel 5 TV. In this case, the digit is treated as if it had no numeric value, and the rules presented previously must be applied to the item specification.

The other method to match numeric data is to use digits. When the item is represented by a numeric value, you can search for forms where the item is greater than, smaller than, or equal to a specified value. In this case, the match specification must begin with one of the special symbols $<$, $>$, or $=$ and be followed by one or more digits. In evaluating a numeric value, pfs:File uses the following rules:

- All characters other than -, ., 0, 1, 2, 3, 4, 5, 6, 7, 8, and 9 are ignored.
- A minus sign (−) appearing before the first digit or after the last digit makes the value negative. All other minus signs are ignored.
- All periods, except the first decimal point, are ignored.

You can also specify a range of values for the match specification by using the two periods (..) in a numeric match. For example, if you want to retrieve the forms for all companies making a salary offer between $19,000 and $22,000, the match specification for the item labeled "Offer:" would be =19000 .. 22000. (Note that currency symbols and commas are eliminated from the search request.)

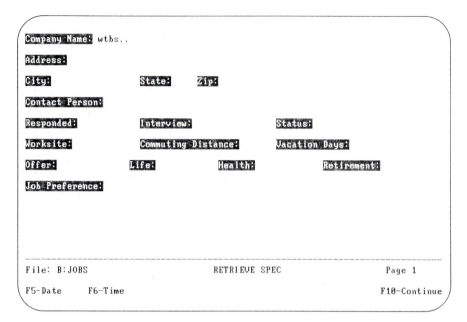

FIGURE 7a.8
Match specification to find the WTBS form

You can begin all of the preceding match specification with a slash (/) character. This character means "not," and it reverses the match specification. For example, the match specification /.. finds all forms with no data entered for the specified item.

To retrieve the form for WTBS Channel 5 TV, enter the match specification in the item labeled "Company Name:" as shown in Figure 7a.8 and press the F10 key. Pfs:File will search the file for a form that meets the match specification and display it on the screen. Once the form is on the screen, use the TAB key to move the cursor to the item labeled "Status:" and enter Rejected. Pressing the F10 key will cause the "Status:" entry in this form to be changed, and the search is continued for other forms that meet the match specification. When the search has been completed, the screen shown in Figure 7a.9 will be displayed. Press the F10 key, and you will return to the FUNCTION MENU.

To enter the data about the offer from First State National Bank, you will again need to use the SEARCH/UPDATE function. Select function 4, press the F10 key, and enter the match specification First State .. for the item labeled "Company Name:." When pfs:File displays the form for First State National Bank, enter the new data as shown in Figure 7a.10. Press the F10 key to save these changes; press the F10 key again to return to the FUNCTION MENU.

Forms found: 1

Press F10 to continue

FIGURE 7A.9
SEARCH/UPDATE completion screen

Company Name: First State National Bank

Address: 302 Central Expressway

City: Dallas   **State:** TX **Zip:** 76243

Contact Person: Ms. Judith Welpit

Responded: 11/30   **Interview:** 01/15   **Status:** Offered

Worksite: North   **Commuting Distance:** 25   **Vacation Days:** 14

Offer: $22,000.00 **Life:** $210.00   **Health:** $325.00   **Retirement:** $2,950.00

Job Preference: 2

File: B:JOBS   FORM 6   Page 1

F2-Print Form   F3-Remove Form   F5-Date   F6-Time   F10-Continue

FIGURE 7A.10
Updated form for the First State National Bank

```
COPY FUNCTION MENU


1   COPY DESIGN ONLY

2   COPY SELECTED FORMS

3   COPY WHOLE FILE



SELECTION NUMBER:

NEW FILE NAME:




                                        F10-Continue
```

FIGURE 7A.11
pfs:File COPY MENU

Eliminating Data from a File — The REMOVE Function

The final change to be made to your file is to remove the forms for companies that have rejected your employment application. There are three methods to accomplish this task through pfs:File. First, you can use the SEARCH/UPDATE function to locate the forms that meet the match specification Rejected for the item labeled "Status:." When those forms are displayed on the screen, press the F3 key to remove each of them from the file. Although this method of removing forms does work, it can take a long time to remove several forms when the file is large.

The second method of removing forms from the file is through the use of the COPY function. This function doesn't actually remove the forms from the file; instead, it creates a new file with the proper forms in it. To use this function, select number 3 from the FUNCTION MENU. Once the COPY MENU is displayed on the screen, as shown in Figure 7a.11, select a function number, press the TAB key, enter the name of the file you want to copy to, and press the F10 key to perform the selected function. If you want to copy the entire file, select function 3. If you want to copy only selected forms, as in the current problem, you will first need to copy the file design (function 1) to the new file. Whenever you copy selected forms from one file to another, the receiving file must already have a file design.

During the performance of the COPY function, only those items that appear in both the sending and the receiving file designs are copied. After the receiving file has a file design in it, you can select function 2 to copy selected forms into the new file. Pfs:File will then display a RETRIEVE SPECification screen like the one used in the SEARCH/UPDATE function, as shown in Figure 7a.7. Now enter the match specifications by moving the cursor to the item labeled "Status:" and entering the text /Rejected for "not rejected." Press the F10 key, and all the forms in the JOBS file that have a status other than "Rejected" will be copied to the new file. You now have two files—the JOBS file, containing the data on all the companies to which you have applied, and your new file, containing only those companies that have not rejected your application.

The final method of removing the forms is to use the REMOVE function, which was designed precisely for tasks like removing companies having a "Rejected" status. From the FUNCTION MENU, select number 6 and press the F10 key. Pfs:File will now display the RETRIEVE SPECifications screen. You will have to move the cursor to the item labeled "Status:," enter Rejected, and press the F10 key. A screen warning you that selected forms are about to be removed will be displayed. Pressing the F10 key will remove the forms and display a screen telling you how many forms have been removed. Pressing the F10 key again will return you to the FUNCTION MENU, and your file will contain only the forms for those companies that have not rejected your application.

Building Reports — Using pfs:Report

Pfs:File has the capability of printing the data in your files through the use of the PRINT function. However, pfs:File cannot do more than simply print all or selected contents of forms; for this, pfs:Report must be used. To use pfs:Report, you will need to exit pfs:File by selecting function 7 from the FUNCTION MENU and replacing the pfs:File disk in drive A with the pfs:Report disk. After entering the command REPORT and pressing the RETURN key, the pfs:Report REPORT MENU, shown in Figure 7a.12, will be displayed on the screen. Before going on with the job hunting problem, it will be helpful to understand what REPORT can do and how it works.

Pfs:Report will print a table consisting of up to 16 vertical columns and an unlimited number of rows. Each column corresponds to an item from the form design in your file or an item you have created in your report. Each row corresponds to a single form from your file. Column widths are determined by the number of characters in the item label or the characters in the item's data, whichever is greater. Although the report can have up to 16 columns, the printer is limited in the number of characters it can print on a line. If the number of characters in one row of your report exceeds the capacity of the

```
                  PFS:  R E P O R T
                  ---------------------


          1   PRINT A REPORT

          2   PRE-DEFINE A REPORT

          3   SET NEW HEADINGS

          4   EXIT PFS:REPORT



          SELECTION NUMBER:

          FILE NAME:



       (C) 1983 Software Publishing Corporation

                                      F10-continue
```

FIGURE 7A.12
REPORT MENU: pfs:Report initial screen

printer, the report will be truncated (the last columns will not be printed).

Pfs:Report automatically sorts the forms being printed, based on the value of the data in column 1. If the data in column 1 is the same for more than one row, those rows are sorted according to the contents in column 2. Only the first two columns are used in the sorting process. If you do not wish to sort your report, then number the first column as column 3. If the data in column 1 is the same for more than one row, it is printed only for the first row. If the data in both column 1 and column 2 is the same, the data is printed only for the first row meeting that condition. The remaining columns of each form will always be printed, even though they may contain the same data from one row to the next.

Finally, pfs:Report allows you to perform column calculations and create new derived columns based on the results of those calculations. For column calculations, special commands are entered into the report specifications to control the way a column is treated, as well as to control the calculations done on that column. Table 7a.1 presents a summary of the column control commands used by pfs:Report. Up to three new columns can be derived from other columns in your report by calculating the values for the derived column from the values in the other columns (including existing derived columns) in the report (the derived columns are counted as part of the maximum of 16 columns permitted for each report).

TABLE 7A.1 Commands (Report Specifications) to Control Columns

Command	Function
N	Numeric — treats the column numerically and lines up the decimal points
A	Average — treats the column numerically and prints an average at the end
SA	Subaverage — gives a subaverage whenever column 1 changes
C	Count — counts the number of entries in a column, whether the information in the column is numeric or alphabetical
SC	Subcount — gives a subcount whenever column 1 changes
I	Total — treats the column numerically and prints a total at the end
ST	Subtotal — gives a subtotal whenever column 1 changes
P	Page break — starts a new page each time the entry in column 1 changes
K	Keyword — prints the same form once for every string of characters in the item selected (can be used only in column 1)
#	Identifies a number as a column number in a derived column formula

Now that you have a general understanding of how pfs:Report works and what it can do, look again at the REPORT MENU. If you select function 3 from the menu, you are given the option of changing the item label that will be printed at the top of a column in your report. Selecting function 2 allows you to predefine a report to be printed from your file. This option is helpful if you are going to be using frequently a particular report format over a long period of time. The steps involved in creating the predefined report are exactly the same as those used when selecting function 1, except that the report specifications are stored for later use rather than cause a report to be printed immediately.

Building a Report with Column Controls

To print the report of companies from which you have received job offers, select function 1 from the REPORT MENU and press the F10 key. Pfs:Report will display the same screen as pfs:File for RETRIEVE SPECifications (shown in Figure 7a.7). Before pressing the F10 key again, enter the match specification Offered for the item labeled "Status:." The next screen allows you to enter the REPORT OPTIONS. Because you are not using a predefined report,

```
                        REPORT OPTIONS



        TITLE: REPORT OF JOB OFFERS
        PRE-DEFINED REPORT NAME:



        OUTPUT TO: lpt1:

        LINES PER PAGE: 66        PAGE WIDTH: 80




                                              F10-continue
```

FIGURE 7A.13
pfs:Report REPORT OPTIONS screen

simply enter the title you want placed at the top of your report, as shown in Figure 7a.13. If you are not using a standard-size paper, this menu will allow you to change the number of lines per page (page length) and the page width.

Press the F10 key, and the REPORT SPECification screen will appear. The job hunting report requires that the list be sorted by zip code. To accomplish this, enter a 1 in the field for the item labeled "Zip:." Remember that the first column is automatically sorted, so placing the zip code in column 1 will sort the report as specified. Now enter the remainder of the column specifications, as shown in Figure 7a.14. Note that the item labeled "Company Name:" has the specification 4c. This specification indicates that the company name should be the fourth column in the report and a "count" of the number of entries in that item should be printed. This "count" specification will tell you the number of job offers you have received. Finally, press the F10 key to produce the report shown in Figure 7a.15.

Building a Report with Derived Columns

The final report you need to produce is a list of job offers that exceed $19,000. This report is also supposed to be in the order of preference, and it should show

Company Name: 4c

Address:

City: 2   **State:** 3   **Zip:** 1

Contact Person: 5

Responded: **Interview:**   **Status:**

Worksite: **Commuting Distance:**   **Vacation Days:**

Offer: **Life:**   **Health:**   **Retirement:**

Job Preference:

File: B:JOBS   REPORT SPEC   Page 1

F7-Derived Columns   F10-continue

FIGURE 7A.14
REPORT SPECifications screen for the report on job offers

```
                        REPORT OF JOB OFFERS

     Zip     City      State        Company Name              Contact Person
    -----   --------   -----   ----------------------------   -------------------------
    76202   Denton      TX     Lewis & Melts Mortgage Co.     Mrs. Roberta Accure
    76234   Dallas      TX     Johnson Instruments, Inc.      Personnel Department
                        TX     Johnson Instruments, Inc.      Personnel Department
                        TX     Johnson Instruments, Inc.      Personnel Department

    76243   Dallas      TX     First State National Bank      Ms. Judith Welpit
    76341   Dallas      TX     Matt's Films, Inc.             Personnel Office
    76907   Ft. Worth   TX     Hormell Texas Chili Company    Mr. Foster Brooks
    79034   Dennison    OK     Ethyl & Jung, DDS              Dr. Emil Franz Jung
    79345   Tulsa       OK     Nephi's Hopi Crafts            Mrs. Carletta Whitecloud

                                ------------------------------------
                        Count:                              9
                                ------------------------------------
```

FIGURE 7A.15
pfs:Report's report on job offers

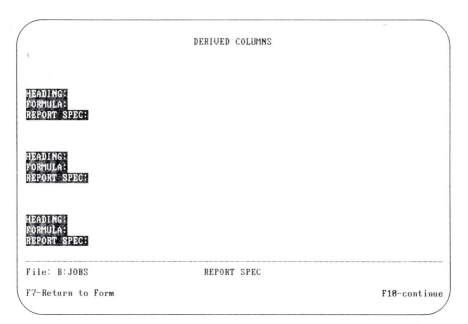

FIGURE 7A.16
pfs:Report DERIVED COLUMNS screen

the "Net Offer" from each company. To produce this report, select function 3 from the REPORT MENU and change the label for job preference to RANK. Without this change, the report will be too wide for the paper and will be truncated. After making the change, press the F10 key, select function 1 from the REPORT MENU, and press the F10 key. When the RETRIEVE SPECifications screen is displayed, enter the word *Offered* for the item labeled "Status:," and enter >19000 for the item labeled "Offer:." Pressing the F10 key will produce the REPORT OPTIONS screen; enter the title REPORT ON COMPANIES MAKING OFFERS MORE THAN $19,000. Pressing the F10 key again will cause the REPORT SPECifications screen to appear. Because you want the report sorted by preference and by company name within groups of preferences, enter 1 for the item labeled "Job Preference:" and 2 for the item labeled "Company Name:." You can now enter the row numbers 3, 4, 5, and 6 for the items labeled "Offer:," "Life:," "Health:," and "Retirement:."

To derive a new column labeled "Net Offer," press the F7 key, and the DERIVED COLUMNS screen, shown in Figure 7a.16, will appear. This screen allows you to enter the HEADING, FORMULA, and REPORT SPEC for each of the three columns you are allowed to derive. For the HEADING, enter the title you want printed above the derived column. If you leave this item blank, pfs:Report will print the formula for the column as a heading.

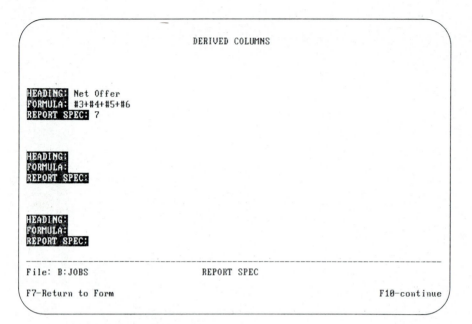

FIGURE 7A.17
REPORT SPECifications for deriving the Net Offers column

To enter a FORMULA, you must add (+), subtract (-), multiply (*), or divide (/) columns in your report. The columns in your formula are identified by number with a # sign in front. Formulas may also contain constants and may use parentheses [( )] to indicate the order of arithmetic operations. To calculate the "Net Offer," enter the formula #3+#4+#5+#6 in the item labeled FORMULA.

The REPORT SPEC item allows you to enter a number to indicate at which column in the report the derived column should be printed. You can also enter any column calculations you want. You can even put the derived column in column 1 of the report, which means that the report will be sorted according to the contents in the derived column.

Once you have entered all of the information in the DERIVED COLUMNS screen, as shown if Figure 7a.17, press the F7 key to return to the REPORT SPECification screen. If, at this point, you have finished entering all of the report specifications, press the F10 key and pfs:Report will produce the report shown in Figure 7a.18.

```
              REPORT ON COMPANIES MAKING MORE THAN $19,000

Rank          Company Name          Offer    Life   Health Retirement Net Offer
-----  ---------------------------- -------- ------ ------ ---------- ---------
1      Hormell Texas Chili Company  19,300.00 164.00 320.00   2,202.20 21,986.20
       Lewis & Melts Mortgage Co.   22,000.00 500.00 600.00   4,400.00 27,500.00

2      Ethyl & Jung, DDS            20,000.00 325.00 950.00   6,000.00 27,275.00
       First State National Bank    22,000.00 210.00 325.00   2,950.00 25,485.00

4      Johnson Instruments, Inc.    19,200.00 135.00 354.00   3,333.00 23,022.00
5      Johnson Instruments, Inc.    19,100.00 135.00 354.00   3,333.00 22,922.00
```

FIGURE 7A.18
**Report on companies making offers
greater than $19,000**

Other Features of pfs:File and pfs:Report

Although all of the features of both pfs:File and pfs:Report have been mentioned in this module, you can perform many database functions that are not supported directly by the packages. All it takes is a little imagination and extra work to achieve a wide variety of results.

The most important feature of pfs:File is that it serves as the centerpiece of the pfs series. Data stored in pfs:File can be read directly by the word processing package pfs:Write (discussed in Module 5a), as well as by the spreadsheet package pfs:Plan (covered in Module 6a), and the graphics package pfs:Graph (see Module 8a). The pfs:File package and the other pfs programs are a very powerful set of application packages.

Lotus 1-2-3 Database

Learning to Use Lotus 1-2-3 Database

Module 6b introduced you to the spreadsheet capabilities of Lotus 1-2-3. This module will investigate how Lotus is used to perform database functions. Because many of the operations performed by Lotus database derive their form from the spreadsheet package, you should be familiar with the material presented in Module 6b.

To use the database capabilities of Lotus, place your Lotus system disk in drive A and enter LOTUS. After the Lotus Access System screen appears, select the 1-2-3 option. Thus, the same procedure used to access a Lotus spreadsheet is also used to access a Lotus database.

Solving the Job Hunting Problem

The remaining sections of this module are devoted to solving the job hunting problem. You may want to refer to the problem statement in the Introduction to Database Modules before you continue. Also, remember that the data used in the problem can be found in Appendix A.

Loading Data into a Lotus Database

Once the spreadsheet skeleton appears on the screen, you may begin to enter data, using the same techniques demonstrated for Lotus spreadsheets. However, if you compare the data presented in Figure 7b.1 with previous Lotus spreadsheets, you will notice that only a single-line heading appears above each column. Each column heading becomes a field name that can be used to identify the data within that column. The difference between "normal" headings and database headings will be explained in the *search criteria* discussion.

Although only a portion of the spreadsheet is shown in Figure 7b.1, all of the job hunting data has been entered—one row per company. (Note that Johnson Instruments was entered three times because you have received three different offers from them.) This format represents one of the weaknesses of Lotus database when compared to other database packages. For example,

```
A1:  ^Company Name                                                    READY

              A                      B                   C
1        Company Name            Address              City
2   ----------------------------------------------------------------
3    Johnson Instruments, Inc.   P. O. Box 1234       Dallas
4    Johnson Instruments, Inc.   P. O. Box 1234       Dallas
5    Johnson Instruments, Inc.   P. O. Box 1234       Dallas
6    Champion Cowboy Supply      126 Hollyhill Road   Garland
7    General Electronics, Inc.   87634 Dynamics Way   Ft. Worth
8    First State National Bank   302 Central Expressway  Dallas
9    Lewis & Melts Mortgage Co.  1 Bank Plaza         Denton
10   Ethyl & Jung, DDS           23 Molar Hill Lane   Dennison
11   Aerospace Education Center  1423 Jupiter Road    Garland
12   ABC Stereo Warehouse        3434 Sound Place     Dallas
13   WTBS Channel 5 TV           9826 Neonoise Court  Plano
14   Hormell Texas Chili Company 1 Hots Place         Ft. Worth
15   Children's Museum           Look Out Point       Ft. Worth
16   FBI                         10-20 Parole Street  Arlington
17   Mosteq Computer Company     1428 Wozniak Way     Farmers Branch
18   Nephi's Hopi Crafts         16 Alma, Suite 34    Tulsa
19   Kelly Construction Company  1414 Jupiter Road    Garland
20   Jana's Management Consultants 2323 Beltline Road Irving
```

FIGURE 7B.1
Creating the original database

dBASE and R:base have the capability of loading data into two or more databases and joining elements of those databases to create other relationships. Lotus database has no such feature.

To correct an entry in the Lotus database, follow the same procedure used for the Lotus spreadsheet. Thus, to change the "Status" of the job offer for WTBS Channel 5 TV from "Ongoing" to "Rejected," simply move the cell pointer to cell I13 and type the new entry, as shown in Figure 7b.2.

To add new information into the database (spreadsheet), simply move to the row you want to contain the additional information and enter the values into one cell at a time. Thus, when new information is received about the job offer from First State National Bank, simply go to row 8 and begin entering the values for "Location," "Offer," "Life Insurance," and so on. Figure 7b.3 shows these values added to the database in row 8.

Performing Search Operations on the Database — Finding Rejected Companies

Your next problem is to locate all companies in the database containing "Rejected" as the job "Status." Then you are to remove the offer information from the database. However, you do wish to retain some information about the company, such as the company name, address, and so on.

I13: 'Ongoing   LABEL
Rejected

	A			Status	Worksite	Distance	Vacation
1	Company Name	1					
2	------------------------	2	------	--------	--------	--------
3	Johnson Instruments, Inc.	3	Offered	South	45	5
4	Johnson Instruments, Inc.	4	Offered	Mid-cities	35	5
5	Johnson Instruments, Inc.	5	Offered	North	25	5
6	Champion Cowboy Supply	6	Ongoing			
7	General Electronics, Inc.	7	Ongoing			
8	First State National Bank	8	Ongoing			
9	Lewis & Melts Mortgage Co.	9	Offered	Mid-cities	35	14
10	Ethyl & Jung, DDS	10	Offered	North	95	14
11	Aerospace Education Center	11	Rejected			
12	ABC Stereo Warehouse	12	Ongoing			
13	WTBS Channel 5 TV	13	Ongoing			
14	Hormell Texas Chili Company	14	Offered	East	53	5
15	Children's Museum	15	Ongoing			
16	FBI	16	Ongoing			
17	Mosteq Computer Company	17	Ongoing			
18	Nephi's Hopi Crafts	18	Offered	East	47	14
19	Kelly Construction Company	19	Ongoing			
20	Jana's Management Consultants	20	Rejected			

FIGURE 7B.2
Changing "Ongoing" to "Rejected" for WTBS Channel 5 TV

Q8: 2   READY

	A			Health	Retirement	Preference
1	Company Name	1				
2	------------------------	2	------	----------	----------
3	Johnson Instruments, Inc.	3	$354.00	$3,333.00	3
4	Johnson Instruments, Inc.	4	$354.00	$3,333.00	4
5	Johnson Instruments, Inc.	5	$354.00	$3,333.00	5
6	Champion Cowboy Supply	6			
7	General Electronics, Inc.	7			
8	First State National Bank	8	$325.00	$2,950.00	2
9	Lewis & Melts Mortgage Co.	9	$600.00	$4,400.00	1
10	Ethyl & Jung, DDS	10	$950.00	$6,000.00	1
11	Aerospace Education Center	11			
12	ABC Stereo Warehouse	12			
13	WTBS Channel 5 TV	13			
14	Hormell Texas Chili Company	14	$320.00	$2,202.20	1
15	Children's Museum	15			
16	FBI	16			
17	Mosteq Computer Company	17			
18	Nephi's Hopi Crafts	18	$425.00	$1,333.00	4
19	Kelly Construction Company	19			
20	Jana's Management Consultants	20			

FIGURE 7B.3
Entering new values for the First State National Bank

```
I28: ^Status                                                          READY

               A                        G       H       I       J
9    Lewis & Melts Mortgage Co.    9    11/30   01/15   Offered  Mid-cities
10   Ethyl & Jung, DDS            10    11/15   11/30   Offered  North
11   Aerospace Education Center   11    11/16   12/13   Rejected
12   ABC Stereo Warehouse         12    11/16   02/22   Ongoing
13   WTBS Channel 5 TV            13    12/03   01/06   Rejected
14   Hormell Texas Chili Company  14    12/05   01/31   Offered  East
15   Children's Museum            15    11/30   01/06   Ongoing
16   FBI                          16    01/03   01/21   Ongoing
17   Mosteq Computer Company      17    12/31           Ongoing
18   Nephi's Hopi Crafts          18    12/09   01/06   Offered  East
19   Kelly Construction Company   19    12/09           Ongoing
20   Jana's Management Consultants 20   01/06           Rejected
21   Bar Four Ranch               21    12/28           Refused
22   Matt's Films, Inc.           22    12/31   01/07   Offered  North
23   Roger, Roger & Ray, Inc.     23    12/15           Rejected
24                                24
25   Search Criterion             25                    Status
26                                26                    Rejected
27                                27
28            Company Name        28    Responded Interview  Status
```

FIGURE 7B.4
Setting up the database for query operations

Before you begin a search operation, it is necessary to set up a Search Criterion. Note that cell I25 in Figure 7b.4 contains the value STATUS, and cell I26 contains "Rejected." These two values could be placed anywhere in the spreadsheet but have been placed below the Status column for convenience. These two values represent the basis of a future search operation. Also note that row 28 now contains a set of headings (field names). These headings signify the data values to be copied when a match for the Search Criterion is found; that is, data that has matching headings can be copied. Although these headings are shown in the same order as the original headings, they may be in any order, some may be eliminated, and others may be added.

The next operation is to provide a Range Name for the set of data to be searched. In Figure 7b.5, the Range function is selected from the primary menu. Next, the Name option is selected, followed by the Create option. Finally, the column of data containing all the job status entries (column I) is identified by the name STATUS; it begins in I1 and ends in I23. Since only a single Name can be provided, this limits the size of column headings.

Now you have completed all of the preparation that is necessary before performing a search operation. You have (1) created a Search Criterion, (2) identified the data to be copied (which is optional), and (3) identified by name and range the data to be searched.

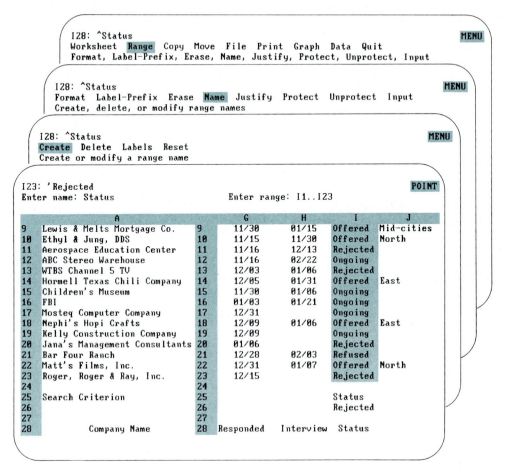

FIGURE 7B.5
Providing a name for a range of data values

To execute the search, select the Data function from the primary menu. The next selection is the Query option from the second menu. This provides the final menu that controls the search process. Note that this menu contains the key words *Input*—identifies all the data to be affected by the search (and move), *Criterion*—specifies the cells in which the Search Criterion appears, *Output*—indicates where copied records are to be placed, *Find*—locates only the records matching the criterion, *Extract*—locates and copies the records matching the criterion from the input area to the output area, *Unique*—locates only a single match, *Delete*—removes records in the input area matching the Search Criterion, *Reset*—establishes a new set of conditions, and *Quit*—returns to the previous menu.

```
I28: ^Status                                                    MENU
Worksheet  Range  Copy  Move  File  Print  Graph  Data  Quit
Fill, Table, Sort, Query, Distribution
```

```
I28: ^Status                                                    MENU
Fill  Table  Sort  Query  Distribution
Find all data records satisfying given criteria
```

```
I28: ^Status                                                    MENU
Input  Criterion  Output  Find  Extract  Unique  Delete  Reset  Quit
Set the range containing data records
```

```
Q23:                                                            POINT
Enter Input range: A1..Q23
```

	A		O	P	Q
4	Johnson Instruments, Inc.	4	$354.00	$3,333.00	4
5	Johnson Instruments, Inc.	5	$354.00	$3,333.00	5
6	Champion Cowboy Supply	6			
7	General Electronics, Inc.	7			
8	First State National Bank	8	$325.00	$2,950.00	2
9	Lewis & Melts Mortgage Co.	9	$600.00	$4,400.00	1
10	Ethyl & Jung, DDS	10	$950.00	$6,000.00	1
11	Aerospace Education Center	11			
12	ABC Stereo Warehouse	12			
13	WTBS Channel 5 TV	13			
14	Hormell Texas Chili Company	14	$320.00	$2,202.20	1
15	Children's Museum	15			
16	FBI	16			
17	Mosteq Computer Company	17			
18	Nephi's Hopi Crafts	18	$425.00	$1,333.00	4
19	Kelly Construction Company	19			
20	Jana's Management Consultants	20			
21	Bar Four Ranch	21			
22	Matt's Films, Inc.	22	$456.00	$5,000.00	4
23	Roger, Roger & Ray, Inc.	23			

FIGURE 7B.6
Selecting and performing database query operations (continued on next two pages)

As shown in Figure 7b.6, the first choice is to select the Input area, consisting of all cells from A1 to Q23 — the entire original database (see p. 375). Next, the Search Criterion is identified as being cells I25 and I26. Then the Output area is identified as cells A28 through I37 (p. 374) — the second set of headings and an additional nine rows. (You do not anticipate that any more than nine companies will have a "Rejected" status.) Extract is now selected (above). This selection completes the "search and copy" operation. Data values for all of the rejected companies have now been copied below the second set of headings. Finally, to remove the rejected companies from the primary part of the database, select the Delete option.

```
I26: 'Rejected                                                        POINT
Enter Criterion range: I25..I26

           A                      G         H         I        J
 9   Lewis & Melts Mortgage Co.   9   11/30     01/15     Offered  Mid-cities
10   Ethyl & Jung, DDS           10   11/15     11/30     Offered  North
11   Aerospace Education Center  11   11/16     12/13     Rejected
12   ABC Stereo Warehouse        12   11/16     02/22     Ongoing
13   WTBS Channel 5 TV           13   12/03     01/06     Rejected
14   Hormell Texas Chili Company 14   12/05     01/31     Offered  East
15   Children's Museum           15   11/30     01/06     Ongoing
16   FBI                         16   01/03     01/21     Ongoing
17   Mosteq Computer Company     17   12/31               Ongoing
18   Nephi's Hopi Crafts         18   12/09     01/06     Offered  East
19   Kelly Construction Company  19   12/09               Ongoing
20   Jana's Management Consultants 20 01/06               Rejected
21   Bar Four Ranch              21   12/28     02/03     Refused
22   Matt's Films, Inc.          22   12/31     01/07     Offered  North
23   Roger, Roger & Ray, Inc.    23   12/15               Rejected
24                               24
25   Search Criterion            25                       Status
26                               26                       Rejected
27                               27
28           Company Name        28   Responded  Interview  Status
```

```
I37:                                                                 POINT
Enter Output range: A28..I37

           A                      G         H         I        J
18   Nephi's Hopi Crafts         18   12/09     01/06     Offered  East
19   Kelly Construction Company  19   12/09               Ongoing
20   Jana's Management Consultants 20 01/06               Rejected
21   Bar Four Ranch              21   12/28     02/03     Refused
22   Matt's Films, Inc.          22   12/31     01/07     Offered  North
23   Roger, Roger & Ray, Inc.    23   12/15               Rejected
24                               24
25   Search Criterion            25                       Status
26                               26                       Rejected
27                               27
28           Company Name        28   Responded  Interview  Status
29                               29
30                               30
31                               31
32                               32
33                               33
34                               34
35                               35
36                               36
37                               37
```

FIGURE 7B.6
(continued)

```
I28: ^Status                                                          MENU
Input  Criterion  Output  Find  Extract  Unique  Delete  Reset  Quit
Copy all records that match criteria to Output range
```

```
I28: ^Status                                                          MENU
Input  Criterion  Output  Find  Extract  Unique  Delete  Reset  Quit
Delete all records that match criteria
              A                   G        H        I        J
 9   Lewis & Melts Mortgage Co.    9    11/30    01/15    Offered   Mid-cities
10   Ethyl & Jung, DDS            10    11/15    11/30    Offered   North
11   Aerospace Education Center   11    11/16    12/13    Rejected
12   ABC Stereo Warehouse         12    11/16    02/22    Ongoing
13   WTBS Channel 5 TV            13    12/03    01/06    Rejected
14   Hormell Texas Chili Company  14    12/05    01/31    Offered   East
15   Children's Museum            15    11/30    01/06    Ongoing
16   FBI                          16    01/03    01/21    Ongoing
17   Mosteq Computer Company      17    12/31             Ongoing
18   Nephi's Hopi Crafts          18    12/09    01/06    Offered   East
19   Kelly Construction Company   19    12/09             Ongoing
20   Jana's Management Consultants 20   01/06             Rejected
21   Bar Four Ranch               21    12/28    02/03    Refused
22   Matt's Films, Inc.           22    12/31    01/07    Offered   North
23   Roger, Roger & Ray, Inc.     23    12/15             Rejected
24                                24
25   Search Criterion             25                      Status
26                                26                      Rejected
27                                27
28           Company Name         28   Responded  Interview  Status
```

FIGURE 7B.6
(continued)

Your screen should now look like the one in Figure 7b.7. First, note that Matt's Films, Inc., originally in row 22, is now in row 19. When the Delete operation was performed, all rows that were below the deleted rows were moved up. Second, as previously indicated, only the rejected companies now appear below the second set of headings.

Producing a Report Containing Only Offered Jobs

You have already been introduced to most of the operations that Lotus database is capable of performing. However, the job hunting problem does involve a few additional situations in which the database function can be useful. Your task now is to locate all of the jobs with a "Status" of "Offered" and produce a report containing only those companies and a count of the total.

As shown in Figure 7b.8, your first step is to alter the Search Criterion so that you find only offered jobs. Thus, cell I26 now contains a new value. Next, select Data from the primary menu and Query from the second menu. Then, check the Criterion selection to make sure it has not changed. You should also

```
B27: 'List of "Rejected" Companies                              READY

                    A                             B                C
14  FBI                           14  10-20 Parole Street    Arlington
15  Mosteq Computer Company       15  1428 Wozniak Way       Farmers Branch
16  Nephi's Hopi Crafts           16  16 Alma, Suite 34      Tulsa
17  Kelly Construction Company    17  1414 Jupiter Road      Garland
18  Bar Four Ranch                18  P. O. Box 92341, Rt. 11  Denton
19  Matt's Films, Inc.            19  P. O. Box 524          Dallas
20                                20
21                                21
22                                22
23                                23
24                                24
25  Search Criterion              25
26                                26
27                                27  List of "Rejected" Companies
28           Company Name         28           Address            City
29  Aerospace Education Center    29  1423 Jupiter Road      Garland
30  WTBS Channel 5 TV             30  9826 Neonoise Court    Plano
31  Jana's Management Consultants 31  2323 Beltline Road     Irving
32  Roger, Roger & Ray, Inc.      32  457 Happy Way          Garland
33                                33
```

FIGURE 7B.7
The result of finding and removing "Rejected" jobs

recheck the Input range. (These items should have been retained from the previous use of the Query function, but it is always a good idea to check that the correct setup is being used.)

Your next operation is to establish a new Output area. Note that in Figure 7b.9, a new set of headings is visible in row 40. These were placed there before entering the Data function but up to now have not been visible. Row 40 is below the companies that were previously "removed" from the primary database, as can be determined by the company names. To complete the process of retrieving "Offered" jobs, select the Extract option, which causes all records matching the Search Criterion to be copied to the Output area.

Now it is time to produce the report. The easiest way to print only those records containing an "Offered" job status value is to save the current database into another file. Then you can delete all rows that precede row 40. This leaves you with only the list of company offers shown in Figure 7b.10. Note that a COUNT of the number of records has been placed in cell C14. (An alternate method of achieving this report that doesn't require producing another file is simply to indicate the part of the database to be printed via Print function options.)

```
I26: 'Offered                                                    READY

I26: 'Offered                                                    POINT
Enter Criterion range: I25..I26
           A                        G        H        I         J
8   First State National Bank    8   11/30    01/05   Ongoing   North
9   Lewis & Melts Mortgage Co.   9   11/30    01/15   Offered   Mid-cities
10  Ethyl & Jung, DDS            10  11/15    11/30   Offered   North
11  ABC Stereo Warehouse         11  11/16    02/22   Ongoing
12  Hormell Texas Chili Company  12  12/05    01/31   Offered   East
13  Children's Museum            13  11/30    01/06   Ongoing
14  FBI                          14  01/03    01/21   Ongoing
15  Mosteq Computer Company      15  12/31            Ongoing
16  Nephi's Hopi Crafts          16  12/09    01/06   Offered   East
17  Kelly Construction Company   17  12/09            Ongoing
18  Bar Four Ranch               18  12/28    02/03   Refused
19  Matt's Films, Inc.           19  12/31    01/07   Offered   North
20                               20
21                               21
22                               22
23                               23
24                               24
25  Search Criterion             25                   Status
26                               26                   Offered
27                               27
```

FIGURE 7B.8
**Setting up the database to find "Offered"
jobs**

Finally, using the standard Print function, print out the report shown in Figure 7b.11. Note that the heading "Companies Making An Offer" has been added to row 1, and the message "Total Number of Offers" has been added to row 14. In addition, only a limited portion of the database is printed by controlling the cell area to be printed (A1 to E14).

Producing a Report for Companies Offering More Than $19,000

Your final task is to create a report for all the companies who have offered you more than $19,000. This report is to include a net amount and should be sorted by job preference.

Your first requirement is to establish a new Search Criterion. As shown in Figure 7b.12, the new criterion is OFFER, where +M2>19000. Although the contents of cell M25 are easy to determine, you must check the status area at the upper-left corner of the screen to determine the actual contents of cell M26.

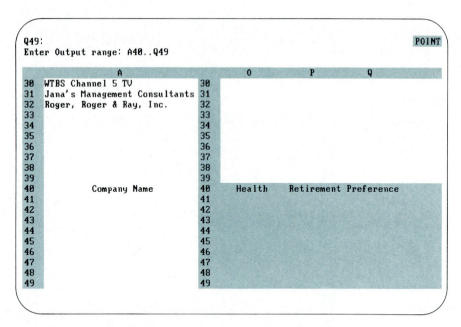

FIGURE 7B.9
Establishing an output area for "offered" jobs

```
C14: @COUNT(C5..C12)                                                    READY

          A                      C       D       E
   1                        1
   2                        2
   3      Company Name      3    City    State   Zip
   4  ----------------------4    -----------------------
   5  Johnson Instruments, Inc.  5  Dallas      TX    76234
   6  Johnson Instruments, Inc.  6  Dallas      TX    76234
   7  Johnson Instruments, Inc.  7  Dallas      TX    76234
   8  Lewis & Melts Mortgage Co. 8  Denton      TX    76202
   9  Ethyl & Jung, DDS          9  Dennison    OK    79034
  10  Hormell Texas Chili Company 10 Ft. Worth  TX    76907
  11  Nephi's Hopi Crafts        11 Tulsa       OK    79345
  12  Matt's Films, Inc.         12 Dallas      TX    76341
  13                        13
  14                        14            8
  15                        15
  16                        16
  17                        17
  18                        18
  19                        19
  20                        20
```

FIGURE 7B.10
List of job offers

```
                        Companies Making An Offer

         Company Name              Contact         City     State   Zip
-------------------------------------------------------------------------
Johnson Instruments, Inc.   Personnel Department   Dallas    TX    76234
Johnson Instruments, Inc.   Personnel Department   Dallas    TX    76234
Johnson Instruments, Inc.   Personnel Department   Dallas    TX    76234
Lewis & Melts Mortgage Co.  Mrs. Roberta Accure    Denton    TX    76202
Ethyl & Jung, DDS           Dr. Emil Franz Jung    Dennison  OK    79034
Hormell Texas Chili CompanyMr. Foster Brooks       Ft. Worth TX    76907
Nephi's Hopi Crafts         Mrs. Carletta Whitecloud Tulsa   OK    79345
Matt's Films, Inc.          Personnel Office       Dallas    TX    76341

                     Total Number of Offers              8
```

FIGURE 7B.11
A report on Companies Making An Offer

What is shown in cell M26 is the result of the logical condition +M2>19000. Zero means the result is false, whereas 1 means the result is true. The character string +M2>19000 is interpreted to mean "the value in cell M2 is greater than 19000." Your final step in this phase is not only to provide a Name for the column of data representing offers but also to make the cells in the "Offer" column a relative range.

The second requirement is to enter the Data function and select the Query option. Check the Input area designation, and, as shown in Figure 7b.12, change the Criterion to identify cells M25 and M26. Next, identify the Output area, as shown in Figure 7b.13. Finally, the Extract operation is performed, and the records matching the Search Criterion are moved to the output area.

Again, it is easiest to proceed from here by saving the original database and then deleting all but those records to be reported. As shown in Figure 7b.14, unneeded fields have been eliminated, a "Net Offer" field has been added, and the records have been ordered by "Preference." Finally, by selecting (and controlling) the Print option, you can produce the report illustrated in Figure 7b.15.

Other Features of Lotus 1-2-3 Database

This module has explained each of the functions available through Lotus 1-2-3 database; no other features are available. However, Lotus does permit the use of *compound search criteria* for more complicated search requests: Search criteria in separate cells are identified, and multiple sets of criteria are designated through the Criteria option of the Data menu. (However, Criterion cells must

```
M26: +OFFER>19000                                           POINT
     Enter Criterion range: M25..M26
```

```
M19: (C2) 18950                                             POINT
     Enter label range: M1..M19
```

	A		K	L	M	N
7	General Electronics, Inc.	7				
8	First State National Bank	8	25	14	$22,000.00	$210.00
9	Lewis & Melts Mortgage Co.	9	35	14	$22,000.00	$500.00
10	Ethyl & Jung, DDS	10	95	14	$20,000.00	$325.00
11	ABC Stereo Warehouse	11				
12	Hormell Texas Chili Company	12	53	5	$19,300.00	$164.00
13	Children's Museum	13				
14	FBI	14				
15	Mosteq Computer Company	15				
16	Nephi's Hopi Crafts	16	47	14	$15,670.00	$250.00
17	Kelly Construction Company	17				
18	Bar Four Ranch	18				
19	Matt's Films, Inc.	19	33	6	$18,950.00	$155.00

```
M26: +M2>19000                                             MENU
     Right  Down  Left  Up
     Each label in range names cell below it
```

```
M26: +M2>19000                                             MENU
     Create  Delete  Labels  Reset
     Create names from a range of labels
```

	A		K	L	M	N
7	General Electronics, Inc.	7				
8	First State National Bank	8	25	14	$22,000.00	$210.00
9	Lewis & Melts Mortgage Co.	9	35	14	$22,000.00	$500.00
10	Ethyl & Jung, DDS	10	95	14	$20,000.00	$325.00
11	ABC Stereo Warehouse	11				
12	Hormell Texas Chili Company	12	53	5	$19,300.00	$164.00
13	Children's Museum	13				
14	FBI	14				
15	Mosteq Computer Company	15				
16	Nephi's Hopi Crafts	16	47	14	$15,670.00	$250.00
17	Kelly Construction Company	17				
18	Bar Four Ranch	18				
19	Matt's Films, Inc.	19	33	6	$18,950.00	$155.00
20		20				
21		21				
22		22				
23		23				
24		24				
25	Search Criterion	25			Offer	
26		26			0	

FIGURE 7B.12
Finding offers that are greater than $19,000

Q49:   POINT
Enter Output range: A40..Q49

	A		O	P	Q
30	WTBS Channel 5 TV	30			
31	Jana's Management Consultants	31			
32	Roger, Roger & Ray, Inc.	32			
33		33			
34		34			
35		35			
36		36			
37		37			
38		38			
39		39			
40	Company Name	40	Health	Retirement Preference	
41		41			
42		42			
43		43			
44		44			
45		45			
46		46			
47		47			
48		48			
49		49			

FIGURE 7B.13
Output area for offers greater than $19,000

C3: (C2) +B3+E3+F3+G3   READY

	A	B	C	D
1	Company Name	Offer	Net Offer	Preference
2	--------------------------	------------	------------	------------
3	Lewis & Melts Mortgage Co.	$22,000.00	$27,500.00	1
4	Ethyl & Jung, DDS	$20,000.00	$27,275.00	1
5	Hormell Texas Chili Company	$19,300.00	$21,986.20	1
6	First State National Bank	$22,000.00	$25,485.00	2
7	Johnson Instruments, Inc.	$19,200.00	$23,022.00	4
8	Johnson Instruments, Inc.	$19,100.00	$22,922.00	5
9				
10				
11				
12				
13				
14				
15				
16				
17				
18				
19				
20				

FIGURE 7B.14
Sorted list of offers greater than $19,000

```
                        Current Job Offers


              Company Name           Offer      Net Offer  Preference
          ----------------------------------------------------------
          Lewis & Melts Mortgage Co.  $22,000.00 $27,500.00      1
          Ethyl & Jung, DDS           $20,000.00 $27,275.00      1
          Hormell Texas Chili Company $19,300.00 $21,986.20      1
          First State National Bank   $22,000.00 $25,485.00      2
          Johnson Instruments, Inc.   $19,200.00 $23,022.00      4
          Johnson Instruments, Inc.   $19,100.00 $22,922.00      5
```

FIGURE 7B.15
Current Job Offers report

be adjacent to each other.) For example, you may decide to search the database shown in Figure 7b.14 for "Net Offer" values greater than $27,000 and jobs that you ranked above three. First, you would establish the search criteria —cell C10 would contain "Net Offer," cell C11 would contain +C2>27000, cell D10 would contain "Preference," and cell D11 would contain +D2<3. Next, you would make sure that the data in columns C and D was identified as range names. Then, you would enter the Data Query procedure and identify the Criterion cells as C10 through D11. After these steps have been completed, other database operations proceed normally.

Finally, Lotus provides a series of special mathematical functions that are related only to database processing. Thus, normal spreadsheet mathematical functions, such as COUNT and SUM, are provided in an additional form (for example, DCOUNT and DSUM) that is related to database operations.

dBASE II and dBASE III

Learning to Use dBASE II and dBASE III

dBASE II and its newer "big brother," dBASE III, are relational database packages that are available on a number of microcomputer systems using a variety of operating systems. dBASE II, one of the oldest microcomputer database packages, is very flexible and easy to use. dBASE III is a newer extension of dBASE II and includes additional powerful features. Although this module deals primarily with dBASE II, many of the functions of dBASE III are the same as or only slightly different from those of dBASE II. The differences between dBASE II and dBASE III will be presented as necessary when they reflect significant variations in the ways the packages work.

Before you start working with dBASE II and dBASE III, you need to become familiar with their terminology. First, a *database* is called a *file*, an *entity* is a *record*, and an *attribute* is a *field*. Thus, if you are familiar with the conventional terminology used in a file management system, you should be familiar with the terminology used in dBASE II and dBASE III.

When you are ready to begin running the package, place a dBASE disk in drive A, type DBASE, and press the RETURN key. When the package has been loaded into memory, it will respond with a "." (period) prompt character. Whenever dBASE is ready to accept a command (whether in the loading process or later on), it will respond with this prompt character.

As is the case with many of the commercially available software packages, dBASE is supported by a "help" function. In dBASE II, if you wish to receive assistance, enter the command HELP [topic], where HELP is the command name and the text enclosed within brackets represents an option. (In the remaining discussion, any text of a dBASE command within brackets can be considered optional.) If HELP is requested without a topic, a listing of the HELP text will begin. The total length of this text is about 65 pages when printed, so you will probably want to supply a topic when you use the help function. When the display screen is full of information, dBASE will pause and ask you to press the RETURN key to proceed with the next screen. If you wish to terminate the HELP function, press the ESCape key at any time and return to the "." prompt. You can use the ESCape key anytime a command is being executed to terminate the command and return to the "." prompt.

The HELP function has been completely revised in dBASE III. To enter the HELP function, you still enter the command HELP. However, dBASE III will respond with a menu of general "help" topics. When you select a general "help" topic, you will be provided with another menu of more specific topics. You may either select one of the indicated topics or return to the previous menu. This approach is much more user friendly, since you have to remember few instructions to receive assistance on any given topic. As long as you can remember "HELP," you should be able to determine quickly what you should do next.

Solving the Job Hunting Problem

The remaining sections of this module are devoted to solving the job hunting problem. You may want to refer to the problem statement in the Introduction to Database Modules before you continue. Also, remember that the data used in the problem can be found in Appendix A.

Building a Database — The CREATE Command

One of the first activities you will want to perform in any database package is to create your own database. To create a new database, enter the CREATE command. The format of this command is CREATE [filename], where the filename is any file name that is legitimate for the operating system in use. Note that only the file name need be specified. dBASE will add the extension ".DBF" (database file) to each file created. Also, unless the default disk drive has been altered, the disk drive should be indicated. In the examples that follow, drive B has been selected for the storage of data. If you do not enter the optional file name when using the CREATE command, dBASE will ask you to enter it. You can also create a new database by using the F8 key, which is usually the default key for the creation process. You should check your system to see if function keys are available and to determine the commands or operations associated with each of these keys. More will be said about function keys later.

To begin the job hunting problem, enter the command CREATE B:COMPANY to represent the company database. When you have finished, you will actually have constructed two separate databases—COMPANY and JOBS. This design was chosen to demonstrate the flexibility of dBASE and to illustrate the means by which the unnecessary duplication of data can be eliminated. (For example, duplication is eliminated by placing the Johnson Instruments, Inc., data in the COMPANY database once, while the JOBS database will contain three separate offers from this company.)

Next, dBASE will ask you to specify the structure for this new database. You will see the following headings produced on the display screen: FIELD, NAME, TYPE, WIDTH, and DECIMAL PLACES. dBASE will automatically

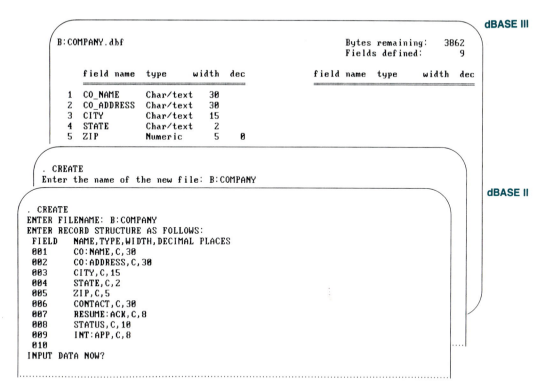

```
                                                                    dBASE III

  B:COMPANY.dbf                                    Bytes remaining:  3862
                                                   Fields defined:      9

       field name  type     width  dec       field name  type    width  dec
       ==========================              ==========================
     1  CO_NAME     Char/text   30
     2  CO_ADDRESS  Char/text   30
     3  CITY        Char/text   15
     4  STATE       Char/text    2
     5  ZIP         Numeric      5    0
```

```
  . CREATE
  Enter the name of the new file: B:COMPANY
```
```
                                                                     dBASE II
  . CREATE
  ENTER FILENAME: B:COMPANY
  ENTER RECORD STRUCTURE AS FOLLOWS:
   FIELD    NAME,TYPE,WIDTH,DECIMAL PLACES
   001      CO:NAME,C,30
   002      CO:ADDRESS,C,30
   003      CITY,C,15
   004      STATE,C,2
   005      ZIP,C,5
   006      CONTACT,C,30
   007      RESUME:ACK,C,8
   008      STATUS,C,10
   009      INT:APP,C,8
   010
  INPUT DATA NOW?
```

FIGURE 7C.1
Creating the COMPANY database with dBASE

number each field (from 1 through the maximum number of fields for each record), and the cursor will be moved under the NAME part of the heading. At this point, you need to supply a field name, descriptive of the data it is to represent. Each field name may be up to 10 characters long and may be composed of letters and digits. In dBASE II, a colon (:) symbol may also be used. [In dBASE III, an underline (_) should be used as a replacement for the colon symbol.] Spaces cannot appear in a field name—use a colon (or an underline) instead of a space to make the name more readable. Thus, as illustrated in Figure 7c.1, enter each field name and other characteristics necessary to describe your file.

In the job hunting example, all the field names are composed of letters and colons (underlines for dBASE III); if you attempt to supply a field name that is not permitted, dBASE will respond with the message BAD NAME FIELD. If this should occur, the field number is repeated, and you are given another opportunity to specify the characteristics of the field. In fact, you will be given

TABLE 7C.1 Allowable Field Types

Field Type	Explanation
C	A character field; a field that will be any combination of letters, digits, and other characters with which no computation is planned
N	A numeric field; a field composed totally of digits (and possibly a decimal point or minus sign) with which some form of computation may be performed
L	A logical field; a field, of a length of one character, that is capable of retaining a "yes/no" type of data, where "T," "t," "Y," and "y" are treated as "true" and "F," "f," "N," and "n" are treated as "false"
D	A date field; a field, of a length of 8 characters, that is capable of retaining a date in a format of "MM/DD/YY," where "MM," "DD," and "YY" represent two-digit values of month, day, and year, respectively (available only with dBASE III)

another chance, regardless of which of the characteristics you specify incorrectly.

Next you must supply the field TYPE. The allowable field types are presented in Table 7c.1. On examining the structure of the example database in Figure 7c.1, you will see that all the field names ("co:name," "co:address," "city," "state," "zip," "contact," "resume:ack," "status," and "int:app") are character fields. (Character is the default type for dBASE III.) They will never be used for computation purposes, and the data in these fields may contain any combination of letters, digits, and other characters. However, Figure 7c.2 shows that the JOBS database indicates that several fields have been recorded as numeric field types. The field names "offer," "life:ins," "health:ins," "commute," "vacation," "retire," and "preference" are numeric fields, and the data in these fields will contain only numeric data. All of these fields *could* be used for computational purposes.

The field WIDTH must be supplied next. What is the maximum number of characters of data you plan to place in the field? dBASE must deal with the maximum field width to be able to store data, even if the field width is a "worst-case" situation. In Figure 7c.1, "CO:NAME," "CO:ADDRESS," and "CONTACT" are all 30 characters long, even though you don't necessarily expect any of the data values to be that long. Specifying that they are 30

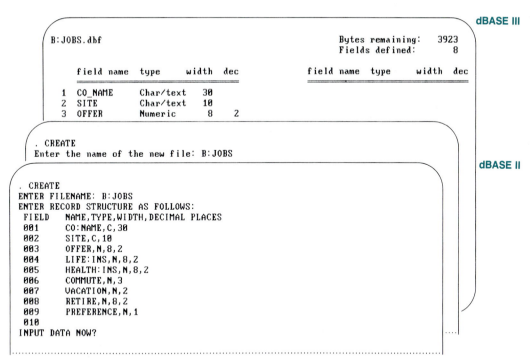

FIGURE 7C.2
Creating the JOBS database with dBASE

characters long allows you to enter a longer piece of data later. Some of the other fields and their widths are "CITY"—15 characters, "STATE"—a 2-character abbreviation, dates ("RESUME:ACK" and "INT:APP")—8 characters, "STATUS"—10 characters, and "ZIP"—5 characters.

Now you have to determine the number of any DECIMAL PLACES necessary in some of the numeric fields. If a numeric field is to contain a decimal fraction, how many digits in the field width follow the decimal point? Look at the field name "OFFER" in Figure 7c.2. Note that the field WIDTH is 8 digits, of which 2 are DECIMAL PLACES. The result of such a definition is that numeric values may be placed into this field in the format of XXXXX.XX, where "X" represents a digit position. Furthermore, note that one position of the field is occupied by the decimal point. Thus, the maximum value that may be placed into this field is 99999.99, and the minimum is −9999.99. Next, look at the "COMMUTE" field. Note that it is also a numeric field but does not contain any decimal digits. Such a field definition indicates that only integers (whole numbers) are permitted in this field. Thus, the commuting distance will be recorded in whole miles.

After all the fields of the database have been entered, simply press the RETURN key when the next field number appears on the screen. When the field name position is blank, dBASE assumes you have completed the definition of the database structure. dBASE will then automatically store the database structure and produce the message ENTER DATA NOW:. If you respond with "N," dBASE will simply return to the "." prompt. If you respond with "Y," you will be presented with a record number and a screen format that identifies each field name specified in the database structure, as indicated in Figure 7c.3. Two colons will follow each field name to indicate the maximum width of the field. This information will be shown in half-intensity (half the normal brightness) on the screen. As you enter data, the data will be shown in full-intensity (full brightness). As you are entering data, if you completely fill the field with characters, you will hear a "beep" tone, indicating the field is full. dBASE will then automatically proceed to the next field. If you are finished with the field but it is not completely filled with characters, proceed to the next field by pressing the RETURN key. If for some reason you need to return to a previous field, use the up-arrow key to go backward through the form. In fact, all the cursor control keys can be used. The left-arrow key can be used to back up within a field, the right-arrow key to go forward within a field, and the down-arrow key to go to the next field. These keys, in combination with the use of the BACKSPACE key, are extremely helpful when it is necessary to correct data. In dBASE III, you can even use the PgUp key to retrieve a previous record or the PgDn key to get the next record. In the case of numeric fields, if the field is not completely full when the RETURN key is pressed, dBASE will automatically right-justify the number(s) in that field. In the case of decimal fields, such as "OFFER," if only the integer portion of the numeric value is supplied, dBASE will automatically supply the decimal point and trailing zeros (".00").

After data has been placed in the last field of the first record, dBASE will clear the screen and automatically present the screen format for the next record. At this point, it is too late to modify the data in the previous record, because you are in the initial input mode. You will have to wait until later to make changes. If you wish to enter another record, proceed as before. If, however, you wish to terminate the input mode, do not enter any data into the first field. dBASE interprets an empty first field as a signal that you are ready to terminate the input operation and return to the "." prompt. All the data entered up to that point is automatically saved in the specified database — in this case, either COMPANY or JOBS.

Finally, suppose you had just finished the COMPANY database and you wished to start the JOBS database. Of course, you would use the CREATE command again, which closes all previously used databases. Thus, you cannot destroy the work you have already completed by getting part of one database into another by accident. However, you can use the commands that appear in the following discussion without creating another database.

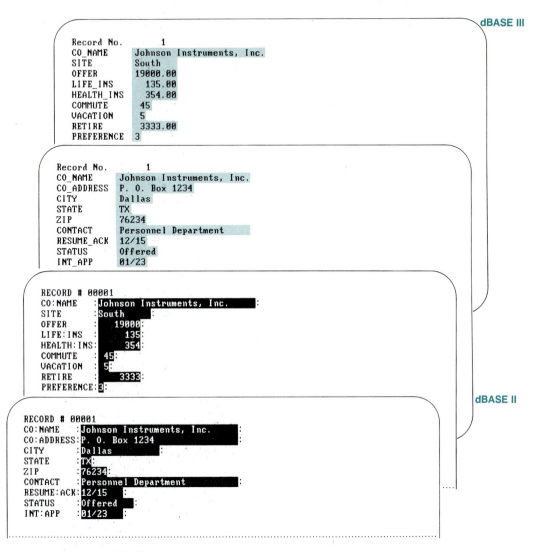

```
Record No.        1
CO_NAME       Johnson Instruments, Inc.
SITE          South
OFFER         19000.00
LIFE_INS        135.00
HEALTH_INS      354.00
COMMUTE        45
VACATION       5
RETIRE         3333.00
PREFERENCE     3
```

```
Record No.        1
CO_NAME       Johnson Instruments, Inc.
CO_ADDRESS    P. O. Box 1234
CITY          Dallas
STATE         TX
ZIP           76234
CONTACT       Personnel Department
RESUME_ACK    12/15
STATUS        Offered
INT_APP       01/23
```

```
RECORD # 00001
CO:NAME   :Johnson Instruments, Inc.    :
SITE      :South          :
OFFER     :     19000:
LIFE:INS  :       135:
HEALTH:INS:       354:
COMMUTE   : 45:
VACATION  : 5:
RETIRE    :      3333:
PREFERENCE:3:
```

```
RECORD # 00001
CO:NAME   :Johnson Instruments, Inc.    :
CO:ADDRESS:P. O. Box 1234        :
CITY      :Dallas         :
STATE     :TX:
ZIP       :76234:
CONTACT   :Personnel Department    :
RESUME:ACK:12/15    :
STATUS    :Offered      :
INT:APP   :01/23    :
```

FIGURE 7C.3
Input formats for dBASE

Starting and Stopping — The QUIT and USE Commands

Assume that you are in a hurry and all that you have time for is to build your databases. To get out of dBASE and return to the operating system, all that is required is to enter the command QUIT.

When you come back later to use the databases you have built, return to dBASE by entering the command DBASE. You will again see the "." prompt. To retrieve the previously generated databases, enter the command USE [filename] [INDEX indexfile1 [,indexfile2] . . .], where filename is the name of a previously created database. (The INDEX option will be described later.) Thus, to retrieve the company database, enter USE B:COMPANY. To retrieve the jobs database, enter USE B:JOBS. Each time a USE command is entered, any previously active databases are normally closed. Thus, it is a relatively simple matter to go from one database to another.

Keeping Track of Where You Are — The LIST and DISPLAY Commands

Now that you have two databases in storage (COMPANY and JOBS), it may be difficult to keep track of what you've done. You may not remember which database you are currently using, or you may not remember the structure of a database that was built a few days ago. Fortunately, there are a number of commands that will permit you to "recall" information about databases and other items.

Two commands, LIST and DISPLAY, are available for such purposes. The formats of the LIST command that are related to databases in general (rather than to fields) are LIST FILES [ON drive] [LIKE skeleton], LIST STATUS, and LIST STRUCTURE. Note that most of the words that appear in dBASE commands can be abbreviated by using the first four characters of the word. Thus, there is no abbreviation for LIST, but DISPLAY may be abbreviated DISP, STATUS may be abbreviated as STAT, STRUCTURE may be abbreviated as STRU, and so on.

The LIST FILES command is similar to the operating system command DIR. In fact, dBASE III permits the command: DIR[ectory] [drive] [LIKE skeleton] to be substituted for the LIST FILES command. These commands allow you to view files that exist on your disks. For example, suppose you forget the name of a database you wish to use. The command LIST FILES will list all the ".DBF" files on the default disk drive. The output from this command consists of the name of the databases, the number of records in each database, and the date each database was last updated. (dBASE III provides the names of the databases, the version of dBASE that created the files, the size of the files, and the amount of remaining space on the disk.) The same result can be achieved by pressing the F4 key, which usually defaults to a LIST FILES command.

If you wish to access the directory of a drive that is not the default disk drive, you can enter a command such as LIST FILES ON B:, which will list all ".DBF" files on drive B, as shown in Figure 7c.4. If you wish to access files other than DBF files, you can use the skeleton option. For example, if you wished to know what index files are available, you would enter a command such as LIST FILES LIKE *.NDX, which would retrieve all file names on the default drive that have ".NDX" as an extension name. In addition, the "?" wildcard option

```
. LIST FILES ON B:
Database files     # records     last update     size
JOBS.DBF                  8       01/01/87         955
COMPANY.DBF              19       01/01/87        3699

   4654 bytes in     2 files.
 291840 bytes remaining on drive.
```

```
. LIST FILES ON B:

DATABASE FILES    # RCDS     LAST UPDATE
COMPANY   DBF     00019      01/01/87
JOBS      DBF     00008      01/01/87
```

FIGURE 7C.4
Identifying the DATABASE — the LIST FILES command

that can be used with the operating system DIR command can also be used with the LIST FILES command. For example, suppose you know part of a database file name but are unsure of the exact spelling of that name: You could use a command like LIST FILES LIKE C??????.DBF, to which dBASE would respond with all database files on the default drive that contain the letter "C" as the first character.

The LIST STATUS command provides you with information about what activities are currently going on, as well as current settings of a number of default parameters. A sample of the output generated by entering this command (or by pressing the F6 key) is provided in Figure 7c.5. Note that the output begins by identifying currently active databases (as well as indexes, if any are in use). The next information provided is related to usage characteristics that may be specified by SET commands. Thus, usage characteristics such as the data disk drive, bell sounding, and so on have certain default settings that can be modified by a SET command. Finally, the LIST STATUS command provides the default setting of all function keys. (*Note:* The default function key settings are slightly different for dBASE III.) These defaults can also be altered by using the SET command.

The final form of the LIST command shown here displays the structure of the current database. By entering the command LIST STRUCTURE (or by pressing the F5 key), the output illustrated in Figure 7c.6 is generated. Not only can you determine which database is currently active, you can also determine other characteristics of the database structure. These characteristics include

dBASE III

```
File search path:
Default disk drive: B:
ALTERNATE   - OFF   DEBUG        - OFF   ESCAPE      - ON    MENU      - OFF
BELL        - ON    DELETED      - OFF   EXACT       - OFF   PRINT     - OFF
CARRY       - OFF   DELIMITERS   - OFF   HEADING     - ON    SAFETY    - ON
CONFIRM     - OFF   DEVICE       - SCRN  HELP        - OFF   STEP      - OFF
CONSOLE     - ON    ECHO         - OFF   INTENSITY   - ON    TALK      - ON
UNIQUE      - OFF

Margin =       0

Function key  F1  - help;
Function key  F2  - assist;
Function key  F3  - list;
Function key  F4  - dir;
Function key  F5  - display structure;
Function key  F6  - display status;
Function key  F7  - display memory;
Function key  F8  - display;
Function key  F9  - append;
Function key  F10 - edit;
```

```
TODAYS DATE         - 01/01/87
DEFAULT DISK DRIVE - C:
ALTERNATE - OFF    BELL      - ON
CARRY     - OFF    COLON     - ON
CONFIRM   - OFF    CONSOLE   - ON
DEBUG     - OFF    DELETE    - OFF
ECHO      - OFF    EJECT     - ON
ESCAPE    - ON     EXACT     - OFF
INTENSITY - ON     LINKAGE   - OFF
PRINT     - OFF    RAW       - OFF
STEP      - OFF    TALK      - ON

FUNCTION KEY ASSIGNMENTS
KEY      ASSIGNMENT
F1       HELP;
F2       DISP;
F3       LIST;
F4       LIST FILES;
F5       LIST STRU;
F6       LIST STATUS;
F7       LIST MEMO;
F8       CREATE;
F9       APPEND;
F10      EDIT #;
```

dBASE II

```
. LIST STATUS

DATABASE SELECTED - B:COMPANY .DBF
PRIMARY USE DATABASE

WAITING
```

FIGURE 7c.5
**Determining current settings and defaults
— the LIST STATUS command**

dBASE III

```
. LIST STRU
Structure for database : B:COMPANY.dbf
Number of data records :      19
Date of last update    : 01/01/87
Field  Field name  Type        Width   Dec
     1  CO_NAME     Character      30
     2  CO_ADDRESS  Character      30
     3  CITY        Character      15
     4  STATE       Character       2
     5  ZIP         Numeric         5
```

dBASE II

```
. LIST STRU
STRUCTURE FOR FILE:  B:COMPANY .DBF
NUMBER OF RECORDS:    00019
DATE OF LAST UPDATE: 01/01/87
PRIMARY USE DATABASE
FLD      NAME      TYPE WIDTH   DEC
001   CO:NAME        C    030
002   CO:ADDRESS     C    030
003   CITY           C    015
004   STATE          C    002
005   ZIP            N    005
006   CONTACT        C    030
007   RESUME:ACK     C    008
008   STATUS         C    010
009   INT:APP        C    008
** TOTAL **              00139
.
```

FIGURE 7C.6
Now what was the structure of the
database? — the LIST STRUCTURE command

the date last updated, the number of records in the database, how the database is used (PRIMARY or SECONDARY), and the characteristics of each field — its field number, name, type, width, and number of decimal places. Finally, you are provided with an indication of the total length of records in the database based on maximum field widths.

Each function of the LIST command is also supported by the DISPLAY command. Thus, you have your choice of wording — LIST or DISPLAY. (Other differences between LIST and DISPLAY are more fully discussed later.)

Changing the Contents of a Database — The BROWSE and EDIT Commands

Among the most important functions of a database is the capability of changing the contents of existing records. After all, it is unlikely that the situations represented by the data will always remain the same. Both the BROWSE and d Base III

```
Record No.        1     company
CO_NAME-------------------------- CO_ADDRESS------------------- CITY----------
Johnson Instruments, Inc.         P. O. Box 1234                Dallas
Champion Cowboy Supply            126 Hollyhill Road            Garland
General Electronics, Inc.         87634 Dynamics Way            Ft. Worth
First State National Bank         302 Central Expressway        Dallas
Lewis & Melts Mortgage Co.        1 Bank Plaza                  Denton
Ethyl & Jung, DDS                 23 Molar Hill Lane            Dennison
Aerospace Education Center        1423 Jupiter Road             Garland
ABC Stereo Warehouse              3434 Sound Place              Dallas
```

d Base II

```
RECORD # :00001
CO:NAME------------------------- CO:ADDRESS------------------- CITY----------
Johnson Instruments, Inc.        P. O. Box 1234                Dallas
Champion Cowboy Supply           126 Hollyhill Road            Garland
General Electronics, Inc.        87634 Dynamics Way            Ft. Worth
First State National Bank        302 Central Expressway        Dallas
Lewis & Melts Mortgage Co.       1 Bank Plaza                  Denton
Ethyl & Jung, DDS                23 Molar Hill Lane            Dennison
Aerospace Education Center       1423 Jupiter Road             Garland
ABC Stereo Warehouse             3434 Sound Place              Dallas
WTBS Channel 5 TV                9826 Neonoise Court           Plano
Hormell Texas Chili Company      1 Hots Place                  Ft. Worth
Children's Museum                Look Out Point                Ft. Worth
FBI                              10-20 Parole Street           Arlington
Mosteq Computer Company          1428 Wozniak Way              Farmers Branch
Nephi's Hopi Crafts              16 Alma, Suite 34             Tulsa
Kelly Construction Company       1414 Jupiter Road             Garland
Jana's Management Consultants    2323 Beltline Road            Irving
Bar Four Ranch                   P. O. Box 92341, Rt. 11       Denton
Matt's Films, Inc.               P. O. Box 524                 Dallas
Roger, Roger & Ray, Inc.         457 Happy Way                 Garland
```

FIGURE 7c.7
Changing the contents of a record — the BROWSE command

the EDIT commands permit the user to examine, and if necessary modify, the contents of records in the database.

The BROWSE command is perhaps the more versatile of the two commands. The format of this command is BROWSE [FIELDS fieldlist]. The simplest form of this statement is BROWSE. The result of entering this command while you are in an active database is illustrated in Figure 7c.7. The BROWSE command is sensitive to the current record position; that is, the screen presentation will begin with the current record position (last record accessed) and will list that record and the records that follow. Thus, it might be necessary to use a command like GO TOP before executing the BROWSE command so that all the records in the database can be viewed. (GO TOP will always cause dBASE to reposition the current record marker to the first record in the database.)

Once records have been produced on the screen, the current record will be highlighted; the characters of the record will be in the normal display mode, whereas all others will be displayed in half-intensity. The record number of the current record will be displayed at the top of the screen, and this number will change as you move from one record to another. In addition, the field names (for example, "CO:NAME," "CO:ADDRESS," and "CITY") will be displayed above the data, followed by dashes to indicate the total width of the field. While you are in the BROWSE mode, if the field name is wider than the field width, characters of the field name are truncated (cut off). Finally, note that only those fields that fit across the 80-column screen will be initially produced for each record, and each record will occupy only one line of the screen. In addition, a maximum of 20 records will be displayed on the screen at one time.

To deal with the limitations imposed by the BROWSE command, dBASE supports a number of functions that permit movement through or examination of the records. For example, while in the BROWSE mode, you are permitted to "pan right" and "pan left." Not all fields of a record are visible (in the example), and you may wish to view the fields on the right of the last field shown. Thus, the BROWSE command permits the use of the control codes that are produced by simultaneously pressing the CTRL key and another key. A list of these control codes and the operations they perform is presented in Table 7c.2.

If you are interested only in certain fields available in each record, you can use the FIELDS option to specify the fields of each record to be displayed. This approach reduces the necessity of panning, allows you to specify fields in any order, and permits fields to appear adjacent to one another even though they are several fields apart in the actual database structure.

What about actually changing the contents of a record? To do this, you will need to use several control codes. The control codes shown in Table 7c.2 are not used only for the BROWSE mode. They apply to all modes (including EDIT) that permit you to modify the contents of a record or other structure. When it is necessary to change an entry, you can use these control codes. However, arrow keys are a bit easier to use than control codes, and you will probably prefer to use them.

When you reach the bottom of the screen, the current records disappear from view, and the next set of records become visible. This operation also works in reverse, should you be viewing records toward the bottom of the database and want to access records that are toward the top.

The functions indicated by data manipulation control codes have no substitute, and the actual changing of the contents of a field is accomplished through this set. For example, if you wish to delete a character from the current field, use CTRL-G (if the cursor currently rests on that character) or the DELete key (if it is the next character). If you wish to delete several characters

TABLE 7C.2 Full-Screen Cursor Movement Codes

Control Code Sequence	Operation Performed
For Cursor Movement	
CTRL-B*	Moves BROWSE window right one field
CTRL-Z*	Moves BROWSE window left one field
CTRL-X, CTRL-F, or down-arrow key	Moves cursor down to the next field
CTRL-E, CTRL-A, or up-arrow key	Moves cursor up to the previous field
CTRL-D or right-arrow key	Moves cursor ahead one character
CTRL-E or left-arrow key	Moves cursor back one character
For Data Manipulation	
CTRL-G	Deletes a character under the cursor
DELete	Deletes a character to the left of the cursor
CTRL-Y	Erases current field to the right of the cursor
CTRL-V	Toggles between the "overwrite" and INSERT modes
CTRL-W	Saves changes and returns to the "." prompt

* This function may be used only with the BROWSE command.

at once, you can repeat these functions. However, if you wish to delete a series of characters, you can use CTRL-Y. This function permits you to delete all characters in the field from the cursor position to the end of the field. To add characters to a field, use CTRL-V. To use this function, position the cursor at the location in the field where new characters are to be entered. This location may be any location in the field. Then press CTRL-V. All characters entered thereafter will appear at the point of the cursor (and to the right). Any characters following the cursor position will automatically be moved to the right. To terminate the operation, press CTRL-V again. This will return you to normal BROWSE mode. Finally, when you have made all the necessary changes and wish to save them, use CTRL-W to write the changes to the database and return to the "." prompt. CTRL-Q can be used to return to the "." prompt, but no changes are saved.

TABLE 7c.3 Control Codes Used for Database Manipulation

Control Code Sequence	Operation Performed
CTRL-U	Toggles the record delete marker "on" and "off"
CTRL-C	Writes the current record to disk and advances to the next record
CTRL-R	Writes the current record to disk and backs to the previous record
CTRL-Q	Ignores changes to the current record(s) and returns to the "." prompt
CTRL-W	Writes all changes to disk and returns to the "." prompt

The EDIT command supports all the full-screen movements and editing commands permitted by the BROWSE command. The format of this command is EDIT [recordnumber]. However, there is a fundamental difference between the EDIT and the BROWSE commands. The EDIT command works on a single record at a time, whereas the BROWSE permits a visual examination of a group of records. To access a record for manipulation by the EDIT command, simply enter the command EDIT (or press the F10 key). In this event, dBASE will respond with the prompt ENTER RECORD # :, to which you should respond with the record number of the record to be edited. However, there is a shorter means of achieving the same result. As noted from the format of this command, you are permitted to enter a record number along with the command name. Therefore, you could enter EDIT 4. Once you have entered the EDIT mode, the content of that record will be displayed in the same form used when you originally entered the data, as shown in Figure 7c.3. You are provided with the record number, the name of each field, the content of each field, and the length of each field (as indicated by the presence and placement of the colons). Movement from field to field is permitted by using either the control codes or the arrow keys. Furthermore, fundamental modifications can be done using the data manipulation control codes identified in Table 7c.2.

There are a number of other control key combinations in the EDIT mode that enable certain functions. These control key sequences are presented in Table 7c.3. The CTRL-U function provides the user with the capability of marking a record for deletion (or removing the deletion marker). The deletion mark takes the form of an asterisk (*) adjacent to the record number. A record marked for deletion is physically retained in the database, but it is essentially eliminated from future "search" requests. If you wish to return a "deleted" record to active status, simply access that record and press CTRL-U. This will remove the deletion marker. More details about deleting records are provided later.

The remaining functions in the list of control codes are primarily for the purpose of accessing the next record by CTRL-C, accessing the previous record by CTRL-R, exiting the EDIT mode (without changes) and returning to dBASE mode by CTRL-Q, and writing the changes and returning to dBASE mode by CTRL-W.

There is a fundamental difference between changes made with the BROWSE command and those made with EDIT. EDIT assumes that all changes made to a record will be saved—that is, unless you choose to exit the EDIT mode by using CTRL-Q—and BROWSE does not. Thus, CTRL-C, CTRL-R, and CTRL-W all save changes. In addition, when you have performed the necessary modifications to the record in the EDIT mode, and you have reached the last field, an attempt to access the next (nonexistent) field will cause the current record to be saved and the prompt ENTER RECORD # : to appear on the screen. Thus, you will not only save the current record but will also be permitted to access any record in the database as the next record for editing.

As you will recall, the job hunting problem requires you to change the job status for several companies in the COMPANY database from "Ongoing" to "Rejected." To perform this operation, you must first access the correct database by entering the command USE B:COMPANY. Then you enter a command that permits you to modify one or more characteristics of the data within that database. Thus, you could select the command BROWSE FIELDS CO:NAME, STATUS. This command produces the screen shown in Figure 7c.8. Note that the status of the job from WTBS Channel 5 TV (RECORD #9) has been changed from "Ongoing" to "Rejected." Your next requirement is to modify the job status of First State National Bank from "Ongoing" to "Offered" and add a job description in the JOBS database. While you are still working with the COMPANY database, all you have to do is access RECORD #4 and change the job status from "Ongoing" to "Offered."

Adding Records to a Database — The INSERT and APPEND Commands

dBASE contains two commands that permit the addition of new records to the database: INSERT and APPEND. The INSERT command is the more versatile of the two, because it allows you to insert a new record anywhere in the database. A record that is APPENDed is added to the end of the database. If it is important to maintain some particular order of records in the database, insertion will probably be your choice. The format of the INSERT command is INSERT [[BEFORE] [BLANK]]. Because the insertion of a new record is based on the location (record #) of the last record accessed (the current

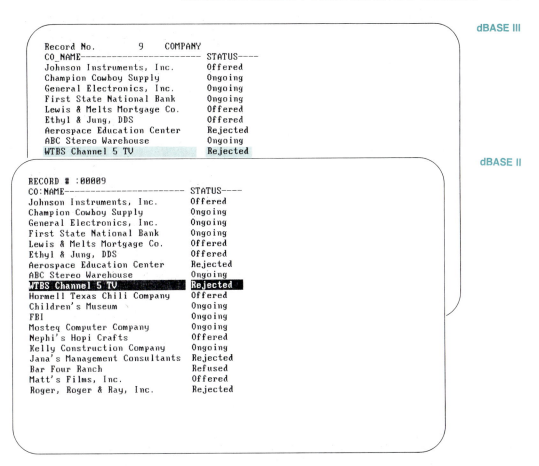

dBASE III

```
Record No.        9    COMPANY
CO_NAME----------------------- STATUS----
Johnson Instruments, Inc.      Offered
Champion Cowboy Supply         Ongoing
General Electronics, Inc.      Ongoing
First State National Bank      Ongoing
Lewis & Melts Mortgage Co.     Offered
Ethyl & Jung, DDS              Offered
Aerospace Education Center     Rejected
ABC Stereo Warehouse           Ongoing
WTBS Channel 5 TV              Rejected
```

dBASE II

```
RECORD # :00009
CO:NAME----------------------- STATUS----
Johnson Instruments, Inc.      Offered
Champion Cowboy Supply         Ongoing
General Electronics, Inc.      Ongoing
First State National Bank      Ongoing
Lewis & Melts Mortgage Co.     Offered
Ethyl & Jung, DDS              Offered
Aerospace Education Center     Rejected
ABC Stereo Warehouse           Ongoing
WTBS Channel 5 TV              Rejected
Hormell Texas Chili Company    Offered
Children's Museum              Ongoing
FBI                            Ongoing
Mosteq Computer Company        Ongoing
Nephi's Hopi Crafts            Offered
Kelly Construction Company     Ongoing
Jana's Management Consultants  Rejected
Bar Four Ranch                 Refused
Matt's Films, Inc.             Offered
Roger, Roger & Ray, Inc.       Rejected
```

FIGURE 7C.8
Using the BROWSE command for selected fields

record), the INSERT command permits you to perform the operation both BEFORE and after the current record. (Because the word "after" does not appear in the format of this command, "after" is the default insertion mode.) If BEFORE is specified, insertion occurs before the current record. If BLANK is also specified, a blank record (a record containing nothing but spaces) is inserted automatically without further user input.

When you think you are ready to INSERT a new record, it is always a good idea to DISPLAY the current record to check your location in the database. If you are not at the desired location, there are a number of commands you can use to adjust the current record position. Of course, GO TOP places you at the beginning of the database. Other formats of the GOTO command include GO

BOTTOM—to reach the end of the database—and GO RECORD n, where "n" represents a specific record number. If you happen to be close to the location where a record is to be inserted, you can use the SKIP command. The format of this command is SKIP [-] [n], where "n" represents the number of records to be skipped while moving forward (down) in the database. The default for "n" is 1. If the "-" symbol is used, you move backward (up) in the database.

When the appropriate position for the insertion of a new record has been reached, you enter the command INSERT, and dBASE will indicate that you are in an input mode by supplying a screen format like that shown in Figure 7c.3. Proceed by entering the values to be associated with the individual field names. After you have entered values for each field, you will automatically return to the "." prompt.

The APPEND command initiates a similar sequence of events. The syntax of the APPEND command is APPEND [BLANK]. As previously mentioned, when the APPEND command is used (or the F9 key is pressed), a new record is added to the end of the database. No prior positioning is required; dBASE knows the location of the last record in the database, so positioning to the last record is unnecessary. When the BLANK option is used, a blank record is added to the end of the database.

For the job hunting problem, you want to add a new record to the JOBS database. Because it makes no difference where you put this job description in the JOBS database, you could use the command sequence USE B:JOBS to gain access to the JOBS database and APPEND to add a record to the end of that database. dBASE will then respond with a screen format like the one in Figure 7c.9. You can verify, by the RECORD #, how many job descriptions are included in the JOBS database.

Getting a Look at the Database—The LIST and DISPLAY Commands

Now that you have built the COMPANY and JOBS databases, perhaps you want to examine the records in one of them. One way to examine a database visually is to use the LIST command. (The LIST command was described earlier, but for different purposes.) The format of the LIST command is LIST [scope] [fieldlist] [FOR expression] [OFF]. As noted from the format, the short form of the command is LIST. This command can be either typed on the keyboard or entered by pressing the F3 key. Either choice produces a complete list of the database—all records and each record's fields. However, a full listing of a database is not particularly useful, especially if your records are longer than 80 characters (the LIST command will "wrap" fields from the end of one line to the beginning of the next line on the screen). Also, the list is produced rather rapidly; so, if the database is long, the top portion of the database will scroll off the screen before you can read it. Note that all the records in the database are listed when only the word LIST is used. This means that the default scope for

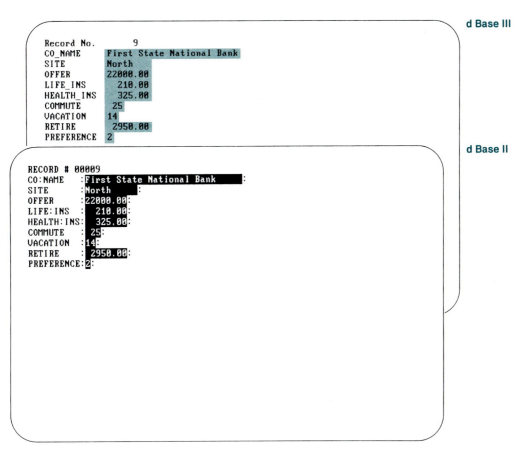

```
                                                                    d Base III

   Record No.        9
   CO_NAME      First State National Bank
   SITE         North
   OFFER        22000.00
   LIFE_INS       210.00
   HEALTH_INS     325.00
   COMMUTE        25
   VACATION     14
   RETIRE         2950.00
   PREFERENCE   2
                                                                    d Base II

   RECORD # 00009
   CO:NAME      :First State National Bank        :
   SITE         :North                 :
   OFFER        :22000.00:
   LIFE:INS     :  210.00:
   HEALTH:INS   :  325.00:
   COMMUTE      : 25:
   VACATION     :14:
   RETIRE       :  2950.00:
   PREFERENCE:2:
```

FIGURE 7C.9
**Using the APPEND command to add a
record—a job description from the First
State National Bank**

this command is for ALL the records in the database. If specified, "scope" indicates the number of records to be listed.

The complement of the LIST command is the DISPLAY command. The format of the DISPLAY command is DISPLAY [scope] [fieldlist] [FOR expression] [OFF]. As with the LIST command, there are multiple forms of the DISPLAY command. What happens when you simply enter the command DISPLAY (or press the F2 key)? With the simple DISPLAY command, only a single record is produced—the current record. Thus, the default scope for a DISPLAY command is 1—the current record. Regardless of which command is used—LIST or DISPLAY—the format of the screen output is the same.

TABLE 7c.4 Options for Indicating "Scope"

Scope Option	Meaning
ALL	Produces all of the records
NEXT n	Produces the next "n" records, where "n" is an integer number; count begins with the current record
RECORD n	Produces only the single record, located at the "nth" position in the database

As mentioned, the first option of both the LIST and the DISPLAY commands is "scope." This parameter identifies how many records of the database are to be produced. "Scope" provides three possibilities, as described in Table 7c.4. Thus, the simple LIST command is equivalent to a DISPLAY ALL. A LIST RECORD n command is equivalent to a simple DISPLAY.

The field list option permits you to identify the fields within a database that you want to see as a result of using the LIST or the DISPLAY command. This option permits you to limit the number of fields produced and indicate the order in which the fields should appear. Obviously, when you need to specify field names, you should be familiar with the structure of the database currently in use. It might be wise to list the structure (LIST STRUCTURE) of the database before trying to identify which fields are to be shown.

Figure 7c.10 shows that you have decided not to use all the fields of the COMPANY database—only a certain subset. The part of the command containing the field names "co:name" and "resume:ack" limits the number of fields produced. (However, the determination of which records are displayed is done through the FOR option, to be discussed shortly.)

Another part of the LIST or DISPLAY command that can be used to limit the length of output for a single record is the OFF option. The OFF option is used to suppress the presentation of record numbers. Use this option when you want to view only the contents of records and not their positions. Note that the OFF option is not used in Figure 7c.10. As a result, the record numbers (7, 9, 16, and 19) are listed in the left margin. When the OFF option is used, the first database field produced occupies the first column on the screen.

Finally, note that dBASE II does not display the field names above the database values with a LIST or DISPLAY command. dBASE III shows the field names above the fields as the BROWSE command does.

```
. LIST CO_NAME, RESUME_ACK FOR STATUS = "Rejected"
Record#  CO_NAME                            RESUME_ACK
      7  Aerospace Education Center         11/16
      9  WTBS Channel 5 TV                  12/03
     16  Jana's Management Consultants      01/06
     19  Roger, Roger & Ray, Inc.           12/15
.
```

```
. LIST CO:NAME, RESUME:ACK FOR STATUS = "Rejected"
00007  Aerospace Education Center         11/16
00009  WTBS Channel 5 TV                  12/03
00016  Jana's Management Consultants      01/06
00019  Roger, Roger & Ray, Inc.           12/15
.
```

FIGURE 7c.10
**Looking at the COMPANY database —
a simple use of the LIST command**

TABLE 7c.5 Relational Operators Used in a FOR Option

Relational Operator	Meaning
>	Greater than (for example, 500 > 300)
>=	Greater than or equal to (for example, 500 > 300; 500 = 500)
=	Equal to (for example, 500 = 500)
<> or #	Not equal to (for example, 500 <> 300)
<=	Less than or equal to (for example, 300 < 500; 300 = 300)
<	Less than (for example, 300 < 500)

The best has been saved for last: the FOR option. The LIST, DISPLAY, and other commands access each record; however, the FOR option permits you to indicate whether the record is to be displayed on the screen. Therefore, with the FOR option, you are permitted to search a database selectively.

The FOR option follows the form for relational expressions presented in the first part of this chapter. The permitted relational operators and their meanings are presented in Table 7c.5.

TABLE 7c.6 Logical Operators Used in a FOR Option

Logical Operator	Meaning
.OR.	Either relational expression may be true for the entire expression to be considered true.
.AND.	Both relational expressions must be true for the entire expression to be considered true.
.NOT.	The first relational expression must be true, but not the second, for the entire expression to be considered true; or the first relational expression must not be true for the expression to be considered true (unary .NOT. — .NOT. relational expression).

In Figure 7c.10, the FOR option is stated as "for status = 'Rejected'." This means that you want to search the COMPANY database and produce the "co:name" and "resume:ack" fields for all records that indicate that your job application has been "rejected." The FOR portion of the expression identifies a field name ("status") associated with the COMPANY database. The relational operator (=) is obvious — equal to. "Rejected" indicates a constant; in other words, you are looking for *all* records with a status of "rejected." Compare the list shown in Figure 7c.10 with the known contents of the COMPANY database. Only those companies that have rejected your application are listed. (Note that WTBS Channel 5 TV is included in the list of company names, because its status was changed earlier.)

The logical operators used to combine relational expressions to create logical expressions in dBASE are shown in Table 7c.6.

Eliminating Records from the Database — The DELETE, PACK, and RECALL Commands

The job hunting problem requires that you remove unwanted records from the COMPANY database. As previously mentioned in conjunction with the BROWSE and EDIT commands, it is possible to "mark" a record for deletion by using the CTRL-U key sequence. However, this isn't the only way to delete records within a database. You can also mark a record for deletion by using the DELETE command. The format of this command is DELETE [scope] [FOR expression] [WHILE expression]. When the DELETE command is entered,

```
. LIST CO_NAME, RESUME_ACK FOR STATUS = "Rejected"
Record#  CO_NAME                        RESUME_ACK
       7 *Aerospace Education Center     11/16
       9 *WTBS Channel 5 TV              12/03
      16 *Jana's Management Consultants  01/06
      19 *Roger, Roger & Ray, Inc.       12/15
```

```
. LIST CO:NAME, RESUME:ACK FOR STATUS = "Rejected"
00007 *Aerospace Education Center     11/16
00009 *WTBS Channel 5 TV              12/03
00016 *Jana's Management Consultants  01/06
00019 *Roger, Roger & Ray, Inc.       12/15
```

FIGURE 7c.11
List of "Rejected" companies marked for deletion

each record identified by the scope, FOR, or WHILE option is marked for deletion. The WHILE option indicates that all records are to be marked so long as the specified expression is true.

There are a number of ways to delete unwanted records from the COMPANY database using the DELETE comand. One approach might be to locate the records to be deleted by using the LIST command, as illustrated in Figure 7c.10. The Aerospace Education Center record is identified as record number 7. Thus, the command DELETE RECORD 7 marks this record for deletion. This operation is then performed for the other records in the list to mark them for deletion. (However, it would be easier to enter the command DELETE FOR STATUS = 'Rejected'.)

Now look at Figure 7c.11. The list of the company names in the database indicates that all "rejected" records appear with an adjacent asterisk (*) — they have been marked for deletion but have not yet been removed. The PACK command can now be used to remove these records physically. After the PACK operation has been performed, the listing of company names shows that the "rejected" records have been removed from the database.

Finally, suppose you make a mistake and mark the wrong record for deletion. This problem is easily solved. If you want to return a marked record to a fully active status, all you have to do is enter the RECALL command. The format of this command is highly similar to the DELETE command: RECALL [scope] [FOR expression] [WHILE expression]. Thus, by using the RECALL command, records that have been marked for deletion can be "unmarked." *Note:* You must use the RECALL command *before* you use the PACK command.

After the PACK command has been used and the records have been deleted, the RECALL command cannot restore them.

If you want to eliminate an entire database, enter the command: DELETE FILE filename. Obviously, you should use this command cautiously. Database files are not marked as are records; they are immediately eliminated. (Of course, you could always remove a file by using the operating system command for deletion.)

Building, Specifying, and Using Indexes — The INDEX, USE, and SET INDEX Commands

Recall that the data in the database has a particular order — the order in which records are entered into the database. However, there are times when it is desirable to access the records in a sequence other than their entry sequence. For dBASE to access the data in an order other than the entry order, an index must first be created and identified, otherwise the data must be actually sorted — that is, physically reordered. This section describes how the indexing process works.

Any number of indexes may be created for a single database and used either individually or jointly. To create an index for a currently active database, the INDEX command is used. INDEX creates a retrieval sequence by which data can be accessed, but, at the same time, the original physical order of the database is not altered. The format of this command is INDEX ON expression TO indexfile. The expression portion of this command identifies the characteristics by which the database is to be indexed. The expression can be as simple as a field name or more complicated (for example, multiple fields added together, such as OFFER + LIFE:INS + HEALTH:INS + RETIRE). For the job hunting problem, a single field will suffice.

The INDEX command produces an index file. An index file is a file name under which an index (a sequence of record numbers) is recorded. An index file may be any file name permitted by the operating system; however, the extension name ".NDX" will be automatically provided by dBASE. Thus, index files are distinguished by their extension name from other files used by dBASE. To illustrate the use of the INDEX command, suppose you entered the following: INDEX ON ZIP TO B:ZIP. Assuming that COMPANY is the currently active database, dBASE will examine the contents of the "ZIP" field and create a sequence of record addresses that will allow you to access records in an ascending order (from smallest to largest), based on the zip code value. These addresses will then be stored in the index file called ZIP.NDX on disk drive B. After the indexing operation has been completed, dBASE will respond with a message such as 00015 RECORDS INDEXED.

The INDEX command generates only an index file. It does not "activate" that file for use. To operate with an indexed database, use one of two commands: the USE command or the SET INDEX command. You will recall that the format of the USE command is USE [filename] [INDEX indexfile1 [,index-file2] . . .]. Previously, this command was used to access a particular database. However, if you are using the INDEX option, you will access the database records in the order of the index file named. Thus, a command such as USE B:COMPANY INDEX B:ZIP would give you access to records in the COMPANY database in zip code order.

Suppose a database is already in use and you want to access the data in an index order. Reentering the USE command is redundant in this case. Instead, you could use the SET INDEX command. The format of this command is SET INDEX TO indexfile1 [indexfile2] . . . . All that is required to establish or change an index file for a currently active database is the SET INDEX command. Thus, a command such as SET INDEX TO B:ZIP could be used to specify an index file if the COMPANY database was currently active.

One final note about the index files that are listed by either the USE or the SET INDEX command: If more than one index file name is specified by the USE or SET INDEX command, only the first index file is used for accessing the records. The other index files are used only in the event reindexing is necessary. Reindexing is necessary after records are added to or deleted from a database. The command to perform this function is REINDEX. When this command is entered, all active indexes are automatically updated (into the current index file names) to reflect the presence of new records or the absence of deleted records.

Now that you can use an index file, how will this help you? Perhaps this question is best answered by examining the effect of an index on the LIST command. Look at Figure 7c.12 (the INDEX and SET INDEX commands are included here only for purposes of clarity). Once an index has been declared, it remains active until another index is identified or the database is closed. Although you are presented with somewhat abbreviated contents of each record (by the FIELDS option), one fact is clear. The records are presented in order by the value of the "ZIP" field. Note that the record numbers are not in order. This is because the record numbers are associated with the entry order of the database, not the indexed order.

An Ordered Database from Old Data— The SORT Command

Perhaps after you have had the opportunity to use a database for a while, you find that the entry order is not to your liking. Or perhaps you entered data into the original database in a haphazard manner, and now that all the data has been entered, you want to create a new database (containing the same data) in a more useful order. For example, you can produce customer invoices in any order. However, in one case, you want the data for the invoices ordered by invoice number; in another situation, you want it in customer-number order. One way to change the order is to use the SORT command.

dBASE III

```
. INDEX ON ZIP TO B:ZIP
     15 records indexed
. LIST CO_NAME, CONTACT, CITY, STATE, ZIP FOR STATUS = 'Offered'
Record#  CO_NAME                        CONTACT                   CITY
     STATE   ZIP
      5  Lewis & Melts Mortgage Co.    Mrs. Roberta Accure       Denton
     TX    76202
      1  Johnson Instruments, Inc.     Personnel Department       Dallas
     TX    76234
      4  First State National Bank     Ms. Judith Welpit          Dallas
     TX    76243
     15  Matt's Films, Inc.            Personnel Office           Dallas
     TX    76341
      8  Hormell Texas Chili Company   Mr. Foster Brooks         Ft. Worth
     TX    76907
      6  Ethyl & Jung, DDS             Dr. Emil Franz Jung       Dennison
     OK    79034
     12  Nephi's Hopi Crafts           Mrs. Carletta Whitecloud   Tulsa
     OK    79345
. COUNT FOR STATUS = 'Offered'
      7 records
.
```

dBASE II

```
. INDEX ON ZIP TO B:ZIP
00015 RECORDS INDEXED
. LIST CO:NAME, CONTACT, CITY, STATE, ZIP FOR STATUS = "Offered"
00005  Lewis & Melts Mortgage Co.    Mrs. Roberta Accure       Denton
     TX  76202
00001  Johnson Instruments, Inc.     Personnel Department       Dallas
     TX  76234
00004  First State National Bank     Ms. Judith Welpit          Dallas
     TX  76243
00015  Matt's Films, Inc.            Personnel Office           Dallas
     TX  76341
00008  Hormell Texas Chili Company   Mr. Foster Brooks         Ft. Worth
     TX  76907
00006  Ethyl & Jung, DDS             Dr. Emil Franz Jung       Dennison
     OK  79034
00012  Nephi's Hopi Crafts           Mrs. Carletta Whitecloud   Tulsa
     OK  79345
. COUNT FOR STATUS = "Offered"
COUNT = 00007
.
```

FIGURE 7C.12
**Creating a database INDEX — using the
"ZIP" field**

The SORT command is capable of accepting data contained in one database, ordering it, and placing the ordered data into another database. The
format of this command is SORT ON fieldname TO filename [ASCENDING/
descending]. When you use the SORT command, you must specify a field name

from the currently active database that represents the sort key—the field by which the data is to be sorted. Next, you must identify the file (by name) into which the sorted data is to be placed. dBASE will create this file (with a ".DBF" extension) when the sorting operation has been completed. Finally, you may need to specify the sorting sequence. As indicated in the format of the command, the default sequence is ASCENDING—from smallest value to largest in the specified field. If you want the reverse order, you must specify DESCENDING—from largest to smallest. The field name can be any field that exists in the database structure, whether the field type is numeric or character.

If you want to produce a database ordered by the "ZIP" fields, the command would be SORT ON ZIP TO B:ZIP. dBASE immediately proceeds to sort the data, based on an ascending sequence of values in the "ZIP" field, in the current (COMPANY) database. When the sorting operation has been completed, a new DBF file, called ZIP, will be created on drive B and dBASE will display the message SORT COMPLETE. To access the new database, you must first indicate that ZIP should be the current database. Thus, enter the command USE B:ZIP. Otherwise, COMPANY will remain the current database.

Note that both a database file and an index file can exist on the same disk, using the same name (for example, ZIP). This is because a database file uses the extension ".DBF," whereas the index file uses the ".NDX" extension. One final note of caution. Several index files have been used in conjunction with the COMPANY database. These indexes are useful only with that database and should not be used in conjunction with the ZIP database. The record sequence of the new database is not the same as that for COMPANY. Therefore, any use of the previous indexes will result in logical sequence errors much the same as those produced after inserting a new record into an existing database but before reindexing.

While dBASE II is limited to a single sort key, dBASE III has no such limitation. In addition, dBASE II must place all records in the current database into the new, sorted database; dBASE III, on the other hand, does not have this limitation. The format of the SORT command for dBASE III is SORT TO filename ON fieldname1 [/A] [/D] [fieldname2 [/A] [/D] . . . [scope] [FOR expression]. Note that in the dBASE III version, the filename has been moved toward the front of the command, followed by one or more sort keys. The first key identifies the major (most global) sort sequence, and other keys (if specified) identify minor keys. The minor key is important only if the major key data value for two or more records is the same. Then the data is ordered on the basis of the minor key for that subset of records. Following each field name is an indication of the direction of ordering—/A for ascending (the default order) and /D for descending. The newer version of the SORT command also provides you with the ability to limit the number of records placed into the sorted database by specifying either a scope or a FOR option (or both).

Note that in Figure 7c.12 the data is ordered (using an index) only by the "ZIP" field. The fact that the city names are grouped (Dallas) is only an accident—based on how zip codes are assigned. Even if you had chosen to create an index by city names and use it as a secondary index, the primary index is the only one that arranges the data. Furthermore, if a SORT was used to order the data (using dBASE II), it would take two separate sorting operations, one on each key, or one sort operation followed by an index operation to achieve a zip code and city sequence. Only with the sort options provided by dBASE III can this operation be performed in a single step.

Building Readable Reports — The REPORT Command

To print reports, dBASE uses the REPORT command. The format of the dBASE II command is REPORT [FORM filename] [scope] [TO PRINT] [FOR expression] [PLAIN]. This command is used to recall a report file name and print the specified report.

Before using the REPORT command, you must build a report file name. If you enter the command REPORT, dBASE II assumes you wish to create a report file. dBASE will then provide a series of prompts (ask a series of questions) directing you toward the creation of a report file (see Figure 7c.13). You will first be asked to provide a file name for the report FORM. Respond with any file name permitted by the operating system, and dBASE will add the extension ".FRM," which designates the file as a report FORM. In this example, the report FORM file name is OFFERS, and it will be stored on drive B.

The next prompt provides you with the opportunity to establish the characteristics of the printed page. If you want to identify the location of the left margin (M), number of printed lines per page (L), or page width (W), you may do so. (The default settings for the options are M=8, L=57, and W=80.) In the example, M=1 indicates that the report is to begin in the first column or at the left margin, and a maximum of 50 lines are to be printed per page (L=50). The default width of 80 characters is also used. (If you enter information for more than one option, you can separate the entries by either a comma or a space.)

The series of prompts continues with the characteristics controlling the appearance of the printed report. The next question asks if you want a heading at the top of each printed page. If you respond with "Y," the next prompt will ask you for the text of the heading. (If you respond with "N" to this or other questions, intermediate prompts are omitted.) In the example, the heading "Current Offers Received" was selected. This heading will be centered at the top of each printed page. If you want to have the report double-spaced, you should respond with "Y" to the next question (the default is for a single-spaced report). If you want totals of particular numeric data items, respond with "Y" to the next question.

The next series of prompts deal with the definition of the fields to be printed. Each field, referred to in the format as a print COLumn, is automatically assigned a number starting with 001, in a manner similar to the way the structure of a database is built. You must supply both the WIDTH of the field (in columns that are to appear in the report) and the CONTENTS associated with each position on the report. The WIDTH may be the same, greater, or smaller than the width of the data to be placed into the field. CONTENTS may be database field names or possibly other identifiers (to be illustrated later) that specify the data to be printed in the indicated position.

In the example, "30,CO:NAME" was supplied for the first field, indicating that you wish the field to be 30 columns wide and you want the data in the database field name "CO:NAME" to appear in this position. Recall from previous discussions of the structure of the COMPANY database that the field called "CO:NAME" can contain data up to 30 columns wide. If dBASE encounters a data value wider than 30 characters when producing the report, it will print the data on two (or more) lines. To make the printed report readable, you should closely examine the WIDTH of each field when designing a report form.

After you have indicated the width and the field name to be used for the first report field, dBASE will ask you for a HEADING. This heading is a column heading to be printed above the corresponding column of data. For the first field, the appropriate column heading could be "Company Name." If you use a heading that is wider than the field, dBASE will automatically chop what you have provided into pieces so that it will fit above the column, even though it may have to be printed on more than one line. (For example, the heading for the last field is "Zip Code," which cannot possibly be printed in 5 columns on one line. Thus, it is broken into two parts and printed on two consecutive lines.) When you have finally completed your description of the report, you will be presented with yet another field number (006 in the example). To conclude building a report form, all you must do is press the RETURN key without entering information related to another field, and dBASE will assume you wish to terminate the report definition.

The dBASE III process of creating a report form is much different. dBASE III uses the CREATE REPORT command to build a report form and the REPORT command to print the form. As shown in Figure 7c.13, once the report form name B:OFFERS has been entered, you are provided with a series of screens designed to assist you in building the report form. The first screen asks you to indicate the page heading and page size characteristics. You are provided with four lines into which the page heading can be entered.

After the page heading and size characteristics have been provided, you will be asked to supply group and subgroup total information. Totals are not required for the current report, and pressing the RETURN key will cause the next screen to appear. However, if totals are desired, you can specify the field names or other conditions on which a group (or subgroup) total is produced (a change in field name value causes the group to be printed). Then you can indicate if the complete report or only the totals are to be printed and if each group is to begin a new page. You can also enter the heading to be printed for each group (or subgroup).

dBASE III

dBASE II

```
. CREATE REPORT
Enter report file name:B:OFFERS
```

```
. REPORT
ENTER REPORT FORM NAME: B:OFFERS
ENTER OPTIONS, M=LEFT MARGIN, L=LINES/PAGE, W=PAGE WIDTH M=1,L=50
PAGE HEADING? (Y/N) Y
ENTER PAGE HEADING: Current Offers Received
DOUBLE SPACE REPORT? (Y/N) Y
ARE TOTALS REQUIRED? (Y/N) N
COL      WIDTH,CONTENTS
001      30,CO:NAME
ENTER HEADING: Company Name
002      20,CONTACT
ENTER HEADING: Contact Name
003      15,CITY
ENTER HEADING: City
004      2,STATE
ENTER HEADING: State
005      5,ZIP
ENTER HEADING: Zip Code
006
```

FIGURE 7C.13
Creating a REPORT FORM file *(above and right)*

The screen that follows the total information is repeated for each field to be printed in the report. You are provided with a complete list of field names and their characteristics at the top of the screen. The field information is followed by a status line, indicating which field you are to describe and the remaining length of the print line. The second part of the status line indicates where the field and its heading are to be printed. You begin your entries on this screen with the specification of the "Field contents." As with dBASE II, a field may be composed of a field name or an arithmetic expression that includes field names. Next, you should indicate if the field contains other than the default number of decimal places and if a total is required for this field. Then you should supply the "Field header" (column heading) for the field. Note that you may use up to four lines to describe the field header. Finally, the "Width" of the report field will default to the width of the field name or the field header, whichever is longer. Although you are permitted to modify the field width, any value smaller than the width of the field name or the field header—whichever is larger—will be ignored. Thus, unlike dBASE II, dBASE III must produce the complete field width—dBASE III does not wrap

Structure of file B:COMPANY.dbf

CO_NAME	C	30	ZIP	N	5	INT_APP	C	8	
CO_ADDRESS	C	30	CONTACT	C	30				
CITY	C	15	RESUME_ACK	C	8				
STATE	C	2	STATUS	C	10				

Field 5   Columns left =   6

Contact Name   City   State ------

XXXXX XXXXXXXXXXXXXXXXXXXXXXXXXXXXXX XXXXXXXXXXXXX XX

Field   ZIP

Structure of file B:COMPANY.dbf

CO_NAME	C	30	ZIP	N	5	INT_APP	C	8	
CO_ADDRESS	C	30	CONTACT	C	30				
CITY	C	15	RESUME_ACK	C	8				
STATE	C	2	STATUS	C	10				

Field 1   Columns left =   90

Field   CO_NAME

Structure of file B:COMPANY.dbf

CO_NAME	C	30	ZIP	N	5	INT_APP	C	8	

Structure of file B:COMPANY.dbf

CO_NAME	C	30	ZIP	N	5	INT_APP	C	8	
CO_ADDRESS	C	30	CONTACT	C	30				
CITY	C	15	RESUME_ACK	C	8				
STATE	C	2	STATUS	C	10				

Page heading:

Current Offers Received

Page width (# chars):   90
Left margin (# chars):   0
Right margin (# chars):   0
lines/page: 50
Double space report? (Y/N):   Y

FIGURE 7C.13
(continued)

the data value or the column heading on multiple lines of the report. However, the report form created by dBASE III can be changed by using a MODIFY REPORT command (dBASE II does not provide this feature).

Immediately on completion of the REPORT prompting sequence, the report itself will be produced on the screen. This will permit you to make a visual inspection of the report form you have designed to decide if alterations are necessary.

Remember that this report form has been saved in a file called OFFERS.FRM on drive B. If you decide to use it again, you don't have to repeat the creation process. All you have to do is call for it. To produce the report shown in Figure 7c.14, the command REPORT FORM B:OFFERS TO PRINT FOR STATUS = 'Offered' for dBASE II and REPORT FORM B:OFFERS FOR STATUS = 'Offered' TO PRINT for dBASE III was entered. Thus, you have recalled the OFFERS report form, indicated that it is to be sent to the printer rather than the screen, and only the record containing a "STATUS" of "Offered" should be printed.

The page number and the current date will automatically be produced at the top of each page — that is, unless you use the PLAIN option. Next, you can see that the report heading is centered and each column of data has an appropriate column heading. Note that the column headings "State" and "Zip Code" could not be produced over the indicated field width, so they have been broken into parts. Also note the data placed under the "Contact Name" heading for the last record. The report definition of this field is 20 characters wide. The database definition of this field is 30 characters. Because the data within the "CONTACT" field wouldn't fit into the indicated print-field width, it was printed on two adjacent lines. Finally, note the order of the data in the report. Although you may not be able to establish exactly the order of the data on the basis of the fields that have been produced, the last time you accessed COMPANY you were using the ZIP index. A careful inspection of the zip codes should reveal that the report is ordered.

Now compare the output produced in Figure 7c.12 with that shown in Figure 7c.14. Which one would you want to use? Both contain exactly the same results, but the report presented in Figure 7c.14 is much more readable.

Making One New Database from Two — The JOIN Command

What do you do when you want to manipulate the data in two (or more) databases at the same time? Depending on how difficult the manipulation is and how often you need the information, you might decide to create a new database based on data in two existing databases. This operation is performed by the JOIN command. The format of this command is JOIN TO filename FOR expression [FIELDS fieldlist]. The JOIN command creates a new database with the indicated file name based on the FOR expression. The new database will be

```
                                                              dBASE III
   Page No.      1

   01/01/87

                             Current Offers Received


   Company Name             Contact Name              City        State   Zip

                                                                          Code



   Lewis & Melts Mortgage Co.    Mrs. Roberta Accure     Denton       TX     76202
```

```
                                                              dBASE II
   PAGE NO.  00001
   01/01/87

                           Current Offers Received

       Company Name             Contact Name        City      St  Zip
                                                              at  Code
                                                              e

   Lewis & Melts Mortgage Co.    Mrs. Roberta Accure  Denton     TX  76202

   Johnson Instruments, Inc.     Personnel Department Dallas     TX  76234

   First State National Bank     Ms. Judith Welpit    Dallas     TX  76243

   Matt's Films, Inc.            Personnel Office      Dallas     TX  76341

   Hormell Texas Chili Company   Mr. Foster Brooks     Ft. Worth  TX  76907

   Ethyl & Jung, DDS             Dr. Emil Franz Jung   Dennison   OK  79034

   Nephi's Hopi Crafts           Mrs. Carletta        Tulsa      OK  79345
                                 Whitecloud
```

FIGURE 7C.14
A printed report produced from a report form

composed of all the fields in the "most active" database, unless the FIELDS option is used to identify which fields should be placed into the new database.

The "most active" database designation depends on whether you are using dBASE II or dBASE III. In dBASE II, you are permitted to have only two databases active at one time. dBASE III allows up to ten active databases at once. A database is activated by employing the USE command. However, if you enter two USE commands in a row, you will have only one active database, because the USE command normally closes all previously opened databases. Thus, you must employ the SELECT command to indicate that you want more than one active database. The format of the SELECT command for dBASE II is SELECT [PRIMARY] [SECONDARY]; the same command for dBASE III is SELECT [number] [filename].

For an illustration of the use of the SELECT command, see Figure 7c.15. The first command in the sequence is USE B:JOBS. Unless dBASE II is instructed to the contrary, B:JOBS is the PRIMARY database. Entering another USE command at this point would result in a new PRIMARY database. However, in the illustration, the command SELECT SECONDARY has been entered. As a result, the next USE command entered will cause the database to be designated as a SECONDARY database. Thus, in the illustration, COMPANY is the SECONDARY database. Based on this use of SELECT and USE commands, the "most active" database is the last one selected. At this point, the most active database is COMPANY. However, this is changed by the SELECT PRIMARY command, which indicates that JOBS is to become the most active database. The SELECT command can be used to switch the activity level between the two databases. If you were using dBASE III, a similar command sequence might be:

```
USE  B:JOBS
SELECT 2
USE  B:COMPANY
SELECT 1
```

or, more simply,

```
SELECT B:COMPANY
SELECT B:JOBS
```

What happens if you have the same field name in two or more databases? In dBASE II, you may "qualify" or clarify a field name by indicating whether it comes from the PRIMARY (P) or SECONDARY (S) database. Again, look at Figure 7c.15. Note that a portion of the FOR option is stated as P.CO:NAME = S.CO:NAME. This indicates that the field name "CO:NAME" appears in both databases. The prefix "P." indicates that you want to reference the field in the PRIMARY database, while "S." indicates a reference to the SECONDARY database field name. To qualify a field name in dBASE III, use the file name followed by the character sequence "->"—indicating that the field name should be referenced from that particular file name. Thus, if you were using dBASE III, this portion of the FOR expression might appear as JOBS->CO_NAME = COMPANY->CO_NAME. (Note that the dBASE III field names are slightly different in that they use an underline rather than a colon.)

dBASE III

```
. USE B:JOBS
. SELECT 2
. USE B:COMPANY
. SELECT 1
. JOIN WITH COMPANY TO B:GOOD FOR CO_NAME = COMPANY->CO_NAME .AND. ;
COMPANY->STATUS = 'Offered' .AND. OFFER > 19000 ;
FIELDS CO_NAME, OFFER, PREFERENCE, SITE, LIFE_INS, HEALTH_INS, RETIRE
```

dBASE II

```
. USE B:JOBS
. SELECT SECONDARY
. USE B:COMPANY
. SELECT PRIMARY
. JOIN TO B:GOOD FOR P.CO:NAME = S.CO:NAME .AND. S.STATUS = "Offered" .AND. ;
OFFER > 19000 FIELDS CO:NAME, OFFER, PREFERENCE, SITE, LIFE:INS, ;
HEALTH:INS, RETIRE
```

FIGURE 7c.15
**Using the JOIN and SELECT commands to
create a new database**

What is the function of the particular JOIN command indicated? Because
the FOR expression indicates that you want to retrieve records that have the
same company names from both databases, only those records that match this
condition will appear in the B:GOOD database. In addition, these records are
to be placed into the new database only if the job "STATUS" is "offered" and
the amount of the "OFFER" is greater than $19,000. Furthermore, note that
the field names identified in the JOIN command come from both databases.
Thus, by this method, one-to-one and one-to-many relationships can be established within dBASE. Finally, note that the FIELDS option indicates only some
of the fields in the JOBS database are copied to the GOOD database.

The final requirement for the job hunting problem is to produce a report containing only "good" offers, ordered by "PREFERENCE" and
"CO:NAME." The ordering is partially achieved by creating an index for the
GOOD database on the "PREFERENCE" field. (The database could be first
sorted on the "CO:NAME" field to guarantee the desired sequence.) Thereafter, a report form is created, as shown in Figure 7c.16. The new report form is
called GOOD. You are permitted to use the same database file name, index
name, and report form name because each has a different file name extension.
Within the report, a "Net Offer" field is created by summing the values of
"OFFER," "LIFE:INS," "HEALTH:INS," and "RETIRE" for each record
reported. Finally, the actual report containing these "good" offers is shown in
Figure 7c.17. Note that although there are several entries in the COMPANY
and JOBS databases, only a few selected records meet all the established cri-

dBASE III

```
Structure of file B:GOOD.dbf

CO_NAME      C  30  │LIFE_INS    N   8  2│
OFFER        N   8  2│HEALTH_INS  N   8  2│
PREFERENCE   N   1  │RETIRE      N   8  2│
SITE         C  10  │

                              Field  4            Columns left =   27
>>>>>>>>>>Company Name         Dollar    Pr ─────────────────────────
                               Offer     ef
                                         .

          XXXXXXXXXXXXXXXXXXXXXXXXXXXXX 99999.99  9

   Field          OFFER+LIFE_INS+HEALTH_INS+RETIRE
   contents
```

```
Structure of file B:GOOD.dbf

CO_NAME    C  30  │LIFE_INS    N   8  2│
```

```
Structure of file B:GOOD.dbf

CO_NAME      C  30  │LIFE_INS    N   8  2│
OFFER        N   8  2│HEALTH_INS  N   8  2│
PREFERENCE   N   1  │RETIRE      N   8  2│
SITE         C  10  │

                    Page heading:

   Preferred Job Offers




                 Page width (# chars):        80
                 Left margin (# chars):        10
                 Right margin (# chars):        0
                 # lines/page:                 50
                 Double space report? (Y/N):    Y
```

dBASE II

```
. REPORT
ENTER REPORT FORM NAME: B:GOOD
ENTER OPTIONS, M=LEFT MARGIN, L=LINES/PAGE, W=PAGE WIDTH M=10,L=50
PAGE HEADING? (Y/N) Y
ENTER PAGE HEADING: Preferred Job Offers
DOUBLE SPACE REPORT? (Y/N) Y
ARE TOTALS REQUIRED? (Y/N) N
COL     WIDTH,CONTENTS
001       30,CO:NAME
ENTER HEADING: Company Name
002        9,OFFER
ENTER HEADING: Dollar Offer
003        2,PREFERENCE
ENTER HEADING: Pref.
004        9,OFFER+LIFE:INS+HEALTH:INS+RETIRE
ENTER HEADING: Net Offer
005
```

FIGURE 7C.16
Creating REPORT FORM for "good" job offers

```
Page No.      1
01/01/87
                          Preferred Job Offers

Company Name                      Dollar Pr   Net Offer
                                  Offer ef



Lewis & Melts Mortgage Co.        22000.00  1    27500.00
```

```
PAGE NO. 00001
01/01/87
                        Preferred Job Offers


        Company Name              Dollar   Pr Net Offer
                                  Offer    ef


Lewis & Melts Mortgage Co.        22000.00  1  27500.00

Ethyl & Jung, DDS                 20000.00  1  27275.00

Hormell Texas Chili Company       19300.00  1  21986.20

First State National Bank         22000.00  2  25485.00

Johnson Instruments, Inc.         19200.00  4  23022.00

Johnson Instruments, Inc.         19100.00  5  22922.00
```

FIGURE 7c.17
Printing the "good" job offers report

teria. Furthermore, notice that both jobs from Johnson Instruments, Inc., are listed—verifying that a one-to-many check has been made between the COMPANY and the JOBS databases.

Other Features of dBASE II and dBASE III

Perhaps while you were examining Figure 7c.12 you noticed that the command COUNT FOR STATUS = 'Offered' was used, and the result of the operation was COUNT = 00007. This represents one of the additional features contained within dBASE. Obviously, the COUNT command counts the records within a database that match a particular set of conditions. The format of the COUNT command is COUNT [scope] [FOR expression] [TO variable], where scope and the FOR option are used in the same way as previously discussed. However, the TO option is new. When this option is added to the command, not only is a count performed but the results of that count are placed into a memory variable (see the following) and can later be recalled for viewing or used in other manipulations.

COUNT is not the only arithmetic command available within dBASE. You may also find the SUM command useful. The format of this command is SUM fieldname1 [fieldname2] . . . [scope] [FOR condition] [TO variable1 [variable2] . . .]. The command permits you to accumulate the values of a field (or list of fields). This total can also be saved as a memory variable.

What are *memory variables*? Memory variables are held in a "scratch pad" area and retained by dBASE, as they are created, for the duration of the dBASE session (or until a CLEAR or RELEASE command is entered). By using memory variables, you can keep track of particular statistics retrieved from a database or simply record "reminders" that you might want to refer to later. Memory variables can be created by the COUNT and SUM commands. However, they can also be created directly by the STORE command. The format of this command is STORE expression TO variable, where the expression may be the name of another variable, a character string, or an arithmetic expression. For example, suppose you entered the following commands while using the GOOD database:

```
COUNT ALL TO NO:OFFERS
SUM OFFER TO TOT:OFFERS
STORE 'Average Offer' TO TITLE
STORE TOT:OFFERS / NO:OFFERS TO AVJ:OFFER
```

This means that you would count the total number of records in the GOOD database, total "OFFER" for all records, store the character string "Average Offer," and calculate and store the average value of an offer.

If you want to recall any of the memory variables for later viewing, all you have to do is enter the "?" symbol, followed by the memory variable name. Thus you might enter ? AVJ:OFFER. In addition, you can use the ? command to perform arithmetic manipulations directly. For example, if you enter the command ? AVJ:OFFER / 12 you can determine an average monthly income. Finally, if you forget the names of memory variables or if you want to retrieve all memory variables and their values, simply enter DISPLAY MEMORY, and all memory variables and their values will be produced on the screen.

A special feature included only in dBASE III is the "Assistance" feature—also known as command ASSIST. The assistance feature converts many of the commands of dBASE III from a command-driven approach to a menu-driven approach. To use this feature, enter the command ASSIST when the "." prompt is the last character on the screen. You will be provided with some preliminary instructions and then a menu of general choices. The selection of a general choice results in a submenu, which usually provides a list of commands. Selections are made by moving the cursor and pressing the RETURN key, and all that is necessary thereafter is to answer prompting questions. To get an idea of how the assistance feature works, examine the report creation sequences shown in Figures 7c.13 and 7c.16.

The last feature of dBASE to be mentioned here is its associated procedural language. dBASE will permit you to enter a series of commands (including many of those previously discussed plus many more) and save them as a procedure, or a program. This enables you to create procedures that will be frequently used, save them, and recall them for execution. Such procedures can eliminate the need for continually reentering the same commands time after time to retrieve frequently needed information. However, because programming is beyond the scope of this text, you should read a dBASE manual if you want more information about this procedural language. The manual also includes information about building screen formats (like report forms) for the data entry or the display of records in a database.

R:base Series 4000 and 5000

Learning to Use R:base

R:base Series 4000, sometimes called R4000, is a powerful single-user database package. R:base is a fully relational database management system that allows you to compare, combine, and manipulate all or part of any relation stored in your database. R:base Series 4000 is only one of a series of database packages available from Microrim. R:base Series 2000 is a limited database that is completely menu driven, with an emphasis on ease of use. R:base Series 6000 is the multi-user version of Series 4000, for large businesses.

R:base Series 5000 is an updated and enhanced version of Series 4000. R:base 5000 has improved menus and makes more use of these menus than does R:base 4000. However, all of the commands used in R:base 4000 are also functional in R:base 5000. Thus, the material presented in this module, while specific to R:base 4000, will also serve as an introduction to R:base 5000.

Before you start working with R:base, you need to become familiar with its terminology and the special options that can be set when first entering the package. This section will introduce you to the vocabulary of R:base and get you started.

In the first part of this chapter, the term *database* was defined as a collection of organized data. In R:base you are allowed to work with only one database at a time; however, you may simultaneously work with up to 40 different relations —tables or files within a database. These relations are made up of attributes, also called *data fields* or *columns.* An attribute is similar to a column heading in a table or a field in a file. A set of attribute values for a relation is called a *row.* A row is the same as a record in a conventional file management system.

Initially, you will need 4 disks to get the R:base package started. The first disk must contain the operating system for your computer (you cannot copy the operating system onto the R:base disk). The second and third disks are the two R:base program disks, and the fourth disk will be used to store your database. To use R:base, your system should have two disk drives; normally drive A contains R:base, and drive B contains the database. Generally, setting up your disk drives in this manner makes working with R:base easier.

To start the R:base package, place your operating system disk in drive A and your database storage disk in drive B, and turn the system on. When the

```
Begin R:base 4000 Version 1.11 MSDOS Serial # ########
For the IBM PC, PC/XT and compatibles (Compaq,Columbia,Eagle and others)
Copyright (C) 1983,1984 by Microrim, Inc.

For assistance type "HELP", for Prompt mode type "PROMPT"
R>
```

FIGURE 7D.1
Initial Screen for R:base Series 4000

system prompt A> appears on the screen, remove the operating system disk in drive A and replace it with the R:base Execute Disk (#1). Now, type RBASE and press the RETURN key. When the computer displays a message asking for the location of RBASE.OVL, remove the Execute Disk from drive A and place the second R:base disk in that drive. Now enter an A, and the computer will display the R:base logo for a few seconds and then change the screen to the display shown in Figure 7d.1. You are now ready to use R:base.

Note that the prompt on the screen is now R> rather than A>. R:base actually uses six different prompts, depending on the functional "mode" you are in. Table 7d.1 provides a description of the different prompts and modes available in R:base.

For the first-time user, the most difficult task in using a new software package is getting the first command to work correctly. To assist the first-time user—and the experienced user who does not remember all the commands available—R:base provides an on-line command reference called HELP.

There are two ways to access HELP information. You can enter the word HELP, in which case you will see a screen listing all of the commands for which assistance is available. While you are in this mode, the H> prompt appears on the screen. To see an explanation for a command in the list, simply type that command name and press the RETURN key. If you already know the com-

TABLE 7D.1 R:base Prompt Modes Table

Prompt	Functional Mode Indicated	Name
R>	Main R:base module	R:base
H>	HELP command	Help
L>	Data loading	Load mode
D>	Database definition	Define
P>	Command prompting	Prompt
+>	Comment or quoted text string from previous line is incomplete (continuation indicator)	Plus prompt

mand for which you need an explanation while still in the R> mode, enter HELP followed by the command name, and the explanation will appear on the screen—bypassing the list of commands. When you wish to leave the HELP mode, simply type END in response to the H> prompt.

Before you start building your database, R:base allows you to set defaults for special characters, to assign values to certain functions, and to create or modify local variables. *Local variables* are internal memory working areas you create to aid in calculations. The SHOW command displays all formats and current default settings. Figure 7d.2 illustrates the SHOW command display, as well as a set of settings recommended by Microrim. Conditions displayed with the SHOW command can be changed using the SET command. Table 7d.2 provides a short explanation of each of the options available through the SET command.

Solving the Job Hunting Problem

The remaining sections of this module are devoted to solving the job hunting problem. You may want to refer to the problem statement in the Introduction to Database Modules before you continue. Also, remember that the data used in the problem can be found in Appendix A.

```
R>show
     Current special characters
       BLANK=            COMMA=,
       DOLLAR=$          SEMI=;
       QUOTES="          PLUS=+

     DATE Format = MM/DD/YY
     LINES per page =    20
     WIDTH per line = 79
     ECHO of input = OFF
     UPPER/lower CASE distinction = OFF
     RULE checking = ON
     NULL value indicator = -0-
     BELL on error = ON
     AUTOSKIP on data entry/edit = OFF
     REVERSE video on data entry/edit = ON
     Diagnostic MESSAGES = ON
R>
```

FIGURE 7D.2
R:base SHOW command, showing special
characters, functions, and variables

Building a Database — The Define Mode

To create databases with R:base, you need to follow two steps: First, *logical design* requires you to determine your needs and structure the database to satisfy those needs. Second, *physical implementation* requires you to express your logical plan in R:base terms. Once you have planned your database, you are ready to define (create) it. You do not need to know how the data will be used or retrieved when setting up a database for the first time. However, you must be able to describe the data fields to be used and how you would like them grouped. For keeping track of the job hunting activities, you will create a database named JOBS. This database will have two relations: COMPANY and OFFERS. You will see which attributes are placed in each relation as the database is defined.

Once you are in the R:base mode R>, begin the define mode by entering the command DEFINE, followed by a database name. This command identifies a new or an existing database to R:base. A database name cannot be longer than seven characters. You may add a disk drive identifier to the seven characters for a total of nine characters. For the job hunting problem, enter the command

TABLE 7D.2 SET Command Options

Option	Function
Special Characters	Special Characters are preset to their most common usage. They can be changed for all command usage of that character. Special characters are blank $ " , ; and +.
Date	The data format can be set to any of the following: MM/DD/YY, MM/YY/DD, DD/MM/YY, YY/MM/DD, YY/DD/MM
Lines	Sets the number of lines per page for data that will be output to the device in use. This does not affect report generation.
Width	Sets the number of columns used per page from 1 to 132
Echo	Causes all commands and data currently being entered to be listed on the current output device in use
Case	If ON, uppercase and lowercase letters are considered separate characters. If OFF, they are considered identical.
Rule	User-supplied rules for checking the values of data as it is entered into the database can be turned ON or OFF (activated or not activated)
Null	Sets the visual representation of a null (no) value. For example, -0- will be displayed if a field contains no value.
Bell	Sets the audible beep ON or Off
Autoskip	If autoskip is ON, when you type the last character allotted to an input field (in an input form), you will automatically move to the next field
Reverse	Sets reverse video (black letters on a white background) ON or OFF
Messages	If OFF, suppresses the display of status messages after a database operation

DEFINE B:JOBS. The R:base package will automatically add the extension n.RBS to the file name when the file is saved. The letter "n" in the file name is a file number used by R:base. The first file (in your case, JOBS1.RBS) is used to hold the data dictionary or database structure definition. The second file (JOBS2.RBS) contains the actual data, and the third (JOBS3.RBS) contains information about the KEY index (explained later).

```
Press [ESC] when done with this data
=================================DEFINE===================================
 The DEFINE command enters the define mode where you can set up a new
 database or add to the definition of an existing one. You must first
 define a database name and drive, then you can create attributes,
 relations, and optionally, passwords and rules for your database. You
 can also define an owner password for the new database. Database names
 are from one to seven characters and can be prefaced by a drive indicator,
 i.e. B:ABC.
=========================================================================

================================PROMPTS==================================
 Remember to include the drive before the database name. (e.g., B:dbname)
 Database name   : B:JOBS
 Owner password  :
```

```
R>define B:JOBS
 Begin R:base Database Definition
D>attributes
D>name text 30
D>address text 25
D>city text 20
D>state text 2
D>zip text 5
D>contact text 25
D>respond text 5
D>status text 10
D>visit text 5
D>site text 10
D>offer dollar
D>life dollar
D>health dollar
D>retire dollar
D>commute integer
D>vacation integer
D>rank integer
D>
```

FIGURE 7D.3
**Database definition using the PROMPT
option and attribute definitions for the job
search database**

If you wish to be guided through the database definition process, use the R:base Prompt option. To use this option, enter PROMPT DEFINE and then provide the information as it is requested. Figure 7d.3 shows the PROMPT DEFINE screen. Once you have entered the required information, press the ESCape key and either Q to quit or G to go to the next page. If you wish to continue in the prompt mode for the database definition, enter the command PROMPT ATTRIBUTE.

The next step in defining the database is to define its attributes. To define attributes without using the PROMPT option, enter the word ATTRIBUTES and press the RETURN key. After entering the ATTRIBUTES command, you must define each attribute by specifying the attribute name and data type (length and key are optional). These are entered in the following order: attribute-name type [length] [key]. The attribute name is the name or the identity of a data field and may be one to eight characters long. Type indicates the type of data to be stored in the data field. Data types may be DATE, which represents the month, day, and year in any of the formats shown in Table 7d.2; DOLLAR, which represents dollar amounts between plus or minus 99 trillion; INTEGER, for whole numbers between plus or minus 999 million; REAL, for numbers with a fractional part; TEXT, which is used for alphanumeric strings up to 1500 characters long; and TIME, used for time in hours, minutes, and seconds.

The length of an attribute must be specified if the data type is TEXT. However, if length is used for numeric data (for example, INTEGER or REAL), it indicates that the attribute is a table and specifies the number of values in the table. Finally, an attribute may be specified as a KEY. This option establishes an index, like that discussed in the first part of this chapter, based on the value of the attribute.

Figure 7d.3 shows the attribute definitions for the JOBS database. Note that the D> prompt indicates that R:base is in the DEFINE mode. Figure 7d.3 (the JOBS database), indicates that all the attributes for both relations have been entered. Later you will place each of these attributes into its proper relation. Also, a number of fields have been recorded as numeric field types — "OFFER," "LIFE," "HEALTH," and "RETIRE" as DOLLAR types, and "COMMUTE," "VACATION," and "RANK" as INTEGER types. "ZIP" could have been identified as a numeric field because it is composed of digits, but it is unlikely that you will ever perform a computation using the zip code. Note that the only attributes that have a length parameter are the ones having TEXT as their type.

Now that all the attributes in the database have been defined, it is time to group them into relations. Enter the RELATIONS command and press the RETURN key. You may also use the PROMPT RELATIONS command to define relations in the prompt mode. Each relation is defined with a single command using the following form: relation name WITH attribute-name1 [attribute-name2] . . .. If the character string representing the relation is over 80 characters long, press the plus (+) key before you reach the right edge of the screen, press the RETURN key, and continue entering the list of attributes.

The relation may be from one to eight characters long. Attribute-name1, attribute-name2, and so on are the attributes that will be combined to form the relation. Each attribute must have been previously defined or must be an attribute name in an existing relation. When you leave the define mode, any attributes not combined into a relation will be deleted. Figure 7d.4 shows the relation definitions for the JOBS database. Note that both the COMPANY and OFFERS relations contain the attribute "NAME." This will allow you to match data in the COMPANY relation with data in the OFFERS relation.

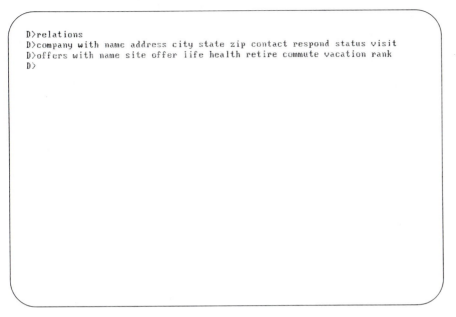

```
D>relations
D>company with name address city state zip contact respond status visit
D>offers with name site offer life health retire commute vacation rank
D>
```

FIGURE 7D.4
Defining relations for the database

Starting, Stopping, and Checking Your Work — The EXIT, OPEN, RENAME, DELETE, REMOVE, LISTREL, and LISTATT Commands

Although there are other options that can be used in defining a database, the JOBS database is now fully defined. The END command is used to exit the define mode. When the END command is entered, R:base automatically saves the structure of the database you just finished entering in the file JOBS1.RBS. If you are in a hurry, perhaps all you have time to do is build the database structure before you quit. To get out of R:base and return to the operating system, all that is required is to enter the command EXIT. When you later start to reuse the database, enter the command RBASE exactly as you did when you first entered the package. To retrieve the previously generated database, enter the command OPEN B:JOBS.

Once the database has been defined, you can change its definition by entering "DEFINE" and making whatever changes you want. Attributes can be added and new relations created by following the steps used in the original definition. If you want to change the names of attributes in relations, enter the command RENAME attribute-name1 TO attribute-name2. To change the name of a relation, use the command RENAME RELATION relation-name1 TO relation-name2. The DELETE attribute-name command is used to erase attributes, and the REMOVE relation-name command is used to delete an entire relation.

You have seen that the structure of a database can be easily changed. Can the structure be easily checked? Visually checking a structure is done with two commands: First, the LISTREL command lists all the relations in the database. For the job hunting problem, the relations are COMPANY and OFFERS. Second, the LISTATT command, shown in Figure 7d.5, lists all the information about the attributes in the database. The information in Figure 7d.5 is the same as in Figure 7d.3, except that the attributes are listed in alphabetical order and the relation that each attribute belongs to is listed. Note that the attribute "NAME" belongs to both relations.

Entering the Data — Creating Forms

Now that you have designed and defined your database, you can load it with data. R:base allows a number of different options for data entry, including:

```
LOAD relation-name
LOAD relation-name WITH PROMPTS
LOAD relation-name FROM filename
ENTER form-name
ENTER form-name FROM filename
```

The LOAD command loads data by row in the same order you defined the attributes for the relation. The LOAD command works with or without prompts and can even be used to load the data from a file that was previously stored on a disk.

R:base also allows you to design customized forms for data entry when using the ENTER command. The same customized screen can also be used to edit your data once it is in the database. To create a form, enter the FORMS command any time you see the R> prompt. The first operation you must perform after entering the FORMS command is provide a form name and tell R:base which relation the form goes with, as shown in Figure 7d.6. A form name may be from one to eight characters long.

After pressing the RETURN key, you will see a blank screen. The entire screen can be used as a "drawing board" to create your form, and you may arbitrarily set up a form to include those attributes you deem necessary. Figure 7d.7 shows an input form for the COMPANY relation. It was created by using the cursor control keys to place the text on the page at the desired position. Once the attribute labels have been entered on the form, press the ESCape key. A message will now appear at the top of the screen asking you if you wish to E(dit), L(ocate attributes), or Q(uit). If you wish to revise your form layout, press E and make whatever changes are needed. If you are satisfied with your form, press L to specify the beginning and end of the location where attribute values are to be entered on your form.

After pressing the L key, R:base will go through the list of attributes belonging to the relation that you have specified for the form. For each attribute, you will be asked if you wish to K(eep), S(et or change), or D(elete) its

```
R>listatt
              Attributes
        Name       Type       Length            Relation   Key
        address    TEXT       25 characters  company
        city       TEXT       20 characters  company
        commute    INTEGER     1 value(s)    offers
        contact    TEXT       25 characters  company
        health     DOLLAR      1 value(s)    offers
        life       DOLLAR      1 value(s)    offers
        name       TEXT       30 characters  company
                                             offers
        offer      DOLLAR      1 value(s)    offers
        rank       INTEGER     1 value(s)    offers
        respond    TEXT        5 characters  company
        retire     DOLLAR      1 value(s)    offers
        site       TEXT       10 characters  offers
        state      TEXT        2 characters  company
        status     TEXT       10 characters  company
        vacation   INTEGER     1 value(s)    offers
    More output follows - press [ESC] to quit, any key to continue




              Attributes
        Name       Type       Length            Relation   Key
        visit      TEXT        5 characters  company
        zip        TEXT        5 characters  company
 R>
```

FIGURE 7D.5
LISTATT — what are the attributes in the database?

location. If you want to keep the attribute where it is or skip it, press the K key. If you want to remove this attribute from the form, press D, and R:base will display the next attribute in the relation. If you want to set the location of the attribute in the form, press S and use the cursor control keys to move to the location where the attribute should begin. When you press S a second time, S will appear on the screen marking the beginning location of the attribute, and the cursor will jump to the last possible position for the attribute, based on the attribute's length. Use the cursor control key again to move the cursor to the desired ending location, and then press the E key to mark the ending position. After you have pressed the E key, the next attribute in the relation will appear at the top of the screen, and you may go through the same procedure to locate it in the form. Once you are satisfied with your form, press the ESCape key followed by Q to quit.

You have now created a new relation, named FORMS, that contains the information about your form. In Figure 7d.6, the form named PLACE was

```
R>forms
Begin R:base forms definition
Enter form name:PLACE
Enter relation name:COMPANY
```

FIGURE 7D.6
Entering the R:base FORMS command

```
E(dit form),L(ocate attributes),Q(uit):
                COMPANY INFORMATION INPUT FORM

COMPANY NAME : S                              E

COMPANY ADDRESS : S                      E

CITY : S                  E     STATE : SE    ZIP: S   E

CONTACT PRESON : S                       E

DATE RESUME ACKNOWLEDGED : S   E

SEARCH STATUS : S          E

DATE OF INTERVIEW : S   E
```

FIGURE 7D.7
The final form for entering COMPANY data

```
E(dit form),L(ocate attributes),Q(uit):
                     OFFERS INFORMATION INPUT FORM

COMPANY NAME : S                                E

SITE : S          E

OFFER : S                        E

LIFE : S          E    HEALTH : S          E    RETIREMENT : S                         E

COMMUTING DISTANCE : S    E    VACATION DAYS : S          E

JOB PREFERENCE : S    E
```

FIGURE 7D.8
Input form for entering OFFERS data

created for use in entering the data for the COMPANY relation, and the form named MONEY, in Figure 7d.8, was created for the OFFERS relation.

After defining a form, the next step is to enter data. Use the ENTER command whenever the R> prompt is displayed on your screen. The command format is ENTER form-name. The form will appear on the screen with the cursor at the first character position of the first entry area. Enter your data in the appropriate areas, pressing the RETURN key after completing each field, and press the ESCape key when all the data has been entered correctly. If you are satisfied with the information you have loaded, press A to Add a new row in your relation. If you press R, a new row is added to the relation, and the information you have entered remains on the screen to be reused in the next row. Once all your data has been entered, press Q to return to the R> prompt. Figure 7d.9 illustrates the entry of the data for the first row in the relation COMPANY using the form PLACE.

Getting a Look at a Database — The SELECT Command

R:base offers three ways to query your database. The first is the very powerful SELECT command. With the SELECT command, you can make inquiries about any or all attributes in a relation, request totals, and specify the column

```
Press [ESC] when done with this data
               COMPANY INFORMATION INPUT FORM

COMPANY NAME : Johnson Instruments, Inc.

COMPANY ADDRESS : P. O. Box 1234

CITY : Dallas              STATE : TX    ZIP: 76234

CONTACT PRESON : Personnel Department

DATE RESUME ACKNOWLEDGED : 12/15

SEARCH STATUS : Offered

DATE OF INTERVIEW : 01/23
```

FIGURE 7D.9
Entering the data for the first company

width for display. The SORTED BY and WHERE options can be used with the SELECT command. The general format of the SELECT command is SELECT ALL FROM relation-name [SORTED BY . . .] [WHERE . . .]. This command produces all the attribute values from the selected relation on the screen or a selected output device. To indicate specific attributes in the SELECT command, use the following format: SELECT attribute-name1 [attribute-name2] . . .] FROM relation-name [SORTED BY . . .] [WHERE . . .].

The WHERE option specifies the conditions that must be met before an attribute is listed. Up to ten conditions may be combined using the logical operators AND and OR discussed in the first part of this chapter. If more than two conditions are specified, they are examined from left to right. Table 7d.3 shows the different forms available to express WHERE clause conditions.

The SORTED BY option specifies up to ten attributes for sorting. If more than one attribute is to be sorted, it is done in the order in which you have entered the attribute names. If there are multiple identical values of the first attribute, rows are sorted on the second attribute. If the second attribute values are also identical, the third attribute is used, and so on. Sorting is done in either ascending [=A] or descending [=D] order. The form of the option is SORTED BY attribute-name1[=A] [attribute-name2[=A] . . .]. If no sorting sequence is specified, the data will be sorted in an ascending order.

TABLE 7D.3 Forms of the WHERE Clause Conditions

Operator	Function	Operator	Function
Comparing Attributes or Local Variables to Values		Comparing Attributes or Local Variables to Attributes	
CONTAINS	Equal to a value or string	EXISTS	Has a value
EQ or =	Equals	FAILS	Has NULL value
NE or <>	Not equal	EQA	Equals
GT or >	Greater than	NEA	Not equal
GE or >=	Greater than or equal to	GTA	Greater than
LT or <	Less than	GEA	Greater than or equal to
LE or <=	Less than or equal to	LTA	Less than
		LEA	Less than or equal to

The column width option of the SELECT command is used to override the default column widths for display. If an attribute exceeds the display width you want, consider specifying a column width. This is done by entering the SELECT command in the following format: SELECT attribute-name1[=w] [attribute-name2[=w]...] FROM relation-name [SORTED BY ...] [WHERE ...], where "w" (width) is the number of characters to be displayed.

The SELECT command can also be used to find totals for specified attributes. Only DOLLAR, INTEGER, and REAL data types may be totaled. For each attribute appended with =s, the sum of the displayed values will be shown at the end of the listing. The format of this SELECT command is SELECT [attribute-name1[=s] attribute-name2[=s] ...] FROM relation-name [SORTED BY ...] [WHERE ...].

For example, you may want an alphabetical list of companies that have made you an offer and are within 50 miles of where you live. Suppose you also want to know the total amount offered by these companies. Enter the command SELECT NAME COMMUTE=2 OFFER=S FROM OFFERS SORTED BY NAME WHERE COMMUTE LE 50. After you have pressed the RETURN key, the result will appear on the screen, as shown in Figure 7d.10.

The second form of inquiry is based on the use of the TALLY command. TALLY produces the distribution of an attribute, displaying each unique value

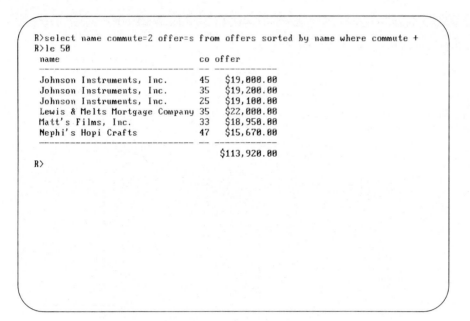

```
R>select name commute=2 offer=s from offers sorted by name where commute +
R>le 50
name                          co offer
----------------------------- -- -------------
Johnson Instruments, Inc.     45 $19,000.00
Johnson Instruments, Inc.     35 $19,200.00
Johnson Instruments, Inc.     25 $19,100.00
Lewis & Melts Mortgage Company 35 $22,000.00
Matt's Films, Inc.            33 $18,950.00
Nephi's Hopi Crafts           47 $15,670.00
----------------------------- --
                                 $113,920.00
R>
```

FIGURE 7D.10
Using the SELECT command to list the companies

and the number of times it occurs in a relation. The format of the command is TALLY attribute-name FROM relation-name [WHERE . . .]. The WHERE clause is optional.

The final form of inquiry is produced by the COMPUTE command. The COMPUTE command calculates values for the selected attribute based on a mathematical function. The COMPUTE operators and restrictions are shown in Table 7d.4. The format of the COMPUTE command is COMPUTE operator attribute-name FROM relation-name [WHERE . . .]. For example, if you wanted to compute the average offer from the companies in the OFFERS relation, you would enter the command COMPUTE AVE OFFER FROM OFFERS, where AVE is an operator or function name.

Changing the Contents of a Database — The CHANGE, ASSIGN, and EDIT Commands

The CHANGE, ASSIGN, and EDIT commands can be used to alter an individual value, several values, or all the values in a relation. The format of the CHANGE command is CHANGE attribute-name TO value [IN relation-name] WHERE . . .. The CHANGE command is used to change the value of an

TABLE 7D.4 COMPUTE Operators and Restrictions

Operator	Definition	Data Types	Length
COUNT	Gives the number of values that satisfy the WHERE clause	All types	No restrictions
MIN	Selects the lowest-valued attribute from the rows satisfying the WHERE clause	All types	20 characters or 1 value
MAX	Selects the highest-valued attribute from the rows satisfying the WHERE clause	All types	20 characters or 1 value
AVE	Computes the arithmetic average of the attribute from the rows satisfying the WHERE clause	DOLLAR, INTEGER, or REAL	1 value
SUM	Adds the attributes from each row satisfying the WHERE clause	DOLLAR, INTEGER, or REAL	1 value
ALL	Computes all of the preceding functional values		

attribute for one or all relations in the database. The WHERE clause is required with the CHANGE command and identifies which of the records are to be changed. The optional parameter IN relation-name is used to specify the relation where changes are to occur. If this parameter is omitted, the value will be changed in all relations in the database using the specified attribute name.

The ASSIGN command changes the value of an attribute by assigning it the value of an expression. The expression may be in any of the following forms:

    attribute-name operator attribute-name
    attribute-name operator value
    value operator value
    value operator attribute-name

The operator may be any of the following:

    + add two items
    - subtract the second item from the first
    * multiply two items
    / divide the first item by the second
    % percent on a given attribute

TABLE 7D.5 Editing Menu Choices

Choice	Meaning
C(hange entry)	[C] indicates that you have made changes to your data. The values you changed are to be updated, and the row is displayed.
A(dd)	[A] indicates that you want to add the row currently displayed on the screen. After you have pressed [A], the row is added, and the current values of the next row are displayed.
R(eset)	[R] signals R:base to ignore any changes made and to return to the original data values for this row.
S(kip)	[S] lets you skip to the next row. If you do not wish to edit a row, press [S] to display the data in the next row.
E(dit)	[E] indicates that you want to edit the row currently displayed on the screen. After you press [E], the message "Press [ESC] when done with this row" will appear.
D(elete)	[D] indicates that you wish to delete the row currently displayed. After you have pressed [D], the message "Push the return key to delete row [ESC] to keep row" appears at the top of the screen.
Q(uit)	[Q] exits the EDIT command. R:base will then show you the number of rows that have been changed and the number of rows deleted.

The format of the command is ASSIGN attribute-name TO expression IN relation-name [WHERE . . .].

There are two forms of the EDIT command. The first edits any or all attributes in a specified relation. The format for this command is EDIT [attribute-name1] [attribute-name2] . . . FROM relation-name [SORTED BY . . .] [WHERE . . .]. You may use the WHERE option to select rows for editing. The SORTED BY clause is used to retrieve rows for editing in a specific order. The second form of the EDIT command is used to edit data using a previously created form. EDIT USING form-name gives you the same editing capabilities as a standard EDIT command. The command format is EDIT USING form-name [SORTED BY . . .][WHERE . . .]. The advantage of using EDIT USING form-name is that you can edit data using a familiar form. Table 7d.5 gives the editing menu choices for both uses of the EDIT command.

Figure 7d.11 shows the EDIT command sequence needed to change the "STATUS" of the offer from WTBS Channel 5 TV from "Ongoing" to "Rejected." You first need to retrieve the row you want to edit by entering the command EDIT STATUS FROM COMPANY WHERE NAME EQ "WTBS

```
R>edit status from company where name = "WTBS Channel 5 TV"


C(hange entry),A(dd entry),R(eset),S(kip),E(dit),D(elete),Q(uit):
status : Ongoing


Press [ESC] when done with this data
status : Ongoing


Press [ESC] when done with this data
status : Rejected


C(hange entry),A(dd entry),R(eset),S(kip),E(dit),D(elete),Q(uit):
status : Rejected


     1 row(s) were changed
     0 row(s) were deleted
     0 row(s) were added
R>
```

FIGURE 7D.11

The EDIT command sequence for changing a data-item value

CHANNEL 5 TV." Then select E from the menu, enter "Rejected," and press the ESCape key. Thereafter, C should be entered to save the change. After making the change, you can check the results by entering the command SELECT NAME STATUS FROM COMPANY WHERE NAME = "WTBS CHANNEL 5 TV" to generate the screen in Figure 7d.12.

Adding Records to a Database

Adding a new record to your database is a simple operation. To add the information about the offer from First State National Bank, use the ENTER MONEY command and add the data to your database, as shown in Figure 7d.13. Don't forget to use the EDIT command to change the "STATUS" of First State National Bank from "Ongoing" to "Offered" in the COMPANY relation.

When You No Longer Want a Record — The DELETE Command

The DELETE command has two uses: The first use allows deletion of duplicate rows from a relation. The format of this command is DELETE DUPLICATES

```
R>select name status from company where name = "WTBS Channel 5 TV"
  name                                status
  --------------------------------    ----------
  WTBS Channel 5 TV                   Rejected
R>
```

FIGURE 7D.12
**Using the SELECT command to check the
change in a data-item value**

FROM relation-name. The second use deletes rows that satisfy the conditions you state in the WHERE clause. This form of the DELETE command is DE-LETE ROW(S) FROM relation-name [WHERE . . .].

To remove the companies that have rejected your employment application from the COMPANY relation, enter the command DELETE ROWS FROM COMPANY WHERE STATUS = "Rejected." To check the COMPANY relation to ensure the deletion was made, enter the command SELECT NAME STATUS FROM COMPANY. The results of using this command are shown in Figure 7d.14.

Building Readable Reports — The REPORT Command

The R:base report writer lets you create reports using the same design capabilities available with the FORMS command. Defining and creating a report is as easy as generating a form for data entry. To begin defining your report, type REPORTS. After entering a report name from one to eight characters long and the name of the relation to be used in the report, you will be presented with the report menu shown in Figure 7d.15.

```
Press [ESC] when done with this data
                  OFFERS INFORMATION INPUT FORM

COMPANY NAME : First State National Bank

SITE : North

OFFER : $22,000.00

LIFE : $210.00      HEALTH : $325.00       RETIREMENT : $2950.00

COMMUTING DISTANCE : 25     VACATION DAYS : 14

JOB PREFERENCE : 2
```

FIGURE 7D.13
Using the ENTER MONEY command to
enter the new offer

To define the variables you are going to use in your report, press D. If you are defining new variables (new to this report), press D again. You may now define up to ten variables per report. The only restriction is that expressions must use attributes or previously defined variables. The rules for creating expressions are the same as those used by the ASSIGN command.

After you have defined your variables, press the E key to begin creating your report. You will be given a blank screen, much like the FORMS creation screen, to work in. In fact, the report is created in exactly the same way you created the input form earlier. When you have finished creating your report form, return to the main menu by pressing the ESCape key and then L to locate the attributes and variables on the report.

Press L again if you are locating new variables or R if you are relocating or deleting variables and attributes that have already been located. After using the S (start) and E (end) to locate the variables and attributes on the report, return to the main menu by pressing the ESCape key. The S (start) and E (end) location works exactly as it did when you created input forms—except that in the case of the report form, you must enter the name of the attribute to be located. If your report uses only a few of the attributes in a relation, entering them by name can simplify the building process.

```
R>delete rows from company where status = "Rejected"
        3 row(s) have been deleted from company
R>select name status from company
name                            status
------------------------------  ----------
Johnson Instruments, Inc.       Offered
General Electronics, Inc.       Ongoing
First State National Bank       Offered
Lewis & Melts Mortgage Company  Offered
Ethyl & Jung, DDS               Offered
ABC Stereo Warehouse            Ongoing
Hormell Texas Chili Company     Offered
Childern's Museum               Ongoing
FBI                             Ongoing
Mosteq Computer Company         Ongoing
Nephi's Hopi Crafts             Offered
Kelly Construction Company      Ongoing
Bar Four Ranch, Inc.            Refused
Matt's Films, Inc.              Offered
Champion Cowboy Supply          Ongoing
R>
```

FIGURE 7D.14
Checking the database after the DELETE operation

```
E(dit report), L(ocate), M(ark), D(efine), S(et), H(elp), Q(uit):

        E - Edit or create report
        L - Locate attributes and variables on the report
        M - Mark the heading, detail, and footing sections
        D - Define or change report variables
        S - Set number of lines per page
        H - Help on creating and changing reports
        ----------------------------------------------------------------

        [F3] - Show attributes and variables
        ----------------------------------------------------------------
```

FIGURE 7D.15
Report menu for creating report forms

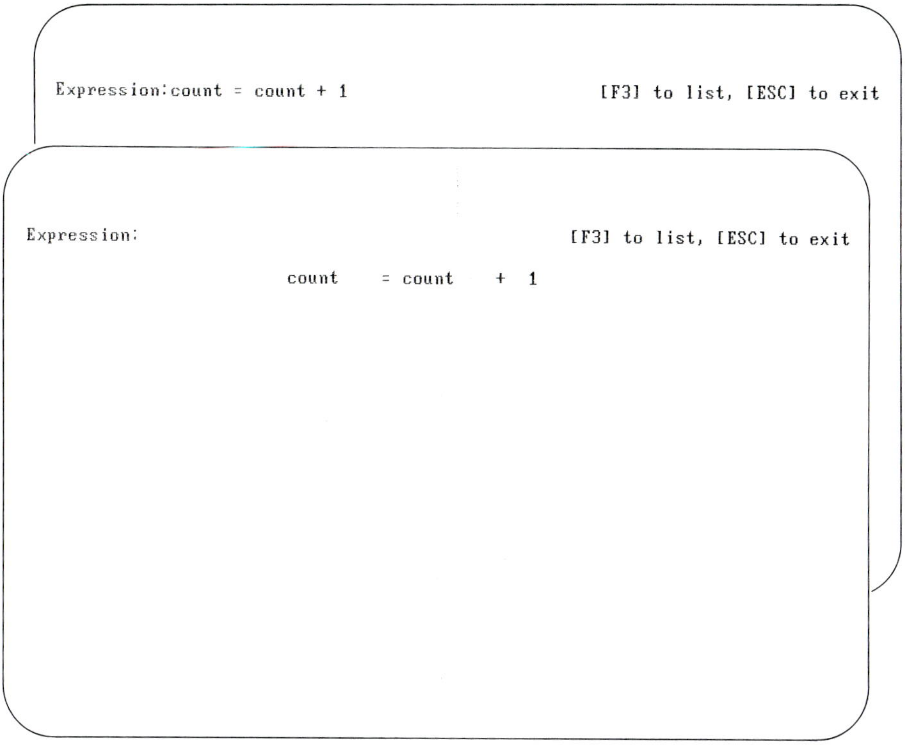

FIGURE 7D.16
Creating variables for the report

Now press M to mark your report layout. You must mark each line of the report with an H, D, or F. H is used to indicate a Heading on the top of each report page. D is used to indicate a Detail line. Each set of D lines is repeated for each row of the database that is reported. F indicates a Footing that appears at the bottom of each report page. Your report is now fully defined. All that remains is to press Q to create a new relation, named REPORTER, containing your reports and return to the R> prompt.

To generate a report of the companies for which offers have been extended, you must first define a variable to count the records to be printed. Press D from the main menu and press D again to define a new variable. Now enter the expression shown in Figure 7d.16 and press the RETURN key. The expression will be recorded in a list at the center of the screen. If you enter several expressions, they are recorded and evaluated in the order entered. When all the expressions you are using in the report have been entered, press the ESCape key to return to the report menu. You can now create the form for

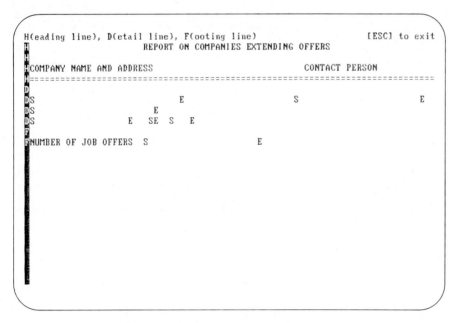

```
H(eading line), D(etail line), F(ooting line)                [ESC] to exit
H              REPORT ON COMPANIES EXTENDING OFFERS
H
HCOMPANY NAME AND ADDRESS                           CONTACT PERSON
H==============================================================================
D
DS                        E                    S                      E
DS                 E
DS               E   SE  S   E
F
FNUMBER OF JOB OFFERS  S                       E
```

FIGURE 7D.17
The final report form for companies
extending offers

your report. Figure 7d.17 shows an example of what a report form for companies extending offers might look like. Note that the COMPUTE operator COUNT was used in this expression. You may use any of the COMPUTE operators shown in Table 7d.4 in the variable definitions of a report.

If for some reason you forget information about a report, query the relation you have just created (named REPORTER) by using the SELECT command. The command format is SELECT ALL FROM REPORTER.

To generate the report—sorted by city and zip code—of companies for which there are still active offers, you can use the report just created. All you need to do is enter the command PRINT REPORT.1 SORTED BY ZIP WHERE STATUS = "Offered." The resulting report is shown in Figure 7d.18. To print this report, enter the command OUTPUT PRINTER before entering the PRINT command.

Making New Relations — The JOIN Command

Relational operation commands give you the power to retrieve and combine information stored in the database relations. Using the six relational commands explained in the first part of the chapter, you can create a new relation

```
                   REPORT ON COMPANIES EXTENDING OFFERS

COMPANY NAME AND ADDRESS                                CONTACT PERSON
=====================================================================

Lewis & Melts Mortgage Company                    Mrs. Roberta Accure
1 Bank Plaza
Denton              TX    76202

Matt's Films, Inc.                                Personnel Office
P. O. Box 524
Dallas              TX    76205

Johnson Instruments, Inc.                         Personnel Department
P. O. Box 1234
Dallas              TX    76234

First State National Bank                         Ms. Judith Welpit
302 Central Expressway
Dallas              TX    76243

Hormell Texas Chili Company                       Mr. Foster Brooks
1 hots Place
Ft. Worth           TX    76907

Ethyl & Jung, DDS                                 Dr. Emil Franz Jung
23 Molar Hill Lane
Dennison            OK    79034

Nephi's Hopi Crafts                               Mrs. Carletta Whitecloud
16 Alma, Suite 34
Tulsa               OK    79345

NUMBER OF JOB OFFERS                        7
```

FIGURE 7D.18

The report on companies extending offers

from existing relations to hold the data needed to answer a particular question. These commands let you specify queries requiring data from more than one relation.

To create the last report, a report of companies with active offers of more than $19,000, you must create a temporary relation that contains the data found in both the COMPANY and the OFFERS relations. From reading the first part of this chapter, you know that the JOIN command is designed to do this. Enter the command JOIN COMPANY USING NAME WITH OFFERS USING NAME FORMING TEMP1 WHERE EQ. The USING clause identifies the attributes in each relation that are to be compared, and the WHERE clause indicates how the attributes are to be compared.

Now that you have created a new relation named TEMP1, you can create a report for this relation. After entering the REPORT command and indicating

```
Expression:                                    [F3] to list, [ESC] to exit

                    sum1    = offer    +  life
                    sum2    = sum1     +  health
                    net     = sum2     +  retire
```

FIGURE 7D.19
Creating the variables for your final report

that the report is for the TEMP1 relation, create the variables shown in Figure 7d.19, followed by the report shown in Figure 7d.20.

To create the report shown in Figure 7d.21, enter the command PRINT REPORT.2 SORTED BY RANK NAME WHERE OFFER > 19000. After printing your final report, be sure to remove the relation TEMP1 by entering the command REMOVE TEMP1.

Other Features of R:base Series 4000 and 5000

R:base has several special features that enhance its capabilities. One of these features is the capability of establishing RULES for data verification when defining the database. These rules can be used to check the conformity of data values being entered. The ability to check the entered data reduces the probability of errors or "bad data" being stored in the database.

To protect your data from outside users, the database may use a PASSWORD. In addition, you can assign passwords to relations, giving them "read only" or "read and write" capabilities. This feature allows other people who know the "read only" password to read your database, but they will be unable to change any of the stored values in it.

```
H(eading line), D(etail line), F(ooting line)                    [ESC] to exit
H       REPORT ON COMPANIES OFFERING SALARIES GREATER THAN $19,000.00
H
H
H==============================================================================
D
D
D   COMPANY NAME : S                                E
D          SITE : S        E
DJOB PREFERENCE : S        E
D
DCURRENT SALARY OFFER :  S                         E
D    NET SALARY OFFER :  S                         E
D
```

FIGURE 7D.20
**Report form for companies offering more
than $19,000 in salary**

R:base also has the capability of interfacing with other microcomputer packages. For example, R:base can read from and write to Multiplan for spreadsheet analysis, as well as communicate with WordStar. Additionally, R:base is capable of producing DIF (data interchange format) files, allowing you to interface with other programs, such as Visicalc and Lotus 1-2-3.

Finally, R:base 4000 has two powerful companion packages: CLOUT and XRW. CLOUT (conversational language option utility) has combined a natural language facility with a database software system. CLOUT "learns" as you go, although it provides you with an opportunity to define terms and phrases that you might commonly use before you start using the package. This type of software characteristic is often called *artificial intelligence.* CLOUT can accept and adapt your plain-English requests for information and generate the desired reports. XRW (the extended report writer) generates complex and detailed reports from R:base files. XRW can be used to retrieve data from multiple relations, perform calculations on ranges of values, and define line and page breaks.

R:base 5000 is also supported by these companion packages, although a new version of the natural language, CLOUT2, is available with R5000. Furthermore, R:base 5000 interfaces with The Application EXPRESS (EXPRESS, for short). EXPRESS provides a method for building R:base 5000 applications

```
REPORT ON COMPANIES OFFERING SALARIES GREATER THAN $19,000.00

================================================================

   COMPANY NAME : Hormell Texas Chili Company
          SITE : East
JOB PREFERENCE :            1

CURRENT SALARY OFFER :              $19,300.00
   NET SALARY OFFER :               $21,986.20


   COMPANY NAME : Lewis & Melts Mortgage Company
          SITE : Mid-cities
JOB PREFERENCE :            1

CURRENT SALARY OFFER :              $22,000.00
   NET SALARY OFFER :               $27,500.00


   COMPANY NAME : Ethyl & Jung, DDS
          SITE : North
JOB PREFERENCE :            2

CURRENT SALARY OFFER :              $20,000.00
   NET SALARY OFFER :               $27,275.00


   COMPANY NAME : First State National Bank
          SITE : North
JOB PREFERENCE :            2

CURRENT SALARY OFFER :              $22,000.00
   NET SALARY OFFER :               $25,485.00


   COMPANY NAME : Johnson Instruments, Inc.
          SITE : Mid-cities
JOB PREFERENCE :            4

CURRENT SALARY OFFER :              $19,200.00
   NET SALARY OFFER :               $23,022.00


   COMPANY NAME : Johnson Instruments, Inc.
          SITE : North
JOB PREFERENCE :            5

CURRENT SALARY OFFER :              $19,100.00
   NET SALARY OFFER :               $22,922.00
```

FIGURE 7D.21
Listing of companies offering salaries greater than $19,000

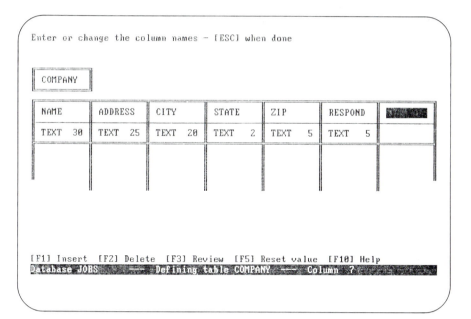

```
Enter or change the column names - [ESC] when done


  ┌─────────┐
  │ COMPANY │
  └─────────┘

  ┌─────────┬─────────┬─────────┬─────────┬─────────┬──────────┬──────────┐
  │ NAME    │ ADDRESS │ CITY    │ STATE   │ ZIP     │ RESPOND  │ ▮▮▮▮▮▮▮  │
  │ TEXT 30 │ TEXT 25 │ TEXT 20 │ TEXT  2 │ TEXT  5 │ TEXT  5  │          │
  │         │         │         │         │         │          │          │
  │         │         │         │         │         │          │          │
  │         │         │         │         │         │          │          │
  └─────────┴─────────┴─────────┴─────────┴─────────┴──────────┴──────────┘




  [F1] Insert  [F2] Delete  [F3] Review  [F5] Reset value  [F10] Help
  Database JOBS    ──   Defining table COMPANY   ──   Column  7
```

FIGURE 7D.22
**Defining the Company Relation (cable) for
the JOBS database using EXPRESS in
R:base 5000**

without having to learn how to enter R:base commands. EXPRESS uses a
visually oriented interface to lead you through the process of building a database structure, application menus, and functions to be executed from these
menus. Figure 7d.22 shows the EXPRESS screen for defining the COMPANY
relationship within the JOBS database.

Summary of Database Modules

This section's modules gave you the opportunity to learn about one (or more)
of the popular database packages available for microcomputers: pfs:File and
pfs:Report (Module 7a), Lotus 1-2-3 (Module 7b), dBASE II and dBASE III
(Module 7c), and R:Base Series 4000 and 5000 (Module 7d). You learned about
the selected database package by solving problems involved in job hunting.

Comparison of Databases

Before using the database package that you have available to answer the questions and solve the problems at the end of this section, take time to compare the different packages. Table 7s.1 presents a quick comparison of the different database packages.

Some of the differences among the packages are quite dramatic (for example, the memory requirements); however, not all of the differences are identified by the table. For example, Lotus 1-2-3 is not really a database system or a file management system; rather, it is a set of record-handling utilities that work with a very powerful spreadsheet. Pfs:File and pfs:Report are a file-handling system rather than a database system. Although these packages are somewhat limited, they will support most database functions if you use your imagination and put in a little extra effort.

There are also price differences among the packages. However, there is such a wide range of prices for each of the packages, depending on where it is purchased, that price comparisons are difficult.

In short, you must compare the capabilities of the different database application packages and find the one that most closely meets your needs. No matter how expensive a software package is, if it doesn't meet your needs, it is worthless to you. Always let your needs determine your software purchases.

Guidelines for the Evaluation of Databases

Before you select a database package for your own use, familiarize yourself with the following questions you should ask about it:

- **Help facility**   How extensive is the Help feature? Does it handle processes such as building, altering, and searching a database? Can it be accessed when needed?

- **Documentation**   How complete is the documentation? Is it written in understandable terms? Is it organized in a useful manner? Does it provide tips or suggestions on how a database should be created, altered, and so on? Does the package come with a tutorial?

- **Package orientation**   Is the package oriented toward commands or menus? Are the commands natural and meaningful to use? Is it obvious which parts of a command are required and which are optional? Under what conditions would they be used? Are menus easy to understand and well organized? Is it easy to get from one menu to another? Are the menus logically related to one another? Are the options easy to select?

- **Creating a database**   What is the database creation process like? Do you have to know how the process works, or does the package lead you through

TABLE 7S.1 A Comparison of Database Packages

Characteristics	Requirements			
	pfs:File	Lotus 1-2-3	dBASE II (dBASE III)	R:base 4000 and 5000
Operating system	MS-DOS or PC-DOS	MS-DOS or PC-DOS	CP/M, MS-DOS, or PC-DOS	MS-DOS, PC-DOS, CTOS
Main memory (RAM)	128k bytes	192k bytes	64k bytes (256 bytes)	256k bytes
Disk drives	1	1	1 (2)	2
Printer (optional)	80- or 132-column ASCII	80- or 132-column ASCII	80- or 132-column ASCII	80- or 132-column ASCII
Command structure	Menu	Multi-level menu or command	Command (multi-level menu)	Multi-level menu or command
Maximum number of files (relations)	1	1	2 (10)	40
Maximum number of records per file	2,200 (disk capacity)	2,048	65,535 (1 million)	2.5 billion
Maximum number of fields per record	3,100	256	32 (128)	400
Maximum number of characters per record	No limit	18,432	1,000 (4,000)	1,530
Maximum precision for numeric fields	No limit	70	10 digits (16 digits)	16 digits
Valid characters in a field name	A-Z, 0-9, !, @, #, $, %, ^, &, (,), _, -, \, ', ~	Any ASCII characters	A-Z, 0-9, : (—)	Any ASCII characters
Interface method	SYLK, print files	DIF, print files	DIF, print files	DIF, print files

the process? How many entities are permitted? How many attributes? What are the limitations on attribute names? What data types (alphabetic, numeric, logical, date) are permitted? What are the maximum lengths for each data type? Are default lengths available?

● **Data entry**   What options are available? Can you create a data entry form into which data can be entered? Does the package automatically prompt you with the attribute name, data type, and length? Can entries be corrected while you are entering them? Are rules available that limit what types of values can be placed into an attribute? Does the package automatically advance to the next attribute once you have finished the one you are working on?

- **Data editing**   Once data has been placed into a database, how difficult is it to change an attribute value? Is there more than one way to change an attribute value? Can entities be added? Can they be added at any location you choose? What is involved to delete an entity? Are the entities simply marked, or are they physically removed?

- **Creation and use of forms**   Does the package support the use of forms for data entry and retrieval? Do you have the option of designing your own forms? Is the design process easy? Is it flexible? Is the form easy to edit? Is the form attached to a particular database, or can it be used on demand? How many forms are permitted? What are the limitations on forms design?

- **Retrieval operations**   What retrieval commands and options are available? Is the format of the retrieval command logical and well laid out? Does it permit the selection of attributes to be listed? Does it permit the use of relational expressions? Logical expressions? Are the expressions easy to create? Are there hidden "tricks" to using the expressions? Does the retrieval operation have a print option? Can you search for partial field contents? Are wildcard operations permitted?

- **Error detection**   Does the package tell you when you have entered a command incorrectly or when it doesn't understand your use of a command or a command sequence? Are error messages readable and useful? Are modifications and corrections obvious on the basis of error messages generated? Does the package warn you that you are attempting to do something that you probably don't want to do, such as accidentally erase a database or fail to save your work?

- **Sorting and indexing**   Is sorting permitted? Do you create a new database through sorting, or is the newly ordered database placed over the old one? Can multiple keys be used in sorting? Can mathematical combination of fields be used as a sort key? Can the order be descending as well as ascending? Is indexing permitted? Can you index on multiple attributes? Can you index on a mathematical combination of attributes? Can an index be in ascending or descending order?

- **Printing reports**   Are report forms available? How easy are they to create and modify? What are the limitations on the size of the report (for example, page length and width)? Are page headings available? Column headings? Page footings? Group breaks? Totals on numeric attribute values? Both horizontally and vertically? What other mathematical operations can be performed during the reporting process? Can working variables be created? Can you view the report on the screen as well as have it printed? Are numeric attribute value editing functions (for example, dollar and cent and date formats) available? Are there any other special features of the reporting process?

- **Database manipulations**   Once a database has been established, can its structure be modified? Can a new database be extracted from an existing database? Can the extraction be conditional? Can a limited number of attributes be extracted? Can an existing database be joined with another? Can this joining operation be conditional? With a limited number of attributes?

- **Extended functions**   Does the package provide a means of security such as passwords? Is the package accompanied by additional capabilities, such as a procedural language? Natural language? Extended processors?

- **Performance characteristics**   How fast can you set up a database? How fast can you enter data? How fast does it sort? How fast does it perform an indexing operation? How fast does it search? As the database gets larger (for example, 200 records), does sorting and searching take considerably longer? How much memory is required? How many disks and how much disk space are required? As entities are added, is extra space required above what is normal for an entity that was originally placed into the database? As entities are deleted, is the size of the database reduced?

What Happened at ACE?

Once the seminar was finished, Chris spent much of the remainder of the weekend thinking about how to solve the inventory problem back at the office. Chris tried to identify the types of requests for inventory information that people would submit, because this would determine the structure of the inventory database.

On Monday, Mr. Jenkins gave Chris some additional insight into the types of requests to be expected. Chris then spent the remainder of the afternoon constructing a structure for the database that would enable it to handle all of the inquiries that would be made. At the end of the day, Ms. Allison was called in to determine which database packages were available for the office microcomputers.

The following day, Chris and the office staff began the long and tedious task of entering the data into the database structure. By the end of the week, they had entered a large portion of the inventory data. However, before they had completed the task, they received the first inquiry request. Luckily, it dealt with information already in the database, and it took just a few minutes to produce the answer. (It would have taken hours to obtain the same result by pulling the records from the filing cabinets.) The database package was already earning its keep!

Module Problems

1. You are still not happy with the job offers you have received. Use the COMPANY database to find all the companies for which negotiations are still "Ongoing" and for which no interview data has been established. You want the list to include company name, address, contact person, and the date on which your résumé was acknowledged.

2. Using the inventory data for ACE, Incorporated (found in Appendix B), set up a database on the store's inventory levels. Use the database to produce a reorder report. A reorder should occur when the reorder point is greater than the current inventory level and there is no outstanding order. The reorder report should include part number, part description, cost per unit, order level, projected total cost (cost times order level), vendor number, and vendor name. The total projected cost of these orders should also be reported. The reorder list should be sorted by vendor number.

    Next, produce a report that indicates the amount of profit for the first quarter (January, February, and March) associated with each inventory item. This report should be ordered on descending values of first-quarter profit (largest first).

3. Set up a database of the books you have in your personal library. (Include textbooks, as well as books you read for personal enjoyment; however, do not include more than 20 books.) This database should contain the following attributes:

    Author (last name first)
    Title
    Edition (for example, 1st, 2nd, and so on)
    Publisher
    Publication date (copyright date)
    Length (number of pages)
    Type (textbook, fiction, nonfiction, and so on)
    Subject area (major topic — for example, "Computers")
    Comments on the content of the book (no more than 50 characters per book)

    Now generate three reports. The first report should list, in alphabetical order by author, all the books in your library. The second report should list all the books in your library that have been published since 1980. This report should include only author, title, and publication date and should be ordered chronologically by publication date. The final report should list author, title, subject area, and comments. This report should be sorted by subject area and include the total number of pages for each subject area. All reports should include a count of the number of books in the list.

Module Questions

1. Select a database package. Describe the creation process for this package's database structure. What are the limitations on attribute names? What data types are available?
2. Select a database package. Are one-to-one relationships supported by the package? One-to-many? Many-to-many?
3. Select a database package. What command(s) can be used to query the database? Do you have control over which attributes are listed as a result of a query? How? What is the name of the option that indicates the relational conditions to be supplied?
4. Select a database package. How do you go about changing an attribute value? What commands are involved? What do you do to add an entity to the database? To delete an entity? Can you "mark" and "recall" deleted entities?
5. Select a database package. What is the process involved in producing a report with this package? How do you control how a report looks? What "extended" controls do you have (for example, page length and width, headings, totals)?

SCENARIO 8

What's Going on at ACE?

One day I discovered that Mr. Jenkins had a problem. He had to make a sales performance presentation during a regional meeting in Dallas the following week, and he needed to get together a set of charts to use during his presentation. However, the art and graphics staff of the advertising department, who had performed this service in the past, were booked solid for the next two weeks.

I remembered hearing something about graphics while learning about spreadsheets. After looking through stacks of notes and manuals, I finally found some material about graphics and explanations on how to do them. Mr. Jenkins eagerly looked over the material and became hopeful that he might get his charts after all. After finding out what Mr. Jenkins wanted his charts to illustrate, I got to work.

Chapter Eight
Applications Software:
Business Graphics

Chapter Objectives

This chapter will introduce you to the foundations of computer graphics, with a focus primarily on business graphics. After you have completed this chapter, you will be able to:

- Describe the general historical development of computer graphics
- Discuss general and business uses of computer graphics
- Describe the fundamental hardware requirements by computer graphics software

- Explain the basic functions of business computer graphics
- Describe probable future developments in computer graphics

Introduction to Graphics

The two previous chapters dealt with methods of calculating (spreadsheets) and storing (databases) large amounts of related data. You are now capable of overwhelming yourself and others with volumes of numbers! For example, suppose you are the manager of an amusement park, and for the past three years you have been recording, on a monthly basis, the average daily gate receipts and the average daily receipt totals for the entire park. At the end of the three years, you would have the data presented in Table 8.1.

Obviously, the data could supply you with some useful information, but the table is hard to read. However, if you present the same data in a graph, as in Figure 8.1, you can quickly see the changes that are taking place from month to month. Putting into words the information in Figure 8.1 would take several pages.

▶

TABLE 8.1 Amusement Park Revenues

Month/Year	Gate Receipts	Total Receipts	Week	Gate Receipts	Total Receipts
1/83	40,000	90,000	7/84	160,000	310,000
2/83	30,000	50,000	8/84	180,000	390,000
3/83	40,000	100,000	9/84	120,000	280,000
4/83	50,000	120,000	10/84	100,000	220,000
5/83	80,000	180,000	11/84	50,000	110,000
6/83	120,000	270,000	12/84	60,000	140,000
7/83	140,000	290,000	1/85	40,000	100,000
8/83	200,000	400,000	2/85	30,000	70,000
9/83	130,000	280,000	3/85	50,000	130,000
10/83	80,000	180,000	4/85	80,000	180,000
11/83	40,000	90,000	5/85	120,000	260,000
12/83	50,000	120,000	6/85	150,000	330,000
1/84	30,000	80,000	7/85	160,000	340,000
2/84	30,000	60,000	8/85	200,000	450,000
3/84	50,000	120,000	9/85	140,000	310,000
4/84	90,000	180,000	10/85	80,000	190,000
5/84	100,000	220,000	11/85	30,000	80,000
6/84	150,000	310,000	12/85	60,000	140,000

Historical Development

When you look at the development of computer graphics, you are really looking at two different paths coming together. The first path is the development of the computer hardware and software needed to perform the graphics. The second path is the increasing use of graphics to share information.

From Mainframe to Microcomputer

Crude computer plotting on hard-copy devices, such as printers, started in the early days of computing. The Whirlwind Com-

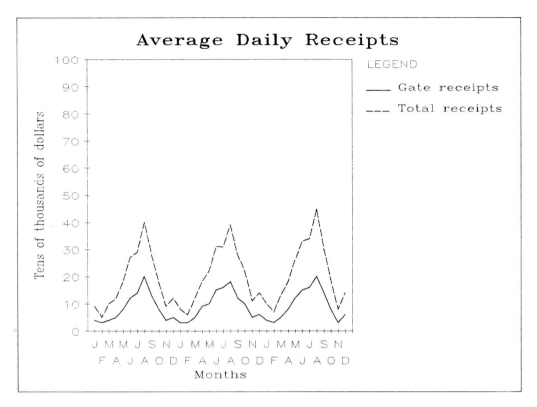

FIGURE 8.1
Graph of average daily receipts

puter, used at MIT in 1950, had a computer-driven CRT display for graphic output. In the middle 1950s, the SAGE Air Defense System used CRT display consoles on which operators identified targets by pointing a light pen at them. This system has since evolved into the Aircraft Identification and Control System used by the air traffic controllers at major airports.

Modern interactive graphics began in the middle 1960s, when Ivan Sutherland published his work on the use of different standard devices to control computer drawing. He also developed many funda-mental ideas and techniques in use today to control the computer's graphic output.

The movement of computer graphics from the mainframe to the microcomputer reads like a map of the technological advancements made in computer hardware. As the capabilities (memory size and speed) of the microcomputer increased, the ability to do graphics moved from primitive point plotting to full-color, three-dimensional drawing. Although many applications still require the use of at least a minicomputer, today most business application graphics can be handled by the microcomputer.

Business personnel, particularly accountants and management scientists, have found that presenting a set of numbers to the other members of a company's management team does not always make the information easy to understand. When information is displayed in a graph, it can be easily and quickly conveyed. For this reason, companies are increasing their use of graphs and charts.

Until recently, a lot of time and effort had to go into producing a meaningful graph. To create an acceptable graph, one had to collect the data, arrange it in the proper order, decide on the method of presentation (what kind of graph to use), and finally hire an artist or draftsman to draw the graph. Of course, if the graph was to be in color, the expense of time and money increased.

With the advent of microcomputers and the availability of additional hardware and software needed to do graphics work, the time and cost required to create graphs have been greatly reduced, and the use of graphs to convey information has increased. When an activity becomes cheaper and easier to do, one tends to find more and more uses for it. This is true of computer graphics.

Graphics Hardware

There are many different types of computer graphics images of varying quality, but they all have one characteristic in common: they are pictures of an object or an idea that are created, manipulated, and stored by a computer. Therefore, you could say that **computer graphics** is the creation, manipulation, and storage of "pictures" through the use of a computer. **Interactive computer graphics** is a special type of computer graphics in which the user controls the picture's content, format, size, and colors on a display screen through the use of special input devices. This doesn't imply that complex graphics cannot be created using standard computer equipment. In fact, the pictures presented in Figure 8.2 were created using a standard line printer. However, to use computer graphics fully, you must know about the special output and input devices that are available.

Output Devices

Chapter 2 introduced you to several output devices. The most frequently used of these devices is the monitor, or display screen. When the monitor is used as an output device for graphics, three types of graphic image are available. The first type of graphic image is called **character graphics,** and it can be produced by all microcomputers. Character graphics uses the various letters, numbers, punctuation marks, and other symbols produced by the computer to create an image.

The second type of graphic image is an expansion of character graphics and is called character **subcell graphics.** Graphics of this type divide the area normally used to display a character into several rectangular areas that use all or a part of the screen area normally devoted to presenting a character. For example, the rectangular area that would be occupied by the letter A might be shown as ■ in subcell graphics. By turning these subcells on or off in combination, one can create an image.

The last type of graphic image is called **pixel graphics.** *Pixel* is an abbreviation for "picture element" and is the smallest unit of a video display that can be used to create an image. The number of pixels available on a display screen varies widely with the com-

FIGURE 8.2
Printer graphics: left to right — bit-mapped, subcell, character

puter and the cost of the graphics equipment. For example, the Apple II microcomputer in **low-resolution** mode has 48 by 40 pixels (that is, 48 rows of 40 pixels each). Newer microcomputers generally have **medium-resolution** graphics of 340 by 200, and a **high resolution** of 640 by 400. Of course, the higher the resolution, the higher the memory requirements for the system and the higher the cost.

Printer output for graphics is frequently done on a dot-matrix type printer. When you are able to control the individual **pins** (printing mechanisms) on the printer to produce the desired picture, you are using **bit-mapped graphics** (when an "on" bit causes a single pin to print).

You will recall from Chapter 2 that **plotters** are used to output graphics. Plotters are of two types: **drum plotters** and **flatbed plotters.** These plotter types are either **single-pen** or **multiple-pen.** The principle of operation is the same, regardless of which type of plotter you have. A plotter is able to move a pen across a piece of paper along two axes. By controlling the length of time the pen is on the surface of the paper and the direction of the pen's movement along the two axes, you are able to produce an image. Figure 8.3 shows how this works using a flatbed plotter.

Input Devices

Chapter 2 discussed most of the input devices; however, because they are also used to produce computer graphics, they need to be mentioned again. Input devices are generally designed to move the cursor from one place to another on the display screen or to mark a position on the screen. For example, one uses a light pen to mark positions by placing the stylus in close proximity to the screen in the position to be marked.

The mouse and mouse-like devices are rolled over a flat surface to control the location of the cursor. In the case of a paddle or a joystick, one manipulates the handle to move the cursor. Buttons on these devices indicate when the activity (for example, icon selection or line drawing) is to begin and end.

Another input device used in graphics is the **graphics tablet,** or **digitizing pad** (also described in Chapter 2). Although microcomputer graphics tablets work in several different ways, the end result is the same. The tablet is divided into a grid (x- and y-coordinates) that is used to indicate positions much the same way that a light pen works. The difference is that a tablet, instead of the display screen, is used as the marking surface. With this type of input device, you can draw a line or a picture on the graphics tablet and watch the computer redraw the same image on the screen.

Functions of Business Graphics

The days of **"stand-alone" graphics packages** (software that produces only charts and graphs) are almost gone. Graphics is becoming a part of existing spreadsheet and integrated packages. However, the stand-alone packages for computer graphics are not going to disappear. They will simply become more versatile and include additional capabilities and flexibility not found in most of the current stand-alone graphics packages.

Despite the increase in the capability of graphics packages and the movement to include business graphics as a part of other packages (for example, spreadsheets), the

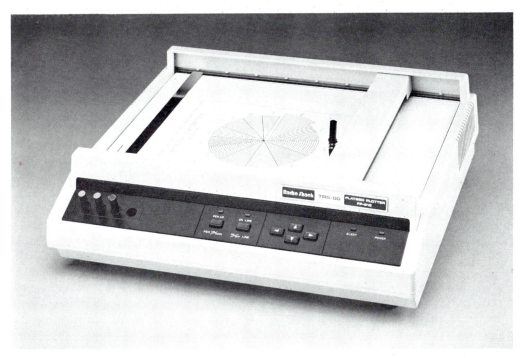

FIGURE 8.3
Flatbed plotter (courtesy of John Windsor)

basic functions of business graphics will remain the same. This section will cover the standard features of a graphics package. Although most of the work involved in creating graphics will be handled for you by the software package, you will be required to make some decisions yourself, and you will need to understand what the computer is doing in order to take full advantage of a package's capabilities.

There are five basic functions of graphics: charting and chart selection; scaling; drawing and painting; doing circles and lines; and labeling. The functions may be performed differently by different software packages, but their purpose and results are the same.

Charting and Chart Selection

Charts are graphic or pictorial representations of data. They are used to show relationships or movements in the data values. The selection of the chart type can be critical to the information being presented.

There are three basic types of charts available to the users of a graphics package: **bar charts, line charts,** and **pie charts.** Some special variations of these charts are also available, depending on the software package you are using. Although each of these chart types can be used to show both relationships and movement, some are more suitable than others for each type of display. Table 8.2 provides an overview of

TABLE 8.2 Best Use of Chart Types

Display	Chart Type		
	Bar Chart	Line Chart	Pie Chart
Relationship	X		X
Movement		X	
Data values clearly and accurately represented	X	X	
Data values quickly understood			X

each basic chart type and the type of presentation for which it is best suited.

Bar charts show relationships among data elements better than any other type of chart. For this reason, and because they are easily understood, they are most often used for management displays. A simple bar chart of the amusement park revenue data is shown in Figure 8.4.

Line charts are the most common type of chart. They communicate movement better than any other type of chart, and they convey the greatest level of detail. Line charts are often called *graphs* because they are built by connecting a set of plotted points. Figure 8.5 illustrates the use of a line chart to display the amusement park data. There are two types of commonly used line charts: The first is a **scatter chart,** shown in Figure 8.6. A scatter chart uses unconnected data points. The second is an **area chart,** as shown in Figure 8.7, which is a line chart with a shaded area under the line.

Pie charts are used to show quantitative data as a percentage of the whole. They are used to show relationships among parts and are primarily used for comparisons. Figure 8.8 is a pie chart showing a comparison of the total annual amusement park revenues for the last three years.

A special option that is frequently available in graphics software packages is the ability to plot more than one set of data values on the same graph. The ability to chart more than one set of data may also allow you to mix the types of charts or stack your charts. Figure 8.9 is an example of a **stacked bar chart.**

Scaling

Scaling is nothing more than the adjustment of the distance between numbers along the vertical and horizontal axes or the adjustment of the range along either axis. Most business graphics packages will automatically scale the vertical (or y) axis according to the data values that are entered. Although some graphics packages will allow for scaling of the horizontal (or x) axis, most do not. When the **linear scale** (equal-sized increments between values) provided does not make for the best presentation of the

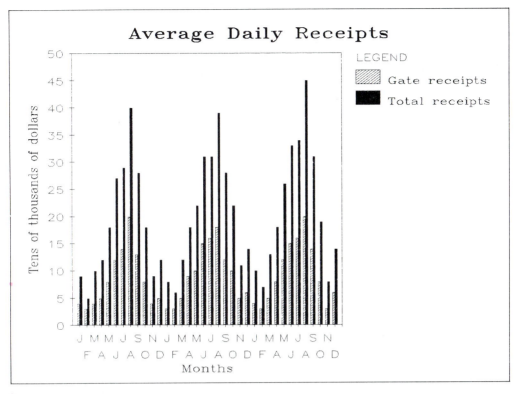

Average Daily Receipts

FIGURE 8.4
**Bar chart of average daily gate receipts
and total receipts**

data, you may be able to improve the quality of the graph. For example, some packages automatically provide alternative scales, such as a logarithmic scale. Most packages allow you to adjust the range of the y-axis yourself to improve the presentation of the data. Such an adjustment was performed on the line chart in Figure 8.5. With a simple adjustment to the scale (by using tens of thousands of dollars rather than single dollar units), the graph provides a better illustration of the revenues of the amusement park.

Drawing and Painting

Although **drawing** is not usually considered a standard feature of business graphics, some packages do give you this capability. Drawing means defining a geometric shape (in the simplest case, a line) and placing (drawing) that shape on the screen. The drawing may be left as an outline of the shape, or you can "paint" it. **Painting** is simply filling the inside of the drawn figure with a color or shading characters like those used in the pie chart in Figure 8.8.

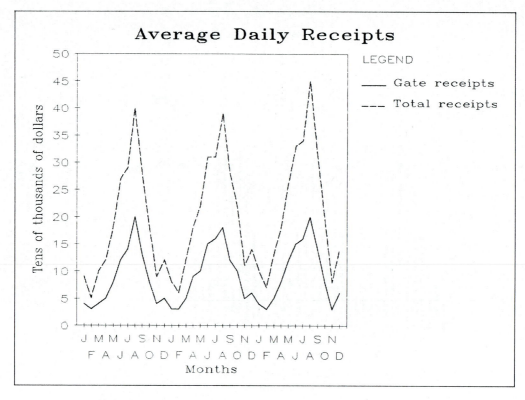

FIGURE 8.5
**Line chart of average daily gate receipts
and total receipts**

Circles and Lines

Drawing circles and lines on a computer is much the same as drawing them on a piece of paper. To draw a circle or part of a circle (an arc), you must define the center of the circle and the length of the radius (its size). (For an arc, you also need to define the angle.) To define a line, you need to specify either the beginning and ending points or the beginning point, the length, and the angle (or direction) of the line. Although it may be entered in different ways, this information is essential for all graphics packages.

Labeling

To be useful, a chart's components must be labeled. **Labeling** a chart consists of naming the chart, naming the vertical and horizontal axes, defining the scales used on both axes, and naming the different elements that are drawn on the chart. Because labels are such an important part of graphics, most graphics packages have a labeling routine that is easy to use and that allows you to define the chart and its properties.

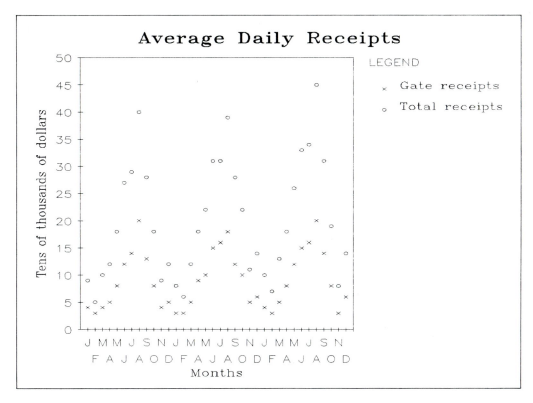

FIGURE 8.6
Scatter chart of average daily gate receipts and total receipts

Other Features

Graphics software packages were developed because people wanted to take advantage of graphics capabilities without having to write programs in a developmental language. However, the developmental languages used with microcomputers usually have some graphics capabilities. The newer versions of the BASIC language are particularly good in this regard. BASIC will allow you to draw circles, lines, and boxes using relatively simple commands, as well as paint the figures drawn (in color, if your microcomputer has the necessary hardware). Additionally, some graphics software will write the data needed to draw a graph in a format that can be read by BASIC. All these features require that you store the programs in BASIC to take advantage of them.

Because many of the business graphics packages in use today are "stand-alone" packages, they need to be able to interface with other packages. If this weren't the case, you would have to enter the values for your charts in the graphics package even though you had already entered them in another package. Because most of the

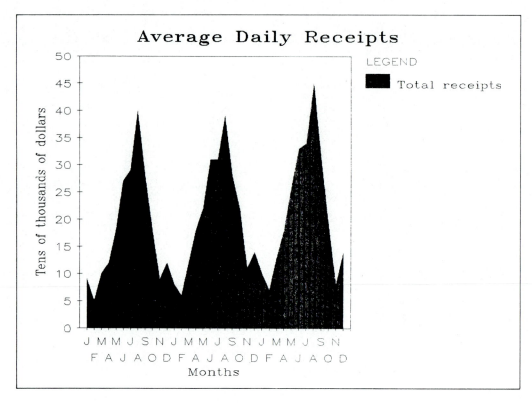

FIGURE 8.7
Area chart of average daily total receipts

charts businesses are interested in use the numbers that have been generated by spreadsheets, most graphics packages have the ability to read data from at least one spreadsheet package. However, because graphics use special characters to create a chart, graphics packages rarely have the ability to move a chart into a word processing document. Some of the new integrated packages, discussed in Chapter 10, attempt to solve this problem.

Some graphics packages have the ability to produce "three-dimensional" charts, graphs, or drawings. A display screen or a printed image cannot show a true "3-D" picture; extra lines are added to give the illusion of depth.

Finally, some graphics packages permit you to manipulate your data mathematically. Count, total, and average functions are generally available, in addition to add, subtract, multiply, and divide operations. Furthermore, some of the more advanced packages provide known geometric graphic functions, such as sine wave, logarithm, exponential, and so on, so that your data can be compared to them.

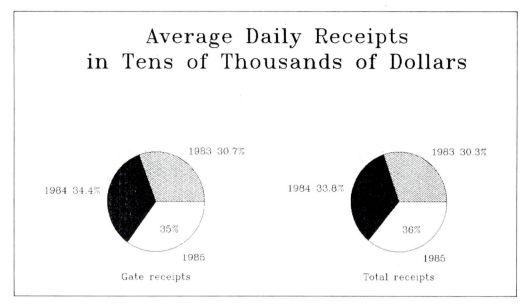

FIGURE 8.8
Pie charts of average daily gate receipts and total receipts

Uses of Graphics

Now that you are acquainted with the history and the hardware and software functions of graphics, let's look at how graphics are being used today.

Movies

Hollywood has been using computer graphics in special effects for years. *Tron* and *Star Trek II* are classic examples of movies that have used computer graphics. Although still in its infancy, computer graphic imaging can create simulated "worlds" that have never existed before. Movies are no longer limited by the physical characteristics of reality; instead, they are as free of limitations as the movie maker's imagination allows them to be.

Industry

"Drafting Dan" is a cross between a typewriter and a drafting board and is used to develop engineering designs for new products. Although "Drafting Dan" has never been built anywhere except in Robert Heinlein's book *Door into Summer* (copyright 1956), a lot of its relatives have been. "Drafting Dan's" relatives are known as **CAD/CAM (c̲omputer-a̲ided d̲esign/ c̲omputer-a̲ided m̲anufacturing)** machines. In the mid-1950s, General Motors was one of the first companies to attempt to use computer-aided design. However, CAD/CAM did not become generally available until the late 1960s. Today, this type of system is used to help design parts, products, and structures from roller bearings and buildings to sophisticated jets, including the space shuttle.

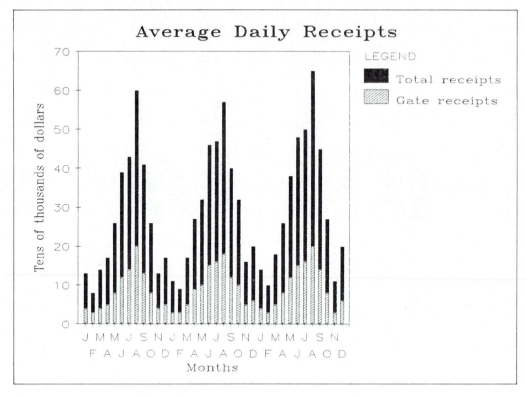

FIGURE 8.9
Stacked bar chart of average daily gate receipts and total receipts

Business

Business graphics are generally divided into two areas: information and presentation. **Information graphics** is the term used to refer to charts and graphs that help one see detailed data in an easy-to-read format. **Presentation graphics** are of higher resolution, usually in color, and more expensive. Although the distinction between the two can be difficult to determine, information graphics are usually too detailed to be used for presentations.

The Wharton School of the University of Pennsylvania in Philadelphia conducted a study that found that speakers were perceived more favorably when they used graphics. Business graphics, therefore, could have a significant effect on your ability to present your ideas successfully.

Chapter Summary

As you have seen in this chapter, business graphics can be an effective method of representing data. It can be used to convey a maximum amount of information with a minimum amount of words and effort.

This chapter discussed the historical development of computer graphics, recognizing that the growth in graphics has followed the growth of the computer industry. Reductions in the cost of microcomputers and software have led to the increased use of computer graphics, which are being used successfully in many businesses, including the movie and manufacturing industries.

Although there are special hardware requirements for advanced computer graphics, graphics work can be done on "standard" microcomputer equipment. Special hardware (such as a laser printer) is required to produce charts that are of high quality (the charts presented in this chapter were created using a standard dot-matrix printer).

The standard functions of business graphics include such important activities as chart selection, scaling, and labeling. Although some of the activities are done for you by the software package, understanding how these functions work and how they can affect a chart is necessary for the appropriate use of the package. This understanding gives you the ability to produce a chart that will convey the maximum amount of information in an easily readable and understandable form.

Chapter Key Terms

Area chart
Bar chart
Bit-mapped
  graphics
CAD/CAM
  (<u>c</u>omputer-<u>a</u>ided
  <u>d</u>esign/
  <u>c</u>omputer-<u>a</u>ided
  <u>m</u>anufacturing)
Character graphics
Computer graphics

Drawing
Drum plotter
Flatbed plotter
Graphics tablet
  (digitizing pad)
High resolution
Information
  graphics
Interactive
  computer
  graphics

Labeling
Linear scale
Line chart
Low resolution
Medium resolution
Multiple-pen
  plotter
Painting
Pie chart
Pins
Pixel graphics

Plotter
Presentation
  graphics
Scaling
Scatter chart
Single-pen plotter
Stacked bar chart
"Stand-alone"
  graphics package
Subcell graphics

Chapter Questions

1. Describe the computer graphics equipment you have available for your class.
2. Discuss how graphics could be used in fields other than those generally associated with business — for example, the health industry, sports, or your school.
3. Describe how scaling can be used to improve a chart.

4. Discuss the type of chart you would use to present information about your school and city in an attempt (a) to convince the state funding agencies to give them more money for the coming year, and (b) to convince people that your school and city are the greatest places in the whole state.
5. Why is labeling considered so important in charting?
6. You are working for a company that

produces five products. Your task is to demonstrate how these five products contribute to the total income of the company. What kind of chart would you select for your presentation and why?

7. You are tracking the price of a share of common stock on a daily basis over a period of three months. You want to compare the price performance of this stock with the activity of the Dow Jones market average. What type of graph would you select and why? Would you attempt to scale the value of your common stock versus the Dow average? Why?

8. You are currently taking five courses, and you have an interim course average for each of these courses. Three of these courses are in your major, and the remaining courses are required courses. You want to compare your performance in major courses with that in required courses. What type of graph would you select and why? Can you alter this type of graph type to obtain an alternative picture of your performance? If so, how?

9. What kinds of input and output devices perform graphics work? Make a list of these devices and briefly explain how each works.

10. Chapter 1 (Table 1.1) provided a table that described the characteristics of decisions made by strategic, tactical, and operational management. Compare the characteristics of strategic and operational management. Which characteristics are best represented by a chart or a graph rather than by a more typical report produced by a spreadsheet or database?

Modules/Chapter Eight
Business Graphics

M8

M8a   pfs:Graph
          Software Publishing Corporation
          1901 Landings Drive
          Mountain View, CA 94043

M8b   Lotus 1-2-3 Graphics
          Lotus Development Corporation
          161 First Street
          Cambridge, MA 02142

M8c   Chart Master
          Decision Resources
          25 Sylvan Road
          So. Westport, CT 06880

Introduction to Graphics Modules

In the modules that follow, you will be given the opportunity to learn about one (or more) of the popular graphics packages available for microcomputers: pfs:Graph (Module 8a), Lotus 1-2-3 (Module 8b), and Chart Master (Module 8c).

Problem Statement for Graphics Modules

Once again, you will use the job hunting problem—this time to learn about graphics packages. You will create and print (or plot) graphs to represent pictorially the data you have been collecting about the companies.

Everyone is interested in keeping track of how well the job hunting process is going and comparing the offers that have been received from the different companies. With this in mind, the following activities were designed to enable you to create charts that can be useful in evaluating the job hunting activities. The data you need for this problem is presented below. (The data is also found in Appendix A.)

1. Create a pie chart that compares the number of companies in each of the "Status" categories in your collection of data. You currently have 21 companies (including the three offers from Johnson Instruments) in your files: negotiations are still ongoing for nine companies, three have rejected your application, you have refused the offer from one, and eight companies have made you an offer.

2. (a) Create a bar chart showing the offers you received from the eight companies. The companies should be listed in alphabetical order.
(b) Create a stacked bar chart showing the Actual Offer from each of the companies. The Actual Offer is the Salary Offer plus the Life Insurance Contribution, the Health Insurance Contribution, and the Retirement Contribution.

3. Create a line chart that charts the Actual Offers (companies listed in alphabetical order) and the Average Actual Offer. (The Average Actual Offer was calculated in the modules in Chapter 6 as $23,470.00.)

The numbers that follow were calculated in the spreadsheet chapter (Chapter 6). The data is summarized as follows:

| Company Name | Salary Offer | Contributions | | | Actual Offer |
		Life	Health	Retirement	
Ethyl & Jung, DDS	$20,000	$320	$950	$6,000	$27,275
Hormell Texas Chili Co.	19,300	164	320	2,202	21,986
Johnson Instruments, Inc. (mid-cities)	19,200	135	354	3,333	23,022
Johnson Instruments, Inc. (south)	19,000	135	354	3,333	22,822
Johnson Instruments, Inc. (north)	19,100	135	354	3,333	22,922
Lewis & Melts Mortgage Co.	22,000	500	600	4,400	27,500
Matt's Films, Inc.	18,950	155	456	5,000	24,561
Nephi's Hopi Crafts	15,670	250	425	1,333	17,678

pfs:Graph

Learning to Use pfs:Graph

Pfs:Graph is the graphics application package for the pfs Software Series of application packages. The package is available for a variety of microcomputer systems using the MS-DOS or the PC-DOS operating system. Pfs:Graph is designed to produce business charts allowing you to represent information visually, to clarify your information, and to enhance its effect in a report. This means that you can produce three types of charts—bar, line, and pie—in a fast, easy, and reliable manner.

Begin with the computer's operating system disk in drive A. If you are using a system that has two disk drives, a disk prepared to hold your graph data should be in drive B. After you have booted your system, replace the system disk in drive A with the pfs:Graph disk, enter the command GRAPH, and press the RETURN key.

When the package is loaded into memory, it will respond by placing the MAIN MENU on the screen, as shown in Figure 8a.1. The MAIN MENU lists the eight main functions provided by pfs:Graph. Whenever you press the ESCape key, pfs:Graph will stop whatever it is doing and return to this menu. When you first use pfs:Graph to create a chart, you must either define the chart or enter the data required by the chart. Usually it is better to start by defining the chart.

Solving the Job Hunting Problem

The remaining sections of this module are devoted to solving the job hunting problem. You may want to refer to the problem statement in the Introduction to Graphics Modules before you continue. Also, remember that the data used in this problem can be found in Appendix A.

What Is the Distribution of Job Status Values? — Creating a Pie Chart

To define a chart, select number 2 from the MAIN MENU. Press the F10 key, and you will see the DEFINE CHART screen. All you need to do to define the pie chart is enter PIE under TYPE for graph A, press the TAB key until the

```
          PFS:GRAPH MAIN MENU
          _____


    1   GET/EDIT DATA       5   PRINT CHART

    2   DEFINE CHART        6   PLOT CHART

    3   DISPLAY CHART       7   CLEAR CHART

    4   GET/SAVE/REMOVE     8   EXIT PFS:GRAPH




          ▐SELECTION NUMBER:▌


  (C) 1983 Software Publishing Corporation

                              F10-Continue
```

FIGURE 8A.1
pfs:Graph MAIN MENU

cursor moves to the input area for CHART TITLE:, and enter the title "Status of Companies in Job Hunt," as shown in Figure 8a.2. The other items on this screen have no effect on a pie chart, and you don't need to enter or change what is already displayed. Finally, press the F10 key to return to the MAIN MENU.

What Are the Values? — Entering Data

Now that you have defined the chart you want to create, it is time to enter the data. Select number 1 from the MAIN MENU and press the F10 key. Pfs:Graph will now display the GET/EDIT DATA MENU shown in Figure 8a.3. This menu can be used to accomplish several different operations. Choosing selection number 1 allows you to enter data for your chart or to edit data you have already entered and that is in memory. Selection number 2 allows you to read data from a VisiCalc spreadsheet file, and selection number 3 reads data from pfs:File.

Press the TAB key to move to the next entry area and select one of the four graph types allowed in a single chart for which data is to be entered. Enter A for the first graph, B for the second graph, and so on. The MERGE (Y/N): prompt is used to indicate whether or not the data being read from a VisiCalc or a pfs:File file should be added to the data already in the graph. The normal entry

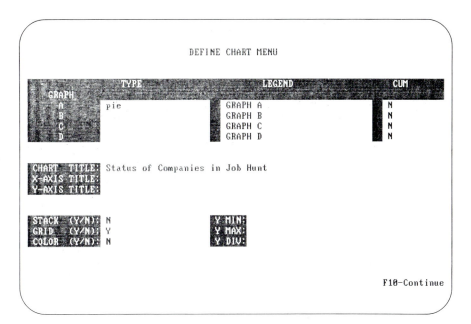

FIGURE 8A.2
DEFINE CHART screen for the pie chart

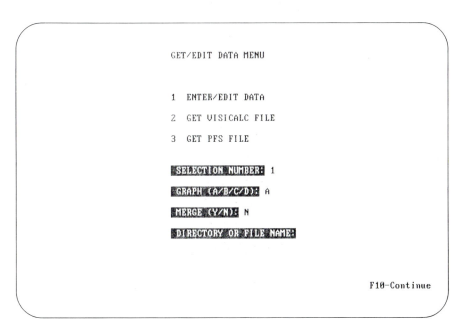

FIGURE 8A.3
GET/EDIT DATA MENU

for this operation is N, meaning that the data entered should replace whatever data is in the graph. The DIRECTORY OR FILE NAME: operation is used to specify which VisiCalc or pfs:File file is to be retrieved.

Because you are entering data for the first time and not reading it from a file, select number 1, and press the TAB key to move to the next entry item. Enter graph A and press the F10 key to continue. Pfs:Graph will now display the DATA ENTRY screen, allowing you to enter the data for your chart.

What Does the Data Look Like? — Indicating Formats

The first item of information you need to provide is the format of the X data in the chart. The X data is used to label the horizontal axis of a chart and the wedges of a pie chart. This data can be formatted in one of three ways: by identifier, number, or date. Entering an I for the X DATA FORMAT: indicates that the X values are identifiers. An identifier may be any string of characters from 1 to 15 characters long. It is advisable to limit the size of your identifiers to just a few characters for bar charts and line charts so that they will all fit across the x-axis (horizontal axis). Because pie charts don't have an x- or y-axis, limiting the size of the identifiers is not necessary.

Entering an N for the X DATA FORMAT: indicates that the X values are to be treated as numbers. An X format of N data type produces only a line graph, because numeric data implies a continuous range of possible values. The values that can be entered for X range from $-1E29$ (or $1E29-$) to $+1E29$ in scientific notation. (This means the digit "1" is followed by 29 zeros or digits if the 29 is positive or preceded by a decimal point and 29 zeros or digits if the 29 is negative — that is, very large or very small values.) More commonly, the numbers used are whole numbers; however, decimal values can be used if they are appropriate.

To specify the X DATA FORMAT: as a date, the letters D for day of the month, M for month of the year, Y for either a two-digit (87) or a four-digit (1987) year, or Q for quarters of the year (three months) can be used. You may even combine the date codes for better labeling. The only valid combinations are YM for year and then month, MY for month followed by the year, QY for quarter and then year, and YQ for the year followed by the quarter. When you enter a date for the X data, you must separate the parts of the date by a nonnumeric character — usually a / (slash), , (comma), : (colon), or a space. The date code D cannot be used with any other date codes, and the date code Q cannot be used with either M or D. If you use an invalid date code, pfs:Graph will choose a date specification that makes sense for use in the data column. For example, if you supply a code such as Q /M, pfs:Graph will alter it to Q /Y.

To enter the data for the pie chart you are creating, enter an I in the X DATA FORMAT: area and press the TAB key to move the cursor down to the X DATA column. Now enter the labels and values shown in Figure 8a.4, pressing the TAB key to move from one entry to the next. When you have entered all of

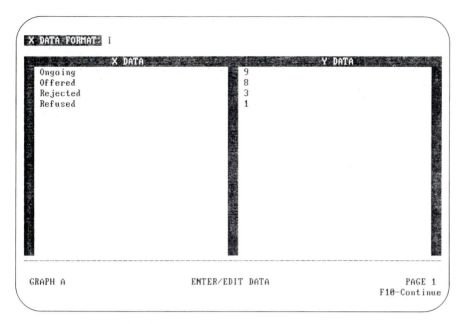

FIGURE 8A.4
Data points needed for the pie chart

the data, press the F10 key to continue, and pfs:Graph will return to the MAIN MENU.

Producing Results — Printing a Chart

Now that you have created your chart, all that remains is to print (or plot) the results. Before you print the chart, take a look at it to make sure it meets your specifications. To accomplish this, simply select number 3 and press the F10 key. Your chart will be displayed on the screen. If the chart is not correct, return to the DEFINE CHART MENU and the GET/EDIT DATA MENU and make the necessary corrections.

Once the chart is ready to be printed, select number 5 from the MAIN MENU and press the F10 key. The PRINTER MENU, shown in Figure 8A.5, is now on the screen. This menu asks what type of printer you are using, what size chart to print, whether you want to list the actual data, and where your printer is connected. Using the TAB key to move through the items, provide the needed information and then press F10 to continue. Actually, the only information you need to be concerned about is the entries for EXPANDED SIZE (Y/N): and PRINT DATA (Y/N):, because the SELECTION NUMBER: and PRINT TO: options are determined by the computer you are using.

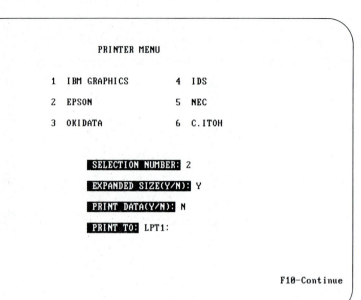

```
                 PRINTER MENU


    1  IBM GRAPHICS         4   IDS

    2  EPSON                5   NEC

    3  OKIDATA              6   C.ITOH



         SELECTION NUMBER: 2
         EXPANDED SIZE(Y/N): Y
         PRINT DATA(Y/N): N
         PRINT TO: LPT1:


                                          F10-Continue
```

FIGURE 8A.5
pfs:Graph PRINTER MENU

If you enter Y for EXPANDED SIZE (Y/N):, your chart will be printed along the length of the page and will fill an $8\frac{1}{2} \times 11$-inch page. If you enter N for this item, the chart will be printed across the page and will be approximately 3×4 inches. Answering Y for the PRINT DATA (Y/N): item will cause the actual data to be printed, whereas entering an N will leave the data off the chart. The chart shown in Figure 8a.6 will be printed if you enter Y for the EXPANDED SIZE (Y/N): item and N for the PRINT DATA (Y/N): item.

How Do Offers Measure Up? — Creating a Bar Chart

Before creating the bar chart, you need to decide what to do with the chart currently in memory. You can save the chart by selecting number 4 from the MAIN MENU and following the save instructions (the save operation is discussed later in this module). Then you should clear the current chart from memory by selecting number 7. After clearing the previous chart from memory, select number 2 from the MAIN MENU to define your bar chart.

Information on a Chart — Labeling

To define your bar chart, fill out the DEFINE CHART menu prompts as shown in Figure 8a.7. Notice that you have used more of the options on this screen

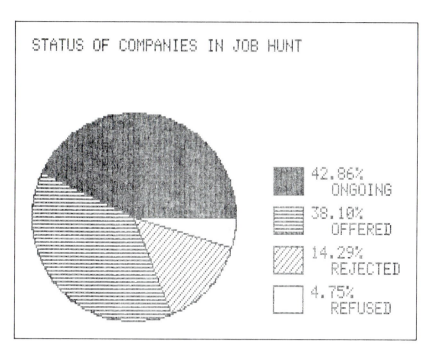

FIGURE 8A.6
Pie chart showing the status of companies in the job hunt

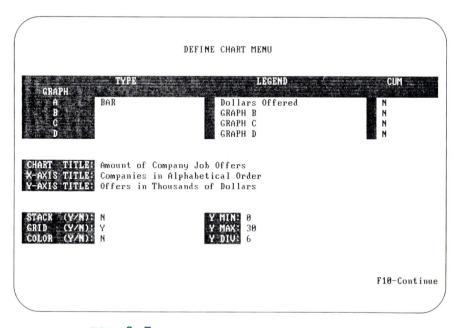

FIGURE 8A.7
DEFINE CHART screen for the first bar chart

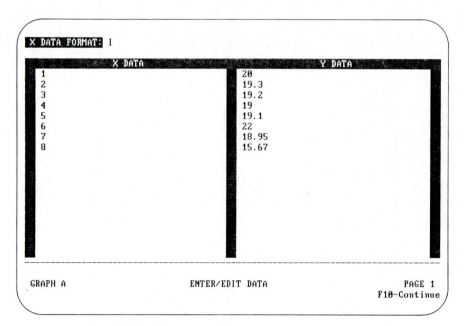

FIGURE 8A.8
Data points needed for the bar chart

than you did for the pie chart. The LEGEND is a set of up to 18 characters displayed at the bottom of the chart that identifies the data from each graph. The CUM column is used to indicate whether you want cumulative values (Y) or actual values (N) plotted. The items CHART TITLE:, X-AXIS TITLE:, and Y-AXIS TITLE: are used to label the chart. The chart title and the x-axis title can be up to 40 characters long, and the y-axis title can be 30 characters long. To stack the bars (plot one on top of the other), enter a Y for the item labeled STACK (Y/N):. An N will use the x-axis as the beginning position or base for all graphs. This option allows you to create stacked bar charts or area charts by stacking line graphs. The GRID (Y/N): item allows you to place horizontal grid lines on the chart, and the COLOR (Y/N): allows you to display or plot the chart in color (if you have a plotter or a color printer).

Producing a "Better" Picture — Scaling

The items labeled Y MIN:, Y MAX:, and Y DIV: are used to adjust the scale of the y-axis. Y MIN sets the minimum value of Y that will appear on the chart, Y MAX sets the maximum value, and Y DIV defines the number of divisions on the y-axis. The maximum allowable number of divisions for the y-axis is ten. If both Y MIN and Y MAX are blank, pfs:Graph will automatically scale the chart on the basis of the data values you enter.

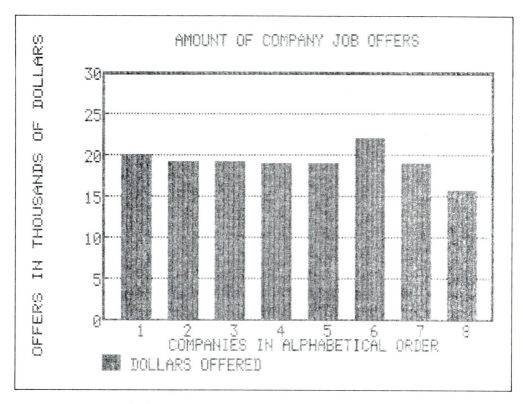

FIGURE 8A.9
**Bar chart showing the amount of company
job offers**

After entering all the information on the DEFINE CHART screen, press the F10 key to return to the MAIN MENU. Select number 1 and press the F10 key to move to the GET/EDIT DATA MENU. Selecting number 1 for graph A and pressing the F10 key will allow you to enter the data points, as shown in Figure 8a.8. After entering the data points, press F10 to return to the MAIN MENU. Now select number 3 and press F10 to display the chart. Once you are satisfied with the chart, return to the MAIN MENU and select number 5 to print the chart shown in Figure 8a.9. Use the same print procedure that you used for the pie chart earlier.

Looking at the Actual Offers — Creating a Stacked Bar Chart

To add the new information about the job offers to the bar chart and print it as a stacked bar chart, return to the DEFINE CHART screen and define the chart

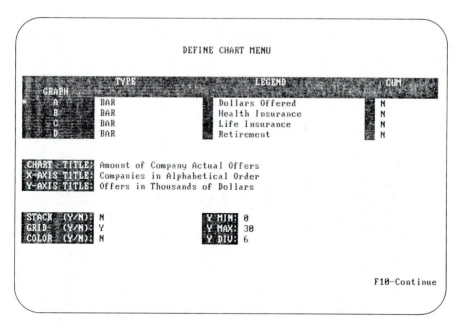

FIGURE 8A.10
DEFINE CHART screen for the second bar chart

as shown in Figure 8a.10 — adding the three new graphs. The asterisk (*) to the left of graph A indicates that the data for this graph is already in memory. Now enter the GET/EDIT DATA MENU and add the data points for charts B, C, and D. When you have finished entering all the data points from the problem description, check the chart by selecting number 3 from the MAIN MENU and print your results by selecting number 5. The stacked bar chart that will be printed is shown in Figure 8a.11.

Comparing Actual Offers with the Average Offer — Creating a Line Chart

You have already created two different types of charts using pfs:Graph, and you can see just how easy it is to generate useful graphics output. To create the final chart, a line chart, clear memory of the current chart information by selecting 7 from the MAIN MENU and press F10 to continue. To define the line chart, select number 2 from the MAIN MENU, press F10, and define your chart, as shown in Figure 8a.12. When the chart is defined, press the F10 key to return to the MAIN MENU, and select number 1 to enter your data. From the GET/EDIT DATA MENU, select number 1 for graph A and enter the Average Offer of 23.47 (the average actual offer in thousands of dollars) for each of the eight companies. After entering these data points, select number 1 for graph B

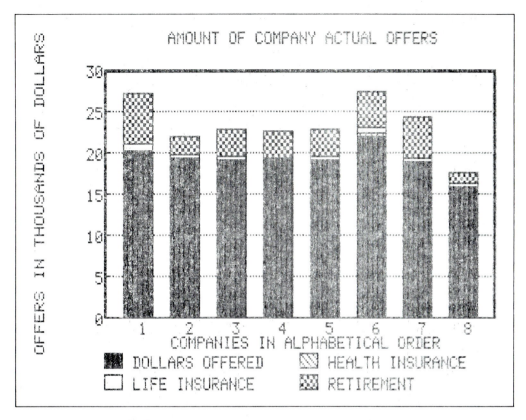

FIGURE 8A.11
**Stacked bar chart showing the amount of
company Actual Offers**

from the GET/EDIT MENU and enter the Actual Offer for each of the companies.

Your line chart is now complete. You should check it for correctness by selecting number 3 from the MAIN MENU. After making sure that the chart is exactly the way you want it, print Figure 8a.13 by selecting number 5 from the MAIN MENU.

Manipulating Files — Saving, Retrieving, and Deleting

Selecting number 4 from the MAIN MENU and pressing the F10 key will produce the GET/SAVE/REMOVE MENU shown in Figure 8a.14. From this menu, you have several options. If you wish to save the information needed to create your chart, select number 2, press the TAB key, and enter the name of the file you want to use to save your chart. The file name may be one to eight

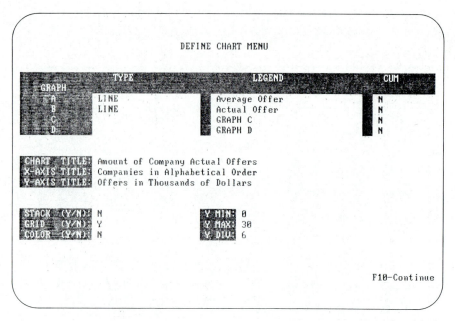

FIGURE 8A.12
DEFINE CHART screen for the line chart

characters long, using the letters A through Z, the digits 0 through 9, and the special characters: $, #, &, @, !, %, ', (,), -, <, >, _, ^, and ~. A file name can also have an optional extension of a period and one, two, or three more characters. If you use an extension in a file name, you must always use that extension when referring to that file. In addition, file names cannot contain spaces, commas, /, or two periods. Finally, the file name can be preceded by a disk drive designation. A disk drive is a letter (A or B) that identifies which disk drive the file is to be saved on. The disk drive designation is followed by a colon (:).

To retrieve a file that has already been saved on a disk, simply select number 1 from the GET/SAVE/REMOVE MENU, press the TAB key, enter the name of the file you wish to retrieve, and press the F10 key. Removing a file is done in much the same manner. Select number 6 from the GET/SAVE/RE-MOVE MENU, press the TAB key, and enter the name of the file you wish to remove. Pressing the F10 key will remove the file from disk.

Other Features of pfs:Graph

From the GET/SAVE/REMOVE MENU, you also have the options of saving, displaying, and printing pictures. Creating a picture of a chart produces a dot

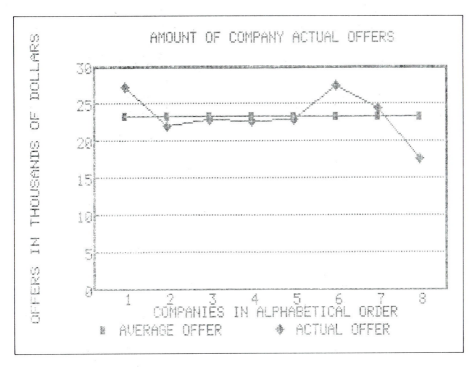

FIGURE 8A.13
Line chart showing the amount of company
Actual Offers and the Average Offer

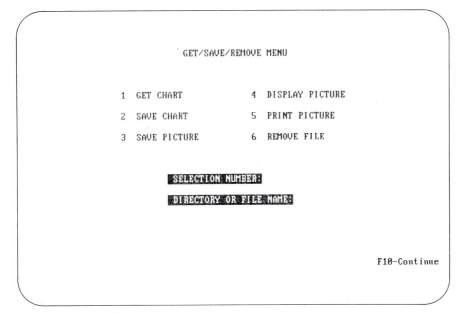

FIGURE 8A.14
pfs:Graph GET/SAVE/REMOVE MENU

image on the screen (320 by 200 pixels). With this function, the chart is treated as a graphics image, not as a data file. You can use a picture file for inclusion in a pfs:Write document, as well as print charts on printers not supported by pfs:Graph. Note, however, that you cannot "get" a picture. A picture file does not contain any data—only the graphics image. Therefore, while you can display and print the picture, there is no data in it to retrieve.

Lotus 1-2-3 Graphics

Learning to Use Lotus 1-2-3 Graphics

This is your third opportunity to examine the capabilities of Lotus 1-2-3. Module 6b presented the spreadsheet capabilities, and Module 7b discussed the database functions of Lotus. In this module, you will investigate the graphics functions available in Lotus. Because the primary operations of Lotus stem from the spreadsheet capabilities of the package, you should have worked through Module 6b. Furthermore, the data on which the graphs in this module are based were produced using the database functions of Lotus in Module 7b. Thus, it is recommended that you review both of these modules before you proceed.

To begin, enter LOTUS and select the 1-2-3 option from the initial screen. After the spreadsheet skeleton appears, retrieve the complete database containing all companies and their present status. Then add the entries shown in the lower right corner—rows 25 through 28—as illustrated in Figure 8b.1. You are now ready to proceed with the graphics operations.

Solving the Job Hunting Problem

The remaining sections of this module are devoted to solving the job hunting problem. You may want to refer to the problem statement in the Introduction to Graphics Modules before you continue. Also, remember that the data used in this problem can be found in Appendix A.

What Is the Distribution of Job Status Values? — Producing a Pie Chart

To enter the graphics mode, select Graph from the Lotus 1-2-3 primary menu (see Figure 8b.1). Then select the Type of graph to be created, as illustrated in Figure 8b.2. You are then presented with a choice of graph types, consisting of Line, Bar, XY, Stacked-Bar, and Pie charts. For your first chart, select the Pie type either by moving the cursor to that position and pressing RETURN or simply by pressing P. You will then return to the primary graphics menu. To select the data to be presented in the pie chart, select data range A. You will

```
I25: 9                                                        MENU
Worksheet  Range  Copy  Move  File  Print  Graph  Data  Quit
Create a graph
             A                     G       H       I      J
9   Lewis & Melts Mortgage Co.  9   11/30   01/15   Offered Mid-cities
10  Ethyl & Jung, DDS           10  11/15   11/30   Offered North
11  Aerospace Education Center  11  11/16   12/13   Rejected
12  ABC Stereo Warehouse        12  11/16   02/22   Ongoing
13  WTBS Channel 5 TV           13  12/03   01/06   Ongoing
14  Hormell Texas Chili Company 14  12/05   01/31   Offered East
15  Children's Museum           15  11/30   01/06   Ongoing
16  FBI                         16  01/03   01/21   Ongoing
17  Mosteq Computer Company     17  12/31           Ongoing
18  Nephi's Hopi Crafts         18  12/09   01/06   Offered East
19  Kelly Construction Company  19  12/09           Ongoing
20  Jana's Management Consultants 20 01/06          Rejected
21  Bar Four Ranch              21  12/28   02/03   Refused
22  Matt's Films, Inc.          22  12/31   01/07   Offered North
23  Roger, Roger & Ray, Inc.    23  12/15           Rejected
24                              24
25                              25  Counts:  Ongoing       9
26                              26           Offered       8
27                              27           Rejected      3
28                              28           Refused       1
```

FIGURE 8B.1
Entering the Lotus graph function

then be asked to specify the beginning and ending cell locations of the first data range. If necessary, move the cell pointer to cell I25, press the period key (Lotus will show ..), move the cursor to cell I28, and press the RETURN key. Figure 8b.3 shows the data to be presented in a pie chart form.

Titles for the Pie Chart—An Initial Look at Labeling

The next step is to provide a series of titles to be presented with the pie chart. Select the X option from the primary menu, and you will be asked to supply the x-axis data values for the pie chart. Because there are no x- and y-axes for pie charts, these values are interpreted to be titles for the individual wedges of the pie. As shown in Figure 8b.4, the range of these values is H25 through H28.

Last, give your pie chart a chart title. To do this, select Options from the primary menu, Titles from the next menu, and First from the final menu. You will then be asked to enter the title for the chart. As shown in Figure 8b.5, you have chosen to name it "Status of Companies in Job Hunt."

```
I25: 9                                                          MENU
Type  X  A  B  C  D  E  F  Reset  View  Save  Options  Name  Quit
Set graph type
```

```
I25: 9                                                          MENU
Line  Bar  XY  Stacked-Bar  Pie
Pie chart
```

```
I25: 9                                                          MENU
Type  X  A  B  C  D  E  F  Reset  View  Save  Options  Name  Quit
Set first data range
```

	A		G	H	I	J
9	Lewis & Melts Mortgage Co.	9	11/30	01/15	Offered	Mid-cities
10	Ethyl & Jung, DDS	10	11/15	11/30	Offered	North
11	Aerospace Education Center	11	11/16	12/13	Rejected	
12	ABC Stereo Warehouse	12	11/16	02/22	Ongoing	
13	WTBS Channel 5 TV	13	12/03	01/06	Ongoing	
14	Hormell Texas Chili Company	14	12/05	01/31	Offered	East
15	Children's Museum	15	11/30	01/06	Ongoing	
16	FBI	16	01/03	01/21	Ongoing	
17	Mosteq Computer Company	17	12/31		Ongoing	
18	Nephi's Hopi Crafts	18	12/09	01/06	Offered	East
19	Kelly Construction Company	19	12/09		Ongoing	
20	Jana's Management Consultants	20	01/06		Rejected	
21	Bar Four Ranch	21	12/28	02/03	Refused	
22	Matt's Films, Inc.	22	12/31	01/07	Offered	North
23	Roger, Roger & Ray, Inc.	23	12/15		Rejected	
24		24				
25		25	Counts:	Ongoing	9	
26		26		Offered	8	
27		27		Rejected	3	
28		28		Refused	1	

FIGURE 8B.2
Beginning a pie chart

Chart Manipulations — Viewing, Clearing, and Saving

Now that you have provided all of the necessary entries, Quit the Options menu and select View from the primary menu. You will then see the chart shown in Figure 8b.6. When you have finished viewing the chart, press any key, and you will return to the primary graphics menu. If you decide to enter changes, all unchanged values (data, titles, and so on) are retained until you change the graph Type or Reset the graph. However, you will probably want to print this graph later, so you should select the Save option from the menu and supply a file name for the chart, as illustrated in Figure 8b.7. Printing graphs is another function that will be discussed later.

```
I28: 1                                                               POINT
Enter first data range: I25..I28

                   A              G       H       I         J
9   Lewis & Melts Mortgage Co.  9   11/30   01/15   Offered   Mid-cities
10  Ethyl & Jung, DDS           10  11/15   11/30   Offered   North
11  Aerospace Education Center  11  11/16   12/13   Rejected
12  ABC Stereo Warehouse        12  11/16   02/22   Ongoing
13  WTBS Channel 5 TV           13  12/03   01/06   Ongoing
14  Hormell Texas Chili Company 14  12/05   01/31   Offered   East
15  Children's Museum           15  11/30   01/06   Ongoing
16  FBI                         16  01/03   01/21   Ongoing
17  Mosteq Computer Company     17  12/31           Ongoing
18  Nephi's Hopi Crafts         18  12/09   01/06   Offered   East
19  Kelly Construction Company  19  12/09           Ongoing
20  Jana's Management Consultants 20 01/06          Rejected
21  Bar Four Ranch              21  12/28   02/03   Refused
22  Matt's Films, Inc.          22  12/31   01/07   Offered   North
23  Roger, Roger & Ray, Inc.    23  12/15           Rejected
24                              24
25                              25  Counts:  Ongoing          9
26                              26           Offered          8
27                              27           Rejected         3
28                              28           Refused          1
```

FIGURE 8B.3
Specifying a data range for job status values

How Do the Offers Measure Up? — Producing a Bar Chart

Now you want to turn your attention to the companies that have made you an offer. Return to the Lotus spreadsheet by entering Quit from the primary graphics menu. Your next problem deals only with companies for which the job status is "Offered." Eliminate all other companies from the spreadsheet. Then re-enter the Graph mode from the primary spreadsheet menu and select Type. Again, your choices are Line, Bar, XY, Stacked-Bar, and Pie. This time, select Bar to produce a bar chart, as indicated in Figure 8b.8. Next, select data range A and enter the range for Offer, as shown in Figure 8b.9.

Titles for the Bar Chart — More on Labeling

After you have supplied the data to be graphed, you should provide titles. Choose Options from the primary menu and Titles from the second menu. As before, select First and enter the title for the chart, which is "Amount of Company Job Offers." This title will appear at the top of the bar chart. Then, choose the X-Axis option and enter the title "Companies in Alphabetical Order." The x-axis title will appear at the bottom of the bar chart. This is

I25: 9   MENU

Type [X] A B C D E F Reset View Save Options Name Quit
Set X-range

	A		G	H	I	J
9	Lewis & Melts Mortgage Co.	9	11/30	01/15	Offered	Mid-cities
10	Ethyl & Jung, DDS	10	11/15	11/30	Offered	North
11	Aerospace Education Center	11	11/16	12/13	Rejected	
12	ABC Stereo Warehouse	12	11/16	02/22	Ongoing	
13	WTBS Channel 5 TV	13	12/03	01/06	Ongoing	
14	Hormell Texas Chili Company	14	12/05	01/31	Offered	East
15	Children's Museum	15	11/30	01/06	Ongoing	
16	FBI	16	01/03	01/21	Ongoing	
17	Mosteq Computer Company	17	12/31		Ongoing	
18	Nephi's Hopi Crafts	18	12/09	01/06	Offered	East
19	Kelly Construction Company	19	12/09		Ongoing	
20	Jana's Management Consultants	20	01/06		Rejected	
21	Bar Four Ranch	21	12/28	02/03	Refused	
22	Matt's Films, Inc.	22	12/31	01/07	Offered	North
23	Roger, Roger & Ray, Inc.	23	12/15		Rejected	
24		24				
25		25	Counts:	Ongoing	9	
26		26		Offered	8	
27		27		Rejected	3	
28		28		Refused	1	

H28: 'Refused   POINT
Enter X-axis range: H25..H28

	A		G	H	I	J
9	Lewis & Melts Mortgage Co.	9	11/30	01/15	Offered	Mid-cities
10	Ethyl & Jung, DDS	10	11/15	11/30	Offered	North
11	Aerospace Education Center	11	11/16	12/13	Rejected	
12	ABC Stereo Warehouse	12	11/16	02/22	Ongoing	
13	WTBS Channel 5 TV	13	12/03	01/06	Ongoing	
14	Hormell Texas Chili Company	14	12/05	01/31	Offered	East
15	Children's Museum	15	11/30	01/06	Ongoing	
16	FBI	16	01/03	01/21	Ongoing	
17	Mosteq Computer Company	17	12/31		Ongoing	
18	Nephi's Hopi Crafts	18	12/09	01/06	Offered	East
19	Kelly Construction Company	19	12/09		Ongoing	
20	Jana's Management Consultants	20	01/06		Rejected	
21	Bar Four Ranch	21	12/28	02/03	Refused	
22	Matt's Films, Inc.	22	12/31	01/07	Offered	North
23	Roger, Roger & Ray, Inc.	23	12/15		Rejected	
24		24				
25		25	Counts:	Ongoing	9	
26		26		Offered	8	
27		27		Rejected	3	
28		28		Refused	1	

FIGURE 8B.4
Creating a legend for wedges of the pie

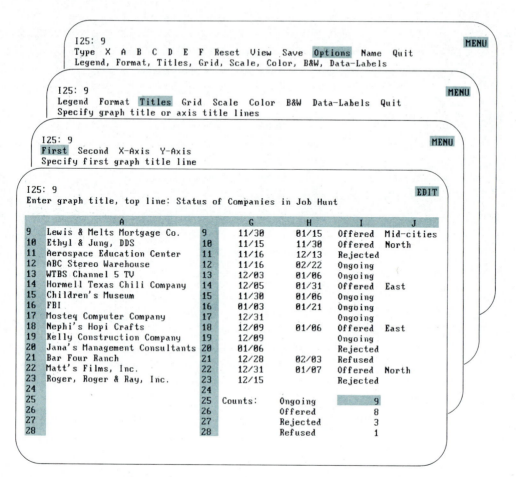

FIGURE 8B.5
Producing titles on the pie chart

followed by selecting a title for the y-axis, which should be "Offers in Dollars." The y-axis title will appear along the left edge of the bar chart.

Finally, as shown in Figure 8b.10, you wish to produce a legend for the job offer amount. Select Legend from the Options menu and select data range A. The title for this legend item is "Dollars Offered." After the legend is in place, you are ready to look at your bar chart. Select Quit from the Options menu and then select View from the primary menu. The bar chart will be produced, as shown in Figure 8b.11. Finally, save this chart so that it can be printed later.

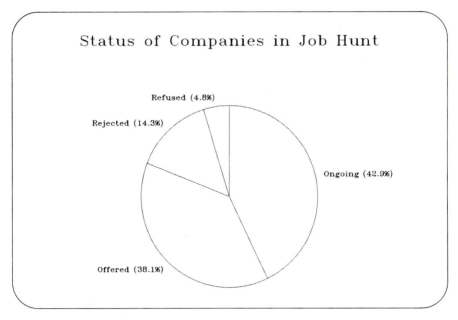

FIGURE 8B.6
The pie chart — distribution of job status values

```
I25: 9                                                          EDIT
Enter graph file name: PIE

        A                        G       H      I        J
 9  Lewis & Melts Mortgage Co.  9   11/30   01/15  Offered  Mid-cities
10  Ethyl & Jung, DDS          10   11/15   11/30  Offered  North
11  Aerospace Education Center 11   11/16   12/13  Rejected
12  ABC Stereo Warehouse       12   11/16   02/22  Ongoing
13  WTBS Channel 5 TV          13   12/03   01/06  Ongoing
14  Hormell Texas Chili Company 14  12/05   01/31  Offered  East
15  Children's Museum          15   11/30   01/06  Ongoing
16  FBI                        16   01/03   01/21  Ongoing
17  Mosteq Computer Company    17   12/31          Ongoing
18  Nephi's Hopi Crafts        18   12/09   01/06  Offered  East
19  Kelly Construction Company 19   12/09          Ongoing
20  Jana's Management Consultants 20 01/06         Rejected
21  Bar Four Ranch             21   12/28   02/03  Refused
22  Matt's Films, Inc.         22   12/31   01/07  Offered  North
23  Roger, Roger & Ray, Inc.   23   12/15          Rejected
24                             24
25                             25  Counts:  Ongoing         9
26                             26           Offered         8
27                             27           Rejected        3
28                             28           Refused         1
```

FIGURE 8B.7
Saving the pie chart for later printing

```
M3: (C2) 20000                                                    MENU
Line  Bar  XY  Stacked-Bar  Pie
Bar graph
```

	A		M	N	O	P
1	Company Name	1	Offer	Life	Health	Retirement
2	----------------------	2				
3	Ethyl & Jung, DDS	3	$20,000.00	$325.00	$950.00	$6,000.00
4	Hormell Texas Chili Company	4	$19,300.00	$164.00	$320.00	$2,202.20
5	Johnson Instruments, Inc.	5	$19,000.00	$135.00	$354.00	$3,333.00
6	Johnson Instruments, Inc.	6	$19,100.00	$135.00	$354.00	$3,333.00
7	Johnson Instruments, Inc.	7	$19,200.00	$135.00	$354.00	$3,333.00
8	Lewis & Melts Mortgage Co.	8	$22,000.00	$500.00	$600.00	$4,400.00
9	Matt's Films, Inc.	9	$18,950.00	$155.00	$456.00	$5,000.00
10	Nephi's Hopi Crafts	10	$15,670.00	$250.00	$425.00	$1,333.00
11		11				
12		12				
13		13				
14		14				
15		15				
16		16				
17		17				
18		18				
19		19				
20		20				

FIGURE 8B.8
Selecting a bar chart

```
M10: (C2) 15670                                                  POINT
Enter first data range: M3..M10
```

	A		M	N	O	P
1	Company Name	1	Offer	Life	Health	Retirement
2	----------------------	2				
3	Ethyl & Jung, DDS	3	$20,000.00	$325.00	$950.00	$6,000.00
4	Hormell Texas Chili Company	4	$19,300.00	$164.00	$320.00	$2,202.20
5	Johnson Instruments, Inc.	5	$19,000.00	$135.00	$354.00	$3,333.00
6	Johnson Instruments, Inc.	6	$19,100.00	$135.00	$354.00	$3,333.00
7	Johnson Instruments, Inc.	7	$19,200.00	$135.00	$354.00	$3,333.00
8	Lewis & Melts Mortgage Co.	8	$22,000.00	$500.00	$600.00	$4,400.00
9	Matt's Films, Inc.	9	$18,950.00	$155.00	$456.00	$5,000.00
10	Nephi's Hopi Crafts	10	$15,670.00	$250.00	$425.00	$1,333.00
11		11				
12		12				
13		13				
14		14				
15		15				
16		16				
17		17				
18		18				
19		19				
20		20				

FIGURE 8B.9
Specifying a data range for offers

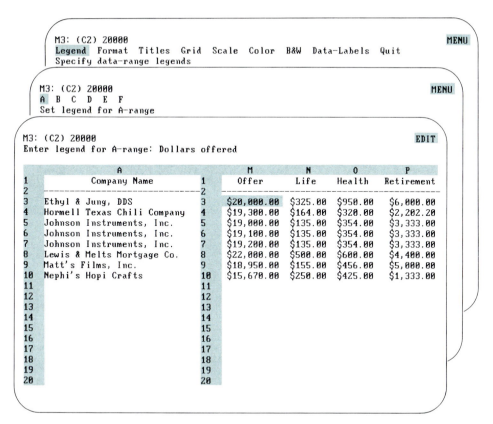

FIGURE 8B.10
Creating a legend for dollars offered

Looking at the Actual Offers — Creating a Stacked Bar Chart

You need to examine further the offers made by each of the companies. First, select the Stacked-Bar chart from the Type option. You already have a beginning for this chart because you have just completed the a bar chart. To create the stacked bar chart, simply add to each stack the elements that represent additional data. As shown in Figure 8b.12, you may begin this process by selecting the B data range and entering the data values from the "Life" column. Then select the C range and enter the data values from the "Health" column. Finally, select the D range and enter the data values from the "Retirement" column.

Now provide titles and legends. Select Options and then Titles. You can keep the x- and y-axis titles previously specified. However, you should change the First title to "Amount of Company Actual Offers." Next, you should provide new legend information. Select Legend from the Options menu and

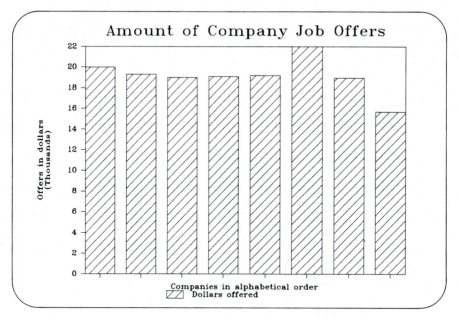

FIGURE 8B.11
The bar chart — amount of company job offers

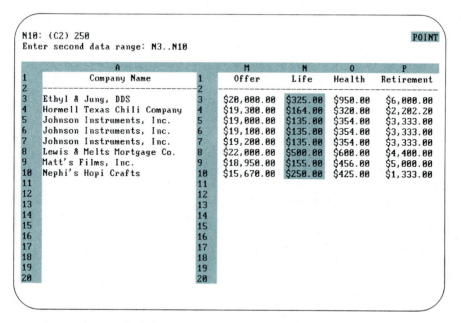

FIGURE 8B.12
Adding data ranges to the stacked bar chart

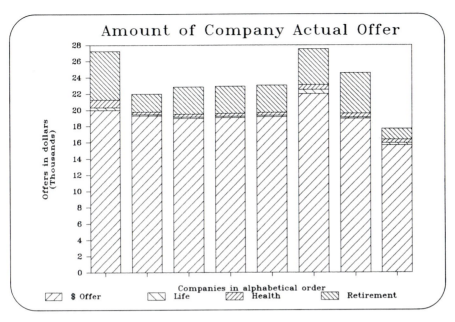

FIGURE 8B.13
The stacked bar chart—amount of actual offers

select data range A. The new legend title for this item is "$ Offer." The legend titles for data ranges B, C, and D are "Life," "Health," and "Retirement," respectively. Now that the chart is complete, Quit the Options menu and select View from the primary menu. After viewing the stacked bar chart, illustrated in Figure 8b.13, save it for later printing.

Comparing Actual Offers with the Average Offer— Creating a Line Chart

Before you create the line chart, you need to return to the spreadsheet and create two new columns of information—"Actual" and "Average," as shown in Figure 8b.14. The actual offer is the total of the offer, life, health, and retirement cells for each company. The values for the average offer are computed for all the actual job offers and simply copied to the cells in the "Average" column. Now return to the Graph function.

To begin the creation of the line chart, select Type and then Line. Next, select data range A and identify the "Actual" data values, as shown in Figure 8b.14. Repeat this sequence for data range B and the "Average" column. Then select Legend from the Options menu. Provide the legend "Actual Offer" for data range A and "Average Offer" for data range B. Now you are ready to view

```
Q10: (C2) +M10+N10+O10+P10                                      POINT
Enter first data range: Q3..Q10
```

	A		P	Q	R
1	Company Name	1	Retirement	Actual	Average
2	-------------------------------	2	---------	--------	--------
3	Ethyl & Jung, DDS	3	$6,000.00	$27,275.00	$23,470.78
4	Hormell Texas Chili Company	4	$2,202.20	$21,986.20	$23,470.78
5	Johnson Instruments, Inc.	5	$3,333.00	$22,822.00	$23,470.78
6	Johnson Instruments, Inc.	6	$3,333.00	$22,922.00	$23,470.78
7	Johnson Instruments, Inc.	7	$3,333.00	$23,022.00	$23,470.78
8	Lewis & Melts Mortgage Co.	8	$4,400.00	$27,500.00	$23,470.78
9	Matt's Films, Inc.	9	$5,000.00	$24,561.00	$23,470.78
10	Nephi's Hopi Crafts	10	$1,333.00	$17,678.00	$23,470.78
11		11			
12		12			
13		13			
14		14			
15		15			
16		16			
17		17			
18		18			
19		19			
20		20			

FIGURE 8B.14
Entering a data range for a line chart

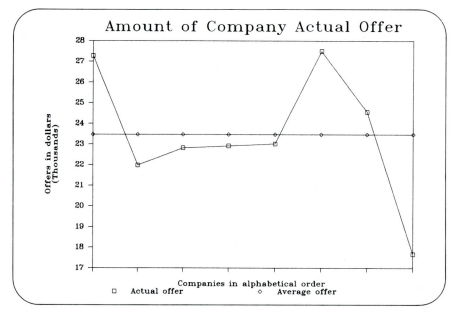

FIGURE 8B.15
The line chart — comparing actual offers to average offer

```
Lotus Access System  V.1A  (C)1983 Lotus Development Corp.        MENU
------------------------------------------------------------------------
1-2-3  File-Manager  Disk-Manager  PrintGraph  Translate  Exit
Enter Lotus Graphics Printing system
========================================================================




                            Thu  01-Jan-87
                              9:19:36am







        Use the arrow keys to highlight command choice and press [Enter]
    Press [Esc] to cancel a choice; Press [F1] for information on command choices
```

FIGURE 8B.16
Selecting the PrintGraph function

your chart. The line chart is shown in Figure 8b.15. Save this chart for later printing.

Printing Your Charts

The spreadsheet function of Lotus does not include an option to print graphs. To produce a graph on a printer, you must Quit the spreadsheet function and return to the Lotus Access System. As shown in Figure 8b.16, one of the choices from this menu is PrintGraph. Once you have made this selection, Lotus will produce a message on the screen asking you to place the Print Graphics disk in drive A. Once this has been done and you have pressed any key on the keyboard, you will see the screen presented in Figure 8b.17. This screen controls the printing of graphs. First, Select a graph for printing. This choice will produce the screen shown in Figure 8b.18. The graph files are indicated along the left side of this screen; mark the one to be printed with the # symbol by pressing the SPACE BAR. In this illustration, the PIE file—the pie chart developed earlier—is to be printed. Then return to the previous screen (Figure 8b.17). From this screen, you are permitted to change the Options (shown below the menu), Configure the printer, Align the paper, advance to a new Page, and so on. To produce the graph on the printer, select the Go option.

```
Copyright 1982, 1983 Lotus Development Corp.  All Rights Reserved.      MENU
----------------------------------------------------------------------------
Select  Options  Go  Configure  Align  Page  Quit
Select pictures
============================================================================
  SELECTED GRAPHS   COLORS            SIZE   FULL          DIRECTORIES

                    Grid:     Black   Left Margin:   .500  Pictures
                    A Range:  Black   Top Margin:    .250  B:\
                    B Range:  Black   Width:        6.852  Fonts
                    C Range:  Black   Height:       9.445  C:\LOTUS
                    D Range:  Black   Rotation:    90.000
                    E Range:  Black                        GRAPHICS DEVICE
                    F Range:  Black   MODES
                                                           IBM/4
                    FONTS             Eject:  No           Parallel
                                      Pause:  No
                    1: ROMAN2                              PAGE SIZE
                    2: ROMAN2
                                                           Length   11.000
                                                           Width     8.000
```

FIGURE 8B.17
Controlling the printing of graphs

```
Copyright 1982, 1983 Lotus Development Corp.  All Rights Reserved.     POINT
----------------------------------------------------------------------------
Select graphs for output

============================================================================
  PICTURE    DATE      TIME    SIZE
----------------------------------------------
  BAR        01-01-87  9:00    2816    [Space] toggles mark on and off
  LINE       01-01-87  9:13    1280    [Enter] selects marked pictures
# PIE        01-01-87  8:41    1024            in the order marked.
  STACK      01-01-87  9:05    5248    [Escape] ignores marked pictures
                                               and returns
                                       [Home] goes to beginning of list
                                       [End] goes to end of list
                                       [Up] moves cursor up
                                       [Down] moves cursor down
                                            List scrolls if cursor
                                            moved beyond top or bottom.
                                       [Graph] draws picture on screen
```

FIGURE 8B.18
Selecting a graph file to be printed

Once the graph has been printed, you may Select another graph for printing. When Quit is selected from the menu, you will be returned to the Lotus Access System screen, from where you may Exit Lotus or re-enter one of the other functions. Remember, you will probably have to change disks to get to most of the other Lotus functions.

Chart Master

Learning to Use Chart Master

Chart Master is a "stand-alone" business graphics application package. The package is available for a variety of microcomputer systems using the MS-DOS or the PC-DOS operating system. Chart Master is designed to produce business charts allowing you to represent information visually, to clarify your information, and to enhance its effect in a report. This means that you can produce three types of charts — bar, line, and pie — in a fast, easy, and reliable manner.

When you are prepared to begin working with Chart Master, start with the Chart Master disk 1 in drive A and the Chart Master disk 2 in drive B. You should also prepare a disk to hold the charts you will create. Keep this disk handy so that it can be used later. When you boot your system, Chart Master will be loaded into your microcomputer's memory.

Once the package has been loaded into memory, it will respond by placing the Chart Master copyright notice on the screen followed by the MAIN MENU, as shown in Figure 8c.1. The MAIN MENU lists the nine primary functions provided by Chart Master. Each of the choices in this menu will provide you with the submenus needed to carry out the activity you have selected.

Solving the Job Hunting Problem

The remaining sections of this module are devoted to solving the job hunting problem. You may want to refer to the problem statement in the Introduction to Graphics Modules before you continue. Also, remember that the data used in this problem can be found in Appendix A.

Creating Titles — Generating Labels for a Chart

To create a chart, select number 1 from the MAIN MENU by either using the arrow keys to move the cursor to CREATE A CHART or pressing the 1 key. Pressing the RETURN key to make your selection will display the TITLES screen. This screen allows you to enter up to four lines of title for the chart you are creating. It also allows you to change the printing characteristics of the title.

504

```
        ◄◄◄  CHART-MASTER MAIN MENU  ►►►

     1  CREATE A CHART

     2  VERIFY CHART

     3  PLOT / PREVIEW CHART

     4  EDIT CHART

     5  STORE / RETRIEVE / DELETE CHART

     6  CHANGE PLOTTING OPTIONS

     7  CHANGE / DISPLAY CONFIGURATION

     8  RUN DATAGRABBER

     9  QUIT MENU
    _____
     ↑↓  Move through choices      ↵  Select
    ============= <F1>  Help ==============
```

FIGURE 8C.1
Chart Master MAIN MENU

In Figure 8c.2, the PgDn key was pressed so that the printing characteristics could be changed, and the FONT was changed to BRM (Bold Roman) by using the up and down arrow keys to move through the list of fonts. Press the RETURN key and then enter the chart title for line 1. Because this is the only title you will need for your chart, press the RETURN key three more times, entering blank lines for title lines 2, 3, and 4.

When you press the RETURN key for line 4 in the TITLES screen, Chart Master will present you with the AXIS LABELS screen. This screen allows you to enter up to two lines of labels for both the x- and y-axes of your chart. However, because you are about to create a pie chart, you will not be using these labels. Press the RETURN key four times to move to the next screen.

Where Do the Values Come From? — Entering Data

The new screen asks for the METHOD OF DATA ENTRY. You will be entering the data manually, so move the cursor to MANUAL and press the RETURN key. The DATAGRABBER option allows you to read data from Lotus 1-2-3, MultiPlan, or VisiCalc files.

After you have pressed the RETURN key, you will be asked to enter the number of variables and the number of observations (number of values per set)

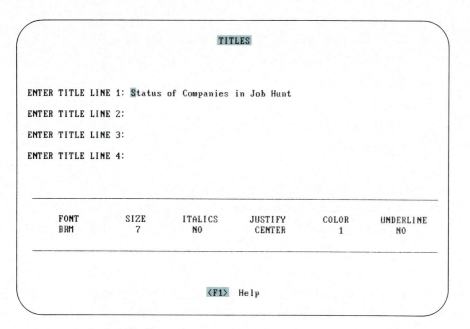

FIGURE 8c.2
TITLES screen for the pie chart

for each variable in your chart. Because you are creating a pie chart of the status of companies in your job hunting activities, enter 4 for the number of variables (the number of different status categories) and 1 for the number of observations. This was done to create Figure 8c.3.

On the VARIABLE LABELS screen, shown in Figure 8c.4, enter the names of each of the variables. Remember to use the PgDn key to move into the print characteristics area, and set the FONT to BRM. After you have entered the last variable label, you will be presented with the OBSERVATIONS LABELS screen. This screen will allow you to label the observations on your chart. However, you are creating a pie chart, so these labels are not needed. Therefore, enter blanks for each of the entries on this screen by pressing the RETURN screen for each observation.

Finally, you are ready to enter the data for your chart. The ENTER DATA FOR ... screen will prompt you for the data for each observation of each variable. Figure 8c.5 shows the data entry for variable 3 ("Rejected"). Once you have entered all of the data, Chart Master will return you to the MAIN MENU.

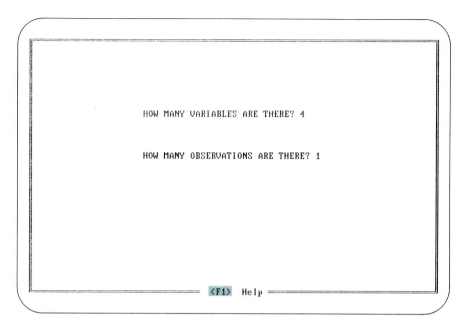

FIGURE 8C.3
The number of VARIABLES and OBSERVATIONS for the pie chart

VARIABLE LABELS

VARIABLE 1: Ongoing

VARIABLE 2: Offered

VARIABLE 3: Rejected

VARIABLE 4: Refused

FONT	SIZE	ITALICS	JUSTIFY	COLOR	UNDERLINE
BRM	4	NO	LEFT	5	NO

<F1> Help

FIGURE 8C.4
VARIABLE LABELS screen for the pie chart

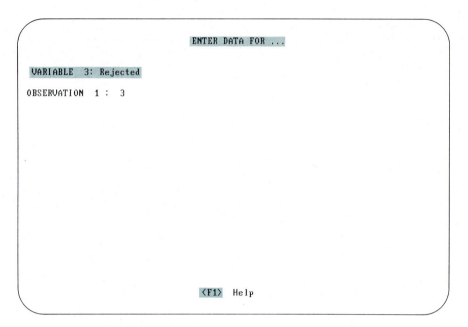

FIGURE 8C.5
Entering the data for the variable "Rejected"

What Is the Distribution of Job Status Values? — Creating a Pie Chart

From the MAIN MENU, you may verify the contents of the chart information, edit the chart if you have made any errors, and plot or preview the chart. To place the chart on paper, select option 3, PLOT / PREVIEW CHART, and you will be presented with the PLOT MENU, shown in Figure 8c.6. Now select option 5 to produce the pie chart. From the PRODUCE CHART ON . . . screen, shown in Figure 8c.7, you can produce the chart on the display screen, if you have graphics capabilities, by selecting option 1, 2, or 3. If you have a plotter available, you can create the chart by selecting option 5. To produce the chart shown in Figure 8c.8, select option 6, PRINTER, and indicate that you want to produce one copy.

How Do the Offers Measure Up? — Creating a Bar Chart

Before creating the bar chart, you need to decide what to do with the chart currently in memory. You can save the chart either by selecting option number 5 from the MAIN MENU and following the save instructions (the save operation is discussed later in this module) and then selecting option 1 to create a new

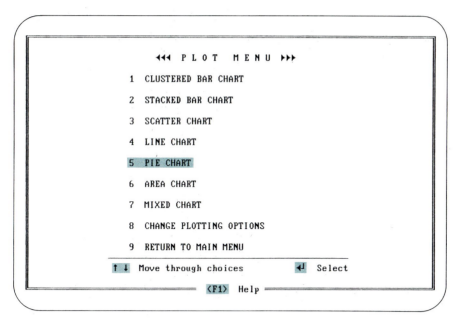

FIGURE 8c.6
Chart Master PLOT MENU

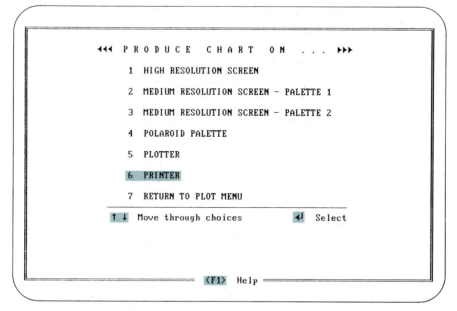

FIGURE 8c.7
PRODUCE CHART ON . . . screen

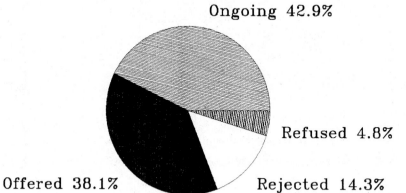

Status of Companies in Job Hunt

FIGURE 8C.8
**Pie chart showing the status of companies
in the job hunt**

chart, or by simply selecting option number 1 to create a new chart. Selecting option 1 will automatically clear the previous chart from memory.

To create your bar chart, enter the title "Amount of Company Offers" for title line 1 and the labels "Companies in Alphabetical Order" and "Offers in Thousands of Dollars" for the x- and y-axes, respectively, as shown in Figure 8c.9. For this chart, you will have one variable and eight observations. After entering this information, label your variable using the VARIABLE LABELS screen shown in Figure 8c.10. This label creates a LEGEND for the chart, which helps to explain its contents. Now, all that remains is to enter blanks for the observation labels and enter the data for the chart.

To produce the chart shown in Figure 8c.11, select the PLOT / PREVIEW CHART option from the MAIN MENU and the CLUSTERED BAR CHART option in the PLOT MENU. Finally, select the printer option from the PRINT CHART ON . . . screen.

MICROCOMPUTERS USED FOR GRAPHICS

A graphics "wand" is used with an IBM PC (25) to enter the coordinates associated with a machine part and with an Apple II microcomputer (26) to outline the shape of the space shuttle. (27) This computer graphics image of the space shuttle shows the shuttle's extended remote manipulator arm.

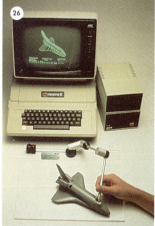

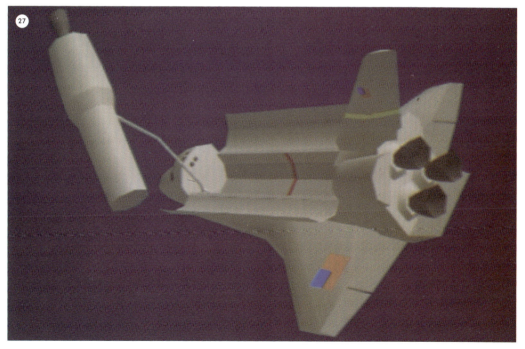

MULTIPLE VIEWS OF THE SAME MACHINE PART

Computer graphics can be used to help in the design of all sorts of machinery. For example, the final assembly view of a ball-type bearing can be produced ㉘, as well as a "cut-away" view ㉙ and an "exploded" view ㉚.

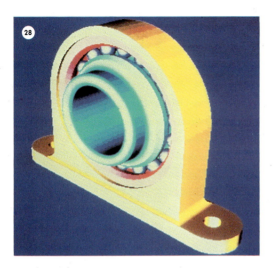

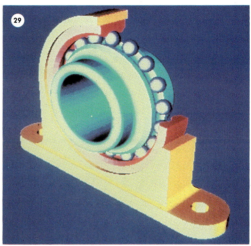

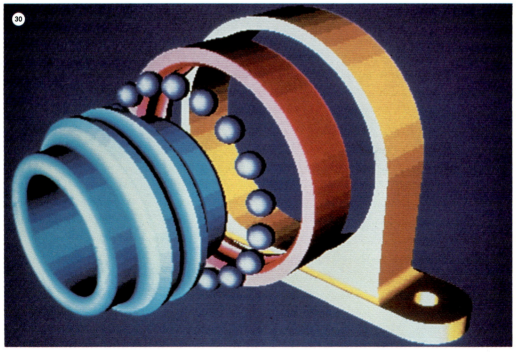

PIES AND BARS

Early microcomputers dealt mainly with text. Recent years, however, have brought many innovations in computer graphics. Presentation graphics software transforms numbers into pictures, making reports more attractive and easier to understand. Pie charts and bar charts are two common presentation formats. (31) More than one pie chart can be produced on the same page by software packages such as ChartMaster. (32) Enhanced pie charts (better resolution, more detail,

sharper colors) produced by more sophisticated systems are especially effective for business presentations. (33) ChartMaster is capable of producing either horizontal or vertical bar charts. (34) Sophisticated systems are capable of producing bars in a variety of colors, as well as a multitude of print fonts. Charts are often captured on film to be used as slides or copied to transparency sheets to be used for overhead projection.

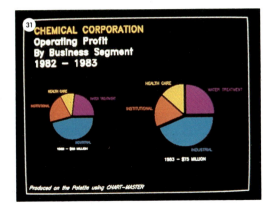

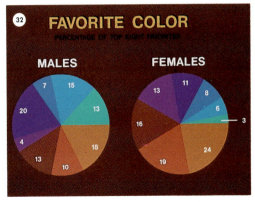

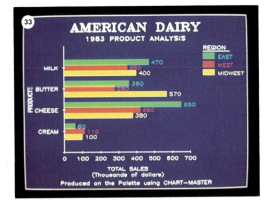

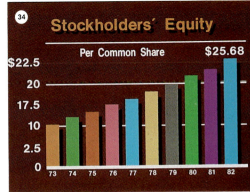

LINES AND SIGNS

Line charts are another common form of presentation graphics. (35) They are frequently used to demonstrate "movement" over time, like this record of an index tracked over eleven years. Most graphics charts are capable of producing line charts along with pie charts and bar charts. (36) SignMaster, a companion package to ChartMaster, is used to create graphics-oriented signs — that is, tables and text that are graphically manipulated—instead of charts. (37) Sometimes charts (such as these more complete pie charts) can be combined with other "pictures" to create a graphic representation of an idea instead of just numbers. (38) Even more sophisticated packages exist in the form of an electronic easel used to "draw" more elaborate graphics. The electronic easel allows its users to select shapes, colors, and patterns as well as determine location, movement, and size of images.

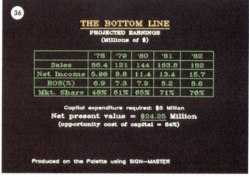

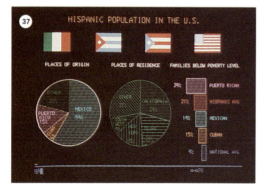

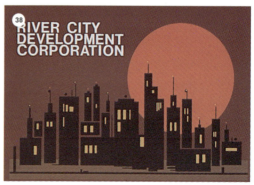

BY LAND

(39) The use of computer graphics allows engineers to simulate the "axle walk" of an automobile over rough terrain. (40) Highly developed graphics systems are capable of producing a relatively high degree of realism in their results, as in this picture of two vehicles passing on a highway. (41) If your objective is to improve safety, you might also want to see a similar scene at night.

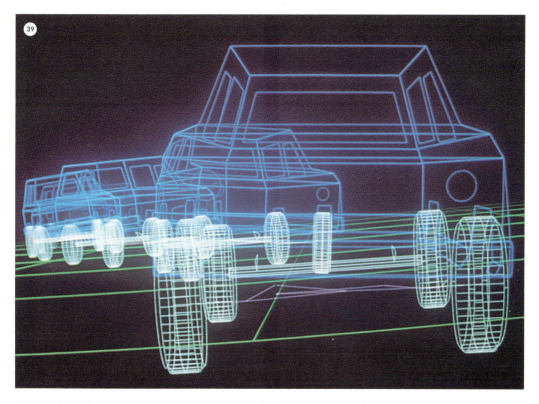

BY SEA

Before constructing the actual product — such as the pleasure craft shown in photo ㊸ — designers can examine a graphic view of the completed product in skeleton form, shown in photo ㊷. After design flaws have been worked out, the product can be placed into production. ㊹ Placing a proposed product in a near normal setting adds realism to this graphics view of a guided missile frigate.

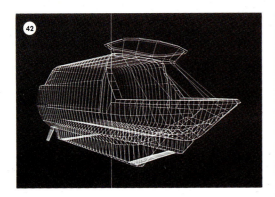

BY AIR

(45) Through computer graphics, architects of this hospital solve highly specific problems and can determine what the completed structure will look like, including the heliport on top. (46) Designing a heliport for an offshore oil rig presents other specialized problems; graphics can help architects antici-pate and solve these problems before they occur. (47) Before entering the cockpit, mili-tary pilots can experience simulated flight by using graphic images of the aircraft they will fly and the environment they will be flying in. In this case, the use of graphics decreases costs and increases safety.

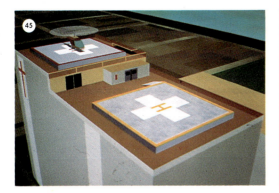

WANT TO KNOW WHAT IT LOOKS LIKE?

(48) Using graphics, you can determine what a proposed building will look like in its surrounding environment. (49) You can also put a robot's arm through its paces and track its movements. Packages capable of producing images of this type frequently permit "movement" around a structure so that it can be viewed from an almost infinite number of positions. (50) Computer graphics allows you to examine the layers of a computer chip to determine if its design is adequate. (51) And you can even see combinations of atoms that exist within a given compound.

The color photographs in this book have shown you that graphics can be one of the most effective ways to communicate information and ideas and to persuade an audience. Computer graphics packages afford us a number of advantages in produc-

ing images that other means of producing images frequently cannot provide. Computer graphics images are often safer, quicker, cheaper, and easier to produce, especially if the image represents a scaled-down reproduction of a physical object. Often the appearance of a graphics image can be easily altered; alternate views can also be constructed.

Graphics can be used to eliminate design flaws before they occur. They can be used to express a concept, an idea that previously existed only in a person's mind, thereby increasing our understanding. In short, if you have a problem that might be solved by the use of a "picture," even a moving picture, you should give computer graphics a try. New hardware and software for computer graphics are increasingly available for business professionals.

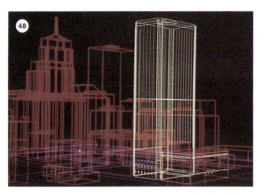

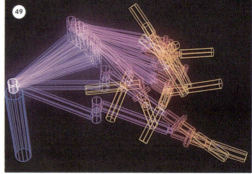

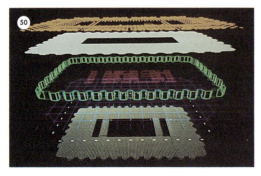

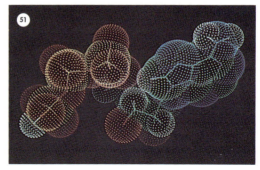

```
                          AXIS LABELS


         ENTER X-AXIS LABEL: Companies in Alphabetical Order

ENTER SECOND X-AXIS LABEL:

         ENTER Y-AXIS LABEL: Offers in Thousands of Dollars

ENTER SECOND Y-AXIS LABEL:

    _____

     FONT        SIZE        ITALICS       JUSTIFY      COLOR      UNDERLINE
     BRM          4            NO           CENTER         1          NO

    _____


                         <F1>  Help
```

FIGURE 8C.9
AXIS LABELS screen for the first bar chart

```
                          VARIABLE LABELS




VARIABLE 1: Dollars Offered






    _____

     FONT        SIZE        ITALICS       JUSTIFY      COLOR      UNDERLINE
     BRM          4            NO            LEFT          2          NO

    _____


                         <F1>  Help
```

FIGURE 8C.10
VARIABLE LABELS screen for the bar chart

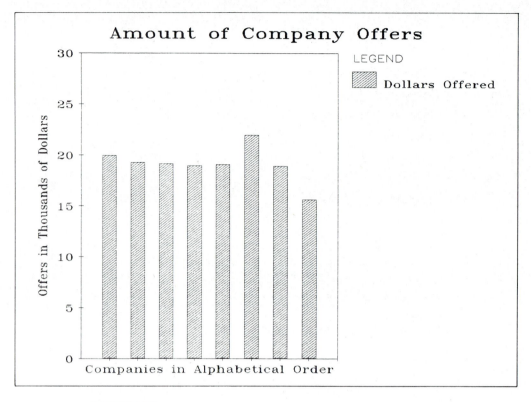

FIGURE 8c.11
Bar chart showing the amount of company offers

Looking at the Actual Offers — Creating a Stacked Bar Chart

To add the new information about the job offers to the bar chart and print it as a stacked bar chart, return to the MAIN MENU and select option 4, EDIT CHART. From the EDIT MENU, shown in Figure 8c.12, select option 5, DATA, and then from the EDIT DATA MENU select option 2, ALL DATA FOR ONE VARIABLE. From the EDIT ALL DATA FOR ONE VARIABLE screen, shown in Figure 8c.13, select option number 1, ADD A VARIABLE, and then select the option ADD VARIABLE TO END OF CURRENT LIST. You will now be asked to enter the name of the new variable and the values of the observations for this variable, using the VARIABLE LABELS screen shown in Figure 8c.10 and the ENTER DATA FOR ... screen shown in Figure 8c.5. Once you have entered the data for the "Life," "Health," and "Retirement" benefits, exit the EDIT MENU and return to the MAIN MENU. Now, select

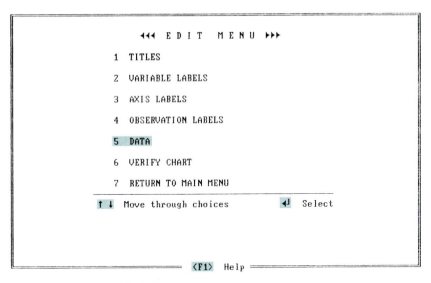

FIGURE 8C.12
Chart Master EDIT MENU

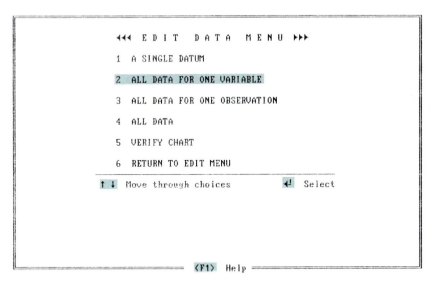

FIGURE 8C.13
EDIT ALL DATA FOR ONE VARIABLE screen

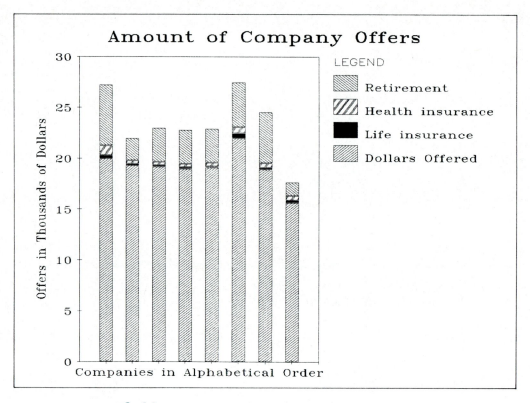

FIGURE 8C.14
Stacked bar chart showing the amount of company actual offers

option number 3, PLOT / PREVIEW CHART, and from the PLOT MENU select option 2, STACKED BAR CHART, to produce the chart shown in Figure 8c.14. Don't forget to edit the title of the chart before it is printed.

Comparing Actual Offers with the Average Offer— Creating a Line Chart

Now that you have created two charts using Chart Master, you can see how easy it is to generate useful graphics output. To create the final chart, a line chart, select option number 1 from the MAIN MENU and enter the title "Amount of Company Actual Offers." Next, enter the x- and y-axis labels "Companies in Alphabetical Order" and "Offers in Thousands of Dollars," followed by the variable labels "Average Offer" and "Actual Offer." After you have entered the data and returned to the MAIN MENU, select option number 6, CHANGE PLOTTING OPTIONS.

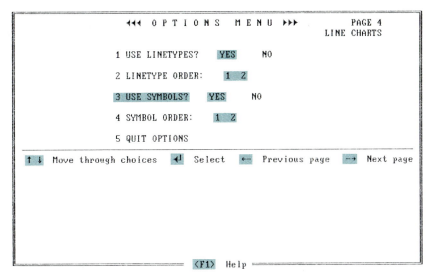

FIGURE 8C.15
Selecting symbols for the line chart

The plotting options menus allow you to change the way Chart Master plots your charts. For the line chart, use the right-arrow key to move to page 4 of the menu, shown in Figure 8c.15, select option number 3, and press the RETURN key. This option tells Chart Master to USE SYMBOLS for the observation values on your chart.

Your chart is now complete. Return to the MAIN MENU and print the chart shown in Figure 8c.16 by selecting the LINE CHART option in the PLOT MENU.

Chart Manipulations — Saving, Retrieving, and Deleting

Selecting option number 5 from the MAIN MENU will present you with the STORAGE / RETRIEVAL MENU shown in Figure 8c.17. This menu allows you to STORE, RETRIEVE, or DELETE charts on your data disk. Additionally, it will allow you to list a catalog of charts that have been saved on the disk and to verify the chart information after it has been retrieved.

Other Features of Chart Master

In addition to allowing you to choose different print characteristics for the chart titles and labels, Chart Master provides an extensive set of special symbols that can be used to greatly enhance the effectiveness of your charts. These

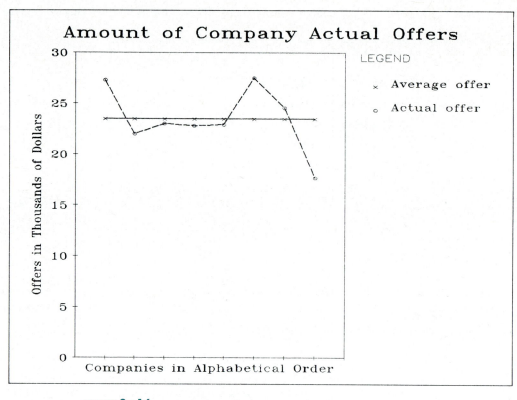

FIGURE 8c.16
Line chart showing the amount of company actual offers and the average offer

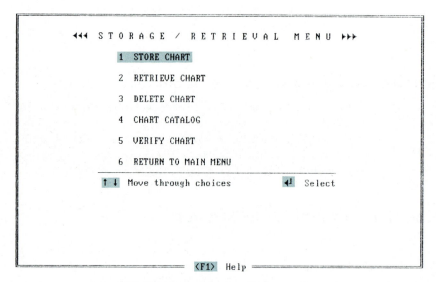

FIGURE 8c.17
Chart Master STORAGE/RETRIEVAL MENU

symbols are available through the SYM (symbol) FONT. You are also able to control, through the OPTIONS MENU, the size, location on the page, and orientation (horizontal or vertical) of the chart.

Finally, among all the other options offered by Chart Master is the ability to calculate and plot regression equations based on the values of the observations you have entered. In fact, the package gives you a choice of using one of five different types of regression calculations.

Summary of Graphics Modules

The modules in this section gave you the opportunity to learn about one (or more) of the popular graphics packages available for microcomputers: pfs:Graph (Module 8a), Lotus 1-2-3 (Module 8b), and Chart Master (Module 8c). You learned about the selected graphics package by solving problems involved in job hunting.

Comparison of Graphics Packages

Table 8s.1 compares the packages presented in the modules. Although all of the packages are relatively flexible, Chart Master provides the greatest flexibility. The reason for Chart Master's flexibility is that it is a "stand-alone" package. Pfs:Graph is a part of the pfs:Software Series, and Lotus Graphics is a part of Lotus. Because pfs:Graph and Lotus Graphics are parts of larger software packages, they give you the choice of creating your data within other portions of the software. (This is your only option with Lotus Graphics.)

Although Chart Master is a "stand-alone" package, it does offer a variety of means of accessing data produced by other packages. However, of the packages presented, only pfs:Graph is capable of directly interfacing with word processing software — pfs:Write. Thus, for the most part, the charts produced by graphics packages are printed or plotted independently of any other software.

Guidelines for the Evaluation of Graphics Packages

Before you select a graphics package for your own use, try to answer the following questions:

● **Help facility**   Is a Help feature available, and, if so, how extensive is it?

TABLE 8S.1 A Comparison of Graphics Packages

Characteristic	Requirements		
	pfs:Graph	Lotus 1-2-3	Chart Master
Operating system	MS-DOS, PC-DOS	MS-DOS, PC-DOS	MS-DOS, PC-DOS
Main memory (RAM)	128K bytes	192K bytes	192K bytes; 256K bytes for printer or slides
Disk drives	1	1	2
Printer (optional)	Dot addressable	Dot addressable	Dot addressable
Graphics hardware	Required	Required	Optional
Command structure	Multi-level menu and function keys	Multi-level menu and function keys	Multi-level menu and function keys; PgDn
Chart types	Pie, bar, stacked bar, line, area	Pie, bar, stacked bar, line, scatter	Pie, bar, stacked bar, line, area, scatter, mixed
Data entry	Independent and pfs:File	Lotus 1-2-3 spreadsheet only	Independent only
Scaling	Automatic and functional	Automatic only	Automatic and functional
Maximum length of titles (characters)	40 — chart and x-axis; 30 — y-axis; 15 — legend	40 — chart and x-axis; 32 — y-axis; 18 — legend	Variable; 16 sizes plus several symbols
Charting controls:			
Size	3 × 4 and 8½ × 11	Variable	Variable
Rotation	Yes	Yes	Yes
Color	Yes; automatic	6; automatic	8; selectable
Shading	4; automatic	6; automatic	8; selectable
Line type	Solid only	Solid only	8; selectable
Symbols	5; automatic	6; automatic	8; selectable
Legends available	Yes; fixed	Yes; fixed	Yes; floating
Font controls	No	4; 2 controls — chart title and remainder of chart	6; 16 sizes; italics; selectable at the character level
Slide show	No	No	Yes
Interface method	DIF, print files	DIF, print files	DATAGRABBER, DIF, SYLK, print files

Does it describe processes such as chart selection, scaling, data entry, and so on? Can it be accessed when needed?

- **Documentation** How complete is the documentation? Is it well written and understandable? Is it well organized? Does it provide helpful tips and suggestions? Does the package have a tutorial?

- **Organization** Is the package command driven or menu driven? Do the commands seem "natural" to use? Are the menus complete and logically arranged? Do you have any difficulty getting from one menu to another? Are there any "holes" in the charting process that are not adequately explained?

- **Graph types** Can you create pie charts? Bar charts? Line charts? Can you pull a "wedge" from a pie chart? Can you produce multiple sets of bars on one bar chart? Can you produce stacked bar charts? Scatter charts? Area charts? What are the limitations on these charts? Is the charting process logical, flexible, and well defined? How easy is the charting process? Can multiple charts be placed into a single viewing area (screen or printer)? Side-by-side? Are the charts relatively accurate and free from distortions?

- **Data entry** Is this graphics function a direct part of a multi-function package? Does the data directly transfer from other functions? Does the package interface with other packages? Do you have the option of entering data into the package directly, even if it interfaces with other software in some way? How difficult is the data entry process? Can you easily modify data that has been previously entered? Can you easily add data? Delete data? Is data entered as pairs (sets) or individually? Can the data be saved? Separated from the chart? Is it retained when creating multiple charts from the same data?

- **Chart modification and storage** Once a chart has been created, can it be easily altered or added to? Is the chart automatically "updated" with each change? Is the chart redrawn from "scratch" each time a change is made? Can one chart be used as an "overlay" for another? Are storage and retrieval of charts easy and natural? What is the process for retrieving and viewing an existing chart? Are charts stored in a form that can be transmitted to other types of packages?

- **Labeling** What kinds of charting labels are available? Titles? x- and y-axis? Legends? Are any of the labels automatically supplied? Do you have a choice of plotting symbols for scatter charts? Do you have any "floating" labels that can be placed where you want them? Are the labels saved as you move from chart to chart?

- **Drawing and painting** Does the package have either of these capabilities? How precise are the drawing controls? Can circles be drawn automatically? Rectangles? Other shapes? Do you have control over line widths? What controls do you have over text production? Do you have any font selections? Can you paint with patterns? Colors? How many colors? How are they selected?

● **Producing output**   Can your graphics be produced on a printer? Plotter? Both? Do you have the right kind of printer to interface with the package? Plotter? Do you have separate size controls when producing a chart on these output devices? Can the charts be rotated? What is the effect of printing colors on a standard printer? On a single-pen plotter? Is the resolution of the printed result similar to that viewed on the screen? How fast is the printing process? Plotting process?

● **Interfaces with other packages**   Does the package directly interface with other software packages? Can the chart be stored in an alternate format (for example, DIF, ASCII, SYLK)? Is it directly integrated with other functions? Can charts be transmitted in a communications environment (presented in Chapter 9).

● **Special features**   Can the package produce three-dimensional charts? Drawings? Can the charts or drawings be rotated? Is there a "zoom" feature? An "invert" feature? Can you "cut and paste" a chart or drawing? Can you produce a "slide show?" What are the timing characteristics? How difficult is it to produce a slide show? How easy it to change? Do you have extended mathematical features? Built-in geometric functions?

What Happened at ACE?

As it turned out, it didn't take Chris much time to do the charts and graphs Mr. Jenkins needed. All Chris had to do was get accustomed to the package. Luckily, the data Chris needed was already in a form the package could use. As a result, Mr. Jenkins's presentation went very well, and even the regional manager commented on the professionalism of his charts.

Module Questions

1. Select a graphics package. What chart types are available for this package? Give an example of how each chart type could be used to illustrate particular types of data. What would be the purpose of each of these charts?
2. Select a graphics package. Is the package a "stand-alone" package, or is it integrated with other software? Describe the process of entering data into this package for use in a graph.
3. Select a graphics package. Can this package produce charts in color? Is shading available? Can you control the assignment of color to particular areas of a chart? Shading?
4. Select a graphics package. Describe the labeling process. How are labels

entered in a pie chart? How are they entered in a line chart? Is there a maximum length for these labels?

5. Write a paragraph describing how graphics may be employed in your chosen profession. List five charts and explain their purposes and what they would contain.

Module Problems

1. You have decided to produce pie charts that demonstrate how each of the actual offers from Ethyl & Jung, DDS, and Lewis & Melts Mortgage Company is broken down into salary offer, life, health, and retirement components. You have also decided to perform a side-by-side bar chart comparison of the offers made by Ethyl & Jung, DDS, and Lewis & Melts Mortgage Company. The bar chart should include comparisons of the salary offer; life, health, and retirement contributions; and the actual offer.

2. Using the inventory data presented in Appendix B, produce a pie chart that demonstrates the number of products in a product group. The product groups are AUDIO, VIDEO, and COMPUTER. The AUDIO group comprises all radios and stereos. The VIDEO group is composed of TVs and VCRs. The COMPUTER group is made up of computers, software, and media. Produce a bar chart that compares the cost, income from sales, and profit for each of these product groups, within classes if possible. Produce a stacked bar chart that demonstrates how each product class contributed to the total profit for that product group during the last 12 months. Finally, produce a line chart that plots the profit for each product group for the last 12 months.

3. An instructor would like to give a report on exam performances to the class during the school term. The instructor has the following information on which to base the report:

Number of	Exam I	Exam II	Exam III	Course Grades
As	5	4	7	6
Bs	15	20	18	17
Cs	12	8	11	14
Ds	3	5	4	?
Fs	5	3	0	1

Produce a pie chart that demonstrates the distribution of grades for each of the three exams. Construct a side-by-side bar chart comparison for each of the three exams and the course grades. Create a line chart that compares all of the data.

SCENARIO 9

What's Going on at ACE?

Shortly after I had completed all the inventory reports for the month, a colleague made a comment that stirred my interest. The person at the next desk said, "The show rooms keep their inventory on a microcomputer at the store. If there is some way we can get that information into our computer instead of having them print it out and send it to us and then reentering it into our computer, it would sure save a lot of time."

I didn't know if this could be done; however, after talking to Mr. Jenkins about it, I knew the process existed and that it was called *telecommunications*. Mr. Jenkins didn't know a lot about it, but he did know that Ms. Allison in the computer center used telecommunications to have ACE's computer use the phone to "talk" to the one in Dallas. Mr. Jenkins asked me to talk to Ms. Allison about using telecommunications to speed up inventory reporting. Ms. Allison said that the computer center was working on the same type of problem for the accounting department, and she invited me not only to join the team working on the system but also to participate in a university extension course on telecommunications.

■

Chapter Nine
Applications Software:
Electronic Communications

Chapter Objectives

When you have completed this chapter, you will be able to:

- Discuss the historical development of electronic communications
- Give a general description of what electronic communications is
- Explain the basic functions of electronic communications
- Describe some of the uses of electronic communications

Introduction to Electronic Communications

Suppose you walk into your first class in political science and are told that your term paper is to be a 25-page report on "The Imperial Presidency." In addition, you are given two weeks to turn in a list of books and articles on the subject, divided into two parts. The first part should be "background" reading, and the second part is to be "current thought."

You are now faced with long hours of library work, looking up books and checking their contents and going through articles in journals just to develop the bibliography. If you had a computer with electronic communications capabilities and access to the commercial bibliographic databases and a data service, such as CompuServe, Dow Jones, or The Source, it would be possible to greatly reduce the time you spend in the library. You could use your computer to search the data service's listings of books, journal articles, and newspaper reports to find material dealing with the "Imperial Presidency." You could then print the list and be ready to do your reading in a matter of minutes rather than days.

Historical Development

One of the problems in communications has always been communicating over great distances. When humans first started to communicate, a great distance meant any distance farther than they could shout. To solve the problem, runners were used to carry messages from one person to another, or, when the people were close enough, smoke signals and mirrors were used to send messages.

No real improvements were made in communications until 1837, when Samuel Morse developed the telegraph. With the telegraph came the ability to communicate over long distances, and Morse code became the first standard for electronic communications. After the telegraph, improvements began to occur more rapidly. The telephone, developed by Alexander Graham Bell in 1876, allowed voice communication over great distances, and the wireless telegraph, invented by Guglielmo Marconi in 1896 and which used Morse code, allowed the sender and receiver to communicate without being connected by wires. The wireless telegraph led to the development of the radio in 1906 by Reginald Fessender; now people could send voice messages through the air. Finally, television, invented by Vladimir Zworykin in 1923, added picture transmission to the world's communication technology.

Data communications between computers is following the same path as communications between people. In the late 1950s, computer users were trying to find ways of working on a computer without leaving their office or home. Because of this need, computer manufacturers began to develop ways of communicating with a computer over distance. By the 1970s it was not only possible for computer users at terminals to communicate with computers, but it was also possible for computers to communicate with other computers. Unfortunately, although almost all computers (in the United States) use ASCII (American Standard Code for Information Interchange) as the code for sending characters and commands, the **protocols** (rules for communications) were developed differently for each computer. This inconsistency has led to an attempt to create a standard for communications. In 1977, the **ISO (International Standards Organization)** developed the **OSI (Open Systems Interconnection)** model, a set of rules for computers communicating with one another. Although the ISO-OSI model has not been universally accepted, it represents a major step forward in standardizing electronic communications.

Today, most computers can communicate electronically. They can be connected together using wires (or cables) in a **local area network (LAN)**, or using telephone wires, microwave, or radio signals (even by satellite) in a **wide area network.** If you are using electronic communications, the amount of data and information available to you at a moment's notice is virtually unlimited.

Definition of Electronic Communications

Up to this point, you have operated a microcomputer in a "stand-alone" mode. However, it is possible to establish a link between microcomputers or between a microcomputer and a larger computer (a minicomputer or a mainframe). This link is

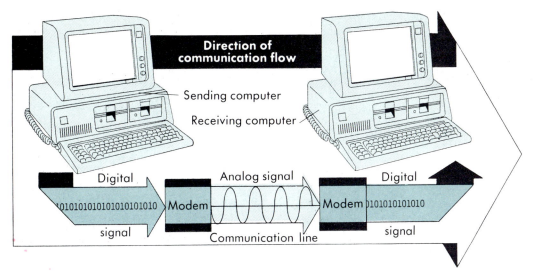

FIGURE 9.1
An electronic communications environment

provided by a communications package. With a communications package, your computer can "talk" with another computer, as illustrated in Figure 9.1.

To establish a communication link between two computers, you must have the appropriate hardware. The first item you will need is a **communications line.** This is a physical line that connects your computer to another. The most widely available communications line is a telephone line—also known as a **dial-up line.** Communication with another computer can be as easy as using your telephone. The kind of communications line called a **hard-wired line** uses a cable installed specifically to run from your computer to another. The hard-wired line is obviously more expensive than a telephone line and usually limited to a rather small geographic area (1,000s of feet). Its primary advantage is that communication can be readily achieved, and the communication speed is usually faster.

The next piece of hardware required (if you are not using a hard-wired line) is a **modem.** A modem (a contraction of "modulation–demodulation") translates the signals transmitted between two computers. Computers operate on a **digital** (0 and 1) basis. However, communications lines operate on an **analog** ("sine"-wave) basis. Thus, a modem attached to your computer is responsible for translating digital signals transmitted from your computer into analog signals (modulation), and a modem at the other end of the communications line is responsible for translating the received analog signals back into digital form (demodulation). Modems come in a variety of types as illustrated in Figure 9.2. For example, you may have a modem with an **acoustic coupler** (a) enabling you to place the headset of the telephone into the modem to establish the communications link. Alternatively, you may have a **direct connect modem** (b), enabling you to plug

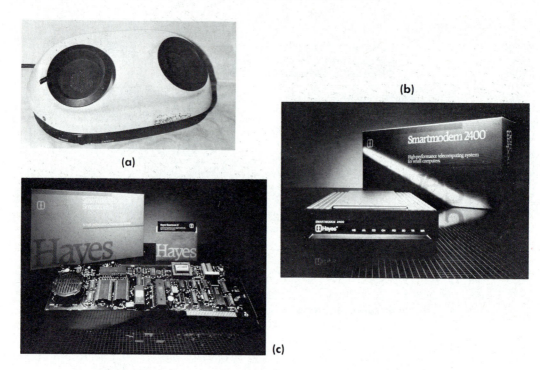

FIGURE 9.2
Types of modems: (a) acoustic coupler (courtesy of John Windsor); (b) external modem (courtesy of Hayes Microcomputer Products, Inc.); (c) internal modem (courtesy of Hayes Microcomputer Products, Inc.)

your computer directly into a telephone line. Both of these are referred to as **external modems,** because they are outside the computer cabinet. An **internal modem** (c) performs the same functions as an external modem from inside the computer cabinet.

Before you establish a communications link between computers, you need to know at least three pieces of information about the two computers involved. You will normally need to supply this information to your communications software package. First, you need to know the communication **baud rate.** A baud rate is simply the speed at which computers transmit data and is interpreted to mean bits per second. Common baud rates are 300, 1,200, 2,400, 4,800,

9,600, and 19,200. To make this a little easier, 300 baud loosely translates into about 30 characters per second. This represents about 350 words a minute—slightly above average reading speed.

Second, you need to know whether you are to operate in **half-duplex** or **full-duplex** mode. *Half-duplex* means that the receiving computer will not **echo** (send back to you) characters as you transmit them from the sending computer. Stated another way, if you are operating in half-duplex mode, characters that are produced on your screen are put there only by your computer. In full-duplex mode, characters are echoed by the receiving computer. For example, if you are in full-duplex mode and you type the letter "A" on your computer, it is sent to the receiving computer and retransmitted back down the communications line to your computer to appear on the screen. Thus, with full duplex, you can more easily determine if there is **noise** (transmission problems or errors) on the communications line.

You can easily determine if your computer is operating in the wrong mode after a link has been established. For example, assume you are the sending computer. If the data to be transmitted does not appear on your screen (you are typing, but nothing appears on your screen), you are transmitting in full-duplex mode and the receiving computer assumes that you are operating in half-duplex mode. (Your computer is assuming that the receiving computer will generate the characters on your screen, and the receiving computer is assuming that your computer is generating them.) If you are typing on the keyboard and you see two of each character on the screen, you are operating in half-duplex mode and the receiving computer is in full-duplex mode.

Third, you need to know how many bits are to be transmitted per character. In Chapter 2, you were shown that most computers operate on the basis of 8 bits per character. However, in a communications mode, some computers transmit only 7 bits per character. Also, you sometimes need to know how many **stop bits** are transmitted per character. These are extra bits that are transmitted to indicate when a complete character has been sent. Generally, if the computers are transmitting 8-bit characters, no stop bits are transmitted. However, computers transmitting 7-bit characters usually send one stop bit for each character.

If your communications package is sophisticated, you may be able to specify other characteristics of the computer link.

For example, if you are operating through a telephone connection, you may be able to program the telephone number to be called. You may also be able to choose whether to operate in an **originate** mode (you establish the contact) or an **answer** mode (the other computer establishes the contact) and to determine on what basis an automatic **disconnect** is to be executed. Furthermore, most communications packages have the ability to **up load** and **down load** files. When you perform an up-load operation, you transmit files through your computer's memory to another computer —you send and the other computer receives. The reverse process is called *down loading;* the other computer sends, and your computer receives and stores the results. By up loading and down loading you are able to share files with other computers, and they are able to share with you.

Data Services and Bulletin Boards

Once you have a computer that is capable of electronic communications, an impressive array of systems and services are available to you. Not only will you have the ability to work on your company's or school's computer from your home and office, but you will also find that many other services that can be fun and useful are only a phone call away. These services include:

- Information utilities
- Encyclopedic databases
- News and specialized business information databases
- Electronic shopping, banking, and barter
- Free computer bulletin board systems (CBBSs)

Some of these services are free; however, most will charge a fee for your use of them. This fee may range from a very low charge for the time you actually use the service to a high subscription charge for being a member of the network.

Information Utility   The term **information utility,** meaning *information service,* is used by the Source Telecomputing Corporation (STC, or The Source), one of the three earliest database information services. The other two are CompuServe Information Service (CIS, or CompuServe) and the Dow Jones News/Retrieval Service (DJNS). These services are designed for the average user, rather than a professional researcher, and provide a wide range of information and associated services.

Encyclopedic Databases   If you want access to information in depth, use an **encyclopedic database.** This type of service has, in the past, primarily been used by professional researchers. However, several of the encyclopedic database services have started to include topics of interest to the average computer user. The major organizations providing this type of service are DIALOG, BRS, and ORBIT.

News and Specialized Business Information Databases   Database services that carry current news reports and newsletters for specific industries and professions are called **news and specialized business information databases.** The main suppliers of this type of service are The Information Bank, run by The New York Times Information Service (NYTIS), and NewsNet.

Electronic Shopping, Banking, and Barter   Comp-U-Card of America, Inc., provides a service called **electronic shopping, banking, and barter.** By accessing Comp-U-Card directly or by using one of the information utilities, you can browse through prices and descriptions of over 50,000 products, place an order, and pay for it all from your keyboard. The information utilities also allow you to place classified ads on their "bulletin boards" so that you can sell, trade, or buy items. Finally, several banks offer full banking services within their banking area through the information utilities.

Computer Bulletin Board Systems (CBBSs)   Services that allow computer users to share information about particular topics or just make contact with other interested people are called **computer bulletin board systems (CBBSs).** These bulletin boards are usually free and can be a lot of fun as well as informative.

Networks

Accessing most of the services discussed above, and the computer at your company or school, is accomplished through the use of a **communications network.** Figure 9.3 illustrates the **hierarchical network,** the simplest way of connecting multiple devices. By this arrangement, all devices are attached to a single computer, called the **host.** The host computer serves as a clearing house for all communication between and among devices. If the devices are video display terminals, then the hierarchical network is actually a **multi-user system** that requires a **multi-user operating system,** as described in Chapter 4. In this case, all the computational power and data reside only in the host computer. The host computer is a **master unit** and all the terminals are **slave units.** If the connected devices are them-

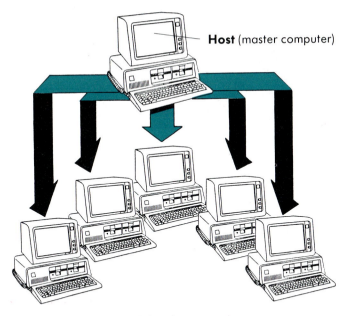

Host (master computer)

FIGURE 9.3
A hierarchical network (or master/slave organization)

selves computers, then computation is performed by the individual computers, although much of the data may still reside with the host computer. Depending on the level of sophistication used in a hierarchical network, it may be possible for each device to communicate with the others. However, all communication is always performed through and under the control of the host computer.

Figure 9.4 illustrates another means of connecting multiple computers. It is called the **ring network.** This arrangement tends to be more sophisticated than the hierarchical network. As shown in the illustration, each of the computers is connected to the next computer in the sequence — creating a circle or ring. In this environment, individual computers perform their own com-

putation, and it is also likely that each retains its own data. However, the data may be shared with any other computer in the network. As noted in the figure, the ring is only one-way — communications flow in a circle in one direction. Thus, the communication signal must pass through all the computers between the two communicating computers. This passing of signals may be performed by a variety of means, but the most popular technique is called **token passing.** By this arrangement, each computer has its own identification code — a token value. The transmitting computer attaches a token to the signal; each remaining computer "looks" in turn to see if the signal contains its token. The computer that has the same token value as the signal accepts the message.

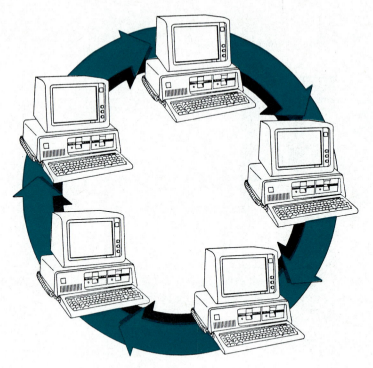

FIGURE 9.4
A ring network

The **star network** is another major computer network organization. As you can see in Figure 9.5, it is called the *star* for obvious reasons. In this configuration, each computer is directly linked to every other computer in the network. Although the star network provides the quickest way to transmit signals to a variety of computers, it suffers from one distinct disadvantage. As computers are added to the network, the number of connections required increases at a very rapid rate. Hierarchical and ring networks do not have this problem.

Hybrid networks are also used in electronic communications. A hybrid network uses more than one type of network in a single, usually large, arrangement. For example, it is possible to have a hierarchical network within which each slave unit is actually a ring network. Of course, other combinations are possible, including hierarchical networks that are part of other hierarchies and rings that are part of rings. The primary objective of combining networks is to create an arrangement of computers (and possibly other devices) that best meets an organization's need to share information.

Tele-conferencing

Earlier, when businesses wanted people in different geographic areas to attend a con-

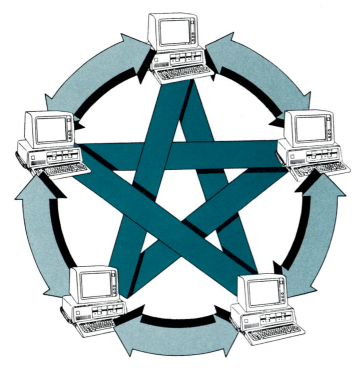

FIGURE 9.5
A star network

ference involving a number of reports and analysis work, they loaded the people on an airplane with all the reports and paperwork and flew them to the meeting place. Now, through the use of networks and a technology called **packet switching** (the process of breaking long messages up into smaller groups called *packets*), the participants never have to leave their offices. All the reports are placed in the computer serving the network and are available to everyone in the conference, no matter where the participants are located.

Tele-conferencing, also called **computerized conferencing,** has become so important that some companies have set up special rooms just for that purpose. These rooms have televisions to carry pictures of the conference rooms being used at the different locations, as well as computer terminals and telephones. In rooms such as these, data communications are available through the computer terminals, voices are carried by the telephones, and pictures of the people involved in the conference are provided by the televisions. Despite the cost of all the electronic equipment, companies have found that tele-conferencing is faster and less expensive than flying everyone to a central location.

Tele-conferencing is also available to the average user through the Electronic Information Exchange System (EIES) and PARTICIPATE. Both systems are available through the information utilities.

Functions of Electronic Communications

Although electronic communications software packages may vary in terms of how they perform specific functions, most of them tend to support the same types of functions. The following discussion covers many of these functions.

Providing Help

As the term implies, the HELP function supports your attempt to use the software package. If you get "stuck" or you simply don't know what to do next, you can ask for help. Obviously, this should be one of the first functions you look for in any software package. Until you learn the package well, the HELP function is an invaluable aid.

Help is made available by topic or function, depending on the software package. For example, some electronic communications packages require you to specify the topic for which assistance is needed. Then, again depending on the package, the software will either provide all information available for that topic or ask you to indicate which of the help elements you wish to view. If help is provided by function, the electronic communications package keeps track of the function you are currently performing and assists with that function. If the function is complicated, you may have to indicate which part of it you want help with.

Setting the Communications Parameters

When you first use a computer to communicate with another computer, you will have to establish the communication parameters or the characteristics to be used. These parameters will generally include establishing full- or half-duplex mode and the baud rate for data transmission. You may also have to establish which **communications port** (a hardware connection that is used to establish a means of transmitting or receiving communication signals—usually a port named "COM1") is going to be used to connect the other computer and whether you are going to originate (call) or answer when the link is made. In addition, all computers will use ASCII code for the characters that are sent and received; however, you will have to specify whether the computer is using 7-bit or 8-bit code and the number of stop bits (0, 1, or 2) used at the end of each character. You will also need to establish the **parity** (error checking) scheme (odd, even, or none) used to check for errors in transmission.

Finally, the computer you are calling may require that your computer "be" a certain type of terminal. If this is true, you will need to enter the parameters necessary for your computer to *emulate* (act like) the required type of terminal.

Saving the Communications Parameters

Because different computers use different parameters for communications, all of the previously mentioned settings must be established before you can begin using the communications link. Because these settings mean entering a lot of information, most electronic communications packages provide you with the ability to save them in a file on a disk. When you need to supply parameters, you simply enter the file name containing the appropriate ones and continue with the communications process.

Making the Call

Once all the parameters have been entered into the communications package, you are ready to call the other computer. If you are using a local area network, you may be directly connected to the host computer, and no telephone call is needed. Simply issue the CALL command, press the RETURN key, and you will be linked to the other computer. If you are not directly connected to the network—for example, if you call the computer at the office from home—you will need to make a telephone call.

When you call another computer using the telephone, you must use a modem. If the modem is the acoustic coupler type, you will have to dial the telephone number, then, after you hear the high-pitched answering signal from the other computer, place the telephone headset in the acoustic coupler and press the RETURN key to establish the link. If you are using a direct-connect modem, simply press the RETURN key when you hear the answering signal and "hang-up" the telephone.

Some direct-connect modems and electronic communications packages provide automatic dialing capabilities, called **auto-dial.** Using this function, the communications package can instruct the modem to automatically dial the telephone number of the computer you wish to call. Additionally, if the telephone number is busy, the communications package can be instructed to redial the number at set time intervals until the link is established. When the link has been made, you can follow the **log-on**

procedures for the host computer and perform whatever tasks are required.

Capturing the Data

Electronic communications packages provide several other useful functions besides allowing your microcomputer to act as a terminal to a host computer. One of the most useful is the ability to down load files. Down loading a file is the high-speed "capturing" of data as it is sent from the host computer to your computer. Using this function, you can copy a file into your computer's memory, onto a disk, or onto the printer so that you can review the data after you terminate communications.

Sending Files

Most communications packages can also up load files from your computer to the host computer. This means that you can use a word processing package to prepare a long and involved report, save the report as a file on disk, and, using communications software, quickly copy it into a network or to a host computer. Of course, any file that you up load must have already been created and stored on disk or in RAM (memory).

When up loading a file, you must understand how the host computer handles the communication process. Otherwise, you may send the host computer more data than it can handle at one time (called "over running the input buffer") or send data that contains control characters that cannot be understood by the host computer.

Other Features

There are several other features offered by communications packages. Some will keep track of how long you have been connected with the other computer and, if you want, automatically disconnect **(log-off)** after a set time limit. Newer communications packages provide for both voice and data communication allowing you to talk to a person at one computer (if the computer has the capability) while sending data to another computer.

One of the most useful features of the more advanced communications packages is the capability of saving commands. This allows you to save the key sequence needed to perform the log-on procedure for your host computer and then execute the entire procedure by simply entering a single keystroke.

Uses of Electronic Communications

The uses of electronic communications are almost limitless. Whenever it's necessary to move data from one computer to another —whether across the room or across the world—electronic communications does it most rapidly.

In Columbus, Ohio, the customer of a particular bank can use a microcomputer to move money between his checking and savings accounts. In addition, not only can bills be paid through the computer without the customer ever having to write a check, but the monthly bills from utility companies and department stores are also received through the computer. This saves both the customer, the bank, and the companies involved the cost of paper, envelopes, and stamps, as well as the time involved in paying bills by mail.

Many industrial sales companies use electronic communications to enter large orders into the computer from the purchasing company's location. Entering orders this way not only speeds up the processing and delivery of the product, but also reduces errors in the order and gives the selling company a competitive advantage in the market place.

At colleges and universities, both students and faculty use bibliographic retrieval services from computers in their libraries to quickly search for books and articles about specific topics. This type of service can quickly identify material on a particular topic, even when it is not available at the local library. In some cases, this service can also identify where the material is located, reducing the amount of time needed to do research.

Newspapers have always been heavy users of electronic communications, particularly of the "wire services." One notable use of electronic communications is by the *Wall Street Journal*. Although the *Journal* is written in New York City, it is printed in several locations around the world. The complete newspaper is transmitted electronically to the printer, typeset, and printed in less than 12 hours so that the customer, located anywhere in the world, can have it at the beginning of the workday.

Electronic communications has reduced the time needed to deliver information, services, and products, and it has also reduced the errors in making those deliveries. Look around you. You can probably identify a dozen ways that electronic communications could be used to solve problems and improve services.

Chapter Summary

This chapter has introduced you to electronic communications. Obviously, long-distance (anything greater than shouting distance) communication has been a problem throughout history. However, the advent of computers, electronic communications software, and networking technology — not to mention the development of telegraph, telephone, radio, and television — has greatly improved people's ability to quickly transfer data from one place to another.

Electronic communications is the term applied to computer networks — that is, computers that can "talk" to one another. The communications network can be of several types: hierarchical (multi-user, master/slave system), ring, star, or hybrid (a combination of one or more of the previous types). The communications line in the network can be the telephone line (dial-up line) or a specially installed hard-wired line. Computers using telephone lines must have modems — either external or internal — which regulate the transmission of signals between computers. Acoustic-coupler modems hold the telephone headset; direct connect modems allow the user to plug the computer directly into a telephone line.

Computer users need to establish certain parameters for the communications system before using a communications package. These parameters include determining the baud rate (speed of data transmission), the use of half- or full-duplex mode, the need for stop bits, and who is to be in answer mode and who in originate mode. Some systems can be set to automatically connect (dial) and save the log-on sequence, and many can up load and down load files, enabling users to share stored data (files).

Electronic communications provides many services through the use of information utilities; encyclopedic databases; news and specialized business information databases; electronic shopping, banking, and barter; and free computer bulletin board systems.

Chapter Key Terms

Acoustic coupler	Communications port	Electronic shopping, banking, and barter	Information utility
American Standard Code for Information Interchange (ASCII)	Computer Bulletin Board Systems (CBBS)	Encyclopedic database	Internal modem
Analog	Computerized conferencing	External modem	International Standards Organization (ISO)
Answer	Dial-up line	Full duplex	Local area network (LAN)
Autodial	Digital	Half duplex	Log-off
Baud rate	Direct connect modem	Hard-wired line	Log-on
Communications line	Disconnect	Hierarchical network	Master unit
Communications network	Down load	Host	Modem
	Echo	Hybrid network	Multi-user system

Multi-user
    operating system
News and
    specialized
    business
    information
    databases

Noise
Open systems
    interconnection
    (OSI)
Originate
Packet switching

Parity
Protocol
Ring network
Slave unit
Star network
Stop bits

Telecommunications
Token passing
Up load
Wide area network

Chapter Questions

1. Name some uses of electronic communications that you are familiar with. Has electronic communications improved the efficiency of the services or companies you have named?

2. What is the major improvement that electronic communications has made in the use of computers? Historically, why was this improvement needed?

3. Some professions use electronic communications more than others. Identify ten professions, professional groups, or job classifications that use electronic communications as a major part of their activity. How might electronic communications be used in your chosen career field?

4. What is the difference between a local area network and a wide area network?

5. What capabilities must an electronic communications software package have to meet your needs?

6. Explain the differences between an acoustic coupler, a direct-connect modem, and internal and external modems?

7. Several different types of data services were discussed. Which do you think is most useful to you as a student? Which is most useful to a college professor? Which ones are designed for the general public?

8. Explain the difference between up loading and down loading.

9. Four types of networks have been discussed. Describe how each of these networks is designed to work.

10. What is the difference between token passing and packet switching?

Modules/Chapter Nine
Electronic Communications

Introduction to
Electronic Communications Modules

In the modules that follow, you will be given the opportunity to learn about one (or more) of the popular electronic communications software packages available for microcomputers. Module 9a covers pfs:Access, Module 9b discusses Crosstalk XVI, and Module 9c presents Smartcom.

Problem Statement for
Electronic Communications Modules

To learn how to use electronic communications packages, you will use the job hunting problem and the information described in Appendix A. When you work through this problem, you will call another computer and retrieve data stored on it.

Everyone who is looking for a job is interested in having up-to-date information about which companies have job openings. The placement service at your school keeps a computerized list of the companies that are interviewing on campus. This list contains the name of the company, the contact person, and the dates they will be on campus. To obtain this information, you need to perform the following tasks:

1. Set up the communications parameters for your electronic communications package so that you can "talk" to the school's computer.
2. Call the school's (host) computer and go through the log-on procedure, so that you can talk to it.
3. List the JOBS.LST file on the host computer, and capture the list on your disk.
4. Again, list the JOBS.LST file on the host computer, and capture the list on your printer.
5. Now that you have a copy of the list, go through the log-off procedure to end your communications with the host computer.

pfs:Access

Learning to Use pfs:Access

Pfs:Access is the electronic communications application package for the pfs Software Series. The package is available for a variety of microcomputer systems using the MS-DOS or the PC-DOS operating system. Pfs:Access is designed to simplify the sign-on (log-on) procedure, as well as the use of any information, communication, or timesharing service. It has many powerful features that allow you to get the most out of your electronic communications operations.

When you are ready to begin working with pfs:Access, start with the computer's system disk in drive A. If you are using a system that has two disk drives, a disk prepared to hold your data should be in drive B. After you have booted your system, replace the system disk with the pfs:Access diskette and enter the command ACCESS. When the package is loaded into memory, it will respond by placing the Main Menu on the screen, as shown in Figure 9a.1. If you are not a subscriber to one of the Main Menu services, press 9 followed by the F10 key to cause the screen to change to the Choose Modem Menu shown in Figure 9a.2. You can return to the Main Menu at any time by pressing the ESCape key. If you press the 6 key and the F10 key, you will return to the Choose Modem Menu.

The pfs:Access package makes use of the function keys to perform special operations. One of these special functions is the HELP command. Later, when you are in terminal mode (connected to another computer), you can press the F1 key for an explanation of scrolling, saving, printing, and sending files. If you are at the Main Menu, Choose Modem menu, or Service Information menu, pressing F1 will cause pfs:Access to display an explanation of the items on that menu. The screen shown in Figure 9a.3 is the HELP screen for the Choose Modem Menu.

Solving the Job Hunting Problem

The remaining sections in this module are devoted to solving the job hunting problem. You may want to refer to the problem statement in the Introduction

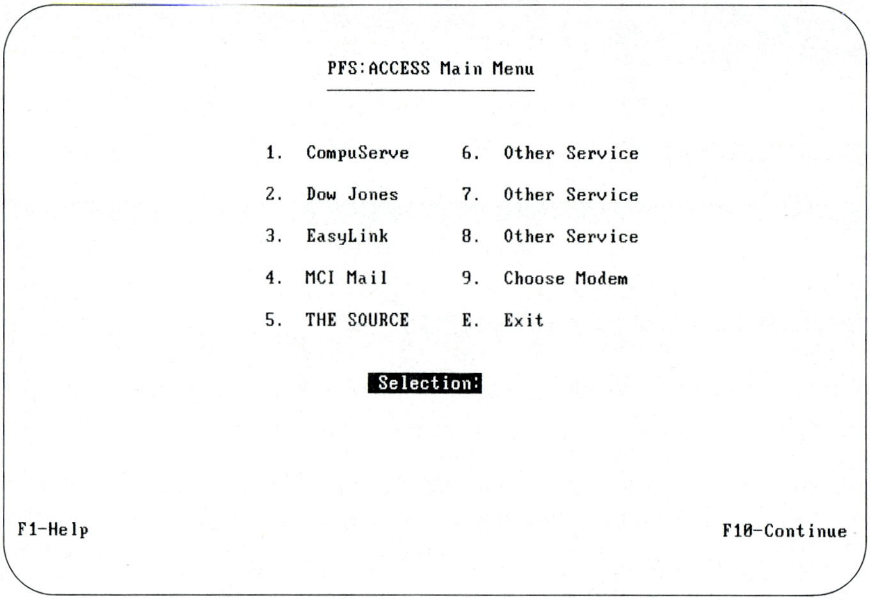

```
              PFS:ACCESS Main Menu
              ─────────────────────

        1.   CompuServe      6.  Other Service

        2.   Dow Jones       7.  Other Service

        3.   EasyLink        8.  Other Service

        4.   MCI Mail        9.  Choose Modem

        5.   THE SOURCE      E.  Exit


                  Selection:




 F1-Help                                    F10-Continue
```

FIGURE 9A.1
The pfs:Access Main Menu

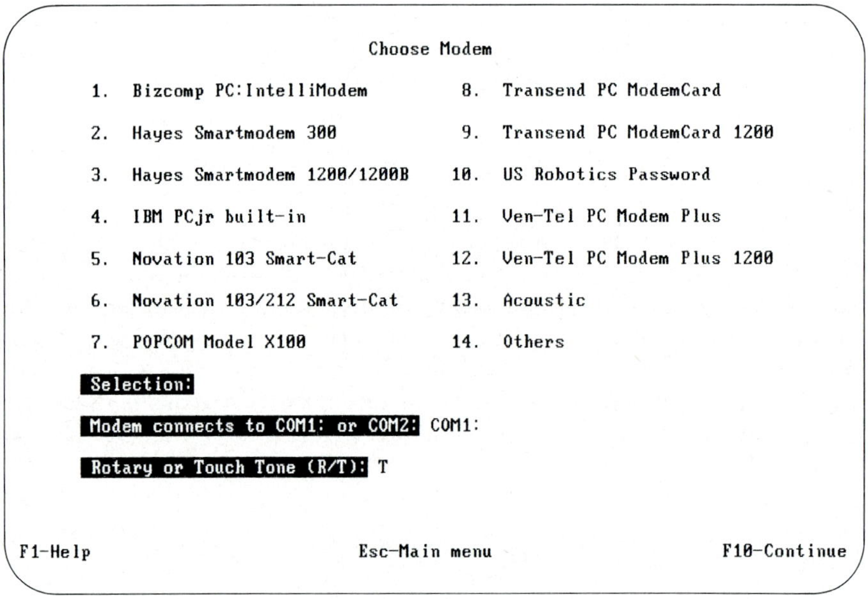

```
                    Choose Modem

    1.  Bizcomp PC:IntelliModem      8.  Transend PC ModemCard

    2.  Hayes Smartmodem 300         9.  Transend PC ModemCard 1200

    3.  Hayes Smartmodem 1200/1200B  10.  US Robotics Password

    4.  IBM PCjr built-in            11.  Ven-Tel PC Modem Plus

    5.  Novation 103 Smart-Cat       12.  Ven-Tel PC Modem Plus 1200

    6.  Novation 103/212 Smart-Cat   13.  Acoustic

    7.  POPCOM Model X100            14.  Others

    Selection:

    Modem connects to COM1: or COM2: COM1:

    Rotary or Touch Tone (R/T): T


 F1-Help              Esc-Main menu            F10-Continue
```

FIGURE 9A.2
The pfs:Access Choose Modem menu

```
                        Choose a Modem


Item                    Enter
----                    -----


Selection:
                The number that corresponds to your modem.

Modem connects to COM1: or COM2:
                The serial port to which your modem is connected.

Rotary or Touch Tone (R/T):
                Enter R if your telephone is a rotary phone; T if
                for a Touch Tone phone.




                Press F10 to continue
```

FIGURE 9A.3
Getting HELP from the Choose a Modem screen

to Electronic Communications Modules before you continue. Also, remember that the data used in this problem can be found in Appendix A and on your host computer.

Setting and Saving the Communications Parameters

To start using pfs:Access, simply press 9 from the Main Menu. After you have pressed the F10 key, the Choose Modem Menu will appear on the screen. Select the modem type you are using from the menu. If your modem is not listed or if you are directly connected to the host computer, select number 14 and press the TAB key to move to the next entry.

The next entry asks whether your modem (or network cable) is connected to COM1 or COM2. These are the computer hardware names for the first and second serial communications ports. For most computer systems, this will be COM1, because they have only one serial communications port. After entering the modem connection, press the TAB key and enter R if you are using a rotary dial telephone or T if you are using a touch tone telephone. Pressing the F10 key will store this information and return you to the Main Menu.

You are now ready to supply the communications parameters needed to talk to your host computer. If you are a subscriber to one of the services listed

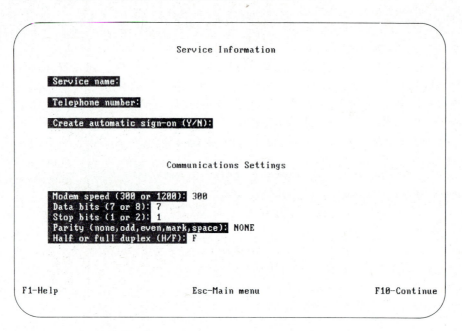

FIGURE 9A.4
The pfs:Access Service Information menu

on the menu, enter the appropriate number, and the Service Information menu for that service—with some of the information already entered—will appear on the screen. If you are going to call a service or host computer not listed on the screen, select 6, 7, or 8 and a blank Service Information menu, as shown in Figure 9a.4, will appear on the screen.

The first item of information you are asked for is the service name/host computer you are going to connect to. This name can be up to 30 characters long and will change the name in the Main Menu from Other Service to whatever you enter. For the problem you are working on, enter the name JOB HUNTING. Pressing the TAB key will move the cursor to the next item to be entered, the telephone number. If you are using one of the modems from the Choose Modem menu, simply enter the digits of the telephone number that must be dialed. Using parentheses, hyphens, or spaces to make the number more readable will not effect the dialing of the number. You can even enter other characters before and after the telephone number for identification. Pfs:Access will ignore these characters. A comma is used in the phone number to cause the package to wait before the next digit is dialed. Each comma causes a wait of about two seconds. This is useful if you are dialing through a telephone

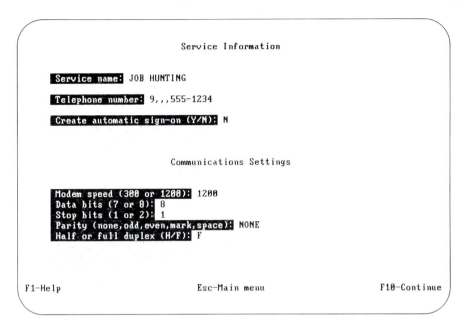

Service Information

Service name: JOB HUNTING

Telephone number: 9,,,555-1234

Create automatic sign-on (Y/N): N

Communications Settings

Modem speed (300 or 1200): 1200
Data bits (7 or 8): 8
Stop bits (1 or 2): 1
Parity (none,odd,even,mark,space): NONE
Half or full duplex (H/F): F

F1-Help   Esc-Main menu   F10-Continue

FIGURE 9A.5
**Setting the communications parameters
for the job hunting problem**

switchboard or using a long-distance service. For example, if you entered the number 9,,,555-1234, pfs:Access would dial 9, wait six seconds, and then dial 5551234. If you are using a modem not found in the Choose Modem menu or if you are directly connected to the host computer, a telephone number must still be entered, even though it will not be used by the package.

Press the TAB key again and enter N to indicate that you do not want to create an automatic sign-on (log-on) file. You are now ready to enter the Communications Settings. (If you had entered Y for this item, pfs:Access would have automatically recorded your log-on process when you made the call and then, when you pressed the F4 key, would have saved the procedure on disk for later use.)

For all the services listed in the Main Menu, the communications parameters are already set with the correct values. If you are connecting with a service or a host computer not listed, you will have to set the parameters according to the standards of the "answering" computer. For the job hunting problem, set modem speed to 1200, data bits to 8, stop bits to 1, parity to NONE, and duplex to F. When you press the F10 key, all the information on the screen shown in Figure 9a.5 will automatically be saved to disk.

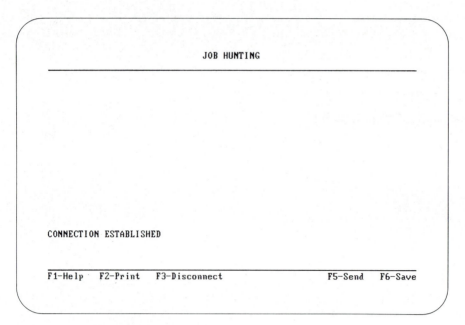

JOB HUNTING
_____

CONNECTION ESTABLISHED

_____

F1-Help   F2-Print   F3-Disconnect   F5-Send   F6-Save

FIGURE 9A.6
The pfs:Access terminal screen

Making the Call

Once you have pressed the F10 key in the Service Information menu, pfs:Access will begin dialing the telephone number that you have entered (provided your modem has an autodial feature and the modem is listed on the Choose Modem menu). As soon as the computer you are calling "answers" your call, the terminal screen shown in Figure 9a.6 will be displayed, and you can start the sign-on procedures for the host computer, if there are any.

If your modem has an autodial feature, but it was not listed in the Choose Modem menu, then you will have to enter the telephone number to be dialed from the keyboard. When the terminal screen appears, it will contain the message Enter modem commands. At this time, enter the commands and the telephone number required by your modem to dial the host computer telephone number and press the F10 key to begin dialing. If you are directly connected to a network, simply press the F10 key for the modem commands.

If you are using an acoustic-coupler modem or if you do not have autodial capabilities, you will need to dial the telephone number yourself. After leaving the Information Service menu by pressing the F10 key, dial the number, and, when you hear a high-pitched tone, connect the headset to the modem and press the F10 key. Once the terminal screen appears you are ready to begin the

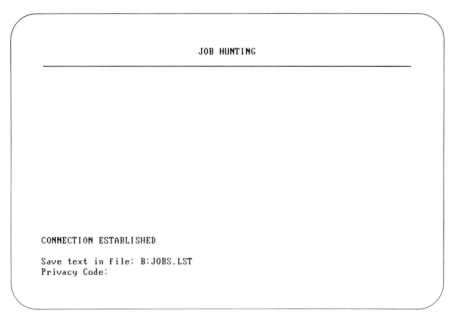

```
                              JOB HUNTING
   _____




   CONNECTION ESTABLISHED

   Save text in file: B:JOBS.LST
   Privacy Code:
```

FIGURE 9A.7
Opening the JOBS.LST file

sign-on procedures, if there are any. (There are no sign-on procedures for the job hunting problem. If you are communicating with another service or host computer, you should use its sign-on procedures.)

Down Loading to Disk

After the terminal screen appears on your monitor, you are ready to capture the information about the company interview dates. To save this information in a file on disk, press the F6 key. When the prompt on the status line appears, as in Figure 9a.7, enter the file name B:JOBS.LST (or a name of your choice) and press the RETURN key. This is the name your computer will use to save the data received from the host computer. Pfs:Access will open a file on the disk in drive B called JOBS.LST and begin saving all the data that appears on the screen into that file. To receive the list of company interview dates, enter the command TYPE B:JOBS.LST (this command may be different depending on the host computer). This is the location and name of the data on the host computer. Once the contents of JOBS.LST are listed on the screen, as shown in Figure 9a.8, they will automatically be saved to disk. Now, simply press the F6 key again, and the file B:JOBS.LST on your computer will be closed and saved for later use.

```
                        JOB HUNTING
_____
>TYPE B:JOBS.LST
Johnson Instruments, Inc.       Personnel Department   09/01 09/03
Champion Cowboy Supply          Mr. Joe Garcia         09/02 09/05
General Electronics, Inc.       Mr. Robert LeTrec      09/02 09/05
First State National Bank       Ms. Judith Welpit      09/02 09/06
Lewis & Melts Mortgage Company  Mrs. Roberta Accure    09/03 09/04
Ethyl & Jung, DDS               Dr. Emil Franz Jung    09/04 09/07
Areospace Education Center       Personnel Department   09/06 09/07
ABC Stereo Warehouse            Ms. Alice Faye Kong    09/06 09/08
WTBS Channel 5 TV               Dr. Jana Willoughby    09/06 09/08
Hormell Texas Chili Company     Mr. Foster Brooks      09/10 09/11
Children's Museum               Pesonnel Director      09/10 09/11
FBI                             Mr. H. Daniel Hoover   09/10 09/12
Mosteq Computer Company         Mr. Peter Hoague       09/15 09/16
Nephi's Hopi Crafts             Mrs. Carletta Whitecloud 09/17 09/17
Kelly Construction              Personnel Division     09/17 09/18
Jana's Management Consultants   Ms. Jana Davidson      10/03 10/04
Bar Four Ranch, Inc.            Mrs. Canda Strong      10/03 10/05
Matt's Films, Inc.              Personnel Office       10/03 10/05
Roger, Roger & Ray, Inc.        Personnel Department   10/03 10/06
_____
F1-Help   F2-Print   F3-Disconnect              F6-Stop Save
```

FIGURE 9A.8
Down loading the JOBS.LST file

It is possible that the host computer will transmit the information to be saved faster than pfs:Access can save it. If this happens, each line will be highlighted as it is saved. Simply wait to press the F6 key to close the file until the highlight reaches the end of the information you want to save.

Down Loading to the Printer

By pressing the F2 key, you can start and stop sending information to your printer at any time while it is connected to a host computer. Your printer must be turned on and be "on-line" before you press F2. To stop sending information to the printer, simply press the F2 key a second time. You can print incoming information and save it to disk at the same time. To print the JOBS.LST file, simply press the F2 key and enter the command TYPE B:JOBS.LST. When the printer stops, press the F2 key again.

Ending Communications

When you have finished working with the host computer, sign off (log-off) by following the host computer's instructions. You can then disconnect from the telephone by placing the cursor on the last line of the terminal screen and pressing the F3 key to return to the Main Menu. To exit the package, select E from the Main Menu and press the F10 key.

Other Features of pfs:Access

Pfs:Access has several useful features that you did not apply to the job hunting problem. Depending on the amount of memory your computer has and the host computer has, the package can save from 15 to more than 50 screens of information. Anytime you are in the terminal screen mode, you can use the HOME, PgUp, PgDn, END, and arrow keys to move through the screens previously transmitted to your computer. Note that you must return to the last line of your session (the last transmission line) before you can issue commands to the host computer.

In addition to being able to review your session, you can print and save files beginning anywhere in the saved screens. Simply move the cursor to the location where you want to start and enter the appropriate pfs:Access commands. Once you press the F3 key to disconnect and return to the Main Menu, all the screens that you haven't saved are erased.

Pfs:Access also allows you do to data encryption using a coding process based on the Data Encryption Standard of the National Bureau of Standards. The process allows you to enter a special code of your choice that will be used to encode your files. You can encode files that you send to the host computer as well as files that you down load from the host computer. Once these files are encoded, only someone who knows the privacy code that you used can decode them.

Finally, pfs:Access also provides a special SETUP program that allows you to select the printer type you are using, turn color off and on, and install the program to a hard disk. The SETUP program further customizes the program to fit your needs.

Crosstalk XVI

Learning to Use Crosstalk XVI

Crosstalk XVI is one of the most popular electronic communications packages produced to date. In part, its popularity is based on the fact that it can be used with IBM PCs and other compatible computers. However, IBM compatibility is not the only reason the package is popular. Crosstalk is one of the more versatile communications packages. Furthermore, it is continually being expanded and improved by its manufacturer.

When you are ready to begin working with Crosstalk, load a copy of the computer's operating system in drive A. Once the operating system has been loaded, replace the system disk with the Crosstalk disk. (You may use drive B for data or to save communications parameters that are established during a Crosstalk session.) With the Crosstalk disk in drive A, type XTALK and press the RETURN key. A Crosstalk logo will temporarily be shown on the screen, followed by the Crosstalk Status Screen shown in Figure 9b.1. The top half of this screen is used to specify communications parameters, the bottom half is used to provide information (such has HELP information), and the last line is used to convey the current status of your operations.

Before you begin to establish communications parameters, press the RETURN key. Note that the (bottom) status line changes to the COMMAND? text (Crosstalk is a command driven package). Crosstalk is now ready to accept your commands.

Solving the Job Hunting Problem

The remaining sections in this module are devoted to solving the job hunting problem. You may want to refer to the problem statement in the Introduction to Electronic Communications Modules before you continue. Also, remember that the data used in this problem can be found in Appendix A and on your host computer.

```
┌──────  CROSSTALK - XVI Status Screen ──────┐          Off line

NAme    Crosstalk defaults                    LOaded    A:STD.XTK
NUmber                                        CApture   Off

┌───── Communications parameters ─────┐    ┌───── Filter settings ─────┐
SPeed 1200   PArity None   DUplex Full       DEbug    Off   LFauto   Off
DAta  8      STop   1      EMulate None       TAbex    Off   BLankex  Off
POrt  1                    MOde   Call        INfilter On    OUtfiltr On

┌───── Key settings ─────┐                   ┌──── SEnd control settings ────┐
ATten  Esc            COmmand ETX (^C)         CWait    None
SWitch Home           BReak   End             LWait    None

┌───────────── Available command files ─────────────┐

1) NEWUSER      2) SETUP      3) STD
```

```
Enter number for file to use ( 1 - 3 ): _
```

FIGURE 9B.1
Crosstalk's Status Screen

Getting Help

To retrieve help information from Crosstalk, all you have to do is enter the command HELP in the command line and press the RETURN key. Your screen will now look like the one in Figure 9b.2. If you haven't already noticed, each command is shown with the first two letters capitalized. This means that commands can be entered by typing only the first two letters, rather than the complete command name. For example, HELP can be abbreviated to HE. To complete the viewing of help topics, press the RETURN key. A complete list of all the commands (or topics) is provided in Table 9b.1.

Setting Communications Parameters

Before you begin to establish communications parameters, you should become familiar with the remaining parameters that can be specified. Enter the command LIST. The screen will now look like Figure 9b.3. Most of the frequently changed communications parameters appear in the top half of the Status Screen. The bottom part of the screen shows Miscellaneous parameters that are less frequently used. (Refer to Table 9b.1 for further information about these parameters.)

TABLE 9B.1 Crosstalk Commands

Command Name	Description
ACcept	Controls caller access to your computer when it is in answer mode.
ANswback	Identifies the code for answering a transmission in a network environment.
APrefix	Provides directions to a programmable modem about the procedure for answering a call.
ATten	Causes a key reassignment that causes ''COMMAND?'' to appear in the control line.
BKsize	Causes larger blocks of data to be transmitted between two machines communicating in Crosstalk.
BLankex	Causes blank lines to be filled with spaces when transmitted.
BReak	Causes a key reassignment of the Break key.
CApture	Causes a received file to be saved on disk or in memory or causes it to be printed.
COmmand	Alters the command key that signals the receiving computer that a command is being sent.
CStat	Used to identify and search files that have been saved in memory.
CWait	Causes a pause in the transmission of characters.
DAta	Indicates the number of bits per transmitted character.
DEbug	Establishes a means of ''trouble shooting'' communications activities while they occur.
DNames	Specifies a number of file names that may be retained in memory.
DPrefix	Instructs a programmable modem to send a specified sequence of characters when dialing another computer.
DRive	Causes a change in the default disk drive.
DSuffix	Instructs a programmable modem to send a specified sequence of characters after a telephone number has been dialed.
DUplex	Indicates whether communication is ''one way'' or ''two way.''
EMulate	Used to specify specific hardware devices or terminal types.
ERase	Removes a file that has been saved in memory.
FKeys	Establishes new values for function keys.
FLow	Indicates the control codes that specify when transmissions are to begin and end.
GO	Causes entry into the communications mode.
HAndshak	Establishes that the link between two systems is based on a hardware connection.
INfilter	Used to eliminate incoming control characters from the sending computer.
LFauto	Causes a line advance on the screen when the sending computer doesn't automatically do so.
LOaded	Causes the retrieval or loading into memory of communications parameter files.
LWait	Causes a pause between transmission of lines.
MOde	Establishes whether your computer is the calling or the answering device.

Command Name	Description
NAme	Specifies a log-on name that appears on a caller's screen when you are in answer mode.
NUmber	Establishes a telephone number for automatic dialing when entering the communications mode.
OUtfiltr	Used to eliminate transmitted control characters sent from your computer.
PArity	Indicates the number of bits per character to be used to check communication accuracy.
PIcture	Saves the current content of the screen into a file to be saved in memory or reviews the lines that have been saved in memory by this process.
PMode	Indicates whether communications exist between two MS-DOS machines or between an MS-DOS and a CP/M machine.
POrt	Identifies which hardware connection or port is to be used during communication.
PRinter	Causes data displayed on the screen to be printed.
PWord	Specifies a password that must be entered by a caller when your computer is in the answer mode.
RDials	Specifies the number of times a telephone number is to be redialed before the dialing process is abandoned.
RQuest	Causes the receiving of a file by one system from another that is operating in Crosstalk.
SEnd	Transmits a file to a receiving computer not operating in Crosstalk.
SNapshot	Determines the number of lines on the screen that are to be saved for review on the screen.
SPeed	Establishes the communication (baud) rate.
STop	Indicates the number of bits per character that signal that the transmission of the character has been completed.
SWitch	Causes a key reassignment for screen swapping between the "Status Screen" and the communications screen.
TAbex	Used to substitute spaces for tab characters when they are transmitted or received.
TImer	Causes the connect timer to be turned on or off.
TUrnarnd	Indicates a signal that is to be sent to a receiving computer when an end of line has been reached.
TYpe	Causes the contents of a file to be placed on the screen.
UConly	Causes all transmitted characters to be converted to upper case.
VIdeo	Specifies the characteristics of the video display screen.
WRite	Causes data that has been captured in memory to be written to a file.
XMit	Causes the sending of a file between two systems that are operating in Crosstalk.

```
            ┌─────   CROSSTALK - XVI Status Screen   ─────┐       Off line

 NAme    Crosstalk defaults                    LOaded   A:STD.XTK
 NUmber                                        CApture  Off

 ┌──────── Communications parameters ────────┐   ┌──────── Filter settings ────────┐
 SPeed 1200    PArity None    DUplex  Full        DEbug    Off    LFauto   Off
 DAta  8       STop   1       EMulate None         TAbex    Off    BLankex  Off
 POrt  1                      MOde    Call         INfilter On     OUtfiltr On

 ┌──────── Key settings ────────┐                 ┌──── SEnd control settings ────┐
 ATten   Esc              COmmand ETX (^C)         CWait    None
 SWitch  Home             BReak   End              LWait    None

 ┌─────────────────── List of Crosstalk commands ───────────────────┐

    NAme        NUmber      ANswback    APrefix    ATten     BReak      DEbug
    DPrefix     DRive       DSuffix     EDit       EMulate   EPath      FIlter
    POrt        PWord       RDials      RQest      SCreen    SNapshot   SWitch
    TImer       TUrnarnd    VIdeo       ACcept     CWait     DNames     FKeys
    GO          INfilter    LFauto      LOad       LWait     MOde       QUit
    RUn         SAve        SEnd        XDos       BKsize    BLankex    BYe
    CApture     CDir        COmmand     CStatus    DAta      DIr        DO

 More to come...    press ENTER: _
```

FIGURE 9B.2
A help screen of commands

Now enter the LOAD command and press the RETURN key. Your screen will now show its original contents, from Figure 9b.1. Examine the contents of this screen. At the top, see that Crosstalk Defaults have been loaded from A:STD.XTK. These characteristics can be reloaded any time you wish by selecting command file 3 (STD) from the list of Available command files, shown at the bottom of the screen. The STD file contains commonly used parameters. However, you can use the STD file and alter parameters as necessary to fit your situation. This is the first of three ways you can specify communications parameters.

The job hunting problem calls for a communications environment using 1200 baud, 8 data bits, 1 stop bit, parity of None, and Full duplex. Coincidentally, these are precisely the default parameters for Crosstalk's STD file. However, you should enter these parameters individually, just to see how to make changes. Assume that none of the default parameters is correct and you have to supply them. The first parameter to set is the baud rate—known to Crosstalk as SPeed. In general, Crosstalk gives you two ways of entering command parameters. For example, you could enter SPeed 1200, which is interpreted by Crosstalk to mean you want to change the speed to 1200 baud. However, you could also enter only SPeed, in which case Crosstalk will prompt you with the

```
┌─────── CROSSTALK - XVI Status Screen ───────┐        Off line

 NAme    Crosstalk defaults                    LOaded   A:STD.XTK
 NUmber                                        CApture  Off

 ┌──── Communications parameters ────┐    ┌──── Filter settings ────┐
 SPeed 1200   PArity None   DUplex Full     DEbug     Off   LFauto   Off
 DAta  8        STop   1    EMulate None     TAbex     Off   BLankex  Off
 POrt  1                    MOde    Call     INfilter  On    OUtfiltr On

 ┌────── Key settings ──────┐         ┌─── SEnd control settings ───┐
 ATten   Esc             COmmand ETX (^C)   CWait    None
 SWitch  Home            BReak   End        LWait    None

 ┌───────────── Miscellaneous parameters ─────────────┐

 DRive   A:              ACcept  Everything   PWord
 DPrefix ATV0X1!~ATDT    DSuffix !            APrefix  ATS0=1!
 PRinter Off             UConly  Off          ANswback On
 PMode   2 (DOS)         BKsize  1            DNames   200
 EPath                   RDials  10           TUrnarnd Enter
 VIdeo   CGA             FLow    ^S/^Q        HAndshak Off


 Command? LIST_
```

FIGURE 9B.3
Additional communications parameters

permitted baud rates, of which you select one (or simply press the RETURN key to keep the current setting). If you were to individually establish all of the remaining communications parameters, you could enter the command sequence DAta 8, PArity None, STop 1, and DUplex Full. Note from the Status Screen of Figure 9b.4 that all of these characteristics are clustered under the heading Communications parameters. These parameters are the ones most frequently changed when users attempt to establish a link with another computer.

Although you will probably use the option for specifying parameters just described, there are two more ways to do this. Again, refer to Figure 9b.1. Note that one of the Available command files is called NEWUSER. As shown in Figure 9b.5, NEWUSER provides an automatic means of supplying communications parameters to many of the frequently used information services. Furthermore, if you select option O (for other services), Crosstalk will provide you with a series of prompts to establish all necessary communications parameters.

The third way to specify communications parameters is to select the SETUP file from the Available command files list. SETUP differs from NEWUSER in that it provides you with more of the Miscellaneous parameters as well as additional descriptions of the parameters to be provided. Also, as shown in

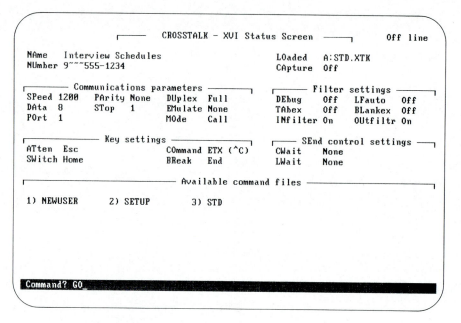

```
 ┌──── CROSSTALK - XVI Status Screen ────┐        Off line

  NAme    Interview Schedules              LOaded   A:STD.XTK
  NUmber  9~~~555-1234                     CApture  Off

  ┌──── Communications parameters ────┐   ┌──── Filter settings ────┐
  SPeed 1200   PArity None   DUplex  Full   DEbug    Off   LFauto    Off
  DAta  8      STop   1      EMulate None    TAbex    Off   BLankex   Off
  POrt  1                    MOde    Call    INfilter On    OUtfiltr  On

  ┌──── Key settings ────┐                  ┌──── SEnd control settings ────┐
  ATten  Esc          COmmand ETX (^C)    CWait   None
  SWitch Home         BReak   End         LWait   None

  ┌──────── Available command files ────────┐

  1) NEWUSER      2) SETUP       3) STD



  Command? GO_
```

FIGURE 9B.4
**Setting up communications parameters for
the job hunting problem**

Figure 9b.6, the Status Screen is always present while SETUP is being used. The
Status Screen temporarily disappears from view when using NEWUSER.

Making the Call

If you want, you can dial the telephone manually to connect Crosstalk to
another computer; however, it's easier to use Crosstalk's autodial feature.
Look at Figure 9b.4, and you will see that the NUmber 9~~~555-1234 has
been entered as a command (in many circumstances, the telephone number
would be much simpler than the one presented)—9 indicates calling for an
outside line, ~~~ specifies that a three-second pause is to follow [each tilde
("~") indicates a one-second pause], and 555-1234 is the telephone number to
be dialed. Hyphens, parentheses (for area codes), and spaces are ignored when
Crosstalk dials a number. However, these symbols are very useful when you are
trying to read a telephone number. (The maximum length of a telephone
number dialing sequence is 40 characters, which also affords you some enhanced readability.) Finally, you may choose to provide a descriptive NAme for

```
                    Choose a service to set up:

                    A - The Source
                    B - CompuServe
                    C - Delphi
                    D - Dow Jones News / Retrieval
                    E - Newsnet
                    F - The Official Airline Guide
                    G - MCI Mail
                    H - LEXIS/NEXIS
                    O - Other service not listed above

                    X - Exit from this program




Please choose a service: _
```

FIGURE 9B.5
Using the NEWUSER file and access to information services

```
             ┌──── CROSSTALK - XVI Status Screen ────┐        Off line

NAme                                    LOaded   A:SETUP.XTK
NUmber                                  CApture  Off

   ┌── Communications parameters ──┐       ┌──── Filter settings ────┐
   SPeed 1200   PArity None   DUplex Full   DEbug    Off   LFauto    Off
   DAta  8      STop   1      EMulate None   TAbex    Off   BLankex   Off
   POrt  1                    MOde    Call   INfilter On    OUtfiltr  On

        ┌──── Key settings ────┐             ┌── SEnd control settings ──┐
   ATten  Esc          COmmand ETX (^C)      CWait    None
   SWitch Home         BReak   End           LWait    None

   ┌                                                                      ┐




Command? _
```

FIGURE 9B.6
Receiving prompts from the SETUP file

the set of parameters you are entering. For the job hunting problem, Interview Schedules was selected.

Now you are ready to actually make the communications connection. Either enter the COMMAND? GO and press the RETURN key, or simply press the RETURN key ("go" is considered the default value). The telephone dialing sequence is then executed, and you should be connected with the host computer. If Crosstalk cannot make the connection (for example, if the phone number is busy), it will ask you if you want to redial now or wait a while. When the connection is established, the Status Screen will disappear, and the bottom command line will be changed to reflect that you are connected to the host computer. If you want to return to the Status Screen, just press the HOME key. Press the HOME key a second time, and you will return to the communications screen. If you are in communications mode and you want to enter a command without returning to the Status Screen, press the ESCape key, and COMMAND? will appear on the command line.

The same type of procedure is used when you are using a direct connect modem or an accoustic coupler. The primary difference is that with a direct connect modem, a telephone number and dialing procedure are needed; with the acoustic coupler, the telephone number must be dialed manually.

Saving and Loading Communications Parameters

Now that the communications parameters have been specified, it is time to save them so that you don't have to enter them again later. Because you want COMMAND? but are probably still in the communications mode, press the HOME key to return to the Status Screen. If COMMAND? is still not visible, simply press the ESCape key. Then enter SAve JOBS or any other appropriate file name. (If you do not provide the file name immediately after entering the SAve command, Crosstalk will prompt you for it.) Crosstalk will save the communications parameters on the default drive under the indicated file name, adding the XTK extension. You could, of course, add a disk drive designation before the file name.

Retrieving a communications parameter file is as easy as creating it. With COMMAND? on the last line of the screen, enter the command LOad and press the RETURN key. The screen will now look like Figure 9b.7. Note that the bottom portion of the Status Screen now contains a list of Available command files—with the JOBS file added to the list. You can retrieve any of these parameter files by entering the number that precedes the file name. You can also enter a command such as LOad JOBS, if you happen to remember the file name.

Down Loading to Disk

Now return to the communications mode by pressing the HOME key. You should still be connected with the other computer. Because Crosstalk lets you

```
┌─────── CROSSTALK - XVI Status Screen ───────┐        Off line

NAme   Interview Schedules              LOaded    A:STD.XTK
NUmber 9~~~555-1234                     CApture   Off

┌──── Communications parameters ────┐  ┌──── Filter settings ────┐
SPeed 1200   PArity None   DUplex Full   DEbug    Off   LFauto    Off
DAta  8      STop   1      EMulate None   TAbex    Off   BLankex   Off
POrt  1                   MOde    Call    INfilter On    OUtfiltr  On

┌──────── Key settings ────────┐  ┌──── SEnd control settings ───┐
ATten  Esc           COmmand ETX (^C)   CWait    None
SWitch Home          BReak   End        LWait    None

┌──────────── Available command files ────────────┐

1) JOBS        2) NEWUSER      3) SETUP      4) STD
```

Enter number for file to use (1 - 4): 1_

FIGURE 9B.7
Loading previously saved communications parameters

adjust communications parameters without having to re-establish the communications link, you can still perform any number of operations. For example, you could modify the baud rate or the duplex setting.

The first step in the down loading operation is to specify that the data to be received from the host computer is to be captured. As shown in the middle of the command line of the communications screen in Figure 9b.8, the file B:JOBS.LST has been identified as the receiving file. Like most of the other commands, the CApture command can be executed from the communications screen. First, press the ESCape key so that COMMAND? appears in the command line. Then, enter the command CApture B:JOBS.LST. (If you switch back to the Status Screen at this point, the screen will indicate that the capture mode is on.)

The next activity is based on the communications capabilities of the host computer. If the host computer is also running Crosstalk, all that is necessary is to press CTRL-C, and you will see that COMMAND? now appears within the communications screen area. You are now ready to send a command to the host computer directly. If you enter the command TYPE B:JOBS.LST, the JOBS.LST file will be retrieved from drive B of the host computer, and it will simultaneously appear on your communications screen while being copied to

```
Johnson Instruments, Inc.        Personnel Department       09/01 09/03
Champion Cowboy Supply           Mr. Joe Garcia             09/02 09/05
General Electronics, Inc.        Mr. Robert LeTrec          09/02 09/05
First State National Bank        Ms. Judith Welpit          09/02 09/06
Lewis & Melts Mortgage Company   Mrs. Roberta Accure        09/03 09/04
Ethyl & Jung, DDS                Dr. Emil Franz Jung        09/04 09/07
Aerospace Education Center       Personnel Department       09/06 09/07
ABC Stereo Warehouse             Ms. Alice Faye Kong        09/06 09/08
WTBS Channel 5 TV                Dr. Jana Willoughby        09/06 09/08
Hormell Texas Chili Company      Mr. Foster Brooks          09/10 09/11
Children's Museum                Pesonnel Director          09/10 09/11
FBI                              Mr. H. Daniel Hoover       09/10 09/12
Mosteq Computer Company          Mr. Peter Hoague           09/15 09/16
Nephi's Hopi Crafts              Mrs. Carletta Whitecloud   09/17 09/17
Kelly Construction               Personnel Division         09/17 09/18
Jana's Management Consultants    Ms. Jana Davidson          10/03 10/04
Bar Four Ranch, Inc.             Mrs. Canda Strong          10/03 10/05
Matt's Films, Inc.               Personnel Office           10/03 10/05
Roger, Roger & Ray, Inc.         Personnel Department       10/03 10/06



Esc for ATtention, Home to SWitch  ‖ Capture to B:JOBS.LST  ‖ On: 00:01:44
```

FIGURE 9B.8
Retrieving the JOBS.LST file

the file B:JOBS.LST (the capture file) on your computer. After this sequence has been completed, you need to "turn off" the capturing process. Press the ESCape key so that COMMAND? appears in the command line and enter the command CApture OFF. This command closes the capture file and returns the capture mode to off.

Down Loading to the Printer

Down loading to the printer is as easy as down loading to a file, perhaps even easier. However, there are two ways of producing the interview schedule on your printer. First, since you already have a copy of the file on your disk, you could simply print that file. This can be done by turning the printer on. To do this, press ESCape so that the COMMAND? prompt is in the command line and enter the command PRinter ON. Then, press ESCape again and enter the command TYPE B:JOBS.LST. This will cause your copy of the interview schedule to appear both on your screen and on the printer. Remember to turn the printer off by entering the command PRinter OFF.

The second way to print data is to simply turn the printer on first by entering the command PRinter ON. All data that appears on the communications screen afterwards will also be duplicated on the printer. Thus, you could enter the sequence CTRL-C TYPE B:JOBS.LST and retrieve and print the host computer's version of the interview schedule. (This approach does not require you to store the data on your disk.) However, remember that everything that is produced on the communications screen also goes to the printer. Don't forget to turn the printer off when unneeded data is to appear on the screen.

Ending Communications

To terminate communications with another computer, first perform the log-off sequence for the host computer. You have three choices when you are ready to perform a disconnect from your end. Of course, before each of these commands can be executed, you must have COMMAND? in the command line. First, you can enter QUit, which terminates the current call and returns you to the operating system. If you enter BYe, you terminate the current call and remain in Crosstalk. This permits you to establish a call to another computer without reentering Crosstalk. Finally, you can enter XDOS, which exits to the operating system without disconnecting the current call. This option allows you to return to the operating system, execute an operating system command or some other program, and return to Crosstalk without interrupting the call that is in progress. However, when you leave Crosstalk in this manner, don't forget you are still connected to the host computer.

Other Features of Crosstalk XVI

You have seen that Crosstalk is a very versatile communications package; however, you have been introduced to only some of the common functions of this software. Review Table 9b.1. This table lists many of Crosstalk's other capabilities. For example, in the job hunting problem, you were required to receive a file from a host computer. Via the SEnd command, you can transmit a file to a host computer. If the host computer is also running Crosstalk, you can send a file using the XMit command and receive files from that computer using the RQuest command.

The job hunting problem assumed that you were the "calling" computer. However, with Crosstalk, you can modify the MOde so that your computer can answer incoming calls from other computers. You can also require calling users to enter a password by executing the PWord command. In addition, you can limit calling users' manipulation of data on your system by employing the ACcept command.

When acting as the calling user, you also have additional opportunities to save data that is being transmitted to you. The job hunting problem required you to save a file on disk and print it, but it is also possible to use the CApture command to save data to memory. You can also add additional material to an existing disk file with the CApture command. Finally, you can save specific display screens to memory and later recall them by using the SNapshot command.

These are only a few of the additional capabilities of Crosstalk. Many of the others are designed to more specifically control the transmission process when the link is not a "near match." Furthermore, Crosstalk lets you build and execute what is referred to as a *Script File,* using additional commands not presented here, and create what amounts to a procedural language that can be interfaced to Crosstalk. It is easy to see why Crosstalk's flexibility, diverse capabilities, and ease of use have made it one of the most popular communications packages.

Smartcom

Learning to Use Smartcom

Smartcom is the electronic communications application package produced by Hayes Microcomputer Products, Inc. It was originally designed to work with the Hayes Smartmodem. The package is available for a variety of microcomputer systems using the MS-DOS or the PC-DOS operating system. Smartcom is designed to simplify the sign-on (log-on) procedure as well as the use of any information, communication, or timesharing service. It has many powerful features that allow you to get the most out of your electronic communications operations.

When you are prepared to begin working with Smartcom, start with a copy of the Smartcom disk containing the operating system in drive A. If you are using a system that has two disk drives, a disk prepared to hold your data should be in drive B. After you have booted your system, enter the command SCOM, and be sure that your modem is turned on. When the package is loaded into memory, it will respond by placing the main menu on the screen, as shown in Figure 9c.1. From this menu, you can select several options. If an asterisk appears before the option, that option is not currently available to you.

The first operation you will need to perform from the main menu is to check the Configuration screen to ensure the package has the correct information about your computer. Press the 6 key while in the main menu, and the Configuration menu, shown in Figure 9c.2, will appear. (You can also move the cursor to option 6 by pressing the left- and right-arrow keys. Once the cursor is at option 6, press the RETURN key, and the Configuration menu will appear.) Pressing the up- and down-arrow keys or the RETURN key will move the cursor through the options on the Configuration menu. The left- and right-arrow keys are used to select the desired value for each of the items on the screen. When all the configuration entries agree with the configuration of your system, you will be asked if you wish to save these settings. Pressing the RETURN key will automatically save the settings and return you to the main menu. No matter where you are in the use of Smartcom, pressing the F1 key will stop what you are doing and return you to the main menu.

The Smartcom package makes use of the function keys to perform special operations. One of these operations is the use of the HELP command. While

```
     Smartcom II              Hayes Microcomputer Products, Inc.

1. Begin Communciation  *. Receive File     7. Change Printer Status  (OFF)
2. Edit Set             *. Send File        *. Select Remote Access   (OFF)
3. Select File Command  6. Change Configuration 9. Display Disk Directory (OFF)
A,B,C - Change Drive                        0. End Communication/Program

                        Press F2 for Help
Enter Selection: 1      Press F1 To Return On-Line


             Dials or answers phone with Smartmodem




12:42 pm          Monday January 5, 1987
```

FIGURE 9C.1
The Smartcom main menu

```
                        CONFIGURATION       Press F2 for Help
PRINTER :                   Port:  PARALLEL
               Serial Protocol:
                        Baud:
        Remove Extra Line Feeds:  NO
                    Add NULs:     0
SMARTMODEM :                Port:  COM1:
             Dialing Method:  TONE
        Pause Time For Comma:   2  (  0-255   seconds  )
          Touch-Tone Timing:  70  ( 50-255   0.001 seconds  )
        Wait For Dial Tone:    2  (  2-255   seconds  )
     Wait For Carrier Signal:  30  (  1-255   seconds  )
     Recognize Carrier Signal:  6  (  1-255   0.1  seconds  )
   Carrier Loss To Hangup Time:  7  ( 10255   0.1  seconds  )
              Speaker Status:  ON UNTIL CARRIER - MED
         Telephone Jack Type:  RJ11
SPECIAL VALUES :     Default Set:  Z
         Available Disk Drives:  ABC
          Monitor and Adapter:  COLOR/GRAPH. DISP. ADPTER/COLOR MONITOR
             Log-on Message:  Smartcom II - IBM Personal Computer
         Direct-Connect Port:  COM1:
          Transet 1000 Port:  NONE

12:42 pm          Monday January 5, 1987
```

FIGURE 9C.2
The Smartcom Configuration menu

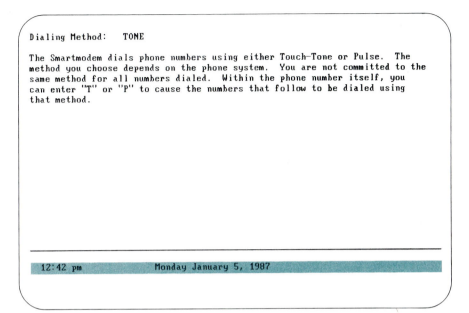

```
Dialing Method:    TONE

The Smartmodem dials phone numbers using either Touch-Tone or Pulse.  The
method you choose depends on the phone system.  You are not committed to the
same method for all numbers dialed.  Within the phone number itself, you
can enter "T" or "P" to cause the numbers that follow to be dialed using
that method.




_____

12:42 pm            Monday January 5, 1987
```

FIGURE 9C.3
Getting HELP when choosing a dialing method

you are in terminal mode (connected to another computer), press the F2 key for an explanation of scrolling, saving, printing, and sending files. If you are at the main menu or one of the option screens, pressing F2 will cause Smartcom to display an explanation of the items on that menu. The screen shown in Figure 9c.3 is the HELP screen for the selection of the dialing method in the Configuration menu.

Solving the Job Hunting Problem

The remaining sections in this module are devoted to solving the job hunting problem. You may want to refer to the problem statement in the Introduction to Electronic Communications Modules before you continue. Also, remember that the data used in this problem can be found in Appendix A and on your host computer.

Setting and Saving the Communications Parameters

To start using Smartcom, simply press 2 from the main menu. After pressing the RETURN key, select S to select the Set of communications parameters you

```
   Smartcom II              Hayes Microcomputer Products, Inc.

1. Begin Communication  *. Receive File       7. Change Printer Status  (OFF)
2. Edit Set             *. Send File          *. Select Remote Access   (OFF)
3. Select File Command  6. Change Configuration 9. Display Disk Directory (OFF)
A,B,C - Change Drive                          0. End Communication/Program
                        Press F2 for Help
Enter Selection: 2      P(arameters, M(acros, R(eprots, C(opy, S(et, B(atch: S
Enter Label: Z

Communication Directory:

A - CompuServe Direct    J - OAG EE Telenet     S - CompuServe Datapac
B - CompuServe Telenet   K - OAG EE Tymnet      T - DJN/R Datapac
C - CompuServe Tymnet    L - OAG EE UNINET      U - KNOWLEDGE INDEX Data
D - DJN/R Telenet        M - THE SOURCE Direct  V - UAG EE Datapac
E - DJN/R Tymnet         N - THE SOURCE Telenet W - THE SOURCE Datapac
F - DJN/R UNINET         O - THE SOURCE UNINET  X - Test Set
G - KNOWLEDGE INDEX Tel  P - Transet Mailbox    Y - Remote Access
H - KNOWLEDGE INDEX Tym  Q -                    Z - Standard Values
I - MCI Mail             R -


 12:42 pm            Monday January 5, 1987
```

FIGURE 9c.4
The Smartcom Edit Set of communications parameters

are going to use. Your screen will now change to the one shown in Figure 9c.4. If you are not a subscriber to one of the services listed in the Communication Directory, press Q to enter your own set of parameters. Note that the Communication Directory items Q and R are blank, which allows two new settings to be entered. You may also change any of the parameter sets already established if you need more than two new settings. After pressing Q (or using the right- and left-arrow keys to move the cursor to Q), press the P key to get a list of the current parameter settings.

You are now ready to supply the communications parameters needed to talk to your host computer. When you call a service or a host computer, you need to enter the parameters used by the host computer or the service you want to contact. If you are a subscriber to one of the services listed on the screen, all of the parameters except the telephone number are already set. Simply enter the appropriate service telephone number and press the RETURN key. After saving the parameters, the package will return to the main menu.

If you are not a subscriber to a service, the first item of information you are asked for is the service name/host computer you are going to connect to. This name can be up to 20 characters long and will change Q in the Edit Set list from a blank to the name you enter. For the problem you are working on, enter the name: JOB HUNTING. Pressing the RETURN key will move the cursor to the

```
                           PARAMETERS
Name of Set: Q - JOB HUNTING              Press F2 For Help

        TRANSMISSION PARAMETERS              KEYBOARD  DEFINITIONS
            Duplex:  FULL             Escape Key:  128 (F1)
   Connection Type:  Bell 1200          Help Key:  129 (F2)
Character Processing:  FORMATTED       Printer Key:  130 (F3)
 Show Control Codes:  NO               Capture Key:  131 (F4)
        Page Pause:  NO           Macro Prefix Key:  132 (F5)
  Show Status Lines:  YES              Break Key:  133 (F6)
      Confidential:  NO             Break Length:   35 (0.01 sec.)
 Include Line Feeds:  NO               Protect Key:  134 (F7)
    Character Delay:     0 (0.001 sec.)
        Line Delay:     0 (0.01 sec.)      PROTOCOL  PARAMETERS
   Character Format:  8 DATA + NONE + 1 STOP   Receive Time-out:   60 (sec.)
          Emulator:  TTY                  Send Time-out:   10 (sec.)
                                  Error-Free Protocol:  Hayes
      TELEPHONE PARAMETERS        Stop/Start- Stop Char:  19 (DC3)
Answer On Ring:    1                      Start Char:  17 (DC1)
  Remote Access:  HAYES  Password:  JOBS  Send Lines- EOL Char:  10 (LF )
  Phone Number:  9,,,555-1234             Prompt Char:  32 (" ")
_____

   12:42 pm              Monday January 5, 1987
```

FIGURE 9c.5
**Setting the communications parameters
for the job hunting problem**

next item to be entered. Figure 9c.5 shows the parameter setting used in the job hunting problem. The last entry asked for is the telephone number of the service or host computer you are going to call. If you are using a direct connect modem with autodial capabilities, you can enter the telephone number here and Smartcom will dial it for you. Using hyphens or spaces to make the number more readable will not affect the dialing of the number. A comma is used in the telephone number to cause the package to wait before the next digit is dialed. Each comma causes a wait of about two seconds. For example, if you entered the number 9,,,555-1234, Smartcom would dial 9, wait six seconds, and then dial 5551234. If you leave the telephone number blank, Smartcom will ask for the number in the main menu when you attempt to Begin Communications (option 1).

After you have made all of the parameter entries, Smartcom will ask if you want to save them to disk. Press the Y key to save them and return the package to the main menu.

Making the Call

Press the 1 key at the main menu, and Smartcom will ask if you are going to Originate, Answer, or Transfer Data. When you press the O for Originate or

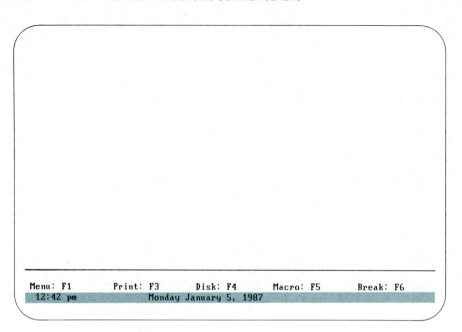

```
Menu: F1        Print: F3       Disk: F4       Macro: F5       Break: F6
 12:42 pm                 Monday January 5, 1987
```

FIGURE 9c.6
The Smartcom Terminal Screen

the RETURN key, Smartcom will begin dialing the telephone number that you entered. As soon as the computer you are calling "answers" your call, the terminal screen shown in Figure 9c.6 will be displayed, and you can start any necessary sign-on procedures for the host computer. If you did not enter a telephone number for the parameter set you are using, then you must now enter the telephone number from the keyboard.

If you are using an acoustic modem, or if you do not have autodial capabilities, you will need to dial the telephone number yourself. After pressing the 1 key, dial the number. When you hear a high-pitched tone, connect the headset to the modem and press the D key. Once the terminal screen appears, you are ready to begin the sign-on procedure, if there are any.

Note that for the job hunting problem, there are no sign-on procedures. The sign-on information needed for Remote Access were set during the parameter selection in Figure 9c.5.

Down Loading to Disk

After the terminal screen appears on your monitor, you can capture the information about the company interview dates. To save this information in a file on disk, press the F4 key. When the prompt on the status line asks for a file name,

```
  Smartcom II              Hayes Microcomputer Products, Inc.

*. Begin Communciation  4. Receive File       7. Change Printer Status  (OFF)
2. Edit Set             5. Send File          8. Select Remote Access   (ON)
3. Select File Command  *. Change Configuration 9. Display Disk Directory (OFF)
A,B - Change Drive                            0. End Communication/Program
                        Press F2 for Help
Enter Selection: 4

         Accepts data via protocol and records to a file on disk




                                      Smartmodem: CONNECT_____1200 BAUD
_____

  12:42 pm          Monday January 5, 1987
```

FIGURE 9c.7
The Smartcom Remote Access screen

enter the name B:JOBS.LST (or a file name of your choice) and press the RETURN key. This is the name your computer will use to save the data received from the host computer. Smartcom will open a file on the disk in drive B called JOBS.LST and begin saving all the data that appears on the screen into that file. To receive the list of company interview dates, enter the command TYPE B:JOBS.LST. (This command may be different depending on the host computer.) This is the location and name of the data on the host computer. Once you have listed the contents of JOBS.LST on the screen, they will automatically be saved to disk. Now, simply press the F4 key again, and the file B:JOBS.LST will be closed and stored for later use.

In the job hunting problem, you are connected to another microcomputer using Smartcom in Remote Access mode. This means that you, the originator of the call, have control over the answering computer. (To perform the down loading operation in the preceding paragraph, follow the instructions in the next section.) Figure 9c.7 shows the screen during Remote Access connection after option 4 (Receive File) has been selected from this screen. Now, simply press the RETURN key, enter the file name, and press the RETURN key to save the file under the selected name on your system, as shown in Figure 9c.8. Smartcom will then save the file on your system, as illustrated in Figure 9c.9. Pressing the F1 key will return your system to the main menu.

```
   Smartcom II              Hayes Microcomputer Products, Inc.

*. Begin Communciation  4. Receive File       7. Change Printer Status  (OFF)
2. Edit Set             5. Send File          8. Select Remote Access   (ON)
3. Select File Command  *. Change Configuration 9. Display Disk Directory (OFF)
A,B - Change Drive                            0. End Communication/Program
                        Press F2 for Help
Enter Selection: 4
Enter File Name: B:JOBS.LST          Same Remote File Name? (Y/N): Y












_____Smartmodem: CONNECT_____1200 BAUD

  12:42 pm          Monday January 5, 1987
```

FIGURE 9C.8
Preparing to receive a file

Down Loading to the Printer

By pressing the F3 key, you can start and stop sending information to your printer at any time it is connected to a host computer. Your printer must be turned on and be "on-line" before you press F3. To stop sending information to the printer, simply press the F3 key a second time. You can print incoming information and save it to disk at the same time. To print the JOBS.LST file, simply press the F3 key and enter the command TYPE B:JOBS.LST. When the printer stops, press the F3 key again.

If you are operating in Remote Access mode, press the 3 key and select P for print file. After entering the file name, press the RETURN key, and the file will be sent to the printer rather than to the screen. Pressing the F1 key will return the package to the main menu.

Ending Communications

When you have finished working with the host computer, you should sign-off (log-off) by following the host computer's own instructions. You can now

```
    Smartcom II                Hayes Microcomputer Products, Inc.

 *. Begin Communciation  4. Receive File      7. Change Printer Status  (OFF)
 2. Edit Set             5. Send File         8. Select Remote Access   (ON)
 3. Select File Command  *. Change Configuration 9. Display Disk Directory (OFF)
 A,B - Change Drive                           0. End Communication/Program
                            Press F2 for Help
 Enter Selection: 4
 Enter File Name: B:JOBS.LST
 Enter File Name: B:JOBS.LST




    ___B:JOBS.LST_____Smartmodem: CONNECT_____1200 BAUD
 Receiving Block 2
    12:42 pm            Monday January 5, 1987
```

FIGURE 9C.9
Down loading the JOB.LST file

disconnect from the telephone by pressing the 0 key and the H to "Hang up" (disconnect) without exiting Smartcom. To exit the package, press the 0 key and the E key while in the main menu.

Other Features of Smartcom

Smartcom has several additional useful features. Depending on the amount of memory your computer has, the package can save from 30 to over 40 screens of information. Anytime you are in the terminal screen mode, you can use the HOME, PgUp, PgDn, END, and arrow keys to move through the screens you have already received.

In addition to being able to review your session, you can print the results of communications beginning anywhere in the saved screens. Simply move the cursor to the location where you want to start and enter the print screen command for your computer. These screens, located in a display buffer, are not lost until you exit from Smartcom.

Summary of Electronic Communications Modules

This section has given you the opportunity to examine one or more electronic communications software packages: pfs:Access (Module 9a), Crosstalk XVI (Module 9b), and Smartcom (Module 9c). You have learned about the selected communications packages by completing tasks involved in the job hunting problem.

Comparison of Electronic Communications Software

Before attempting to answer the questions and solve the problems at the end of this section, take the time to get an overall grasp of the capabilities of each of the electronic communications software packages. Table 9s.1 provides a quick comparison of the different electronic communications packages discussed in the preceding modules. While there are similarities among the packages (for example, each one can be used with only one disk drive), there are also a number of distinct differences. (The table covers only a few of these differences.)

Some of the communications packages are easier to use than others. Some packages also have more flexibility than others in setting the communications parameters used for linking computers. Thus, you should determine which package to use based on the type of communication needed to solve your problem.

Guidelines for the Evaluation of Electronic Communications Software

Before you select an electronic communications package, answer the following questions:

- **Hardware Required**   Will the electronic communications software package run on your microcomputer? Does it work with your brand of modem, and is it able to use the full capabilities of the modem?

- **Parameter Entry**   How easy is it to enter the communications parameters? If a menu structure is used (this is most common), are parameters clearly identified? Is it clear what the possible values are for the parameters? Can the values of the parameters be changed during linkage? Is it possible to save the parameter settings in a file so that they can be reused?

TABLE 9S.1 A Comparison of Electronic Communications Packages

Characteristic	Requirement		
	pfs:Access	Crosstalk XVI	Smartcom
Operating system	MS-DOS, PC-DOS	MS-DOS, PC-DOS	MS-DOS, PC-DOS
Main memory (RAM) (minimum)	64k	96k	192k
Disk drives	1	1	1
Printer (optional)	80- or 132-column ASCII	80- or 132-column ASCII	80- or 132-column ASCII
Help function	Yes, at any time	Yes, at any time	Yes, at any time
Automatic dialing	Yes	Yes	Yes
Automatic sign-on	Yes	Yes	Yes
Baud rates	300; 1,200	110; 300; 600; 1,200; 2,400; 4,800; 9,600; 19,200	110; 300; 600; 1,200; 2,400; 4,800; 9,600;
Programmable keys	No	Yes	Yes
Up loading	Yes	Yes	Yes
Down loading	Yes	Yes	Yes
Data bits	7, 8	7, 8	7, 8
Stop bits	1, 2	1, 2	1, 2
Parity	None, odd, even	None, odd, even	None, odd, even
Duplex	Half, full	Half, full	Half, full
Emulation	TTY	TTY, TVI920, VT52, IBM 3101, VT100	TTY, VT52, VT100

- **On-screen Help**   Does the package provide on-screen help? Can the HELP menus be accessed during linkage? Are the HELP screens informative and useful, or are they very difficult to understand?
- **Baud Rates**   Does the package support the baud rates and communication standards that you will be using? If you are using your system in a local area network and are directly connected to that network, you will probably want to operate at 9,600 baud or above. Is this baud rate supported?

- **Automatic Dialing and Local Mode**   Does the communications package support both automatic dialing and manual dialing of the telephone numbers? Will the package dial using either pulse or touch-tone modes? (Although most telephone systems are now touch-tone, there are still some pulse dialing systems in operation.)

- **Programmable Procedures (Command Files and Text Files)**   Is it possible to create and save command files, containing communications parameters, and text files, containing log-on and log-off procedures? (These files should be executable using only one or two keystrokes. Their use can save time and effort if you are constantly signing-on to the same computer service.)

- **Down Loading**   Does the communications package allow you to down load files from the host computer to your disk and/or printer? (If you do not have this capability, your telephone will be busy most of the time while you read the output and hand copy the information you are trying to get from the host computer.)

- **Up Loading**   Does the communications package allow you to up load files from your computer to a host computer? (Although this feature is more dependent on the host computer's communication procedures than down loading is, once mastered, it can be a great time saver.)

- **Protocols Supported**   What protocols does the communications package support? (Not all computers use the same protocol. For a communications package to be useful, it should support several different protocols, as well as the one currently used by your host computer.)

- **Emulation**   Is this communications software package capable of emulation of different terminal types? (Some host computers look for certain types of terminals, with particular capabilities. If you are able to emulate these terminals, you can take advantage of the full capabilities of the host computer.)

- **Color Graphics**   Is your communications package capable of using color graphics? (If your computer has color graphics capabilities, you can use color to make the screen easier to read and to indicate that certain options are being used without adding additional text to the monitor.)

What Happened at ACE?

Chris attended the course at the university and became part of the team working on the communications problem at ACE. After several months of work, the team set up the computers at the stores to handle electronic communications. After a couple of training sessions, the store employees were ready to try the system out.

Chris called each store and established the computer links. It took only one day to down load all of the inventory data to Chris's computer. This certainly was an improvement over the one-and-a-half weeks it had taken to gather the data previously! As a result, it took less than a week to do the monthly inventory reports.

Module Questions

1. What electronic communications software package are you using? Is it command driven or menu driven? Does it have a help function? How is the help function used?
2. Read your electronic communications package's documentation to find out what special features are available to you. How do you use them (as part of a command file or during execution)?
3. How are the file management operations (opening, closing, naming, deleting, and saving of files) handled by your communications package? (Automatically, or must you perform some or all of these operations?)
4. Is your communications software package capable of up loading files from your computer to a host computer? What controls do you have during the up loading process?
5. What other electronic communications software packages (besides the one you are using) can be used on your microcomputer? (*Note:* Use the library or your local computer store to find the answer to this question.)

Module Problems

1. When a company in the job hunting problem announces the date it will be interviewing on campus, the placement office begins setting up an interview schedule. Two weeks before the company is to start its campus interviews, the schedule is placed in a file on the placement office's computer. As the time slots are requested, a notation is made in the file changing the entry next to the appropriate time slot from OPEN to CLOSED. You have decided to interview with Johnson Instruments, Inc., First State National Bank, and Hormell Texas Chili Co. Use your communications software package to down load the files JOHNSON.SCH, FSNBANK.SCH, and HORMELL.SCH to printer and select an interview time.
2. You are to prepare a report on the inventory levels of all audio equipment in your district for ACE. Inventory is carried in the files on each of the store's computers and at the central warehouse. There are five stores in your district, and the files are AUDIO.S1, AUDIO.S2, AUDIO.S3, AUDIO.S4, AUDIO.S5, and AUDIO.CW. Call the host computer(s) and down load to disk on your computer the current inventory levels for each store and the central warehouse. When you are done, list these files on your printer.
3. Using the electronic communications package available for your microcomputer, call another microcomputer (a host computer) and down load the results of a check of the space available on drive B of the host computer. Now down load a directory listing of the contents of both drive A and drive B of the host computer. Print the results of these operations.

SCENARIO 10

What's Going On at ACE?

Although I had learned a lot about using microcomputers during my first few months at ACE, a continuing problem interfered with my ability to use ACE's software packages efficiently. The problem was sharing the data. I often spent hours setting up spreadsheets only to have to re-enter much of the same data to use a database. I thought that there ought to be a better way.

Then Mr. Jenkins, my boss, announced that ACE was going to have a complete inventory analysis at the end of the month. On top of that, he said that Ms. Fullerton liked the work I had done earlier so much that she wanted a report on inventory activities every month. Now, I really began to worry about the time needed to re-enter the data for each analysis.

Right about this time, I overheard a conversation between Ms. Allison, of Computer Services, and Ms. Robertson, of Accounting. They were talking about something called "integrated systems." It sounded as though there *was* a way to enter data into the system and then access it in a word processing mode, a spreadsheet mode, a database mode, and so on. I was interested and called Ms. Allison later to find out more about "integrated systems." Ms. Allison then invited me to attend a training seminar on integrated systems that one of her staff was planning for the accounting department.

Chapter Ten
Applications Software:
Integrated Systems

Chapter Objectives

When you have completed this chapter, you will be able to:

- Define the term *integrated system*
- Describe the types of processes used in integrated systems
- Describe the method used to achieve integration
- Identify the means by which data is shared by applications packages

Introduction to Integrated Systems

Any time you are dealing with data or information that must be analyzed and reported to someone else, you will need to use the full range of capabilities of the computer. For example, suppose you are managing a health club. You want to keep records of all your members including data about height, weight, and other general health considerations. Because you want to continually update the data at set time intervals and record it, you use a database. To analyze the data and turn it into useful information, you use a spreadsheet. To present the information to the members of the club, you use a word processor and a graphics package. If each of these packages operates independently, you have to re-enter the data every time you want to manipulate it. Obviously, there should be a better way, and there is—integrated software. If you are using an integrated software system, you can enter the data into a database, extract the data needed to do the analysis in the spreadsheet, use the data to create the appropriate charts, and finally use the word processing function to bring all the work together to print your report.

Historical Development

The idea of integrating software occurred in the early 1960s, with the growth in use of large mainframe computers. The development of Lotus 1-2-3 in the early 1980s focused attention on the integration of microcomputer software. Microcomputers commonly in use before the development of Lotus had severe limitations—primarily in terms of internal memory—relative to today's machines. Thus, with more advanced microcomputer hardware came the opportunity to expand the capabilities of microcomputer software. By the mid-1980s, several firms were producing what are referred to as totally integrated software packages. Symphony is an example of such a package.

Definition of Integrated Software Systems

You are already familiar with the concept of "stand-alone" packages. Application packages such as WordStar, Multiplan, dBASE II and III, and Chart Master are "stand-alone" packages; that is, they are specifically designed to perform a single process, and data entered into these packages is not designed to be easily shared with other packages. In other words, these applications don't directly *integrate* (share data) with other packages.

In a management information systems (MIS) environment, you would expect data that was used in one application to be frequently used in others. For example, you have seen that the company names in the job hunting problem have been used in word processing, spreadsheet, and database packages. The job offer amounts have been used in spreadsheet, database, and graphics applications. However, each time you needed data for a new application, you probably had to re-enter it. Thus, "stand-alone" applications, although extremely useful, have not solved (or have only partially solved) problems that require the manipulation of data in different ways.

Integrated software systems are designed to support multiple application areas. Once data has been entered into an integrated system, it can be accessed by a variety of processes. For example, data entered into an integrated system can be manipulated in a spreadsheet form and later reported by using a word processing facility. Data can be manipulated by a database processor, and graphic presentations of the data can be generated later.

There are three primary and very different means by which word processing, spreadsheets, databases, and so on are integrated with one another—by **file exchange, primary feature,** or **design.** Integration by file exchange means that each function operates independently of the others, and integration is achieved by sharing data through files. Integration by primary feature means that one function of the integrated system has been selected for special treatment, and all other functions interface with that function. Integration by design represents a fully integrated system. The modules that follow Chapter 10 cover each type of integration.

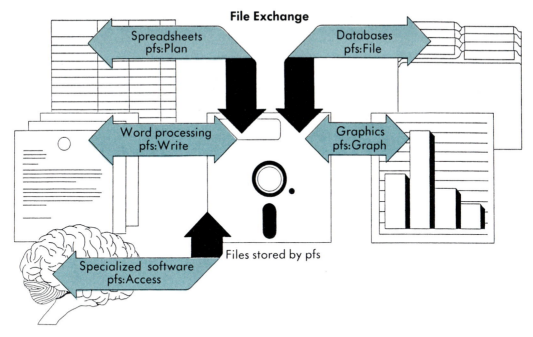

FIGURE 10.1
pfs:Series — integration by file exchange

Integration by File Exchange

The first type of integration is achieved through the exchange or sharing of files. As shown in Figure 10.1, the pfs:Series (covered in Module 10a) is organized around the use of common files. For example, when a file is produced by pfs:File, it can be accepted by pfs:Write. The same is true of the other features of the pfs:Series. Because of its design, the pfs:Series has one primary advantage over the other integrated packages — each piece can be purchased separately and operated independently.

Integration by Primary Feature

Lotus 1-2-3 represented one of the first attempts at integrated software packages. It is an example of a package that achieves integration through the use of a primary feature — the spreadsheet. As you might already have noticed, Lotus has been used as a spreadsheet in Module 6b, as a database in Module 7b, and as a graphics package in Module 8b. Thus, Lotus represents another type of integration. As shown in Figure 10.2, Lotus is integrated around the spreadsheet, with all other functions of secondary importance (and treatment). (Its spreadsheet function is very well developed; however, the database and graphics functions are a bit more Spartan.) If you are

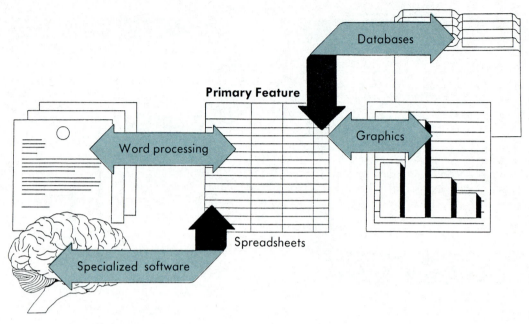

FIGURE 10.2
Lotus 1-2-3 — integration by primary feature

primarily interested in spreadsheets and have only occasional uses for databases and graphics, then Lotus may be perfectly suited to your needs.

Integration by Design

Packages that have been integrated by design represent some of the most recent advances in microcomputer software. Integration by design means that all of the functions of the package are supplied as one piece of software: each of the functions is available on request (see Figure 10.3). You may go from one function to another with little or no difficulty. In fact, the package might provide for multiple windows, whereby each window provides a different "picture" of the data — one window being used for word processing, another for a spreadsheet, still another for a database,

and so on. Module 10c discusses Symphony, an example of integration by design.

Because packages that have been integrated by design are typically the newest type of software, they are also among the most expensive. Furthermore, because all functions are combined into a single piece of software, you have access to all functions whether you want them or not. Finally, these packages are usually rather large and require more internal memory (and perhaps some hardware enhancements) than is typical of most other software packages.

Functions of Integrated Software Systems

Typical integrated software systems support a variety of processes. However, the

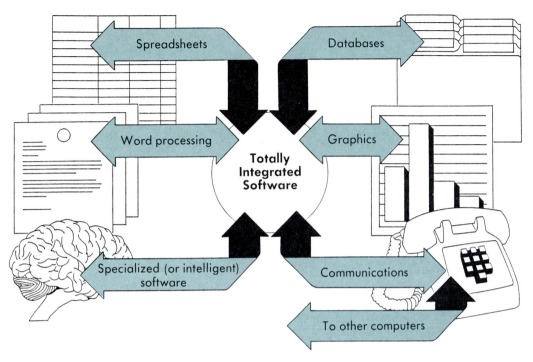

FIGURE 10.3
A totally integrated system — integration by design

Word Processing

Chapter 5 described the types of functions normally supported by word processing packages. Most of these functions are supported by "stand-alone" packages; however, integrated packages usually support only the basic word processing functions. For example most "stand-alone" word processing systems support print enhancements such as boldface and underline, but some integrated packages do not provide these options. Other features that may not

degree of support may not be as sophisticated as that provided by "stand-alone" packages.

be available with an integrated system are page headings and footings, find and replace, and spell checking. In fact, some of the more limited integrated systems provide extremely limited word processing capabilities — for example, word wrapping may not be available. Thus, word processing is not usually a strong point of integrated systems.

Spreadsheets

Although some integrated systems are not well suited to word processing uses, almost all of them provide ample support for spreadsheets. Because spreadsheets are one of the most popular types of software (see Chapter 6), an integrated package that does not support spreadsheet use has a very limited buyer's market. Thus, the spreadsheet function is one of the best developed functions in integrated systems. You should not only be able to develop a spreadsheet and perform computations based on the contents of groups of cells, but you should also be able to use formulas, mathematical and statistical functions, row and column copying, row and column movement, and so on.

Databases

Integrated systems are usually designed to support almost all the database functions mentioned in Chapter 7; that is, databases can be created, altered, and searched. However, if an integrated system does have a limitation, it will likely be in the area of combining two or more databases into a new one. Thus, features like the join function may not be available. Furthermore, integrated databases are likely to be file oriented rather than a true relational database.

Graphics

Most integrated systems are capable of producing a wide range of graphic displays (see Chapter 8). Pie, bar, and line charts are the most prevalent. However, extended functions such as stacked bar charts and selectivity in creating titles and legends are sometimes not included. Thus, you may not be able to produce all kinds of graphics or control the graphics output as easily with an integrated system as you can with a "stand-alone" system.

Communications

Integrated software is supposed to eliminate the need for other software packages;

it is not designed to eliminate the need to communicate with other computers. However, most integrated packages go beyond simply providing communications capabilities (see Chapter 9). They will capture and store the data coming from other computers in a form that is immediately usable by the integrated system. In addition, they provide the flexibility to set baud rate, parity, and stop bits as well as allowing up loading and down loading.

Specialized Functions and "Intelligent" Software

Some integrated systems go beyond supplying the capabilities of word processing, spreadsheets, databases, and graphics. For example, Lotus 1-2-3 can create and store macros. You will recall that macros are used to save and execute frequently used spreadsheet procedures. (Other types of difficult or very involved procedures can also be saved as macros.) Creating a macro involves using a procedural language to save a sequence of selected commands. After the commands have been saved, they can be executed anytime the macro is selected; the use of one command—the macro—can execute a large number of saved commands. However, special functions of this type are not unique to Lotus or even to integrated systems in general. For example, dBASE II and III and R:base 4000 and 5000, as well as many other spreadsheet packages, include a procedural language that can be used to create, save, and execute procedures or functions. With the procedural language, you can even write application programs or complete application systems, as described in Chapter 3.

Other integrated packages provide templates. As mentioned in Chapter 6, templates are special functions or procedures that are generally used in spreadsheets to customize the package. For example, templates can be used with Lotus to solve engineering or mathematically oriented problems. Templates can also be used in graphics packages to draw program flowcharts or house plans.

Although integrated packages provide the capability of both data processing and information processing functions (see Chapter 1), to offer a complete management information system (MIS), they must also include decision support system (DSS) functions. For microcomputers, this area might be called "intelligent software." R:base—described in Module 7d—is linked to a companion piece of intelligent software known as Clout. Clout provides a means of interacting with a database using a natural language, such as English. Thus, Clout provides the means for creating an English vocabulary of frequently used words and phrases that can be entered in place of more direct, less English-like database commands. In addition, Clout represents a first attempt to provide artificial intelligence capabilities. This means that your computer can "think" on a limited basis. In the case of Clout, the computer "thinks" by making associations within the natural language that you have not supplied. For example, you might enter a phrase that does not exist in the Clout vocabulary. Clout will attempt to determine what you mean based on its existing vocabulary and might respond with a phrase like "do you mean . . . ?" Clout represents only the beginning of the use of natural languages and artificial intelligence. In the future, you can expect computers to perform a higher level of "thinking" than represented by a "do you mean" response. Someday, in the not-too-distant future, you can expect to see phrases on your video screen like "It looks to me as though you have a _____ problem. Did you think about solving it by the _____ method?" "Did you notice that there is a _____ relationship between _____ and _____?" or "Don't you think it's about time to _____?"

Interfacing with Other Application Packages

Almost all packages have a means of reproducing file contents in at least a partially shareable form; that is, some—but not all—other packages should be able to use the files. Thus, it is possible for "stand-alone" software to interface (share data) not only with integrated systems, as shown in Figure 10.4, but possibly among "stand-alone" packages as well.

The use of ASCII (American Standard Code for Information Interchange) files, or "print" files, (files composed totally of characters) is the most popular way to facilitate data sharing. ASCII is the most popular microcomputer character coding scheme, and it can be used by almost all application packages. As you know, many packages can print reports on the printer or save them in a disk file. When data is placed in a file of this type, using ASCII, it is stripped of all special symbols or coding used by the package. Thus, an ASCII file is a pure text file—a file composed of only the text or characters that you would see if you printed the file.

The second most popular way to share data is through the use of data interchange format (DIF) files. The data placed in a DIF file is fundamentally different from that placed in an ASCII file. DIF files are composed of rows and columns, which makes these files a natural means of transferring spreadsheet data between packages. (Some database packages can also produce and ac-

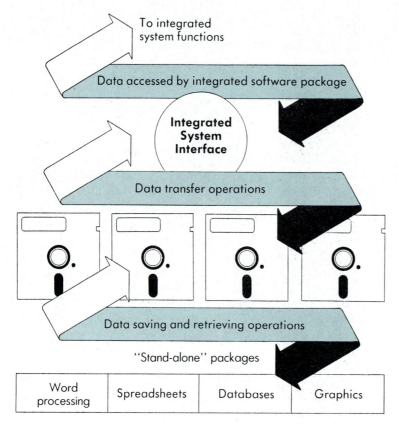

FIGURE 10.4
Interfacing with "stand-alone" packages

cept DIF files.) However, only data can be transferred when DIF files are used. For example, the translation of data in a spreadsheet package into a DIF file results in the translation of formulas and expressions into the values they represent. Not all formulas and expressions can be translated into a meaningful form for a DIF file. Thus, every element within a package may not be translated.

The primary disadvantage of using DIF files is that the data transfer may only work in one direction. You may be able to

transfer data from a database to a spreadsheet, but you may not be able to perform the reverse operation.

The third type of file that can be used in data sharing is the symbolic linkage (SYLK) file. The SYLK file is the least-used format for data exchange. When data is placed into this format, not only is the data saved, but so are any special characteristics of the data, including format, formulas, expressions, and so on. Data stored in SYLK files can be transferred in both directions between the packages capable of producing and accepting the SYLK file format; that is, data can be manipulated in a spreadsheet package, transferred to a SYLK file, entered into a database package, manipulated in the database, transferred to another SYLK file, and transferred back into the spreadsheet package.

Most "stand-alone" packages are capable of producing files in at least one of the preceding three data-exchange formats. Some "stand-alone" packages can interface with two of the formats, and a few are capable of interacting with all three. Integrated systems may be capable of accepting all three formats; however, some integrated packages provide no data sharing or conversion options because the packages themselves are supposed to encompass all the necessary functions.

Uses of Integrated Systems

Obviously, integrated packages are useful if you need to process data in a variety of ways. In addition, the extended capabilities of integrated packages may solve problems that "stand-alone" packages cannot solve.

In a business office, for example, a secretary could use an integrated package's word processing feature to produce letters and other business correspondence while an accountant is using the spreadsheet feature to produce an office budget. When the accountant needs an accounting report, the spreadsheet information can be transferred to the secretary for inclusion in a report.

At the same time, an inventory control manager could manipulate an inventory database and pass summary information about the database to the accountant's spreadsheet. Perhaps the office manager needs to make a presentation to the district manager and wants to use a graphic format

to display the activity associated with the inventory database, as well as a graphic display of how the office budget is allocated.

Because integrated software packages for microcomputers are relatively new, they are not yet in common use. However, a local telephone company in the western United States has found that it can operate its entire inventory control and reporting system using integrated software. The inventory levels of each item based on sales, usage, items returned, and orders received are kept current using the database feature. The history of sales (depletion from inventory) of an item and its current inventory level are used in a spreadsheet to calculate the quantity to order. Orders and reports on inventory activity are produced using the word processing function of the package. Graphics are used to display the inventory activity in the reports. Finally, the telecommunications capabilities of the package are used to get sales information from the computers at regional stores.

Chapter Summary

Integrated software systems support a variety of applications—including word processing, spreadsheets, databases, and graphics—and they may have certain special features—for example, templates, macros, and artificial intelligence. These systems can be integrated by file exchange, by primary feature, or by design. It is clear that integrated software packages will gradually replace the collection of "stand-alone" packages being used today. This replacement will be fastest in the areas where the same data must be treated in many different ways.

Chapter Key Terms

Artificial
intelligence

American Standard
Code for
Information
Interchange
(ASCII)

Data interchange
format (DIF)

Data processing

Decision support
system (DSS)

Design integration

File exchange
integration

Information
processing

Macro

Management
information
system (MIS)

Natural language

Primary feature
integration

Print enhancement

"Stand-alone"
system

Symbolic linkage
(SYLK)

Template

Window

Chapter Questions

1. What is an integrated system, and how does it differ from a "stand-alone" system? What functions are generally found in an integrated system?

2. Describe the three different methods of achieving integration. How does each of these three methods influence the design of the integrated system?

3. Describe three different ways data can be shared by application packages. How do these methods differ from true integrated software?

4. What is natural language? What problems do you see for the development of integrated software that uses a natural language?

5. Explain the difference between templates and macros. How might each be used in an integrated software package?

6. What capabilities must an integrated software package have to meet your needs? Would this package eliminate your need for any other software packages?

7. Name five professions that could use an integrated software package. How would each of these professions use the package?

8. What data processing functions are performed by integrated software systems? What information processing functions are performed by (or may soon be performed by) integrated software systems?

9. Why would the use of windows be important in an integrated software system?

10. Will integrated software systems replace "stand-alone" systems? Under what conditions would you expect this replacement to take place? Under what conditions would you not expect this to occur?

Modules/Chapter Ten
Integrated Systems

M10

M10a pfs:Software Series Integrated
Software Publishing Corporation
1901 Landings Drive
Mountain View, CA 94043

M10b Lotus 1-2-3 Integrated
Lotus Development Corporation
161 First Street
Cambridge, MA 02142

M10c Symphony
Lotus Development Corporation
161 First Street
Cambridge, MA 02142

Introduction to Integrated Systems Modules

In the modules that follow you will be given the opportunity to learn about one (or more) of the following popular integrated systems packages available for microcomputers: pfs:Series (Module 10a), Lotus 1-2-3 (Module 10b), and Symphony (Module 10c).

Problem Statement for Integrated Systems Modules

You will use the job hunting problem to work through the functions of the integrated package—that is, to perform database queries, perform spreadsheet manipulations, generate a graph, and produce a memorandum through word processing.

As students go through the job hunting process, they may be assisted by the school placement service. The placement service is responsible for inviting companies to come on campus, providing job candidate credentials, and setting up on-campus interviews. At the end of the recruiting season, the placement service frequently asks job candidates to provide an evaluation of their success in the job hunting process.

The recruiting season is now over, you have found the right job, and your placement service has just requested a report on your success. The data needed for this problem is presented in Appendix A. The following list represents some of the ways you can use an integrated systems package to prepare your report.

1. Enter the data provided in Appendix A into a single file or database.
2. Perform a count of the number of companies in the list.
3. Evaluate the "status" of the list of companies, and produce a pie chart illustrating the number of companies in each "status" category.
4. Create a table showing the location of each company (location and city) from which an offer was received, the amount of the dollar offer, and the amount of the total offer (the dollar offer plus all fringe benefits).
5. Compute an average for both the dollar offer and the total offer.
6. Produce a memorandum to the placement service, as illustrated below:

MEMORANDUM

TO: Placement Service

FROM: (your name)

DATE: 03/15/8X

SUBJECT: Report on job offers received during the
         past interview season

During the past interviewing season, I had
contact with 21 companies. The attached chart
illustrates the offer status of these contacts.

The table below provides a summary of the offers
that I received. The second and third columns
show the approximate location of each company.
The fourth column represents the actual salary
offer by each company. The fifth column
represents the amount of salary plus all fringe
benefits. The average dollar offer and the

average total offer are shown at the bottom of the fourth and fifth columns, respectively.

Company	Location		Offer	Total Offer
1	South	Dallas	$19,000.00	$22,822.00
2	Mid-cities	Dallas	$19,200.00	$23,022.00
3	North	Dallas	$19,100.00	$22,922.00
4	North	Dallas	$18,950.00	$24,561.00
5	Mid-cities	Denton	$22,000.00	$27,500.00
6	North	Dennison	$20,000.00	$27,275.00
7	East	Ft. Worth	$19,300.00	$21,986.00
8	East	Tulsa	$15,670.00	$17,678.00
		Average	$19,152.50	$23,470.78

I deeply appreciate the help and cooperation you have given me during the past interview season. Your efforts have been instrumental in helping me to find employment with just the right company.

Thank you.

Attachments (1)

pfs: Software Series Integrated

Learning to Use pfs as an Integrated System

Modules in previous chapters introduced you to the various packages that make up the pfs: Software Series. Module 5a examined the word processing package (pfs:Write and pfs:Proof), Module 6a presented the spreadsheet package (pfs:Plan), Module 7a covered the database package (pfs:File and pfs:Report), and Module 8a presented the graphics package (pfs:Graph). This module will examine the integration of these packages into a complete information system that will meet most, if not all, of your data or information needs.

In general, the pfs: Software Series represents a system that is integrated through the ability to share files. In fact, the series actually shares two types of files. First, the word processing package can read print files that have been saved on disk by the other packages in the series. This means that you can include the output of one of the other packages in the series in a document (a report or a letter) created in pfs:Write.

The second type of file shared by the all of the packages in the series is the SYLK file created by pfs:File that contains the data entered in the database. This means that in most cases you need enter the data you are going to use only once through pfs:File to use it in any of the other packages in the series.

Before you proceed with this module, review Module 5a (pfs:Write and pfs:Proof), Module 6a (pfs:Plan), Module 7a (pfs:File and pfs:Report), and Module 8a (pfs:Graph). The following presentation is based on the assumption that you are familiar with each of these independent packages in the pfs: Software Series.

Start with the computer's system disk in drive A. If you are using a system that has two disk drives, a disk prepared to hold your data should be in drive B. After you have booted your system, replace the system disk with the disk containing the program in the pfs: Software Series that you want to use.

Solving the Job Hunting Problem

The remaining sections in this module are devoted to solving the job hunting problem. You may want to refer to the problem statement in the Introduction

to Integrated Software Systems Modules before you continue. Also, remember that the data used in this problem can be found in Appendix A.

Loading Data into pfs — pfs:File

To begin the job hunting problem, you need to load data. Because this data is to be used for multiple purposes, it should be entered in the package that has the highest capability to share the data — pfs:File. Module 7a explains how to build your files and enter the data needed for the job hunting problem. However, because you are now planning to use this data in the other packages in the pfs series, you must enter the data a bit differently.

Because all of the other packages in the series are going to access the data stored by pfs:File, the identifying fields in each record should be unique. One of the identifying fields used is the Company Name. Johnson Instruments, Inc., appears in the data three times for three different job offers at three different locations. Because the name is repeated three times, it is not a unique identifier. To overcome this problem, simply enter the Company Names as Johnson 1, Johnson 2, and Johnson 3.

Also, recall from Module 6a (pfs:Plan) that the column widths of a spreadsheet cannot exceed 25 characters. Therefore, you should truncate the name of any company that exceeds 25 characters. (The Company Name Lewis & Melts Mortgage Company should be entered as Lewis & Melts Mortgage Co, and the Company Name Hormell Texas Chili Company should be entered as Hormell Texas Chili Co).

One of the requirements of the job hunting problem was to report the number of companies contacted. The simplest way to generate this number is to choose option 4 (SEARCH/UPDATE) from the PFS:FILE FUNCTION MENU and press the F10 key when the RETRIEVE SPEC screen is displayed. Pressing the F10 key every time a record is displayed will result in the screen shown in Figure 10a.1, which shows a count of the number of records in your file. Of course, you could also generate a report using the COUNT function described in Module 7a.

Integrating the Database and the Graphics Functions — Preparing a Pie Chart

One of your first reporting requirements is to indicate the distribution of the offer status for the companies contacted. A pie chart is the most useful form for this presentation. To produce the chart, exit from the pfs:File package by choosing option 7 in the PFS:FILE FUNCTION MENU. Then replace the pfs:File disk with the disk containing the pfs:Graph package, and load pfs:Graph into memory by entering the command GRAPH.

Pfs:Graph can read data directly from files created by pfs:File. To do this, simply choose option 3 in the pfs:Graph GET/EDIT DATA MENU. Specify the

```
                          Forms found: 21


                          Press F10 to continue
```

FIGURE 10A.1
Counting the companies contacted

name of the file where the data is located and press the F10 key. You will then be presented with a pfs:File RETRIEVE SPEC screen. Enter the retrieval specifications exactly as you would in pfs:File. Because you want to retrieve all of the records in the file, press the F10 key. You will next be presented with the GRAPH SPEC screen, where you indicate the fields to be used for the X and Y variables in the chart.

To indicate which field is to be used for the X variable and its format, enter an X next to that field name followed by two dashes (--) and the data format code (N for numeric, I for identifier, and so on as explained in Module 8a). For the pie chart, enter X--I next to the field labeled STATUS.

Next, indicate which field is to be used as the Y variable by entering a Y next to that field name. The field used for the Y variable must be numeric. If you do not specify a Y data item, pfs:Graph will count the number of forms that exist for each status category and enter the count as the Y value of that category. The graph specifications needed to retrieve the data for the pie chart are shown in Figure 10a.2.

Press the F10 key, and the package will retrieve the requested data. You may now define the chart and display it exactly as described in Module 8a. This time when you are ready to save the chart, choose option 3 (SAVE PICTURE) in the GET/SAVE/REMOVE MENU and indicate the file B:CHART as the

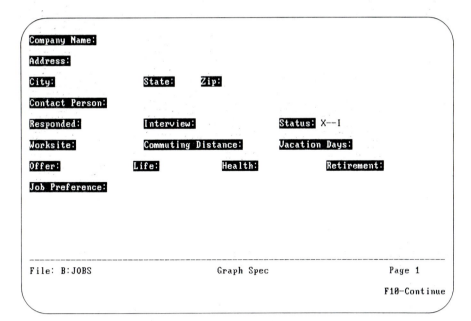

Company Name:

Address:

City: State: Zip:

Contact Person:

Responded: Interview: Status: X--I

Worksite: Commuting Distance: Vacation Days:

Offer: Life: Health: Retirement:

Job Preference:

File: B:JOBS   Graph Spec   Page 1

                                                        F10-Continue

FIGURE 10A.2
Entering the graph specifications

name of the file to be used to save the chart. The new pie chart can now be used by pfs:Write as part of your memorandum.

Integrating the Spreadsheet and the Database — An Analysis of Job Offers

The next activity to be performed is to produce a table containing information about only those companies from which a job offer was received. To do this, exit the pfs:Graph package and replace that disk with the disk containing the pfs:Plan package. Now load pfs:Plan into memory and use the information presented in Module 6a to design the spreadsheet shown in Figure 10a.3.

This spreadsheet has been set so that the minimum column width is ten characters and the global format is 2,$. The column titles entered, besides the group title LOCATION, are OFFER, TOTAL OFFER, LIFE, HEALTII, and RETIREMENT. In addition, the formulas for AVERAGE COMPANY and TOTAL OFFER have also been entered. The only operation left to do is to enter the data into the spreadsheet.

To enter the data, press the ESCape key, return to the PFS:PLAN MAIN MENU, and select option 2. When the GET MENU appears on the screen, select option 3. Then press the TAB key and enter the name of the file where

```
                           ┌──────Location──────┐
          Headings         │  Site  ││  City    ││  Offer  ││Total Offer ║
COMPANY
Johnson 1                   South     Dallas
Johnson 2                   Mid-cities Dallas
Johnson 3                   North     Dallas
Matt's Films, Inc.          North     Dallas
Lewis & Melts Mortgage Co   Mid-cities Denton
Ethyl & Jung, DDS           North     Dennison
Hormell Texas Chili Co.     East      Ft. Worth
Nephi's Hopi Crafts         East      Tulsa

AVERAGE




 F1-Help    Working Copy                    Replacing    2% Full    R1    C1
```

FIGURE 10A.3
Designing the spreadsheet

```
 Company Name: R

 Address:

 City:              State:      Zip:

 Contact Person:

 Responded:         Interview:              Status:

 Worksite:          Commuting Distance:     Vacation Days:

 Offer: CV          Life: CV        Health: CV          Retirement: CV

 Job Preference:




 ─────────────────────────────────────────────────────────────────────
 File: JOBS                   Plan Spec                   Page 1

 F1-Help                    Esc-Main Menu                 F10-Continue
```

FIGURE 10A.4
Entering the plan specifications

```
Currently defined views:              (None)

              View to define/edit: PRINT

View ------->      +        +         +         +
  :           ------Location------
  ↓ Headings    Site  ‖ City  ‖  Offer  ‖Total Offer‖    Life
     COMPANY
       1       South    Dallas  $19,000.00 $ 22,822.00 $    135.00
       2       Mid-cities Dallas $19,200.00 $ 23,022.00 $    135.00
       3       North    Dallas  $19,100.00 $ 22,922.00 $    135.00
       4       North    Dallas  $18,950.00 $ 24,561.00 $    155.00
       5       Mid-cities Denton $22,000.00 $ 27,500.00 $    500.00
       6       North    Dennison $20,000.00 $ 27,275.00 $    325.00
       7       East     Ft. Worth $19,300.00 $ 21,986.20 $    164.00
       8       East     Tulsa   $15,670.00 $ 17,678.00 $    250.00


     AVERAGE                     $19,152.50 $ 23,470.78 $    224.88




                 Use "+" to include, OR "-" to exclude
  F1-Help    Working Copy                    Replacing    2% Full    R1    C1
```

FIGURE 10A.5
Defining the PRINT view of the spreadsheet

your data is stored. When the pfs:File RETRIEVE SPEC screen appears, enter >0 next to the field labeled OFFER. This will cause all companies that have made you an offer to be retrieved (including the companies you have refused). Pressing the F10 key will cause the PLAN SPEC screen to appear.

Using this screen, enter three items of information for the fields being used in the spreadsheet. Label the fields used to match the row headings with an R, the fields used to match the column headings with a C, and the fields that contain the values to be read with a V. The labels R and V can be used together, as can the labels C and V. However, R and C may not be used together. If you enter the plan specifications as shown in Figure 10a.4 and press the the F10 key, your spreadsheet will appear on the screen with all the calculations completed.

To make the final adjustments to your spreadsheet, replace the company names with numbers and define the view that you want to print. To define a view with pfs:Plan, press the F8 key and enter the name of the view to be defined and a plus sign (+) above the columns to be included in the view, as illustrated in Figure 10a.5.

To print the spreadsheet to disk so that it can be included in the memorandum you are sending to the school's placement service, select the PRINT

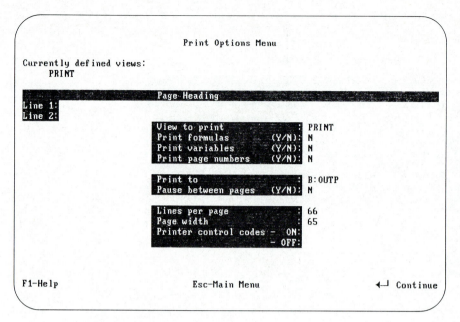

FIGURE 10A.6
Entering the Print Options for the spreadsheet

OPTIONS MENU and enter the information shown in Figure 10a.6. Note that the view of the spreadsheet to be printed has been specified, the Print page numbers option has been turned off, and "Print to" location has been entered as a disk file B:OUTP, and the Page width has been set to 65. If your file is to be read by pfs:Write, the page width must be 78 characters or less. Now press the RETURN key to print your spreadsheet.

Integrating Word Processing — Creating the Text Part of the Memo

To begin the entry of text, exit pfs:Plan and replace that disk with the disk containing the pfs:Write package. Using Module 5a as a guide, begin entering the memorandum until you reach the end of the first paragraph, where you will insert the pie chart you created using pfs:Graph. To do this, enter the print instruction *GRAPH b:chart*, as shown in Figure 10a.7.

At the end of the following paragraph, insert the spreadsheet you created using pfs:Plan. This can be done by entering the print instruction *JOIN B:OUTP* or by pressing the F9 key to append the file B:OUTP, as was done in Figure 10a.7.

```
During the interview process, I had contact with 21 companies.  The
chart below illustrates the offer status of these contacts.
*GRAPH b:chart*
The table below provides a summary of the offers that I reveived.  The
second and third columns show the approximate location of each company.
The fourth represents the actual salary offer of each company.  The
fifth column represents the amount of salary plus all fringe benefits.
The average dollar offer and the average total offer are shown at the
bottom of the fourth and fifth columns respectively.


                    ------Location-------
                      Site      City       Offer     Total Offer
                    ---------- ---------- ----------- -----------
          COMPANY
             1       South      Dallas    $19,000.00  $ 22,822.00
             2       Mid-cities Dallas    $19,200.00  $ 23,022.00
             3       North      Dallas    $19,100.00  $ 22,922.00
             4       North      Dallas    $18,950.00  $ 24,561.00
             5       Mid-cities Denton    $22,000.00  $ 27,500.00
             6       North      Dennison  $20,000.00  $ 27,275.00
             7       East       Ft. Worth $19,300.00  $ 21,986.20
```

```
MEMO                 Inserting                5% Full    Line 27 of Page 1
F1-Help
```

FIGURE 10A.7
**Getting the graph and the spreadsheet
into the memo**

Now finish the memorandum and send it to the printer using the instructions in Module 5a. Figure 10a.8 shows the completed report. Remember to indicate on the PRINT MENU that you are joining a pfs:Graph to the document. Also, don't forget to save the document if you want a permanent record of what you have done.

Other Features of the pfs Series

In addition to providing a proofreading package (pfs:Proof, discussed in Module 5a), pfs:Write can also join a file created from pfs:File and use selected fields to print form letters and other documents.

Pfs.Access (Module 9a) can be used to communicate with other computers. The package will dial the telephone for you, "sign on" to the computer called, and send it files created by the other packages in the series. In addition, pfs:Access will allow you to save on disk or send to the printer the data being sent to you by the other computer. Pfs:Access will even encrypt a file using a privacy code of your choice so that only someone who knows your privacy code can read it.

```
                    M E M O R A N D U M

TO:   Placement Service
FROM:      (your name)
DATE:      03/15/8x
SUBJECT:   Report on job offers received during the past interview
           season

During the interview process, I had contact with 21 companies.  The
chart below illustrates the offer status of these contacts.

  STATUS OF COMPANIES IN JOB HUNT
```

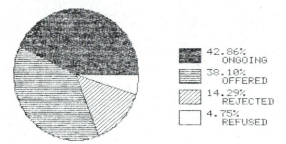

```
                       42.86%
                        ONGOING
                       38.10%
                        OFFERED
                       14.29%
                        REJECTED
                       4.75%
                        REFUSED
```

```
The table below provides a summary of the offers that I received.  The
second and third columns show the approximate location of each company.
The fourth represents the actual salary offer of each company.  The
fifth column represents the amount of salary plus all fringe benefits.
The average dollar offer and the average total offer are shown at the
bottom of the fourth and fifth columns, respectively.
```

| | ------Location------- | | Offer | Total Offer |
	Site	City		
COMPANY				
1	South	Dallas	$19,000.00	$ 22,822.00
2	Mid-cities	Dallas	$19,200.00	$ 23,022.00
3	North	Dallas	$19,100.00	$ 22,922.00
4	North	Dallas	$18,950.00	$ 24,561.00
5	Mid-cities	Denton	$22,000.00	$ 27,500.00
6	North	Dennison	$20,000.00	$ 27,275.00
7	East	Ft. Worth	$19,300.00	$ 21,986.20
8	East	Tulsa	$15,670.00	$ 17,678.00
	Average		$19,152.50	$ 23,470.78

```
I deeply appreciate the help and cooperation you have given me during
the past interview season.  Your efforts have been instrumental in
helping me to find employment with just the right company.

Thank you.
```

FIGURE 10A.8
The job offers report

Lotus 1-2-3 Integrated

Learning to Use Lotus as an Integrated System

Previous modules covered the various functions of Lotus: spreadsheet (Module 6b), database (Module 7b), and graphics (Module 8b). This module covers the integration of these functions of Lotus as well as its word processing capabilities.

Lotus's primary strength is the spreadsheet function. Indeed, this function is better developed in Lotus than it is in most other packages. The second most powerful feature of Lotus is graphics. Lotus has most of the features of "stand-alone" graphics packages. One of the weaker functions of Lotus involves database manipulations. Finally, the weakest of the standard functions is word processing. It might be said that Lotus does not handle word processing, but rather text editing. As you will see later, when compared to those of "stand-alone" packages, the word processing capabilities of Lotus are rather primitive. As mentioned earlier in Chapter 10, Lotus represents a package that is integrated according to a primary feature — the spreadsheet function. Thus, many of the operations performed will be visible on the screen in what appears to be a spreadsheet mode.

Before you proceed, review Module 6b (Lotus 1-2-3 Spreadsheet), Module 7b (Lotus 1-2-3 Database), and Module 8b (Lotus 1-2-3 Graphics). The following presentation is based on the assumption that you are familiar with each of these somewhat independent features of Lotus.

When entering Lotus, you should have a Lotus system disk in drive A and a data disk in drive B. To start the software, simply enter LOTUS. As a result, you will see the Lotus Access System Menu, as shown in Figure 10b.1. In previous Lotus modules, you performed most of the operations by selecting 1-2-3 from this menu. The same situation applies to using Lotus as an integrated package. (Your only other exposure to using the other selections in The Access System Menu was in Module 8b, when you selected PrintGraph to produce charts on the printer. You will have an opportunity to become familiar with the functions associated with the other options later in this module.)

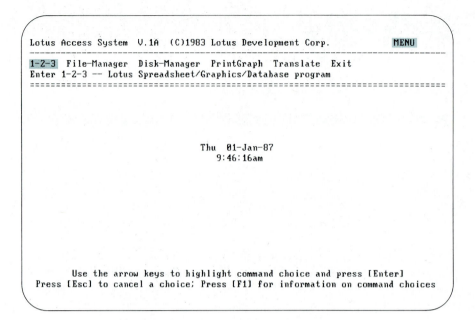

```
Lotus Access System  V.1A  (C)1983 Lotus Development Corp.        MENU
----------------------------------------------------------------------
1-2-3  File-Manager  Disk-Manager  PrintGraph  Translate  Exit
Enter 1-2-3 -- Lotus Spreadsheet/Graphics/Database program
======================================================================




                          Thu  01-Jan-87
                             9:46:16am







          Use the arrow keys to highlight command choice and press [Enter]
       Press [Esc] to cancel a choice; Press [F1] for information on command choices
```

FIGURE 10B.1
The Lotus Access System Menu

Solving the Job Hunting Problem

The remaining sections in this module are devoted to solving the job hunting problem. You may want to refer to the problem statement in the Introduction to Integrated Systems Modules before you continue. Also, remember that the data in this problem can be found in Appendix A.

Loading Data into Lotus

To begin the job hunting problem, you need to load the data. Because the data is to be used for multiple purposes, it should be entered according to the most limiting function based on the data—the database function. Recall, from Module 7b, that you had a limitation of one row on the column headings when the database functions were to be used. Thus, as shown in Figure 10b.2, the data has been entered in a format that is suitable for manipulation by the Lotus database function.

In the job hunting problem, you were asked to report the number of companies contacted. Figure 10b.3 indicates, in cell I25, that 21 companies have been contacted. Although there are a number of ways to obtain this count,

```
A1:  ^Company Name                                              READY

            A                        B                  C
 1      Company Name              Address              City
 2  -----------------------------------------------------------
 3  Johnson Instruments, Inc.   P. O. Box 1234       Dallas
 4  Johnson Instruments, Inc.   P. O. Box 1234       Dallas
 5  Johnson Instruments, Inc.   P. O. Box 1234       Dallas
 6  Champion Cowboy Supply      126 Hollyhill Road   Garland
 7  General Electronics, Inc.   87634 Dynamics Way   Ft. Worth
 8  First State National Bank   302 Central Expressway Dallas
 9  Lewis & Melts Mortgage Co.  1 Bank Plaza         Denton
10  Ethyl & Jung, DDS           23 Molar Hill Lane   Dennison
11  Aerospace Education Center  1423 Jupiter Road    Garland
12  ABC Stereo Warehouse        3434 Sound Place     Dallas
13  WTBS Channel 5 TV           9826 Neonoise Court  Plano
14  Hormell Texas Chili Company 1 Hots Place         Ft. Worth
15  Children's Museum           Look Out Point       Ft. Worth
16  FBI                         10-20 Parole Street  Arlington
17  Mosteq Computer Company     1428 Wozniak Way     Farmers Branch
18  Nephi's Hopi Crafts         16 Alma, Suite 34    Tulsa
19  Kelly Construction Company  1414 Jupiter Road    Garland
20  Jana's Management Consultants 2323 Beltline Road Irving
```

FIGURE 10B.2
Entering data

```
I25:  @COUNT(I3..I23)                                           READY

            F                 G          H         I         J
 6  Mr. Joe Garcia          01/10               Ongoing
 7  Mr. Robert LeTrec       11/15     12/24     Ongoing
 8  Ms. Judith Welpit       11/30     01/05     Ongoing
 9  Mrs. Roberta Accure     11/30     01/15     Offered   Mid-cities
10  Dr. Emil Franz Jung     11/15     11/30     Offered   North
11  Personnel Department    11/16     12/13     Rejected
12  Ms. Alice Faye Kong     11/16     02/22     Ongoing
13  Dr. Jane Willoughby     12/03     01/06     Ongoing
14  Mr. Foster Brooks       12/05     01/31     Offered   East
15  Personnel Director      11/30     01/06     Ongoing
16  Mr. H. Daniel Hoover    01/03     01/21     Ongoing
17  Mr. Peter Hoague        12/31               Ongoing
18  Mrs. Carletta Whitecloud 12/09    01/06     Offered   East
19  Personnel Division      12/09               Ongoing
20  Ms. Jana Davidson       01/06               Rejected
21  Mrs. Canada Strong      12/28     02/03     Refused
22  Personnel Office        12/31     01/07     Offered   North
23  Personnel Department    12/15               Rejected
24
25                                               21
```

FIGURE 10B.3
Counting companies contacted

```
I26: @DCOUNT(STATUS,0,H25..H26)                                      READY

            F                 G            H           I           J
10   Dr. Emil Franz Jung     11/15        11/30     Offered   North
11   Personnel Department     11/16        12/13     Rejected
12   Ms. Alice Faye Kong      11/16        02/22     Ongoing
13   Dr. Jane Willoughby      12/03        01/06     Ongoing
14   Mr. Foster Brooks        12/05        01/31     Offered   East
15   Personnel Director       11/30        01/06     Ongoing
16   Mr. H. Daniel Hoover     01/03        01/21     Ongoing
17   Mr. Peter Hoague         12/31                  Ongoing
18   Mrs. Carletta Whitecloud 12/09        01/06     Offered   East
19   Personnel Division       12/09                  Ongoing
20   Ms. Jana Davidson        01/06                  Rejected
21   Mrs. Canada Strong       12/28        02/03     Refused
22   Personnel Office         12/31        01/07     Offered   North
23   Personnel Department     12/15                  Rejected
24
25                                    Status        21    Percent
26                                    Ongoing        9     42.86%
27                                    Offered        8     38.10%
28                                    Rejected       3     14.29%
29                                    Refused        1      4.76%
```

FIGURE 10B.4
Using database and graphics commands to determine status

in this case the function @COUNT(I3..I23)—a spreadsheet counting function—has been used.

Integrating the Database and the Graphics Functions— Preparing a Pie Chart

One of your first reporting requirements in this module is to indicate the distribution of the offer status for the companies contacted. A pie chart is the most useful form for this presentation. However, before attempting to produce the pie chart, you need to establish the data to be diagrammed—how many companies are "ongoing," how many made you an "offer," how many you "rejected," and how may offers you "refused." As shown in Figure 10b.4, the values for each of these status categories is presented in rows 26 through 29. In Module 8b, these values were created on a "manual" basis—you simply counted them. However, in this illustration, you have used another counting function—a database counting function. To use this function, you must establish an input range—all the status values in column I (a search criterion)—shown as cells H25 and H26, and an offset—the number of columns to the right of the input range to be searched. By varying the value in cell H26 (from

```
A31: ^Company Name                                           MENU
Input  Criterion  Output  Find  Extract  Unique  Delete  Reset  Quit
Copy all records that match criteria to Output range
              A                    B                    C
20  Jana's Management Consultants 2323 Beltline Road    Irving
21  Bar Four Ranch                P. O. Box 92341, Rt. 11 Denton
22  Matt's Films, Inc.            P. O. Box 524         Dallas
23  Roger, Roger & Ray, Inc.      457 Happy Way         Garland
24
25
26
27
28
29
30
31        Company Name            Worksite                 City
32  Johnson Instruments, Inc.     South                 Dallas
33  Johnson Instruments, Inc.     Mid-cities            Dallas
34  Johnson Instruments, Inc.     North                 Dallas
35  Lewis & Melts Mortgage Co.    Mid-cities            Denton
36  Ethyl & Jung, DDS             North                 Dennison
37  Hormell Texas Chili Company   East                  Ft. Worth
38  Nephi's Hopi Crafts           East                  Tulsa
39  Matt's Films, Inc.            North                 Dallas
```

FIGURE 10B.5
Extracting companies from which offers have been received

"ongoing" to "offered" and so on), you can easily determine the number of companies in each category. The values associated with the column labeled "Percent" are not necessary for this problem, but rather demonstrate another selectable data format. (The actual value in cell J26 is based on the formula I26 / I25, which produces a numeric value of .4286—that is, 42.86 expressed as a percentage.)

Once the data values (9, 8, and so on) and labels ("Ongoing," "Offered," and so forth) have been developed, you may proceed to graph the results. As shown in Figure 10b.4, you have selected Graph from the primary Lotus menu and Type from the initial graphics menu. From this point on, the process of creating the pie chart is a repetition of the procedures covered in Module 8b, so it will not be reproduced here.

Integrating the Spreadsheet and the Database — An Analysis of Job Offers

Next you need to produce a table containing information about only those companies that offered you a job. In Figure 10b.5, a database Extract operation has been performed to produce a list of companies from which job offers

```
E2: (C2) @SUM(D2,F2..H2)                                          READY

                     A                  B        C       D          E
 1              Company Name         Location         Offer      Total
 2  Johnson Instruments, Inc.     South Dallas   $19,000.00  $22,822.00
 3  Johnson Instruments, Inc.  Mid-cities Dallas  $19,200.00  $23,022.00
 4  Johnson Instruments, Inc.     North Dallas   $19,100.00  $22,922.00
 5  Lewis & Melts Mortgage Co.  Mid-cities Denton  $22,000.00  $27,500.00
 6  Ethyl & Jung, DDS             North Dennison  $20,000.00  $27,275.00
 7  Hormell Texas Chili Company   East Ft. Worth  $19,300.00  $21,986.20
 8  Nephi's Hopi Crafts           East Tulsa      $15,670.00  $17,678.00
 9  Matt's Films, Inc.            North Dallas    $18,950.00  $24,561.00
10
11
12
13
14
15
16
17
18
19
20
```

FIGURE 10B.6
Creating job offer totals

have been received (a value of Offer that is greater than zero). This is a typical database operation, as previously illustrated in Module 7b. In summary, this result is achieved by the following steps: (1) A search criterion is established (Offer > 0); (2) the status column is Labeled, and a relative Range of cells is identified for this label; (3) a series of headings are indicated (row 31); (4) the Data function is selected from the primary menu, and Query is selected from the next menu; (5) an Input range is selected (the entire top portion of the spreadsheet); (6) an Output range is identified (row 31 and at least the next eight rows thereafter); and (7) the Extract function is executed.

Note that in the results, the Company Name field is the first column of the output area. This will later be changed to Company, and the actual company names will be replaced with company numbers. The second column is Worksite. This column actually appears after the third column, City, in the primary spreadsheet—confirming that the positions (columns) of extracted data may be arranged differently from those in the original spreadsheet. (Later, Worksite and City will be reformatted and a new heading supplied.) Finally, note that the values under Offer appear as asterisks. This means that although data is present, it is numerically larger than will fit into the present column size. It should also be noted that during the extraction process, the column headings for Life, Health, and Retirement were also present in the output area.

```
F12: (C2) @AVG(F3..F10)                                              READY

     A        B          C        D          E              F
1            Company       Location       $ Offer       Total
2            ───────   ──────────────   ────────────   ────────────
3               1         South Dallas   $19,000.00   $22,822.00
4               2      Mid-cities Dallas  $19,200.00   $23,022.00
5               3         North Dallas   $19,100.00   $22,922.00
6               4      Mid-cities Denton  $22,000.00   $27,500.00
7               5        North Dennison  $20,000.00   $27,275.00
8               6        East Ft. Worth  $19,300.00   $21,986.20
9               7          East Tulsa    $15,670.00   $17,678.00
10              8         North Dallas   $18,950.00   $24,561.00
11
12                          Averages    $19,152.50   $23,470.78
13
14
15
16
17
18
19
20
```

FIGURE 10B.7
Finishing the job offer table

Now you can begin to manipulate the part of the spreadsheet that is important for your report. The easiest way to proceed from here is to save the current spreadsheet, retrieve it, and then delete all of the "nonessential" rows. The result of this type of process is shown in Figure 10b.6. Note that in this figure the column headings for Worksite and City have been replaced by a Location heading. The Worksite values have been right-justified. The width of the Offer column has been expanded so that the values are now visible. A Total column has been added and formatted with a Currency presentation, and data values have been created. The spreadsheet function @SUM(D2,F2..H2) has been used to create the data values for Total (cell pointers for this type of command may consist of a range of cells as well as a list of cells). Cell D2 contains the Offer values, and cells F2 through H2 contain the values for Life, Health, and Retirement, respectively.

The next step is to create an average value for the Offer and Total columns. These averages, and the means by which they were created, are illustrated in Figure 10b.7. In this table, the Company Name column has been changed to Company, company numbers have replaced actual company names, and the numbers have been centered under the column heading. The final alteration is extremely important. A new column that is currently blank has been added to the left of the table. This column, Column A, will be used for word processing.

```
A12: 'During the past interviewing season, I had contact with 21 compan    MENU
Format  Label-Prefix  Erase  Name  Justify  Protect  Unprotect  Input
Adjust width of a column of labels
                                       A
 1                         M E M O R A N D U M
 2
 3   TO:   Placement Service
 4
 5   FROM:   (your name)
 6
 7   DATE:   03/15/8x
 8
 9   SUBJECT:   Report on job offers received during the past interview
10              season
11
12   During the past interviewing season, I had contact with 21 companies.
13   The attached chart illustrates the offer status of these contacts.
14
15
16
17
18
19
20
```

FIGURE 10B.8
Adjusting text to fit a specified line length

The addition of this column is done to avoid altering the composition of the table — you want the table to be reproduced exactly as shown, and you want the word processing function to be achieved as easily as possible.

Word Processing with Lotus — Creating the Text Part of the Memo

Keep two extremely important points in mind when you begin the entry of text within Lotus: First, Lotus allows you to enter text into a cell that is longer than the width of the cell. This is how you achieve the placement of the Location column heading over both the worksite and city columns. Furthermore, if the trailing cell(s) are blank, text in the first cell will appear in the second (third, and so on) cell to the right. You will take advantage of this characteristic to have both textual and spreadsheet material appear on the same printed page. Second, Lotus does not perform a word wrapping function on textual data. Thus, to have textual data placed within given "margins," you have to adjust the written material so that it fits into the width of the specified column.

To begin the entry of textual material into Lotus for the job hunting problem, first expand the size of column A to 65 characters, as is illustrated in Figure 10b.8. Note that the only column identifier in this figure is column A. The cell width of 65 was selected to provide for text that is ultimately no wider than 65 characters. Thus, this value established the maximum length of a line and, consequently, left and right margins. Next, before entering the beginning of the memo, be sure to insert sufficient rows through the worksheet function to accommodate the text you are about to enter. (If you don't, you will find that your table is to the right of the first few lines of your memo.)

To begin the memo, enter the text MEMORANDUM in the first row. Then proceed to Center the Label-Prefix through the Range function of the primary menu. Then skip to row 3 and enter the text as shown in Figure 10b.8, through the end of the first paragraph. Unless you were very careful, you probably have lines that are longer than 65 characters. As shown in Figure 10b.8, this problem can be fixed by selecting the Justify option from the Range function. The purpose of the Justify option is to insure that the length of data within a cell is no longer than the cell width. This is the primary reason for expanding the size of column A to 65 characters. If the text within a cell is too long, Lotus will scan the text from right-to-left until a blank is encountered, and all the characters to the right of that position will be added to the next row. If the row is not full, Lotus will add characters from the following row to fill it. After selecting the Justify option, you will be asked to supply a range of cells to be adjusted. This range of cells should include the entire first paragraph. In some cases, you would also indicate an additional row or two, just in case the adjustment of the text requires more "lines" that the current text. Thus, after the Justify procedure has been completed, the first paragraph has been "reformatted" into a 65-character line.

Now you are ready to enter the second paragraph, as illustrated in Figure 10b.9. The text, as shown, has already been adjusted to a cell width of 65, and the width of column A has been reduced to 5 characters. This should place the job offers table within the current window so that it appears to be indented 5 columns (the width of column A) relative to the paragraph above it. The primary objective of reducing the width of column A is to confirm the placement of the table relative to the text. Depending on how many rows you inserted initially, it may be necessary to insert more rows or delete unneeded rows to achieve the vertical spacing shown.

After you have verified the location and spacing of the table, change the cell width of column A back to 65 characters and move to the second line below the table. Then, enter the remaining text of the memo, as shown in Figure 10b.10. (The table has again "disappeared" from the current window.) Note that the words "and cooperation" have been omitted from the contents of row 37. To fix this problem, press the F2 key to enter the Edit function. The Edit function will permit you to modify the contents of the current cell without completely retyping them. Once Edit has been selected, you may use the left- and right-arrow keys to move forward and backward within the line. As you type additional characters, they are inserted into the line at that position, and the trailing characters are moved to the right. If you press the BACKSPACE key, characters will be deleted from right-to-left, beginning at the position immedi-

```
A35:                                                                    READY

        A       B         C          D          E          F
16  The table below provides a summary of the offers that I
17  received.    The second column shows the approximate location of
18  each company.    The third column represents the actual salary
19  offer of each company.    The fourth column represents the amount
20  of salary plus all fringe benefits.    The average dollar offer
21  and the average total offer are shown at the bottom of the third
22  and fourth columns, respectively.
23
24      Company          Location       $ Offer      Total
25      _____     _____  _____  _____
26         1            South Dallas   $19,000.00  $22,822.00
27         2        Mid-cities Dallas  $19,200.00  $23,022.00
28         3            North Dallas   $19,100.00  $22,922.00
29         4        Mid-cities Denton  $22,000.00  $27,500.00
30         5           North Dennison  $20,000.00  $27,275.00
31         6          East Ft. Worth   $19,300.00  $21,986.20
32         7             East Tulsa    $15,670.00  $17,678.00
33         8            North Dallas   $18,950.00  $24,561.00
34
35                         Averages    $19,152.50  $23,470.78
```

FIGURE 10B.9
**Entering the second paragraph and
checking the table placement**

ately to the left of the cursor location. If you use the DEL key, characters will be removed from the line from left-to-right, beginning at the cursor location. Thus, you should be able to easily manipulate the contents of all cells within a Lotus spreadsheet (including formulas, functions, and other contents) without retyping everything.

Before producing the printed version of the memo, you must first adjust the final paragraph using the Justify option. Then, to "recover" the table, you must reduce the width of column A to 5 characters. After this has been done, select the Print option from the primary menu. Before actually printing the results, shown in Figure 10b.11, you should limit the range of cells to be printed so that the cells following column F are not printed. To produce the pie chart, you must exit the 1-2-3 function and select the PrintGraph function from the Lotus Access System Menu (see Module 8b).

Other Features of Lotus

You have already seen that selecting 1-2-3 from the Lotus Access System Menu accesses the primary functions of Lotus and that selecting PrintGraph allows

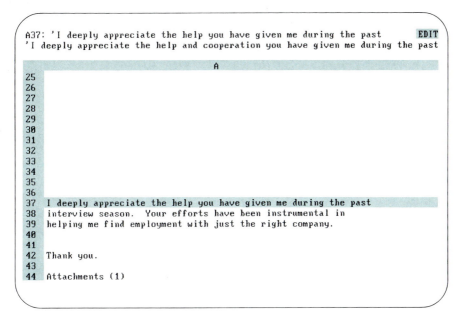

```
A37: 'I deeply appreciate the help you have given me during the past        EDIT
'I deeply appreciate the help and cooperation you have given me during the past

                                    A
25
26
27
28
29
30
31
32
33
34
35
36
37  I deeply appreciate the help you have given me during the past
38  interview season.  Your efforts have been instrumental in
39  helping me find employment with just the right company.
40
41
42  Thank you.
43
44  Attachments (1)
```

FIGURE 10B.10
Editing the contents of a cell

you to produce a printed copy of charts developed during a 1-2-3 session. However, other options are available from the main menu.

The File-Manager option allows you to manipulate disk files. Figure 10b.12 shows that among the functions available through File-Manager are Copy (produce a duplicate of a file on the same disk), Erase (remove a file from a disk), Rename (provide an alternate name for an existing file), Archive (make a backup copy of a file on another disk), Disk-Drive (change the default disk drive), Sort (reorder the list of file names), and Quit. When File-manager is selected, the File-Manager menu and a list of files in alphabetic order are produced on the screen. However, Figure 10b.12 illustrates the use of the Sort function to reorder the list of files. (The sequence of files shown is ordered by descending values of EXT and by ascending values of FILENAME.) You can use the up- and down-arrow keys to move through the list of files. The highlighted file name identifies the file on which the selected function (for example, Sort) is to be performed.

The Disk-Manager option of the Lotus Access System Menu permits manipulations at the disk level. As shown in Figure 10b.13, the functions of Disk-Manager include Disk-Copy (make a duplicate of a complete disk), Compare (determine the differences between the contents of two disks), Prepare

```
                    M E M O R A N D U M

TO:  Placement Service

FROM:  (your name)

DATE:  03/15/8x

SUBJECT:  Report on job offers received during the past interview
          season

During the interview process, I had contact with 21 companies.
The attached chart illustrates the offer status of these
contacts.

The table below provides a summary of the offers that I
received.   The second column shows the approximate location of
each company.   The third column represents the actual salary
offer of each company.   The fourth column represents the amount
of salary plus all fringe benefits.   The average dollar offer
and the average total offer are shown at the bottom of the third
and fourth columns, respectively.

        Company        Location        Offer        Total
        -------   -------------------  -----------  -----------
           1        South Dallas      $19,000.00   $22,822.00
           2      Mid-cities Dallas   $19,200.00   $23,022.00
           3        North Dallas      $19,100.00   $22,922.00
           4      Mid-cities Denton   $22,000.00   $27,500.00
           5        North Dennison    $20,000.00   $27,275.00
           6      East Ft. Worth      $19,300.00   $21,986.20
           7        East Tulsa        $15,670.00   $17,678.00
           8        North Dallas      $18,950.00   $24,561.00

                       Average        $19,152.50   $23,470.78

I deeply appreciate the help and cooperation you have given me
during the past interview season.   Your efforts have been
instrumental in helping me find employment with just the right
company.

Thank you.

Attachments (1)
```

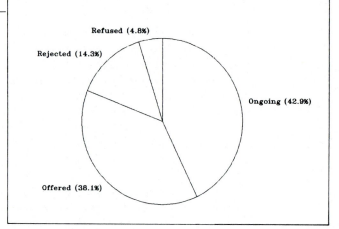

Status of Companies in Job Hunt

Refused (4.8%)

Rejected (14.3%)

Ongoing (42.9%)

Offered (38.1%)

FIGURE 10B.11
The job offers report

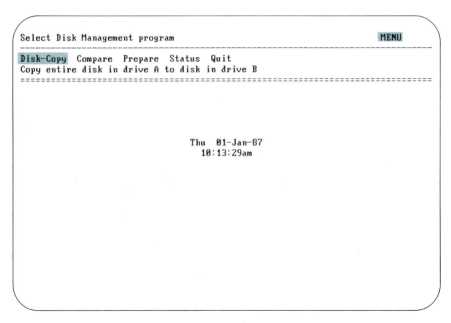

```
LOTUS File Management System V.1A (C)1983 LOTUS Development Corp.    MENU
----------------------------------------------------------------------------
Copy  Erase  Rename  Archive  Disk-Drive  Sort  Quit
Sort the directory entries.
============================================================================
   FILENAME EXT    DATE     TIME    SIZE
   JOBS     WKS  01-Jan-87  11:12am  2560
   COMPANY  WKS  01-Jan-87  9:50am   4992
   PIE      PIC  01-Jan-87  8:41am   1024
   BAR      PIC  01-Jan-87  9:00am   2816      Current Drive:      B
   STACK    PIC  01-Jan-87  9:05am   5248      Number of Files:    20
   LINE     PIC  01-Jan-87  9:13am   1280      Total Bytes Used:   71680
   PREF     NDX  01-Jan-87  1:06am   1024      Total Bytes Free:   290816
   ZIP      NDX  01-Jan-87  1:12am   1024
   GOOD3    FRM  01-Jan-87  1:02am   1990
   GOOD     FRM  01-Jan-87  10:54am   512
   OFFERS3  FRM  01-Jan-87  1:08am   1990
   OFFERS   FRM  01-Jan-87  10:33am   512
   JOBS     DBF  01-Jan-87  9:47am   1154
   JOBS3    DBF  01-Jan-87  10:09am  1034
   COMPANY3 DBF  01-Jan-87  10:43am  3584
   GOOD3    DBF  01-Jan-87  8:55am    703
   COMPANY  DBF  01-Jan-87  9:51am   3302
   COMPANY  BAC  01-Jan-87  9:51am   3302
```

FIGURE 10B.12
The Lotus File-Manager facility

```
Select Disk Management program                              MENU
----------------------------------------------------------------------------
Disk-Copy  Compare  Prepare  Status  Quit
Copy entire disk in drive A to disk in drive B
============================================================================




                        Thu  01-Jan-87
                           10:13:29am
```

FIGURE 10B.13
The Lotus Disk-Manager facility

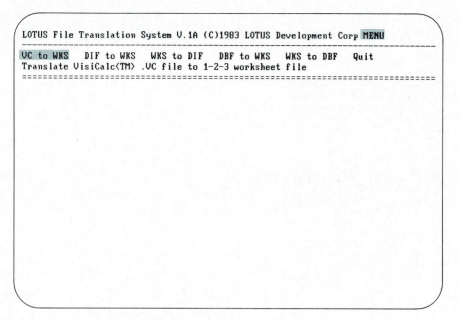

```
LOTUS File Translation System V.1A (C)1983 LOTUS Development Corp MENU
--------------------------------------------------------------------------------
VC to WKS   DIF to WKS   WKS to DIF   DBF to WKS   WKS to DBF   Quit
Translate VisiCalc<TM> .VC file to 1-2-3 worksheet file
================================================================================
```

FIGURE 10B.14
The Lotus Translate facility

(format a disk), Status (determine the current disk drive in use and the amount of available space on the disk), and Quit.

The final option of the Lotus Access System Menu is Translate. By using the Translate option, you are able to exchange files between Lotus and other application packages. Figure 10b.14 illustrates that among the file-interchange capabilities of Lotus are VC to WKS (translate from a VisiCalc file to a Lotus worksheet file), DIF to WKS (from DIF file to Lotus worksheet), WKS to DIF (from Lotus worksheet to DIF file), DBF to WKS (from dBASE II or III file to Lotus worksheet), and WKS to DBF (from Lotus worksheet to dBASE II or III).

Symphony

Learning to Use Symphony

Symphony is a relatively new software package from the same people who created Lotus 1-2-3. It is a fully integrated package based on the Lotus 1-2-3 software package. However, Symphony's capabilities are so much greater than those of Lotus 1-2-3 that it is hard to think of Symphony as merely an extension of Lotus.

Symphony provides you with the ability to select one of five work environments: SHEET for spreadsheets, DOC for word processing, FORM for database manipulations, GRAPH for graphics, and COMM for communications. The SHEET environment provides you with all the capabilities of Lotus spreadsheets. The DOC environment provides complete word processing capabilities, including a special print command for boldface and underline as well as the ability to create page headings and footings. The FORM environment provides additional capabilities and also creates a database in spreadsheet form much like the one created by Lotus database. Finally, the GRAPH environment provides easy access to the Symphony graphics features, and COMM lets you talk to other computers.

After you have booted Symphony, you should set the environment within Symphony to SHEET and go through the material presented in Module 6b (Lotus 1-2-3 Spreadsheet), Module 7b (Lotus 1-2-3 Database), and Module 8b (Lotus 1-2-3 Graphics). The following presentation is based on the assumption that you are familiar with each of these somewhat independent features of Lotus and, consequently, the Symphony SHEET environment.

When you enter Symphony, the Symphony Program disk should be in drive A and a data disk should be in drive B. To start the software, all that is necessary is to enter ACCESS. The result will be the Access System menu shown in Figure 10c.1. The majority of your work will be performed by selecting Symphony from this menu. The PrintGraph selection is used to produce charts on the printer and works exactly like the PrintGraph feature in the Lotus package (see Module 8b). The Translate function is used to convert data files created by VisiCalc or dBASE II or data files stored in DIF format into Symphony format files. It will also convert symphony files to DIF and dBASE II format. This feature also works exactly like Lotus (see Module 10b).

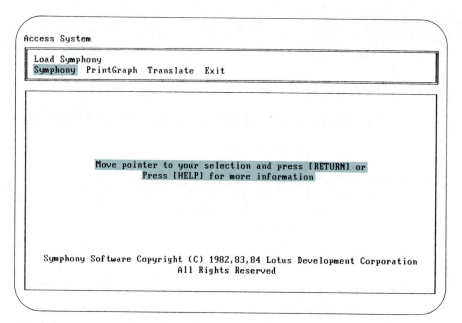

```
Access System

┌─────────────────────────────────────────────────────────────┐
│ Load Symphony                                                 │
│ Symphony  PrintGraph  Translate  Exit                         │
├─────────────────────────────────────────────────────────────┤
│                                                               │
│                                                               │
│                                                               │
│                                                               │
│                                                               │
│          Move pointer to your selection and press [RETURN] or │
│                Press [HELP] for more information              │
│                                                               │
│                                                               │
│                                                               │
│                                                               │
│    Symphony Software Copyright (C) 1982,83,84 Lotus Development Corporation │
│                     All Rights Reserved                       │
│                                                               │
└─────────────────────────────────────────────────────────────┘
```

FIGURE 10c.1
The Symphony Access System Menu

Press the RETURN key twice to get through the Symphony messages, and you will be presented with a screen in SHEET mode that is exactly the same as the Lotus spreadsheet screen. If you have reviewed the material presented in the Lotus modules, you are ready to go on with the material in this module. If you have not reviewed the material in the Lotus modules, please do so at this time.

The Symphony command structure is very similar to that found in Lotus, except that there are two types of command menus. The first type, activated by pressing the F9 key, contains the general services of Symphony and is called the SERVICES MENU, or just SERVICES. These services are available in all five Symphony environments and are used for global (overall) control of the work space. The second type is the environment command menu called MENU. This menu, activated by pressing the F10 key, applies specifically to the environment you are working in. In the SHEET environment, you can also obtain this menu by pressing the slash (/) key—just like in Lotus.

To change the environment of your work space, press the ALTernate and F10 keys and then use the arrow key to select the desired environment. Pressing the ALTernate and F9 key will switch the work space environment back to its previous type without going through the selection process. Symphony uses all of the function keys, although the keys' functions may vary according to the environment of the work space. These keys will be covered as they are needed in the module. However, it will help you to know now that the F1 key is the HELP key. It will provide you with help messages based on the current environment of your work space.

The Symphony work space is 256 columns wide and 8,192 rows deep, and it is set up as cells, much like the Lotus work space. This means that there are over two million cells available for the user. (The actual number of cells available to you will depend on the size of your computer's memory.) At any particular time, you can have only one work space in memory. If, as with the jobs problem, you want to perform several different tasks using different environments, you will need a way to integrate your data and its presentation. One way to do this is through the use of windows (see Chapter 6).

In Symphony, it may be useful to think of windows as basically the same as the Lotus windows; however, do not carry the similarity too far. A window is nothing more than a view of a work space. The one to four windows that can be created in Symphony all look at the single work space in the computer's memory. Each window has its own "view" that does not affect the overall "picture" of the work space and is independent of all other windows. However, changes to cells in one window will change the corresponding cells in all the other windows. After all, the cells are all in the same work space; they are just being viewed differently in each window.

The GRAPH environment uses a special region of the work space to draw its charts. Therefore, the actual drawing of a chart does not affect the rest of the work space. The DOC environment uses editing commands that affect the entire area that has been specified as the DOC region. Because of this, normal word processing activities can change the values in cells throughout the work space. To overcome this problem, you will have to "restrict" the region of the work space that is used for word processing to only that window.

For the jobs problem, although it is not totally necessary, start by dividing the screen into four windows as illustrated in Figure 10c.2. This is accomplished by pressing the F9 key to activate the SERVICES menu, selecting the Window option, selecting Pane, and finally selecting Both. You now have four windows on the screen, each with a SHEET environment and each showing the same region of the work space. The windows are currently labeled as MAIN (center of the screen), 1 (center right), 2 (lower right), and 3 (lower center). You can move the cursor — and, therefore, the environment you are working in — from window to window by pressing the F6 key. If you are going to be doing a lot of work in a single window, press the ALTernate and F6 keys to Zoom the window in which your cursor is located. This window will now fill the entire screen and will reveal a much larger area of the environment. To return to the view of all four windows, press the ALTernate and F6 keys a second time.

To complete setting up the windows for the jobs problem, change the name of the MAIN window to BASE. This area of the work space will be used for database operations, including creating and entering data and performing

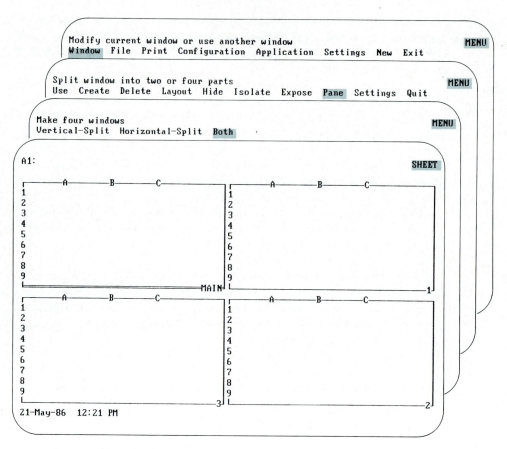

FIGURE 10c.2
Establishing the windows in your work space

search operations. Use the F6 key to move the cursor to window 1 and change its name to CHART and its environment to GRAPH. This area will be used to draw your charts. Because GRAPH uses a special region of the work space to draw its charts, the column and number labels disappear in this window. Now move to window 2 and scroll down so that row 100 is at the top of the window. This can be done by pressing and holding the down-arrow key until row 100 is at the top of the window, by pressing the PgDn key, or by pressing the F5 key for the GOTO command and entering 100. By performing this operation, you will create sufficient space for the other environments so that work spaces for each window will not overlap. You should name this window OFFERS and set its environment to SHEET. You will do your computations in this area.

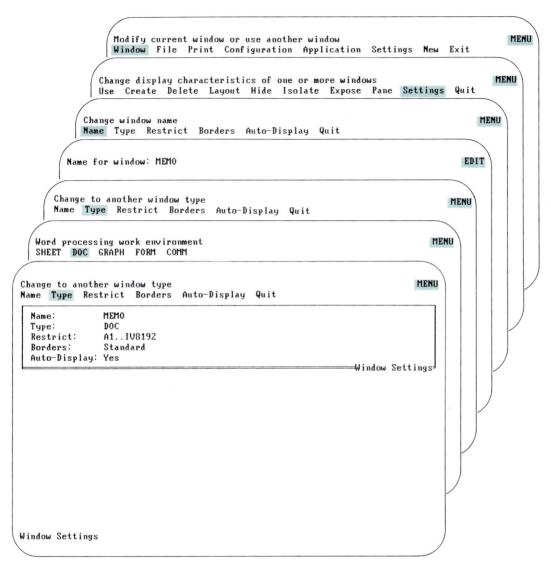

Modify current window or use another window   MENU
Window File Print Configuration Application Settings New Exit

Change display characteristics of one or more windows   MENU
Use Create Delete Layout Hide Isolate Expose Pane Settings Quit

Change window name   MENU
Name Type Restrict Borders Auto-Display Quit

Name for window: MEMO   EDIT

Change to another window type   MENU
Name Type Restrict Borders Auto-Display Quit

Word processing work environment   MENU
SHEET DOC GRAPH FORM COMM

Change to another window type   MENU
Name Type Restrict Borders Auto-Display Quit

Name: MEMO
Type: DOC
Restrict: A1..IV8192
Borders: Standard
Auto-Display: Yes
                                                    Window Settings

Window Settings

FIGURE 10c.3
**Setting the Name and Type for the DOC
window**

Moving to window 3, scroll down to row 115 and follow the illustration in
Figure 10c.3 to change the settings in this window. This area will ultimately
contain the memo portion of the jobs problem. From the SERVICE menu,
select the Window option followed by the Settings option. Now select the Name

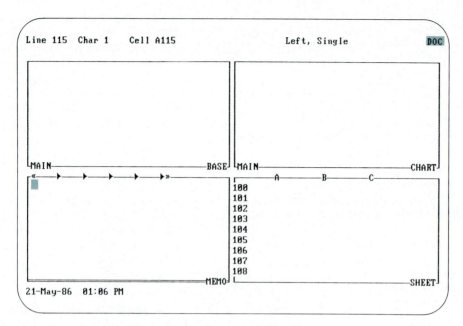

FIGURE 10c.4
All four windows established on the screen

option and enter the name of the window ("memo"), and finally select the Type option and use the arrow keys to select the window type you desire (DOC). Press the ESCape key or the Q key twice, and your screen will look the same as the one shown in Figure 10c.4.

Solving the Job Hunting Problem

The remaining sections in this module are devoted to solving the job hunting problem. You may want to refer to the problem statement in the Introduction to Integrated Systems Modules before you continue. Also, remember that the data in this problem can be found in Appendix A.

Loading Data into Symphony

To begin loading the data into Symphony, return to the BASE window, press the ALTernate and F6 keys to Zoom the window to full screen, and change its Type to DOC by pressing the ALTernate and F10 keys and selecting DOC. Now enter the defining information for the database. Using one line for each field, enter the name of the field followed by a colon (:), the type of field (L for label

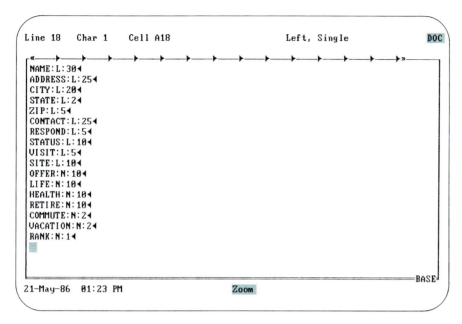

FIGURE 10c.5
Defining the database form

or character data, D for date, N for number, T for time, and C for computed) followed by a colon (:), and the length of the field. The results of entering this information for the jobs problem are shown in Figure 10c.5.

Follow the sequence of commands in Figure 10c.6 to create the database and enter the first record. From the Type menu select FORM, then press the F10 key to activate the FORM Menu, and select Generate. Now press the RETURN key to select Label as the default field type, press the RETURN key again to select the default field length of 9, and then enter the name of the database settings sheet as SCREEN before pressing the RETURN key a third time. Next you will use the arrow keys to indicate the range of field names to be used in generating the database. Pressing the RETURN key again will present you with a blank form, and you can enter the required data. You may use the up- and down-arrow keys to move through the form or the RETURN or TAB keys to move to the next field.

Once the record has been completely entered, you can use the cursor control keys to move around the form to correct any errors that you made while entering the data. You may also press the END key to end the data-entry operation and enter the editing mode to correct any errors. Pressing the PgDn key will move you to the next record. If this record contains data, you will be in the editing mode. If the record is empty, then you can enter new data.

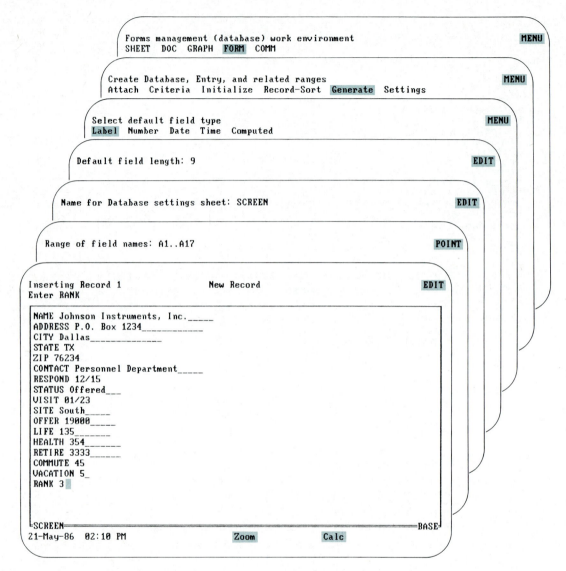

FIGURE 10C.6
Generating the database and entering data

After all of the data has been entered, you can move around the database by pressing the HOME key to move to the first record. To move to the last record, press the END key. You can also move sequentially through the records by using the PgUp and PgDn keys. There are many other options that can be

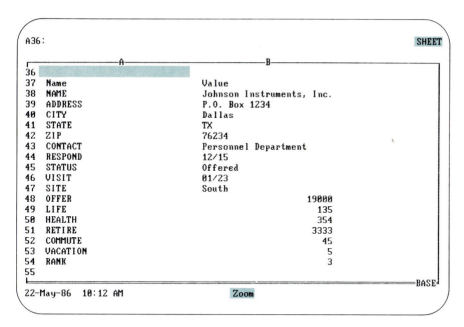

```
A36:                                                              SHEET
┌─────────────A─────────────────────────────B─────────────────────┐
36
37  Name                      Value
38  NAME                      Johnson Instruments, Inc.
39  ADDRESS                   P.O. Box 1234
40  CITY                      Dallas
41  STATE                     TX
42  ZIP                       76234
43  CONTACT                   Personnel Department
44  RESPOND                   12/15
45  STATUS                    Offered
46  VISIT                     01/23
47  SITE                      South
48  OFFER                                          19000
49  LIFE                                             135
50  HEALTH                                           354
51  RETIRE                                          3333
52  COMMUTE                                           45
53  VACATION                                           5
54  RANK                                               3
55
└───────────────────────────────────────────────────────────BASE─┘
22-May-86  10:12 AM              Zoom
```

FIGURE 10c.7
The database definition SHEET

used in the FORM environment, some of which you will use later; however, at
this point you should look at the other areas of your work space to see what has
been done.

Press the ALTernate and F9 keys to Switch the window back to the SHEET
environment, and use the down-arrow key to begin scrolling down the work
space. Immediately under the record definition you will find a copy of a blank
entry form. In row 37, after the blank form, you will find the data used to define
the entry form and the database itself, as illustrated in Figure 10c.7. Below this
is the data from the first record you entered. On row 59 are the titles of the
fields you entered followed by blank rows through row 63. This region is
actually the query specification area used for database operations. Finally,
beginning in row 64, you should find all of the records you entered, now in
spreadsheet format. This area, shown in Figure 10c.8, may be used to do
database operations in a spreadsheet mode exactly like the operations done
using Lotus in Module 7b.

In the job hunting problem, you were asked to report the number of
companies contacted. When you were in the FORM environment and looking
at one of the records, a message appeared at the top left corner of the screen
indicating that there are 21 records in the database. If you do not remember

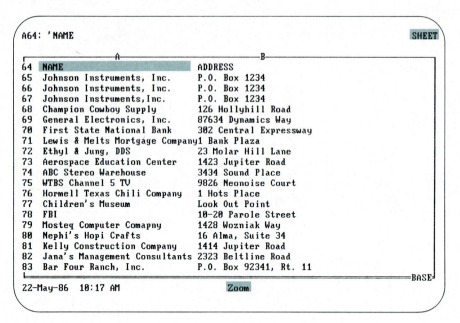

FIGURE 10c.8
The actual database in the SHEET environment

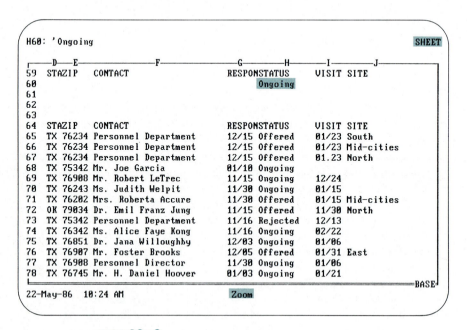

FIGURE 10c.9
Setting the query criterion

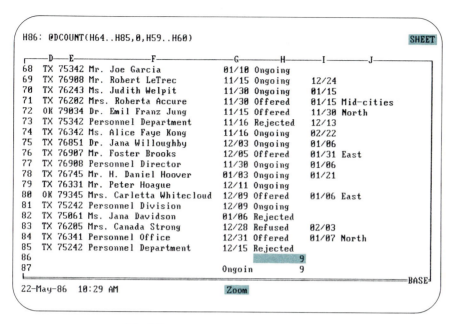

FIGURE 10c.10
Counting the number of "ongoing" companies

this, press the ALTernate and F9 keys to Switch back to the FORM environment and check the number of records in the database. Of course, you could always perform a @COUNT, as was done in Lotus.

One of your first reporting requirements in this module is to indicate the distribution of the offer status for the companies contacted. To get the needed data, a database count can be performed on the records for each of the categories in the STATUS column. To perform this count, move the cursor to cell H60 and enter the query criterion "Ongoing," as illustrated in Figure 10c.9. The additional blank cells in this column (rows 61, 62, and 63) are also used to establish query criteria; however, because none of the records in the database contains blank fields, the records will be ignored. Now move the cursor down to cell H87 and enter the command @DCOUNT(H64..H85,0,H59..H60). Finally, move the cursor down one row and enter a label in column G and enter the number in cell H87 in cell H88, as illustrated in Figure 10c.10. This operation saves the results of the @DCOUNT function.

Figure 10c.11 shows the work space after repeating this process for the other three categories ("Offered," "Rejected," and "Refused") and erasing the criterion in cell H60. The numbers entered in column I are Hue information to be used in the pie chart you are going to create. They control the cross-hatching pattern that will be used when the chart is produced.

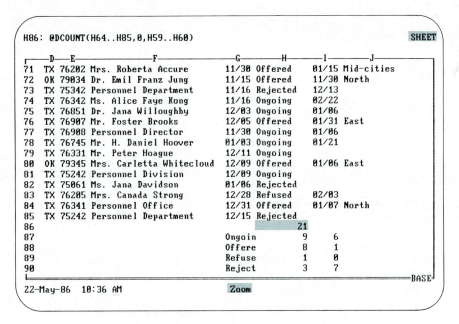

H86: @DCOUNT(H64..H85,0,H59..H60)   SHEET

	D	E	F	G	H	I	J
71	TX	76202	Mrs. Roberta Accure	11/30	Offered	01/15	Mid-cities
72	OK	79034	Dr. Emil Franz Jung	11/15	Offered	11/30	North
73	TX	75342	Personnel Department	11/16	Rejected	12/13	
74	TX	76342	Ms. Alice Faye Kong	11/16	Ongoing	02/22	
75	TX	76851	Dr. Jana Willoughby	12/03	Ongoing	01/06	
76	TX	76907	Mr. Foster Brooks	12/05	Offered	01/31	East
77	TX	76908	Personnel Director	11/30	Ongoing	01/06	
78	TX	76745	Mr. H. Daniel Hoover	01/03	Ongoing	01/21	
79	TX	76331	Mr. Peter Hoague	12/11	Ongoing		
80	OK	79345	Mrs. Carletta Whitecloud	12/09	Offered	01/06	East
81	TX	75242	Personnel Division	12/09	Ongoing		
82	TX	75061	Ms. Jana Davidson	01/06	Rejected		
83	TX	76205	Mrs. Canada Strong	12/28	Refused	02/03	
84	TX	76341	Personnel Office	12/31	Offered	01/07	North
85	TX	75242	Personnel Department	12/15	Rejected		
86					21		
87				Ongoin	9	6	
88				Offere	8	1	
89				Refuse	1	0	
90				Reject	3	7	

22-May-86   10:36 AM   Zoom   BASE

FIGURE 10c.11
A count of all the companies by STATUS

From Database to Graphics — Preparing a Pie Chart

A pie chart is the most useful form for presenting the status-count data you just obtained from the database. To produce the pie chart, use the F6 key to move to the CHART window, and then press ALTernate and F6 to Zoom this window. Now that you are faced with a blank GRAPH work space, press the F10 key to get the graphics menu and select 1st-Settings. From this submenu, select Type followed by Pie to indicate that you want to produce a pie chart. Now select Range and, following the example in Module 8b, select the X range as the labels for the chart, the A range as the values to be used, and the B range as the cross-hatching to be used for the chart, as shown in Figure 10c.12.

Finally, select Switch to access the 2nd-Settings, Titles to enter the title of the chart, and enter the title: Status of Companies in Job Hunt, as illustrated in Figure 10c.13. Now press the Q key twice, and you will see the chart on the screen. All that remains is to enter the graphics menu one more time, select Image-Save, and enter the file name B:CHART to save the image in a file on the disk in drive B. For a more detailed explanation of the graphic capabilities of Symphony, refer to Lotus 1-2-3 Graphics in Module 8b.

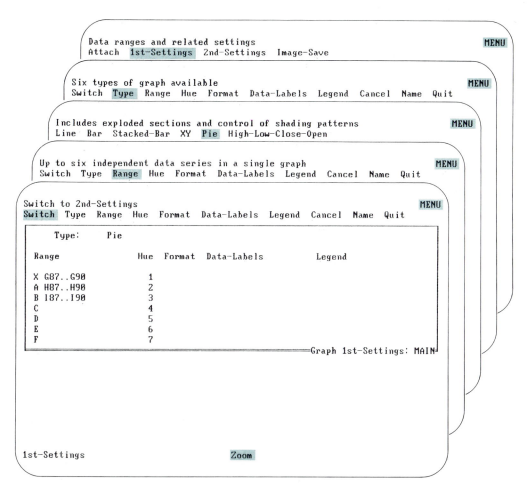

Data ranges and related settings   **MENU**
    Attach 1st-Settings 2nd-Settings Image-Save

Six types of graph available   **MENU**
    Switch Type Range Hue Format Data-Labels Legend Cancel Name Quit

Includes exploded sections and control of shading patterns   **MENU**
    Line Bar Stacked-Bar XY Pie High-Low-Close-Open

Up to six independent data series in a single graph   **MENU**
    Switch Type Range Hue Format Data-Labels Legend Cancel Name Quit

Switch to 2nd-Settings   **MENU**
    Switch Type Range Hue Format Data-Labels Legend Cancel Name Quit

          Type: Pie

    Range   Hue   Format   Data-Labels   Legend

    X G87..G90   1
    A H87..H90   2
    B I87..I90   3
    C   4
    D   5
    E   6
    F   7
                                                  Graph 1st-Settings: MAIN

    1st-Settings   Zoom

FIGURE 10c.12
Defining the pie chart

From Database to Spreadsheet—An Analysis of Job Offers

The next problem requirement is to produce a table containing information about only those companies that offered you a job. In Figure 10c.14, the F6 key was used to return to the BASE window, and then the ALTernate and F6 keys were used to Zoom the window to a full screen. Next, the ALTernate and F9 keys were used to Switch the window to the FORM environment. Finally, the F10 key activated the FORM menu, Criteria was selected, Edit was selected, and the criterion +OFFER>0 was entered in the criterion record for the field

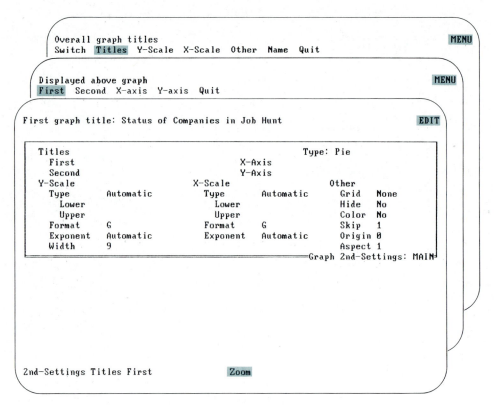

FIGURE 10c.13
Entering a Title for the chart

labeled OFFER. Entering the criterion here actually places this logical selection criterion in row 60 under the OFFERS column for use by the database facility. You will use this criterion to Extract the records from the database belonging to the companies that have made offers and place them in a new spreadsheet region so that you can perform the necessary calculations.

To finish entering the information needed to perform the extraction, use the ALTernate and F9 keys to Switch back to the SHEET environment, move to cell A100, and in row 100 enter the titles of the columns you want to extract from the database. These titles are NAME, SITE, CITY, OFFER, TOTAL OFFER, LIFE, HEALTH, and RETIRE. (TOTAL OFFER, although it does not currently exist in the spreadsheet, will be used in later computation and has no effect on the extraction operation.) Press the F10 or slash (/) key to activate the spreadsheet MENU. Figure 10c.15 illustrates the selection sequence needed to finish entering the extraction information. Select Query, Settings,

```
┌──────────────────────────────────────────────────────────────────┐
│   Control use of record-selection criteria              MENU       │
│   Attach  Criteria  Initialize  Record-Sort  Generate  Settings    │
│ ┌────────────────────────────────────────────────────────────────┐ │
│ │ Revise contents of Criterion range              MENU            │ │
│ │ Use  Ignore  Edit                                               │ │
│ │ ┌──────────────────────────────────────────────────────────────┐│ │
│ │ │ Editing Criterion Record 1 of 1                 CRIT          ││ │
│ │ │ Enter NAME                                                    ││ │
│ │ │ ┌──────────────────────────────────────────────────────────┐ ││ │
│ │ │ │ NAME _____                           │ ││ │
│ │ │   ADDRESS _____                             │ ││ │
│ │ │   CITY _____                                  │ ││ │
│ │ │   STATE __                                                  │ ││ │
│ │ │   ZIP _____                                                 │ ││ │
│ │ │   CONTACT _____                             │ ││ │
│ │ │   RESPOND _____                                             │ ││ │
│ │ │   STATUS _____                                         │ ││ │
│ │ │   VISIT _____                                               │ ││ │
│ │ │   SITE _____                                           │ ││ │
│ │ │   OFFER +OFFER>0__                                          │ ││ │
│ │ │   LIFE _____                                           │ ││ │
│ │ │   HEALTH _____                                         │ ││ │
│ │ │   RETIRE _____                                         │ ││ │
│ │ │   COMMUTE __                                                │ ││ │
│ │ │   VACATION __                                               │ ││ │
│ │ │   RANK _                                                    │ ││ │
│ │ │ └──────────────────────────────────────────────────────────┘ ││ │
│ │ └SCREEN═══════════════════════════════════════════════════BASE┘ │ │
│ │   Criteria Edit                      Zoom                        │ │
│ └────────────────────────────────────────────────────────────────┘ │
└──────────────────────────────────────────────────────────────────┘
```

FIGURE 10c.14
Setting the extraction criterion

and Basic, and the Output range as: A100..I113. Now press the Q key twice and select Extract from the Query submenu.

To begin work on the spreadsheet, use the F6 key to move to the window labeled SHEET and Zoom this window so that it occupies the entire screen. Note that this is the output area for the extraction function you just performed, and the NAME field is the first column of the output area. This will later be changed to COMPANY, and the actual company names will be replaced with company numbers in the memo. The second column is SITE. This column actually appears after the third column, CITY, in the database—confirming that the positions (columns) of extracted data can be arranged differently from those in the database. (Later, SITE and CITY will be reformatted and a new heading supplied.) The values under OFFER appear as asterisks. This means that although data is present, it is numerically larger than will fit into the present column size. Note that the column under TOTAL OFFER is blank,

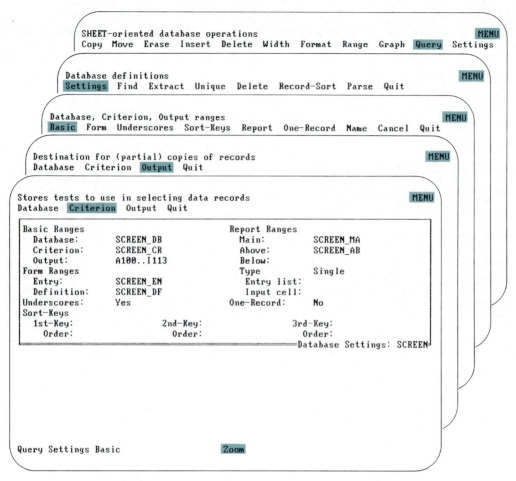

FIGURE 10c.15
Performing the extraction

indicating that this column was not in the database. Note also that during the extraction process, the column headings for LIFE, HEALTH, and RETIRE were also present in the output area.

Now you can begin to manipulate the spreadsheet to get the information necessary for your memo. The easiest way to proceed is to start by adjusting the column widths so that they are large enough to hold all of your data. These changes affect only the current environment and will not affect the column widths in the rest of the work space.

Figure 10c.16 shows the results of all the spreadsheet manipulations. Note that in this figure all the titles have been centered, the column con-

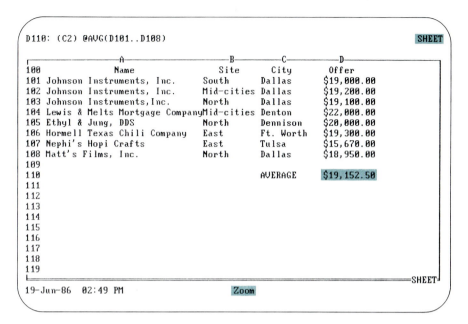

D110: (C2) @AVG(D101..D108)   **SHEET**

```
┌─────────────────A────────────────B──────C──────────D────────┐
100                  Name           Site      City      Offer
101 Johnson Instruments, Inc.       South     Dallas    $19,000.00
102 Johnson Instruments, Inc.       Mid-cities Dallas   $19,200.00
103 Johnson Instruments,Inc.        North     Dallas    $19,100.00
104 Lewis & Melts Mortgage CompanyMid-cities Denton     $22,000.00
105 Ethyl & Jung, DDS               North     Dennison  $20,000.00
106 Hormell Texas Chili Company     East      Ft. Worth $19,300.00
107 Nephi's Hopi Crafts             East      Tulsa     $15,670.00
108 Matt's Films, Inc.              North     Dallas    $18,950.00
109
110                                           AVERAGE   $19,152.50
111
112
113
114
115
116
117
118
119
└──────────────────────────────────────────────────────SHEET┘
```
19-Jun-86 02:49 PM   Zoom

FIGURE 10c.16
The job offer table

taining the SITE data has been left-justified, and the spreadsheet has been formatted for a CURRENCY presentation. The spreadsheet function: @SUM(F101..H101,D101) has been used to create the data values for TOTAL OFFER. Cells F101 through H101 contain the values for LIFE, HEALTH, and RETIRE respectively, and cell D101 contains the OFFER value. Finally, an average value was calculated for the OFFER and TOTAL OFFER columns by entering the function @AVG(D101...D108) (for OFFER).

Your spreadsheet is now ready to be used in the DOC environment of Symphony. Further changes to the spreadsheet will be done at that time and in a different window. In this way you will save your work space and be able to access the data in each step of the process without having to recreate it. For more complete coverage of most of the capabilities of the Symphony spreadsheet, refer to Lotus 1-2-3 Spreadsheets in Module 6b.

Word Processing with Symphony — Creating the Memo

To begin word processing with Symphony, use the F6 key to move from the SHEET window to the MEMO window, and then Zoom the window so that it uses your entire screen. One of your first tasks is to move the spreadsheet in the SHEET window into your current window. Remember that the windows are

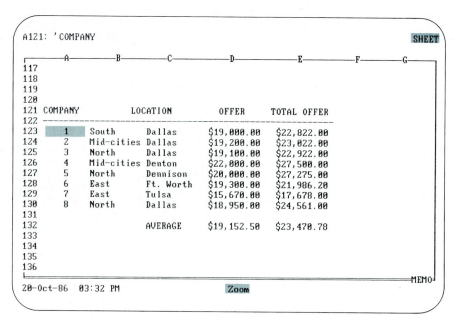

FIGURE 10c.17
The job offer table in the memo

just different views of the same work space. Therefore, the easiest way to move the spreadsheet into the area you want to use for the memo is to press the ALTernate and F9 keys to Switch the window environment from DOC to SHEET and copy rows 100 through 110 for columns A, B, C, D, and E down to rows 121 through 132. Figure 10c.17 was created by performing the copy operation, replacing NAME with the title COMPANY, removing the company names and entering numbers, and inserting a new row at row 122 filled with a dashed line (enter \- in each column). Finally, the titles SITE and CITY were erased, the title LOCATION was entered in cell B121, and all column widths were adjusted (including spaces) to reflect these changes. (*Note:* Use of the COPY command will cause an arithmetic error in the Total Offer column.)

Now that the spreadsheet is in the area you plan to use to create your memo, you are ready to set up the window for word processing. Remember from earlier discussions that some of the commands you will use during the word processing operations will affect other parts of your work space. To protect the rest of your work space and to protect the MEMO area from changes you might make in the rest of the work space, you need to restrict the window. First, use the ALTernate and F9 keys to Switch the environment back to DOC, and then press the F9 key to activate the SERVICES menu. From this menu, select the Window option, followed by the Settings option, the Restrict

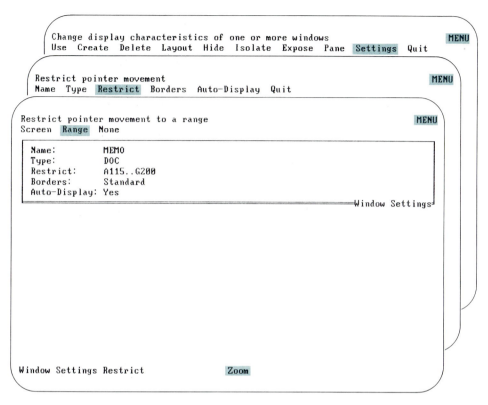

Change display characteristics of one or more windows   MENU
Use Create Delete Layout Hide Isolate Expose Pane Settings Quit

Restrict pointer movement   MENU
Name Type Restrict Borders Auto-Display Quit

Restrict pointer movement to a range   MENU
Screen Range None

    Name: MEMO
    Type: DOC
    Restrict: A115..G200
    Borders: Standard
    Auto-Display: Yes
                                              Window Settings

Window Settings Restrict   Zoom

FIGURE 10c.18
Restricting the DOC window

option, and finally the Range option. Now use the arrow keys to enter the range A115 through G200, as shown in Figure 10c.18. The lower-left corner of the range is not critical except that it must be more than 65 characters to the right of A115, and the area specified should be large enough to hold the memo.

After pressing the RETURN key, you are ready to enter the document setting for this window. To do this, press the F10 key to activate the document MENU, and select the Format option. Next select the Settings option, the Right option, select Set, and enter the Default right margin of 65, as illustrated in Figure 10c.19. Now your document has a right margin of 65 characters. However, in the first line of the memo you want the word MEMORANDUM to be centered. This means that the first line in the document needs to be reformatted. To do this, reenter the document MENU and again select the Format option. This time select the Create option, as shown in Figure 10c.20. When you are asked on what line to insert the new format press the RETURN key and select the Justification option and finally the Center option. Now press the

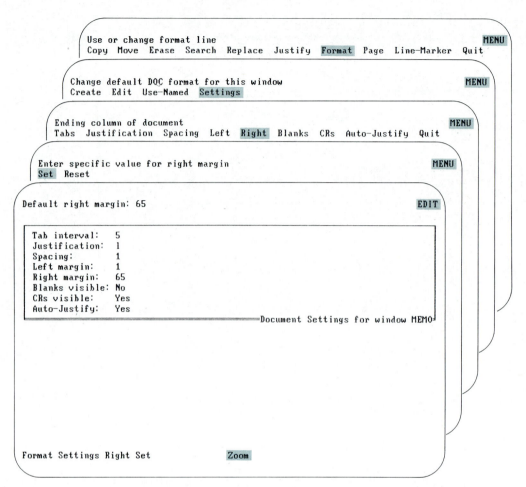

FIGURE 10c.19
Setting the Format for the memo

RETURN key and enter the word MEMORANDUM. Note that MEMORAN-DUM was entered with spaces between the letters. Note also that the CTRL (control) and B keys were pressed to mark the beginning of a special printing feature to be used with the word MEMORANDUM. The second character entered indicates the feature to be used (B for boldface, I for italic, U for underline, and so on). In this case, a 0 was entered for bold italic print. After the word was entered, the CTRL and E key were pressed to mark the end of the print feature. After the RETURN key was pressed, the up-arrow key was used to move the cursor up one line and the F2 key was pressed to justify (in this case Center) the text.

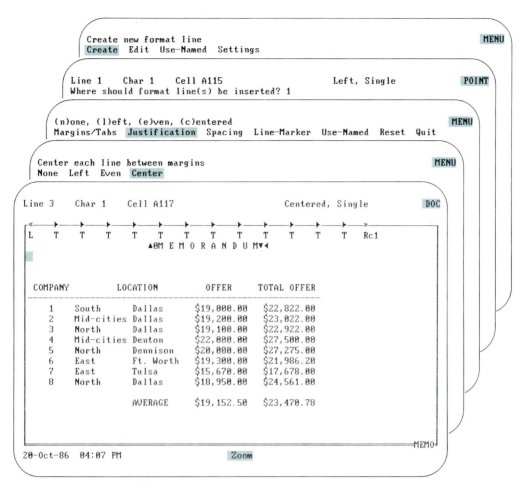

FIGURE 10c.20
Formatting the first line to center the table

To continue the memo, the line format needs to be set back to left-justified by following the procedure you just finished. Now simply type the text of the document. As long as you are in the insert mode (this is the default setting and may be changed by pressing the INSert key), the spreadsheet will be moved down the page and the word wrap feature of the DOC environment will automatically move you to the next line, as illustrated in Figure 10c.21.

When you have finished entering the second paragraph of the memo, use the DELete key to remove any extra blank lines between the paragraph and the spreadsheet. Now use the down-arrow key to move a couple of lines below the spreadsheet and finish entering the memo, as shown in Figure 10c.22. Once

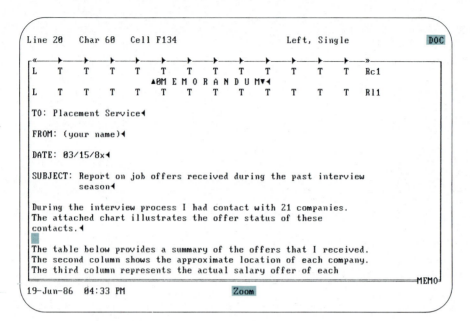

FIGURE 10c.21
Entering the memo

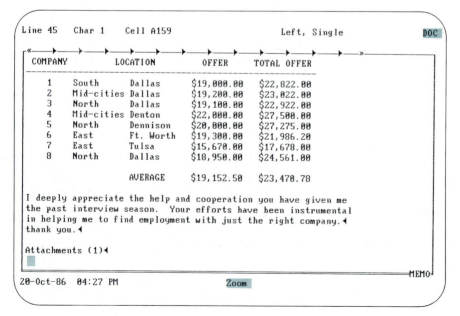

FIGURE 10c.22
Finishing the memo

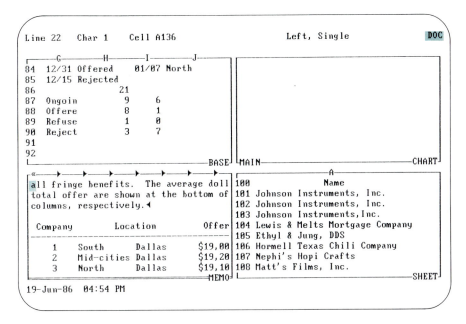

FIGURE 10c.23
The work space after completing the jobs problem

you have finished the memo, press the ALTernate and F6 keys to show all four windows on the screen. Your screen should look something like the one shown in Figure 10c.23.

To save your work space, press the F9 key, select the File option, then the Save option, and enter a file name. You are now ready to print your memo. To do this, simply press the F9 key to activate the SERVICES menu and select the Print option. When you are presented with the print setting and menu, position the paper on your printer and press the RETURN key to print the memo in Figure 10c.24. If the default settings do not meet your needs, you can use the menu at the top of the screen to change them. Finally, be sure you are in the MEMO window when you issue the print command; otherwise, the rest of your work space will be printed, not the memo.

To print the chart in Figure 10c.24, you will need to exit from Symphony by pressing the F9 key and selecting the Exit option. Be sure you have saved your work space before you answer YES to the question at the top of the screen; press the RETURN key. Once you are back in the Symphony Access menu, select the PrintGraph function to print the pie chart you created. For details of this process, see Module 8b (Lotus 1-2-3 Graphics).

```
                    M E M O R A N D U M

TO: Placement Service

FROM: (your name)

DATE: Ø3/15/8x

SUBJECT: Report on job offers received during the past interview
         season

During the interview process I had contact with 21 companies.
The attached chart illustrates the offer status of these
contacts.

The table below provides a summary of the offers that I received.
The second column shows the approximate location of each company.
The third column represents the actual salary offer of each
company.  The fourth column represents the amount of salary plus
all fringe benefits.  The average dollar offer and the average
total offer are shown at the bottom of the third and fourth
columns, respectively.
```

COMPANY		LOCATION	OFFER	TOTAL OFFER
1	South	Dallas	$19,000.00	$22,822.00
2	Mid-cities	Dallas	$19,200.00	$23,022.00
3	North	Dallas	$19,100.00	$22,922.00
4	Mid-cities	Denton	$22,000.00	$27,500.00
5	North	Dennison	$20,000.00	$27,275.00
6	East	Ft. Worth	$19,300.00	$21,986.20
7	East	Tulsa	$15,670.00	$17,678.00
8	North	Dallas	$18,950.00	$24,561.00
		AVERAGE	$19,152.50	$23,470.78

```
I deeply appreciate the help and cooperation you have given me
during the past interview season.  Your efforts have been
instrumental in helping me find employment with just the right
company.

Thank you.

Attachments (1)
```

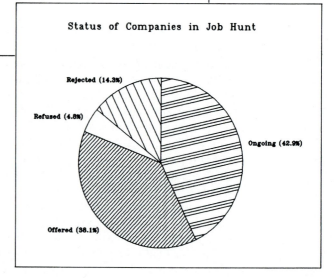

FIGURE 10c.24
The job offers report

Other Features of Symphony

Completing the job hunting problem has only scratched the surface of Symphony's capabilities. For a more detailed explanation of the basic capabilities found in the SHEET environment, review Module 6b; for the database capabilities of the SHEET environment, read Module 7b. For more details about the GRAPH environment and the PrintGraph function, read Module 8b.

The DOC environment of Symphony, although not as comprehensive as MultiMate (Module 5b) or WordStar (Module 5c), is a very powerful and easy-to-use word processor. In addition to having great flexibility in formatting documents, the DOC environment also provides an extensive list of special printer controls. Finally, the DOC environment supports the Search, Replace, and Move operations found on most modern word processing systems.

Through the use of the File option in the SERVICES menu, Symphony provides you with the capability to manage your files on disk and in the work space. As implied by the name of the option, you are able to Save and Retrieve files stored on disk. Additionally, you can save and retrieve parts of your work space and files by selecting the Xtract or Combine options. You can even create a Table in your work space containing all the file information on a disk. The File option allows you to manage your data disks by checking the number of Bytes free, displaying the Directory, giving a List of files by type, and providing the capability to Erase any of your files.

The SERVICES menu also provides you with the opportunity to use APPLICATIONS. An application is a program that has been created using Macros or the Symphony command language. The APPLICATIONS function will let you load applications into memory and execute them within the Symphony environment.

You will recall from the beginning of Module 10c that Symphony has more than four environments: the fifth environment is COMM. This window allows you to communicate with other computers through Symphony. The COMM MENU, displayed in Figure 10c.25, gives you the choice of having Symphony automatically Phone (dial) another computer or hang up after you have finished the work you want to do. Symphony will even go through the Login procedures needed to connect you with the other computer. It will send data from your work space or a file stored on disk (up-load) as well as place incoming data in the work space or file on disk (down-load). You can change the Settings in the window so that it can communicate with almost any type of computer. In fact, you can even set up the COMM environment so that it behaves like a regular computer terminal, rather than a powerful microcomputer.

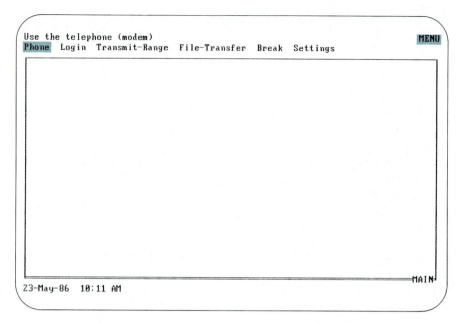

Use the telephone (modem)   MENU
Phone   Login   Transmit-Range   File-Transfer   Break   Settings

                                                                         MAIN
23-May-86   10:11 AM

FIGURE 10c.25
The Symphony COMM menu

Summary of Integrated Systems Modules

The preceding modules have given you the opportunity to examine one or more integrated software systems: the pfs:Series (Module 10a), Lotus 1-2-3 (Module 10b), and Symphony (Module 10c), the newest breed of integrated software.

Table 10s.1 provides a summary overview of these packages and will help you to compare them. However, only your direct involvement with one of these packages will tell you if it is the most practical one for your application. Each presents its own unique advantages.

A Comparison of Integrated Software Systems

The pfs:Series is a set of individual, "stand-alone" application packages that can be purchased separately. Thus, you can select the particular components that suit your needs. The pfs:Series is an example of an integrated system based on file sharing. Lotus 1-2-3 represents a "middle-of-the-road" form of inte-

TABLE 10S.1 A Comparison of Integrated Software Systems

Characteristic	pfs:Series	Lotus	Symphony
Main memory	128K	192K	320K
Disk drives	1	1	2
Type of integration	By file sharing	By central function	Total integration, but spreadsheet based
Word processing	pfs:Write full function boilerplating spell checking	Very limited	Adequate for most general applications
Spreadsheet	pfs:Plan slightly restricted 48 × 20 matrix	Full function 2048 × 256 matrix	Full function 8192 × 256 matrix
Database	pfs:File/pfs:Report single file somewhat restricted	Single spreadsheet, very restricted	Multiple-window spreadsheet, somewhat restricted
Graphics	pfs:Graph relatively flexible graph can be inserted in text material	Relatively flexible, stand-alone printing	Relatively flexible, stand-alone printing
Communication	pfs:Access somewhat restricted	None	Special function, relatively complete
File sharing/ exchange	DIF, SYLK, print files	DIF, print files, special link to VisiCalc and dBASE	DIF, print files, special link to VisiCalc and dBASE
Manufacturer's documentation	None for full integration; for individual packages only	Adequate, but somewhat difficult	Not intended for the novice

gration, and all of its functions center on the spreadsheet facility. If your needs can be met by a strong spreadsheet package with relatively good graphics capabilities, Lotus 1-2-3 might be your choice. Finally, Symphony, the "big brother" of Lotus, provides a complete range of functions in one package and is typically viewed as a totally integrated system. Its advantages stem from this total integration; however, it is a bit more expensive and complex than many of the individual pieces of software you could otherwise select.

In the final analysis, "beauty is in the eye of the beholder." Each of these packages is capable of solving a rather wide range of complex problems. You should choose the package that best fits your problem.

Guidelines for the Evaluation of Integrated Software

- **Word processing**   Use the evaluation guidelines found in the Word Processing Module Summary.
- **Spreadsheets**   Use the evaluation guidelines found in the Spreadsheet Module Summary.
- **Database**   Use the evaluation guidelines found in the Database Module Summary.
- **Graphics**   Use the evaluation guidelines found in the Graphics Module Summary.
- **Communications**   Use the evaluation guidelines found in the Communication Module Summary.
- **Integration**   How is the integration of software achieved? (Remember that integration by files can cause a lot of extra work changing disks.) How large is the program? That is, what are the memory requirements to run the package, and what are the space requirements to store the package?
- **Complexity**   Is the system easy to use? Can the commands be remembered and entered easily? Will you have problems trying to execute database commands in the spreadsheet function?
- **Documentation**   Is the documentation for the integrated software system complete? Is it easy to read and understand?
- **Support**   Is there a number that you can call to have questions about the software answered? Is this a local number or a long-distance number? Because integrated software systems can require you to learn a lot of material all at one time, is local support available?

What Happened at ACE?

The problem actually turned out to be easy to solve. Chris used an integrated package for some of the work Mr. Jenkins had assigned. After discovering how the package worked, Chris realized that although it wasn't as powerful as the "stand-alone" packages, it still had some excellent features. Chris moved all of the inventory reports into the integrated system. There was a slight reduction in the time needed to produce the reports, and the whole process became easier. Additionally, the secondary reports—reports supplying specially requested information—were much easier and faster to produce.

Module Questions

1. What integrated software system are you using? Is it command driven or menu driven? Does it have a help function? How is the help function used?
2. Compare the capabilities of each of the functions in the integrated software system you are using with the capabilities of the "stand-alone" packages you used. Which has the greatest capability?
3. How does the integrated software system you are using achieve integration? Does this add to or detract from the usefulness of the package?
4. Check your integrated software system's documentation to find out what additional features are available. How do you use them (separate programs or parts of the integrated system)?
5. What other integrated software systems (besides the one you are using) can be used on your microcomputer? (*Note:* Use the library or your local computer store to find the answer to this question.)

Module Problems

1. Using the data available for the job hunting problem, prepare a class presentation concerning the availability of jobs in the area. Your presentation should include (a) an introduction, (b) getting ready for the initial interview, (c) the follow-up or on-site interview, (d) a listing of where jobs are likely to be found, (e) a comparison of salary offers to total offers (including fringe benefits), and (f) a description of how a microcomputer can be useful in maintaining and processing information about interviews and job prospects. You should also use a pie chart to show a breakdown of jobs (from your database) indicating the number of job prospects by city. Then create a stacked bar chart to compare fringe benefits. This chart should be based on four companies from your database for which the job status is "offered."
2. Use the inventory information in Appendix B to solve the following problem. You are to provide your boss with information about the sales performance of all audio equipment. First create a list of all inventory items in this category, the total sales for each item, and the vendor supplying the item. Next produce a pie chart comparing the number of inventory items in each category of audio equipment. Finally, produce a line chart that compares the past year's performances of the worst-selling and the best-selling audio items (based on units of sales).

3. Use the inventory data in Appendix B to create a report that demonstrates the sales performance, based on total profit, for each inventory category. Your report should first present a comparison based on the inventory items in each inventory category, followed by a comparison of categories. Your comparisons should be presented both in table form and in bar charts. The tables and charts should be produced individually and numbered (add titles and table or figure numbers), and these numbers should be referred to in your writeup. Your writeup should identify the best and worst profit performances in each category. The summary should identify the best and worst categories in your analysis.

EPILOGUE

Now that you have been introduced to the use of microcomputers in conjunction with a selection of software packages, it is time to reflect on what you've learned, what the future of microcomputers and software holds, and what effect microcomputers and computers in general will have on society.

Reflecting on What You've Learned

You have seen that microcomputers and software can save you time, enabling you to tackle tasks that otherwise would not be possible and providing you with answers to questions that otherwise would not be available. Not only have you examined the hardware characteristics of microcomputers (Chapter 2), but you've also been introduced to a number of software products and packages. You learned that an operating system (Chapter 4) is an essential element of the total software mix. You were also introduced to word processing (Chapter 5) and learned how computers can be used to process text—letters, reports, manuals, and so on. In Chapter 6, you handled "what if" questions and numeric manipulations of data through the use of spreadsheets. When it comes to storing volumes of quickly retrievable data, computers using database software (Chapter 7) have few peers. Databases can't be beat in the areas of flexibility, speed, storage, capacity, and reporting ability. Chapter 8 introduced you to new ways of presenting data in a graphics mode. Chapter 9 showed you how to use electronic communication to share the results of computer processing with other computers. Finally, in Chapter 10, you learned about integrated software, which attempts to give you all the various applications of software in one package.

What's Going On at ACE?

Chris had just finished the last project when Mr. Jenkins walked into the office with a smile on his face. Looking very proud, Mr. Jenkins informed Chris that he and Chris had been invited to come to the Dallas regional office to explain all the work they had done to use a microcomputer to solve inventory problems. Mr. Jenkins indicated that Ms. Fullerton had mentioned their work to the regional manager the last time she was in Dallas. Mr. Jenkins also mentioned that if their presentation went well, Chris might be asked to take a temporary assignment in Dallas to set up a microcomputer inventory system there and at the other district offices in the region. Chris was very proud of the progress they had made on the inventory system and looked forward to the possibility of a new assignment and new challenges. It was hard work setting up the inventory system, and it looked as though some of that hard work and dedication was about to pay off.

The Future of Microcomputer Processing

You can expect to see further advances in both hardware and software. The physical dimensions of future microcomputers will probably not shrink dramatically when compared to today's models, but the capabilities housed in those cabinets are likely to improve substantially. Currently, many microcomputers operate on a 16-bit basis. (The CPU of some current microcomputers operate internally on a 32-bit basis, but transfer data on a 16-bit basis.) In the future, microcomputers are likely to become "baby" mainframes—using full 32-bit processing. They are not likely to expand beyond this point, however, because most of today's mainframes process on a 32-bit basis. Of course, with additional improvements in CPU "horsepower," the speed of

microcomputers will increase: Future microcomputers may be as much as 10 times faster than today's microcomputers. This increase will likely be partially the result of using hardware "multiply/divide" or math "coprocessor" devices that are frequently available today as "add-on" features. Finally, advances in both mainframes and microcomputers will result in "use transparency"—you won't be able to easily determine which computer you are using as hardware and software become more directly compatible.

The standard configuration of many of today's microcomputers includes 256K bytes of internal memory, not including any "on-board" ROM devices. As CPUs improve, you can expect improved performance from all memory devices, including ROM. Furthermore, additional memory capacities in excess of 1M byte will probably become standard with internal expansion to 5M or 10M, as new software is designed to take advantage of these higher capacities. In addition, further uses will be made of ROM to include larger memory capacities and many of the most-used software packages.

Of course, you can expect further enhancements of peripheral devices. Many of these enhancements will be in the human interface area. For example, display screens will become more versatile, less fatiguing, and easier to use, and more use will likely be made of flat-screen or plasma displays that not only take less space but should produce a higher quality image with less eye strain. One of the major limitations of computer systems has been keyboard-entry speed. Improvements in this area will include keyboard designs with a better "feel," more special function keys, and a more natural keying motion. The keyboard will remain one of the major human links to the computer, but the use of voice-driven devices will increase as that technology improves. These devices may also include headsets for both voice response and tracking of eye movement. Printing devices should become quicker, quieter, and more versatile. For example, future printers should be able to easily produce dozens of fonts in a variety of sizes directly under the control of software. The quality of the printing should also be near typeset quality. These printers will likely include a variety of color arrangements and schemes vastly superior to today's models. Printing combinations of text and graphics should also be possible.

Secondary storage should also improve. The use of disk will become less important as the price of hard-disk units continues to fall (even though the capacity of these units will increase). Disk formats will also become much more standardized, allowing easy transfer between machines made by different manufacturers. Disk capacities exceeding 1M byte should also be expected, and, although additional improvements in backup devices should be produced, floppy or semi-floppy disks should become a more practical medium for backup purposes. In addition, the need for many secondary storage devices may be reduced by the installation of high-density, nonvolatile internal memory devices. Finally, installing and connecting these devices should become much easier as standard connection choices narrow and as the need for physical wires between devices is minimized or eliminated.

The most drastic change in software will be the elimination of specific package applications; that is, total integration — already available in a few packages — will likely be the predominate software format. Thus, word processing, spreadsheets, databases, graphics, communications, and other functions will all be part of a single package, and these functions will surpass the capabilities of current "stand-alone" packages. These packages will be produced in a standard format that can be tailored by the user to meet individual needs. This tailoring will include creating user menus, forms, functional sequences, definitions, and so on. Thus, these packages will be able to develop a "personality" that more closely fits the user and the user's needs. They will be available for all computers and will easily interface with other highly specialized application areas for which the user has a direct need or interest. Future integrated packages should also include a "universal" data format that is easily exchanged between packages.

The Effect of Computers on Society

As you know, the use of microcomputers and software is growing at a rapid rate. No one can tell for sure what the future will hold. However, if the past is any indication of the future, microcomputers may well become an appliance as common as the telephone. Not only will the microcomputer be used in the work place to enhance the performance of the work force, but microcomputers are likely to invade the home as well. Although microcomputers have been available for home use for over a decade, the home uses have been mostly trivial — not justifying the expense of having a microcomputer. In fact, many microcomputers were purchased as "toys" and are now gathering dust, both because they were not used and also because they were not very useful. You should expect the rebirth of interest in the microcomputer for home use, but you should expect this home use to become almost completely redefined.

In the future, microcomputers may be referred to as "home service centers." A new approach to microcomputers in the home could easily entail their use for environmental control (heat, air conditioning, lighting, humidity, air purification, and so on), security (access sensors, break-in detection, notification of police, fire, and so forth), entertainment (TV program and channel selection, music control, movie and other program listings), financial services (banking, purchases, payments, orders, and the like), and obtaining information (travel services and tourism information, news services, library source retrieval, and so on). Some of these services are already available through commercial data services. However, improvements in both the services and computer systems will make their daily use commonplace.

You have already seen that the computer and software can greatly enhance your performance capabilities in job-related activities. However, this improvement also involves a certain amount of risk. Think back over your performance while using a software package. Did you ever make a mistake? What do you think the effect would have been if you hadn't caught the mistake? Even though most computer experts have spent years receiving training on how to avoid mistakes, they still make them. That's why you hear stories of someone receiving a telephone bill for hundreds of thousands of dollars or receiving an excessive amount on a social security check. Now think about the bills you receive every month? Do they come from a computer? Do you check their accuracy? We often think that just because results are produced by a computer, it has to be correct. This is not always true. Because of your experience level, you are likely to make more mistakes than the experts. So you should be exceedingly careful to fully check what your computer (and others) is doing or telling you.

Many organizations maintain information about people. Credit histories, personal information, criminal records, and so on are maintained and used by these organizations. More than likely, there are several organizations that have some type of information about you. In most cases, these are large, well-recognized organizations using large computers. These organizations must abide by current laws that pertain to the invasion of personal privacy, and many of them are required by law to let you examine information they have that pertains to you. Although these laws are reasonably enforcable for large organizations because these organizations are easy to identify, such is not the case for small organizations performing the same types of operations on microcomputers. Thus, there is the ever-present danger of "secret" or nonpublic information being maintained about you and other members of society.

Could the use of microcomputers have any direct effect on large organizations such as ACE? As you read about what was going on at ACE, you should have been aware that information was being changed from a generally accessible format to a more restricted one. For example, when the inventory files were converted from a room full of filing cabinets into a microcomputer database, they were no longer available to anyone who happened to walk into the file room. The inventory data became accessible only to those who knew how to use the microcomputer and the software, provided they had access to the system.

Even large organizations must evaluate the value of microcomputers and software for their applications. If certain types of data are created, manipulated, maintained, and accessed only on a microcomputer, it may not be available for others to use. Furthermore, if someone is copying data from a large machine to a microcomputer, the microcomputer copy will be only as current as the last time it was copied. Thus, if the data is updated on the large computer, the microcomputer user may be unaware of the changes. This could cause problems when decisions are made based on the microcomputer's data.

There are certain risks and dangers associated with the use of any tool or device. If you operate your automobile unsafely, you are at physical risk. If you operate a microcomputer "unsafely" or inappropriately, you could incur a personal or financial risk. However, if you operate your automobile safely and prudently, you will enjoy the many benefits associated with enhanced mobility. If you operate your microcomputer wisely and with forethought, you will be able to reap the benefits associated with letting the computer do the work to assist you in quickly making appropriate decisions.

The Challenges

You have learned quite a lot since you began this book. You have learned something not only about how the computer works, but also about many of the popular software packages. However, this text is only a starting point; there is much more to learn. You are faced with two challenges. First, if you don't plan to use what you've learned right away, you should "play" with it every so often so you don't forget what you've learned. Second, be aware that new products are manufactured and new software is written almost every day. Current technology in both hardware and software quickly becomes obsolete. Thus, you should periodically examine new material related to microcomputers and software. You might find that one of the many microcomputer magazines will help you keep current.

We hope you have enjoyed learning about microcomputers and software. We think that you will find that microcomputers and software will help you be more productive, regardless of your chosen profession or career. We know that learning and applying this material has taken effort on your part. Now it's time for your hard work to pay off. Good luck!

APPENDIX A

Job Hunting Data

For even the most experienced person, job hunting can be a confusing time. This is particularly true of a student who is looking for a job that he or she hopes will turn into a career. The student in this problem has decided to organize a record of all the activities involved in looking for and evaluating job offers.

The problem presented here will be used in each module to give you an introduction to each of the software packages covered in the text. All of the data needed to solve the problems presented in the Module Introductions is presented in Table A.1, Companies Applied To, and Table A.2, Offers From Companies.

The problem situation is this: The following information is collected for each company to which an application is made.

Company Name	Date the Résumé Was Submitted
Address	Date the Company Responded
City	Date the Interview Is Set for
State	The Status of Negotiations
Zip Code	Contact Person

When a company makes you an offer, the following data is added:

Work Site
Salary Offered
Life Insurance Paid by the Company
Health Insurance Paid by the Company
Retirement Benefits Paid by the Company
Commuting Distance
Number of Vacation Days
Subjective Rank (Job Preference) of How Well the Student Likes the Offer

You will be asked to initiate contact with the company (word processing), evaluate the various offers (spreadsheets), organize the information in a database, and graphically display information needed in the job hunting process.

TABLE A.1 Companies Applied To

Company Name	Address	City	State	Zip Code	Contact Person	Date Résumé Sent	Date Company Responded	Job Status	Date of Interview
Johnson Instruments, Inc.	P.O. Box 1234	Dallas	TX	76234	Personnel Department	11/01	12/15	Offered	01/23
Champion Cowboy Supply	126 Hollyhill Road	Garland	TX	75342	Mr. Joe Garcia	11/02	01/10	Ongoing	
General Electronics, Inc.	87634 Dynamics Way	Ft. Worth	TX	76908	Mr. Robert LeTrec	11/02	11/15	Ongoing	12/24
First State National Bank	302 Central Expressway	Dallas	TX	76243	Ms. Judith Welpit	11/02	11/30	Ongoing	01/15
Lewis & Melts Mortgage Company	1 Bank Plaza	Denton	TX	76202	Mrs. Roberta Accure	11/03	11/30	Offered	01/15
Ethyl & Jung, DDS	23 Molar Hill Lane	Dennison	OK	79034	Dr. Emil Franz Jung	11/04	11/15	Offered	11/30
Aerospace Education Center	1423 Jupiter Road	Garland	TX	75342	Personnel Department	11/06	11/16	Rejected	12/13
ABC Stereo Warehouse	3434 Sound Place	Dallas	TX	76342	Ms. Alice Faye Kong	11/06	11/16	Ongoing	02/22
WTBS Channel 5 TV	9826 Neonoise Court	Plano	TX	76851	Dr. Jana Willoughby	11/06	12/03	Ongoing	01/06
Hormell Texas Chili Company	1 Hots Place	Ft. Worth	TX	76907	Mr. Foster Brooks	11/10	12/05	Offered	01/31
Children's Museum	Look Out Point	Ft. Worth	TX	76908	Personnel Director	11/10	11/30	Ongoing	01/06
FBI	10–20 Parole Street	Arlington	TX	76745	Mr. H. Daniel Hoover	11/10	01/03	Ongoing	01/21
Mosteq Computer Company	1428 Wozniak Way	Farmers Branch	TX	76331	Mr. Peter Hoogue	11/15	12/11	Ongoing	
Nephi's Hopi Crafts	16 Alma, Suite 34	Tulsa	OK	79345	Mrs. Carletta Whitecloud	11/17	12/09	Offered	01/06
Kelly Construction Company	1414 Jupiter Road	Garland	TX	75242	Personnel Division	11/17	12/09	Ongoing	
Jana's Management Consultants	2323 Beltline Road	Irving	TX	75061	Ms. Jana Davidson	12/03	01/06	Rejected	
Bar Four Ranch, Inc.	P.O. Box 92341, Rt. 11	Denton	TX	76205	Mrs. Canada Strong	12/03	12/28	Refused	02/03
Matt's Films, Inc.	P.O. Box 524	Dallas	TX	76341	Personnel Office	12/03	12/31	Offered	01/07
Roger, Roger & Ray, Inc.	457 Happy Way	Garland	TX	75242	Personnel Department	12/03	12/15	Rejected	

TABLE A.2 Offers From Companies

Company Name	Location	Salary Offer	Contributions			Commute Distance	Vacation Days	Job Preference
			Life Insurance	Health Insurance	Retirement			
Johnson Instruments, Inc.	South	19000.00	135.00	354.00	3333.00	45	5	3
Johnson Instruments, Inc.	Mid-cities	19200.00	135.00	354.00	3333.00	35	5	4
Johnson Instruments, Inc.	North	19100.00	135.00	354.00	3333.00	25	5	5
Matt's Films, Inc.	North	18950.00	155.00	456.00	5000.00	33	6	4
Lewis & Melts Mortgage Company	Mid-cities	22000.00	500.00	600.00	4400.00	35	14	1
Ethyl & Jung, DDS	North	20000.00	325.00	950.00	6000.00	95	14	2
Hormell Texas Chili Company	East	19300.00	164.00	320.00	2202.20	53	5	1
Nephi's Hopi Crafts	East	15670.00	250.00	425.00	1333.00	47	14	4
First State National Bank	North	22000.00	210.00	325.00	2950.00	25	14	2

APPENDIX B

ACE Company Inventory Data

Welcome to Ace, Incorporated. It's time for you to become familiar with your job and learn how the microcomputer can be used to help make your work easier. To this end, data for the company has been organized so that you can use it to help your boss, Mr. Jenkins, and showroom managers deal with the day-to-day operations.

You will find two tables of information on the following pages, Table B.1, ACE Company Inventory Data, and Table B.2, ACE Company Supplier Data. These tables contain data about the district's inventory items and the sales for the last 12 months.

With your knowledge of the company and the information you will gain about the microcomputer and the application packages, you will be expected to become involved with all phases of the company's operations. The data presented here will be used to give you an example of how to use each of the software packages discussed in this text. You will find that each of the "What's Going on at ACE?" sections of the chapter presents realistic problems that might be encountered in operating a business. By using the information provided by the modules, you should be able to solve the Module Problem #2 in each set of modules.

TABLE B.1 ACE Company Inventory Data

Item			Per Unit		
Number	Description	Class	Price	Cost	Vendor
15268	Magnavox 19 inch Clr w/Remote	TV	$499.99	$250.00	468
659237	Bender 14-Day Programmable	VCR	$750.00	$450.00	202
896527	Mitsubishi 15 in Clr w/Remote	TV	$650.00	$400.00	698
965842	Westman AM/FM Portable	RADIO	$25.99	$10.00	221
128965	TI AM/FM Clock Alarm, Snooze	RADIO	$35.99	$15.99	221
756420	TI 64K Internal, 1 Dsk Drive	COMPUTER	$2,595.00	$1,500.00	100
978562	Windsor 7-Day Programmable	VCR	$500.00	$300.00	202
859642	Magnavox 13 inch B/W	TV	$299.00	$100.00	468
789541	Thames 8 inch Portable B/W	TV	$200.00	$100.00	698
323456	RCA 25 inch Clr Programmable	TV	$975.00	$750.00	698
454987	GE AM/FM Auto Alarm	RADIO	$32.99	$15.00	221
164587	RCA 19 inch Clr w/Remote	TV	$499.00	$300.00	468
184973	Bender 19 inch Clr Stereo	TV	$600.00	$450.00	468
615468	COMPAQ Portable 128K 9 inch	COMPUTER	$2,995.00	$2,000.00	100
256840	Chameleon 128K, 2 Drives	COMPUTER	$1,995.00	$1,500.00	100
586497	Micro Mart Diskettes	MEDIA	$3.95	$2.00	100
568912	TI AM/FM Portable	RADIO	$9.99	$3.00	525
894572	Nashua 5 inch Floppy Diskette	MEDIA	$3.95	$2.00	100
897512	Zenith 25 inch Color w/Cabinet	TV	$1,020.00	$700.00	100
865425	Magnavox Portable B/W	TV	$299.00	$186.00	256
120548	Magnavox Console Color	TV	$700.00	$550.00	256
879542	Marantz System, 100 Watts	STEREO	$1,500.00	$1,000.00	202
485762	Marantz, 30 Watts	STEREO	$650.00	$500.00	202
546824	Apple MacIntosh System	COMPUTER	$3,000.00	$2,000.00	106
846597	Commodore CPU	COMPUTER	$199.00	$100.00	193
549768	Commodore System	COMPUTER	$700.00	$550.00	193
546872	Mitsubishi 50 inch, Rear Proj.	TV	$3,000.00	$2,150.00	468
849756	Haba Spreadsheets	SOFTWARE	$350.00	$236.00	200
846590	Apple Database	SOFTWARE	$375.00	$250.00	200
845672	RCA Portable Color	TV	$300.00	$210.00	128
796541	RCA Console w/Remote	TV	$699.00	$550.00	128
846582	Sharp 13 inch Color w/Remote	TV	$425.00	$300.00	256
541245	Pioneer 45 Watts	STEREO	$650.00	$525.00	202
542160	Sansui	STEREO	$700.00	$600.00	12
542864	Fisher 50 Watts	STEREO	$488.00	$350.00	12
468524	Dow Jones Word Processing	SOFTWARE	$500.00	$379.00	200
845624	Apple Accounting Program	SOFTWARE	$575.00	$485.00	200
222010	Apple Game Program	SOFTWARE	$20.00	$9.50	200
200193	RCA Console 25 inch	TV	$600.00	$525.00	128
526554	Sansui Speakers	STEREO	$250.00	$175.00	12
584621	Sharp 19 inch Color	TV	$499.00	$350.00	878
854689	KCB 2-Tape VCR	VCR	$675.00	$500.00	964
854629	Micro Soft Spreadsheet Program	SOFTWARE	$275.00	$200.00	427
526889	Fisher Stereo, Portable	STEREO	$125.00	$84.00	427
876542	Marantz 75 Watt Stereo	STEREO	$1,200.00	$975.00	878
876540	Telos Database Program	SOFTWARE	$220.00	$150.00	200
541856	Radio Shack AM/FM Alarm	RADIO	$15.99	$9.99	221
287900	Cobra AM/FM Alarm Phone	RADIO	$99.99	$65.00	128
72186	Cobra Message Phone AM/FM	RADIO	$149.99	$99.00	128

TABLE B.1 ACE Company Inventory Data *(continued)*

On Hand	Order Level	Order Point	Date of Order	Jan	Feb	Mar	Apr	May	Jun	Jul	Aug	Sep	Oct	Nov	Dec
	Units								Unit Sales						
12	15	10		1	2	3	5	3	3	2	3	2	8	6	10
5	10	5	07/10/8x	2	1	2	0	3	2	1	0	2	1	3	8
12	10	10		3	2	3	4	3	5	1	2	3	2	4	7
44	25	20		4	5	7	6	8	6	7	5	3	4	16	25
12	50	35		5	8	6	7	8	12	9	11	7	9	78	29
5	10	5	07/25/8x	0	1	2	2	1	0	2	4	5	2	4	6
25	10	5		1	2	1	1	2	1	0	3	2	2	3	4
12	15	10		3	4	2	3	5	5	2	4	5	3	6	12
0	15	10	07/08/8x	2	3	6	5	4	4	5	2	3	4	8	10
10	10	5		0	1	2	1	3	2	0	3	3	2	4	5
22	25	15		4	3	4	6	7	3	4	8	7	5	15	20
12	10	10		2	3	1	2	4	2	1	3	3	4	5	5
8	10	10		1	2	3	2	3	3	2	1	2	3	5	4
3	10	5	07/08/8x	0	1	2	2	0	3	2	3	4	3	4	3
2	10	5	07/25/8x	0	1	2	1	2	1	1	0	4	2	3	4
496	750	500		199	220	322	234	265	122	186	145	356	252	386	358
52	150	100		32	34	21	22	45	46	55	53	34	22	42	58
304	750	500	06/30/8x	203	208	342	255	203	210	200	182	246	302	200	303
5	10	5	07/10/8x	0	1	1	2	2	3	2	0	1	2	2	5
25	15	10		3	5	4	5	2	6	5	2	4	3	6	7
0	10	5	07/16/8x	2	1	1	2	1	2	1	2	1	3	4	4
4	10	5		0	1	1	0	2	3	2	1	3	4	4	5
8	10	10	07/06/8x	2	3	2	3	2	3	3	1	3	3	4	5
4	5	5	07/02/8x	0	1	0	1	1	0	1	0	0	0	2	5
18	10	10		3	2	3	2	1	4	0	2	5	4	3	7
12	10	10		1	2	3	2	3	2	0	2	2	5	3	5
3	5	1		0	0	0	0	1	0	0	0	1	0	1	1
8	15	10	06/30/8x	3	2	5	2	1	4	0	3	7	4	4	6
12	10	5		0	2	1	3	4	2	0	1	2	3	4	4
5	10	10	05/31/8x	2	3	2	1	3	2	3	4	3	2	2	6
2	5	5	05/31/8x	0	1	2	1	3	1	2	0	1	0	1	2
8	10	5		2	3	3	2	2	1	2	1	2	4	2	3
11	10	5		0	1	2	1	2	3	1	2	2	3	3	5
10	5	5		0	0	0	1	1	0	0	0	1	1	0	2
5	10	5	06/21/8x	2	1	0	2	1	3	2	1	2	3	4	4
8	10	10		1	2	3	4	2	3	2	4	3	4	4	5
10	10	10	06/20/8x	2	3	3	6	1	2	1	3	2	3	4	4
150	125	80		20	25	31	40	26	24	32	63	42	38	61	73
7	10	5		1	3	4	4	3	2	1	2	0	3	2	4
7	10	5		0	1	2	1	3	2	2	1	3	2	3	3
13	10	10		2	1	3	2	1	3	2	2	3	4	3	6
3	5	1		0	1	0	0	1	0	0	0	1	0	0	1
8	5	5		1	2	1	1	2	2	1	0	2	2	1	2
20	20	10		2	8	5	6	4	7	3	5	4	6	5	10
6	5	5		0	0	1	0	1	0	1	0	1	1	2	0
10	15	10	06/22/8x	2	3	2	5	4	3	2	4	3	4	5	6
21	40	25	07/30/8x	5	8	10	12	9	11	8	18	20	16	22	15
23	25	15		3	4	3	6	5	7	6	8	7	8	9	16
20	20	15		2	3	5	4	5	6	8	6	6	9	4	13

TABLE B.2 ACE Company Supplier Data

Vendor Number	Vendor Name	Vendor Address	Vendor City	Vendor State	Vendor Zip Code
100	Carl's Computers	20014 Dallas Parkway	Dallas	TX	76002
106	R. J. E. Corporation	528 Ocean Blvd.	Carson	CA	53208
468	Carrington, Inc.	52410 Gremlin Avenue	Boston	MA	46358
202	Bender, Inc.	2214 Parkside Avenue	Denver	CO	20896
698	R. E. Thames Corporation	1428 Kendolph Blvd.	Miami	FL	85213
221	Quaisianni, Inc.	2024 Redbird Parkway	Phoenix	AZ	52147
525	Nicholas Distribution	2516 Christine	Houston	TX	78062
256	Bannasch Electronics	6518 Clay Circle	Philadelphia	PA	66864
193	Commodore Computers	5842 Oakland Avenue	St. Louis	MO	47521
200	Jon's Software	2215 Bent Tree Drive	Memphis	TN	22584
128	RCA Unlimited	21456 Armstrong Avenue	Seattle	WA	25014
012	Westman & Associates	25416 21st Street	New York	NY	10052
878	K. C. B. Corporation	21054 34th Street	New York	NY	10165
964	North Lakes Corporation	21054 Lakeshore Drive	Des Moines	IA	20548
427	Steele Operations	25412 Steele Drive	Detroit	MI	35214

GLOSSARY

Absolute address a specific cell reference within a spreadsheet, such as row 3 of column D

Acoustic coupler a modem that converts analog signals to digital signals; used to transmit data along voice telephone lines using a normal telephone headset as the input device for a computer system (*see* **Modem**)

Activity specification identifying the operations that should be executed by a software package and their sequence (*see also* **Programming**)

Address bus parallel connections (hardware circuits) used to carry binary addresses from the CPU to memory; part of a system bus

Algebraic precedence the order by which arithmetic operators (for example, + and −) are evaluated by the computer to determine an arithmetic result of a formula

Alignment the way right and left margins are treated; margins may have a *ragged edge*, indicating that lines do not end flush with the margin, or they

may be *right-justified* or *blocked*, indicating that words begin and end flush with the margin (*see also* **Left-justified** *and* **Right-justified**)

Alphanumeric data *see* **Character data**

Alternative(s) one of a number of possible choices that guide the process of decision making; different ways in which a problem can be solved

American Standard Code for Information Interchange (ASCII) a standard binary notation for numbers, letters, and special characters; also, when dealing with files, a standard method for the storage of data on a disk

Analog a system in which the output signal bears a continuous relationship to the input signal, as opposed to the discontinuous, or discrete signals, used by digital systems

Answer mode the use of special frequencies by the computer to indicate it is answering a call made by another computer

Application a particular task for which programs need to be

written or are presently available

Application generator developmental software designed to automatically produce, at some level, applications programs

Applications software a program or series of programs written to perform specified tasks (*see also* **Packaged software**)

Area chart a line chart with a shaded area bounded by the line (*see* **Line chart**)

Arguments a list of one or more items, such as cell references, that appear in mathematical and logical functions

Arithmetic/Logic Unit (ALU) the *arithmetic unit* and the *logic unit* combined; one of the essential components of a microprocessor; carries out arithmetic and logic operations on data

Arithmetic operation the computer function of performing some type of numeric manipulation of data

Arithmetic unit *see* **Arithmetic/Logic Unit**

Artificial intelligence a field

653

of study within computer science attempting to design a computer system (including software) that allows the computer to operate certain functions on its own; for example, learning, adaptation, simple reasoning, improvement, and optimizing

ASCII *see* **American Standard Code for Information Interchange**

Assembly language a relatively low-level language that is frequently used to develop systems software

Attribute (field, data item, or **data element)** a property of an entity; represented by a name and a set of values

Autodial a feature in modems that enables them to dial phone numbers in the phone system without the use of a telephone transmitter

Background a term used in connection with computer operating systems; it implies that there are programs with varying levels of priority; the lower priority levels are run in background—that is, in the computer's spare time or unused memory locations; the more important, higher priority jobs are run in foreground

Backup a copy or copies of programs or data for archival or security purposes (*see also* **Disk backup, File backup**)

Bar chart a graphics presentation represented by vertical (or horizontal) rectangles plotted against *x-y* axes

Bar code readers input device used to read bar codes, usually the *Universal Product Codes*

Baud rate the number of binary digits transmitted per second

Bernoulli Box *see* **Hard disk drive**

Bidirectional printer *see* **Printer**

Binary system a two-state system that uses only two digits —1 and 0—to represent the turning on and off of electric current; a digit, or a bit (for binary digit) is interpreted by the computer as part of a data character

Bit binary digit; a single binary digit is 1 or 0; basis on which data is created, manipulated, and stored by a computer

Bit-mapped graphics a process used by software capable of producing high-resolution printed output, whereby a single pin of a dot-matrix printer is struck independently of the other pins

Blank a space; the character that normally appears between words; a blank may be a *soft blank* that can be ignored by the word processor if it is at the beginning or end of a line, or it may be a *hard blank* that cannot be ignored

Block an area of text that has the same format; this may be a user-defined area of text, large or small

Block buffer a special area in memory used to temporarily hold a user-defined block of text that is being moved or copied from one place in the document to another

Branching operation the computer function that causes an instruction other than the next sequential one to be performed

Boilerplating creating one text by combining stored textual elements

Boldface a print control that causes a letter or group of letters to be overprinted several times (typically three or four times), thus giving a dark, or bold, appearance

Boot (booting; bootstrap) a technique or device designed to initiate itself; for example, a program whose first few instructions are sufficient to bring the rest of itself into the computer from an input device; can be used as a noun or a verb to describe the device or the process; loading the operating system

Business applications software typically designed for business uses, characterized by minimal computation activity and rather large amounts of input-output activity

Byte a usable unit of data; eight consecutive bits treated as an entity; byte and character are often used synonymously

CAD/CAM (computer-aided design/computer-aided manufacturing) sophisticated graphics systems (including both hardware and software) designed to assist in product design and production

Calculating the data manipulation function of performing mathematical alterations

Camera ready copy high-quality printed output that can be photographed rather than typeset for publication

Cathode ray tube (CRT) *see* **Display**

Central processing unit (CPU) the heart of any computing system, made up of the arithmetic/logic unit (ALU) and the control unit; in a microcomputer, this unit is sometimes called a *microprocessor* and referred to as an *MPU*

Character the lowest level in the data or word processing hierarchy; the smallest building block or element of a document; usually one letter or one digit

Character data (alphanumeric data)   data usually composed of combinations of letters, numbers, and other symbols that are not to be mathematically manipulated

Character graphics   a form of graphics that uses the various letters, numbers, punctuation marks, and other symbols produced by the computer to create an image

Chip   *see* **Miniature circuit; Very large scale integration**

Circular reference   a spreadsheet error that occurs when the recalculation of the contents of a cell references another cell, which in turn references itself

Classifying   the data manipulation function of categorizing items into groups

Clock   the internal timing mechanism of a computer, sometimes called the *internal clock*

Cold boot   a system start-up following a lengthy period of inactivity; an initial start-up

Column-width format   the spreadsheet function that permits widths of columns to be adjusted to the number of desired characters

Command bus   parallel connections (hardware circuits) used to carry a binary signal or group of signals to start or stop an operation; part of a system bus

Command driven   a type of software package structure; entering a command causes the package to perform a given action

Command language   a series of instructions designed to control the operation of a software package

Communications line   a wire or cable used to enable computers to communicate with one another

Communications network   the interconnection of processors and peripheral devices that allows them to communicate with one another

Communications port   a connector that provides electrical access to or from a computer system

Compiler   a system software program designed to translate a group of instructions written in a developmental language (source code) into machine language (object code); all instructions are translated at one time (for example, a COBOL compiler)

Computer bulletin board systems (CBBS)   the name of what is generally acknowledged to be the first bulletin board system; also a generic term for all computer bulletin board systems, regardless of the particular software they run

Computer generations   terminology used to keep track of the type and state of the art of technology used in a computer system; modern computers currently use fourth-generation technology

Computer graphics   the creation, manipulation, and storage of "pictures" through the use of a computer

Computerized conferencing   the process of using a computer network to carry on a conference in which the participants are physically separated

Computer software   *see* **Program** *and* **Software**

Computer system   a collection of all the devices needed for data and information processing, including a processing device and peripheral devices (output devices and input devices)

Conceptual view   an examination of a database based on what data is needed by the organization

Concurrent processing   multiple executions of the same program at the same time; usually used when more than one user is executing the same program on the same computer

Control character   special character used to control the actions of a printer, or special functions in a word processing package

Control key   *see* **Keyboard**

Control(ling)   the management function of supervising the use of an organization's resources

Control program   software designed to control the functions of a computer (*see also* **Monitor** *and* **Operating system**)

Control unit   the section of the central processing unit that performs the control functions

Copy   a standard function of applications packages that duplicates data from one location to another; an operating system function of duplicating a file

CP/M (control program for microprocessors)   an operating system developed by Digital Research in 1972, originally designed for 8-bit microcomputers

Currency   a representation of numeric data whereby values appear in a fixed point format with two decimal positions; value is preceded by a $ symbol

Cursor   a position indicator that enables the user of a video display screen to see exactly where the next character is placed and to track position; a visual indicator analogous to the place on the paper when typing; the ability to place the cursor anywhere on the screen is called *cursor addressing*

Cursor addressing   *see* **Cursor**

Cursor control key   *see* **Keyboard**

Cut and paste   a standard function of a word processing package that moves text from one area of a document to another

Daisy wheel printer   *see* **Printer**

Data   symbols, such as letters or digits, that describe or represent a person, place, or thing; the raw material from which information is produced; facts and figures

Database   the accumulation of all related data; an integrated collection of cross-referenced computer data files

Database management system (DBMS)   software that provides the linkage between the logical view of the user and the physical view of the hardware; software that allows the user to access and manipulate data stored in a database

Database structure (model)   the manner in which entities or attributes are related to each other in terms of organization and design of a database (*see* **Hierarchical structure, Network structure,** and **Relational structure**)

Data bus   a group of connecting paths (hardware circuits) that convey data to and from the central processing unit, memory storage, and peripheral devices; part of a system bus

Data editing   the process of examining and altering data or data values

Data element   *see* **Attribute**

Data hierarchy   the relationship among elements of data including characters, fields, records, files, and databases

Data independence   the difference between how an element of data is stored and how it is used (separate processes)

Data integrity   means that the data is complete, accurate, and not misleading

Data item   *see* **Attribute**

Data management   a common function of all operating systems, it controls the movement of data within the computer

Data management Systems (DMS)   a forerunner of database management systems that focused on the storage of fields within a record rather than the records themselves

Data processing (DP) system   a transaction processing system; a computerized system that manipulates data primarily initiated by a transaction, such as the sale of an inventory item

Data redundancy   the unnecessary duplication of data

Data types   forms of data representation; in spreadsheets these forms are generally text or character data (sometimes called *labels*) and numeric data, such as dollar or quantity values

Date code   a special control character that places the operating system date at a specified location in a document or file

Debugging   the process of searching for and eliminating sources of error in the operation of a computer; the term is attributed to Commodore Grace Hopper, USN Ret., after insects interfered with the operation of the MARK I

Decimal-point alignment (decimal tabs)   the alignment of decimal points in a column of numbers by shifting the numbers either left or right; a special tab stop in word processing

Decision making   the process of determining an appropriate course of action based on available information and alternatives

Decision model   a mathematical, computerized procedure that is used to approximate an existing business environment or anticipated situation

Decision support system (DSS)   a computerized system designed to help managers, especially strategic managers, make decisions; the highest level within a management information system

Dedicated system   a system designed to perform one function only, such as a dedicated word processor

Default drive   the disk drive that is read first by the computer; also the disk drive where the computer expects to find the operating system, applications software, or data

Default settings   the settings (for both hardware and software) that are present whenever a computer system or software package is first activated

Design integration   a method of developing integrated software whereby all functions are available in one software package and are available on request; total integration

Developmental language   a language that is used to develop application programs

Dial-up line   a telephone line

Dictionary   the file in a spelling verification routine that contains the list of correctly spelled words; there are usually two dictionaries—the main dictionary provided by the package and a personal dictionary built by the person using the system

DIF (data interchange format) a common method of storing files and documents on a disk (in rows and columns) that allows other software packages to access them

Digital a system that requires information to be transmitted in the form of separate binary signals, as distinct from an analog system, which receives a continuous signal

Digitizing pad (*see* **Graphics tablet**)

Direct-connect modem a modem that connects directly into the telephone line without using a telephone transmitter

Direct file a file storage method that stores records at unique locations (addresses) on disk, whereby each record can be accessed independently of the others

Directory (*see* **Index; Volume table of contents**)

Direct (random) access an addressing mode characterized by the ability to reach directly any point in memory or a storage device such as a disk; going directly to the location of the data

Disconnect the process of breaking the link between computers in a communications environment

Disk drive designation the part of a full file name that indicates the disk drive on which the file is to be found

Disk(ette) backup the process of backing (copying) the contents of a disk; in some cases, this operation will format the receiving disk

Disk operating system (DOS) an operating system for disk-based computers; an operating system in which certain functions are placed into memory while others reside on disk

Display the face of a *cathode ray tube (CRT)* or monitor, on which output can be viewed; also called a *video display terminal (VDT)* or *screen;* the display may also be single color (monochrome) or full color (sometimes called *RGB* for red, green, blue); newer technologies also include plasma screens and liquid crystal display (LCD)

Display format *see* **Number format**

Document the highest level in the word processing hierarchy, also called a *file;* it represents the complete unit of text that is stored on a disk

Domain/key normal form in relational databases, the primary keys that uniquely specify each entity record

Dominant entity an entity in a hierarchical database that acts as a superior or controlling entity to a number of subordinate entities in a one-to-many relationship

Dot addressable printer *see* **Printer**

Dot matrix printer *see* **Printer**

Doublestrike a print control that causes a character or group of characters to be printed twice to make the characters appear darker

Double underlining a control in printing that causes a character or group of characters to be printed with a double underline

Down load the telecommunications process of capturing information sent to the calling computer by the answering computer, as opposed to letting it disappear as it scrolls off the screen; receiving and saving data

Draft quality a high-speed print of a document that is generally done with one pass of the print head of a dot matrix printer

Drawing defining a geometric shape and placing that shape on the screen

Drum plotter a plotter that moves the graphics paper attached to a cylinder and moves the pen(s) only laterally to produce the graphics image (*see* **Plotter**)

Dvorak keyboard a keyboard that is designed to increase typing speed by placing the most often used keys where they are easiest to press

Echo the display of characters that have been entered at a local computer, sent to a remote computer, and returned to the local screen

Edit to revise a document or file (*see also* **Data editing**)

Electronic shopping, banking, and barter a computer-based service that allows you to buy and sell merchandise and services and provides full banking services

Embedded character a character that has been entered into a document but does not appear on the screen or on the printed document

Encyclopedic database a specialized database providing in-depth information on specific topics

Entity any identifiable object, concept, or activity belonging to an organization for which data is to be stored

Entity record a collection of fields or attributes that represent a set of data values within a database (*see also* **Attribute, Database, Entity, Record**)

Export   creating and storing a document or file in a format that can be accessed by another software package

Extension   a set of characters (usually three) appearing after the label in a file name, commonly used to indicate the file type

External information   information that is produced primarily outside an organization, such as information about competitors

External modem   a modem that is not a part of the primary computer cabinet.

Feedback   reported results of a decision

Field   a group of related characters, such as the letters in your name; can also be one independent character (*see also* **Attribute**)

File   a group of related records, such as an employee file containing all data about employees

File backup   the process of backing up (copying) the contents of a single file

File exchange integration   a method of developing integrated software whereby each function is available within its own software package but data is shared by allowing for the common access of files

File management system (FMS)   a self-contained system integrating all of the facilities needed for file handling

Find   a special word processing function that searches a document for occurrences of a sequence of letters; a database function that searches a file for specified attribute relationships

Firmware   a piece of hardware (for example, a ROM chip) that contains software

(for example, a machine monitor program)

Fixed point   a representation of numeric data whereby values appear in a decimal-point form with a specified number of decimal positions, which do not necessarily fill the cell or field in which the data resides

Flatbed plotter   a plotter that keeps the graphics paper in a fixed position and moves the pen(s) both horizontally and vertically to produce the graphics image (*see* **Plotter**)

Floating point   a representation of numeric data whereby values appear in a decimal-point form with sufficient positions following the decimal point to completely fill the cell or field in which the data resides

Floppy disk(ette)   a combination of magnetic tape and disk technologies, it is a flexible, oxide-coated disk (similar in appearance to a 45-RPM record) used for relatively permanent storage; capacity varies depending on the number of sides used (single-sided or dual-sided), the physical size of the floppy disk (3.5″, 5.25″, or 8″), the number of tracks (recording circles) on each side of the disk (40 or 80 tracks), the number of sectors (recording segments) per track (usually 8 or 9), and the recording density (single-density, double-density, or quad-density); floppy disks can currently hold up to 1.2 megabytes of data; all floppy disks usually have an external label, a write-protect notch, a read-write head notch, and a track sense or timing hole

Font   a set of characters of the same size and shape; a term that describes the size and style of printed material—for ex-

ample; 10 pitch italic, or 12 pitch Gothic bold

Forced end-of-page   a special function in word processing that forces the printer to begin printing at the top of a new page

Foreground   the partition of computer memory in which the highest priority tasks are executed (*see also* **Background**)

Formatting   the process of setting up a disk so that it can be used by an operating system (and the computer); the operation typically puts label information at the beginning of each track, the beginning and end of each sector of a track, and erases any data contained on the disk; the process of forcing the text of a page or paragraph (usually a block) to conform to the margin and tab stop setting of the word processor

Form letters   a set of letters having the same format and text that have been created from a single document; only minor items like name and address have been changed

Full-duplex mode   simultaneous transmission over a communications channel or series of wires in both directions

Function key   a special keyboard key that—when pressed—executes a specified activity (*see also* **Keyboard**)

Game paddle   a hand-controlled input device used to move the cursor to different positions on the screen

Garbage-in, garbage-out (GIGO)   a saying that means that the quality of data received from a system is no better than the data entered into that system

Graphics tablet (digitizing pad)   a flat slate with sensors laid out in a grid (*x*- and *y*-coordinates) used to mark different positions on a screen; by marking different positions in a continuous sequence, circles, lines, and other graphics can be drawn

Half-duplex mode alternate transmission over a communications channel in both directions

Hard blank *see* **Blank**

Hard disk drive a hard disk is made of a rigid alloy plate coated with mylar and it has a much greater storage capacity than a floppy disk; if the disk and the read-write heads are sealed in an air-tight case, then the hard disk is using Winchester technology; hard disks are usually nonremovable—however, several removable technologies exist, such as the Bernoulli Box

Hardware the mechanical, electromechanical, magnetic, and electronic devices that make up a computer system; the physical equipment

Hard-wired line a communications line connected directly to the computers without the use of a modem

Hard tab *see* **Tabs**

Hashing algorithms mathematical manipulations that produce storage locations in direct files; the manipulations to create storage locations are performed on the fields within each record

Help function a special function available on most commercial software packages that provides a description and instructions on how to use a command; this information is usually provided through the use of a help screen

Help screen *see* **Help function**

Hierarchical network a computer network that uses a "master (host) and slave" organizational setup

Hierarchical (tree) structure a means of organizing a database based on a rigid one-to-many relationship between dominant and subordinate entities

High-level language developmental software designed to assist programmers by removing many of the details associated with programming in a lower-level language

High resolution a mode of pixel graphics in which a large number of light dots appear on the display screen (for example, 640 rows of 400 pixels each)

Host *see* **Master unit**

Hybrid network an integrated network consisting of more than one type of network

Impact printer *see* **Printer**

Import to access a document or file that was created by another software package

Index (directory) an extra portion of an **indexed-sequential file** that is produced when the file is created and that contains the location of each record in the file based on its primary key (*see* **Indexed-sequential file** and **Primary key**)

Indexed-sequential file a method of storing data sequentially in an ascending order with an associated index, whereby records can be accessed either sequentially or in a direct-access manner (*see* **Index**)

Information data that has been manipulated or processed to have meaning or value

Information Center an orga-

nizational unit responsible for providing computer resources to users

Information graphics business charts and graphs that help one see detailed data in an easy-to-read format

Information processing the use of a computer to generate information from data

Information processing (IP) system a computer system that generates information from data

Information utility a term used to describe a general information database service

Ink jet printer *see* **Printer**

Input device allows data to be put into the computer

Input-output operation the computer function that causes data recorded on a peripheral device to be transmitted to internal memory or that causes data recorded in internal memory to be transmitted to a peripheral device

Inquiry *see* **Retrieve**

Integer a representation of numeric data whereby values appear as whole numbers (without decimal fractions)

Interactive having the property of enabling the computer and its user to communicate; when a computer immediately responds to its user

Interactive computer graphics a special type of computer graphics in which the picture's content, format, size, and colors are produced on a display screen under the direct control of the user through special input devices

Internal information information that is primarily produced within an organization, such as sales information

Internal memory also called *primary storage* and *internal storage*; the part of the computer that stores data and information; internal memory is either random access memory (RAM), which stores data that can be both read and changed, and read-only memory (ROM), which the computer can only read (not change)

Internal modem a modem that is in the primary computer cabinet

International Standards Organization (ISO) an international organization set up to establish standards in electronics and computing

Interpreter a system software program designed to translate a group of instructions written in a developmental language (source code) into machine language (object code); individual instructions are translated as they are executed (for example, a BASIC interpreter)

Insert the entering of new text into a document or file without destroying the existing data; usually the existing data is shifted (to the right or down) as new data is entered

Install program a special set of computer instructions, typically used only once, that permits a user to tailor packaged software to particular configurations of hardware or specific uses of the software

Instruction a specific operation that can be executed by a computer

Instruction set the combination of all operations that are available within a particular programming language

Job control language instructions, interpreted by an operating system, that control the fundamental operations of a computer (for example, a command that instructs the computer system to list the contents of a disk

Job management a common function of all operating systems, it controls the loading and scheduling (setting of priority levels) of programs

Joy stick a hand-controlled lever that can be rotated 360 degrees; used to move the cursor to different positions on the screen

Key in a direct-access file, a field within a record that uniquely identifies it; an attribute that uniquely identifies the attribute values of an entity record in a database

Keyboard an input device that contains keys much like those on a typewriter; typically, a keyboard will contain the common typewriter keys plus special function keys — usually programmable and used to send commands to the computer, a numeric key pad — used for the quick entry of numbers, cursor control keys — used to move the cursor to different positions on the screen, and control keys — used to send special commands to the computer

Label a part of the full file name that identifies the file by a particular name (in common usage the label is called the *file name*); the label is usually between one and eight characters long and begins with an alphabetic character

Labeling the process of naming a chart — naming its vertical and horizontal axes, defining the scales used on both axes, and naming the different elements that are drawn on the chart

Label name identifying name

that is attached to groups of spreadsheet cells, such as all or part of a row or column

Language *see* **Programming language**

Laser printer *see* **Printer**

Left-justified the adjustment of a data value in a cell or field such that the first character of the value occupies the first character position of the cell or field, with sufficient spaces added to the right to completely fill the cell or field

Letter quality (near letter quality) an option provided by some dot matrix printers and word processing packages; each line is printed twice with a small shift in the print position of the print head so that the document approximates the quality achieved by a daisy wheel printer

Light pen a pencil-shaped input device containing a photoelectric cell at its tip; generally used in conjunction with a CRT having a sensitized screen surface

Liquid crystal display (LCD) *see* **Display**

Line the text entered between the left and right margins of a page in a single row

Linear scale a measurement with equal-sized increments between values (for example, 1, 2, 3, and so on, or 500, 1000, 1500, and so on)

Line chart a graphics presentation represented by data points plotted on *x-y* axes and then connected by a line or lines

Local area network (LAN) a general-purpose network that provides interconnection of a variety of data communicating devices within a small geographic area (1000s of feet)

Logical condition an expression of the form "value1 relational-operator value2"; used in find and retrieve operations

Logical expression a combination of relational expressions using the logical operators AND or OR (*see* **Relational expression**)

Logical function a special spreadsheet routine capable of testing the relationship between two values, such as "value1 greater than value2," to determine whether the result is true or false; also available in some database packages

Logical operator a connector between two or more logical conditions on the basis of key words, including AND, OR, and NOT

Logical view an examination of a database based on how data is used or examined

Logic operation the computer function of making decisions regarding the relationships between two pieces of data

Logic unit *see* **Arithmetic/ logic unit**

Log off (out) the process of exiting a computer system; also the process of disconnecting a peripheral device; procedure for disconnecting from a host computer

Log on (in) the process of entering a computer system; also the process of connecting a peripheral device; procedure for connecting to a host computer

Low resolution a mode of pixel graphics in which a few light dots appear on the display screen (for example, 48 rows of 40 pixels each)

Machine cycle the amount of time elapsed in one clock unit; may be thought of as the amount of time it takes the computer to perform a single activity

Machine dependent having the property of not being transportable from one computer to another, if those computers are produced by different manufacturers

Machine language the lowest-level programming language; a set of instructions that is executed directly by a computer without translation; object code; machine code

Macro a sequence of commands or keystrokes that can be stored, retrieved, and executed; used to replace keyboard entry of commands or keystrokes

Macro language a set of instructions attached to a software package that are used to construct an activity specification sequence

Mail merge a special feature of word processing packages that will merge items from a file—such as name and address—into a separate document to create a form letter.

Mainframe the largest and most powerful type of computer; also the generic name given to the earliest computers produced by IBM and other large computer manufacturers; requires extensive and sophisticated operating systems or shared use of the computer to enable economic use

Management information system (MIS) a collection of systems designed to assist in the running of an organization; includes manual processing systems, data processing systems, information processing systems, and decision support systems

Manual processing system a means of manipulating and maintaining data without the use of a computer

Many-to-many (m:m) relationship when entity #1 of a database references many values in entity #2, and a value in entity #2 relates to many values in entity #1

Margin settings the number of print, or character, positions from the left edge of the paper that the text of a document begins (left margin) and ends (right margin); the white space that borders the text unit

Master unit a host computer that controls communication in a network

Mathematical functions special spreadsheet routines capable of performing specific mathematical operations on numeric data, such as totals, averages, logarithms, sines, and so on; also available in some database packages

Matrix data combined in a pattern of rows and columns

Matrix arithmetic mathematical operations that are performed on sets of values at the same time, such as matrix inversion and determinants (not performed by spreadsheet packages)

Medium resolution a mode of pixel graphics in which an intermediate number of light dots appear on the display screen (for example, 340 rows of 200 pixels each)

Megahertz (Mhz) a measure of clock speed, in millions of cycles per second

Member record a subordinate entity in a network database structure

Menu a list that appears on the screen that shows actions that may be taken; it is a list either of commands that may be entered or options that may be selected

Menu driven structure of the type of software package that allows the user to control the activities of the software by making selections from a menu

Meta language a set of instructions attached to a software package that is structurally similar to a programming language

Microcomputer a collection of devices that includes a microprocessor, memory, and associated interface circuits to communicate with peripheral devices or other circuits; the smallest type of computer

Microprocessor the central processing unit in a microcomputer

Miniature circuit commonly called a *chip*, this is the technology used for third- and fourth-generation computers; small pieces of silicon etched with copper lines to conduct electricity

Minicomputer the medium-sized computer; the distinctions between minicomputers and mainframes have blurred with the acceleration in the development of new technologies, but a mini is usually smaller and slower than a mainframe; a mini is generally called a *mini* because its manufacturer calls it a *mini;* the size difference between a mini and a micro is more obvious, as are the differences between their speed and performance

Mnemonics letter codes that are attached to particular machine language instructions to make them easier for a programmer to remember

Model *see* **Database structure**

Modem a modulator/demodulator; transforms a digital bit stream into an analog signal

(modulator) and vice versa (demodulator)

Monitor in operating systems, the program that provides the initial instructions to start the "bootstrap" process (*see also* **Display**)

Mouse a hand-held input device that is rolled around on a flat surface to move the cursor to different positions on the display screen, mark those positions, and select certain functions

MS-DOS (MicroSoft disk operating system) an operating system developed by Microsoft in 1981; it was originally developed to work on 16-bit microcomputers

Multiple column a document format where the text is present in more than one column on a page (similar to a newspaper); the text is read completely down one column and then to the top of the page, next column to the right

Multiple-pen plotter a plotter that produces a graphics image with a number of pens that are exchanged on command by the graphics software (*see* **Plotter**)

Multi-tasking refers to operating systems that can run a number of programs or subroutines at the same time; actually, the processor schedules tasks and takes them in order to service several users in a time-sharing environment

Multi-user system a real-time computer system, often designated as time-sharing, which is established to serve a group of separate and unrelated users

Natural language a computer language that is relatively close to a native language, such as English

Network structure a means

of organizing a database into set types based on flexible one-to-many relationships and many-to-many relationships between an owner record and member records

News and specialized business information database a database that provides information about current events

Noise unwanted signals that combine with and distort the signal intended for transmission and reception in a telecommunications environment

Nonimpact printer *see* **Printer**

Nonprocedural language a set of computer instructions that may be used to construct a program without completely identifying the logical sequence of activities to be performed

Number format the means by which the representation of numeric values can be altered to present a more useful appearance

Numeric data data composed of a combination of digits, with the possible inclusion of a decimal point and a plus or minus symbol, that can be mathematically manipulated

Numeric key pad *see* **Keyboard**

Object code the translated version of source code; machine code; that which might be executed by a computer without translation

One-to-many (1:m) relationship when a value in one entity of a database relates to many values in the second entity; however, a value in the second entity can relate to only one value in the first

One-to-one (1:1) relationship when a single value in one entity of a database can be related to only a single value in a second entity, and a single value in the second entity relates to only one value in the first

Op code (operation code) specifies the activity to be executed within a computer instruction

Open Systems Interconnection (OSI) the ISO standard for communication among computer systems (*see* **International Standards Organization**)

Operands the identifiers for data to be manipulated within a computer instruction

Operating system the main supervisor programs resident in memory that provide the instruction needed for the computer to perform its tasks; the common parts (and functions) of operating systems are monitor, job management, task management, and data management

Operating system software fundamental program used to control the activities of a computer system (*see* Chapter 4; *see also* **System software**)

Operational management line management; the lowest level of management within an organization; accepts the directives and decisions of tactical management and supervises procedural personnel

Organizing the management function of collecting or arranging an organization's resources

Originate mode the use of special frequencies by a computer to indicate it is making the call to another computer

Output device allows the computer to transmit and report results of computerized processing

Overstrike a special printer control function that causes a particular location in the text to be printed twice, usually with two different characters —for example, 7 and ñ

Owner record a dominant entity in a network database structure

Package a group of one or more programs

Packaged software programs created by software manufacturers for specific purposes and available commercially

Packet switching a method of transmitting messages through a communications network, in which long messages are subdivided into short groups or packets

Page the text that appears on one page of printed material (approximately 55 lines of text —page length is usually 66 lines)

Page footer a running text that appears at the bottom of each page in a document; a footer may appear on all pages, only on even-numbered pages, only on odd-numbered pages, or two different footings may appear on alternate pages

Page formatting *see* **Pagination**

Page header a running text that appears at the top of each page in a document; a header may appear on all pages, only on even-numbered pages, only on odd-numbered pages, or two different headings may appear on alternate pages

Page number code a special character used to count pages and place the current count at a particular location in the text —for example, within a page header or footer

Pagination (page formatting) the process of forcing the text of a page to conform to the margin, tab stop, and page length setting of the word processor

Painting filling the inside of a drawn shape with a color or shading (*see* **Drawing**)

Paragraph in word processing, the text that appears between consecutive RETURN key entries

Parallel in communications, sending all the bits of a character simultaneously by transmitting each one through a separate wire; the technique is faster than serial communication

Parity a check digit (bit) appended to an array of binary digits to make the sum of all the binary digits, including the check bit, always odd or always even

Partition an addressable area of memory needed to carry out a task, or execute a program or subroutine

Password a means of providing security for a database or other software; a series of characters that the user must successfully enter before using a package

PC-DOS (Personal Computer Disk Operating System) the IBM version of MS-DOS developed for IBM by Microsoft in 1982

Peripheral device external equipment attached to the computer by wires

Physical view an examination of a database based on how data is stored on physical devices such as disks

Pie chart a graphics presentation represented by a circle in which data is represented in terms of segments or wedges of the circle

Pins the printing mechanisms of dot-matrix printers;

usually seven to nine pins, arranged horizontally are fired (struck) in a particular sequence as the print head moves across the paper to create the desired characters

Pitch   the number of characters per inch of a particular font; most dot matrix printers will support 10, 12, and 16 pitch; most daisy wheel printers will support 10 and 12 pitch

Pixel   abbreviation for "picture element"; a picture element or single dot on the screen; the software's ability to turn on and off individual picture elements is referred to as *pixel addressing*

Pixel addressing   *see* **Pixel**

Pixel graphics   a form of graphics that uses the light dots that appear on the display screen (*see* **Low resolution, Medium resolution,** and **High resolution**)

Planning   the management function of anticipating future uses of an organization's resources; the establishment of goals and the means to achieve them

Plasma screen   *see* **Display**

Plotter   an output device that converts signals from the computer into graphics; plotters may be single-pen or multipen, and the surface used to hold the paper may be flat (flatbed) or curved (drum)

Policy formulation   the management function of specifying rules and procedures to be followed by the organization's members

Portable   the property of being able to transfer software or data from one computer to another, with little or no conversion

Presentation graphics   high-quality (high resolution and color) business charts and graphs produced for general information or educational purposes

Primary feature integration   a method of developing integrated software whereby the different functions are treated as add-on features to a main or primary feature of the software package

Primary key   the most important field used to directly access a record in a direct-access file; a field used to sort a file (*see* **Key**)

Print enhancements   the collective name of the printer controls used to change the appearance of a character or a group of characters

Printer   the second most common form of output device; can be impact (dot matrix and daisy wheel) or nonimpact (ink jet and laser) and can print either in one direction (unidirectional) or in both directions (bidirectional); if a printer is capable of printing a single dot within a portion of a character space, then the printer is dot addressable

Printer stop   a special printer code sent to the printer to stop the printing operation, usually so that a print wheel can be changed (daisy wheel printer), or so a new sheet of paper can be put in when using cut paper

Printing   the process of reproducing the contents of a document on paper; the control characters in the document control the way the document is printed

Procedural language   a set of instructions that may be used to specify the complete logic and sequence of a computerized task

Procedural personnel   workers; individuals within an organization who carry out the instructions or directives of management

Processing device   a device that manipulates data (*see* **Central processing unit**)

Processor   *see* **Central processing unit**

Program   a complete, logical, step-by-step series of instructions given to a computer to perform a specified task

Programmer   a person that uses a developmental language to translate the specifications for a procedure into a program

Programming   the act of using a developmental language to create a program (*see also* **Activity specification**)

Programming language   a set of instructions used to create a program

Prompt   a special character used by a computer system to indicate that the system is ready for input from the user

Proportionately spaced   right-justified or blocked margin alignment achieved by equally adjusting both the space between letters and the size of the letters

Protocol   a set of rules used by a computer to communicate with peripheral devices and other computers; serial data transmission must rely on a defined protocol; there are several internationally accepted protocols

Protected   a change or alteration of all or part of a software package that reduces or eliminates its risk of being reproduced in an unauthorized manner

Query   *see* **Retrieve**

QWERTY keyboard   a keyboard originally designed to avoid mechanical problems with movable keys in early typewriters; currently the most common design of a keyboard, it is named after the letters appearing in the top row typed by the left hand

Ragged right *see* **Alignment**

Random-access memory (RAM) internally stored information and data that the computer can both read and alter

Read-only memory (ROM) internally stored information and data that the computer can only read and not alter

Read-write head notch *see* **Floppy disk**

Record a group of related fields, such as a completed personnel form (*see also* **Entity record**)

Relational expression the condition on which an entity record is to be retrieved during a query operation

Relational operator a statement of relationship between two (attribute) values, such as greater than, less than, or equal to

Relational structure a means of organizing a database based on associations of tables of attributes and the relationships between those tables

Relationship the way two pieces of data (in a database) are tied together (*see* **One-to-one relationship, One-to-many relationship,** and **Many-to-many relationship**)

Relative address a cell reference within a spreadsheet relative to the position of another cell; for example, if your current cell reference is row 3 of column D, an indication such as "up 2, right 3" would place you at row 1 of column G

Replace removing text from a document by typing over (replacing) with new text material

Reporting the manipulation function of presenting or producing information

Reserve word a series of symbols that have a particular meaning and purpose within a programming language and that may not be used for any other purpose within that language

Retrieve (Query or **Inquiry)** the database function that causes selected pieces of data to be made available for viewing by the user

Right-justified the adjustment of a data value in a cell or field such that the last character of the value occupies the last character position of the cell or field, with sufficient spaces added to the left to completely fill the cell (*see also* **Alignment**)

Ring network a local network in which computers are attached in a closed loop

Roller ball a hand-manipulated input control device that uses a rotating ball to move the cursor to different positions on a screen; typically found on computer arcade games

Ruler a line appearing at the top or bottom of the screen displaying the right and left margin settings as well as the current tab stop settings for a document in word processing

Scalar arithmetic mathematical operations that take place between two values, such as addition, subtraction, multiplication, and division

Scaling the adjustment of the distance between numbers along the vertical and horizontal axes of a graph or the adjustment of the range along either axis

Scatter chart a line chart with unconnected points (*see* **Line chart**)

Scientific applications software typically designed for scientific uses, characterized by minimal input-output activity and rather large amounts of computation activity

Scratchpad an alternative name for a spreadsheet

Screen *see* **Display**

Scrolling the process of changing the view of a document or file by moving text off the top (or bottom) of the screen so that new text is displayed at the bottom (or top) of the screen; scrolling not only moves a view of the document or file up and down but also right and left within the document or file; the appearance of spreadsheet movement across the screen

Secondary key a less important field used to access a record in a direct-access file; a second field used for sorting (*see* **Key**)

Secondary storage *see* **Storage device**

Sector *see* **Floppy disk**

Security a means of controlling or limiting access to a database or other software package (*see* **Password**)

Sentence the text that appears from the first character encountered after the end of a sentence until next end-of-sentence punctuation is encountered (for example, !, ?, or .)

Sequential access the process of reading data from memory or disks in sequence from first to last

Sequential file one of the first methods of handling data; data is stored in either ascending (smallest to largest) or descending (largest to smallest) order, by a selected field within a record; each subsequent record can be accessed only by retrieving the records that precede it

Serial in communications, the transmitting of data one bit at a time

Set type the classification of relationships between an owner record and member records in a network database structure

Single-pen plotter a plotter that produces an image with only one pen at a time (*see* **Plotter**)

Single-user system a computer system that is capable of executing only one program at a time

Slave unit the computer that calls a master (host) computer in a network

Soft blank *see* **Blank**

Soft tab *see* **Tabs**

Software computer programs of all types; "instructions" for the computer

Software engineer *see* **Systems analyst**

Software house a company that produces and sells packaged software

Software package *see* **Packaged software**

Sorting the data manipulation function of arranging data in a desired order

Source code instructions written in a developmental language

Spelling verification a feature of a word processing package that checks the spelling of words within the document

Split screen the ability to divide the screen in half, either vertically or horizontally, to provide two different views of a document or file

Spooling an acronym of arguable parentage; one definition is simultaneous peripheral operations overlap—it refers to one method of improving a computer's operation by allowing printing to occur while simultaneously performing other work on the computer

Stacked bar chart a bar chart in which multiple data items are represented in a single bar (*see* **Bar chart**)

"Stand-alone" graphics package computer software that produces only charts and graphs; a package that is not integrated with other computer applications or functions

"Stand-alone" system a computer system (or microcomputer system) that needs no additional hardware or software to perform a task

Star network a local network in which each computer is connected to every other computer

Status area an area on the screen that gives the status of the software or document—usually including the current line number, character position, margin and tab setting, page number, and document or file name

Status line a single line containing the status area information

Stop bits the signaling bits attached to a character used to indicate the end of the character in a communications environment

Storage device (secondary storage) a medium or device that can store data relatively permanently but that is not part of the computer's internal memory

Stored-program concept the idea that computer programs can be temporarily saved within the computer's memory while being executed, rather than being fed to the computer one instruction at a time

Storing the data manipulation function of saving data for later use

Strategic management the top level of management of an organization, charged with directing the organization as a whole

Strike through a special printer-control function that causes a particular location in the text to be printed twice: once with any character and a second time with a-—for example, THIS IS A STRIKE THROUGH

Structured programming the techniques and philosophy of software design that entail the development of programs as a series of modules that conform to particular standards

Subcell graphics a process of creating graphics output whereby a "cell" is represented by a single character position; graphics are created by using all or part of the cell area

Subdirectory a directory that represents a part of the entire storage space on a disk; frequently used with hard disk systems to divide large numbers of files into groups

Subordinate entity one of a number of entities that are related to a dominant entity in a hierarchical database structure

Subscript a letter, number, or other symbol entered slightly below and to the right or left of a character; can also be directly underneath the text character

Summarizing the data manipulation function of reducing the amount of detail

Superscript a letter, number, or other symbol entered slightly above and to the right or left of a character; can also be directly above the text character

Supervisor a program that controls the activities of the computer; system software

Symbolic code instructions that provide directions to the computer by means of symbols; typically, numeric instructions that have meaning in machine language

Symbolic Linkage (SYLK) a common method of storing files and documents on a disk that allows other software packages to access them

Synchronized movement in a spreadsheet operation, movements linked together in two or more windows such that a movement in one window causes a corresponding movement in other windows

System bus a network of paths (hardware circuits) inside the computer that facilitates data and control flow

Systems analyst a person who analyzes problems and designs and creates software

System software programs that control or extend the capabilities of a computer system; programs that are used directly by the computer system

Tabs (tab stops) position markers set up to stop the movement of the cursor across screen when the "tab" key is pressed; a tab may be a soft tab that can be ignored by the word processor if it is at the beginning or end of a line, or it may be a hard tab that cannot be ignored

Tactical management middle management; personnel within an organization who accept the directives of strategic management, implement strategic management decisions, and supervise operational management

Tape streamer the device that powers and controls the movement of magnetic tape past the read-write head; tape streamers operate at very high speeds and record at a high density and are used as backup devices for hard disks

Task management one of the common functions of all operating systems, it controls the execution of a program

Telecommunications electronic communications between computers using telephone wires

Template (model) specialized software that, when used in conjunction with a standard spreadsheet package, is capable of quickly and easily solving specific types of problems for which spreadsheets are suitable

Text character data used to identify titles or labels within the spreadsheet work space, frequently used as row or column headings

Text area the area on a screen that displays the text entered into a word processor document

Text file a file that is used to store text material, usually in ACSII format

Time slicing the process for breaking the computer's processing time into specific time intervals that can be used by different users, memory partitions, or peripheral devices

Token passing a control technique for ring networks used to identify the computer that is to receive a message

Touch screen a relatively new input device that uses a grid of photosensors across the surface of the display screen to sense where the screen is touched, thereby marking the cursor position

Track *see* **Floppy disk**

Transaction process system *see* **Data processing system**

Transparent the data characteristic of being "invisible" to either the user or the software; for example, records marked for deletion may not be retrieved by (are invisible to) query activities of a database package

Truncate to shorten, cut down; to eliminate characters within a data field so that no more than the maximum field length is retained

Tuple a group of related attributes in a relational database; a row in a relational database attribute table

Underlining a printer control that causes a character or group of characters to be printed with an underline

Unidirectional printer *see* **Printer**

Unsychronized movement in a spreadsheet operation, movements in windows that are independent of one another, such that a movement in one window does not cause a corresponding movement in other windows

Up load the process of sending information from one computer directly from memory or disk to another computer

User (or End User) a person who uses a computer system to solve problems

User friendly having the property of being easy to use, particularly related to non-technical or novice users; a software package that, through a series of questions and answers or by simple English-like instructions, allows beginning or novice users to access data and perform data manipulations

Utility program a program, sometimes accompanying an operating system, that performs very specialized functions that are infrequently needed by the user

Very large scale integration (VLSI) chips containing a minimum of 5,000 integrated circuits, or more than 16,000 memory bits

Video display terminal (VDT) *see* **Display**

Visiclones software packages, created after the VisiCalc package, that emulated the idea of spreadsheets

Voice output device a voice synthesizer; an electronic device used to generate sound that approximates the human voice, based on the output of a computer

Voice recognition equipment an input device that converts the human voice into electronic signals that can be used by a computer

Volume search the process of searching the contents of an entire volume (disk)

Volume table of contents (VTOC) a special record on a disk that lists the names and addresses of all the files on that disk

Warm boot a system restart following a very brief period of inactivity; virtually an immediate restart; this process is used to clear memory and "reload" the operating system without turning off the computer system

Wide area network a general-purpose network that provides interconnection of a variety of data communicating devices within a wide geographic area (100s of miles)

Wildcard special symbol(s) used in a file name to designate an unknown character or set of characters

Winchester technology *see* **Hard disk drive**

Window a separate screen work area (up to eight) that (1) in a spreadsheet, permits the splitting of the screen to enable the user to view two or more widely separated parts of the spreadsheet at the same time; (2) in an integrated software package, allows the user to see different views of the same application area or views of several different applications; (3) in a word processing package, allows the user to view different areas of one document or areas in different documents at the same time

Word the text that appears between blank characters

Word origination the process of entering text into a word processing document area

Word processing the manipulation of alphabetic or alphanumeric data; usually to create, edit, and print documents

Word processing system the hardware and software need to do word processing

Word wrapping the process of automatically moving text to the next line in a document, without splitting a word, when the right margin of a document is encountered

Worksheet an alternative name for a spreadsheet

Work space an area of internal memory into which a spreadsheet is placed and manipulated; an area divided into rows and columns

Write-protect notch *see* **Floppy disk**

INDEX